D0458919

The
Complete
Guide to
WRITING
NONFICTION

The Complete Guide to WRITING NONFICTION

by the American Society of Journalists and Authors

Edited by Glen Evans

Writer's Digest Books

Cincinnati, Ohio

Library of Congress Cataloging in Publication Data

The complete guide to writing nonfiction.

 Includes index.
 1. Authorship. I. Evans, Glen. II. American Society of Journalists and Authors.
PN145.C73   1983   808'.02   83-16935
ISBN 0-89879-117-0

Design by Hal Siegel

CREDITS AND PERMISSIONS

We gratefully acknowledge the assistance of the following in the preparation of this book.

American Society of Journalists and Authors, "Code of Ethics and Fair Practices"; "On Work Made for Hire: A Statement of Position"; and "Suggested Letter of Agreement" (New York, 1982)

Judith Applebaum and Nancy Evans, *How to Get Happily Published* (Harper and Row, New York, 1978)

Jefferson D. Bates, *Writing With Precision: How to Write So That You Cannot Possibly Be Misunderstood* (Acropolis Books, Ltd., Washington, D.C., 1981)

Shirley Biagi, *How To Write and Sell Magazine Articles* (Prentice-Hall, Inc., Englewood Cliffs, New Jersey, 1981)

Julian Block, *Tax Saving: A Year-Round Guide* (3rd ed., Chilton Book Company, Radnor, Pennsylvania, 1983)

Hal Borland, *How to Write and Sell Non-Fiction* (Greenwood Press Publishers, Westport, Connecticut, 1973)

Walter S. Campbell, *Writing: Advice and Devices* (Doubleday, New York, 1958)

Claudia Caruana, "Reference Books For Your Bookshelf" (*Writer's Digest*, May 1982. Appeared in slightly different form under the title "Get the Most Out of Your Research Time")

Curtis Casewit, *Freelance Writing: Advice From the Pros* (Collier Books, New York, 1974)

Kay Cassill, *The Complete Handbook for Freelance Writers* (Writer's Digest Books, Cincinnati, Ohio, 1981)

Chet Cunningham, "The Partial Road to Complete Writing Success" (*Writer's Digest*, June 1979)

Jolee Edmonson, "Out of the Rough and into the Green" (*Writer's Digest*, October 1980)

Connie Emerson, *Write on Target* (Writer's Digest Books, Cincinnati, Ohio, 1981)

David W. Ewing, *Writing for Results: In Business, Government, the Sciences and the Professions* (2nd ed., John Wiley and Sons, New York, 1979)

John Fischer, *The Stupidity Problem: And Other Harassments* (Harper and Row, New York, 1964)

Brendan Gill, *Here at the New Yorker* (Random House, New York, 1975)

Stephen Goldin and Kathleen Sky, "Working with an Agent" (*Writer's Digest*, April 1982)

Alex Haley, "On Becoming a Writer," *ASJA 30th Anniversary Journal* (New York, 1978)

Frances Halpern, *Writer's Guide to Publishing in the West* (Pinnacle Books, New York, 1982)

Hayes B. Jacobs, "So You're Going to Take a Writing Course" (*Writer's Digest*, May 1981)

David Lambuth (and others), *The Golden Book of Writing* (Viking Press, New York, 1964)

Colman McCarthy, *Inner Companions: A Personal Encounter with Enduring Thinkers* (Acropolis Books, Ltd., Washington, D.C., 1978)

Scott Meredith, *Writing to Sell* (2nd rev. ed., Harper and Row, New York, 1974)

Harry E. Neal, *Nonfiction: From Idea to Published Book* (Funk and Wagnalls, New York, 1967)

Sally Wendkos Olds, "Write a Query—Get an Assignment" (*The Writer*, August 1977)

————"First Magazine Article Sales" (*The Writer*, August 1973)

Vance Packard, "Writers as Explorers," *ASJA 30th Anniversary Journal* (New York, 1978)

Kirk Polking and Leonard S. Meranus, *Law and the Writer* (Writer's Digest Books, Cincinnati, Ohio 1981)

Paul R. Reynolds, *The Non-Fiction Book: How To Write and Sell It* (William Morrow, New York, 1970)

Nora Sayre, "How Free is the Free-Lance Writer?" (*Mademoiselle*, March 1968)

Art Spikol, *Magazine Writing: The Inside Angle* (Writer's Digest Books, Cincinnati, Ohio, 1979)

Alden Todd, *Finding Facts Fast: How to Find Out What You Want and Need to Know* (Ten Speed Press, Berkeley, California, 1975)

Alvin Toffler, "Future Flak," *ASJA 30th Anniversary Journal* (New York, 1978)

Stanley Vestal, *Professional Writing* (Macmillan Publishing Co., New York, 1938)

Myra Waldo, "Have Typewriter, Will Travel," *ASJA 30th Anniversary Journal* (New York, 1978)

Mort Weisinger, *A Treasury of Tips for Writers* (Writer's Digest Books, Cincinnati, Ohio, 1965; rev. ed. 1981)

ACKNOWLEDGMENTS

Books don't write themselves. "Who casts to write a living line, must sweat," wrote Ben Jonson. For this book many people across America have sweated. I'd like to thank them, one and all. They include:

Past ASJA Presidents Grace Weinstein and Sally Wendkos Olds, for helping to develop the book's concept and set it in motion; 1982-83 President June Roth, for helping to see a long and ambitious project through; and to Vice-President Dodi Schultz for invaluable editorial assistance and expert counsel in ironing out wrinkles of contract and procedure.

I'm deeply indebted to the many friends and colleagues from ASJA, without whose selfless and talented assistance this project would never have come to fruition. They are identified by name in the Author Biographies at the end of this book.

A hearty thank-you must go to my dedicated editors, editor-in-chief Carol Cartaino (whose idea the book was), Barbara O'Brien, Anita Buck, and Beth Franks (who lived with a 900-page manuscript for six months), as well as editor Kirk Polking and the many other helpful people at Writer's Digest Books—all of whom have been of tremendous assistance with writing, editing, and research.

And a special thanks is in order to Marylyn St. Clair and Sharon Meli, for tireless—and, sometimes, I'm sure, tiresome—typing services and administrative work.

Last, but far from least, I underline my debt to my wife, Margie, and my daughter, Lisa, for support, tolerance, and abundant good humor along the way.

For all this, to all these, my thanks.

—G.E.

ACKNOWLEDGMENTS

ABOUT THE ASJA

No editor could have asked for a more competent group of writers to call on for this project than the professional freelancers of ASJA. Beginning in 1948 as the Society of Magazine Writers (SMW) with a "handful of loners," the New York-based Society today has active regional chapters in the Midwest, Southern California, Northern California, New England, and Washington, D.C.

The Society's name was changed some years ago to reflect the broadened interests of its members. "ASJA works steadily," explains past president Grace W. Weinstein, "to raise the standards and rewards of magazine journalism; it applies the same efforts in the realm of book publishing. ASJA's Code of Ethics and Fair Standards, Model Letter of Agreement for magazine articles, and Position Statement on Work Made for Hire have all had a positive effect on the industry, improving conditions for all writers. And its periodic Conscience-in-Media Award recognizes distinctive contributions by any journalist in any medium."

ASJA has also been in the forefront of the fight against any and all forms of censorship. In the fall of 1981, the group launched a concerted nationwide campaign against attacks by special-interest groups on First Amendment rights. This important work continues.

Professionally, our primary interest will always be the constant refinement of the nonfiction craft. Our annual writers' conferences, currently held in New York City, Southern California, and Madison, Wisconsin, are designed to share our wealth of knowledge.

Books such as this are yet another way we share our skills and experience with other writers, writing instructors, and students. The first edition of *A Treasury of Tips for Writers,* published in 1965, became a classic in its fifteen-year life. (A revised and updated version was issued in 1981.)

We believe that *The Complete Guide to Writing Nonfiction* will prove even more valuable, since it draws on a broader spectrum of our members' talents, and gives readers a more complete picture of today's world of nonfiction writing. As professional freelancers and members of the American Society of Journalists and Authors, we feel a special responsibility to the community at large—and to the writing community in particular. This work is but one more means of meeting that essential responsibility.

—G.E.

CONTENTS

"People want to write. The desire to express is relentless. People want others to know what they hold to be truthful. They need the sense of authority that goes with authorship."

—Donald H. Graves
Papers on Research About Learning
(New York, Ford Foundation, 1978)

INTRODUCTION

"The man is most original who can adapt from the greatest number of sources."
—Thomas Carlyle

Many years ago, writers often began an article, an essay, or a book with a poem or a quotation. Such leads today are considered passé, if not a bit hokey. I've always liked Carlyle, however, and I'm a nut on quotations. And if the learned Scot was on track, I'm a most original editor—because this books owes a debt to every single member of the American Society of Journalists and Authors, past and present.

In these pages, you are invited into the minds and hearts of 107 professional writers. All are accomplished freelancers whose special talents and experience will help you plot the course of your own writing life.

Nonfiction—the staple of the freelance career, the steady seller most writers depend upon to pay the bills—has experienced sweeping changes in the past twenty years. Writing styles (e.g., the so-called "New Journalism") and requirements have changed; indeed, the whole magazine landscape is altered. We see this book as a detailed map and atlas of the inviting but demanding new world of nonfiction.

Until now, there has been little guidance for those who wanted to try their hands at—and master—one or more of the specialized writing fields. Likewise, only limited instruction was available for nonwriting professionals in various pursuits who increasingly need to communicate via writing. And the specialized information that does exist has never been assembled into a single volume.

None of the areas covered in this book is new. What is new, however, is the conviction that something needed to be done to call attention to the full range of challenge and opportunity that nonfiction affords freelance writers today. In accord with the move to specialization in nonfiction writing, we have tried to provide a total package of specialized writing and marketing know-how. We hope it will benefit those wishing to acquaint themselves with the whole spectrum of specialized writing—beginners who would like to specialize in a particular field or fields, as well as professionals who would like to broaden their expertise (and supplement their income) with additional options.

As the hole is intrinsic to the doughnut, however, ASJA members know well the necessity of learning the ABCs of writing—no matter what nonfiction field you pursue. They know, because in the course of their careers, all have learned the hard way that you must crawl before you walk. And you must walk before you can run. And even then you must learn *how* to run.

For this reason, Part One deals with what might be called the verities, the essentials of the writing craft. These are the fundamentals that can spell the difference between success and failure for both part- and full-time writers. This section, called "Writing to Sell," provides hard-learned, practical techniques and tips for launching and managing your writing career—and avoiding the pitfalls that have turned many a writer's dream into a nightmare.

You'll learn how to research, write, and sell solid articles and books that meet the needs of widely differing markets. Also included is a lively chapter that debates the pros and cons of the question: Should I specialize? We felt such a panel-in-print was necessary if writers were to get a comprehensive look at the concept of concentrating their efforts in specific areas of nonfiction.

Part Two moves to the nitty-gritty of writing for the individual specialties that make up the bright new world of nonfiction. Today's most vital and significant areas are fully covered here. In each of these fifteen key sections ASJA professionals put their skills and techniques into your hands, and provide expert insights and sidelights on their specialties. They write lucidly and honestly about their experiences and explain the limitations, as well as the advantages, of that particular field. You'll learn the requirements of each field, the full range of freelancing opportunities—including the range of remuneration. You'll discover how you can best use the expertise of authorities as well as the secrets of bringing a subject to life. We have appended a list of organizations and associations that can provide you with further information, usually free upon request, to assist your research in your chosen field.

In these pages, we have gathered a wealth of know-how to help you achieve your goals—by learning to write about what interests you or what you know best. The authors quoted here have bruised their backsides along with their egos in the course of their careers; their candor and shop savvy will help you direct your own professional life. Set yourself the task of learning the methods they know work in this business.

We hope we have given nonfiction writing the blend of responsible reportage and creativity it deserves, to encourage and guide the writer-explorer of today and tomorrow.

—Glen Evans, Editor
Stamford, Connecticut

PART ONE

WRITING TO SELL

Chapter One

BECOMING A FREELANCE WRITER

I've been a full-time freelance writer for some twenty-two years and have survived to tell the story.

It wasn't easy at first. When I think about it, it's not all *that* easy to-day. Freelancing's a tough, fiercely competitive, modestly paying business with its full share of atrocity stories. To even approach success, you must be disciplined, industrious, a little eccentric, politely aggressive, and able to suffer setbacks galore. In fact, if you can't take rejection, don't even consider being a freelance writer—full-time or any time.

Moreover, the freelance writer faces many pitfalls aside from rejection: loneliness, deadlines, difficult research, endless revisions, crabby editors who aren't sure what they want, collaboration, writer's block (yes, Virginia, there is. . .), writing on speculation, slow pay, no pay, unanswered phone calls, and irate landlords, to name a few.

Why, then, do we take it on? The reasons are as distinctive and varied as the personalities of ASJA's members, and they will give you their views in the pages of this book. But one thing is certain—none of us does it for instant big bucks. I'll hazard another theory: the *real* pay-off to the writer, whether as a part- or full-time freelancer, comes not in the form of money but in a sense of self-worth and autonomy. Maybe, as author Nora Sayre said in "How Free is the Freelance Writer?" (*Mademoiselle*, March, 1968), it's because ". . .the freelance writer can do one thing that is impossible for almost any other professional: take a walk at 3:30 in the afternoon."

The reason for discussing this with students, beginning writers, and even struggling professionals is twofold. First, we want this book to present a realistic picture of the writing and publishing business as it exists today; second, by removing the mystique from the craft of freelance writing, we hope to help you avoid the common mistakes and Cinderella strategies that can wreak havoc with anyone's writing goals.

FACING THE FINANCIAL FACTS (OR, SNAKES IN THE GARDEN)

The James Micheners, Erma Bombecks, and Herman Wouks not-withstanding, there are those among us (whose sole occupation is writing) who don't make all that much money. For every Art Buchwald or Gail Sheehy there are thousands who don't make it in this business. However, were you to attend one of our monthly ASJA meetings, you'd soon learn that we compensate with the subjective conviction that our plight is usually someone else's fault.

To put the whole matter into perspective, the median annual earnings from writing for book authors—as determined by a recent survey conducted for the Authors Guild Foundation by Columbia University's Center for the Social Sciences—was $4,775. *Newsweek* (June 22, 1981) assessed the situation as: ". . .a fascinating—if somewhat ema-ciated—profile of that often romanticized figure, the writer. In 1979, he earned an estimated hourly wage of $4.90—that is, less than half of what bricklayers, painters, and construction workers make. . . .The $4.90 figure places most writers below the government's estimated 'poverty threshold' for 1979."

A sobering but misleading picture. For one thing, 46 percent of those who responded to the Authors Guild survey have paid positions other than freelance writing. They write only part-time. For another, of the 2,239 respondents, many write *only* books—nothing for maga-zines, trade papers, journals, and no teaching or lecturing. This neces-sarily restricts their annual "writer" earnings.

In the ASJA, where 67.1 percent of the members write full-time, the 1980 median gross earnings from freelance writing were $17,500. The median figure for full-timers was $20,000; more than one third grossed over $25,000. And even for those members who devote only half their working time (i.e., between 40 and 60 percent) to freelancing, the median gross earnings from freelancing in 1980 were $12,000. Not great, to be sure, but certainly not as depressing as the Authors Guild statistic.

Nevertheless, for you who seek instant fame and fortune from a writing career, yes, there are snakes in the freelancer's garden. And constant financial concern is one of them (unless, as one wag suggested, "you die young, preferably in a tragic manner").

Tens of thousands of men and women all over the country are trying to earn all or part of their income from writing in the uncertain eighties. Who better to give an initial overview on "The Freelance Mystique" than Betty Friedan, author of the bestsellers *The Feminine Mystique, It Changed My Life,* and *The Second Stage?*

In this interview, which appeared in the ASJA's *30th Anniversary Journal* (May, 1978), Friedan discusses freelancing with another ASJA member, Margaret Markham.

Markham: Nonfiction writers have recently been making headlines as superstar bestsellers, giving rise to the impression they have gained new and favored economic status. Is this mere ballyhoo?

Friedan: For the most part, yes. The public has been led to believe that if a writer has one hit book, two things automatically follow: the author can always command a six-figure advance, and the one hit book has overnight moved the writer into the same bracket as the Rockefellers. This is pure mystique. Nobody tells it like it is. Supposing one does get a six-figure advance. In the first place, it's not net. Out of that must come taxes, overhead costs, and everything in the process of producing a book—from typists and duplicating expenses to interview-transcribing and travel. And, of course, one's own living expenses. And the advance may have to support the writer for anywhere from two to five years. The advance I got for *The Feminine Mystique* was approximately $3,000—and it took me some five years to put the book together.

My next book, *It Changed My Life,* I wrote over a span of ten years, in the sense that parts of it included events and writing I had done during the last decade, but in the strict sense of a concentrated effort, it cost me close to two years to put it together in final shape. And I did not have a six-figure advance for that either.

As for my latest book, *The Second Stage,* it has taken two years of research to pull together the material I need, and another two years to write it. And there's no special fee to cover the research time and costs. As for the travel needed in connection with it, I have to rely on my lecture tours to subsidize that or dip into my own pocket for it.

So if you amortize even a six-figure advance over the time it takes to finish a book, minus costs and taxes, you're left with more mystique than money. In any case, how many nonfiction writers are likely to get a six-figure advance? And, unlike the fiction writer, they stand very little chance of spin-offs like movie sales.

Markham: What about the magazine field? Has it taken an upturn for the better?

Friedan: It's not a glowing situation there, either. Often big magazines do pick up the tab for travel, at least on major assignments, and that's a help. But the magazine market, in contrast to other communications media, has not increased the prices it pays for articles, not even the top scale, to any significant extent over what they were paying when I first started writing for them a quarter of a century ago. When you match this against the rise in cost of living over those twenty-five years, it's far from impressive.

Moreover, many magazines that paid top prices have folded in the last couple of decades. What is mushrooming is a slew of smaller magazines for special audiences, though they often don't pay very well.

For a writer struggling to support a family—even if it's a spouse responsible for only partial support—freelancing can offer a very grim prospect. When my own children were growing up and I was only a partial contributor to the family income, it wasn't so rough. I could take on assignments pretty much at my own pace. But these days, when two full incomes are often a dire need, or when more and more women are going it alone, often largely supporting their children as well as themselves, it's another matter.

In any event, I don't think it's easy for a freelance nonfiction writer, man or woman, to be self-supporting through freelance work alone. It's almost mandatory, at least from time to time, to take a stint in some allied field, like lecturing or teaching. It's through a combination of such professional roles that I support myself.

Markham: Do you think freelance nonfiction writers have been shortchanged by society's failure to support their efforts?

Friedan: Definitely. Today's serious nonfiction writer is important to society because from a solid background of social sciences, combined with the journalistic skills of a reporter, one moves beyond the reporter function to the front edge of our emerging society. This is a critical role because all too often those actually involved with special issues, and those locked into specific disciplines, miss the broad social implications of questions vital to our times.

Our type of nonfiction writer—who is not apt to be the fine-tuned "writer's writer"—is generally not a member of the academic "club." This means we are not in line for a Guggenheim grant or similar support needed to subsidize in-depth research. There is government support for the performing arts, for instance, and it's easier to find money to underwrite the research for a book on ancient Japanese calligraphy than the pressing current problems most of us nonfiction writers deal with. I'm in that boat right now, trying to find foundation support for the research that is essential to my next book. I can't expect my publisher to underwrite that.

Despite the perils of survival as a freelancer, I still firmly believe that this is a fine field. It is ever-changing; it leaves no room for boredom. Every time I tackle a new book, I get a new lease on life. It's exhilarating to plunge into a subject when I'm far from knowing all the answers. Anyone who can take the relative insecurity—and today, the economic challenge is the same for women and men—and can function in an unstructured situation that requires self-generating activity can bask in the special benefits that accrue from this kind of life.

Betty Friedan, who at this writing is teaching and lecturing at Harvard University, makes a significant point: that the work of writers is not rewarded monetarily—not as it should be, anyway, especially considering the overall contribution to society freelance writers make.

However, don't overlook the other key point Friedan makes: that the ultimate payoff to dedicated writers who have something important to say comes less in the form of money (nice as that always is to receive) and more in the writer's sense of self-esteem and shared conviction.

I like, too, what Walter S. Campbell had to say on the subject in *Writing: Advice and Devices* (Doubleday, 1958):

"It seems incredible that anyone capable of writing should refuse to do it, the rewards of the writer are so many and so great.

"To begin with, prestige. As Dr. Samuel Johnson declared, 'The chief glory of every people arises from its authors.'

"Yet the writer's greatest reward is not fame (a somewhat doubtful advantage), or money (always a by-product in the arts), but rather the great satisfaction of trying to contribute something of value, of sharing experience, the joy of expressing one's self and having one's work appreciated."

Most professionals will tell you substantially the same thing.

If a painful payment-rate structure (which hasn't changed much since gasoline was 30 cents a gallon and a new car cost $3,500) is one snake for writers to contend with, another is their failure to understand that writing is a business, a trade with more commercial mechanics than mystique.

Many ASJA members freelance full-time, but as you'll discover in Part II, most started out part-time. Writers generally agree that although finding the time to work on your own projects can be a challenge when you're holding down a full-time job, it's definitely easier to concentrate when you aren't worried about where your next meal is coming from. Writing in any form—full-time profession or leisurely avocation—is a structured, hard-nosed business, and writers, if they're to succeed, must consider their manuscripts as merchandise. To sell merchandise you need to understand marketing techniques. You must keep up-to-date on current publishing (both book and magazine) needs and prices—as well as editorial staff changes. You must follow industry trends, know the different kinds of periodicals and journals, and always keep the reader's interests and your abilities (specialties) in focus.

No matter how well you write, freelancing is still a business involving people, ideas, research, interviews, travel, organizing, time, filing, taxes, negotiation, accounting, contracts, fees, libel suits and, yes, *writing*.

The serious writer quickly learns this and understands that freelancing is a commercial craft calling for sensible business strategies and practices. But most novices usually work their way through the maze to the markets by trial and error. Because of inexperience—and not a few misconceptions—they need reputable counsel and guidance.

In the remainder of this chapter—indeed, the rest of this book— you'll learn some basics about the mysterious things a writer is expected to do. And equally important, you'll discover what a writer is *not* supposed to do.

Beware of "They"(Along the Way)

"They" include the baker, the music maker, and the next-door neighbor. *Especially* the next-door neighbor. "They" all went to the same nonexistent journalism school, or worked on their high school paper, or got an A in composition in seventh grade, and formed an opinion on every writing and publishing matter that exists. And if the matter doesn't exist "they" have an opinion anyway.

The amount of misinformation "they" manage to masquerade under the cloak of truth is boggling. Professional freelance writers, editors, publishers, and agents have a difficult time competing with the "theys." Most of you have, I'm sure, heard some of their myths and misconceptions: "If you don't live in Manhattan, forget about ever selling to the major magazines." "When you submit your book manuscript to a publishing house, always glue a couple of pages together. That way, see, if the two pages come back unseparated, you know nobody even looked at your book!" "Take your article to the magazine's office yourself and make certain you personally hand it to the editor-in-chief. Otherwise your idea's gonna get stolen, for sure!" "Don't bother with those writing workshops or conferences. They're all ripoffs."

That's just a smattering of the advice so willingly dispensed by the "theys." I can only beseech "them" to stop peddling their old wives' tales and old boys' notions and private prejudices about complex processes they don't understand. Fortunately, *they* are their own worst enemies and will trip over their own misguided views.

KEEPING BANKRUPTCY AT BAY

How do people usually get started as freelance writers? Not very shrewdly or efficiently; most fledgling freelancers are like so many Don Quixotes foolishly charging windmills.

Here's some advice to help you avoid windmill tilting. It doesn't concern writing as such, but it's crucial to success. I'm talking about start-up costs, such as writer's materials and equipment. Here's what Kay Cassill says about them in *The Complete Handbook for Freelance Writers* (Writer's Digest Books, 1981):

"I know of no other business in the world where the first question prior to venturing into the blizzard of competition—'what will it cost?'—isn't primary. So many writers start out with just the shirts on their backs to keep them warm, it's a wonder we don't find more frozen bodies along the wayside. We all know about the big successes in this profession because the headlines are dazzling when they happen. What those banners don't report so often is how the ones who didn't make it are managing to survive, if indeed they are.

"To avoid calamity, make a checklist of your probable start-up costs for your first two years as a freelancer. Begin with the following list and add to it any special expenses, such as child care, that you know you can expect.

proper stationery and business cards	business gifts
professional tools and equipment	taxes
	insurance
local transportation	personal library and subscriptions
records and bookkeeping	office and equipment rental
part-time help	photocopying costs
postage and shipping	telephone and answering machine
dues for professional organizations	office furnishings
educational seminars and meetings	special clothing if necessary
	promotion publicity
travel and entertainment expenses	legal costs
	miscellaneous

"In your first months," says Cassill, "you won't need to fork over cash for everything listed. That would be foolhardy. Ask yourself what you absolutely must have to start out. Be relatively hard-nosed about your answers, since you will be competing with freelancers already out there with steady incomes and more or less balanced budgets. You should appear as professional as possible in your start-up with the minimum of the essentials you'll be able to afford.

"You need a place to work. You need a desk, a chair, a functioning typewriter, paper and supplies, and good-looking business stationery. You should start with a simple but expandable bookkeeping method. You'll discover you need some sort of files. Again, if you arrange to keep track of your papers properly at the outset, you'll reap many benefits later. So make sure the method you choose is easily expandable. When you've toted up the minimum costs for these (after some telephoning around town for price estimates on second-hand furnishings and office equipment rental costs), round out the figures a bit, add ten dollars a month to each category for good measure, and multiply by six months. Now you have a figure to measure by. If your savings or other available monies match your six-months' figures, you're in pretty good shape to start off. Not that you won't have to hustle to replenish some of that dough within those six months of writing and marketing—you will. But with such a cautious start, you'll have far less to worry about.

"When considering what you have in reserve, it's not prudent to forget your outstanding debts. They'll be eating away at your budget if you do.

"Take your calculations and ask a friendly bookkeeper, businessperson, or accountant whether the picture seems realistic. Or speak to someone at the Small Business Administration. Such people may give advice that sounds all too stern, but remember, they're used to hearing about new business start-ups and subsequent failures. They may know very little about the freelance business, however, so also try to talk to someone closer to your field—an editor or reporter for the local paper who moonlights as a freelancer, for example—about your planned necessary expenses.

"If you have no penchant for keeping accounts, be particularly resourceful at the outset. Check your list again for accuracy of your estimates. This practice with figures—receipts and expenditures and hidden costs—will prepare you to better analyze every phase of your business, now and later on. And you'll be much happier at tax time when you discover you've successfully wrestled the financial tiger into line.

"Next, prepare a tentative budget for each month, using your estimated figures. Allot time in a regular schedule for review and updating. You may find you have to examine figures more often at the beginning, but as in most anything, practice, happily, leads to perfection.

"Obviously, there are a number of qualifications necessary to working successfully on your own, aside from the ability to write, not the least of which is the ability to deal with money, managing your daily work, and marketing. Even though these three elements might seem alien to the creative spirit, they are often the ones that spell the difference between success and failure in the independent life of freelancing."

Freelancer, Know Thyself

How do you really know if writing is the life for you? Nora Sayre says you can discover whether you're a natural freelancer by spending five minutes alone with your temperament. "The most suitable freelance writers are eccentrics," says Sayre. "Loners and renegades, they like to travel, like their own company and the discovery that life can change radically within a week. They are nourished by sudden surprises, but are apt to be fiends for privacy. (For them, the friendly inter-office visit is an outrageous interruption, as is the coffee break. The telephone is not their instrument for affectionate intercourse: 'I just rang up to say hello' will make them furious.) The freelancer simply doesn't like organizations, and the safety they provide adds up to feet-in-cement for her (and him). The unfettered life is simply a necessity—no less, no more."

Whether or not you agree with Sayre, many of us do choose to freelance because we want to be free of corporate constraints, of management by fourth-quarter numbers and computer printouts. That, in fact, is what happened in my case. I'd done a lengthy stint as editor of a company business magazine. Then came a day when I got tired of the rat race. I found it increasingly hard to understand why the company's sour cream always seemed to rise to the top, why lifelong friends would slit each other's throats for a nodding smile from the boss, or why I should have to tolerate being forever locked into what was then called the "gray-flannel syndrome."

Yet we all soon learn, if we want to stick around as freelancers, that the business of writing, like any other, has its own restrictions, its own constraints. And, as Kay Cassill says, "To keep them from becoming shackles, you'll have to work very, very hard. Start out right. Begin by learning all you can about the perils and pitfalls before you take the big leap."

According to the Small Business Administration, "The single biggest reason for failure is lack of experience in a chosen field. People are attracted to a business for a variety of reasons—almost always without the necessary understanding of the business side." There it is again, writers—the need to focus on such dull, rational matters as filing systems and bookkeeping, not to mention the nagging necessity of a comfortable cash flow.

Here, as set forth in Kay Cassill's no-nonsense book, are some hard but necessary questions you must put to yourself (or to yourself and your partner if you have one) before you quit your job and step out on your own—unless, of course, you have married big money. Do you:

- try to make limited capital stretch too far?
- handle creditors too tolerantly?
- let material get backlogged, not getting it to its market in a timely fashion?
- concentrate on markets that pay too little?
- lack training and preparation for the particular areas of freelancing you want to enter?
- have an inadequate understanding of the markets available to you?
- wait too long to update your equipment, bottlenecking your productivity?
- lack financial savvy, lack knowledge of sources of available funds or how to use them to the best advantage?
- have little or no record-keeping skill, little familiarity with accounting methods?
- get so involved in the pressure of day-to-day details you never take time out to analyze the situation?
- fail to seek help when you need it?
- become frustrated by changing, competitive conditions—unable to evaluate or cope with them?
- lack understanding of the basics of business management?

"To succeed in today's competitive world of communications, a freelance writer must wear a number of hats: creator, editor, interviewer, researcher, secretary, salesperson, public relations executive, bookkeeper, cost accountant, bill collector, general manager, and sometimes designer, promoter, and publisher as well. With such a list of responsibilities (and I'm certain to have left out a few), there is little room for the lackadaisical or nonprofessional attitude. Unlike many businesses, freelance writing naturally attracts creative people who, often proudly, claim they 'have no head for business.' Freelancing success, however, is based on handling business details in a businesslike fashion."

What Cassill says may make the road to freelance success seem truly forbidding. But you must recognize the inescapable business facts of life: the stork isn't going to bring you your rent or mortgage money, and you won't find a new typewriter under a cabbage leaf. Once you face the facts and deal with them sensibly, however, you'll find they aren't half bad.

The Bottom Line

While your creative spirit would wish it otherwise, publishing is a tooth-and-nails business. Publishers (of magazines and books alike) and their stockholders are necessarily interested in short-run profits. They must turn a dollar—the sooner the better.

Reduced to its simplest terms, the publisher's goal is the same as yours: to do as much business as possible while holding operating costs to a minimum. That's why editors you deal with will try to buy your product—articles, books, photographs—for as little money as possible. This doesn't make the editor an ogre, necessarily. We all deal with editors who are ex-freelancers themselves, who are sympathetic to the realities of the writer's life, however, there's not much you can do about the rates their publishers pay. But there are a few exceptions: you can bargain, you can ask for expenses where they're not normally paid, you can insist on kill fee protection (of at least 50 percent), you can ask for more money if the editor requests a *second* rewrite, or you can let your agent handle it.

If you question this withering situation, just do a little research into the fees paid by magazines or advances given by book publishers (a handful of "blockbusters" to the contrary notwithstanding) ten, even fifteen years ago. Then compare those figures with what the same houses are paying today. Most publications and publishers not only haven't increased their fees or advances to freelance writers but, in some instances, are actually paying *less*. A number of magazines that pay about the same rates as a decade ago now pay writers upon publication instead of upon acceptance—and that's no way to have to work.

It's true that publishers are victims of inflation, like everyone else. Everything from staff salaries to postage rates has risen continually. It's also true that the advertising rates of these magazines have skyrocketed, and consumers now pay almost double what they did a decade ago for the same publications, whereas editorial budgets (at least the purchasing portion of those budgets) have remained pretty much the same.

Why this heartless state of monetary affairs for freelancers? How can publishers get away with such Scrooge-like tactics?

Well, it's as basic as it is sad: the book and magazine marketplace, like any other market, is governed by the law of supply and demand. With an estimated half-million people in the United States freelancing either part- or full-time as writers today, and thousands more who want to be writers, supply is outstripping demand. In short, it's a buyer's market.

There are many New York book publishers that receive from 5,000 to 10,000 *unsolicited* manuscripts a year, out of which they may publish two or three. The average big-circulation magazine receives about 200 to 250 manuscripts each week. For every freelance writer who is selling manuscripts regularly, scores of others are trying desperately to get one piece accepted and paid for. This keeps prices low; and too often, if the writer doth protest too much, there's the implied threat, "If you can't do the article for our rates, we've got a wagonload of writers waiting who can—and will!" In some cases this has resulted in a sort of literary Gresham's law, with the bad manuscripts driving out the good. There's no law, however, preventing any writer from moving on to more productive pastures.

For aspiring writers, or even for most established writers, the odds of selling either magazine articles or books might seem all but impossible. But that's not necessarily so. Again, Kay Cassill explains: "For the thoroughly competent writer, the chances of selling are far greater. Perhaps only 20 of those 200 manuscripts will be good enough for an editor to take the time to read. Bear in mind that the flood of material that washes over editors' desks in publishing houses and magazine offices, in newspaper and syndicate offices, in television and movie producers' studios, consists mostly of badly written material. Well-conceived, well-written, and well-targeted material is scarce. Currently marketable material is even less available. The trend-setting story or article series is an absolute rarity."

Cassill adds: "Keep the following thought uppermost in your mind as you approach each new and potentially successful day: the many benefits of the freelance life and riches from your writing efforts, like the gold that lies under the mountains, come to those with the knowledge and ability to dig in the right places, the proper tools, and the overriding ambition to find it despite the often back-breaking, ego-mangling work that's required."

CRAFTSMANSHIP

If you would write what sells—and sell what you write—you must constantly develop your writing ability. It may be, as Mark Twain once remarked, that anyone can write because all the words are in the dictionary. However, crafting words is more complicated than just setting them down in rows upon paper. Hal Borland says, in *How to Write and Sell Nonfiction* (Greenwood Press Publishers, 1973), "Craft represents the skill with which tools [e.g., words, grammar, sentence, the paragraph] are used to shape and fashion raw materials into something useful and valuable."

All serious writers have studied their craft, and most of them continue their study throughout their lifetimes. Just as someone who practices medicine without going to medical school is a quack, so a writer who hasn't intensively studied and practiced writing is a hack. Another word for a writer who thinks he was "born with the gift" and needs no practice is an *amateur*.

Washington columnist-author Colman McCarthy said in *Inner Companions* (Acropolis, 1978): "Writing is like walking blindfolded: instinct will carry you far, but not always where you want to go. Before long, the instinct-guided writer, like the blinded walker, bumps into things."

One of the most organized and self-disciplined writers I've ever known is humorist Max Shulman, creator of *Dobie Gillis* and more recently the TV series *House Calls*. In an interview for *Writer's Digest* several years ago, Shulman told me: "Like all professionals, writers must know how to use the tools they're working with, how to spell without looking up most of the words, what the words mean, and how sentences and paragraphs become what they are. The more you work at the craft of writing—and this is true of all writing, fiction or nonfiction—the more skilled you become in the use of words and the better able you are to express yourself. To put it simply: you become a writer by *writing*. You practice it constantly. I know of no other way."

Can Writing Be Taught?

Can good writing be taught? And if so, where does the student go for instruction? Are writing courses the answer, considering the cost? What's the real value of correspondence courses, seminars, workshops, and adult education classes? Aren't most writing teachers or instructors failed writers?

Valid questions. Significant questions. I think the answers depend on what kind of writing you're interested in doing. Do you want to follow in Thomas Wolfe's or Tom Wolfe's footsteps? Are your wants and needs those of the great novelist or the celebrated practitioner of the New Journalism? Jefferson D. Bates gives some sound advice in his book, *Writing With Precision* (Acropolis Books Ltd., 1981):

"Admired literary figures such as James Joyce, Ernest Hemingway, and John Steinbeck did not learn to write the way they did by listening to learned professors or participating in classroom discussions. Their kind of writing (for simplicity, let's call it 'creative' writing) does not come out of academic exercises or textbooks on composition or rhetoric."

Bates, who has been teaching seminars in effective writing throughout the country for many years, adds: "But if you are talking about writing as a craft rather than writing as an art, that's another story. If you are concerned with what we might describe as 'practical' or 'useful' writing—writing that is clear, precise, well organized, easy to read and understand—the answer to your question is Yes."

Certainly the skills and techniques of good nonfiction writing can be taught (and learned). Any good course—whether by correspondence or in a classroom or workshop—can expose the beginning nonfiction writer to rules, practices, habits, styles, and ideas. The rest, of course, depends upon you. Writing what will sell in today's highly specialized, money-tight marketplace is hard, exacting labor.

Hayes B. Jacobs, veteran columnist for *Writer's Digest* and head of the largest college writing program in the country, the Writing Workshops program at the New School in New York, offers the following tips for those of you considering classroom instruction—at your nearest college or university, or at your local "Y" or community center.

"Do some *investigating*, wherever you go; don't just fall under the spell of a seductive ad or catalog course description. If a catalog supplies no biographical data on instructors (and most don't, beyond listing degrees, which can mean a lot, or nothing much), inquire of the department chairman or counseling office. Check biographical and other reference works (such as *Readers' Guide, Contemporary Authors,* and *Who's Who)* in the library. Consult any editors you may know, and any professional writers. Try to read some of the instructors' published work.

"In searching for a teacher, look for a pro, an active writer, editor, or agent, who will not only guide your writing but also help you learn to publish. 'Publication,' said J.D. Salinger, 'is the function usually omitted in writing courses.'

"Recognize that good writing is an art, and that in art, tastes differ. No teacher's views are The Last Word.

"Speak up in class! Don't sit, nodding assent. Don't be afraid to challenge any teacher's opinions, and don't be intimidated by classmates' statements regarding your writing.

"Write regularly. No teacher can help you without seeing what you can do. Get work in early in the term, so your problems will show up in time for the teacher to help you.

"Don't try to turn your teacher into a collaborator by asking for 'progress' reports on fragments. Submit only completed manuscripts.

"Do the required or suggested reading. Most teachers structure courses with strong emphasis on outside reading.

"Don't expect any writing course to transform you quickly into a professional writer. (Ever heard a violinist after his or her first twelve lessons?)

"The object of any course should be to teach you to do without a course; prepare, right from the start, for graduation; learn to make it on your own.

"While enrolled in a course, don't show your work to friends matching their views with the teacher's; the confusion will overwhelm you.

"Never, never take two writing courses simultaneously. Nobody can do enough work to do justice to more than one course at a time.

"You are entitled, in any course, to *full criticism*—not quickly written labels: 'Excellent,' 'Weak,' 'Pretty good.' "

This advice comes from Jacobs' article "So You're Going to Take a Writing Course," *(Writer's Digest,* May 1981). Jacobs stresses reading—and reading lists passed out as part of classroom work. "I ask students to read books on style, craft, technique; I look for books that will tell them about the business aspects of publishing; they read (I hope) the memoirs of writers, editors, publishers; they read the writers' magazines, and *Writer's Market;* they read the quality periodicals, and good newspapers . . ."

As David Lambuth notes in *The Golden Book of Writing* (Viking Press, 1964), "After all, good writing is like good social usage. It is learned by constant association with those who practice it, and it must be instinctive and unselfconscious before it is of the slightest value. That is why you can learn how to write well only by reading well. Therefore, read . . . read . . . read . . . and still read."

The Truth About Workshops

What about the myriad seminars, workshops, and conferences held each year for writers? Are you going to learn anything? Are these writer gatherings worth the expense and the time spent away from your typewriter (or word processor)? Or are they simply a means for literary hucksters to make money, while paying for vacations *al fresco,* by preying on the hopes and dreams of would-be writers?

Many professional writers do feel seminars are a waste of money and valuable writing time. One writer told me, "Writing conferences are like watches—the worst is better than none, and the best cannot be expected to run quite true."

I disagree. Good workshops and conferences invite working editors, agents, and professional writers to lecture, counsel, and serve on panels and in craft sessions, such as the annual writers' conferences held by the American Society of Journalists and Authors and by Women in Communications. (See the May issue of *Writer's Digest* for an annual listing of conferences.)

ASJA member and author Curtis Casewit, who teaches a writing course at the University of Colorado in Boulder, says in *Freelance Writing: Advice From the Pros* (Collier Books, 1974):

"An experienced pro can also function well as a teacher at your elbow. It is true that he cannot write the articles or books *for* you. But he can give the beginner an overview. He can coax you into better craftsmanship, explain some of the rules, or point out important flaws in your work. . ."

And that's not all. Casewit adds, "An experienced professional may come up with fresh, constructive ideas. He may even suggest that you change directions. To illustrate:

"John Malo, an Illinois high school principal, had been receiving rejection slips for years. He was so frustrated that he almost gave up. His teenage sports stories just wouldn't sell. The novel was not his cup of tea, either. Then he attended a summer seminar for budding writers. The instructor had a long talk with Malo, who was an expert canoeist. Almost at once he discovered the man's real interests. Malo had a swath of time each summer. He was interested in outdoor activities, especially canoeing. So the ex-principal was advised to switch to nonfiction. As a result, Malo garnered a contract to write a book about canoeing; it sold eventually to two book clubs, and was reprinted in paperback. Within two years, Malo sold many thousands of copies. All thanks to a summer writers' seminar." [Editor's note: Malo has a piece in Part II of this book.]

Many conferences focus on special fields of writing. The Mystery Writers of America, for example, conduct periodic workshops for persons interested in writing detective and suspense short stories and novels. Likewise, the annual ASJA conference is primarily (though not entirely) for those who want to write nonfiction—both magazine articles and books.

At other conferences, some dedicated to writing for religious publications, others to juvenile or young adult books, and still others specializing in business writing, you meet experts working exclusively in a particular field. Your choices are varied and endless: conferences for black writers, photojournalism, travel, poetry, science fiction—even a writing workshop for people over fifty-seven (the Council on Aging, Ligon House, University of Kentucky at Lexington 40506). And, if it's your bent, you can "Write Yourself Into American Literature" at Emerson College in Boston, where programs in professional writing and publishing are offered.

While the quality of conferences and workshops may vary, there's one thing you can count on: you'll at least get rid of some of the loneliness that plagues writers. You'll be comparing problems and disappointments with fellow writers who share your concerns, interests, and ambitions. And that can be therapeutic, if nothing else. It's a good way to blow off steam—you have a captive audience (but don't become a boor by inflicting yourself upon anyone who'll listen).

A final word on the subject of seminars, conferences, workshops, and writing courses: if you're going to get your money's worth, get involved in the proceedings. After all, teachers and instructors function best when students show interest, enthusiasm, and attentiveness. But don't accept everything you hear as gospel, a common failing of eager beginners. As Hayes Jacobs says, "Teacher knows! Sometimes teacher doesn't."

Learning by Mail

We've all seen the ads in popular and writers' magazines for writers' correspondence schools. But how good is the instruction provided by such schools and teachers? Most writing authorities seem to feel that it isn't too bad. The consensus is, like most things, that you get what you pay for. The Writer's Digest School (WDS), which is directed by successful editor-author Kirk Polking, charges from $125 up to several hundred dollars (this includes materials, tuition, and registration fee). The WDS has sound, sensible courses in three categories: articles, short stories, and effective writing. The WDS gives the student individual attention and insists on a staff of competent writers as instructors. All are practicing professionals in the subject they teach. The School also offers updated selling advice and marketing information.

Some correspondence schools advertise aptitude tests; they claim such tests weed out aspirants who aren't qualified for enrollment. Most professional freelancers scoff at these tests—and these claims. A New York agent-friend of mine dismisses them as "a sales hype to get money out of bored widows and retired colonels." She believes that the schools "will never be able to devise a test that can satisfactorily determine a person's aptitude for writing anything more than a letter home."

This seems a little shortsighted. The tests I've seen currently being used by such schools can give a general idea of writing aptitude *if the evaluation is honest.* Whether or not this is always the case—whether the schools actually use them to screen out incompetents—I can't say.

Writing Clubs—
Are They Worth It?

Students and other emerging writers will usually find kindred spirits in a local or regional writers' club. Many of these groups are made up of other struggling novices, most of them without a sale as yet. Some, on the other hand, accept only members who have been published. Such organizations often specialize; there are groups for poets, for garden writers, or for women. But most clubs are open to anyone interested in writing.

Skeptics say that writing groups or clubs are a classic example of the blind leading the blind. In some instances I'm sure this is true. Still, who's to say that newcomers to the writing business can't learn together—even, as Curtis Casewit says, "by making mistakes and jointly correcting them."

After all, Casewit contends, among the ranks of these local clubs there might well be a few individuals who've studied writing in college or worked on a regional magazine or local newspaper—writers who have a talent for teaching others. No one should discourage the writer who is serious, who is willing to work long and hard to get ahead, and who needs the support such a group affords.

When you've been at the business for a time and earned your stripes, you'll want to join one or more professional writers' organizations. Why, if you're already fairly successful? Again, listen to ASJA's Casewit: "All such organizations will supply you with a useful press card, an interesting list of people you can respect and with whom you may become friends, and a periodic newsletter containing inside information. Some organizations appeal to specialists like outdoor writers, Christian writers, western writers, and dramatists. If you have written a book, you're eligible to join the Authors Guild. The Guild has campaigned for better copyright laws, better book contracts, and other items affecting writers, and has done much to influence legislators."

There are other topflight professional writers' organizations for both part- and full-time freelancers. Many have chapters throughout the country. And most have annual or even monthly meetings and conduct periodic workshops for members. Their newsletters alone are often worth the annual dues fee. These organizations have been—and remain—one of the better ways for beginners and seasoned pros to meet, compare notes, and exchange ideas and information about the business in their special interest areas. Key writers' organizations are listed in the Additional Resources section following each chapter in Part II.

Ruth Winter, past president of ASJA, answers the writers' club question this way: "You learn from one another's failures and successes and mutually set new goals. In such groups, it's possible to be understood and encouraged as only one freelance writer can understand and encourage another.

"This all adds up to a camaraderie that reinforces our inner conviction that we would rather be freelance writers than anything else in the world—despite the impracticality of our profession on a day-to-day basis, despite its indigenous drawbacks, hazards, and downright frustrations."

YOU ARE WHAT YOU READ

Before you can be a selling freelancer you must be an effective reader. Learn, as you read, to analyze and make notes on what interests you. Nothing is more vital to your writing career than reading; that goes for seasoned professionals as well as beginners.

Any aspiring writer will be wise to regard every article, every book, as a potential guideline, not merely a means of entertainment. Serious writers soon find themselves reading critically, watching for methods, techniques, ideas, structure, styles, and other devices. Through reading and analysis, writers learn how best to improve their own work. They spot new and different ways to handle leads, sentences, paragraphs, words, dialogue, point of view, conclusions—even errors to avoid making themselves.

In addition, through reading, you learn what subjects are being published by magazine and book editors, which ideas sell. "To know what to write," says ASJA member Shirley Biagi in *How To Write and Sell Magazine Articles* (Prentice-Hall, 1981), "you must know what sells. This sounds too simple, but the most common mistake beginning freelancers make is that they decide to write without understanding the market."

When you read magazine pieces you'll want to study the mechanics of writing, and then do a market analysis of the magazine itself. How to do a marketing analysis will be discussed in detail in Chapter 4, but for now remember that only after you know and understand what magazines are publishing (and for what audience) can you start sensibly developing ideas for your own articles.

Yet another reason writers are among the most prolific and voracious of readers is that it's still the best way I know to cultivate and foster good ideas. Whether you write articles or books, fiction or nonfiction, the daily newspaper is probably your best source of ideas. In its pages and columns you'll find information—the latest word—about topics and subjects from every locale imaginable. Your newspaper records the struggles of people throughout the world and from every walk of life—all yours for the reading. There's nothing like a good metropolitan newspaper for teaching a writer how other people live and what they think. Kenneth Grahame, author of *The Wind in the Willows*, once said a few words that might well be framed above every writer's desk: "The most priceless possession of the human race is the wonder of the world."

One *caveat:* don't read another writer's work merely to copy it. Instead, learn from other writers in order to adapt your own style and method. When you find a passage that strikes your fancy, study it. Determine how the writer did what you haven't been able to do with a similar idea. Technical competence—as well as as hackneyed writing—can be studied to benefit you in future work.

If you are to be a selling writer, you must learn to read the professionals and inventory their arsenal of technical devices and methods. In *Writing: Advice and Device*, Oklahoma University's Walter S. Campbell says, "There is no secret about the craft of writing. All its magical effects are achieved with words on paper. And so every device a writer ever used lies there under your nose plainly set down in black and white."

FREELANCERS ARE BORN FREE

No introduction to freelance writing would be complete without a few words from Maurice Zolotow, the ASJA's first president when it was formed in 1948 as the Society of Magazine Writers. One of the nation's premier freelance writers, Zolotow specializes in articles and books about the celebrities and personalities of the entertainment world. He lives and works in Hollywood and is a contributing editor for *Los Angeles* magazine. Says Zolotow:

"The freelancer's life is often hard and insecure. And sometimes the money isn't there and then sometimes there is too much of it all at once and it goes to your head. But it is the best life I have ever had and I would not have lived any other. The elation, the sense of liberty is still as true for me today as forty-one years ago.

"There is the same sweet satisfaction in the research, the writing, the moment of acceptance, and the joyous sequence of events until publication.

"The most aggravating things about the life of freelancing are the financial uncertainty and the loneliness. Those of us who started meeting in Phil Gustafson's apartment in the London Terrace Flats (in New York City) that spring of 1948 thought we could overcome the isolation by meeting, gossiping, and exchanging market news. Sometimes we had nothing to exchange but our company. Other times it was sad and bitter tales. Editors who deceived us. Publishers who paid only on publication. Ill treatment of one sort or another. Recently I spoke with one of those old companions and learned that collecting money from one of those old villains is still a problem.

"Some of those old-time magazines died, some were revived, and new ones came along. Yet the problems and pleasures of freelance writing have remained fundamentally the same. But what has happened is that through the growing membership of our Society, through our newsletter, and through our responsible leaders, we have given our profession some sense of stability and helped improve writer-editor relations. Murray Teigh Bloom, the late Mort Weisinger, Norman Lobsenz, Jack Pollack, among many others, gave so much of their time and energy to fight the battle for all of us, to set standards of pay and responsibility on both sides.

"Sometimes I sit at the meetings of the Southern California chapter with some of the members as obscure as we were a couple of decades ago, and I hear complaints about low-paying markets, payment only on publication or six months later. About freelancers who have to take part-time jobs in teaching, public relations, or advertising just to hang on. Yet I am quietly grateful that even through some very hard years I have been able to hold on to all the freedom to which I'm entitled. I also know that among these obscure young women and young men, struggling to get their emotions down on paper, are going to be future movers and shakers of the world.

"We, the freelancers, represent a very important phase of publishing. Always have. Always will. Magazines will and should staff their offices. Book publishers will and must try to tell writers what to write and how to write. It is inevitable that computer scientists and efficiency experts will try to reduce the trade to predictable outcomes. But we are unpredictable. Because we are free. Nobody could have predicted the degree of fame that would come to Fielding's *Guide to Europe*, Friedan's *The Feminine Mystique*, Packard's *The Hidden Persuaders*, or Toffler's *Future Shock*." [Editor's note: All of these writers are ASJA members.]

Clearly, then, to produce writing that sells, to enjoy the benefits and satisfactions of a steady career while suffering the slings and arrows, you must have the desire to write every single day and the determination to stick with it. I sold my first feature article in college; it was six years later that my next piece was purchased by a commercial magazine editor.

The aforementioned Dr. Walter Campbell, whose courses in professional writing at the University of Oklahoma were considered among the country's best, held that if you wish to write well, two things are required of you:

"First, that you learn to see and understand the problems every writer must solve, and second, that you learn how the best masters have solved such problems."

SYLLABUS FOR SURVIVAL

To the professor's qualifications I would add a third requirement; that you read the following "Syllabus for Survival" by Murray Teigh

Bloom—another ex-president of ASJA—who has sold as many major magazine articles and books as any other living nonfiction writer. Bloom's ten-point program for developing a professional attitude toward your career will keep you on track and out of the cracker factory.

"1. Paranoia is to the freelancer what narcissism is to the actor—a territorial tag-along. There *are* crooked publishers out there. And larcenous editors. And plagiarists, and so on. But if you try to be bushytail quivering alert all the time, you'll paralyze your writing functions. The freelancer's secret radar is trained instinct. If you've survived three years, your instincts on an editor or a new publication should be trustworthy. You don't have to be the first kid on the block to sell a hot new mag. Some writers think the only way to make it in this business is to seek out and be in on every *new* magazine. Their whole approach (and income) is selling to start-up publications.

"2. There are agents who will lend you money, drink with you, socialize, and even become your second-best friend. But if you *need* an agent for any of these functions, you're in trouble. The agent's *only* real job is to get you more money with less hassle than you could on your own.

"3. Most book projects will take longer and give you more headaches. But books can be a bountiful joy. Just make sure you're getting enough up front.

"4. Sure, you might be making more money than the editor you write for. But why mention it, let alone joke about it?

"5. During the couplings, no one wants to ask: 'Who will pay for the possible abortion?' And few of us want to ask what happens if the piece doesn't work out. But the professional freelancer knows there are worse things than asking. *Not* asking.

"6. How dependable is a stranger's written promise to pay you $10,000 in two years—when you finish the book? If a book publisher or magazine accounts for more than a third of your income, you ought to know as much about it—finances, power structure, prospects—as your bank would know about you if it agreed to lend you a few thousand without collateral.

"7. The freelancer is always at risk in relations with editors. But the writer who submits material on a pay-on-publication basis is not only revealing insecurity but paying a premium to earn an editor's contempt.

"8. The necessary art of freelance survival is never mastered, only practiced. Five-year hash marks don't ensure fifteen, let alone twenty. Drink and marital misery are big spoilers, but the worst is the writer's frequent lack of sense about money.

"9. The writer who thinks ten $100 pieces are the same as a $1000 piece can't add. Worse, this helps multiply editors who divide writers with contemptuous monetary terms.

"10. Writers sometimes badmouth each other because the loneliness and fears can foster despair and envy. You don't have to love or admire every fellow writer. Just remember that together we form a powerful amalgam, a miracle bonding that makes us better writers, reinforces our confidence, and deters our enemies."

Not for nothing has Murray Teigh Bloom for years chaired ASJA's important Editor-Writer Relations Committee. His efforts often bring order out of the chaos left by agreements gone awry, tardy payments by editors, broken contracts, and generally shabby treatment of freelance writers by certain wheeler-dealer publishing types.

By now you must see that the publishing industry is as much business as it is writing. But write you must. Someone once remarked that he didn't especially like to write—rather, he enjoyed having written. A lot of us feel that way some mornings when the daily 1,000 to 1,500 words loom like a James Clavell novel.

It was Pliny the Elder who said, "Cobbler, stick to your last," or words to that effect. Anyway, it's good advice for freelancers. Author and freelance writer Peter Benchley did just that, even after sending the *New Yorker* something between fifty and one hundred stories before they bought one. Says Benchley: "You have to keep writing, keep submitting, and keep *praying* to the god of whimsy that some editor will respond favorably." By persisting despite a flood of rejections, Peter Benchley finally hit the commercial jackpot with *Jaws, The Deep,* and *The Island*.

So read on; we have a troupe of tightrope artists who've long enjoyed the challenge of this craft. They'll tell you how to perform even after a slip or a fall, how you can get published—without perishing. I commend to you the first law of motion—a body in motion tends to remain in motion. Therefore, "Get started!"

Chapter Two

THE FIRST STEP— RESEARCH

Writers who don't learn the essentials, the ABCs, of good writing will not be capable of producing salable work. What we mean by the ABCs are those fundamentals that Marvin Weisbord, editor of *A Treasury of Tips For Writers* (Writer's Digest Books, 1965), calls "the scaffolding"— the basics that spell the difference between success and failure in this business. This doesn't mean you must have one eye cocked toward a textbook, or half your brain always trying to remember Rule 33. Good writers cannot write by rule—in fact, the skilled professional soon learns that most rules are made to be broken. But the pro also knows you only break rules sensibly when you understand their reason for being.

"Easy writing," Hemingway once said, "makes hard reading." The point is worth remembering. Professionals have practical work plans and techniques that you will find not only helpful but necessary to writing an easy-to-read article or book (or business letter). That, to me, is why writing nonfiction is a craft, not an art. Like Hal Borland, I believe that "if there is an art to writing, it is the art of thinking." But before you can communicate the results of thinking you must learn how to communicate. When you try to practice the craft without making use of the scaffolding, you may end up with an amorphous mess.

IN THE BEGINNING—THE IDEA

One plus about writing articles is that ideas are all around you. After you've been writing for a few months you'll discover there are more ideas than you have time for—the trick is one of selection. You need to find the right ideas for *you*, ideas you are comfortable with, ideas that literally beg to be written. At first, you may have difficulty deciding which are best for you, but soon you'll develop a "sixth sense" for those you'd enjoy working on.

Sally Wendkos Olds wrote to 267 fellow ASJA members asking about their first sales and the sources of their ideas. Following is an excerpt from her article "First Magazine Sales," which appeared in *The Writer*. "I felt that some knowledge about their first plunges into the sometimes refreshing, sometimes icy waters of freelance writing could prove useful to the new writer of today. From the 101 replies I received (the others must have been too busy meeting deadlines), some valuable points emerged.

"In the beginning is the Idea. Despite one respondent's wry observation that 'you can always write a better article unhampered by knowledge,' the greatest single source of ideas for first articles was some personal experience of the writer. Forty-six of the 101 attributed the idea for their first article to something they had done as a hobby, as a volunteer, in the home, or on the job.

"One writer was a 'stage mother,' who modeled her pet cat for TV commercials; she sold an article about modeling pets to *TV Guide*. An 'airplane bug' wrote about a squadron of the Civil Air Patrol. A PTA mother wrote an article for the local Sunday supplement about a gardening project at her child's school. A bridge player sold his first article to a bridge magazine, developed a daily newspaper column about bridge, and eventually cracked the slick magazine market with pieces about—guess what—bridge. 'Once having demonstrated that I could write,' he says, 'I was able to branch out into general articles on a wide range of topics.'

"A young woman who took her mother on a canoe-and-camping trip recalls, 'My mother's old-lady way of coping with the wilderness amused me, so I wrote a story about it.' The story appeared in a women's magazine.

"Some new writers used information gleaned through their daily work. An engineer on a WPA job sold an article on his project to the *New Republic;* an advertising copywriter wrote an article for an advertising publication about working harmoniously with art directors; a college student who was working high on the catwalks of the San Francisco Bay Bridge sold his experiences to *Esquire;* and several homemakers turned child care, decorating, and cooking experiences into full-fledged articles. Some of the many personal experiences that ended up as articles included amusing a child with water play, comforting one who has awakened with a nightmare, constructing an unusual record cabinet, building a six-story mouse house, living in a women's hotel in New York, fishing in Canada, and eating mushrooms in France.

"Sometimes interesting people whose lives had crossed those of the writers inspired magazine articles. One writer's father had been ruined by publicity; another writer had gone to a dinner party, where he sat next to a reform mayor trying to battle the long-standing corruption in his small town; another came across a black janitor in a southern college who had absorbed an education from the blackboards he erased and the lectures he eavesdropped on. All these unusual personalities sparked lively articles.

"Personal travel is another idea lode. A college student planning a summer's trip to Mexico contacted several magazines before he left to propose articles on various facets of Mexican life. When he came back, he sold fifteen stories based on this one trip. Not surprisingly, he is now a top travel writer. One young woman's first article was inspired by her experiences on a youth hosteling trip in post-World War II Holland; a veteran studying in France under the GI Bill wrote about the tumultuous political situation in Morocco; another, vacationing in Turkey, ran across a story about a sexy sultan, which he sold to a men's magazine.

"Two writers sold articles as by-products of research they were doing for books. One took time out from a children's biography to make her subject an 'Unforgettable Character' for *Reader's Digest*. Another came across material about a protégé of the historical personage he was really focusing on; he sold an article about the protégé—but his full-length biographical manuscript languishes in his desk drawer.

"Seven of my respondents got their first article ideas from items they spotted in newspapers and magazines—still a favorite source for many of us. One 'Saturday handyman' came across an obscure newspaper paragraph about an unusual invention, dug up other 'wacky inventions,' and sold his first article to *Mechanix Illustrated*. Another saw a brief newspaper story about an unusually high suicide rate among New York policemen, did in-depth research, and came up with a moving magazine article. Writers who live outside the New York area have a great advantage here, since the stories they see in their local papers are not likely to be spotted and acted upon by New York-based established writers or by editors who assign their own staffs to cover them. So keep your eyes open for stories about interesting people, heartwarming personal experiences, community projects, or profitable business ventures."

Olds's idea for the article you just read resulted from research she did for a talk on the "Sales for Beginners" panel of a nonfiction writing workshop at the New School for Social Research. So there's another source for ideas—turning speech and lecture material into nonfiction magazine pieces.

I know of one editor-in-chief at a major women's magazine who had his young staff members submit twenty-five article ideas every Monday. Having to produce that many ideas each week developed a habit of awareness in new editors; they couldn't walk down the street or ride the subway without consciously storing up impressions, observations, bits of dialogue, scenes, attitudes, and dozens of things they learned to turn into articles for their magazine.

Ideas, Ideas Everywhere

Uncovering fresh, salable ideas becomes second nature to writers. The ways and means of discovering commercial writing ideas are as varied as the people looking for them. As Sally Olds makes clear, your travels, homemaking activities, hobbies, family interests, chance acquaintances—even your job—often provide enough material to launch a freelance career.

Again, however, the best way to spot ideas for magazine pieces (books, too) is to read newspapers. Besides your hometown paper, read the *New York Times*, the *Chicago Tribune*, or the *Washington Post*, especially the Sunday editions—their coverage is extensive and in-depth. Read everything with a microscopic eye, because often seemingly obscure items contain solid article ideas. Read the columns, the editorials, the Op-Ed pages. Watch the wire stories from remote corners of the world, and keep an eye out for celebrities and personalities in the news.

Weekly news magazines are good sources for article ideas, too. *Time, Newsweek,* and *U.S. News and World Report* are tillable soil for topical ideas. Read carefully their departments on science, money, education, medicine, religion, and other subjects. Many writers also make a practice of reading periodicals and journals focusing on a particular industry, business, or technical field. This, of course, depends on whether you think you might concentrate on a specialty—and are ready to handle specialized subjects.

If, for instance, you can make technical or scientific topics clear and digestible for the average reader, you're a sure bet for a successful freelance career. Why? Because in this nuclear age nearly all editors use some scientific articles, and science-oriented magazines continue to flourish, yet few freelance writers handle these pieces effectively. The same thing goes for medical ideas. Few writers have the technical knowledge to write accurately *and* readably about these vital and complex subjects.

Remember that an idea won't be rejected merely because it isn't new. The idea may be old as the editor you're querying, but the presentation of it *must* be fresh. This calls for an observant eye, a keen imagination—and long, hard hours of digging. As Emerson said, "All life remains unwritten still." But you'll have to come up with a different angle, a unique slant, see the common in the uncommon, the universal in the parochial, the colorful in the drab.

Other sources for magazine article ideas include TV, newspaper, and magazine advertisements (you'd be surprised how quickly trends are reflected in ads); government bulletins, booklets, and pamphlets; newsletters (a bullish field today); college and university specialists; public speakers or panelists; movies; and, most certainly, books.

After you've had several articles published, you'll come to realize another source: spin-off ideas from pieces you've written. Read over your published pieces from time to time for possible new slants or angles, variations on a theme. For example, several years back I did a piece on the importance of having a will. While watching TV one night I learned of a new gimmick: video wills. I did some quick research, located the company that pioneered the video-will concept, queried *Parade* (the national Sunday supplement), got the assignment, and did a piece—based both on my new research and information I'd used in the original article.

Slant for Success

You can slant the same basic idea to several different markets. This is where market studies and analyses come into play. Because this important topic will be discussed later, at length, suffice it to say here that multiple markets should be your goal for every idea you write about. As Shirley Biagi says in *How to Write and Sell Magazine Articles*, "Why should you do extensive research, spend a month or more of your time, just to sell one article? A better approach is to find topics that will satisfy more than one buyer."

Biagi, who is on the journalism faculty at California State University, Sacramento, says on the subject of slanting:

"A successful topic that can fit into more than one category, for example, might be an article about women who lift weights as part of a university physical-fitness experiment. This can be written from a news angle for a local newspaper ('This is what these women are doing now'), from a sports angle for a sports magazine ('This experiment may help women become better athletic competitors'), or for a science magazine ('This controlled documented experiment may tell us something about how women respond physiologically to regular heavy exercise').

"With three different market categories you can take three different article approaches with just one central topic. Each approach is called a 'slant.' This means you will tailor your article precisely to fit each of the different types of magazines.

The nonfiction writer must have the highest respect for both the facts and the audience; and keep both in mind at all times. There have been, for example, scores of articles on the fascinating subject of phobias. I did a humor piece on the idea for *Girl Talk* in the early seventies; since then I've done phobia pieces for *Boys' Life, Essence, Beauty Digest, Dynamic Maturity, Passages,* and *TWA Ambassador* (and the *Boys' Life* piece was picked up for use in an anthology). One idea, one subject—eight paychecks!

A serious mistake many aspiring freelancers make is not understanding the difference between subjects, ideas, and topics. ASJA defines an *idea* as a topic (or subject) combined with an approach (or slant). Shirley Biagi explains:

"When you say 'I want to write an article about television news,' your concept is too broad. A magazine editor approached with this idea will reply: 'What do you want to say about television news?'

"If you are an able freelancer, your reply will be something similar to an article entitled 'Disco News,' an analysis of the deterioration of local television news by Edwin Diamond in the *Washington Journalism Review*.

"A general idea is always less appealing to an editor than a specific one. An editor may spend time with a veteran contributor to refine an idea into a topic, but will be less patient with newcomers. Your idea must be refined when it reaches the editor.

"To test whether you have an idea, state it as a question and an answer. If one question and one answer cover your idea, you probably have a satisfactory topic. The question asked by Diamond's article is 'What is the current quality of local television news?' The answer, according to Diamond, is that television news is 'practically all entertainment, and practically zero information.' "

While article ideas aren't hard to come by—once you get the hang of things—you'll need to support your topic and theme with substantive facts. You cannot merely sit back and applaud your cleverness—unless and until you've unearthed enough material to write a complete story with a unique slant or angle. If every article begins with an idea, it comes to a screeching stop without the information supplied by nuts-and-bolts research.

HOW TO RESEARCH EFFECTIVELY

Research—getting facts and opinions from the world outside yourself—is the foundation of nonfiction writing. Thorough research helps give you and your article or book ideas the authority to convince readers and assure would-be critics that what you've written is both reliable and current. (Unless, of course, you're doing a think piece or personal experience article—and even then you limit yourself if you haven't visited a library or picked up a telephone.)

Editors' return mail is voluminous partly because writers don't do an effective job of digging for facts. Magazines, particularly the bigger ones, employ researchers to check manuscripts. Sometimes these "checkers" uncover errors or aspects of a piece you haven't bothered to investigate, and such errors and omissions are the kiss of death, especially if the magazine staffers find the correct information readily available. Your research was sloppy, it wasn't thorough; your data weren't fresh. The editor will not only kill your article but drop you as a writer who didn't do his or her homework.

Thus research is not only *important* to writers—of narrative nonfiction, factual magazine articles, and even fiction—it's *essential*. Why? Because you're handicapped if the scope of your writing is limited by your own knowledge. "Write about what you know" doesn't mean the writer must have had personal experience in every field or subject. If that were the case, little or no medical nonfiction would be written, few articles about advanced technology would be published, there would be almost no sports books, and only writers who had spent a lifetime in James Beard's kitchen could write good cookbooks.

To make up for a lack of firsthand experience, writers research. Marc Rose, late senior editor of *Reader's Digest*, used to advise writers to gather twice as much material as they would need, "so that a selection can be made from a wealth of material." If your facts are scanty your article will be thin.

Realizing that research is a key part of their work doesn't prevent many writers from being intimidated by the process. I know some who are actually fearful of the task, and still others who consider it drudgery. These people make research more difficult than it is because, in most cases, they simply haven't bothered to learn common-sense fact-finding techniques.

These poor souls could save themselves hours researching articles and books (or, in the case of students, reports and term papers) if they knew what Alvin Toffler, author of the bestsellers *Future Shock* and *The Third Wave*, knows. Says Toffler: "The shortest path between two facts may well be Alden Todd."

Todd, a veteran of the writing wars and longtime ASJA member, is author of an excellent book on research means and methods. Called *Finding Facts Fast* (Ten Speed Press, 1979), the book is subtitled *How To Find Out What You Want and Need to Know*. According to Todd, who has taught the course "Research Techniques and Fact-Finding" at New York University since 1966, a good researcher-writer has qualities of a reference librarian, a university scholar, an investigative reporter, and a detective. Says he: "There's no reason for you to learn everything that these four specialists should know in order to do their jobs well. But the excellent researcher should learn certain essential skills used by each, and combine them so they support one another. If you learn well, you come out with a broader and more generally useful range of abilities than any single one of these specialists commands.

"By combining these abilities," he says, "you can become a skilled specialist in research."

Todd believes that more than anyone else, the fictional detective Sherlock Holmes taught us the value of "thinking a research problem through first—and then looking in the places that offer the greatest promise."

Here's Alden Todd on why writers should first think through their research plan:

"It was only after wasting considerable time in research for my own professional writing that I recognized the importance of thinking through a research project and planning in general lines before digging in. The beginner often makes the mistake of rushing to the first possible source of information that occurs to him, when he should take a few minutes to consider several possible sources, then choose carefully the best order in which to follow them.

"In research in history, biography, and events of the recent past, particularly when you are looking for printed material, you can frequently get results if you play detective and ask yourself:

"Who would know?

"Who would care?

"Who would care enough to have put it in print?

"By following this procedure, the researcher might quickly come up with conclusions like these in specific cases:

"What was the dollar value of the property loss in a recent big fire or hurricane? Because insurance companies paid the property loss claims, they cared enough to compile their loss records. And because several companies must have been involved, the total loss figure is likely to have been compiled by the trade association of insurance companies—the American Insurance Association.

"Another case: Where should I look for biographical material on a distinguished American architect who died a few years ago? First, in the obituary pages of the daily newspaper in the city where he lived, because the local paper usually carries a more detailed obituary than papers in other cities. Second, in the pages of the periodical or journal of the special group of which he was a member—in this case the official organ of the American Institute of Architects."

Todd stresses that five minutes may do the job, but do the job you must if you're to save wasted hours and even days. He also details four ways writers can discover what they need to know. Let him explain:

"Research is not all paperwork, or reading. There are four basic ways to find out what we want to know, and *Reading* [Editor's note: Todd classifies the use of all audiovisual equipment—films, tapes, photographs, etc., under *Reading*] is but one of them. The others as I classify them are:

"**Interviewing,** or asking other people, both orally and in correspondence.

"**Observing** for yourself.

"**Reasoning** what must be the fact from what you have learned by other means.

"In some research projects, using only one or two of these methods is sufficient to reach your desired end. But it is always worthwhile to remain alert to all four methods, in order to make sure that you have not overlooked a fruitful source or an important part of the story. Consider the four methods briefly:

"**Reading.** Most of what people want to know has already been put on paper—somewhere, sometime. The difficulty for most of us lies in our not having the means, or the knowledge, to find the right books, articles, manuscripts, and other written materials. We do not have *universal* subject indexes and in many parts of the country it is difficult to obtain some written materials about which we know.

"**Interviewing the expert or source-person.** When facts we want have not been put in writing, at least not to our knowledge, we can try to find the people who know and ask them. (Example: the survivors of a disaster of years ago that has not been fully documented; or intimates of a political figure, now dead, who can discuss the behind-the-scenes action of their late friend or relative.) The interviewer's written account of what such source-people tell him then may become the first document on the subject.

"Interviewing and reading are closely connected, and they complement each other. Reading can lead the researcher to the source person who can fill in gaps in the written record. And those we interview can often point us toward written sources we have not yet used. (Example: biographers who track down a subject's surviving relatives or friends often discover valuable documents that have long lain unknown and untouched in attic or basement.)

"**Observing for ourselves.** When what we want to know has not been put satisfactorily in writing, and when we cannot find anyone who can tell us, we must sometimes observe for ourselves, using our own eyes and ears. This is the method of research basic to the natural sciences and to exploration, such as the space flights of the astronauts, or Robert E. Peary's trek by dog sled over the Arctic ice to the North

Pole, or Columbus's voyages across the Atlantic Ocean. In research for books of history, biography, and even for fiction, the writer often finds it useful to immerse himself in his locale in order to gather information of an atmospheric nature—how things look, feel, sound, and smell. Such direct observation is interwoven with reading and interviewing.

"**Reasoning from what we have learned.** Concluding what must have happened, or what must be the case now, from facts we have learned by other means is the most elusive and dangerous method of fact-finding. It is heavily employed by vertebrate paleontologists, archaeologists, and geologists, whose science rests on reasoned conclusions from evidence in the earth. It is the method most *misused* by historians and biographers. (Example: the many so-called 'lives' of William Shakespeare rest shakily on the skimpiest of documentation, and are pasted together with presumptive terms such as 'probably,' 'can be assumed to,' 'perhaps,' 'is supposed to,' and the like.)

"Reasoning from the known to the unknown in research is best used as a method that leads to new documents and sources, and therefore to finding more than standard bibliographies and other sources have provided. It is a method that should be used from the beginning in drawing up a research plan, in order that the *most likely* sources are covered before those that are merely *possible* sources."

Todd also makes the key point that freelancers, students, and aspiring writers must be realistic about their research purpose, time, and cost. It goes without saying that if a book or magazine piece is to stand up against both editor and reader scrutiny, the competent freelancer will make sure to gather reliable and current data. "On the other hand," adds Todd, "the hack writer will crank out books and articles simply by reading and reorganizing what more conscientious researchers have written from original sources."

In any research project, according to Todd, the "desired result, or purpose, should bear some sensible relation to the time and money spent in research. A busy professional in the thirty-thousand-dollar-a-year class should spend twenty dollars without hesitation for Xerox copies that will save him a day's work, whereas a student of age twenty-one might well choose to save the money. Or if a few dollars' worth of long-distance telephone calls will speed up a committee chairman's work by several days, the money is well spent."

THE COMPLEAT RESEARCHER

Now let's suppose that you've come up with a fresh article or book idea that may become a salable manuscript. Before you begin even preliminary research for an article query or book proposal there is one other essential the serious writer must consider: What to *do* with all the material you are about to uncover? How on earth do you handle the sheer volume? Harry E. Neal, one of ASJA's most prolific and versatile members, suggests you consider the following:

"Keep research notes together. Before you begin your research, devise a method for keeping notes together. Don't combine your research notes with those of the 'daily journal' type. Some writers use loose-leaf pages in three-ring binders, some use ruled pads, and others make research notes on 5x8-inch index cards, sorted according to chapter headings in the book outline. [Editor's note: If researching an article, sort material according to your best guess as to what will be the lead, the theme, the body or main portion of the piece, and the conclusion.] Some authors use typewriter paper and keep numbered pages in folders or envelopes that can also hold newspaper clippings, pamphlets, and other pertinent printed material—one envelope or folder for each chapter of the book.

"Me? I use both stenographic notebooks and loose-leaf fillers and binders. I'm fortunate to be able to write shorthand, and for a long time I wrote shorthand notes in a stenographer's notebook, then transcribed them by typewriter on loose-leaf pages without attempting to sort them. For ready reference I typed two or three words in the left margin opposite each paragraph or series of related paragraphs, and then when I was ready to work on my manuscript I hunted through the typed pages to pick out the sections I needed to fill in my outline or chapters.

"Subsequently, however, I found it easier to affix adhesive index tabs (the 'make-yourself' kind, available in any stationery store) to loose-leaf dividers, each tab bearing an abbreviation of a chapter heading, or the chapter number. I then arranged my various typed pages in the appropriate sections, so that when I began to write the book my research material for each chapter was all in one place. I found this to be more efficient and convenient, and I recommend it to you for trial. If you devise a system that is better for you, use it."

Neal also suggests you take time to make sure that necessary research material is accessible to you for what you want to write, and that you can sensibly invest whatever time and money is required to obtain it. Both Todd and Neal, plus every other writer I know, also carry a pocket-sized notebook or pad at all times. And they use them! What goes into such notebooks? "Fleeting thoughts, the fresh impression, the stray idea," says Neal, "because any or all of these may be forever lost if the writer depends upon memory alone to preserve them." Classic examples are found, Neal points out, in W. Somerset Maugham's *A Writer's Notebook* (Doubleday, 1949) and *The Crack-Up*, by F. Scott Fitzgerald (New Directions, 1945), both of which are recommended reading, especially for beginning book writers, of both fiction and non-fiction.

THE HOME LIBRARY

For most nonfiction articles and books, library research is a must. The writer can save many trips to the local public, school, or college library—and therefore much time and money—by stocking his or her own home library with certain essential reference books. Professional writers know that a carefully chosen collection of reference books will quickly pay for itself. One such writer is Claudia M. Caruana, an instructor of magazine journalism at St. John's University, in Jamaica, New York. The following is a helpful listing of reference books you ought to consider owning—and why.

REFERENCE BOOKS FOR *YOUR* BOOKSHELF
by Claudia M. Caruana

Every serious writer, whether of fiction or nonfiction, needs a home library that can supply basic information. A well-chosen home library can save you the trouble of visiting the public library for basic facts—as well as provide you with an interesting source of ideas for new stories or projects.

The following were selected after talking to freelance writers and reference librarians. These books aren't particularly expensive—all of them would total less than $200 if purchased, a small price for the convenience and security of having information at your fingertips when you need it.

Finding Facts Fast: How to Find Out What You Want and Need to Know, by Alden Todd. (2nd ed., Ten Speed Press, P.O. Box 7123, Berkeley, California 94707. $3.95 paper.)

This may well be the best of the how-to-do-research books on the market today. Todd is a research pro who gives readers the benefit of his expertise. *Finding Facts Fast* provides a working knowledge of library resources and other means of obtaining information: fact-gathering techniques, such as finding experts, interviewing elusive sources, eliciting oral histories, obtaining government documents, and enlisting the aid of your congressperson. 123 pages.

The New York Times Guide to Reference Materials, by Mona Mc-

Cormick. (2nd ed., Popular Library, 1515 Broadway, New York, New York 10036. $1.95 paper.)

McCormick, a former *New York Times* librarian, details the various reference sources that writers, students, and researchers might have to consult in their work. She describes reference books by type and then devotes the second half of the guide to reference books in a variety of subject areas—science, philosophy, religion, art, books, literature, education, politics, government, history, current events, and others. 224 pages.

Reference Books: A Brief Guide, by Marion V. Bell and Eleanor A. Swidan. (8th ed. Not available at bookstores. Order from the Enoch Pratt Free Library, 400 Cathedral Street, Baltimore, Maryland 21202. $3 paper; price includes postage and handling; $1 more for special handling; eight to ten weeks delivery.)

Like the Todd and McCormick books, this volume belongs on every serious writer's bookshelf. Found here is an annotated bibliography of the most-used reference sources. This includes encyclopedias, yearbooks, indexes, guidebooks, atlases, periodicals lists, biographical sources, and government publications. 179 pages.

Reference Books for Small and Medium-Sized Libraries, by the American Library Association. (3rd ed. Order from the ALA at 50 E. Huron Street, Chicago, Illinois 60611. $9.)

Although this book is designed for librarians, many writers find it extremely helpful. There are more than 750 annotated listings of reference sources, some of which are certain to touch on the writer's fields of interest. If you don't want to purchase your own copy of this book, ask the reference librarian at your local library if you can use his or hers while you're there (this book usually is kept behind the desk, not on the shelf).

A standard almanac.

There are several of these annuals on the market today. Usually costing less than $5, they provide a wealth of information.

A standard yearbook.

Like almanacs, yearbooks hold information that can lead you to other sources. Yearbooks published by encyclopedia companies, such as the *World Book Yearbook* and the *Americana Yearbook,* can be more expensive than you're willing to pay for an at-home reference source (especially since they're in the reference section of most local libraries) but you could consider other, less expensive ones such as the *Facts on File News Dictionary* ($14.95), updated annually, or the *Facts on File Yearbook* ($19.95).

Miscellaneous Reference Books

Statistical Abstracts of the United States. (Order from the U.S.

Government Printing Office, Washington, D.C. 20402, or purchase from a federal government bookstore, often located in a federal office building in major American cities. $10 paper, $13 hardcover.)

Need to know how many pounds of beans were produced in Idaho last year or the number of Americans who have master's degrees? Chances are you'll find the numbers in *Statistical Abstracts*. Published annually since 1880, the statistical information here is provided by the U.S. Bureau of the Census. Data regarding government agencies, business, finance, population, etc., are contained in the statistical tables. Sources for those statistics are also given.

United States Government Manual. (Order from the U.S. Government Printing Office, Washington, D.C. 20402, or purchase from a federal government bookstore.)

This volume, updated annually, describes all government agencies, gives names and telephone numbers of press officers in these agencies, and provides background information on agency and government functions. It also lists the members of Congress, their party affiliations, etc.

Guinness Book of World Records. (19th ed. Bantam Books, 666 Fifth Avenue, New York, New York 10103. $3.50 paper.)

Need to know which country produces the most bauxite or which is the fastest animal in the world? For these types of questions, this book is a great starting point. 255 pages.

Writer's Market. (Writer's Digest Books, 9933 Alliance Road, Cincinnati, Ohio 45242. $18.95 hardcover.)

This annual provides relatively detailed, up-to-date information about magazines and publishers that purchase material from freelance writers.

Literary Market Place. (R.R. Bowker Company, 1180 Avenue of the Americas, New York, New York 10036. $35 paper.)

This annual directory lists the address and principal editorial staff of most U.S. magazine and book publishers. It also lists many agents, writers' organizations, book manufacturers, public relations outlets, writing conferences, and awards. Most public libraries keep this volume on hand in the reference section.

Bartlett's Familiar Quotations. (15th ed. Little, Brown and Company, 34 Beacon Street, Boston, Massachusetts 02106. $24.95.)

Not the only quotation book on the market but a good choice for literary, political, and historical quotations.

Oxford Dictionary of Quotations. (3rd ed. Oxford University Press, 200 Madison Avenue, New York, New York 10016. $29.95)

A good alternative to *Barlett's*. Note, however, that there are many collections of quotations and you might find one with a specific theme more appropriate to your needs.

The Information Report, by Washington Researchers. (Order from Washington Researchers, 918 16th Street, NW, Washington, D.C. 20006. Yearly subscription, published monthly, $39.)

This newsletter is especially valuable to the writer who needs information the government or other organizations provide free or for a minimal fee. Recent information included the telephone numbers of all federal libraries in Washington, D.C.; fact-finding by telephone; Washington "hotlines"; and others.

How to Use the Federal FOI Act: A Concise and Complete Do-It-Yourself Guide for Print and Broadcast Media, Authors, Scholars, Students, Researchers, Writers, and Teachers, a joint project of the Society of Professional Journalists (Sigma Delta Chi) and the Reporters Committee for Freedom of the Press. (2nd ed. Order from the FOI Service Center, c/o Reporters Committee, 1125 15th Street, NW, Washington, D.C. 20005. $1.)

Mandated by Congress in 1966, the Freedom of Information Act has allowed writers and scholars to uncover a variety of otherwise unobtainable facts on such issues as FBI harassment, automobile design defects, consumer product testing, international smuggling operations, CIA spying, and more; using the FOI Act could easily be the subject of an entire chapter. Since it is not possible to go into specifics here, suffice it to say that this is a low-cost, important addition to any home library, because the FOI Act provides invaluable leverage for getting hard-to-obtain data held by various U.S. government agencies. Included here are sample letters, forms, and lists of directories.

Facts on File Student Research Guide. (Facts on File, 460 Park Avenue South, New York, New York 10016. 25¢.)

Basic but valuable, this four-page booklet gives information on essential references and how to use them.

Telephone directories from major American cities.

As long as they're still free and you have room to store them, get on the phone and have Ma Bell send the directories you believe you'll need. They can be valuable reference sources. You know the problem when you're trying to find addresses of out-of-town companies, potential sources, or government agencies: telephone information doesn't always provide addresses. So even if you want to write a letter, you might have to plunk down money to call a firm for its address, or trek to the library to find its listing in a directory. Obviously, you can save yourself some change if the directories are at hand. The Yellow Pages are worth having around for the same reasons, especially if you're seeking a category of services or products in another city.

Reference book catalogs.

Without even stepping outside your home, you can become acquainted with many reference sources if you obtain descriptive literature from publishers. Catalogs are free. Major reference publishers are: Gale Research Company, Book Tower, Detroit, Michigan 48226; R.R. Bowker Company, 1180 Avenue of the Americas, New York, New York 10036; Facts on File, Inc., 460 Park Avenue South, New York, New York 10016; The H.W. Wilson Company, 950 University Avenue, Bronx, New York 10452; Marquis Who's Who, 200 E. Ohio Street, Chicago, Illinois 60611.

Other handy references include the *Directory of Publishing Opportunities*, Marquis Academic Media, 200 East Ohio Street, Chicago, Illinois 60600; and the *Standard Periodical Directory*, Oxbridge Publishing Company, Inc., 1345 Avenue of the Americas, New York, New York 10019.

THE DEWEY DECIMAL JUNGLE

If you can't find the facts you need in Claudia Caruana's suggested home library, then it's time for you to leave your den and take up the hunt in a public or other library. Here is Caruana's guide to finding your way through the labyrinth of stacks and getting the most out of your research time.

TACTICS FOR LIBRARY SURVIVAL
by Claudia Caruana

You're almost on deadline—no need to worry, though. The assignment from the health magazine seems simple enough: a 1,500-word story on beans and ten recipes that use legumes "creatively."

But something is wrong, and you know it. The historical facts about beans you culled from your daughter's encyclopedia are neither adequate nor appropriate for a health-conscious audience. Moreover, the piece could use some updated information on protein complementing and the views of a nutritionist on the value of legumes in today's diet. There is the nagging question: "Are beans *really* popular in the United States?" After you ponder that one and try to decide who could give you the answer you seek, you ask yourself: "Who could provide me with free photographs so I won't have to go to the bother or expense of taking them myself?" Simple assignment, right?

Your piece could be about anything, of course. It could be the article you put aside in despair yesterday, annoyed that you didn't have all the information needed to complete it. Perhaps you decided it just would "take too long," or worse yet, you didn't know precisely where to begin looking for the information.

No one needs to tell you that the line between an article idea and a finished manuscript isn't usually a straight one. In fact, it may not be a line at all, but a jagged journey laced with many false starts, diversions, and dead ends. Often the finished piece (if you decide to complete it) is entirely different from what you originally planned because your research, or lack of it, changed things. "Research," as one Long Island librarian puts it, "is more than the cornerstone of most pieces—it is usually the foundation."

But if you find your foundations are weak or faulty, take heart. You are not alone; there are many other writers who secretly suffer from the "I don't know where to find it" syndrome. The cure is simple: take the time *now* to learn how to find information. You will then have more time for your most important task—writing.

When in Doubt, Ask

For starters, reacquaint yourself with your local library. "The best reference tool of all," says Andrew M. Hansen, executive director of the Reference and Adult Services Division of the American Library Association, "is a librarian. He or she is an information specialist who can quickly lead you to the information you need. Moreover, librarians are acquainted with the newest research tools and techniques, making *your* work easier." He strongly suggests that writers talk to librarians about their specific information-gathering problems, emphasizing that "no question is so insignificant that it shouldn't be asked."

Like Hansen, Joseph Mathewson, public information director for the New York Public Library System, believes that asking questions is important. "No one should be apologetic about asking questions. Librarians are paid to answer questions." Rochelle Yates, Division Chief of the Brooklyn New York Public Library's Telephone Reference Service, whose staff answers more than 1,000 telephone calls per day, reports that most writers she has worked with are "good with questions." She believes that the writer should "not be afraid to describe why the information is being sought." This way, she explains, the librarian often has a better grasp of just how much information will be needed.

Most librarians agree that writers should have a good handle on what's available in the library. The library tour during college orientation many years ago may not be sufficient for your needs now, Hansen says. He advises writers to ask for a quick tour of the reference area if the library doesn't already schedule guided tours.

What happens if the reference or lending material in your local library is sparse, or geared to the general reading public and doesn't meet your specialized needs? Instead of throwing up your hands in despair (which writers have been known to do), more productive options are available.

First, talk with the reference librarian. Mary Pradt, a Time-Life, Inc. reference librarian who also teaches a research course for writers in New York City, advises library users to discuss the need for a particular book with the library staff. She recalls that when she was working for a public library outside Manhattan several years ago, one request for a book often resulted in its purchase.

Another often overlooked resource is interlibrary loan. Interlibrary loan privileges at your local library allow you to receive a copy or photocopy of the material you need from associated libraries. Remember, however, that if you're on a tight deadline, the time involved in obtaining material (delivery problems or a lengthy wait if the book is circulating) could be troublesome.

If you live in or near a big city, locating a specialized library that has the information you seek is simple enough. Often, the information you need can be obtained by letter or a telephone call. To find such a special library or collection, check any one or all of the following: *American Library Directory* (American Library Association), which lists American, Canadian, and some overseas libraries and special collections they may have; *Special Collections* (R.R. Bowker Company), which details more than 70,000 special collections and subjects found in 16,000 American and Canadian libraries; *Directory of Special Libraries and Information* (Gale Research Company), which describes more than 14,000 special libraries and special collections; and the *Special Libraries Directory* for your state, published by the Special Libraries Association. (For the address of your state's Special Libraries office write national headquarters at 245 Park Avenue South, New York, New York 10016.)

If you cannot find any of these directories listed in the library's card catalog or reference printout, Pradt suggests that you check with the reference librarian. There's a good chance he or she may have an office copy of one or all of them for staff use and will let you thumb through it while you're there.

Writers often obtain permission to use college or university libraries while working on a special project. Often, all that's required is a letter from the writer or publisher and some background information detailing the reasons for needing the facilities. In other cases, the writer might be required to pay a special fee or make a donation to the library. Membership in certain professional organizations—the American Management Association and the Magazine Publishers Association are two examples—often entitles the member to use their special reference collections and services. There are also some professional organizations that will open their reference collections to the general public upon advance (written or telephoned) request.

Dial-an-Answer

It never hurts a writer to become acquainted with other professional services the community library offers. In addition to providing typewriters during the day, and "quiet space" for writers to work, write, think, or read, many participate in community law-enforcement programs to protect property (remember your trusty typewriter) by lending engraving equipment. But perhaps the most treasured ancillary service provided by many libraries is telephone reference service. This service, often referred to as "tel ref," has answered innumerable questions for countless writers on tight deadlines. The New York City Public Library tel ref service, for example, has a full-time staff of four librarians and answers more than 1,000 calls per day. The tel ref staff works on the telephone exclusively from 9:00 to 5:00, six days a week, and will field any question that can be answered within five minutes. This service is not computerized; consequently, the librarians work out of a large reference room with more than 1,500 encyclopedias, directories, clippings, and reference volumes. A similar service operates out of two other New York boroughs—Queens and Brooklyn. For questions that plague people after hours, the Brooklyn library system provides Library on Call from 5:00 to 10:00 four nights a week, plus weekend hours.

For questions that cannot be answered within the allotted time, the caller is told what references have already been checked and where else to check on his own. For example, when I called the New York tel ref service to locate the author of a quotation, the librarian on duty checked several quotation books without much luck. Her suggestions included looking up the original Greek words, as well as contacting the university that used the quotation on its official seal. (I got the answer from the college.)

Yates points out that in cities where tel ref is not available many librarians, as part of their service to the community, answer questions over the telephone. It is not uncommon, either, for writers in cities without tel ref to telephone a library in a city that does have the service.

If you have a series of reference problems that you must resolve before completing a project, Hansen suggests that you "call ahead and make an appointment with a member of the reference library staff." This practice, which is becoming more common in many communities, benefits both writer and librarian. First, writers don't have to wait behind a queue of high school students needing the librarian's assistance at the same time. Second, if the librarian is notified in advance that someone is coming to do a project on XYZ, he or she can block out a non-hectic time and have various sources of information ready.

Computer reference service is also available in many libraries, especially those affiliated with colleges and universities. Often, the user must pay a fee for computer services, but the fee is sometimes waived, Hansen says, depending on specific library regulations. These services are especially beneficial if you are seeking a list of references for a book, a bibliography on a specific topic, current references in your field of interest, or a faster method of searching printed indexes.

Digging It Out Yourself

Librarians are the best people to consult before starting any research project, but unfortunately today's library budget cutbacks, reduced hours, and smaller staffs have made it increasingly important for writers to personally take the "search" out of research. Often, too, some writers prefer to obtain the basic information they need and ask for assistance only when they are confronted with an advanced research problem.

"There is much a writer can do to help himself," says Pradt. She suggests you become acquainted with one or several how-to-do-research books. "Guides can help you get a 'feel' for the type of reference sources found in libraries and other places, and how to approach your particular research problem," she adds.

Before you start any project, however, follow the adage, "plan your work and work your plan." Just as you can *usually* determine how much time should go into writing and rewriting (although it might not always be an accurate guess), you should try to estimate how much research a project is going to need. Obviously, a five-generation saga beginning in the early 1800s will require more time than a short piece on exercise. Be flexible, however. Some twist or turn in your findings could result in a different approach—or even another project.

"Research overkill" is sometimes a problem, especially with new freelancers. Writers faced with an intimidating writing assignment, or suffering from writer's block or a severe case of procrastination, often enthusiastically root out more information than they need to avoid actually writing (or completing) a manuscript.

When some clearcut parameters can be drawn as to the scope and extent of your research, Pradt recommends that the required information be broken down into manageable sections.

For instance:

What questions can be answered by topical materials—newspapers, scholarly journals, magazines, or pamphlets?

What information can be answered by reference directories or books?

What information can be answered by government data or government experts?

What information can be obtained from "experts in the specialty" or by interviewing other sources?

Reference directories and periodicals are discussed later in this chapter. And for questions that cannot be answered by using reference books, either in your library or on your own, it's always best to consult a librarian.

Anybody Know an Expert?

Need to find an "expert" who can give you a quote for your piece? If you don't already know someone in the field, it would be wise to check the *Encyclopedia of Associations.* Many trade organizations have spokespersons who are willing either to talk with writers or lead them to knowledgeable people. Another idea is to contact trade magazine editors in the discipline where you need an authority and ask them about industry leaders or others who might be good sources.

Corporate public relations professionals are also good information sources. Often, they can arrange for you to see company executives as well as provide you with background details. *O'Dwyer's Directory of Public Relations Firms* (J.R. O'Dwyer, 271 Madison Avenue, New York, New York 10016) lists the clients of many public relations firms. You can also write directly to the public relations, public affairs, or information department of a company.

Public information officers in government agencies can often give you the names, telephone numbers, or addresses of government personnel who can answer questions either for attribution or for background research. Another source of expertise is college professors. Check the *National Faculty Directory* (Gale Research Company) or *Directory of American Scholars* (R.R. Bowker Company). Experts in academia can also be found through university "speakers bureaus" which provide the community and press with a listing of personnel and their areas of expertise. If the college or university you'd like to contact doesn't maintain such a speakers bureau, check with the school's news bureau or public information office for suggestions and referrals.

Other sources of experts include (but are not limited to) public information personnel in hospitals, medical centers, foundations, embassies, and chambers of commerce; librarians; other writers; or even your family or neighbors.

You Have Friends in Washington

The federal government publishes more material than any other organization in the United States (although this may change with continuing federal cutbacks). At this writing, the U.S. Government Printing Office alone publishes more than 25,000 titles annually. Most libraries carry the *Monthly Catalog of U.S. Government Publications*, which lists these documents. You can write the Superintendent of Documents (U.S. Goverment Printing Office, Washington, D.C. 20242) for a shortened version, *Selected List of U.S. Government Publications*. This list (available for a small charge) includes more than a hundred publications in each issue.

Admittedly, it can take a long time to receive publications from the government. Moreover, you can't browse through the book or pamphlet to decide if you really need or want it when you purchase material by mail. One way of cutting the time it takes to receive publications (and have an opportunity to browse through them) is to check if a federal government bookstore (located in such cities as Atlanta; Birmingham, Alabama; Boston; Chicago; Cleveland; Columbus, Ohio; Dallas; Denver; Detroit; Houston; Jacksonville, Florida; Kansas City; Los Angeles; Milwaukee; New York; Philadelphia; Pueblo, Colorado; San Francisco; and Seattle) has it in stock.

Using the U.S. Library of Congress (which could fill a chapter all its own) is necessary for some complicated research projects. If the information you need is located only there (your community librarian can tell you that after searching through the *Union Catalog*) you can write directly to the Library of Congress. There is no guarantee that you will hear from them, however. Sometimes, it can help if you write your representative, spelling out your research needs and stating that only the Library of Congress can help you. Often the assistance of such an official will give you access to the material you require.

Need to find out about pending legislation? Check with the *Congressional Record Index*, which describes the actions of all congresspeople and indexes where to find the information in the *Congressional Record*. An excellent synopsis of what is happening on the Hill is *Congressional Quarterly's Weekly Review*. Two other sources are the *Washington Monitor's Congressional Yellow Book* and *Federal Yellow Book*. Both these loose-leaf directories, available in many libraries, provide up-to-date information about members of Congress, House and Senate leadership, and members' staffs and legislative responsibilities. The firm also publishes the *Congressional Record Scanner*, which, as its name implies, is a quick way of going through the *Congressional Record* to find out the status of legislation.

LEGIS, a computerized data base housed in the Library of Congress, records all legislation since the Ninety-second Congress and can be reached at (202) 225-1772. This telephone service, when given a key word such as "pension reform," will provide through your home or library computer a printout of current and past legislation, legislation drafters and sponsors, or the status of new legislation. (And again, your own representative in Congress can be helpful, especially if you simply want to know about recent or current legislation on a single topic.)

The courses offered by Washington Researchers are an excellent guide through the Washington information maze (918 16th Street, N.W., Washington, D.C. 20006; 202/833-2230). Their prices are steep ($225 at this writing—tax deductible) but they do offer concrete instruction and an insider's view of how to get the information you need out of the tangled red tape of bureaucracy. The Researchers provide two books with their "Washington Information Seminar": the *Washington Information Workbook*, and the *Researcher's Guide to Washington*. The firm also gives a seminar on research tools for business researchers (you get *How to Find Information About Companies* with this course) and publishes the *Business Researcher's Handbook*. All books can be purchased separately; they are updated frequently.

Professional Research Services

Many writers dream of the day when all their information will be at their typewriter, ready for creative handiwork. That dream comes true for writers who hire professional researchers. According to Enid Klass, a professional researcher who works in New York, many writers who are working on several projects simultaneously or who need information that can only be found in New York are among her clients. "These writers need to spend as much time as possible at their typewriters. For them, a professional researcher can get to the sources and provide a report of the findings much quicker than they themselves can. A researcher often has cultivated sources at a variety of places, and some of these sources might be difficult for a writer to locate in a short period of time." Klass contends that working with a researcher is beneficial for the writer in another way. "Since so often a writer is working alone, he or she needs someone else to talk with about the project." If the occasion arises and you do need a professional researcher, check the editorial services section of *Literary Market Place* or ask a reference librarian for suggestions.

One of the most pleasing moments in a writer's life (other than receiving a hefty check in the mail) is knowing that all the pertinent information is in the piece, that what's been written is accurate, timely, and more important, relevant. At those moments you might feel like the

Syracuse University founders who coined the school's motto: "Knowledge crowns those who seek her."

Some Reference Selections of Special Interest to Writers

All writers must have a basic knowledge of reference materials if they're to be successful. Listed below is a sampling of directories, indexes, and reference sources described by the librarians interviewed for this article as being particularly useful to writers. Remember, *this is only a sample.* For specific answers to reference questions not listed here, consult a reference librarian.

For current events and general information

• *The New York Times Index,* 1851 to date. As its name implies, the *NYT Index* categorizes all the stories that have appeared in this world-respected newspaper. It is an important as well as a useful reference tool because it identifies trends, events, and news personalities. Moreover, it briefly summarizes major news items. Since you can obtain a "time frame" on an event—i.e., all the stories that appeared over a period of time—you get a complete (or near-complete) outline of the event (or personality or trend) and can track down other sources that might provide additional information.

• *Facts on File,* 1940 to date. This weekly digest of world news, like the *NYT Index,* has a semi-monthly cumulative index. The firm also publishes the *Facts on File Five Year Index,* which lists, in one volume, all world events that occurred during specific five-year periods, i.e., 1946-1950, 1951-1955, 1956-1960 and so on through 1980; and *Editorials on File,* which is a semi-monthly compilation of editorials and editorial cartoons on various topics in the news. The editorials are selected from more than 140 U.S. and Canadian newspapers.

• *Public Affairs Information Service,* 1915 to date. Better known as *PAIS,* this weekly subject guide indexes periodicals and pamphlets, as well as government documents. Annual compilations of the weekly indexes are available in many libraries.

For magazines, scholarly journals, and other periodicals

• *Readers' Guide to Periodical Literature,* 1900 to date. Indexes approximately 180 periodicals, mainly general or popular in nature.

• *Popular Periodical Index,* 1973 to date. Indexes approximately 40 periodicals that are usually not indexed by *Reader's Guide.*

• *Alternative Press Index,* 1980 to date. Indexes more than 100 alternative and activist magazines, newspapers, and journals.

• *Business Periodicals Index,* 1958 to date. Indexes approximately 270 business, trade, and special-interest publications.

• *Education Index,* 1929 to date. Indexes approximately 300 periodicals in this subject area.

• *Social Sciences Index,* 1974 to date. Indexes approximately 260 periodicals in this subject area.

• *Humanities Index,* 1974 to date. Indexes approximately 250 periodicals in this subject area. This and the *Social Sciences Index* (above) together were called the *Social Sciences and Humanities Index* from 1916 to 1974.

• *Art Index,* 1929 to date. Indexes approximately 150 periodicals in this subject area.

• *Biological and Agricultural Index,* 1964 to date. Indexes approximately 200 periodicals in these subject areas; titled *Agricultural Index* from its inception in 1916 until 1964.

• *Index Medicus,* 1879 to date. Indexes approximately 2,600 medical journals worldwide.

• *Index to Legal Periodicals,* 1908 to date. Indexes approximately 375 English-language periodicals published in the United States, Canada, Great Britain, Australia, New Zealand, and Ireland.

Encyclopedias

If you need general background information regarding a topic before you research the specifics or interview a potential source, encyclopedias, such as the ones below, can be helpful.

• *Encyclopaedia Britannica,* first published in 1771.

• *Encyclopedia Americana,* first published in 1829.

• *The World Book Encyclopedia,* first published in 1917.

To find copies of articles

If you need information about specific publishers, magazines, newspapers, or periodicals—for copies of articles that may not be available at your local library, or to research markets for your work—check some of the following:

• *N.W. Ayer and Son's Directory of Newspapers and Periodicals,* 1880 to date (N.W. Ayer Company). Updated annually. Publications (including magazines and trade papers) are listed by location.

• *Editor and Publisher International Yearbook,* 1920 to date (*Editor & Publisher*). Updated annually. This volume provides a comprehensive listing of daily and weekly newspapers, including names and positions of key personnel.

• *Magazine Industry Market Place* (R.R. Bowker Company).

Available since 1979. Updated annually. Provides names and addresses of magazines, suppliers to the industry, and manufacturers.

• *Ulrich's Quarterly* (R.R. Bowker Company). This is a quarterly update of *Ulrich's International Periodicals and Irregular Serials and Annuals*. It lists approximately 2,500 publications that have editorial offices outside the United States.

• *Working Press of the Nation* (National Research Bureau). This annual directory consists of five volumes: newspapers; magazines; radio and television; feature writers, photographers, and syndicates; and international publications.

• *International Directory of Little Magazines and Small Presses,* edited by Len Fulton and Ellen Ferber (Dustbooks, P.O. Box 100, Paradise, California 95969). This paperback book lists more than 3,000 markets for fiction and nonfiction, including information on a wide range of smaller publishers. Its subject and regional indexes are helpful in solving placement problems.

• *Writer's and Photographer's Guide to Newspaper Markets,* by Joan and Ron Long (Helm Publishing Company, P.O. Box 10512, Costa Mesa, California 92627). This spiral-bound book, which many writers now keep on their own bookshelves, lists American and Canadian newspapers that buy articles and photographs from freelance writers and photographers.

• *Standard Periodical Directory* (Oxbridge Communications, Inc., 183 Madison Avenue, New York, New York 10016). Lists 65,000 U.S. and Canadian periodicals, arranged by subject matter. It is revised biennially.

• *Bacon's Publicity Checker* (Bacon's Publishing Company, Inc., 14 E. Jackson Boulevard, Chicago, Illinois 60604). Three volumes: magazines; newspapers; and radio and television. Updated monthly with new entries or changes that can be pasted over the earlier ones, these reference sources are especially valuable for names of editors in individual departments or on special-assignment desks. New volumes are issued yearly.

• *Gebbie's All-In-One* (Gebbie Press, P.O. Box 1000, New Paltz, New York 12561). Similar in scope to *Bacon's* with the exception that all media are listed in one spiral-bound volume.

For information regarding books

In addition to the library's card catalog of its collection or the *Union Serial Catalog,* which lists all the books particular libraries hold, consult with the following for books still in print as well as books that are soon to be published. Note that many bookstores also have these volumes for customer use.

• *Books in Print* (R.R. Bowker Company). Revised annually, these volumes index (by title, author, and subject) close to 585,000 books in print.

• *Paperbound Books in Print* (R.R. Bowker Company). Issued twice yearly, this reference source lists more than 400,000 books in print.

• *Subject Guide to Forthcoming Books* (R.R. Bowker Company). Indexes by subject books to be published in the United States during the next five months. Issued bimonthly.

• *Forthcoming Books* (R.R. Bowker Company). Issued bimonthly, this volume indexes, by author and title, books scheduled for publication within the next five months.

(The last two books are of particular interest to writers because, in addition to knowing if new information on your research area is in the works, you also have an idea of what topics are not being covered. Eureka—another idea for a book!)

For information about people in specific fields

• *Current Biography* (H.W. Wilson Company). This periodical provides information about people in the news. Each article is approximately 2,000 words long; a bibliography is included.

• *Directory of American Scholars* (R.R. Bowker Company). This volume gives brief biographical sketches of scholars in a variety of fields. It is a good source of experts.

• *National Faculty Directory* (Gale Research Company). This is a two-volume set providing an alphabetical listing of more than 495,000 names and addresses of college educators in the United States and Canada. Another good source of experts.

• *Who's Who in America*, 1899 to date (Marquis Publishing Company). This volume is updated biennially. The Marquis firm also publishes *Who's Who* in other areas: science, art, education, etc. Check the reference section card catalog, reference printout, or with a librarian for additional information about these volumes and other reference sources that provide similar data.

• *Contemporary Authors* (Gale Research Company). A multi-volume set that includes biographies of 66,000 authors living or deceased since 1960. Writers in all nontechnical genres, as well as prominent persons in communications, are represented. New volumes in the series are published periodically.

Reference sources of special interest to writers

• *Awards, Honors, and Prizes* (Gale Research Company). Fourth edition, Volumes 1 and 2, gives the names and addresses of U.S. and Canadian (Vol. 1) and foreign (Vol. 2) organizations that sponsor competitions.

• *Directory of Directories* (Gale Research Company). An annotated guide to more than 5,100 directories published in the United States and Canada.

• *Encyclopedia of Associations* (Gale Research Company). This indispensable volume lists names, addresses, and functions of more than 14,000 national organizations. A good source for locating experts in a variety of fields.

• *Gadney's Guide to 18,000 International Contests, Festivals, and Grants in Films and Video, Photography, TV-Radio Broadcasting, Writing, Poetry, Playwriting, and Journalism* (Festival Publications, P.O. Box 10180, Glendale, California 91209). This directory lists awards in the communications field, as well as their requirements and how to apply for them.

• *Guide to Theses and Dissertations* (Gale Research Company). An annotated bibliography of 2,000 theses and dissertations arranged by subject. The guide's index is arranged by subject, title of dissertation or thesis, and name of the college or university issuing the writer's degree.

• *Research Centers Directory* (Gale Research Company). This volume details 6,000 research centers in the United States and Canada; periodic supplements are added to each edition. Indexed by research center and subject, it is an excellent way of locating experts in your field of interest.

• *Standard Directory of Advertising Agencies* (National Register Company, Inc.). Three volumes annually; a helpful source if you need to know which advertising firm is representing which company.

• *Thomas' Register of American Manufacturers* (Thomas Publishing Company). This four-volume series, updated annually, gives information on who manufacturers what. There is also a section on trademarks and who owns them; names and addresses of manufacturers and their subsidiaries are provided.

• *Famous First Facts* (H.W. Wilson). Need to know what to call a young partridge? Chances are you'll find that and other interesting "firsts" here. [Editor's note: A young partridge, in a pear tree or not, is a *squeaker*.]

• *The Wall Street Journal Index* (Dow Jones Books). A recognized source for information on corporations and business trends. Probably the most extensive coverage on a daily basis of any publication in America.

• *Standard and Poor's Register of Corporations, Directors and Executives* (Standard and Poor Corporation). This volume, updated annually, lists corporations and their executive officers as well as headquarters sites.

● *The American Book of Days* (H.W. Wilson). Need to know what happened on September 3, 1945? You'll find out if you check through this book.

● *What Happened When* (Washburn Publishers). This handy reference is out of print, but your library may have a copy. Lists events of historical and human-interest importance that may be valuable in your search for information.

● *Gallup Opinion Index* (Scholarly Research Incorporated). Need to know what Americans thought about former President Carter's performance during the Iranian crisis? If the Gallup organization did a poll on it, you'll find it indexed here. This is a reliable source for national trends.

I think you'll agree, having read Claudia Caruana's three Rs of research, that there's no lack of source material for your writing. Let me stress, however, that change is the one constant of the writing and publishing business. Magazines change addresses, editors, publishers, policies—and you must be among the first to learn such trade news. Most of the reference materials Caruana has surveyed are revised at regular intervals and should be checked carefully to insure that you're using the most recent edition.

YOUR PRIMARY SOURCE—THE INTERVIEW

Until now we have been discussing what scholars call "secondary" sources of research. That means making use of facts uncovered and published, at least once, by somebody else. But when you've done your bookwork and have a background of information at hand, it's time to move on to *primary* sources—something that hasn't been written down before. Those sources are *people,* and you gather the material you need from them by means of the *interview.*

You cannot avoid the interview. You need people for original material—the astonishing fact, the fresh quotation—that will make your writing truly valuable to editors. But for many writers the interview is the most difficult—even frightening—part of their work.

The art of interviewing is an elusive one and mastered only by doing. Master it you must, however, if you want to become a professional writer. One excellent book is John Brady's *The Craft of Interviewing* (Writer's Digest Books, 1976). Another is Bob Baker's *Newsthinking: The Secret of Great Newswriting* (Writer's Digest Books, 1981). Read on for three seasoned professionals' insights into interviewing.

We will first hear from ASJA's Paul Friggens. For many years a roving editor for *Reader's Digest*, he now lectures to Reader's Digest-University sponsored writers' workshops across the country. Here's what he has to say on the importance of interviewing.

ON INTERVIEWING
by Paul Friggens

In my lectures to writers' workshops across the country, I cover "The Art of Interviewing," and indeed I consider interviewing not only an art when well done, but the keystone of our profession. The most insightful and valuable contributions to journalism today result largely from effective interviewing.

How do you conduct an interview? Let's discuss some fundamentals, and the first is this:

(1) *You must establish friendly rapport and win confidence. Sell yourself.* To begin with, dress inconspicuously; and as Red Barber, that veteran of thousands of sports interviews, counsels, "Display good manners." But the real essentials of this business are to have an insatiable curiosity and to like people.

The best interviewers like people—all kinds of people—and they establish rapport easily. They put people at ease. Distinguished interviewer John Gunther sums it up: "You need to get the interviewee relaxed, to make him really talk instead of just answer questions."

Your job is to build an atmosphere of mutual trust and respect. This is something you may have to work at, depending on your personality and feeling for other people. I have only two rules or guidelines:

First rule: I try to *understand* people, to walk in the other fellow's shoes, to see things the way he or she sees them, to feel the way others feel; and I realize that every person is my superior in some way.

Second rule: I never *compete* with the experts. In fact, I have an abiding fear of "experting" about anything. To be sure, I do my homework and try to punch in with knowledgeable questions. But I never argue with or debate the interviewee as so many reporters do today. Instead, I listen, ask questions like a child and, in effect, sit at the feet of the master, who tells me. I keep in mind the old Chinese proverb: "He who asks a question is a fool for five minutes, and he who does not is a fool forever."

There is another indispensable step to winning confidence, and that is to carefully prepare for the interview. The more time you devote to that preparation, the better. One very able interviewer I know spends at least three days getting ready for an interview, learning all he can about a person. As the veteran political reporter and Washington columnist Roscoe Drummond says, "You can't get the right answers unless you know the right questions to ask."

I like to work around my subject in advance. That is, I talk to as many people as I can who give me an assessment, an accurate picture, of the individual. In the case of political figures, educators, and scientists, I gather their speeches and writings beforehand. These materials provide not only invaluable background and insights, but tips for possible discussion—the right questions, as Drummond says—and they give me a familiarity with the subject that wins confidence and respect.

Well, you've got your feet inside the door. You've sold yourself and won confidence. Now let's go on to the second fundamental:

(2) *Use the best interviewing techniques.* Here are some general observations you will find helpful in conducting an interview:

The best place for an interview. I'd say most anyplace except over lunch. It's too busy and distracting. The best place may be home, office, in a car, an airplane, boat, on horseback, or just trailing the subject around all through the day. In this way, you get action and insight and flavor.

How to open an interview. Techniques differ. Some writers like to ask the softball questions first and put the interviewee at ease. If I have time, I like to get acquainted, to ask a few revealing questions about the topic at hand, thus building rapport before I lead into my major questions. On the other hand, time may be short, and your subject tough and seasoned. That's when I toss out my hardball questions right at the start to show that I know my business. If it's a hard, spot news interview, I don't visit.

However you do it, your job is to be in complete command and to steer the interview. Personally, I prefer to interview in a gentlemanly, fair-minded, and informed style, rather than to boldly confront and rudely probe, like a prosecuting attorney. This more restrained technique has worked best for me through the years. I ask tough questions, but never dirty questions. I don't think it's good journalism.

Some tips that will pay off. In the case of a well-known person or celebrity, don't waste time by asking questions or background you should have researched in advance.

Remember that you set the tone of your interview by your very first question—whether you ask something banal and shallow, or thoughtful and stimulating.

You should strive to get behind the public image, to get inside your subject. What makes the man or woman tick, what are his or her biases, great passions, particular philosophy? In all of this, you should strive to be fair-minded and objective. Keep your own opinions and personal feelings out of it.

You should respect a person's time. An hour interview is long enough at one time, and two hours or more is fatiguing and probably counterproductive.

When you have finished your key questions, or if the interview seems to lag, just pocket your notes and chat. Your subject will relax and may give you some of your best quotes.

I come to my third fundamental of interviewing:

(3) *You should learn to listen.* There is no greater art than to be able to listen sensitively and intelligently to others, and then communicate their thinking. To be a good interviewer, you must listen with total concentration.

Let the interviewee do the talking. Steer him or her with a few well-timed questions, keep 'em on the track, but *listen.* Don't be a gabby reporter.

You can frequently loosen people up by getting them to talk about themselves, about what really interests them. Then listen. Often, I trigger people by asking them what they do on a typical day or at their job—from dawn to bedtime. You'd be surprised how they open up.

Listen for nuances of expression and look for gestures. Listen, but don't hesitate to break in with a quick follow-up question. Remember to steer the interview and follow new avenues that provide fresh insights and illumination.

Now an important point:

If the interviewee makes some startling disclosure, sensational statement, or controversial opinion, *just listen.* Don't betray your surprise or show special interest. That may well shut off the interview. Instead, draw out your subject and then carefully check your quotes at the close. Never assume anything to be off the record, unless you have agreed in advance.

Keep looking for your lead, the main thrust of the interview, as your subject talks and you mentally edit your story. (Admittedly, this practice is tricky and takes experience, a feel for what's important and what's not.) If you don't seem to be developing anything compelling or memorable, dig deeper—and just listen.

And, by all means, listen for the choice anecdote or lively quote in your interviewing. It is this ear for dialogue that puts vitality and life into an interview and brings the subject to life. Listen for the *quotable* and the *memorable.*

You should listen so closely and carefully that at the end of the interview you can scan your notes and say to the subject: "Now let me summarize and recap; from our interview, it seems to me, you said thus and so." Your subject may agree, or go on to clarify and fortify and, as noted before, perhaps give you your best quotes. You will have greatly strengthened your interview and will be vastly more accurate and fair, assuming that you've carefully checked every fact and quote.

This is the art of good interviewing, and I know of no greater challenge and satisfaction for the freelance writer than bringing off a lively, informative interview.

LONG DISTANCE INTERVIEWS

For most writers, the telephone becomes Robert Lynd's "greatest nuisance among conveniences, the greatest convenience among nuisances."

I like what humorist Robert Benchley had to say on the subject of telephones: "There is something about saying 'okay' and hanging up the receiver with a bang that kids a man into feeling that he has just pulled off a big deal, even if he has only called up Central to find out the correct time."

The much-maligned telephone is to freelancers what CB radio is to truckers. The phone interview, for example, can be time- and money-saving, and is particularly effective when doing "round-up" pieces, for which information must be collected from sources scattered across the country, or world. A case in point:

In May, 1971, I did a round-up article for *True* magazine. The piece, entitled "What To Tell Your Kid About Pot," required that I talk with prominent Americans to see what they'd told their youngsters about experimenting with marijuana. Since I had a tight deadline, and since time was money, I taped my talks instead of concentrating on writing down answers (and losing my train of thought). In less than two working days, I phoned, interviewed, transcribed, and wrote the piece. I not only made a fast $2,000, I got to chat with Benny Goodman, Melvin Belli, the late Whitney M. Young, Jr., Art Buchwald, George Wallace, Joan Bennett, Charles Schulz, and Dr. Michael De Bakey, not to mention novelist Shirley Ann Grau, Muppet's creator Jim Henson, and then-U.S. Attorney General John Mitchell. Oh yes, also a governor of California, the concerned parent of four children, who told me, "Cop-outs don't solve problems—they create them. Problems can only be solved by those who are willing to face reality. A mind fogged by chemicals, drugs, marijuana, or alcohol contributes nothing to the fight against injustice, the protection of the environment, or the achievement of a lasting peace." My obliging interviewee was Ronald Reagan.

If I'd had to write the twenty-six well-known people whose views were used in the article, it would have taken weeks, perhaps months, to get replies and complete the piece. As a result, it would not have been topical. (Yes, *True* paid phone expenses plus travel to and from my home in Connecticut and a couple of sumptuous lunches!)

Make Pay Phones Pay

The late Mort Weisinger, one of ASJA's former presidents and most enthusiastic, aggressive, and ingenious freelancers, theorized that calls from a pay phone couldn't be ignored. Writing in *A Treasury of Tips for Writers*, Weisinger said:

"Do you have trouble bearding VIP lions in their dens for quotes? Soliciting celebs via the mails is hazardous; a secretary will reply with a letter of polite refusal; often your letter will lie in limbo and never be acknowledged. During the past several years I have developed a sure-fire gimmick that works nine out of ten times. I simply ensconce myself in a public telephone booth with a stack of quarters and dimes. Then I phone the celebrity at his office, person-to-person. When I reach him, the operator invariably says: 'I have your party. Please deposit $3.25.' Then I go into my ritual of inserting 13 quarters.

"Can you imagine the reaction of the subject at the other end? When I identify myself as a freelance writer, he knows I have invested $3.25 of my own hard-earned money (not a big magazine's!) and he immediately feels obligated. If I had phoned him from my home phone, he might curtly tell me he's busy and to send him a letter. But when he knows I've shelled out hard cash, a fact that has registered via the tolling of the coins, he is sympathetic, helpful, and cooperative. He regards me as an underdog and becomes quite loquacious. (Once when I phoned Senator Robert Kennedy and my time ran out, he told the operator to charge him for the extra minutes.)

"Should you decide to experiment with this technique, make it a point to phone your subjects during the lunch hour. Usually, their secretaries will be out for lunch. I have found that most famous folk are so busy they usually send out for their lunch and eat at their desk. Consequently, they will answer the phone themselves when you call. But be careful to check on the time zone differences!"

Hold the Phone!

Many ASJA members—in fact, most—use telephone-answering machines to prevent calls while they're writing. When they've finished the day's writing, they return any calls they've received in that period. (Most writers find that four hours of straight, uninterrupted writing at their typewriter or word processor is about all they can handle before their work begins to deteriorate.)

A few writers successfully query editors on article ideas by phone. They are the exception, however. A good rule of thumb: check the market listing for a magazine before you telephone the editor or any of the staffers. Some editors are amenable to phone queries, but most are not. Many *Writer's Market* listings for various publications state, "No phone calls accepted." (And *never* stroll into an editor's office for a social visit. If you have important business get an appointment on the phone.) As both an editor of a corporate magazine and a freelance writer, I've dealt with many publishing people I knew only by phone—or through the mails.

There are two primary purposes for the telephone interview. One is to get factual information that can be had only from a certain authority who is too busy to see you at the time or is otherwise inaccessible. The other is to save travel time and money. ASJA member Isobel Silden, a successful California freelancer with a background in public relations, explains.

THE TELEPHONE INTERVIEW
by Isobel Silden

Please don't tell my editors, but I've never set eyes on many of the famous people I have interviewed over the years.

This is not because I don't want to see them, or they don't want to see me, but because often it is inconvenient for a face-to-face interview. And so I rely on the telephone. God bless Alexander Graham Bell and all his inventions—not to mention the tape recorder and the handy device that suctions onto the phone to tape phone conversations.

It is entirely possible that I invented "phoners," as I've dubbed them. Step backward in time to the 1950s, when television was a mewling infant. TV critics on daily newspapers were just being assigned that beat, and press tours as we now know them were not held as frequently as they are today. A press tour, in case you care, is an assemblage of TV critics in New York or Hollywood to interview stars and executives of upcoming shows. Since no network can or would bring in a group of critics for every important show, the phoner was born.

At that time, I was an account executive of one of the largest independent public relations firms in the world. I was head of the TV department, and I realized long before it became a phone company slogan that I could let my fingers do the walking, or in this case, publicizing. I called up TV critics and said "How'd you like to talk to Lorne Greene, or Robert Young"—or whomever I was pushing that particular day.

Without hesitation the journalist would say okay. The call would be completed, he'd get a good story, write it, and I'd get good free space in leading newspapers around the country.

It seemed logical to continue similar procedures when I began freelancing. Obviously, you'll get a better interview if you can sit down with George Burns or Danny Kaye in his living room, and I have. But in the case of Michael Learned, I couldn't.

It was raining buckets. Radio announcers insisted that people stay home. And I wanted to. But I was also on deadline for a story with Learned. I called the network and asked if we could do it by phone. The program executive in charge of her show called Learned. Well, certainly, was the response. She didn't want me in her house any more than I wanted to drive up into the Hollywood Hills. Her roof was leaking in a dozen places. There were buckets all over the house. One of her dogs was sick, and she'd worked very late the night before.

That did it. I phoned her, fastened the suction cup onto the phone, started the tape recorder and—important point here—*told her I was taping the conversation*. There are laws in most states that you *must* tell people they're being taped—and if you don't, not only are you dishonorable and even somewhat rotten, you're also making it more difficult for those of us who are honorable and do say we're taping.

My technique with Learned, or any show business personality, was to set the scene, in order that the reader might feel with me on the interview. I asked her to describe the room in which we'd be sitting if I were there for an in-person interview. I needed to know what her home looked like, the furniture, decorations, etc. I then asked what clothes she'd have worn for such an interview, how much makeup, how her hair would have been dressed. Had she served me coffee or tea and if so, what kind of cup and saucer was I holding?

Everything was described down to the most minute detail and if she thought I was wacko for asking those questions, well, too bad. When I felt totally at home in that house, we began the interview. It went swimmingly and I got a fine story.

I have done phoners with actors on location, when time was an element or the location was difficult for me to get to. One actor called me from a phone booth near a freeway. The sound effects were dreadful, but I got the story, and lent authenticity to it by describing how his dressing room trailer was parked near a freeway and how the conversation was being punctuated by traffic noises. True, every word of it.

Obviously, if I have an assignment of national scope I must interview authorities all over the country, and phoners are mandatory. It's tough calling cold; wouldn't you hate it if a stranger turned up on your phone saying he wanted to interview you on X subject right then?

Generally I call ahead, introduce myself, say what I need and then ask when it would be convenient for me to call back. Once in a while the subject says "Let's do it now," and we do. Often I let the person think about the topic for a few hours or days and then call back.

But, you may ask, "What about those phone bills?" They're not as steep as you might think. When I'm doing a show business story, the network or studio involved will let me charge the calls to their number. If I'm going to recharge the publication, I establish the fact with the assigning editor going in. I always time my long distance calls. I have a stopwatch to remind me that it isn't a local call and I can't play "Chatty Cathy."

Since I live in Los Angeles, I try to place my calls before 8:00 in the morning or after 5:00 in the afternoon to take advantage of the lower rates. I haven't felt it necessary to buy those long-distance phone services, since I don't have to pay for too many of the calls. [Editor's note: There are presently several new cost-saving phone services available; check the Yellow Pages of your local directory.]

A journalist friend who is West Coast editor of a film-oriented magazine does call all over the country interviewing subjects for his publication, and he's found the alternate phone service has cut his bill in half.

To each his own.

Only a ninny would go off on an interview without a list of prepared questions. It is even more important to have good questions when doing a phoner, to avoid those dreary periods of "dead air time," while you're thinking but the subject thinks you've gone away.

Don't rely too heavily on your tape recorder. It is a machine, and machines go awry on occasion. It happened to me recently. The subject was a terrific interview, bright, funny, and very quotable. The tape recorder was going, the suction cup was on the phone, and I didn't bother taking notes.

You got it. Blank tape. I don't know what happened. I do know I didn't have my story, and I didn't have the nerve to call the man back and ask him to repeat an hour's conversation. What to do? I remembered some salient points that I wanted to include in my story. He wasn't the sole person I was interviewing for this piece, a story on cable TV production.

I called his executive assistant and told her the tape recorder had malfunctioned at the point where Mr. X had told me the titles of those shows he was producing. Could she give them to me again? Of course, she could, she did, and I had less than half my great interview.

But who'd admit to the stupidity of not taking notes as insurance to tape? Not this craven coward. The tape recorder can make you very lazy if you rely on it too much. It can also be instrumental in botching a story, as it did in this instance.

What I now do is let the tape go, and I write down much of what the subject is saying, as fast as I can. I'm not going to get it all, true, but enough so that the tape will embellish and add to what I've missed.

It is also a timesaver, because I don't have to type up the entire tape. We repeat ourselves so much in conversation, and I'm sure you've all seen transcriptions of tapes typed by a professional typist—who doesn't know what's important and what isn't and so types every cough and hmm. When you type your own tape, you can remember from the notes what you want to keep and what can whirl by.

I'll often pick up a colored marking pen and make a note next to important quotes in my notebook, so when I get to that point on the tape I'll know to listen carefully and type that portion.

Sure it's tedious, sure it's tiring. I typed a tape of an actress and her husband, nonstop, for five hours one Sunday. When I finished, I knew I could always earn a living as a professional typist. I knew too I was exhausted, and that I had a terrific story. To make big bucks, it's worth working hard. And it's wondrously gratifying; there aren't that many big bucks in this business.

My telephones are every bit as important to me as a freelance journalist as my typewriters. So you can imagine my consternation one day when the phones were silent for an unusual stretch of hours. I picked up one and heard nothing. I picked up the other. Ditto.

I HAD NO PHONE SERVICE! I was almost hysterical. My umbilical cord had been cut. I was shut off from the world. Who knew how many editors were dying to give me assignments that particular Tuesday? And they couldn't reach me.

I called repair service from a neighbor's phone. I was assured my phone service would be fixed before the end of that day.

Could I work, uninterrupted by calls? Of course not. I was picking up phones every five minutes to see if they'd been reconnected. There is no sound more threatening than hearing nothing on your telephone. Take it from me . . . take it from any writer.

Finally, about 5:30 that afternoon, one of the phones rang. It was the repair supervisor. Everything had been fixed in the main office, and I could reach out and touch someone, ANYONE in the outside world.

I had come through the crisis. I survived. I was alive. Then why were my hands shaking?

It had been a profoundly stressful experience, that's why. As a result of that awful day, I have plans to initiate a "Be Kind to Telephones Week." I know every freelancer in America will applaud.

Should You Get Pushy?

A word about telephone interviews and egos. Trying to get interviews can be hazardous to your self-esteem, especially when you're confronting staff assistants trying to protect bosses from "the media." This is especially so in the case of business, government, and political pooh-bahs. They have lieutenants whose job is to shield them from the dread horde of journalists (until they try to snow you with a propaganda hand-out issued for their own specific purpose).

During President Jimmy Carter's term I accepted an assignment to interview Charles Kirbo, the chief executive's closest personal friend and adviser outside the White House. Thinking it would be a breeze, I called Kirbo's Atlanta law firm, King and Spalding, one of the most prestigious in the South. I hadn't counted on Kirbo's extreme reticence where writers are concerned—his special friendship with James Earl Carter going back years made him extremely protective of the man.

No amount of charm and good manners on my part could convince the President's trusted friend to grant me a personal interview. I had to settle for submitting a list of questions (some of which he refused to answer) in writing, getting the famous counselor's views by return mail. It was a blow to my professional ego—the only in-person interview I've missed on—and made for a less-than-sparkling piece, since Mr. Kirbo reached his kitchen-cabinet conclusions deep within the confines of his impenetrable law office. He gave me the information *he* wanted me to have rather than the other way around.

Barbara Walters has established a reputation (with salary to match) for being an aggressive, no-holds-barred interviewer on television. Oriana Fallaci has similarly made her mark in print. Their male counterparts might be David Frost and Mike Wallace. No one would deny the skills of this quartet of interviewers. And certainly no one would say their success resulted from being shy or sensitive.

Yet, those very traits—plus a couple of others—stand in good stead one of the best interviewers I've ever met. Alex Haley is a very quiet-spoken man, who leads you on so subtly that you divulge your opinions not only on his stated question, but on many other things as well. Charles Kuralt of CBS is another.

PUTTING IT TOGETHER

Turning the fruits of your researching and interviewing into writing is our next writer's subject.

Nearly any nonfiction article you ever write will require interviewing to make it work—but no other form of article depends more completely on a good interview than the profile piece. Here Shirley Biagi takes a close look at this popular article type.

WRITING THE PROFILE
by Shirley Biagi

When you write a profile, you create a word picture. With each paragraph, your readers discover a nuance, a dimension of character they did not know before. Your ultimate goal is to turn that word picture into a fully developed word sculpture.

Writing a profile involves three interrelated tasks: researching, interviewing, and writing.

Researching Before the Interview

Crucial to any profile is the research behind and before the interview. If your interviewee is fairly well known, or even if he or she isn't particularly noteworthy, the best way to learn whether there is any previously published biographical material is to check the *Biography and Genealogical Master Index*, published by Gale Research Company. This volume lists (alphabetically) anyone who is included in any biographical index.

If, for example, you were to check a listing for Edward M. Kennedy, the *Master Index* would tell you which indexes list Senator Kennedy. Then you could go to each of those indexes (found in almost any public or school library) to uncover background information on the senator before interviewing him.

Marquis Who's Who is perhaps the best-known biographical index. Actually, it is a series of biographical indexes, updated regularly and separated into indexes such as *Who's Who in the West* and *Who's Who in Boxing*. All the *Who's Who* listings are included in the *Master Index*, but listings in the companion publication, *Who Was Who*, are not. *Who Was Who* lists once-prominent people who have died; it can even provide background information on deceased spouses of people who are listed in the *Master Index*. Many biographical indexes also list notable people's home addresses, or at least their agents.

If your profile subject is not listed in any biographical index, you should check further in the major periodical indexes to see whether any magazines previously have profiled your subject. The most familiar periodical index, of course, is *Readers' Guide to Periodical Literature,* but do not overlook the specialty indexes to other publications, such as *Business Periodicals Index,* or the *Popular Periodicals Index,* which indexes many widely read periodicals that *Readers' Guide* omits.

For newspaper articles that might provide background, check the *New York Times Index,* the *Wall Street Journal Index,* and *Newspaper Index* (which indexes several newspapers, including the *Los Angeles Times* and the *Washington Post).*

If your interviewee doesn't show up in any of these listings, check your local library—which often indexes the local newspaper—and, finally, ask your interviewee when you make the interview appointment if there is any background material that would be helpful. Pick up the material *before* the interview so you aren't in the position of asking the interviewee basic questions (such as, "Exactly how do you spell your name?") during the interview, which wastes valuable time—and makes you sound unprofessional.

Interviewing

Unlike the artist who uses only the sense of sight to create a two-dimensional black silhouette, you must capture a multi-dimensional subject during your interview. You must use all five senses— sight, hearing, smell, taste, and touch. Add to this a sixth sense, which I will call your sense of *digestion.*

Sight. Visual observation sets the scene for your reader. Your job is to place the reader in your seat, to discover for the reader through your profile what you discover about your subject, therefore *seeing*—not just looking—is very important. Try to arrive at the interview a few minutes early, and perhaps while you're waiting you can note interesting details that will flesh out your profile. My first and most difficult interview was with Shirley Boccaccio, a woman who had decided to have children but not to marry, for the article "San Franciscan Devoted to Role of Mother, Not Wife." Boccaccio chose a candidate to father her three children and legally they agreed that he would accept no further responsibility for them.

Boccaccio was very cooperative, but what made the interview difficult was that there was no background information available except for one article in the *San Francisco Chronicle,* which is where I learned about her. Thus when I entered her Haight-Ashbury apartment, visual information was unusually significant. The children were chasing the family cat across the hardwood floor, and the front-room windows were covered with crayon marks. So that is where the finished article began:

The slim, black cat jumped off the dining room table where he had been napping. He walked across the room and hopped up on the sofa next to the window, searched around until he found a spot where the stuffing wasn't coming out, then nestled near the arm of the couch.

Outside, through the red crayon marks on the windows, it was a dank, rainy San Francisco afternoon. The second floor flat sits on a hill in the midst of what was once the Haight-Ashbury phenomenon, a neighborhood which now houses an assortment of students, homosexuals, lesbians, minorities, young marrieds, single parents, and children.

Hearing. Obviously, the answers to your questions are of primary importance during an interview, so listen more than you talk. Many interviewers think they must dominate the conversation; you are talking too much if you are talking more than 10 percent of the time.

Second, remember to listen to what is going on around you. I once was interviewing the police chief of a small northern California town. Physically, he looked like every stereotypical Southern sheriff you have imagined, with a pear-shaped stomach and a habit of stuffing his thumbs in his belt when he talked.

He was shy, however, and would only give me the one- or two-word answers that are an interviewer's nightmare. "How do you feel about the severe budget cuts that face your department?" I asked. "Terrible." "What will you do if you have to cut your force in half, as projected?" I asked. "Make do."

This pattern showed no promise of improving, until the radio in his office blurted a bulletin about a lost little girl. When I asked him, "How would the cutbacks affect your ability to handle cases such as this, where lost children are involved?" he responded with an emotional, focused answer that was the best he gave all day. The radio bulletin gave me a cue to phrase my question specifically—and this specific focus helped him overcome his shyness.

Smell and Taste. These two senses often go together. (Some scientists say they *are* the same in some respects.) The smell of pipe smoke is a cue, as is the coffee or tea the interviewee offers. You can look for a pipe collection, or see whether your subject prefers herbal tea or decaffeinated coffee.

When I interviewed a food flavor chemist, smell and taste became essential to the story. This chemist's job was to make unappealing but nutritious substances taste good so people would want to eat them— making seaweed taste like hamburger, for instance. In fact, the man's long-term research goal was to help ease, if not solve, the world hunger problem.

His laboratory was my smelling and tasting test. He led me to a machine that was extracting the "essence" of bananas—that is, what it is that makes bananas taste and smell like bananas. If he could capture this essence, he could make anything taste like bananas. So the scientist led me around the room smelling and tasting. I made sure the profile I wrote was permeated with these sensations. I hoped the reader could taste those bananas too.

Touch. Pay attention to the way your interviewee approaches you—with a firm handshake or a weakly dropped hand. Is your interviewee a Grabber—who uses one hand to shake yours and the other to grab your elbow—or is he or she standoffish, distant? Then there is the Stroker—who fondles your arm—and the Tapper—who repeatedly pats your hand. All of these motions should be projected throughout your profile.

Pay close attention to the postures of the people you interview. Do they lean into their voices, or back away from your voice? Your goal should be to keep them from placing barriers between you, so try to lure a businessperson out from behind the desk to sit in the office chairs, or lead a scientist from the laboratory to the university's garden. Any tactic you can use to relax your interviewee will make your interview, and your profile, warmer and more revealing.

Digestion. Digestion is a sort of sixth sense that all good interviewers possess.

If you are interviewing someone, and you can't digest an answer—either because it doesn't agree with something someone else has told you, or you cannot understand the interviewee's explanation of a situation or a problem—ask follow-up questions to help you understand the answer before you leave. Don't go on to a new point or question until you fully understand the answer to the matter at hand.

Writing. Well, you've had all the fun; now comes the work. It's important to organize the mass of information and interview material before you start writing. Some writers work best with an outline, a listing of the sequence they will use to reveal their subject's personality. No matter how you organize, however, all profiles depend on two elements—quotes and description.

Quotes. The best profiles are filled with candid, original quotes, so be listening for them while you are interviewing. You'll want to use *significant* statements your interviewee has made, not the ho-hum or the ordinary. Call attention to material that reveals your interviewee's intellect or emotions.

If your interviewee says, "I was born in Washington, D.C.," you don't need to highlight this with quotation marks. You can easily paraphrase this information. But if your interviewee says, "Fifty steps from the Capitol, my mother went into labor. I was the first baby ever born on the Capitol doorstep," you have uncovered anecdotal material that only your interviewee could provide.

Try to avoid asking questions that can be answered "Yes" or "No"; they won't get you good quotes. Instead, ask "How do you feel about . . .?" "What do you think about . . .?" or "How do you evaluate . . .?" Answers to these types of questions will be more speculative and more useful.

Description. If you have used all six interview senses, you will have collected almost photographic notes about the interview setting and the interviewee's idiosyncrasies and mannerisms. Weave those throughout your interview so the reader will absorb them almost unconsciously between quotable passages. In an article I wrote about a one-man television station in California's gold country, "The Walter Cronkite of San Andreas," the pattern of description and quotations from station owner Bob Akin resulted in these two paragraphs:

Akin can interrupt his station any time with any programming he chooses. Occasionally he shows an hour and a half of Little League baseball or conducts his version of "Meet the Press" with the county supervisors.

"Sometimes I go on a story, and the best I can drum up is an interview with a rabbit," he says jokingly. "But other times, everything fits into place. For instance, at this year's Calaveras County Frog Jump, a baby was sitting on the ground eating an ice cream cone, and this baby lamb walked up to the infant and lay down. The next thing I knew, the baby was sharing the ice cream with the lamb. And we had it all on film. It was terrific!"

From Silhouette to Sculpture

With the use of all six senses, and a careful choice of quotes and description, your finished profile will reveal with each sentence a different facet of the subject's appearance or personality or both. You will have created not just a silhouette, but a complete word sculpture.

Get It Right

One last thought on the matter of doing interviews. Whether for a factual article or a profile, whether the subject is a shy professor of pediatrics at Podunk U. or a pompous performer from Las Vegas, *never* condense or change a quote that alters the content or meaning of the person quoted. If you think it's unusable as is, why tempt trouble and use it? Out-of-context quoting is tricky stuff and tags you as an irresponsible journalist. When you quote an interviewee on a question of fact or opinion, get it down fully and correctly.

Don't trust your memory. Either write everything down or get it on tape—you can always junk it later. Exceed the 55-mile-per-hour speed limit, run around with people who smoke unfiltered cigarettes, cheat at solitaire—but *never* rely on your memory. I stress this again and again, because it's an ever-present danger.

WHAT YOU SHOULD KNOW
ABOUT PHOTOGRAPHY

For the writer-photographers among you, *research* includes getting photos to illustrate your articles. And if you aren't a writer-photographer now, you might want to consider becoming one. The writer who is a competent photographer increases his or her chance for sales. Your own photos sent along with an article often help convince an editor to buy the total package—especially for certain kinds of articles (travel features and how-to-do-its, for example).

BETTER PHOTOGRAPHS FOR YOUR ARTICLES
by Claudia Caruana

It's no secret that good photographs beef up a magazine article's marketability. But if you've never even considered becoming a photographer because you thought the dynamics of shooting good photographs were hopelessly mired in technical jargon, perhaps it's time to rethink your position. Here's a brief, uncomplicated explanation of what goes into effective photographs—photographs you can take to accompany your own articles.

Good photographs don't require years of photographic experience or top-of-the-line camera equipment—any medium-priced 35mm single lens reflex (SLR) with built-in light meter will do. And all you need to know is: how to operate the camera you have; simple, portable lighting techniques (described in detail in many beginning camera texts); what to pack in your camera bag; and how to use your auxiliary equipment effectively.

Begin at the library. Check the photography section for simplified camera manuals, basic texts, and photography magazines. Read them thoroughly.

Know the camera equipment you have with you and how to use it properly. Remember, the time to test your camera skills is at home—not out on the story. If your photography skills are rusty or nonexistent, sign up for the low-cost lessons often given by high school continuing education programs, YMCAs or community groups.

Have an idea of what you are going to shoot before you arrive at your destination, but don't eliminate the surprise factor. Pros know that some of the best pictures happen spontaneously. Your camera should be loaded, however, and a well-organized camera bag with your auxiliary lenses and accessories will prevent you from fumbling with equipment.

If you're shooting informal portraits of people for your article, have them do something related to their work or their everyday activities. A few obvious examples: a musician at his piano, a writer in her office, a teacher in a classroom filled with children. (Be sure to get signed model releases when there are recognizable people in your pictures.) When using flash, pose your subject at least six feet away from the background for a more flattering shot. Watch out for (and avoid) unsightly backgrounds. Always take several shots of each scene or pose; you may not get a second chance.

For site shots (actual location shots of buildings, boats, lakes, whatever), look for interesting camera angles and use a telephoto or wide-angle lens for a variety of perspectives. Many photographers shoot each picture as both a horizontal and a vertical, to give the editor a choice.

Use an all-pupose film such as Kodak Tri-X, a black-and-white film that can be used in a variety of lighting situations. If color is required, use transparency film, not print film. And remember, daylight-balanced color film is not compatible with fluorescent *or* incandescent lighting—so unless you shut off the lights, use color-corrective filters, or film specially balanced for such lighting conditions, your subject will be green- or orange-faced. [Editor's note: About 75 percent of all photos used by consumer magazines today are 35mm color transparencies, but trade publications use mostly black and white.]

Flash photographs on your agenda? Make certain your flash unit is operating. Bring an extra set of batteries as insurance. If the flash unit is held to the side of the camera, or if the flash is bounced off a white ceiling instead of simply being placed above the camera, you'll usually get more flattering and better-illuminated photographs. There are situations, too, where you don't set out to take flash photos but discover that flash is your best bet (even though there are options such as available light). Always bracket flash exposures and practice taking flash photographs at home, using friends or family members as models.

Windows or bodies of water can cause unwanted glare in your photographs; solve this problem by attaching a polarizing filter to the lens to minimize or eliminate the glare. If you don't have a polarizing filter, try to move the subject or change your angle to do away with the glare.

No skills or inclination to develop and print your black-and-white film? Then go to a custom photo lab; the technicians there have the professional expertise you lack. They can make a "proof" or "contact" sheet (an 8x10 print of all the frames you shot on one roll) from which you choose the frames you want enlarged.

Selecting a Professional Photo Lab

The time arrives in almost every writer's career when the photographic services of the corner drugstore (or discount outlet or photo kiosk) are no longer adequate to acompany the article at hand. When the editor wants to see a contact sheet or several versions of one frame, it's time to hire the services of a professional photo lab.

A professional or custom lab gives you access to the same technical expertise and quality available to professional photographers. This means flexibility, not only in size and quantity of prints, but in such special services as contact sheets, cropping, special effects, negative manipulation, "pushing" film speed, and cropping frames for printing. In other words: making the best of your exposed film.

If you are not acquainted with a particular custom lab fellow writers or friends may be using, and are happy with, call up a local camera club or the photography or publications department of a local college for their recommendations. You can also check the local telephone directory, and—as a last resort—photo magazines such as *Popular Photography* or *Modern Photography* for custom lab ads. Mail-order transactions with a competent lab are advisable if you live in a rural area without custom photo services, or when local labs offer poor or erratic service.

After you have a list of laboratories that you want to consider using, check for the following:

Compare prices and services carefully. Look for prices that are comparable for the services offered. Bargain-basement prices might result in bargain-basement quality and service. Usual laboratory service time is somewhere between forty-eight and seventy-two hours for developing film and making contact sheets. The same holds true for print orders. Some labs assure film developing *and* contact sheets within twenty-four hours. This might be important if you're asked to reshoot certain photos (or take shots not included at first) for an assignment or if an editor is in a hurry for the photos or contact sheet. Rush service costs double the standard fee (or more) at most labs.

Other services that custom labs provide include special borders, print mounting, keeping your negatives on file in the office, and delivery. (The latter two usually involve an additional fee.) Spotting—the careful elimination of minor dustmarks or scratches on the negative that will appear on the finished print—should be included in the regular price; extensive spotting or air-brushing may call for an additional fee. Sure signs of a sloppy lab are fingerprints, scratches, and dust on negatives they've processed. Other warning signals are work not completed as scheduled, misplaced or lost negatives, and poor-quality prints from properly exposed negatives. If your lab gives you shoddy work more than once, find another one.

Is there a minimum charge for orders? How much? Remember, not all publications require 8x10 prints; you could save yourself a bundle by submitting 5x7 prints instead. Be aware, too, that double-weight paper fares better in the mails and on the editor's desk than single-weight paper. Double-weight paper costs more, but always ask for it—it's worth it. You will usually be asked what type of finish you want on your prints. Most publications prefer either an engraver's matte or a glossy finish; check with your editor for his or her preference.

Will you be receiving personalized service or is the laboratory just a place to drop off your order Monday and pick it up on Thursday? You should expect more. The staff should be willing to answer your questions, and offer suggestions for the best use of your negatives, or how they (the laboratory) can improve or salvage a poorly composed or exposed frame. If the laboratory staff seems uninterested or only wants to work with professional photographers or people generating a lot of business, you may want to find a lab with more cooperative personnel.

Just as your written work reflects your professionalism, so do the photographs or transparencies you submit. Make certain the lab processing your work takes the same care that you would if you were doing it yourself.

Finally, *Writer's Market* and *Photographer's Market*, along with freelancer's guidelines from specific magazines, will tell you what a client pays for photos. Some good books for the beginner: *The Amateur Photographer's Handbook*, 8th ed., Aaron Sussman (Thomas Y. Crowell, 1973); *Photographer's Market* (Writer's Digest Books, annual), and *Sell and Re-Sell Your Photos*, Ron Engh (Writer's Digest Books, 1981).

One note of caution and reassurance: if you're not a photographer already, or if you feel no particular inclination toward becoming one, you shouldn't feel you won't be able to sell articles without photos. For many types of articles, photos *will* help you make a sale, but if you're just starting out as a freelancer you might be better advised to put your time, energy, and disposable income into writing and research instead of fiddling with a camera. Remember that a top-notch national magazine is likely to be skeptical about the quality of a stranger's photos, and that local magazines usually have staff photographers on salary who need to be kept busy; often the editor isn't happy to pay additional fees for photos the staff could have taken.

Try teaming up with a photographer in your area. Ask around among your writer and artist friends, or contact a good local photography school or the art department of your area university (both faculty and advanced students are possibilities). If you've developed a good working relationship with a local magazine or newspaper photographer, he might well be eager for some freelance work to expand his list of credits.

No matter what kind of arrangement you work out, chances are that any experienced photographer will take better photos—and waste less film doing so—than you can, at least at first. So think the writer-photographer option over carefully before you plunge into it.

Chapter Three

THE SECOND STEP—WRITE

Aspiring writers tend to ask the same questions. Those heard most often, according to Kirk Polking, director of the Writer's Digest School, are: "How can I keep editors from stealing my ideas?" "How can I get an agent?" and "How can I use real people and events in my story or article without getting sued?" My experience at workshops, seminars, and writer's conferences confirms this. Other regularly asked questions include: "Whom shall I let publish my book?" (No, I'm not kidding.) "Shall I copyright my manuscript?" "When will I get paid?"

Notice anything wrong with the questions? If you don't, go back to page one and reread to this point. And as you read this time constantly be mindful that every suggestion and observation is made in light of market needs. You want to sell what you write. But, have you asked the essential question: "What makes for a salable article?"

Many beginning writers seem relatively unconcerned with the nuts and bolts that spell the difference between manuscript acceptance and rejection. The mechanics of writing articles and books that sell mysteriously take a back seat to such fascinating concerns as worrying about movie contracts, book club percentages, and foreign rights. Many beginners would rather play at being Philadelphia lawyers, it seems, than become honest-to-God freelance writers. It's no wonder that entire forests are wiped out to provide pulp for their rejection slips.

I say forget thieving editors (you're not likely to meet one), agents, and kill fees—at least for the time being. Wait until you're being published on a regular basis to stew about such refinements as copyright laws and publishers' dirty tricks. Learn first how to build an article or book that will increase your sales—and reduce the number of your rejection slips. And save a few precious trees!

Here, then, are the essentials that spell the difference between stories that sell and those that are turned down. They are fundamental to any nonfiction article. They are the work of Berniece Roer Neal—author, lecturer, teacher, and one of the ASJA's most respected freelance writers.

THE BASICS OF A SALABLE MAGAZINE ARTICLE
by Berniece Roer Neal

So you have a great idea for an article.

Hooray for you. The world is full of people with great ideas for articles. But only a few of those articles are ever written, and only a fraction of those that are written see print. After latching onto an idea that you're *sure* (well, 95 percent sure) editors have been praying would cross their desks, now comes the hard part: transforming your gossamer thoughts into a persuasive query, then doing your research (including interviews), and finally, turning that pile of research into a manuscript that sells.

How do you beat the odds? That's a question that puzzles published and aspiring writers alike.

The answer, as with many things in life, is to *organize*, to take one step at a time in a planned sequence. And the sequence in a well-planned article is: *title, beginning, middle, end.*

The Title

Your title might well be the bait that lands your manuscript on the senior editor's desk.

Believe me, your manuscript is going to need some kind of red flag or blaring trumpet or eye-catching element to receive serious attention. I have a letter from *Family Circle* magazine lying on my desk that states in part ". . . we receive over 10,000 manuscripts and article suggestions a year." Many publications receive more.

Certain professional writers' bylines are well enough known to cause an editor to welcome those writers' manuscripts—and often to buy them. But if your name isn't yet a household word, a tantalizing title is well worth the time necessary to create it.

Before you work on your title, though, let's back up a bit. Are you certain you have *one* sharp idea to present, or are you still doubtful about your topic? In editing articles for aspiring writers I've found that what they thought was one idea turned out to be a mixture of ideas too formless for the reader to grasp immediately.

All the "labor" of writing doesn't happen on a machine: much mental work gets done when no one dreams you're wearing your writer's cap. You must spend time mulling and mumbling over your subject matter before you begin the actual writing. You need to extract the essence of your material and express it in *one sentence*.

Then you're ready to create a title that will catch an editor's attention.

Professional writers speak of hooking the reader, snagging the reader, of luring readers into the piece. In the case of the title we're interested primarily in catching the editor's eye—if only for a short time. We know it's common practice for editors to change writers' titles without asking consent. And what does it matter, really, what title is eventually used as long as we've sold the editor and will see our *ideas* transmitted to thousands and thousands of people? The publication is our soapbox, and the editor is the middleman or middlewoman who sets it up for us.

You may be wondering, "Which is better, a long or short title?"

Because of the countless words that come under an editor's scrutiny, I try for a title on the short side. I was recently intrigued by the heading of an article about the history and sport of the boomerang—"Boomerang-ang-ang-ang!"

Today it's important for a title to appeal to the eye as well as the mind and the heart.

How about this title for an article concerned with gift-giving? "Gift-Rapped" says it all—well, almost. But it was enough to get me to read the article. Another, a bit longer—"A Man's Car Is His Hassle"—was an eye-catcher that promised a bit of sympathy.

Almost any old familiar saying can be switched around—using inverted word play—to create an upbeat title. One that comes to mind is "The Chance of a Ghost" A similar device is the play on words: "Edifice Complex" and "Going for Baroque" titled articles about architecture. The chic publication *W* carried a garden article under the title "The Garden of Eatin'." "No Free Launch" topped a newspaper story on the sober subject of air space use.

Titles cannot be copyrighted. But caution is necessary. You couldn't title a novel *Gone With the Wind*—you might be found guilty of violating what lawyers call "fair trade practices"—but there is a book called *Gone With the Windsors*.

Remember above all else that your title should make the editor want to read your story. I once heard the editor of *Saturday Review* remark that he was about to publish an article titled "The Supreme Court: Observations and Reflections." But after some thought the editor changed it to "Has the Supreme Court Abandoned the Constitution?" Subsequent letters revealed a large reader response. So, a particular title *can* cause an article to be read.

Remember that editors and scanners notice titles if nothing else. That's why magazine publishers try to cram all those titles on the covers. You can't personally introduce every article to its would-be publisher, so you must use the title as your foot in the door. Perhaps I should say "oar in the door," for according to H.L. Mencken, "In the duel of editor versus writer, the editor fights from a dreadnought and the writer from an open raft."

Even though you've come up with a good strong title, keep your one-sentence idea in mind as you get on with the other basics of a salable article. It can prevent you from wallowing about in generalities. And editors *hate* generalities.

The Beginning

Mood. Decide on the mood of your piece. Out-and-out humor? Serious? General? Mood, of course, is usually determined by the type of piece you're writing: personal experience, factual, think piece, essay. This doesn't mean that a factual article can't contain some humor, or that there aren't serious moments in a humor piece. But the overriding mood is primarily a result of the kind of article you're working on.

The mood of a piece may also depend upon the magazine you're targeting for. There's quite a difference between the humor written for *Playboy* and for, say, *Reader's Digest*—even though they may deal with similar subjects.

Viewpoint. It may be necessary to write your article from the first person viewpoint. Or, in a combination of "I" and "you." But most published articles are written in the third person with a generous sprinkling of the second person "you." And if you *must* use the first person, there's no better way to begin than by bringing the reader into your idea right away: "I was the head of a girls' boarding school for twenty years—and lived to tell about it."

Outline. Whether you use a very formal outline or merely a few phrases to help keep you within your idea frame depends upon your own personality. This is what makes writing so interesting and challenging. You should read voraciously how selling writers got where they are. But no one is compelled to carry on in like fashion. Take what you wish from established writers, then do the rest *your* way. As for outlines, I've always used the simple but workable "circle."

It goes like this. The beginning curves down into the middle, which then curves upward to unite the ending with a summary or final anecdote that ties in with the beginning. *Voilà!* The reader experiences a sense of completeness in your article.

Recently I read some advice from James Reston that improves upon my circle. He said "Write your stories in the shape of a 'Q.' Write all the way around the subject. When you come back to the beginning, give it a twist." Shades of O. Henry!

The beginning should show what your idea is about. It could be expressed in the form of an anecdote or be a direct statement of your idea. It could also be in multiple-choice form, inviting the reader to play a little game with you. The old rule of three applies here: don't have more than three choices, or three questions if you choose a question-and-answer format. After three your reader is thinking, "Okay, let's get on with it."

As you read published articles, get into the habit of analyzing why a particular beginning caused *you* to read the article.

The shorter your beginning, the better.

If you haven't enticed the editor with your title, this opening paragraph or two is probably your last chance to stay the hand that drops the manuscript back into its self-addressed, stamped envelope.

An editor, after all, isn't waiting with bated breath for the opportunity to read your manuscript. That same editor's eyes are no doubt tired, his or her back weary. In many, many ways this beginning is the most important part of your work, and I'm convinced that the short but intriguing beginnings of my articles have played a large part in my selling them.

Don't be misled by those closely packed beginnings you'll find in many published articles. Note that in most instances there are photos or some kind of graphic to grab the reader in the first place. In this age of electronics editors are aware that something more exciting than small black letters on plain white paper is needed to persuade people to read. When you send in your beautifully brief beginning, you've got to attract that editor. Later, he or she may wish to condense it further to make room for the graphics.

In other words, *our* task is to sell to the *editor.*

The editor's task is to sell to the *public.*

The beginning should, along with other techniques used by the writer, work to entice readers.

The key word is "entice." That doesn't mean "mislead." For instance, "Is the President getting a divorce?" followed shortly by "Of course not. But divorces in our culture are soaring."

No one appreciates that kind of trickery.

The Middle

This is where you tell your story. With your intriguing beginning, you've persuaded the "glancers" that if they will stay with you, there's an important and interesting idea that's theirs for the reading.

But that hard-won attention must be sustained all the way through the body of your article. Writers don't have readers—we have *potential* readers.

If you have difficulty getting into your idea at this point, pretend you're explaining it to someone. Say something aloud. Type it. You'll find you can usually go on from there. Later, during your rewrite, you can perhaps improve upon those sentences. Throughout your article strive to make the reader feel you're speaking directly to him or her.

You don't necessarily have to communicate your whole idea in chronological order. Something that happened some time ago may be inserted to accentuate or explain your present-day situation. This is what we call a flashback, an interruption in a normal sequence to introduce past events. When you come out of the past and enter the present again be sure to do so smoothly and clearly. Often just a word or two will suffice. "Today . . .," or "Nowadays . . .," etc.

On the whole, a chronological tale is easier to understand and enjoy. Otherwise you have one more danger zone where your reader could become weary while striving to keep up with your flashbacks and flashforwards, switching into and out of complicated time zones. It's easier for the reader to switch on the TV and find information and entertainment through that audiovisual medium.

But writers still have a few devices to capture the attention of those elusive readers, devices that can lure with a "read me" look. Call it concrete prose, call it visual writing—it's our best defense against the more glamorous forms of communication.

Lists, for instance. Readers love them. Lists suggest a quick and painless method of getting information. The white space attracts. (Not too long a list, of course, because publishers cannot afford *too* much white space.) Anyway, here's a list for you, *my* reader:

1. **Concrete nouns.**

Instead of "shoes," write "sneakers" or "slip-ons," etc. And isn't "cows munching in a meadow of buttercups" better than "livestock eating in an uncultivated area"?

2. **Active verbs.**

Sentence constructions vary, but when possible think: "A did something to B." For example, "The burglar punched the owner as he fled the house."

3. **Similes and metaphors.**

The greatest tools in a writer's bag. There is no more effective elixir with which to mix your word magic. But a word of caution. Similes and metaphors must be fresh, or seem fresh. And they must fit the situation.

Fresh: "The prof spoke at a mud-pouring pace." "The kitchen exuded a teacozy warmth." "The teacher motherhens her students in the museum."

In *Catcher in the Rye*, Holden Caulfield says that dancing with old Marty was like dragging the Statue of Liberty around the floor.

Very fresh: "Her eyes were as big and bittersweet as Godiva chocolates." (Wish I'd said that.) "He was just the sort of adventurer you'd expect to meet on the Appalachian Trail, tall as a tree and nearly as talkative." (Wish I'd said that, too. Great characterization.)

Seemingly fresh: In "The Bear," William Faulkner says that fear tasted like brass.

Fitting the situation. "The Mexican desert spread out flat as a tortilla." (Instead of, "The Mexican desert spread out flat as a pancake.")

4. Contrast.

Writers often achieve startling effects by comparing things that are strikingly different. The contrast between good and bad, or thick and thin, rich and poor, for example. (A reviewer once described a mediocre play that was given an elaborate, no-holds-barred production, as "Like putting béarnaise sauce on Spam.")

5. Onomatopoeia.

The use of words that fit a sound to a sense, like this: *K'nip k'nop k'nip k'nop"* as the sound of a ping-pong game. Or "The puppy's tongue lapped steadily at the water—*shlup, shlup, shlup."* *Bang, fizz, burp, flop,* and *sneeze* are onomatopoeic.

6. Punctuation.

Periods. Use them—after a declarative sentence, or after an imperative sentence (unless an exclamation is called for), and when a question is stated as a polite command. Example: "Will you please read Chapter Five for tomorrow."

Semicolons. Indicate a greater break in thought than the comma but less than the period—the comma is equal to, say, an eighth rest in music, the semicolon equal to the quarter rest, the period to the half rest. Semicolons are used to separate independent clauses ("The boys were late; this wasn't unusual") as well as for clarity, usually in a series.

Commas. Don't overwork them. Harold Ross, former editor of the *New Yorker,* encouraged his writers to use commas according to the rulebooks. Such as "the red, white, and blue." (James Thurber said all those commas made the flag look rained on.)

Strunk and White, those peerless authorities, agree with Ross that the comma before the *and* is important for clarity. If you disagree, watch what happens when the comma is left out of this example:

"Write name, address, age, sex and housing requirements."

Then there was Oscar Wilde, who said, "I'm exhausted. I spent all morning putting in a comma and all afternoon taking it out."

Commas are necessary and sometimes useful for a kind of rhythmic quality in prose. But if there's no good reason to use a comma, forget it. It does no harm to bend rules once in a while as long as we retain an overall respect for our beautiful English language.

Dashes. Dots. Exclamation points. There's a tendency to overuse all three of these forms of punctuation. Some writers use them, it seems, to avoid having to decide what punctuation mark to use. Still, each has its uses.

Dashes and dots can transmit moods. Three dots suggest unexpressed but continuing thought. A dash illustrates an interruption, or it can accent a word or phrase that follows. A dash has more flair than a comma and it doesn't slow down the action or the reader.

Exclamation points transmit dramatic qualities: the famous play was not *Oklahoma* but *Oklahoma!* An exclamation point can change the entire meaning of a sentence. Note the difference in "Why not?" and "Why not!" However, exclamations lose their strength through overuse.

These are only a few of the basic rules and are not a complete guide to the science of punctuation. To learn to use punctuation correctly—and professionals are expected to—you must keep a good stylebook at hand, *and use it*, as you write. The aforementioned Strunk and White's *Elements of Style* is one such book. Another, one that is *the* accepted modern style authority and is likely to be on your editor's desk as well, is *The Chicago Manual of Style* from the University of Chicago Press. It's a book no writer should be without.

7. **Anecdotes.**

Short narratives relevant to your article involving people in action—to illustrate an idea—constitute perhaps one of your most important tools. Example: "Is technology the cause of unemployment? Years ago, two workmen watched with awe the performance of a huge steam shovel, which took up many tons of earth in one bite. Said one, 'If it wasn't for that blasted scoop, five hundred of us might be working with shovels.' 'Yes,' said the other. 'And if it wasn't for our shovels, a million of us might be working with spoons.' "

8. **Quotations.**

Like anecdotes, of which they are often a part, quotations pep up your writing and give readers a feel for the people in your article. Use them correctly, and use them often.

9. **Alliteration.**

It's the repetition of the same sound at the beginning of two or more consecutive words or of words near one another.

Examples: "A ladybug, small and spotted, seated on a leaf of gold," which I read somewhere. Or "soot and cinders cover the city sidewalks." In a rewrite for a recent article I changed "She patented a color for the bedroom walls" to "She coined a color for the bedroom walls." These precious pieces of prose are fine on occasion but don't use them too often—as many writers are prone to do.

10. **"You."**

For practical purposes you should start to think of that little pronoun as the name of your reader. It permits the writer to be friendly with readers without being too familiar. It is one of the best methods you have for creating a one-on-one relationship with your readers. And it more easily allows readers to identify with you and what you're trying to say.

Naturally the use of "you" will depend upon the particular kind of article. *You* cannot always incorporate it—for example, in the "I" piece, the personal experience or "it happened to me" article.

11. **Style.**

An aspiring writer once asked a professional the definition of "style." The reply was, "Your style is *you*."

Don't be afraid to allow *you* to come through in your writing. I'm referring to *your* you, not the reader's *you*. Dare to experiment with some of your original ideas by displaying a unique—"You-nique"—style.

We cannot and need not incorporate those eleven items—or other techniques I haven't the space to mention—in every article we write. And we need not even *worry* about them during the original process of connecting all those tenuous strands of thought into one taut line that we'll reel out during the writing process.

That's why rewrites were born—to give writers a better chance at a byline and a check.

The Ending

This is the point where your circle (or "Q") closes.

My advice for the perfect ending:

1. Save something special for the end. Something with clout.

2. Come back to the beginning in some fashion.

3. Have only one ending. Don't be like the boring speaker who has four or five conclusions.

That done, ask yourself, "Did I say in my article what I was going to say in that one-sentence idea?"

It's surprising how easily a writer can allow an original train of thought to get switched off on a sidetrack. It's all right there in your head, so it's easy to assume that the complete idea has been transmitted clearly to the public. Alas, not necessarily so.

My own antidote for that is to take a page at a time, scan it, ask myself what I said on that page, jot it down in a sentence, then continue the same exercise with the following pages of manuscript. You cannot actually visualize an entire manuscript as an artist does a canvas. But you *can* see the overall concept if it's written in condensed form, one sentence per page.

By now many of you may have decided—and rightly so—that there's a lot more to the writing craft than you thought. You may be wondering if you'll ever be able to write a literate article about a serious idea and stand a chance of selling it. Well, you can—but only if you write, revise, rewrite, condense, expand, insert, and rewrite again.

Why? Because—and it bears repeating—we must compete with the ever-expanding technology of communication. Lois Gould expressed it thus: "The audience which responds to television no longer can glue its eyes to a page of gray type." She added that word people have already lost much of their audience because they don't understand that.

A recent item in the *Washington Post* began this way: " 'A Nation of Readers,' the exhibit now playing at the Library of Congress, is perhaps less noteworthy for its admirable contents than for its wishful title. Ours is a nation of many things, but 'A Nation of Readers' it is not."

And it may be in the process of becoming even less so as the more exciting forms of communication continue to attract our young people.

That is why, after you've put the basics of your article together, you must tackle the chore of the rewrite. (Sometimes *rewrites*.) This is where you can improve the syntax, check for accuracy, and clear up foggy passages.

Does it all sound difficult? Well, it isn't easy. If it were, everyone would be a writer and then editors would go mad trying to choose among us. It is work, but as with other creative endeavors, the feeling of accomplishment is fantastic when you see your byline over the finished product.

And who knows? That great idea of yours may be what Thornton Wilder had in mind when he wrote (in *Centaurs*), "The stuff of which masterpieces are made drifts about the world waiting to be clothed in words."

Your words.

Any professional who stays out of singles bars and sauna baths will vouch for Berniece Roer Neal's words. Her basics are the keys that unlock editorial doors—and basics are mainly responsible for the many published credits of each person whose work appears in this book. If you want to be published, make use of Neal's essential elements for a salable article.

This doesn't mean that you won't sell an occasional piece that *doesn't* include one or possibly two of these basics. You will. Sometimes you can peddle a piece with a less than intriguing title. But you can bet the editor will come up with a catchy caption before the article sees print. There'll be times, too, when your style is a little sickly. But the good editor will punch it up before publication. (As the *New Yorker*'s Wolcott Gibbs once noted in a memo on editing, "Try to preserve an author's style if he is an author and has a style.")

However, the writing that consistently works will contain the fundamentals Neal has discussed. It doesn't make any difference into what category the article happens to fall. Your piece can be about people, about things, or about ideas and opinions—the basics are the same. Keep them in mind always to help you sell your writing.

TEN TYPES OF MAGAZINE ARTICLES

Having mastered the basics, you still must decide what *kind* of article to write—the same idea can be handled in different ways. Shirley Biagi classifies articles within ten categories: informational, how-to, profile, historical, personal experience, inspirational, humor and satire, travel, investigative, and point of view. She says that none of these categories is exclusive; sometimes categories overlap—you could do a historical travel piece, for instance, or an inspirational profile. Obviously, other writers and editors may classify articles differently, but Biagi's theory is that once you have some concept of the options available, you can match your idea with the markets that buy those kinds of articles.

Certain types of articles appeal to different editors and readers more than others, of course. Your job is to propose an article that is slanted for a particular magazine—and for high readership appeal. Here's what Biagi has to say about her ten magazine article categories:

"**Informational article.** This is the most common. An informational article may sketch a runner's map for your town, describe a medical procedure, or detail parts of a 1936 Ford engine. It must include accurate information, explained in easy-to-understand language. Verify and recheck every detail.

"**How-to.** The recipe is an easily recognizable how-to. However, recipes for solar water heaters are just as much how-to's as recipes for hot Texas chili, and more marketable. How-to's are a good choice for the beginning freelancer. Offer step-by-step instructions and if possible, duplicate the process you're discussing, watching for holes in your description. Think of yourself as a teacher explaining an experiment that you expect the class to duplicate. Be careful to avoid words that might confuse the beginner.

"**Profile.** In the twenties, the *New Yorker* popularized the idea that a magazine article could sketch a word portrait of a personality, and that section of the magazine was called 'Profile.' Interviews with notable people are always salable, but a profile of someone in your community with an unusual hobby or profession or someone who has accomplished an interesting feat is just as marketable. This is another good choice for the novice.

"**Historical.** This type of article is not confined to historical events or people, but may simply have facts arranged chronologically, whether you are describing the history of the hot dog or chronicling the events that caused the 1929 stock market crash.

"**Personal experience.** The pronoun 'I' is an element in any personal experience article since the storyteller is usually the central observer. Everyday personal experiences often make good fiction when told well, but for nonfiction you are more likely to sell an adventure that few people have shared.

"**Inspirational.** This is a variety of the personal experience article, although the experience may be a friend's or a relative's. A moral message is crucial here. The purpose of this article is to uplift the reader. Avoid negative ideas and create the feeling that hope always exists. Remember that hope sometimes grows out of a feeling of hopelessness or despair. The emotions of the experience are central to the inspirational article.

"**Humor and satire.** This is a difficult form, mastered by few. If you want to try, do not write a letter to an editor asking whether he or she would be interested in your humor; send the entire article. This is different from all other types of articles, for which you query the editor first.

"**Travel.** Visiting Waikiki may have been fascinating for you, but asking a travel editor to buy 6,000 words about 'gorgeous white sand beaches' is an insult. The successful travel writer chooses the offbeat, photographs the unusual, visits the out-of-the-way.

"**Investigative.** An evolutionary form of what was called 'muckraking' at the turn of the century, investigative articles are time-consuming and rely heavily on detailed research. The beginning freelancer probably should avoid this type of article, as the markets are limited and the payment you receive for your article may not compensate for the time and money you must spend gathering statistics. However, if you are already a specialist in a subject area, have completed the research as part of another project, and know that no investigation of the same type has been published, this can be satisfying and lucrative.

It's the kind of piece that often leads to a nonfiction book contract, too.

"**Point of view.** The Letters to the Editor column of every newspaper contains someone's point of view. If you want to sound off on a topic, write a letter to the editor and do not expect to be paid for it. In this category, editors are especially impressed by credentials. Freelancers should avoid this type of article unless they have extraordinary backgrounds and are themselves experts or have personal access to experts they can quote. Marketable point-of-view articles usually contain opinions of people specially qualified to state those opinions."

But no matter what kind of article you decide to write, you must begin with a solid structure. Some writers are able to think through an article thoroughly and see the sequence of their piece so clearly that they can then sit down and start writing or typing. Others must make a detailed outline and then write from it. Still other writers do a first draft of the piece and concentrate on structuring during a second or even third draft. I know many good writers who never do their leads and conclusions until all else is written and in order.

How you do it is up to you, of course. The important thing is to leave the reader feeling that the order is right, if not inevitable.

UNITY, COHERENCE, EMPHASIS

No discussion of the anatomy of a magazine article would be complete without a word or two about the key elements of *unity, coherence,* and *emphasis.* They are the mortar that holds together the structural bricks of beginning, middle, and end. Successful writers use the principles of unity, coherence, and emphasis to build logical, readable articles.

1. **Unity,** the first principle, is simply singleness of purpose, consistency of theme. One writer has called it the piece of string on which the writer's thoughts and facts are strung. It means staying on track, avoiding deviation from the thesis.

2. **Coherence,** principle number two, is the cement of your piece and holds your words, sentences, and paragraphs together so that they achieve unity. Without coherence, your article won't move smoothly from one thought to another.

3. **Emphasis,** the third basic principle of structure, means stressing key parts of your article so they stand out and take on special importance for the reader. No emphasis, no highs or lows in your piece, results in writing as dull and monotonous as soap opera dialogue. Emphasis allows your reader to grasp ideas in the order of importance you intended when you structured the article. Here are some ways to give

emphasis to a piece: by flat statement (usually from an authority); by building up one topic or one person over others; by means of style (i.e., *how* you say what you say); by relative positioning of certain facts, ideas, or thoughts; by repetition; or by a sidebar (the trade term for what the text refers to when it says "see box") or a special information paragraph (e.g., when magazines or newspapers set a paragraph in heavy black type known as boldface).

There is another constant in writing, and that is organization. As Francis Bacon wrote four centuries ago, "If it be done without order the mind comprehendeth less that which is set down; and besides, it leaveth a suspicion, as if more might be said than is expressed."

ORGANIZING THE MAGAZINE ARTICLE

The structure of a magazine article is just the opposite of a newspaper story. The structure of the newspaper piece resembles an inverted pyramid. All the important facts are crammed into the beginning—the lead. The details (which in a magazine are threaded into the fabric of the article) are included in a sequence of descending importance. This is done so that as succeeding editions of the paper come out and other news takes precedence, the editor can cut the story from the bottom without losing the main facts.

The magazine article's structure, on the other hand, resembles an upright pyramid, with the lead, theme, body, and conclusion following in more or less orderly fashion throughout the article, held together by the mortar of unity, coherence, and emphasis.

Why the difference? Yesterday's newspapers are for wrapping fish; magazines stay around longer on the coffee tables or in doctor's offices. Magazine articles are usually—if you've done your job—read through to the end.

If you study published articles you will see that with only slight variations, they use the pattern of progression discussed here by Paul Friggens, who in Chapter 2 gave us his insights into interviewing. If you don't remember anything else in this book, store somewhere in your memory bank what this freelance writer-author-lecturer has to say about the importance of organization.

STRUCTURING YOUR ARTICLE
by Paul Friggens

If I had to put down some basic rules for all writers in search of a successful career, "Organize your material" would top the list. It would probably top many editors' lists, too, since they complain most often about writing that lacks organization.

Lack of organization shows early on in an article, because the writer fails at the beginning to tell readers exactly what the piece is about, where it's going, and why it is important that it be read. The writer fails to carry out the stated intention—to talk about what he or she was supposed to talk about, in the right order.

How do you achieve this organization?

It begins with effective gathering of your materials, and the first imperative is to *think your article through*—that is, decide what your central message is and then how you intend to document it. As you think your story through, you should also choose an accurate, compelling title. Some writers disagree with me, but I find that I'm not really ready to compose until I've thought through the piece and written a good working title.

So now, let's assume you've decided on a compelling title. What's next?

You should set down clearly, and in the right order, the main points or ideas that will sustain and document your title. You can do this one of three ways:

1. *You can outline in detail what you wish to say.* I know this sounds elementary, like high school English. But you can't write clearly until you know, even before you start, precisely where you're going and where you will stop.

Your outline should include the principle ideas and/or subheads under your title. These main ideas are signposts to guide the reader through your piece.

And just how should you organize these signposts?

Many writers use 3x5-inch cards, noting one point (or signpost) on each card. Those who use this method then group all the cards covering a single point together.

Next, they arrange the cards—their main points or signposts—in the most logical sequence to effectively tell the story. In so doing, they know what they want to say and where they want to take the piece before they have even begun to write.

2. *You can draft a short, simple (informal) outline.* This may include just a paragraph or two systematically setting down your signposts in whatever sequence you deem most effective for telling the story. Having sorted out this set of directions in brief outline form, you're ready to write.

3. *Or you can do as I do* (but I don't recommend this procedure for everyone): think your story through (your mental planning) and choose a compelling title; type only the story's major points on one 3x5-inch card—and do your first draft largely from memory.

In effect, you write a letter and thus achieve a fluidity in your narration. You construct a beginning, a middle, and an ending. Invariably, I know how my story is going to end before I ever start to write.

Admittedly, this first draft is loose, inaccurate, and usually omits or overlooks some pertinent materials. But it does provide some sense of structure, a point from which you can now go back and insert precise quotations, statistics, and other source materials in a second draft.

After you pull your material together in this second draft, you're ready to condense, expand, insert—in short, revise in whatever ways are necessary to produce what I call *marching copy* (i.e., it moves right along). Then you write the third (and perhaps final) draft. But the best articles are written and rewritten, and you may wish to do four or five drafts before you're satisfied with your piece.

If there's any secret to this business of writing articles, stories, or books, it's to stick to those main ideas, those signposts.

You're taking readers on a trip, to a definite destination. So first, let them know where they are—and where they're going—as the journey gets underway. Then make sure you've set up signposts at each fork in the road. Though readers may not be aware of it, you're actually leading them by the hand through a maze of materials. But, if you've properly organized those materials, you do it so skillfully—much like the slow emerging of a clearing from dense forest—that the readers don't realize you've stripped away the underbrush and are safely guiding them out of the woods.

Each of these signposts, of course, introduces a new aspect of your article. The value of good organization is that you then take up each aspect, discuss it, dispose of it, and go on to the next point.

This demands a smooth transition, naturally, and a clear-cut signpost. But I have found that organizing my material in this orderly fashion, and proceeding in the script from copy block to copy block, greatly facilitates my writing. Then, at the end, I bring it all together—preferably with a strong conclusion—and I have thus delivered the reader to the destination.

Like all writers and editors, I've struggled hardest with this problem of organization. The trouble is that we fail to think our stories through, to recognize the main points or set up our signposts. Each night, after travel and interviewing on *Reader's Digest* assignments, I would go back over my day's notes to see how I was progressing and ask myself these questions: Did I really know where I was going? Just what *was* the story, what were the principal elements, what should I be developing in order to bring home all the essential points and, ultimately, bring off a sound, balanced article?

Each night, I'd do a brief running outline of my story, listing the signposts as they seemed to be pointing—and noting, as well, whatever questions, quotes, and evidence I appeared to be lacking. In this way, I came home with the whole story; frequently I had formulated a compelling title, lead, and ending even before I had studied my notebooks, documents, and great stacks of source materials.

This is the essence of organization, and no writer can competently lead a reader by the hand through the subject until he or she has first thought the story through.

Experience and practice—which translates to constant revision of your work—alone will help you refine your techniques of organizing and writing. There will be heartaches along the way, but persistence can turn them into satisfaction.

REVISIONS & REWRITES

The late Paul Reynolds, well-known literary agent, thought that any first-draft manuscript could be improved by revision. The *New Yorker's* famed Genet (Janet Flanner) admitted that "I keep going over a sentence, I nag it, gnaw it, pat and flatter it."

Some—in fact, most—serious writers go over their work with great care. They weigh every paragraph, every sentence, often every *phrase* with a view to improving their first, second, and subsequent drafts. Many would-be writers seem surprised to learn that professionals revise and rewrite over and over to achieve the result they're after. It's easy when you're just starting out to be so smitten with your precious prose that you're blind to its abuse or misuse. And you're so happy to have completed an article that little or no thought is given to such mundane matters as length and pace or even readability.

Samuel Johnson wrote, "An old tutor of a college said to one of his pupils: 'Read over your compositions and whenever you meet with a passage you think is particularly fine, strike it out.' " It hurts, sure. Sometimes it hurts like hell—but revise, cut, perform surgery until you're convinced you've done your best with the manuscript.

You can revise in several ways. The most common is by simply editing your first draft by hand, with pencil or pen. Some writers do rewrites on their typewriters. Others use scissors and paste to cut and rearrange sections of a manuscript. What's best is what works for *you* as you condense, expand, insert, and rewrite.

Revision may be one of the hardest acts of writing for you, but it is also one of the most necessary. You must be willing to run your manuscript through the typewriter time and again. Only when you are conditioned to throw away pages and rewrite your beloved prose are you beginning to learn your craft. T.S. Eliot—with the help of Ezra Pound—

revised "The Wasteland" several times. Author Rosemary Rogers is reported to have rewritten her bestseller *Sweet Savage Love* twenty-three times! Bruce Catton, the highly sucessful historian, admits to constant revision of his work.

If you are fortunate enough to make a sale to one of the mass-circulation magazines, plan on doing a rewrite. As they say, it goes with the territory. This is especially true with tough-to-sell markets such as *Playboy* or *Reader's Digest*, both noted for asking writers for one or more altered versions of accepted manuscripts.

Accept the fact that you will often have to rewrite to make the sale. Do it, and count your blessings. You're in a highly competitive field and arguing with editors about revisions or rewrites won't endear you to them. And you'd be surprised how effective and widespread the grapevine is in this business; it's easy to get a reputation for being surly and uncooperative. Besides, you aren't going to change the editor's mind about a proposed revision (or rewrite), because he or she usually has a better idea of what's wanted for the magazine's readers—and knows the magazine's space requirements. Change the piece as that editor suggests and get it back to the magazine—fast. And get on with your next project.

When this happens to me, as it does to us all, I send a cover letter with my revision thanking the editor for suggesting changes that made my manuscript acceptable. In my experience, editors not only appreciate such an attitude but think favorably of you next time an assignment is in search of a writer. Ego aside, a good article that impresses the reader is the result of collaboration, of close work between you and your editor.

You can, however, get caught up in a vicious rewrite syndrome. I've known writers who spent too much of their valuable time revising, rewriting, and polishing their material. After a while, you lose any objectivity you might originally have brought to the piece. It starts to bore you. A little common sense will serve you well here. While you're reworking any manuscript, ask yourself: Can I say this more simply, more aptly? You may discover that it doesn't need to be said at all! Then be done with it. In William Zinsser's words, "There's not much to be said about the period except that most writers don't reach it soon enough."

Many writers claim they do their best writing while revising. Some professionals say they let a manuscript rest for several days or weeks before getting to their revisions or rewrites. Dorothy Aldis, the children's writer, says she lets a manuscript rest six months before doing any revision. This allows thoughts to jell and the writer can approach the piece fresh, with a more detached point of view. Usually good writers are also good readers. They can spot someone else's bad writing.

Revising or rewriting is being able to discipline yourself sufficiently to apply the same critical standards to your own material.

I like what *Writer's Digest* columnist Art Spikol says in *Magazine Writing: The Inside Angle:*

"Who's right? There is no right. Different strokes, as they say. If you can do it in one draft, you're either good enough to get it right the first time out, or you don't have enough taste to realize that you really should've done three drafts. If you do six drafts as a matter of course, you might be heading for an ulcer. Or a nervous breakdown. Or the Nobel Prize in literature."

As Spikol says, each writer must finally work out his own revision and rewrite routines. What works for you may not work for me. But one thing's certain: all writers will need to do considerable amounts of both revising and rewriting.

Whichever methods you employ (and you'll experiment with all of them if you're wise), don't despair. Experience and practice—and this means constant revision of "completed" articles or books—are the best teachers. As painful as rewriting may be for you, sooner or later you'll discover that revision equals sales. Or, as Kurt Vonnegut says, "This is what I find most encouraging about the writing trades: they allow mediocre people who are patient and industrious to revise their stupidity, to edit themselves into something like intelligence."

One ASJA member told me, "I'm not at all happy when I have to revise, but I'm a helluva lot more unhappy when I don't have to."

This final suggestion comes from Kay Cassill: "If you still need help, get an editorially talented, hard-nosed friend, sibling, or spouse to criticize your work from time to time. Your prose will improve, and so will your ability to undergo the editorial blue pencil without getting the blues."

A FEW WORDS ABOUT SEXISM

Recently another salvo was fired in the battle against sexism in the English language. This one came from Professor W. Kenneth McFarlane of Temple University. In search of a new genderless pronoun, the good professor says he is "continually exasperated by expressions like 'he or she,' the unpronounceable 's/he,' or by the alternative of constructing sentences like, 'Every student in the laboratory must collect that student's own data.' "

And until a new pronoun is invented, the concerned academic has a suggestion: we might—just might, mind you—replace the "h" in "he," "him," and "his" with the "s" from the feminine pronoun "she." Thus McFarlane's sample sentence would become: "Every student in the laboratory must collect *sis* own data."

Why he didn't take the easy way out is beyond me. All he had to do is use a *plural* form of the word up front, as the subject, then he could legitimately use *their* as the pronoun. Thus, "Students in the laboratory must collect *their* own data."

Of course, I realize this device doesn't always work. But in those few instances where it won't, there are other ways. You can, for example, refer to a person by job title or organizational position, rather than referring to the person's sex: instead of saying "The woman in our New York office will give you the information," say, "The executive secretary in our New York office will give you the information."

You can often write around the pronoun. For example, instead of writing, "Sales will only result if the writer himself has worked to earn them," try saying "Sales will only result from the writer's own efforts . . ."

Some publishing houses suggest you use a slash between the two gender-related pronouns, if there's no other way to handle it. "Each reader must make his/her own judgment." I'd still use the plural "readers" here, but admittedly there are times when the plural won't be appropriate—or accurate.

I don't think Professor McFarlane's neuter singular pronoun is going to be a winner. Neither do I think beginning writers—or any other writers—should let this sort of problem keep them awake at night. Many times in this book I have used "his or her" and that gets unwieldy and awkward. (I have even let writers get away with using (s)he once or twice—but I was quoting them and that's what *they* said!) You'll note that I've stuck with *his* most of the time, even though I'm aware my traditional remedy for the *he/she* dilemma may bring down the wrath both of my fellow ASJA members and the editors at Writer's Digest Books.

I could have alternated *hims* and *hers* and *hes* and *shes*. But that would only have drawn further attention to the problem.

All this is not to say feminists aren't justified in pointing out that our language has long since assumed that everybody was male unless proven otherwise. Nor am I necessarily arguing against the need to de-gender the language. The language, after all, must sooner or later get into step with social change.

Sexism is a problem you must deal with in your daily work. And if you're wise, you'll not get caught up in the sexist language snarl. You won't let extremists on either side of the fence keep you from your appointed time with the typewriter. Just be careful not to write such things as "Everyone should hold on to *their* notes." (The pronoun *their* is obviously plural, and does not agree with its antecedent in number.) Simply say, "Writers should hold on to *their* notes."

There's no need for exaggeration in handling sexism in your writing, a few inflexible and humorless reformers notwithstanding. It's foolish to use such word-contraptions as "herstory" for *history* and "wo/manual" for *manual*. Still, an awareness of sexual equality does demand certain logical changes. David W. Ewing offers the following rules excerpted from his book *Writing For Results* (John Wiley and Sons, 1979):

"1. *Be consistent in your manner of referring to males and females.* If you refer to men by their last names, refer to women by their last names, also. If you use only the first names of men, use only the first names of women. If you call the women *girls*, call the men *boys*. If you put *Mrs.* or *Ms.* before a woman's name, put *Mr.* before a man's name.

"2. *Do not describe a characteristic of women that you would not describe if the people were men.* Referring to Maxwell as a *buxom blonde*, or to Esposito as a *grandmother of three* is inappropriate if you would not think of calling Tamoshunas a *broad-shouldered guy* or Andrews a *grandfather of three*.

"3. *Avoid patronizing references to women.* For instance, don't refer to the *fair sex* or the *weaker sex*; say *women*. Don't write *authoress, poetess,* or *Jewess*; write *author, poet,* or *Jew*. The term *housewife* is in disfavor; use *homemaker* instead.

"4. *Recognize that decision makers in most fields today are male and female.*

"5. *Use nondiscriminating occupational terms.* (For example, *chairperson* or *chair* instead of *chairman, spokesperson* instead of *spokesman, firefighter* instead of *fireman*.)

"6. *Don't go to ridiculous extremes.* (One wag claims that the next term we will have to learn is *person-person* instead of *mail-man*.)"

We all have read humorous pieces about the *person* suffix kind of lunacy in which the writer lets *his/her* imagination run wild, pursuing bizarre examples of locutions such as Norseperson, personhole cover, personpower, personslaughter, personly, and so on. Don't be entrapped by pompous patterns and precedents (leave those to William Safire or Edwin Newman). Some of these matters resolve themselves, in time. Years ago everyone called Amelia Earhart an "aviatrix." Today "aviator" is the accepted term, whatever the flier's sex. Emily Dickinson was a "poetess," although today she's remembered as a "poet." Yet men are still "waiters." Women are not—they're "waitresses." Men and women are both "authors" but women actors are actresses. And, it should be added, men or women who take care of your food, drink, and other needs on planes are "flight attendants."

How do writers learn to recognize sexist language patterns and remove them from their writing? Some publishing houses have written guidelines to help their writers over the shoals of sexism. An excellent book on the subject is *The Handbook of Nonsexist Writing* by Casey Miller and Kate Swift (Lippincott & Crowell, 1980). And remember that editors are ever swift to clean up your chauvinistic copy.

STYLE? WHAT'S A STYLE?

Without question, the most controversial and elusive of the basic elements of a salable article is style. There are as many variations of style as there are definitions of what it is. Swift said style is putting "proper words in proper places." Schopenhauer believed "style is the physiognomy of the mind, and a safer index to character than the face." Matthew Arnold wrote: "People think I can teach them style. What stuff it all is! Have something to say, and say it as clearly as you can. This is the only secret of style." *The American College Dictionary* defines style as "characteristic mode of writing or speaking, as determined by period, literary form, personality, etc."

Style in writing is each writer's own personal way of expressing something. Writing styles, like styles in dress or architecture, vary with the times. As the late Bergen Evans noted, the writer must listen to the way people actually talk, must know every shade and nuance, so that without his readers in the least perceiving *how* he does it, he can speak to them in words and phrases that move them.

Most professional writers and editors seem to agree that the best writing styles are the most natural styles. Many of our better writers think and talk much the same way they write.

The trend in the U.S. for some years now has been toward simple, conversational, informal writing. Sentences (and articles) grow shorter each year, especially if you want to sell to the mass-circulation magazines and newspapers. Write as if you were talking to your reader in person. Dr. Evans believed that "a student should adapt himself to the conversational style by seeking models who have mastered that style—writers like Twain, Hemingway, Lardner—and by checking the conversational quality of his work by reading it aloud to himself."

One way to make your writing easier to read is by sentence variety. This involves using question and answers, mixing short sentences with your longer ones, and taking care that no sentence is made exactly like the one before. Another way is to use familiar, comfortable words. Mark Twain once said: "I never write *metropolis* for seven cents when I can get the same price for *city*."

Style is what Chesterton chose to call "the dress of thought." It's you, the writer, who must choose how you wish to clothe your thoughts—and that choice will determine your style. Style will come with practice. One key point to remember: don't consciously adopt someone else's style. As Voltaire wrote: "All styles are good that are not tiresome."

ORGANIZING THE NONFICTION BOOK

Writers of nonfiction books face problems comparable (but proportionately bigger) to article writers in writing and selling their wares. They conceive an idea, research the market, refine the idea, get it down on paper and, once satisfied the job is done, send the manuscript to an agent or appropriate publisher and await results.

Between getting that brilliant idea and delivering that sparkling manuscript, however, comes the all-important ingredient Paul Friggens wrote about for articles: organization.

The same basic principles apply when organizing a nonficton book as with an article. You must think your project through from start to finish, mentally sorting out your ideas and putting them in logical order as you do your preliminary research. When you've done this, you will probably (I say probably because different writers, different strokes) want to prepare an outline based on your research and mental sorting.

Not Like You Learned in School

When an editor says "Let me see an outline and a sample chapter," he or she doesn't mean the old college method of beginning with "I. Introduction" and following with endless subjects such as "A, A1, A1a." What the editor means is, "Describe your book and tell me what's involved and how you're planning to treat the material."

Writers outline using many forms and approaches. Some are more formal than others; many outline in their minds only. But in book writing, outlines help most of us as we sift and sort through our welter of source material. And shuffling ideas and facts and setting them down in 1-2-3 order is easier *before* we begin to write than after we're several chapters into our book. Based on the substantial foundation of an outline, what you ultimately build will be a book of sounder and surer structure.

One of the simplest methods for organizing your book—and one many writers I know use—is to write out your chapter titles, using separate cards for each one. Then, start adding cards as various subjects occur to you until you can't think of any more. That done, go through all your subject cards, arranging them by chapters in a logical order. (You can always add new cards if gaps in your sequence appear.)

It also helps to research the market for a book (i.e., check *Books in Print* and publishers' catalogs) before you begin writing it. You may find that you'll want to reslant your topic according to what's already in print or what likely publishers you turn up, or perhaps scrap the idea altogether. In any case, the less work you have to redo or throw out based upon market findings the better. And convincing marketing conclusions can only strengthen your proposal in an editor's eyes.

Having completed your outline you will see that you've pretty thoroughly planned the book itself. You've thought the project through from start to finish, you've located pertinent sources of information, begun to compile material from key sources, and sorted and digested what you've already assembled.

Now you're ready to write a sample chapter or two, which you'll include as part of your proposal package. (Proposals are discussed in detail in Chapter 4.) Which chapter should you write? Many authors prefer to start with the first, introductory chapter, to demonstrate how they will capture the reader's interest immediately, and many editors like to see the first chapter for this reason. But also write a chapter you're really excited about—your enthusiasm may help sell the editor on your idea.

WRITING IN TANDEM—COLLABORATION

To close this chapter, let's take a look at another important part of nonfiction work, one that is somewhat mysterious to most fledgling writers, since its professional practitioners often do their work in obscurity. I'm talking about collaboration, that tricky area of writing in which two heads can be better than one—or worse than none.

The merits of collaboration can be vouched for by many ASJA writers: Patrick M. McGrady Jr. (*The Pritikin Program for Diet & Exercise*, with Nathan Pritikin; see Chapter 9 for McGrady's views); Dodi Schultz (*The First Five Years*, with Virginia E. Pomeranz, M.D.); and Terry Morris (*A New You: How Plastic Surgery Can Change Your Life*, with James O. Stallings, M.D.) are just a few.

Perhaps the best-known collaborators in our organization are Judi K-Turkel and Franklynn Peterson, who have worked as a successful writing team for years. They explained their work methods, which apply to books and articles alike, at an ASJA craft session.

"One of us writes the first draft and does all the research. Then the other edits the first draft, asking for clarification or amplification where needed, making suggestions, cleaning up the language, and typing the second draft. That way, we find that by the time we send our completed manuscript to the publisher, there's little for the copyeditor to do. Because the 'uninvolved' partner approaches the manuscript cold, we know that if (s)he understands and is entertained, the book does what we've set out to do. Our writing has improved since we've joined forces, because we hold each other to high standards."

But collaboration, like croquet or watching Phil Donahue, is not for everyone. It can be as tricky as riding the New York City subway. For one thing, there has to be a certain chemistry between the two persons. Even then, there are special problems and considerations, and if you don't resolve these at the outset, your partner (usually a celebrity or an expert in a special field) can send you screaming to the cracker factory.

In other words, choosing to collaborate with somebody on a book—or even an article—is serious business, since you'll be working closely and intensely with that person for six months or a year or more. You are investing your writing skill, experience, contacts, and time— and gambling your hard-earned reputation—on your co-worker's reliability and integrity.

To explain collaboration, with its many pluses as well as pitfalls, I can think of no ASJA writer more suited to the task than former ASJA president Norman M. Lobsenz. A highly successful and prolific writer, Lobsenz collaborated on the bestseller *No-Fault Marriage*. Currently, he has another smash hit, *Nobody's Perfect*, which he wrote with Hendrie Weisinger, and at this writing, yet another collaboration (with the co-author of *No-Fault Marriage*, Marcia Lasswell), *Equal Time*, has just been published.

Here are some points to consider, according to Lobsenz, before you commit yourself to collaborating with anybody—whether it be an expert from one of the professions or your identical twin.

THE COLLABORATION FACTOR
by Norman Lobsenz

Nonfiction collaborations, especially in the book field, seem to be highly productive. As I write, four of the ten top titles on the current bestseller list carry double bylines. But collaborations can also turn sour, be depressing, infuriating, unrewarding. They can start friendships, but they can also end them. How a collaborative writing project works out depends on how well you are aware of—and can guard against—the problems that so often appear.

For example, a writer I know embarked on a major project some years ago in collaboration with a well-known sociologist. The writer spent a great deal of time preparing a detailed outline, which was approved by the collaborator. But when the writer received the first packet of research material which was to provide the content of the first chapter, he was horrified to find that it consisted only of half a dozen pages of scribbled notes. When the same thing happened with succeeding chapters, the writer ultimately decided to abandon the project and return his share of the advance to the publisher. "It was," the writer said, "a nightmare."

The experienced writer will ask himself several key questions before agreeing to enter into a collaboration:

1. Will the other person's idea or personal experience be of wide enough popular interest—or a unique enough specialized project—to be worth my investment of time and energy? I've often been approached by would-be collaborators who are convinced their idea is important; but when I look into it in any detail, it becomes clear that there is a limited audience for it.

2. Assuming the idea has substance, does the collaborator have enough supportive material (facts, theories, statistics, anecdotes, case histories) to flesh it out to book length? Recently I was asked to work with a psychologist on a book that would help parents answer children's questions about sensitive topics. The material from which I was supposed to produce this book turned out to be one tape cassette with some generalized comments by the expert, plus a packet of index cards—each of which carried a scribbled "typical" question.

3. Will the collaborator give me enough of his or her time? Too many "experts"—physicians, therapists, lawyers, etc.—imagine that talking to you for a few hours, or turning over a handful of files and clippings, fulfills their share of the task.

4. Is the collaborator reasonably knowledgeable about the business of writing? Most are not. They have *un*reasonable expectations about how long it takes to produce a finished manuscript, how long it takes to turn that manuscript into a finished book, how much the book is likely to earn, etc. When reality does not meet their expectations they are likely to blame you for it.

Ground rules: There are *no* set rules that govern such touchy areas as who has the last word on the manuscript, how the byline will read, how the earnings (if any) will be divided. You and your collaborator must set your own ground rules in each case. In many instances the writer and the collaborator actually draw up a written agreement spelling out these guidelines in detail. Whether you opt for a written agreement or not depends on your relationship with your collaborator: Is he or she a friend? Can the other person be trusted to share the load?

Written or not, you and your collaborator need to agree on several essential points:

Who controls what the book says? In my own experience working with experts in the field of psychology and counseling, the expert has the last word on content and I have the last word on organization and style.

What is the working schedule? How often will you meet for interviews? Will each of you prepare drafts of the material, or will one of you do the original version and let the other concentrate on rewriting and revising?

What happens if one of you fails to maintain the writing schedule and thereby threatens to delay the manuscript past its deadline?

What happens if the project falters through no fault of yours? Are you recompensed for your time? Can you take the idea and seek another collaborator?

How will the byline read? In a true collaboration, the byline usually reads, "By Dr. John Jones *and* Norman Lobsenz." A collaborator who resists sharing credit to this extent may want the byline to read "By Dr. John Jones *with . . . .*" or *"as told to . . . ."* Also, if it's necessary to use the first person singular— e.g., "As I said to one of my patients"—a *with* byline makes the most sense. (If you are ghosting a manuscript, of course, you will get no byline credit at all.)

Finally, how will the earnings be divided? There are probably as many ways to split the income from a collaborative project as there are collaborations. Here are some of the options:

All monies earned will be split 50-50.

All monies earned will be split in different proportions—60/40, 75/25, etc.—depending on whether the collaborators agree on which of them is contributing more to the project.

The writer gets all (or the bulk) of any advance against royalties, and then shares (in varying percentages) in whatever royalties are earned once the advance has been recouped. This arrangement is a reasonable one to propose if: a) the collaborator is wealthy and/or not concerned about earning money from the project; or b)the collaborator continues to earn his or her normal income while the writer must forgo other income-producing projects while concentrating on the one at hand.

In instances where the writer gets all or most of the advance, the collaborators can agree that the expert will receive all (or most) of any royalty payments until both parties have earned an equal amount.

Sometimes one or the other of the collaborators brings such a special knowledge or skill to the joint project that he or she is entitled to more of the return from certain subsidiary rights. If, for example, you are writing someone's life story that may well have movie potential, your collaborator may reasonably ask for a larger share of money from the motion picture or television rights. After all, it *is* his or her life story. On the other hand, since a first serial sale often depends on how well something is written than on actual content, you may be able to hold out for a larger share of those rights.

While all these points are important to discuss, negotiate, and agree on, they are really secondary.

The truly important touchstone for a collaboration is to work only with someone whose ideas you respect, whose project interests you beyond the elements of financial return, and whose temperament meshes with yours. Ultimately, a collaboration is much like a marriage: it stands or falls on mutual trust, respect, and liking.

Finally, one thing I should point out—and it's no small consideration—is that the big advantage for the writer in a collaboration is that you don't feel so damned lonesome all the time!

Chapter Four

THE THIRD STEP—PUBLISH

We've said before that only a few of the manuscripts stacked on any editor's desk are publishable. The fact you must now face is that *even competently written manuscripts are rejected*. The research is solid, the words well chosen, yet the piece comes back with a rejection slip. Why?

Because writing is not enough. Think of what you write as a product. As with any product, you must put as much effort into sales as into manufacturing. And, as with a car or toaster or whatever else you want to sell, the product must *be attractive* and *reach the right buyer*.

DRESS (YOUR MANUSCRIPT) FOR SUCCESS

From time to time I run into freelance writer Stuart James in the ground floor coffee shop at the Greenwich, Connecticut Library (one of the finest in the country for a town of 65,000). James has fought the good fight from both sides of the publishing desk—he has worked at various times as editor of *Show* magazine, executive editor of *True,* and as editor of *Rudder.* I hated to see him start freelancing, because he had bought a number of my articles.

When we meet it's always shop talk, naturally, and a little gossip about people in the trade to keep things humming. On one occasion James remarked, "I was always shocked by how many writers—many of them old pros—totally ignored the mechanics of our business. I don't know if it was naîveté, artistic temperament, or just plain laziness."

He said it was unbelievable how sloppy many otherwise competent writers were. "Manuscripts arrived mangled on my desk, and not because of the postal service. I mean disheveled, with a scribbled note for a cover letter. Sometimes with no paper clip, a typewriter ribbon that hadn't been changed since Prohibition was repealed, and every color and weight of paper you could imagine. I often wondered where they found some of the materials they used—and why there was such a shortage of stamps and envelopes."

The award-winning former editor went on to ponder why so many otherwise meticulous writers were guilty of the sin of sloth where their work was concerned. "They'd come in the Fawcett offices dressed for a party and throw manuscripts on my desk that looked like they had spent weeks in a Dempster dumpster."

Many editors and agents have confirmed this unfortunate fact. If it's a truism that there's opportunity for everyone in this business, it's also true that even greater possibilities exist for those who pay strict attention to preparing their work for market.

If the following points of mechanical detail seem too high-schoolish to you, remember (and it can't be repeated often enough) that editors receive manuscripts by the scores every day that violate one or more of them:

1. Use 8½x11-inch (standard) white bond typing paper (16- or 20-pound is best). Avoid "corrasable" bond (erasable) because it smudges.

2. Use only one side of the paper.

3. Double-space and type neatly. Never single-space copy and never send anything handwritten (despite those romantic stories you've heard about Thomas Wolfe or William Faulkner).

4. Use black typewriter ribbons (that's solid black, not gray as Stuart James mentioned). Editors read typed material constantly, and a faded typewriter ribbon will *not* help your cause.

5. Type your name, address, and phone number in the upper left corner of the first page; in the upper right corner put the approximate text length (e.g., 2,000 words).

6. Center the title and your name about halfway down the first page. This leaves ample space for editorial notations, printer's labels, etc., if they're buying the article. If not, most editors won't mark up your manuscript—most, that is, but not all.

7. Number each page of your manuscript in the upper right corner and type your last name in the upper left corner.

8. Leave margins of about two inches on the left side of your typed manuscript and at top and bottom, and roughly one inch on the right.

9. Never staple manuscript pages; use only a paper clip.

10. Never, ever, send in a dog-eared or coffee-smeared manuscript—particularly one with a sloppily typed, battered first page. It's your entree, the first impression (and you know what they say about first impressions). If necessary, retype the page until it looks perfect.

11. Always enclose a self-addressed, stamped envelope. I know you've read arguments to the contrary. My view, and that of 90 percent of the editors I've polled on the question, is that SASEs are always necessary when you're sending a query or an unsolicited manuscript. This is especially true, particularly in today's economy, for newcomers or writers unknown to the editorial staff.

12. Send a brief cover letter with your manuscript telling a little about yourself and listing your best (or most recent) credits. Again, some pros disagree with this and consider it unnecessary. Different strokes, once more.

13. Don't fold the pages of a long article or section of a book. Mail them flat, with cardboard backing. However, it's acceptable to mail queries, letter-type outlines, and very short articles (fewer than five pages) folded.

14. Send your material—articles, book chapters, or photographs—First Class mail. It travels fast (that's what the Postmaster General says) and is handled with greater care. You're trying to sell a $1,000 to $2,500 manuscript, or even a $300 to $500 one, so isn't First Class justified? And *always keep a carbon or a photocopy of everything you put in the mail.*

What has been said about article manuscripts also goes for book manuscripts—with a few exceptions. Never bind your nonfiction book pages; leave that to the publisher if it's accepted. The manuscript should be mailed loose in a proper-sized box (e.g., a ream-size paper box) and, again, no binding or transparent tape or red ribbons. If you prefer, many bookstores and stationery stores sell padded bag-like mailers for sending manuscripts or books by mail. To ensure safe return of your book script, enclose a self-addressed label and necessary postage in stamps clipped to the label. (Don't send a check since the amount is too small and a nuisance to the accounting department.) The package may be mailed Fourth Class Manuscript Rate if time isn't a factor—which it usually is! This can be very slow and tougher on your package. If you use Fourth Class and include a letter, so state (e.g., Fourth Class, Letter Enclosed) on the outer wrapping and add necessary postage to the manuscript postal rate. Most professionals stick with First Class; the service is both safer and speedier. You may save money by using United Parcel Service (usually even less costly than First Class mail), but only if you're near the UPS depot and can drop off the manuscript yourself. Warning: UPS cannot legally carry First Class mail, so you'll have to send your cover letter separately and hope that both reach the editor or agent at approximately the same time. You should check with UPS in your area—it may or may not hold cost benefits for you. (Cost depends upon package weight and delivery distance.)

KNOW THE BUYER— ANALYZE THE MARKETS

Seldom will you find an area of this brain-bending business where there's a consensus among writers. One exception is "study the markets"; it's an income imperative. You can be the greatest idea person in town, but you'll still fail as a freelancer if you're weak in the marketing department. Most writers—and this includes many otherwise sensible professionals—waste gobs of time and money sending material to the wrong magazine.

Why? How can anyone not see the folly of trying to sell articles without first analyzing markets? The reasons are: simply not realizing you must match ideas to markets, then tailor the article for the publication (this applies to beginners); and—for those who've been around a while—lack of discipline, and plain old-fashioned laziness.

By material appropriate to a specific magazine, I mean a piece that has reader interest and correlates to the overall editorial content of the publication. This is why the ability to slant and to focus ideas can help you sell what you write. For example, *Catholic Digest* would not have been a likely market for a piece I did entitled "Give Me a Sex Represser Just Like the One They Gave to Dear Old Dad." But this humor article about the dread substance saltpeter—suspiciously linked in every serviceman's life to reduction, if not obliteration, of his sexual urges—was a natural for *True*.

I did a piece for *TWA Ambassador*, "The Beleaguered Business Lunch." Ideal for that in-flight magazine, since a good chunk of their readership is business executives concerned with this modern tribal ritual, *Savvy*, the magazine for women executives, would also have been a potential market for a piece on business lunches. But not *Sports Illustrated* or *Decorating and Craft Ideas*.

Admittedly, both examples are extreme. But the point is clearly made: magazine editors are hungry for ideas—ideas suitable for *their* publications. And the only way you can possibly know what is appropriate for them is to study their magazines and their competition.

In other words, before you even so much as think about trying to sell any articles to a magazine (or newspaper or trade periodical or business journal), study the publication carefully—its writing style, its favorite topics, the columns it runs, photographs, artwork (or lack of it), anecdotes (both how they're used and how many), and quotes, and any clues offered in the foreword, which editors or publishers often use as a platform to sell an issue or idea. Check the magazine's masthead; study the staff hierarchy. If necessary, make a phone call to find out which editor should get your query. Finally, analyze the advertisements in magazines you wish to sell. You'd be amazed at the extent to which a publication's ads affect the editorial content. It's sad but true that as a freelance writer you won't place a hard-hitting, in-depth indictment of the liquor industry in *Esquire* or *Penthouse*. Nor will you get to first base knocking wood stoves if you direct such a piece to *Country Journal* magazine.

Connie Emerson, in her book *Write on Target* (Writer's Digest Books, 1981), says: "The degree to which advertising influences the copy in a magazine depends both on the advertising agencies involved and the magazine's decision makers. Since advertising is often a magazine's life-blood, editors use editorial copy as bait to entice potential accounts. They solicit these customers on the basis of articles they plan to run in upcoming issues. Their advertising salespeople approach a prospective client armed with a printed sheet that lists future articles, one or several of which are on subjects of interest to the people that client wants to present his message to."

As you study a magazine's ad and editorial content, keep in mind one bedrock fact: if you're trying to sell a piece that would antagonize an advertiser, you're wasting time and postage.

The business of market analysis before trying to sell may offend those with idealistic notions of their writing. I can only ask those folks, "Whom are you writing for?" If the answer is "Well, everyone," they're in trouble. You write for yourself and not some monumental mass audience. (Besides, such a bird doesn't exist because each reader is a different person.) You write for yourself in terms of doing the kinds of work you enjoy, you're interested in, and understand.

But, and here's what certain aesthetes fail to realize, once written, that piece *must* be sent to the proper magazine or it won't see the light of publication. Crass? No. Too commercial, like peddling pots and pans? Not entirely, though writers *are* entrepreneurs.

The point is, once again, that writing is a business and you are a professional craftsperson. You must first master the essentials, the tools of your craft. The next process is selling what your labor has produced. To do that, you must know the marketplace.

To sell your house, you first determine who the likely buyers are and who will pay the best price. A real estate agent does the same thing. A magazine article (or a nonfiction book) is simply a commodity like your house, and as a serious freelancer you must figure out who are your appropriate buyers and what price to ask and expect.

Magazine market analysis is the common-sense way to focus your article ideas. Effective analysis tells you whether or not the magazine you've targeted for your article has just run a similar piece. It teaches you whether your topic has been overworked in the past couple of years, whether even a new angle on an old idea should, perhaps, be tried elsewhere or put to pasture for a period.

Multiple Markets

As you do your magazine analysis, look for ways to multiply your markets. As Shirley Biagi says, "Why should you do extensive research, spend a month or more of your time, just to sell one article? A better approach is to find topics that will satisfy more than one buyer."

Multiple markets are the desserts of freelance writing. They represent those spin-off sales to secondary and what Biagi calls "tertiary" magazine markets. Study guides like *Writer's Market, The Writer's Handbook,* or *Magazine Industry Market Place* and you'll see how each divides publications into market categories—health, juvenile, and religious magazines, for example. Says Biagi, "A good magazine article is one you can sell in more than one market category and to more than one magazine in each category."

Let me give you an example based on recent experience. I read a newspaper article about the rapid increase in the U.S. of various forms of legalized gambling. Did this, I wondered, apply to all segments of the population—both women and men? It did; teenagers, too. I sold three informational articles on the general subject, each slanted to a specific market category: one to a women's magazine, another to a young people's magazine, and the third to a fraternal organization's publication. I took three different article approaches with one central topic—gambling—and each approach had a slightly different angle or slant. The piece for *Kiwanis* theorized that legal gambling was a bad bet for both the government and the betting public; the *Woman's World* article showed how more and more homemakers were gambling compulsively; and in *Seventeen* I pointed out how thousands of teens were now gambling illegally. Each magazine fell within a special, non-competing market category.

What's more, the piece entitled "Teenage Gambling" was ultimately reprinted by two other publications—markets with smaller audiences than that of my primary market, *Seventeen.* Such magazines can't pay the money the primary-market publications do, but they sometimes (though not always) accept reprinted material, as well as old material—i.e., researched but not used in a completed article—with a slightly different angle. (Often only a new lead is required.) Another plus in dealing with these secondary-market magazines: because they have small editorial staffs, less material is written in-house; thus, they buy more freelance articles than many primary markets—albeit at lower fees.

Some examples of these spin-off markets where your articles can be recycled include religious magazines, publications targeted for certain age groups (such as retirees or adolescents), and local newspapers. In their book *How to Get Happily Published* (Harper & Row, 1978), co-authors Judith Appelbaum and Nancy Evans say: "The single best key to financial success in writing is recycling. Both the materials and the skills that go into creating a piece of written work can be reused in a great variety of profitable ways, and while those who've written books have the widest range of recycling options, everyone who's written anything should be able to make it at least double duty for pay. Or triple. Or quadruple. Or more."

A word of caution: before you start trying to sell an article reprint, check your agreement or contract to make sure you control the rights. If not, you'll have to obtain clearance from the original magazine market to resell it elsewhere. It's my view that beginning writers don't need to be *too* concerned about reselling, but as they gain experience they can put more energy into it.

So, systematically study your potential magazine markets, learn how to focus ideas for those magazines that interest you, then write pieces that are appropriate to the primary publication in a given category. It's not a matter of crystal ball gazing or mind reading—it's down-to-earth, detailed market study. As New York literary agent Donald MacCampbell says, "The two words for you to always bear in mind are *slant* and *query*. Otherwise you may be wasting your time and the time of a busy editor who has a pile of rejection slips in the drawer of his desk."

QUERIES:
THE SALES PITCH

The query letter is without doubt the magazine article writer's most vital sales tool. It is to the freelancer what the sample case used to be to the country's traveling salesman. The Jewel Tea Company operated for years using the idea of door-to-door salesmen carrying hefty cases filled with enticing product samples. Fuller Brush did the same quite successfully—and today a legion of Avon representatives also employ the effective point-of-sale sample technique.

That's what querying is for freelancers: getting a foot in the door, putting an appealing article "sample" on the desk of an editor in search of ideas—a sample so loaded with "sales pitch" that the editor places an order in the form of an assignment.

There are reasons for querying and there are cardinal rules to remember about how to write and submit a good one. Sally Wendkos Olds, an ASJA past president and one of the country's top-selling journalists and authors, discusses the importance of customized queries to all freelance writers.

WRITE A QUERY—GET AN ASSIGNMENT
by Sally Wendkos Olds

Most editors of major magazines are urging writers to query them first, instead of submitting completed manuscripts. It's solid advice. A good query can often get an unknown writer a go-ahead to write for a top magazine. It's the route I took to get my first article assignment for *Parents* magazine in 1967. And today I still take this route to get assignments.

For the new writer, this form is often shrouded in mystery. You cannot go to the newsstand and see what kinds of queries editors like best. There is no compilation of "The Fifty Best Query Letters of 1980." The only people who see queries—also called "proposals"—are the writers who write them and the editors who receive them. So let's bring the query out of the closet.

What Can a Query Do?

The query letter is a sales tool. You use it to sell your idea and to sell yourself as the one person who's best equipped to write this particular article for this particular magazine.

A query can save you time and effort by sounding out a magazine on your idea before you invest your blood, sweat, toil, and tears in the complete article. You might write the best article in the world about a revolutionary medical discovery—and then find that the magazine you wrote it for already had an article in inventory on the exact same subject. It can't publish two articles on the same topic; so no matter how good yours is, it will be rejected. A query letter, which might have taken a couple of days of preliminary research, could have saved you the weeks or months of research you invested in your article.

At those magazines that still do read manuscripts that come in "over the transom," a query letter will be read by a highly placed editor instead of the reader who first goes through the articles in the "slush pile." And when a query letter is successful in getting you the assignment, you and your editor can exchange views about the direction your article will take; the final result is likely to be stronger for your two heads getting together.

How to Write a Query

Now that you're convinced you should write the query, *how* should you write it? Write it well. The query letter is a sample of the way you think and the way you write. If your proposal is ungrammatical, dull, poorly organized, long-winded, or full of clichés, the editor will assume that your article will be the same. Your query should showcase the best writing you can do.

Form

An article proposal can be set up as a letter or as an outline sent with a covering note. The letter is more personal. The editor who receives it will get the feeling that you have designed your proposal specifically for his or her publication.

The outline is not the number-and-letter affair we all learned to write in school, but a proposal on a separate sheet of paper that indicates where you plan to go with your article. It is more practical than a letter, since you will not need to retype it if it is rejected by the first editor you send it to, unless it comes back wrinkled and dirty. Signs of rejection—the indentation of the paper clip, the curled edges, the coffee spots, the erased notations—are all obvious clues that your proposal has taken a previous trip. And no editor likes to catch a spurned offering on the rebound. So examine your outline before sending it out again as carefully as you would check your appearance before setting off for a job interview.

Either style of proposal should look professional—typed single-space on white bond paper or business stationery. If you don't have a printed letterhead with your name, address, and telephone number, be sure to give that information in your letter; you want to make it easy for the editor to find you. It is courteous—and often conducive to a quick reply—to enclose a stamped, self-addressed envelope.

Address your letter to a specific person, *by name:* the articles editor, features editor, managing editor, or executive editor of the magazine. Find the name of the individual by looking at the masthead in a current copy. (Do *not* get the name from an old, tattered copy. Editors move frequently.) For magazines that are not readily available, check the current edition of *The Writer's Handbook* or *Writer's Market* in the reference room of your local library.

Be sure you're accurate. If you were an editor, what would *you* think of the research skills of a writer who misspelled your name or got the name of the magazine wrong or addressed a query to a person who left the staff five years ago?

Length

Editors are usually bright, but they are not clairvoyant. So don't be too brief, giving only the lead paragraph and assuming the editor knows where you're going from there. Nor should you be too wordy, going on for three or four pages. The ideal query runs one to two single-spaced pages—long enough to develop your idea, short enough to be read through quickly.

Title

A catchy heading—which an editor may see as a cover line that can help to sell the magazine—may sell your idea. It pays to put some time into thinking of a lively title, which you can suggest either at the top of your outline or in the body of your letter.

Lead

Start out your query letter with a strong opening paragraph, just as you would begin your article. Don't write your query until you have thought of your lead. You can change your mind later and use a different opening for the article, but the fact that you have a strong lead in your proposal attracts the editor's interest by showing that you can attract the reader's. Keep this lead to one or two paragraphs.

My husband and I used the following lead to begin a proposal for an article (published in *LI, Newsday*'s Sunday magazine, and reprinted in *Catholic Digest*) that we titled "The Weekend That Changes Marriages":

The weekend began badly. By the time F. Whitman Haggerson, 29, and his 28-year-old wife, Ingrid, had arrived at Cor Maria Retreat House in Sag Harbor, Long Island, they had fought vociferously throughout dinner and in the car about the packing of suitcases, about Whit's having come home late from work, and about the best route to take to the retreat house.

But by Sunday night, Ingrid and Whit, who had been married for six and a half years and were the parents of five-year-old Fritz and two-year-old William, felt like newlyweds again. "I can't remember exactly what we said and did on that weekend," says Ingrid today. "We were in a big daze by the time we got home. I just know we held hands for the whole ride back. And, of course, I know now that these were the most important couple of days in either of our lives."

Central Idea

State your idea in a nutshell, proposing a specific aspect of your topic. You would not, for example, say that you want to write an article about marriage. This is too general. You need to find a narrower focus.

You also need to make clear the angle you will take. "The Weekend That Changes Marriages," about Marriage Encounter, could be handled several different ways. A writer could appear in the first person, drawing on his or her personal experiences and attitudes. A factual report about the overall growth of the movement could be written. Since we had already seen articles about Marriage Encounter that followed these two patterns, we proposed a profile of the Haggersons as a typical "team couple" and leaders in the movement. Here's how we suggested this:

That weekend in March of 1971 was the Haggersons' introduction to Marriage Encounter, a movement founded in Spain in the 1950s by a priest and a devout Catholic couple, and brought to this country in the summer of 1967 by Father Charles Gallagher, a Long Island-based Jesuit priest concerned about the ever-weakening state of American marriage. The movement's growth has been dizzying. About a thousand new couples a month are now swelling the ranks of the 25,000 American couples who, in the past five years, have gone on Marriage Encounter weekends to learn a special technique for drawing closer together.

Ingrid and Whit Haggerson have gone on to use this technique, known as Dialoguing, on virtually a daily basis ever since they "made" their first encounter. Now, as one of about 700 specially trained volunteer "team couples" around the country, they go out regularly on weekends to teach other couples how to Dialogue.

The success of the Marriage Encounter movement is in large part attributable to the enthusiasm and dedication of its team couples. They attend encounter weekends about every 6-8 weeks, leaving their children with relatives or with other "encountered couples." They attend numerous meetings that last till the early hours of the morning, write their own presentations that draw heavily on experience from their own marriages, and do a considerable amount of administrative work. During the encounter weekends, they share intimate details about themselves and about their own marriages. They also participate fully in each weekend, making a new encounter each time.

THE THIRD STEP—PUBLISH   113

You need to make clear your point of view. Are you positively enthusiastic about your topic, indignantly opposed to it, amused by it, or
are you setting out to write an objectively balanced report of it? We indicated our viewpoint later in the query:

Not every couple who makes an encounter will find their entire
lives—or even their marriages—completely changed, as the Haggersons' have been. But we, the authors of this article, made our own encounter last July, and we agree with Ingrid Haggerson when she says,
"I can't imagine any couple not being able to get something from Marriage Encounter. . .Every couple can grow in their marriage."

Details

Give some clues as to what your article will contain. Weave in an
anecdote or a case history if you did not use one in your opening. Toss
out a handful of intriguing facts. Include relevant statistics.
In the query for the Marriage Encounter piece quoted above, we
did some of this in the third paragraph.
Somewhere in your proposal, you need to provide a sketchy plan
of the way you will organize your article. Here's one way:

Through an in-depth profile of Ingrid and Whit, we could explain
why a happily married couple would make an encounter in the first
place. We could briefly tell the story of the movement. We could then
go on to explore the reasons for the Haggersons' deep involvement,
the effects of their participation on their children, and their feelings
about making new encounters every couple of months—don't they
run out of things to say?

Timeliness

Why should the editor publish this article *now*? Why would readers want to read it *now*? If you can, give some reason why your article is
timely—a new scientific discovery, a tie-in with current news events,
recently released statistics that indicate the popularity of a phenomenon.
As you can see, you need to do some preliminary research before
you can even begin to write a query. You have to demonstrate that you
know your subject and that you know where to go for more material.

Who Are You?

By this time the editor should be so impressed by the professional
way you have put your proposal together that she or he will want to

know something about you. Introduce yourself. If you have professional writing experience, indicate what it has been. If not, say nothing. (Don't say, "I'm only a beginner, but . . .")

If you have relevant personal experience, give that, too. The editor will want to know that the author of an article about part-time jobs manages an employment agency, or that someone proposing an article about "tennis elbow" is an orthopedist *and* a tennis player. But keep it relevant. The editor doesn't care that your analyst feels it would be therapeutic for you to write about your relationship with your mother.

If you have special skills—for example, you are a photographer who can illustrate your own story—say so. If you have special access to a unique resource—such as a prominent person who does not ordinarily grant interviews but has agreed to speak to you—mention it.

By this time, you've said it all, and it's time to end your query simply, with the brief, pointed question, "Are you interested?"

This note, addressed to Silvia Koner, then articles editor of *Redbook,* is typical of the cover letters I usually send along with article proposals, such as the one reprinted below.

Dear Ms. Koner:

I am enclosing a proposal for an article that I feel would be right for the readers of *Redbook.*

In connection with my research for my books, *A Child's World* (McGraw-Hill, 1975), a college-level textbook on child development, and *Helping Your Child Learn Right from Wrong* (Simon & Schuster, 1976), I have heard many parents of young children express their concern about their children's moral development. My proposal offers practical advice for such parents from two of the nation's leading spokesmen in the field of moral education.

I hope you're interested.

Sincerely,
Sally Wendkos Olds

Article proposal

Helping Children Learn Right from Wrong

One day while I was cleaning my eight-year-old daughter's room, I found a half-empty, very large bag of candy underneath a pile of Jane's school papers. I was surprised to find the candy, both because this was something my husband and I never bought and discouraged our children from buying, and also because Jane had recently complained that she didn't have enough money to get something else she wanted.

When I questioned Jane about the candy, she first looked at me blankly, then stammered a couple of weak replies, and finally admitted she had stolen it from the 5&10. I tried not to overreact, even though my fantasies of my daughter's turning into a shoplifter and eventually a hardened criminal terrified me. I wondered how my husband and I had failed as parents. Why didn't our child know right from wrong?

How *can* parents help their children to make moral judgments? When does learning about values begin? We all come into this world as amoral creatures, not knowing anything about the concepts of right and wrong, and not caring. But beginning in infancy, moral issues begin to fill our lives. The nursing baby bites her mother's nipple and causes pain; how should the mother react? When toddlers get together, they squabble over toys and throw sand in each other's faces; how can parents help them learn to share and keep from injuring each other? Very young schoolchildren are in situations that test their loyalty to friends, that tempt them to cheat on tests, that make lying seem the easy way out; what can parents and teachers do or say?

In this instance with Jane, my husband and I sat down with her that evening. "Why did you take that candy?" I asked her.

"I don't know," she shrugged.

"Did you want it so very badly?" my husband asked.

"I didn't even eat most of it. I gave it to some friends in school," she said. Somehow, in Jane's mind, this fact seemed to help absolve her from guilt.

"What do you think we should do now?" I asked.

Another shrug, accompanied by an unintelligible grunt.

The conversation was less than satisfactory.

We adults finally decided that Jane would withdraw $1 from her bank account to pay for the candy. I accompanied her to the 5&10—and felt like an ogress as my very small, very chastened, and very embarrassed daughter held out the dollar bill and the few coins to Mr. Burns at the register. When he asked her what it was for, there was no way she could bring herself to say a word in explanation. I mumbled something about this being money that Jane owed the store, a flicker in his eyes let me know that he understood instantly, and Jane and I walked out, both sighing with relief that the ordeal was over.

At the time, my husband and I did what we thought best.

Today, we might handle the situation somewhat differently. If we had spoken to Dr. Lawrence Kohlberg, for example, we might have approached the incident in this way: (Here I would construct an imaginary scenario, based on what Kohlberg would tell me in an interview.) Kohlberg, professor of education and social psychology at Harvard University, is the most prominent contemporary theorist about children's moral development. After following pre-adolescent and adolescent boys for twelve years and tracing their thinking about morality, he concluded that children's moral thinking proceeds in a definite sequence from doing the right thing because they are afraid of being punished, to doing it to gain the approval of others, to doing it because of their own internal standards of right and wrong.

If I had spoken to Dr. Sidney B. Simon, we might have handled Jane's candy stealing along these lines: (Here would be another imaginary scenario, based on Simon's Values Clarification philosophy.) Within the past few years, Simon, professor at the Center for Humanistic Education at the University of Massachusetts, has carried his message about Values Clarification to thousands of parents, teachers, and other adults who work with children. Under this approach, adults use an assortment of specific techniques, including game-like exercises, to help children think about values and determine which ones they want to live by. It gives practical application to the theories of Kohlberg and others.

My article about children and morality would use lively anecdotes to show the ways Dr. Kohlberg's theories apply to young children and what this means in terms of parents' day-to-day dealings with them. It would also illustrate with actual examples the ways Values Clarification techniques can be applied to deal with such issues as honesty, willingness to help other people, "white lies," and other values issues.

The article that resulted from this query appeared in *Redbook* under a slightly altered title, "Teaching Your Child Right from Wrong." It had a different opening, because before going ahead with it I checked with my daughter, who told me she would not like me to write about her. That's why her name has been changed here. (Since I have three daughters, her identity can remain a mystery.) I found a similar incident to lead off the article.

When Should You
Expect a Reply?

Queries are usually answered sooner than finished articles. If you write to Rebecca Greer, articles editor of *Woman's Day,* you should get an answer within a week. More typically, you can expect one within four weeks. If you have not heard by then, write or phone the editor to ask whether your proposal has been received. Since we all have our favorite horror stories with the mails, it's perfectly acceptable to follow up in this way to be sure your proposal did not go astray. Then you may ask whether the editor has come to a decision about your proposal. Indicate that if your idea is still under consideration, you will be happy to allow more time.

If the editor's answer is "no," don't try to talk him or her out of it and don't ask why. You can make better use of your time and energy by sending the idea somewhere else. Try again with this editor some other day.

A professional freelance writer has to be profligate with ideas. The only way you can protect yourself from being paupered by the loss of one is to keep coming up with so many more that your stockpile won't be depleted. And remember, an idea is just an idea unless you do something with it—think about it, develop it, write it up, send it out—and then, upon getting the assignment, transform it from a proposal into a full-fledged article.

WRITING ON SPECULATION
VS. ASSIGNMENT

As you study the markets and send out your queries, keep in mind that there are assignments. . .and then there are assignments. Specifically, there are real, firm, honest-to-God assignments, and there are assignments "on spec."

When you agree to work "on speculation" it means simply "You take the risk." The magazine editor has no obligation to buy the finished article. Read the small print on the contents page of most magazines and you'll notice a line that says the publication cannot be responsible for unsolicited manuscript submissions. It's not there to fill white space; it's there to let you know the risk is all yours when you put something into the mail for that magazine.

If you are a new freelancer without any credits, almost any assignment you get from the bigger—mass-circulation or quality—magazines is probably going to be on spec. They can't afford to take the chance on having to pay a full fee to a writer whose work is of unknown quality. You may have a brilliant idea and present it in a superb query, but that doesn't mean you can deliver what the editor wants in the way of a finished article. At least that's the rationale behind working on spec.

On the other hand, a firm assignment from the magazine editor means that you are guaranteed the publication *wants* your piece—or one that closely resembles the piece you've pitched in your query. But even this doesn't mean the editor is going to buy the finished product you finally turn out. What it does mean is that if for some reason your piece proves unacceptable to the editor (or editorial committee), you will still receive a "kill fee'" (a consolation payment) for your effort. The logic here is that you have at least kept your promise to deliver a finished article you believe is like the one you queried the editor on. If for various reasons (often seemingly incomprehensible to you) the piece just doesn't work, it doesn't mean you haven't. So you're paid for at least part of your effort. And you can still sell the piece somewhere else.

Not all magazines, however, have a kill fee arrangement. And even those that do vary considerably in the amounts they will guarantee. I've only had two paid me in my years of freelancing (and that's two more than I wanted): one was for a quarter of the fee originally agreed to, the other for one-third the full assignment fee. Most ASJA members tell me a minimum of one-third the fee is customary, although some admit they've had to accept kill fees of only ten percent.

I've heard some heated discussions among writers on the business of writing on speculation vs. writing on assignment. Most agree that for newcomers, on spec is usually their only hope for making a few sales and establishing a reputation. Others argue it just isn't professional to work without a firm assignment based on a written agreement. But all writers agree that no freelance writer should *ever* consent to do a full book-length project on sheer speculation. If it's worth publishing in the first place, the book deserves a reasonable cash advance. Yet, there are a few trade publishing houses that continue to ask you to do a book with a paltry advance or even *no* advance. They would like the writer to gamble on royalty payments alone. When confronted by a publisher of that ilk, walk fast to the nearest exit. Even the rankest beginner should be infuriated by such a non-offer. (The exception here might be university presses, who consider only completed manuscripts.)

Few professional writers will ever sit down at their typewriters to do an article on speculation. They've long since passed working that side of the tracks. But the beginning writer, whether part- or full-time, must pay his or her dues and must earn enough credits to ask for an assignment. Even then, certain magazines will only give written assignments grudgingly. Other publications ask that anyone—even writers with solid credentials—who has never worked for them do a first article on speculation. You must decide for yourself if this is what you want to do. Though working on spec is not exactly a fun way to do business, the novice can turn it to advantage, and quickly. How? By doing four things:

1) Keep your end of the bargain by giving the editor a hard-hitting piece of agreed-upon length, on schedule.

2) Make sure your manuscript is free of errors, neatly typed, and professionally packaged.

3) Include an SASE.

4) Send along a brief cover letter thanking the editor for the opportunity to work with him or her—and suggest another idea or two you'd like to propose if given the green light. (If you get a go-ahead on several query ideas, can assignments be far behind?)

The more professional you are in your approach, the more likely it is that you'll soon be getting serious assignment consideration from any editor.

In this business, Murphy's Law certainly applies: whatever can possibly go wrong, will. Therefore, be warned that there are a few deadbeats out there. And, in fairness, a lot of honest but harried editors who aren't as well organized as you are. All by way of saying that when you've reached the assignment stage, you'll occasionally get one by phone. Follow the conversation *immediately* with a confirming letter of assignment, detailing the discussion by including article topic, length, agreed-upon fee (including expense allowance), delivery date, and a professionally polite "Thank You."

The American Society of Journalists and Authors offers a "Suggested Letter of Agreement" originating with the writer to be used when a publication doesn't issue its own written confirmation of assignment. See Appendix.

Getting Paid . . . Someday

The subject of assignments brings us to that scourge of all freelance writers, the dread dregs of the publishing world—magazines that pay on publication. Deal with these publications and you're begging for headaches or a trip to the psychiatrist's office, or both. Why? Because many (in fact I'd say most) times "pay on publication" translates "several months or more after publication." By then you may have wasted considerable time and money on telephone calls or postage trying to collect your fee. And unfortunately, more magazines are now adopting a pay-on-publication policy—even some fairly large-circulation ones. It's a trend that disturbs all writers and not a few editors, who don't like to have to follow such policies.

I grant you the most important goal for the beginning writer is always to get published—and most city and regional magazines, where aspiring writers are likely to make initial sales, pay only on publication. But if you insist on dealing with the manuscript muggers at the pay-on-publication magazines who don't really pay *on* publication, you're going to get published the hard way. They'll often cost you more in aspirin than you'll receive for your article. Except for spin-off articles requiring little or no work, I'd strongly advise you to ignore these markets. Neither your pocketbook nor your pulse can take the punishment.

If, however, you're still determined to deal with these people and you find yourself unpaid for a piece several months after publication, your only recourse is to send a registered letter advising that you intend to take the magazine to small claims court. (You probably won't, because the amount involved is too small, but it does let them know they might be in for some adverse publicity.) You could appeal to the editor's business sense by billing by invoice indicating you're going to charge interest on the unpaid account, just as you're charged if you become delinquent in your bill payments. You won't receive the additional amount, but you just might jar loose what is owed you in the first place. If the magazine folds and you never get paid, you are, of course, free to submit your material to other markets.

ARTICLE OR BOOK?

Many writers first break into print by selling short articles and fillers. Why? Because it's a good field for beginning writers who would like to see their work published quickly. The market is limited only by the writer's ingenuity and imagination, as are the subject matter and kinds of treatment. Moreover, there's almost no competition from the established professional writers.

After a time, however, you graduate to longer, more in-depth articles. You've learned technique and you've developed the disciplines that keep you working at your craft. Besides, both inspiration and money (rare commodities for many writers) insist that you shoot for better markets.

Finally, you write and sell several of the major magazines. And those $1,500 or $2,000 checks are a dream come true! When I began to freelance full-time in 1960, I never dreamed that I would sell nonfiction articles to such big-name magazines as *True, Travel & Leisure,* or *Family Circle.* In those days I was satisfied to see my byline in any magazine (though I confess several times I used a pseudonym for pieces that appeared in *Dapper, Jaguar, Fling,* and *True Woman*).

Then one day you realize that your competition—your freelance friends—are not only writing and selling articles to the big-name periodicals, they're also writing nonfiction books. And a number of those books first appeared in print as magazine articles.

That's one of the pluses that nonfiction writers enjoy. While writing and selling magazine pieces you start to see definite similarities between writing articles and writing books. For example, the research for an article is much the same as for a book—there's just less of it. The same sources are often used for both. Also, interviews for bigger magazine pieces become increasingly involved, and usually provide you with information that would be worthwhile for a book. In short, the working methods and writing techniques for articles and books are not all that different. What you have to offer in both instances is the same: technical knowhow; discipline; experience in researching, interviewing, and organizing facts. . . . So why not write a book? Why not, indeed.

However—and there's always a however—there are a few fundamental differences between a nonfiction book and an article. A book idea must be considerably bigger in scope than an idea for a magazine piece. It must have breadth and depth and widespread interest and appeal (particularly an idea for a general trade publisher; this is not always the case with specialized publishers). This is not to say many articles in the mass-circulation magazines don't have that bigness of concept. They do. But in an article you're limited by strict space requirements. It's one thing to explain the hazards of tension in a magazine piece—as ASJA member Ruth Winter has—and another to write a book entitled *Triumph Over Tension* (Grosset, 1976)—as Winter also has done.

Another difference: the writer makes a sustained effort over a much longer time. And certainly the structure of a book differs somewhat from that of an article, since the project involves more in-depth probing and detailed discussion.

Discovering The Difference Firsthand

I learned by experience that it's one thing to present a subject in 2,500 words for a major women's magazine and quite a different task to expand the idea into a 240-page book, even though the idea proved suitable and had potential for both. In early 1977, several pieces of good fortune fell my way (there's no escaping the fact that freelance earnings are governed by the gods of happenstance). The chance reading of a brief newspaper article led to a $2,500-plus (expenses including travel) magazine article assignment that led to a profitable book contract ($10,000), which, in turn, led to several spin-off magazine pieces and a special National Endowment for the Humanities grant—all within a year's time. And it all started with my reading one ten-paragraph AP news release in my hometown newspaper.

Inspired by the AP release, I sent a query to Judith Ramsey, then an editor-at-large for *Family Circle* magazine. I proposed an article that would cover the burgeoning self-help movement in the U.S. and Canada, and how self-help therapy had become the nation's biggest human-service industry. I would also attempt to explain *why* this social phenomenon was exploding on the American scene.

Arthur Hettich, longtime editor of the service-oriented magazine, talked to me about the assignment at length one afternoon. As I was leaving his office, he casually said, "By the way, you do realize you have a book here, don't you?"

When I'd read the newspaper piece I immediately sensed an article in the making. But I confess it wasn't until Hettich's remark and a talk with my agent that I knew the answer to the veteran editor's question was a resounding, "Yes!" The perceptive Hettich showed me that there was sufficient ammunition to persuade a book editor that the self-help movement was strong and diversified enough to justify a full-length nonfiction book.

Moreover, I now realized, the topic was timely. In fact, everyone involved was puzzled by the lack of such a book for the general public (there were a couple of scholarly books for social science professionals). The upshot of all this: *The Family Circle Guide to Self-Help* (Ballantine Books, 1979).

But the story doesn't end there, because the book made me something of a specialist. My months of research into the subject not only resulted in the book and various commissioned articles, but I've been acknowledged by those in the field. Through publicity in newsletters and papers published by many self-help organizations across the country, I've been invited to speak before their groups, and have established a slender reputation in the human services sector.

The climax came in the form of an invitation from President Jimmy Carter's office to deliver a paper on "Self-Help and the Family" for the Research Forum for Families, the White House Conference on Families, in Washington, D.C. And *that* didn't hurt my résumé.

All this is told here to show you how article ideas expand into book concepts. Admittedly, even with all that's happened, I'm earning less than Richard Simmons. But I have been provided with dividends—a second book contract and, just as important, feelings of self-worth and accomplishment. I've received letters from many readers thanking me for such a helpful book. Still do. And those commodities can't be bought.

BOOK PROPOSAL BASICS

The road from articles to books I have just described is a well-traveled one. You may take that same route yourself someday. If so, don't let yourself get sidetracked by faulty marketing techniques.

The working methods of the book-publishing business are different from those of magazine publishing. The first thing you must realize is, when you send a proposal to a book editor, you're asking that editor to commit thousands of the company's dollars to a product that exists only in your mind. It's a difficult sale to make. Second, you must realize that even if the editorial staff loves it, *they* have to sell your book to marketing managers and advertising directors and other company bigwigs. Sometimes that's an even harder sale.

These facts ought to suggest to you that you must pull together every ounce of creativity and craftsmanship you possess when writing a book proposal.

The major objective, of course, is to prepare a clear, orderly proposal that grabs the editor's attention quickly and explains why this particular book will be a profit-maker for all concerned.

A nonfiction book proposal can sell a book before you write it. Many publishing houses will offer an advance to the writer on the strength of a proposal alone—usually paying half the advance upon your signing the contract, the other half upon receipt of a satisfactory completed manuscript.

Book proposals can be submitted either to agents or directly to an editor of the publishing firm. (An agent will often accept you as a client having read your promising proposal. We'll discuss the agent business later in this chapter.) Just as every word of an article query has one purpose—to get the assignment—so, too, is the book proposal directed to getting you a publishing contract. The essential points made in a query apply to the proposal. You must include details in your proposal that will persuade an editor and other members of the editorial and marketing committee to recommend that the publisher approve a contract.

Here are the basics to include if your proposal is to appeal to an editor's imagination and commercial sense:

1. Title.

Have a working title that is at once distinctive, catchy, and, to use Friggens's term, "compelling." And keep it as short as possible. *Passages* and *Roots* and *Future Shock* have all done well with brief titles.

2. Market potential.

Describe your book idea briefly but clearly to *sell* the editor (and all those committee colleagues to follow) on its marketing possibilities. Offer facts that demonstrate the book's sales potential—and to which audiences. Identify those blocks of readers from special-interest groups (e.g., physicians, nurses, human-service workers, paramedics, laypersons interested in volunteer health work, etc.).

3. Significance and uniqueness of the book.

Show how and why your book is fresh and different. Include a couple of anecdotes that underline your theme (your point of view) and its importance to today's reader. These anecdotes *show* what you want to say about the topic.

4. Competition.

Discuss other books on your subject, explaining why and how your book either differs from or does better what has been published recently.

5. Personal credentials.

List your writing (or other) credentials—that is, publishing credits and/or significant professional experience or training relevant to your book project.

6. Promotion and publicity potential.

Briefly explain the book's features that lend it to media publicity and promotion such as reviews, interviews, bookstore tie-in promotions, etc.

7. Suggested table of contents.

Include chapter titles and a brief explanation of the main points you'll be covering in each, showing how you will develop your book. Also, let the editor know where you intend to get your information, primary sources for reliable data, statistics, and quotes.

8. Sample chapter.

It needn't be the first or last; it should be whatever you feel is most likely to sell an editor on your book idea and writing style. Some editors prefer two or three finished chapters, not necessarily in sequence.

9. **Cover letter.**
A short, simple letter to establish or reestablish business contact with an editor or agent.

Also, include with your proposal any photographs, slides, illustrations, charts or graphs that support what the book proposal is selling. Anything you've obtained through reliable research sources and have permission to reproduce in your proposed book may be included. Such material should be there only to show why your book will sell, not as self-serving evidence of your being a good photographer or having met Andy Warhol at the Russian Tea Room. Make sure photos or drawings are protected by a stiff cardboard backing; a plastic sleeve should hold 35mm slides—and mark the outside of your envelope "Photos—Do Not Bend" (there's no guarantee these words will be heeded, however).

Writers take many different approaches and there are surely as many writers who will disagree with this book proposal structure as will agree. There is no one approach that will guarantee success. This one has worked for many top-flight nonfiction authors, however, and is offered here for beginners as a blueprint for a sound nonfiction book proposal.

A few other comments about book proposals: I've said nothing here that will teach you how to arrange your words to capture an agent's or editor's attention. However, your proposal should work much as the lead does in an article—a succinct, irresistible opening that will attract book buyers (and that includes editors, marketing directors, sales managers, and the general public). Each word must help sell your concept. Resist the desire to tell editors how great you are and how wonderfully you write. Stick to words and facts that sell your proposal, not your *self*. A proposal should be as short as possible, yet long enough to make your sales talk effective.

What's next? If the editor likes your proposal and manages to sell your idea to the powers-that-be (usually, the marketing department), instead of that bulky, self-addressed package with your manuscript and a "Sorry, not right for us at this time" note, you'll receive a thin envelope with a contract enclosed. But before you rush to sign it, there are a few things you should know.

BOOK CONTRACTS: FIRST, THE GOOD NEWS

The book contract is a legal instrument so couched in complicated terms that its detailed, convoluted jargon will have you questioning your sanity. (The contract that launched the book you are reading was sixteen pages long!)

Briefly, the contract says you give the publisher legal authority to print, distribute, and market your book. It binds both parties—you and the publisher—to its provisions. Bear in mind, however, that all contracts are not necessarily alike, and that even if you're represented by an agent or a lawyer who's familiar with publishing, you should by all means force yourself to wade carefully through the contract to know and understand its essential provisions—and be able to suggest any changes you'd like made before signing it. You'll probably have to read the contract more than once, unless you have a background in law and feel at home with circumlocution and cagey clauses.

You will, of course, want to query your agent or attorney (or sometimes your editor or publisher) if there's anything in the contract you don't fully understand. But, as Judith Appelbaum and Nancy Evans say, "Comprehension of a contract's basic provisions is about all a writer can hope to achieve on his own. Common sense has no place in the highly stylized negotiations of the usual contract quadrille."

It's important for the writer, particularly a new writer caught up in the drama and excitement of that first book sale, to realize one basic thing: book contracts are written primarily for the publisher's protection and advantage—not the author's. If an astute, though honest, publisher knows that you are unrepresented and overjoyed by your initial book deal, you'll be expected to accept the contract as printed. And you probably will.

I strongly urge you not to do it. If as a neophyte you decide, for whatever reason, to conduct negotiations yourself, apply immediately for membership in The Authors Guild (234 West 44th Street, New York, New York 10036) and get a sample contract form. The 6,000-plus member organization, along with ASJA, has long lobbied for fairer contracts and more forthright consideration for authors in matters such as advances, royalties, subsidiary rights, etc. The Authors Guild maintains a competent staff of professionals who can assist you by providing surveys, bulletins, symposiums and, of course, their definitive book contract—used by most serious writers who've been through the negotiation battles time and again. Moreover, Authors Guild members are automatically members of the Authors League of America, which forms, in its words, "a family with its two component organizations— the Dramatists Guild and the Authors Guild." Both Guilds act in concert through the umbrella League on matters of joint concern to over 10,000 authors and playwrights: copyright protection, taxation, legislation, freedom of expression.

Granted, your hot salable book property and a little sales savvy are prime assets when negotiating a contract. But you must still have a working knowledge of the intricacies of book publishing contracts. The Authors Guild agreement will help you by serving as a strong, sensible contract guideline.

Only when you're dealing with the small publishing houses, also called "small presses," can you usually negotiate the contract without the help of an agent or a lawyer. Scores of these firms have sprung up in the past decade. They normally use a simple, straightforward trade book contract and you seldom have to deal with more than a two- or three-page agreement—and a one-person publishing team. Otherwise, be advised to stay alert to the ever-changing publishing scene. And stay abreast of the latest developments in book contract chicanery so that you don't sign away the rights you're entitled to. You've got to be aware of your options and let your agent or attorney know that you know what the best terms are that can *reasonably* be expected.

If you have a strong, salable manuscript (or proposal) there's always room for sensible negotiation, although first-book authors are seldom in a strong negotiating position. Book publishing is often the result of a little talent, a lot of energy, and the instincts of a riverboat gambler. Most contracts, moreover, are still the result of old-fashioned bargaining. In Paul Reynolds's words, "Publishing is no longer an occupation for a gentleman."

Unless you write a bestseller, don't expect to make a lot of money on your book beyond the advance. This is particularly true if the potential audience is specialized and small. For example, a professional—say a scientist—who writes a book on a highly technical topic often is writing for love of the subject and may receive no more than $500 to $1,000 for the effort. It's a good idea to compare contracts and experience with other professional specialists who have published. And be wary of contracts that limit your rights—now and future—as a writer.

SHOULD YOU PUBLISH IT YOURSELF?

Until now we've been discussing *trade* publishers—those that edit, print, distribute, and advertise your book for you and pay you a royalty. Most of you have also seen the "Publisher In Search of Author" ads and understand that these are placed by *subsidy*—also called *vanity*—publishers. These companies expect you to pay them to publish the book. A ripoff? Sometimes, sometimes not. If you're considering a subsidy press, first send for a free reprint of "Does It Pay to Pay to Have It Published?" from *Writer's Digest* (9933 Alliance Road, Cincinnati, Ohio 45242; include SASE).

There is yet another option—self-publishing. It's still your money, but now *you* are the publisher. If you don't want to edit, proofread, and run the presses yourself, then you contract to get the work done. But it's all your show.

Self-publishing is an honorable, and sometimes profitable, alternative to selling your manuscript to a trade publisher. Just keep in mind that putting money into publishing a book is as much a speculation as drilling for oil. Don't go into it unless you have the capital to spare.

Here is ASJA's Harry Milt with his own success story.

HOW TO SELF-PUBLISH YOUR BOOK
by Harry Milt

There is money in self-publishing and you don't have to be a technical or business wizard to become your own publisher. The required know-how can be acquired quite easily. What you do need, however, is a book for which there is a decided need or demand in a specialized market—one you know is going to sell. A well-heeled publisher can take a chance on a book that may or may not pay off. As a writer with limited resources, you have to be sure of the product before you begin—unless, of course, you are willing to risk your resources and credit.

My venture began about fifteen years ago and is still alive today. In this time I have netted about $150,000 on two softcover books and one 36-page pamphlet. Since this article is concerned with books, I will not discuss the pamphlet, and, to keep the bookkeeping straight, I will deduct $15,000 earned by the booklet; that gives us $135,000 earned by the books.

When this all started, I was working as director of public information for the National Association for Mental Health. In that role, I had turned out a mountain of leaflets and booklets on mental illness—the different types of mental illness, the causes, the course of development, treatment, treatment facilities, personnel, and so forth. What was still lacking was a comprehensive book on the subject, one that would be useful to professionals who needed to know about mental illness for their work—physicians, teachers, lawyers, court and law enforcement personnel, clergy, and others. When I suggested to my organization that it publish such a book, the directors felt it might require a financial risk they weren't willing to take. So I obtained their permission to publish it myself, privately. I knew there was a need for this book—a definite ready-made market—and I therefore had no hesitation about proceeding.

If You Want It Done Right . . .

First, I got in touch with one of the printing firms that did a good deal of work for my organization. I asked if they would take on a small book—about 100 to 125 pages—and whether they would give me credit in the range of $5,000 to $10,000. Since they had been working with me for more than ten years, they knew I was a very good risk and agreed to become the printer for my newly created publishing firm, Scientific Aids Publications. Why I chose that name is not important. It could have been anything—Ace Publications, Arrowsmith Publishers—anything I wanted as long as the name didn't already belong to somebody else.

That taken care of, I began to write the book, evenings and weekends, and, when it was finished, edited it myself. Had I not been sure about my capabilities as an editor, I would have called a writers' or editors' association and asked to be put in touch with a freelance editor.

The next task was to get the book designed—how many pages, what size pages, what style and size of type, the number of lines on a page, the width of each line; the kind and size of chapter heads and subheads; the table of contents; the weight and shade of paper and weight, color, and design of the cover; and other such technical concerns. Again, I had acquired the necessary know-how as part of my public information job at the mental health organization. But I wouldn't have been lost without it. I could have hired a freelance graphics expert or asked my printer to suggest one. Many printers have an in-house graphics staff and are quite happy to do the design and layout for you and include it in the cost of the whole printing job. Printers who lack this kind of talent within their organization almost always have access to freelancers.

The Bottom Line

It was now time for some difficult decisions. "How much is this job going to cost me?" I asked the printer's representative. "That depends," was his answer. "Depends on what?" "On the number of copies you want to print."

I had known he would need a quantity from me, but I hadn't yet tackled figuring it. He told me he'd need the answer several weeks before he could start the job, since he needed to know how much paper and cover stock to buy. He also had to line up a slot—an opening when the presses were free—and for that he had to estimate the length of time my press run would take; that, of course, depended on quantity. And he had to work out similar arrangements with the bindery—binding being a separate step in the operation.

That night, I went home and did some hard thinking. How many books did I think I could sell the first year, the first two years, the first five? Up to this point, it had all been a glowing fantasy that went something like this: *The Basic Handbook on Mental Illness* was going to sell tens of thousands of copies, maybe even hundreds of thousands of copies—if not the first year, then in two—certainly in five. This was the book they were all waiting for—doctors, nurses, lawyers, teachers, clergy, psychology students, social workers, mental hospital volunteers, adjunct mental health professionals, and others. It might even make its way into bookstores and become a popular seller among the self-help books.

That was Harry Milt the author fantasizing; Harry Milt the publisher was a different fellow entirely. This is what he was thinking: "You've got to be kidding. You'll be lucky if you sell 5,000 altogether. What makes you think they'll even be interested in your book? What about all the other books on mental illness? What does your book have that the others don't? The competition is going to be tough and you'll probably lose your shirt on the deal. It isn't too late to quit now."

Harry Milt the author and Harry Milt the publisher engaged in a long and painful struggle that lasted through a sleepless night. By morning, they had reached an aggreement. The book had good prospects for selling about 25,000 copies within five years—maybe better, but 25,000 sounded reasonable. But that answered only one question. The next question that had to be answered was, "How many are you going to print on the first run?"

Fixed Costs, Variable Costs

I was already well acquainted with this rule of thumb: the more you print on your first run, the lower your cost per unit will be. Here's how that figures. There are certain fixed costs that stay the same whether you print 100 copies or 100,000. These fixed costs include layout and design; setting type, putting the type in galleys, correcting and editing the galleys, setting up the corrected type in pages; indexing; preparing pages for camera, and making negatives and plates; and putting the plates on the press.

Then there are the variable costs. These include running the press; paper, cover stock, and ink; binding, packaging, and delivery.

As you move up the scale in your estimated press run, you cut down on your unit cost two ways. First, you distribute the fixed costs over a greater number of copies. Second, you get a better price on your variable costs. The printer will be able to get a much better price on paper, cover stock, and ink by buying them in larger quantities and can pass the savings along to you. He can also economize the same way in paying for binding, packaging, and delivery, and that savings, too, gets passed along to you.

That being the case, why not print the whole 25,000 on the first run and cut my unit cost way down? Because that would be taking too much of a chance. Suppose my forecast has been too rosy and the book didn't sell the way I thought it should. That could mean I would be stuck with maybe 15,000 or more books that cost me about $1 each to produce. Then why not go the other way and print only 2,000 or 3,000? That way I wouldn't be taking much of a chance; certainly I would be able to sell that many. The reason I didn't go that way was that it would make the cost per unit too high. The idea, therefore, was to print as many copies on my first run as I safely could, safely meaning as many as I thought I could surely sell within the first two years. That would be somewhere between 5,000 and 25,000. I decided on 10,000—not for any scientific reason but because that's a figure I felt comfortable with.

Now it was possible for the printer to give me a price. With a 10,000 quantity the cost to me would come out to $6,500 or 65 cents a unit. Credit was arranged on the following terms: I would pay the printer $1,625 on delivery, another $1,625 within 120 days, and the balance within twelve months. These were very lenient terms, especially since he didn't charge me interest. (Those were the good old days.) Had I not been able to work out my credit entirely with the printer, I could have managed a personal bank loan with savings accounts as security.

The next item to decide was how much to charge for each copy of the book. I knew that most of my sales were going to be to institutions, schools, and organizations and that they were going to be in lots of 5, 10, 15, 100 and upward. That meant I needed to set a sliding scale of prices. There would, of course be some single copy sales, and the basic price would be the one set for a single copy. The quantity sales would be scaled down from there. How much to charge for a single copy? The only way I knew was to see what comparable books in other fields were bringing and charge about the same. I looked around and found that $1.75 a copy was what books of this size (100 pages or thereabouts) were bringing and that was the price I fixed for my *Basic Handbook on Mental Illness*, scaling it down to $1.35 a copy in quantities of 100 or more.

Marketing It Myself

Now that I had made the necessary arrangements to produce and finance the book and had worked out a scale of prices, my next task was to work out a system of distribution and sales. I had already identified my potential customers as professionals who needed sound knowledge about mental illness in their work. I knew there were hundreds of thousands of them, but how was I going to reach them? The way was through (1) organizations and agencies already in the business of disseminating information about mental illness; (2) the professional oganizations to which my prospective customers belonged; and (3) the facilities in which they were working. The distribution network was already there, consisting of mental health associations; state and local government mental health departments (particularly the health educators in those departments); state mental hospitals, private mental hospitals, and mental health clinics; and state and local health and welfare departments.

In the health and welfare field, there are all sorts of directories and lists of agencies and organizations complete with subdivisions, department chiefs, and the like. Most of these were free or cost very little. I pulled them together, compiled my master mailing list, produced a promotional piece with an order form, got a bulk mailing permit and a post-office box, then sent out several thousand flyers.

The promotional piece contained a brief overall description of the book and its coverage; the table of contents, with a capsule summary of the subjects covered in each chapter; a listing of the professions, agencies, and institutions who would find the book useful; endorsements by several well-known authorities in the mental health field; and, of course, the price list and order form.

Good Reviews Help

How did I get the endorsements? When the book was still in typescript, I sent out a couple of dozen copies to experts, many of whom I knew personally through my work with the National Association for Mental Health. Some didn't respond at all. Some responded with casual interest. Some responded enthusiastically, and there were enough of the latter to give me some fine promotional blurbs, which went not only on the promotional piece but also on the back cover of the book. In addition, I had the book reviewed (in galley) by the major organizations in the field—the American Medical Association, the American Psychiatric Association, and the National League for Nursing. Favorable reviews in these organizations' publications gave me additional endorsements, which went into the promotional piece and on the front cover of the book.

It wasn't two weeks before the orders started trickling and then flooding in. I knew then that the book was going to be a success.

In the meantime—while the promotional piece was out in the

mail—I had set up a combination warehouse, shipping room, and office in my home basement, the whole occupying a space of about ten by twenty feet. My work force consisted of Wayne Tate, our neighbor's 17-year-old son. (I paid Wayne twice the going rate for babysitters.) The books arrived and I stacked them along the walls. Wayne picked up the orders at the post office, filled them, packed them, mailed them, and sent out the bills. Since about 99 percent of the orders came from organizations and agencies, I didn't have to worry about payment. In the past fifteen years, with a gross sale of several hundred thousand dollars, I have lost only about $500 in uncollected bills.

By the end of the eighth month, I had sold all but 1,000 of the 10,000 books and ordered another 10,000, estimating that the new shipment would be in just at about the time that my inventory was exhausted. I have gone into many reprints over the years. Of course, sales today are not as ample as they were at the beginning. And of course, I have raised the price several times to keep up with costs.

Spinoff Success Stories

A couple of years after the start of my venture, I got a contract from the National Institute of Mental Health—a government agency—to write a monograph on alcoholism. After I finished it and turned it in, I had the makings of a book on alcoholism and so proceeded to write and publish *The Basic Handbook on Alcoholism*, going through exactly the same procedure I had followed with the first book.

Shortly thereafter, I left my job with the National Association for Mental Health and went into freelance writing full-time. My publishing continued, requiring no more than four or five hours a week of my time.

That is not quite yet the end of the story. About seven years ago, Scribner's was looking for a book on mental illness. A good friend recommended my *Basic Handbook on Mental Illness* to the publisher's science editor. The editor liked the book very much and asked if I would do an updated version for them. I agreed—but on condition that I be permitted to continue to publish my own version. The condition was accepted and so I had two books going at the same time. The reason Scribner's accepted the proposition was that we were reaching two different, non-competitive markets. Their hardback and trade paperback was going into bookstores; my book was going to institutions and agencies.

Shortly after the Scribner's edition of my mental illness book came out they became interested in my book on alcoholism, and we made the same kind of deal for that book as for the mental illness book.

Both my books are still selling today. The Scribner's edition of my mental illness book went out of print about a year ago; their edition of the alcoholism book is still selling.

In the course of the past fifteen years, I have revised and updated each book several times. I have also mailed out numerous promotional flyers to announce the revisions and to sustain interest.

I probably could have made lots more money on these two books, and possibly some other books, if I had put more time into the publishing venture. But the truth is, I just couldn't muster enough interest to give it more than I was giving. There were just too many creative things I liked to do more than I liked the business end of publishing.

We offer this account of Harry Milt's experiences not as a recommendation to self-publish, but to give you some idea of what it involves. There are several (self-published) books on the subject. These include *The Publish-It-Yourself Handbook,* by Bill Henderson (Pushcart Press, rev. ed. 1979); *The Encyclopedia of Self-Publishing,* by Marilyn and Tom Ross (Communication Creativity, 1979); and *The Self-Publishing Manual,* by Dan Poynter (Para Publishing, 1979). Learn all you can before taking the plunge.

MULTIPLE SUBMISSIONS: BEYOND TRADITION

Whether you write magazine articles or books, you will find that you must stay on top of constant fluctuations in the market. Editors change jobs. Magazine and book publishers go bankrupt; new companies are born. Marketing methods change, too, though more slowly.

The practice of sending completed articles or book proposals simultaneously to several potential markets was once taboo, but today, multiple submissions are fairly common among freelancers. This is especially true for certain kinds of magazine pieces and book proposals. However, there is one unwritten rule you should observe: be candid about what you're doing. Let editors know that others are looking at the same material—at the same time. But honesty and all, many editors won't like what you're doing.

Many ASJA members continue to avoid multiple submissions like the Jersey Shore in August. Reason? "Too many editors of top-paying slick publications still don't accept the practice," says one, "especially when they know you've sent queries or articles to competing magazines." These editors resent being asked to spend time considering a query or manuscript they may have to compete for if they decide they want it.

Other writers consider the practice not only legitimate but necessary in today's competitive market. They shrug off the notion of losing editor friends while selling others. "There's nothing dishonest about it," says one writer. "I play fair and tell all my editors I'm offering the piece to several others at the same time."

Will you get blacklisted at a particular magazine because the editor doesn't approve of multiple submissions? It isn't likely. If that editor receives an idea he's ecstatic about, he'll probably forget and forgive in his rush to get you on the phone.

The decision is yours.

In book publishing, where it often takes several weeks or even several months to get a decision on a proposal, single submissions simply don't make sense. Life is too short. Besides, the four or five publishers you send your book proposal to today may be gobbled up by the same conglomerate tomorrow.

Author Chet Cunningham reported in an article on the subject for *Writer's Digest* that he routinely submits multiple book proposals:

"Multiple submissions are simply good merchandising. You send out a partial [book], say, to Avon. Avon says no thanks, but it takes two months. If you got two-month service from six different publishers, one at a time, with your original, it would take you a year to cover all six. By sending out six partials at once you can cover the same publishers in two months, and get your product to eighteen publishers in only six months! This is especially important if you have a subject that is topical or tied in with the news. In a year the idea might be so out of date the book would not be worth publishing."

Again, as with magazine queries or completed articles, when sending off book proposals, avoid using the words "multiple submission." As Judith Appelbaum and Nancy Evans say in *How To Get Happily Published*, those words "act as a red flag to many editors." They add, "Formulations like 'several publishers have expressed interest,' or 'I'm exploring publication possibilities with a number of houses' should serve to keep editorial dispositions relatively unruffled."

Incidentally, the book auction, until recently held only for the big-name authors, is commonplace now. These manuscript auctions (not likely in the sale of a first book) are often conducted from single-page outlines as well as a few complete chapters; and, they've resulted in highly inflated prices. Some hardcover publishers refuse to take part in these often frenetic auctions by agents. (Ironically, these same publishers are constantly auctioning reprint rights of their own hardcover properties to paperback houses.)

The book auction, first pulled off by super-agent Scott Meredith, works this way: the agent submits the manuscript (or whatever) to several publishers simultaneously, announcing by cover letter (or phone call) that there's a deadline for acceptance or rejection. Usually there's a floor (a minimal amount for considered offers) announced up front. The best publisher offer is accepted, usually involving advance money plus special contract terms covering paperback rights, royalties, movie sale rights, promotion, and publicity—the total package.

It should be pointed out that while most of us may drool over such "blockbuster" deals as those made via book auctions, we must realistically accept that today's book advances usually run between $5,000 and $10,000. In fact, for a first-time author, it might well be less—or nothing, from a small press. An advance over $10,000 is still the exception to the rule, and $25,000 is a rarity.

In deciding to make multiple submissions of books or articles, let your idea—especially a topical one—and your conscience be your guide. (Keep in mind that multiple submissions or queries work best in non-competing markets with sales of one-time rights.) And, in any case, be sure to enclose a self-addressed stamped envelope with your inquiry—otherwise you can't be certain of receiving a reply and you'll never know if the reason was multiple submission or just mediocre writing.

STALKING THE LITERARY AGENT

"Will you need an agent? In a word, no. Agents rarely work with beginning freelancers and usually handle magazine articles only in conjunction with an upcoming book from which the agent can market excerpts."
—Shirley Biagi in *How to Write and Sell Magazine Articles*

"My best advice to beginners is to send these highly subjective ('creative') articles out on their own and hope for the best. If you should make some big sales, agents will be asking you to let them have a chance at selling your work."
—Marjorie Holmes in *Writing the Creative Article*

"Your chances of finding an agent who will handle you are slim until you've put together a track record in major magazines or have sold your first book."
—Nancy Edmonds Hanson in *How You Can Make $20,000 A Year Writing*

"The agent is never a necessity. If an author cannot sell his book, the reason for his failure is not the lack of an agent."
—Paul R. Reynolds in *The Non-Fiction Book: How to Write and Sell It*

"When a beginning writer asks, 'Shouldn't I have an agent? Wouldn't an agent help me get established?' The answer to both questions is a firm No."
—Hal Borland in *How To Write and Sell Non-Fiction*

Writers—especially beginning writers—have always had a "thing" about literary agents; it's a sort of Freudian love-hate affair. I sometimes think aspiring writers are more concerned about agents than about learning their craft. Maybe it says something about agents' Svengali-like ability to keep themselves uppermost in writers' minds. I'm not sure.

I *am* sure that getting an agent seems to many writers like getting a first job: the employer tells the young job-seeker to come back "when you have more experience." Yet if you cannot land a job, you can't get the experience. It's a standoff.

Perhaps Kay Cassill's chicken-and-egg analogy is more apt. She says, "If you haven't published, you can't get an agent. If you can't get an agent, it's almost impossible to get a book published." The key word here is "almost."

A past edition of *Writer's Market* (1982) pointed out that many writers—among them, novelists John Updike and Joseph Wambaugh—prefer not to have an agent. Say the editors, "They do their own deal-making, hire an attorney for contract review, and keep the 10 percent—or, increasingly, the 15 percent—for themselves." According to a 1981 survey of ASJA members, 48.7 percent—fewer than half—were represented by agents; and of *those,* only a quarter (25.3 percent) were so represented on all their writing (another 46.7 percent of agented members were represented on all books), the remainder only on certain projects.

The fact is, it's quite possible to negotiate the book marketing minefield entirely on your own. Many successful writers have done it and are doing it today. Having said that, I must admit that if you're going to try to sell your book, it's less treacherous if you have the guidance and expertise afforded by a reputable agent.

Why? Because publishing today is a very complicated business. For one thing, conglomerates are everywhere, and you could conceivably spend half your writing time just following the acquisition-merger parade. Another reason is that MBAs are calling most of the shots these days, and it takes a shrewd agent or lawyer to stand up for your rights with these wizards of the bottom line. As Hayes Jacobs says, "Contracts for foreign rights, paperback rights, etc., can become complicated, and difficult to negotiate, and a good agent can take all that worry off your hands, and in many cases, negotiate for a more profitable deal than you will be able to swing."

If you're shopping for an agent (and you probably shouldn't bother to until after you've made a reasonable number of article, story, or book sales on your own), there are several ways to go about it. Get yourself recommended to an agent by an acquaintance who happens to be an author, editor, or working in the publishing business. That's not as farfetched as it may sound, or as simplistic.

For example, I know a writer who had a photographer friend. Over the years, the photographer had done many book-jacket portraits of famous authors, and she recommended the writer—based on a nonfiction manuscript she'd read—to a well-known New York agent. The agent agreed to see the writer's work, took her on as a client, and her first nonfiction book was published and sold moderately well. She has since published a second book and is busy working on a third.

You'll sometimes meet literary agents at writers' conferences and seminars. Don't hesitate to talk with them, show them your credentials, and ask about your chances with their agency. Agent Donald MacCampbell says you may want to inquire of publishers themselves. He makes the point that most publishers have lists of agents they do business with, but for ethical reasons won't usually recommend a particular agency. You should also write to the Society of Authors' Representatives (225 W. 12th Street, New York, New York 10011) and request they send you an excellent pamphlet titled "The Literary Agent" (free in return for a #10 SASE). It explains the agent's role, how best to get an agent, and lists the current SAR membership. Also contact the newer Independent Literary Agents Association (c/o Elaine Markson Literary Agency, 44 Greenwich Avenue, New York, New York 10014).

Some agents specialize. You can obtain a listing of play agents, for instance, by writing the Dramatists Guild, 234 W. 44th Street, New York, New York 10036. Other ways to locate agents that specialize include checking the individual agency listings in *Literary Market Place*. Also watch *Publishers Weekly, Writer's Digest,* and *The Writer* magazines for announcements of new literary agency openings.

What can—does—a literary agent do for you? In *The Non-fiction Book: How to Write and Sell It* (William Morrow, 1980), the late Paul R. Reynolds, for years a highly respected literary agent, explains:

"The primary function of the literary agent is to handle the literary business of the professional writer. The agent negotiates contracts for the author, collects the money, retains 10 percent [Editor's note: A few now retain 15 percent] as a commission, and pays 90 percent to the author. The agent is a businessperson, a negotiator, and a bargainer who sells the various rights to an author's work at the highest possible prices and at the most advantageous terms. Every sale the agent makes, every contract the agent negotiates, is subject to the author's approval."

All writers, but especially those new to the business, should beware of fee-charging agents: most of the suede-shoe pseudo "agents" have less contact with editors and publishers than you do. Few even bother to offer material or their services and those who do have reputations so spotty they rarely if ever make a sale. As Reynolds warns, "An author with a poor manuscript might as well throw his money down the drain as to pay it to these pseudo-agents. And a good manuscript is under a cloud when in the hands of one of these people." These operators make their money from reading, criticism, and editing fees—not from sales to publishers.

Some of these people make unethical deals with certain vanity publishers. For example: a vanity publisher may agree to pay the agent a commission—$250 to $300—if he recommends that the author sign up with that publisher. That's akin to asking the fox to kindly guard the hen house. The pseudo-agent has already collected a reading fee from the hapless author—and will now collect an additional fee to tout and make a sale for the vanity publishing house.

There are legitimate fee-charging agents. They are usually members of large well-established firms. They explain their practice by noting that it's time-consuming and costly to read and properly critique a manuscript (this is true, of course). They rationalize that the agent has no guarantee a sale will result and that even if it does it often doesn't cover the agent's time and expertise. "By charging a minimal reading fee," one such agent told me, "I can at least make enough money to open my agency's doors to promising beginners who might not otherwise be able to find an agent." Unlike the pseudo-types, these agents usually dispense with the fee (some even return it) after a few sales— and then handle the author's work on a regular commission basis.

In their comprehensive article "Working With an Agent" (Writer's Digest, April 1982), Stephen Goldin and Kathleen Sky say, "Most established writers and commission agents look down their noses at these procedures—and most editors distrust submissions from these fee agents because they're not as selective about the material they represent as a commission agent is. Even the large, respected agencies that charge fees for beginners segregate their fee-charging operation from their normal business."

If the beginning writer wants professional criticism—and who doesn't?—there are other, less expensive ways, of getting it. I've already mentioned writers' conferences and seminars or workshops where you can have your work read and critiqued. Also, we've discussed high school and college writing courses, plus the many adult education, Y, or extension courses. In addition, there's the Writer's Digest Criticism Service, where manuscripts are reviewed and criticized—which includes advice on where to submit your material—by discerning professional writers who know what editors look for.

As Goldin and Sky observe, "You get an agent the same way you get a bank loan: by proving you don't need one." Many serious freelancers will agree with them, too, in the judgment that "—unless you can get an agent to handle you on a regular commission basis, you're probably better off marketing your work yourself."

Deciding whether and when you actually need an agent is a major step for most writers, not unlike deciding whether or not to get married. That's because, as the super-successful agent Scott Meredith says, "They [authors] call me for tea and sympathy, money, and plot discussions. I'm a good friend who can also be objective. I'm part salesman, part lawyer, part literary critic, and part Father-confessor. I get calls from clients who are drunk or who have been arrested for beating their wives. One writer called from a neighbor's to tell me his house was on fire and all his manuscripts were burning. Why did he call me? Because he wanted to talk to someone who would be sympathetic—and I was."

Not a few writers have dropped their agents for lawyers who specialize in matters literary. They work pretty much the same way an agent does, except more often than not they ask for a monthly retainer fee. Some work for a flat fee, share royalties with the writer, or negotiate other terms. Most of these attorneys reside in New York, Chicago, or Los Angeles, and are contract specialists. They are also expensive. As Donald MacCampbell notes: "Happily for agents, few writers can afford to be handled by lawyers, and fewer still are good enough at business to conduct their own auctions or to get the kinds of deals that are offered when properties are submitted through agency channels."

No literary agent or lawyer can teach you to write, and most will not have time for detailed criticism of your work. In most cases, however, an agent can save you many heartaches, especially after you've begun to sell books, and the agent's commission is usually covered by the advances obtained for you, not to overlook the additional monies secured from the sale of subsidiary rights, etc. Finally, with today's complex book contracts—drawn up always to protect the publisher, not the writer—good agents will be even more in demand, if not indispensable. And writers, whether newcomers or old pros, will surely continue to scramble for their services. An estimated 90 percent of everything published commercially today is being handled by the business middlemen we call agents.

But if an editor sends you a contract and offers you an advance on your book project, you'll be amazed how easy it is to get a literary agent to represent you. I've never known a writer with contract in hand who was rejected as a client by an agent. It's the nature of the breed. And it's the writing business, with the operative word being "business."

SEE YOU IN COURT

Ours has become a litigious society, and legal troubles have plagued many talented writers in recent years. As Kirk Polking, co-editor with Leonard S. Meranus of *Law and the Writer* (Writer's Digest Books, 1978 and 1981) says, "The time to learn about laws affecting the written word is *before*, not after, you find yourself in the midst of a legal battle."

The following piece is written by ASJA member John W. English, writer and instructor at the University of Georgia's School of Journalism. Writers should consider it as preventive medicine. English's to-the-point explanation will familiarize you with the most common legal mistakes *before* you fall into such traps.

Granted, there's no substitute for having both a good agent and a lawyer experienced in publishing to protect the writer. But even they can get careless. Smart freelance writers will avoid most legal snarls by acquainting themselves with potentially troublesome areas. Then, for a fuller understanding of laws relating to those major areas of concern—freedom of speech, copyright, libel, permissions, the Freedom of Information Act (FOIA), literary contracts—read *Law and the Writer*. Other good books on the subject are *Making it Legal: A Law Primer for the Craftworker, Visual Artist & Writer* (McGraw-Hill, 1979) and Tad Crawford's *The Writer's Legal Guide* (Hawthorn Books, 1977).

Now, on to John W. English's valuable insights into the essential legal points that govern your day-to-day writing work.

LEGAL MATTERS
by John W. English

Neophyte writers often tremble when discussions of legal matters commence. Such terror usually stems from the fact that laws are written in legalese that requires an attorney to translate it into simple English. In addition, few writers ever study the laws that apply to their work. Most get their "education" from case studies relayed by old-timers, who learned what they know the same way—there are few legal experts among writers. Laws vary so much from state to state that knowing what is permissible in one liberal state may have little to do with restraints in a nearby conservative one, and since writing for books and national magazines crosses state lines, the unhappy writer sometimes finds himself being sued in a state whose laws differ considerably from those in his own! To make matters worse, the law constantly evolves and you must always keep up with it.

Another cause of writer panic when the word *litigation* is mentioned stems from recent cases in the news: lawsuits involving libel, invasions of privacy, hoaxes, plagiarism, and even contractual disputes between authors and publishers now involve megabuck settlements, often in favor of the plaintiff. Typically these lawsuits pit an outraged celebrity offended by some fabricated gossip against a less-than-ethical writer who was sloppy in "research" and whose sensationalistic article reads like a poison-pen note. The cases arise because of bruised egos and the prospect of trial publicity and huge cash settlements for damages. The cautious writer should keep in mind that the climate of opinion among judges and juries is often against writers, who are sometimes perceived as snoops making money out of other people's lives. But few such suits would have a legal claim if writers acted responsibly.

There's little reason to worry about being sued by anyone if you write and research with diligence and care in controversial matters. For example, it's wise to have two or three sources. Some basic knowledge of the laws affecting writers can also help you avoid trouble spots. In fact—taking a positive approach—press law actually protects writers and their products and makes the practice of their craft easier.

For example, no one questions a journalist's right to report these days. It is an established principle that writers can publish what they uncover in interviews and from various sources. Indeed, the Freedom of Information Act permits writers to sue the government for access to classified materials when there is no alternative.

So writers *aren't* boxed in by stringent press laws? No, not really. The laws governing the press allow rather liberal interpretations of the public's right to know. Accordingly, it is almost impossible to libel, slander, or invade the privacy of a public figure—a performer, government official, or anyone who has thrust himself into (or accidentally landed in) the news spotlight. (Be careful, however, about focusing too closely on people who become public figures for a short time purely by accident, especially if a crime is involved.)

The legal principle of fair comment and criticism allows you to write about any aspect of someone's public or professional life, as long as what you say is relevant to the discussion or content and it is true. (Relevance is usually determined by whether or not you stick to the topic you're writing about as it relates to the person being discussed.)

It is possible, therefore, to say in an article that a public official is an alcoholic and that the disease affects the official's job performance. But don't do it unless you can prove it—as you'll have to if you're sued. It is also possible to disclose the contents of confidential papers that reveal corrupt practices or incompetence on the part of officials, including those who manage publicly held corporations.

The private lives of public people are considered newsworthy, say many editors, and any decision on whether to publish something has to depend on whether that information is relevant to a particular article. Ask yourself, "Does the person have the right to be left alone in this case?" If the matter involves accountability to the public, the answer is no. Questions regarding taste (e.g., sexual proclivities, personal biases, etc.) also have to be considered.

The media are charged with keeping the public informed; that usually means poking around in people's lives. The messy details need not always surface, but occasionally they must. Sometimes the publication of certain facts will embarrass folks, but that isn't cause enough for a lawsuit. It is only a writer who knowingly communicates gossip, rumors, or lies about someone and has not thoroughly checked facts who has no defense and is vulnerable legally—and should be.

In the late 1970s the courts tended to favor an individual's right to privacy over the public's right to know, and this had a decidedly restrictive effect on reporting. Another common court clash of the era was between the public's right to know and the accused's right to a fair trial, including access to all possible exonerating evidence, which led to subpoenas of reporters' notes. Publications still have considerable latitude in writing about people, events, issues, the whole spectrum of life. Press freedom is *not* dead, although reporters may be asked to break promises of confidentiality with other sources as they are drawn into the legal process. They may also have to decide whether to destroy their notes and tapes so that they cannot be subpoenaed, or to keep them for defense against a future libel suit. The guidelines for writers remain the same, but you must weigh the repercussions or public value of what you're saying more precisely than ever. If you can defend it, go with it, say the aggressive press lawyers. If you have doubt, go over the portions of your story that might have legal ramificatons for you and your publication with your editor. Consult before baring all.

The legal responsibility for publication rightfully rests with both author and publication. To formally establish that bond, *Texas Monthly* magazine insists that all authors sign a form specifying the legal obligations of the author. The form, sent at the time the manuscript receives its final edit, is designed to assist both the writer and the magazine should any libel or other suits be filed in connection with the story. Payment for the story is sent only after the signed form is received. Briefly, the form insures *Texas Monthly* that:

1. the manuscript is solely the work of the author (protecting us against plagiarism);
2. the author has used all reasonable care to check facts and

statements (to insure we have not been negligent);
3. the author agrees to keep all notes, tape recordings, and working papers relating to the manuscript for two years (so we will be able to reinforce court testimony with source material);
4. the author will cooperate with *Texas Monthly* should publicaton of the story result in a lawsuit (assuring us that you and your story source materials will be available to our attorney).

Is it necessary to get releases from sources? Generally, no. But in investigative journalism involving allegations of corruption or malfeasance, prudent reporters always ask sources to sign controversial and/or accusatory statements to prevent these sources from denying them later or claiming they were misquoted, if a court case later materializes. Stories using unidentifiable sources also demand especially careful treatment. Reporters have to study the company the source keeps, motivations, and reasons for asking for confidentiality. Such requests should not be routinely granted; it may be better to interview someone who will talk on-the-record. Some reporters, in fact, refuse to interview anyone who won't speak on the record.

Libel insurance, for publishers as well as for individual writers, is now available, albeit at very high premiums. (Some book publishers have begun extending house libel coverage to their authors.) Generally, if you have done a thorough and accurate job of reporting, it is unnecessary for most stories.

Protect Your Rights

Writers should also know about legal protection of their work. The question is, protection from whom? Unscrupulous editors and publishers. It is no secret that relations between magazine writers and magazine editors are frequently adversarial, though not necessarily hostile. (The adversarial relationship is rather less so in book publishing.) The two have diametrically opposed goals: the writer wants to produce an acceptable article with the least amount of work for the biggest paycheck; the editor also wants the best possible article from the writer, but wants the maximum amount of work for the smallest fee. That means hassles involving rewrites, story angles, editing changes, and fee negotiations. Sometimes these contested areas have ended up in court battles. Hence, a network of laws has been created to help protect the writer.

The federal Copyright Act of 1976 revised earlier statutes to give the writer more protection. For example, the new law gives authors copyright protection of their work from the time of creation, not just publication. You can establish the time of creation from carbon copies of query letters sent to editors, by registering a work immediately with the U.S. Copyright Office (simply send $10, a complete copy of the work, and Form TX to the Library of Congress, Washington DC 20559) or by the traditional precaution of sending yourself a copy of the manuscript by registered mail at the same time you send a copy to the editor and not opening it once it arrives. Obviously the safest is official registration, but it's also time-consuming and expensive and not worth the effort in most cases. Publication in a copyrighted publication constitutes virtually the same protection.

Some writers routinely put a copyright notice on their stories, even though they have not officially registered their work. They figure such a notice will deter most editors from tampering. Copyright notices simply state who holds the copyright and the year it was created or first published. A typical notice would read: ©Copyright 1983 by John W. English. Copyright protection for authors was also extended by the Copyright Act of 1976 from a maximum of 56 years under the old law to the lifetime of the author, plus 50 years, under the new.

Beginning writers often worry that editors will steal their ideas from manuscripts or proposals, especially the latter. Editors who pirate and plunder never stay in business very long, so most don't attempt it. Writers cannot copyright ideas or facts—only their unique style of expression or approach to those ideas or facts. There is always risk that some other writer will get "your" idea into print first, but when that happens, it becomes "his" idea, so you must proceed with all due speed in order to be first in a highly competitive business.

Another pre-publication point that authors must understand and establish is what rights you are selling. Many periodicals ask only for "First North American Serial Rights," which means you retain the right to sell in Europe, Japan, or elsewhere, as well as to reprint markets in the U.S. (You are selling only first rights and not *all* rights; you should be able to profit from subsequent publication or reprints.)

The Copyright Act of 1976 has a loophole in this area that authors are lobbying to amend. It concerns what has come to be called write-for-hire clauses or "Work Made for Hire." By including this phrase in standard authors' agreements, publishers legally acquire *all* rights to future use of the material without paying for them. The work-for-hire tactic violates the intent and spirit of the new Copyright Law, which is to protect creators and to permit them to profit from their work.

The obvious reason why writers don't want to sell all rights to material they have generated is its potential resale value—either to reprint in another magazine, a book, or perhaps selling the story idea for adaptation to either television or the movies—i.e., multiple use. To protect yourself, you should specify what rights you are selling and indicate that preference in the upper right-hand corner of the first page of the manuscript. Check *Writer's Market* to see what a particular publication usually expects, but be prepared to negotiate if you have other preferences. Obviously you cannot sell first rights to more than one publication in any region.

There are several areas in which authors need protection but the law is not very precise or helpful. One involves editing and rewriting. Writers are entitled to have their creations protected from mutilation or distortion by editors. The best publications take an enlightened approach to the editing process and make it a real dialogue. *Texas Monthly* specifies in its guidelines for writers: "The editors' function is to make the magazine as readable and unimpeachable as possible, and we will work with authors to improve stories. We consult with the author about editorial changes whenever possible. The author has the option to withdraw the story if agreement on points of editing cannot be reached. Your editor will continue to work with you until the manuscript reaches its finished form." The author should expect to read galley proofs of the edited article and make any final corrections at that stage, so that what appears in print is not a surprise or at variance with what was written.

Similarly, if the publication does not get around to publishing an author's material within a reasonable amount of time, the author has the right to ask for its return for possible publication elsewhere. Authors write to be published, not just for money. Sometimes they must exercise that right of publication by withdrawing an article from one editor's purview (demanding a kill fee, of course) and submitting it to another.

To specify agreements between writers and editors over expenses such as travel, telephone calls, photocopying, and the like, it is advisable to put the details down in writing. Some editors balk at formal contracts, but others—such as the Times Mirror Magazines group—insist on them. A short informal letter to your editor with the details of how many words are required on your topic and what the agreed fee and deadline will be, whether you are to assist or provide illustrative material or a manuscript only, will suffice. If you send two copies of these terms to your editor, both signed by you, and ask the editor to sign one copy and return it to you, you essentially have negotiated a binding contract for that article. Generally, the rule is that the more you have in writing that is agreed upon by both parties, the easier it will be to sort out disagreements later. Many writers now keep telephone logs, in which they jot down the details of conversations wth editors, just in case they need to refer to that discussion later.

Reputable writers do not steal from other writers. They either make "fair use" of someone else's work (*briefly* quoting and crediting the source) or they obtain written permission (often paying a fee for secondary use). In both cases, the original source must be cited and the author given credit. Such a citation might read, "Tom Wolfe, in the February issue of *Harper's*, wrote . . . " Fair use means just that, that you do not exploit the value of the original or diminish its reprint worth by using too large a portion of it. There's an often-cited rule of thumb regarding what constitutes fair use. Many writers believe that any quotation of fewer than 250 words from a full-length book—again, used with credit—would not constitute copyright infringement. Use of another's work without credit (or permission) constitutes plagiarism or outright piracy.

The exceptions to this fair-use rule, for which you should always obtain permission before using, include song lyrics; lines from plays, movies, or TV shows; letters; theses; poetry; and most graphic material such as charts, illustrations, or photographs. But opinions on the hazy area of fair use vary, so, if in doubt, consult your editor (who in turn can consult the house lawyer).

Facts and ideas, of course, cannot be copyrighted, so the details of any story can be used as long as you tell them in your own words. As an additional precaution, write from more than one source to avoid paralleling the thoughts in the other works. Don't forget that the same law that protects other's works also protects yours, so utilize the principle of the Golden Rule and you should have no problem.

RECORD KEEPING

Throughout this book we've talked about the need for you to take a businesslike approach to freelancing. This is because writers, as a group, tend to give short shrift to even the most basic business details. An example: keeping suitable records.

After you've sent out several queries and proposals and made an article sale or two, you'll soon discover the importance of keeping track of your output. As your numbers of submissions, sales—and yes, alas, rejections—increase, it'll become impossible for you to remember the details of all your transactions.

Also, when income tax time rolls around, you'll be painfully aware of the necessity for keeping detailed records—and this includes both income earned and expenses paid—for the IRS. This means keeping a day-to-day account of business expenses (mileage, memberships, education, telephone calls, photo supplies, typewriters, maintenance, word processors, pencils, paper, mailing costs—you name it) that are a must for any freelancer. Even beginning writers will learn from others and through trial-and-error how to take advantage of certain business deductions. In fact, most fledgling freelancers will discover that their allowable expenses (deductions) actually exceed their writing income for perhaps a year or two. This, of course, means they can declare a net loss for their businesses—if they've kept good records and can provide documentation to support their claims. Such documentation, incidentally, includes rejection slips (see, they *do* serve some purpose), query and assignment correspondence, and sales receipts for actual earnings.

You'll discover, too, that even though freelancers may be able to take advantage of many tax write-offs, they can't fail to report their magazine sales. Publishers, you see, must pay taxes too and are required to file an earnings report with the Internal Revenue Service each time they pay a freelance writer more than $600 in a single calendar year. And since I see that sparkle in your eyes, be advised that many magazines report *all* such income to the IRS—no matter how small the check may have been.

First, however, let's consider your own marketing system for keeping records. These records, after all, can prove helpful the following April when the tax man cometh.

Your Personal Marketing Records

There's no one surefire method I'd recommend by saying, "This is it—and only this." Simply find the method you're most at ease with and stick with it. Your system should enable you to tell at a glance what your current marketing situation is.

All you need is a record of query or article submissions and return dates, sales, date of payment, and publication date. Some writers prefer to note this information on the carbon copy of the article (or the cover letter). Others use 3x5 index cards for recording all the above-mentioned manuscript marketing information. Still others keep an elaborate loose-leaf notebook, using dividers for types of articles and a separate sheet of paper for each manuscript, inserted either by title or subject. On the individual sheets they record all the necessary market data and follow-up information.

One of the best systems I've seen—and the one I use—is a simple but organized permanent record provided under the section "Record of Submissions" in the back of the Writer's Digest Diary (available each year). It provides a space for date, title, market, editor, photo submission, acceptance date, amount paid and date, whether pictures were used and returned, tearsheets received, and expenses incurred while doing the assignment. It's all laid out for you in one place, it's easy to use, and makes record keeping almost pleasant.

Marketing, as you've come to realize, is a time-consuming but vital part of our business. Most freelancers estimate that it takes roughly 40 to 50 percent of their work time. And that can become frustrating, if not downright maddening, for the creative person. So why complicate the process further by failing to keep simple, accurate, organized records? That's why we never cease hammering home the point that freelance writing, even for fiction writers and some poets, is a business—a business that demands you pay strict attention to keeping detailed records. You must reconcile yourself to the commercial aspects of freelancing, do your marketing work, and back it up with your simple but sound record system. It'll take less time and go easier for you if you do it right, and right from the start of your career.

A caveat: I know writers who are reliable, skillful, and able record-keepers—but they get so caught up in the business of keeping beautiful records that they overlook their writing obligations. Don't let this happen to you; do a workmanlike job of record keeping and get on with the business of writing. Otherwise, you won't have the satisfaction of doing either.

Writing doesn't pay enough for a freelancer to afford *not* to deduct every possible item—mileage, business lunches, phone calls, etc., all add up. These same freelancers are masters at combining their work and personal lives, for instance, having friends (who are contacts) to dinner, or scheduling vacations to coincide with a travel assignment or a writer's conference.

If many people are unable to live with the uncertainty of the freelancer's income, the IRS is unable to live with the uncertainty of the freelancer's sloppy record keeping. (For one thing we are at once suspect because our income tax is not deducted from our paychecks.) ASJA member and tax specialist Julian Block, author of *Tax Saving: A Year-Round Guide* (Chilton, 1981), from which the following material was adapted, explains tax records for freelancers.

HOW LONG TO KEEP TAX RECORDS
by Julian Block

You need no reminder to hold on to your tax records in case your returns are questioned by the Internal Revenue Service. But just how long do you need to save those old records that clutter up your closets and desk drawers? Unfortunately, there is no flat cutoff. The IRS says the answer depends on what's in those records and the type of transaction involved.

Although the IRS doesn't even require you to keep copies of your returns, it warns that supporting records must be kept "for as long as their contents may become material in the administration of any Internal Revenue law." In plainer language, hang on to receipts, cancelled checks, and whatever else might help support income, deductions, or other items on your return at least until the statute of limitations runs out for an IRS audit or for you to file an amended return should you find an error after filing.

As a general rule, the IRS has three years from the filing deadline to take a crack at your return. For example, a return for 1983, with a filing deadline of April 15, 1984, remains subject to an audit until April of 1987.

Incidentally, a return filed *before* its due date is treated as having been filed *on* its due date. In the case of a return for 1983 that is filed in January of 1984, the three-year period still does not elapse until April of 1987. Conversely, should you obtain a filing extension, the three years are calculated from the date on which you file your return.

Once the three-year period runs out, it's usually safe to dispose of your receipts and other supporting records. But there are exceptions to the general rule, and they can be significant. The tax code gives the IRS *six* years from the filing deadline to begin an examination if you omit from the return an amount that runs to more than 25 percent of the income you reported on it. And there is *no* time limit on when the IRS can begin an audit if you fail to file a return or you file one that is considered fraudulent.

You should keep copies of your old tax returns for at least five years. If you decide to take advantage of income averaging because your income rose sharply, you will need your returns for the previous four years. And even if you do not need them for averaging, they are always helpful as a guide for making out future returns.

Copies of your returns can also prove helpful in case the IRS claims you failed to file them. If you want to really nail things down at filing time, you can hand-deliver a return to your local IRS office, which will stamp the receipt date on both the filed copy and the copy you keep. That way, there should be no question that your return was filed.

If you need copies of old returns, you can get them by filing IRS Form 4506, "Request for Copy of Tax Form." A separate form must be filed for each return requested. If you have moved, send the form to the IRS Service Center where the returns were filed, not the Service Center for your current address. The IRS will bill you when it sends the copies. The charge for copies is $1 for the first page and ten cents for each additional page. (The IRS doesn't keep returns as long as you should. It usually destroys the originals six years after the filing date.)

It's wise to hold all cancelled checks for tax payments. And before you mail any check to the IRS, make sure the following information is on it: the reason for the payment, plus the form number and year of the return for which the check is being sent—for instance, the balance due on Form 1040 for this year—and your Social Security or employer identification number.

Also, the IRS asks that you use separate checks and note the necessary information on each one when you pay two different taxes at once—say, past due income taxes and interest for an earlier year, and an estimated tax payment for this year. Doing that will make it much easier for the IRS to identify and credit you with the payment if it becomes separated from the accompanying correspondence or return.

Overlooking this simple step may confuse the computers and, at a minimum, direct attention to your return and require otherwise avoidable correspondence. Even worse, it may cause those relentless computers to erroneously charge you with a penalty for failing to make a timely payment—and interest to boot.

More than one person has learned the hard way that it's important to save copies of returns and cancelled checks. For instance, the IRS charged that a lawyer had not filed his returns. The lawyer argued that he had filed, but was unable to produce copies of the returns, cancelled checks, or any other records to back up his claims. The Tax Court refused to believe him and he was nailed for additional taxes, interest, and late-filing penalties.

Fortunately, the IRS doesn't always have the last word. In another case, the court held that just because the IRS couldn't find any records of a particular return didn't necessarily mean the taxpayer had failed to file it. The court found he had been a regular filer before and after and refused to impose any penalties. Moreover, the judge noted that IRS "faith in the perfection of their system is commendable, but the court is not persuaded that IRS index records are the only man-made records free from error."

In addition to copies of returns and cancelled checks, which should be saved for at least five years, there are other records that should be kept until they can no longer affect a future return, which may be far longer than five years. For instance, you should retain records of what you paid for stocks or other investments, not only because you may need them for an IRS audit, but because you need them to figure your profit or loss on a sale that may not take place until many years later.

Finally, unless you have expertise in tax matters, you'd be wise to consult your tax preparer or the IRS. And, once again, be warned to keep all records (including correspondence) that will identify you as a professional writer.

Chapter Five

THE WRITING LIFE—STICKING IT OUT

When John Fischer, former editor-in-chief of *Harper's* magazine, was a näive young editor, he made a study of the performance records of some two hundred writers. He sought common characteristics that would distinguish "the good risks from the bad." Fischer admitted his findings proved less than revolutionary, but he did discover that all successful writers had two things in common. These were, in his words, "an abnormal supply of simple animal energy, and an overcharged ego."

Surprised that Fischer didn't mention talent? Don't be. All the talent in the world won't see you through the tough years of learning and rejection. All the talent in the world won't guarantee that you can stick it out.

This chapter is devoted to a little shoptalk about the writing life. First, we'll get some insight into writers from the point of view of editors and publishers. Then we'll hear from writers who will discuss what keeps them going. You may want to reread this chapter whenever your career seems to have come to a halt. We hope it helps.

The following piece by ASJA member Frances Halpern was excerpted (and rearranged for this book) from her incisive *Writer's Guide to Publishing in the West* (Pinnacle Books, 1982). I think that all writers, professional and aspiring, will benefit from reading what Halpern has to say in "Publishers Talking."

PUBLISHERS TALKING
by Frances Halpern

Most publishers, when asked to talk about themselves, the industry, and their relations with writers, jump at the chance to plead their cause, clear the air, and in general respond to the universally held theory that writers and publishers are natural enemies. (Well, probably they are. All you have to do is check with both unpublished writers who never get near a publisher and successful authors who deal with them constantly and in a majority of instances, you'll not hear a good word about publishers from either group.)

So we asked a number of editors and publishers to address this issue and discuss anything else they had in mind. They perceive themselves as wide open, willing to listen, wanting to cooperate with writers (and many of them are). They say they spend their waking hours in holy pilgrimage seeking the fresh story, the beautifully written word, and the commercial property to put between two pieces of plain or fancy cardboard, call it a book, and ship it to market. And they all agree that most writers are incredibly ignorant about the business of publishing.

Whatever else they are, writers are not an endangered species. Camped like a hostile army outside the walls, they hurl thousands of queries and manuscripts at besieged publishers, a less numerous species, who survive by trying to anticipate the habits of the reading public, a third species far from extinct, but certainly erratic in its response. Meanwhile, the writers gather 'round campfires to tell one another horror stories about the enemy behind the wall. Waving form letter rejections, they complain: "Those lousy, insensitive shoemakers don't recognize a piece of literature when it's rubbed into their eyes." And, "When we do get a contract, it's filled with insidious small print calculated to make them (the publishers) rich and keep us poor. They mangle our prose, allow the printer to get away with hideous mistakes, then bury the book in a warehouse in Minneapolis."

But Jeremy Tarcher, of J.P. Tarcher (Los Angeles)—now a subsidiary of the vernerable Boston publisher Houghton Mifflin—insists, "Publishers are lovers. We see a manuscript that captures our fancy and think, 'Let's do it,' despite the fact that seven out of ten books lose money and one in ten supports the whole system."

Bantam Books editor Charles Bloch has been working with writers in the Los Angeles area for years. He calls the editor/writer relationship a negative yin and yang. "I try to avoid the arrogance that comes with making life-and-death career decisions deeply affecting another person and I wish I could dispel the paranoia among writers," says Bloch. "Most writers don't realize that when they create a book it's theirs and the publisher is only buying the right to publish it in a certain form."

"When the dream is realized and a book contract is signed, almost inevitably the hostility between writer and publisher begins," says Evelyn Grippo, senior editor of Harlequin Books West. "I don't understand why writers are always complaining about their contracts," she adds. "The same people who dissect a cookbook recipe with great care will not invest the time or energy to study their book contracts. We always urge authors to take the contracts to agents or lawyers."

Carole Garland, a Pinnacle Books editor, suggests, "The biggest problem between the editor/publisher and writers is 'The Great Expectation Syndrome.' It happens again and again, and is born out of an author's ignorance of the publishing business, mixed with fantasies about being another Judith Krantz and/or Ernest Hemingway." Garland explains, "We contract to publish a first novelist. We're delighted because we have discovered and nurtured a new talent. Then the book is published, and the author is mad as hell! The complaints include, 'You didn't promote my book! Why isn't my book in the bookstores? Why aren't I on the bestseller list?' "

According to Garland, "Publishers don't promote or advertise every book. They do recognize their responsibility to get the book to the marketplace with the best package possible. Then it's up to the public. We can't force booksellers to order a particular title, or make the public buy it. Perhaps it is necessary for authors to have tremendous faith in their work and dream about fame and riches to keep them at the typewriter day after day. But when the creative process is finished, the writer must face reality. It takes time to build a name in the marketplace and few first- or even second-time authors, particularly novelists, will break into the big time or earn enough to support themselves."

L.L. (Larry) Sloan of Price/Stern/Sloan, publisher of humor and gift books, says, "I can empathize with writers. I'm a writer myself, and yet I am still astonished at an author who sends an 800-page novel to this house. What can writers be thinking about, to know so little about who publishes what?" Sloan also confesses to getting carried away when he comes across a special talent who needs direction. "It's rare," he admits, "but we have nursed writers along who finally produce for us." A big problem for a publisher like Price/Stern/Sloan is the writer who thinks he or she has come up with an original concept and doesn't realize that the same idea has been submitted forty times.

Publishers on Rejection

Publishers insist that writers are needlessly suspicious about not getting a good (or any) reading of their manuscripts and they like to remind writers, "Editors don't get rewarded for rejecting manuscripts. It's a game of discovery and we need writers. We all bring manuscripts home and plow through hundreds of submissions looking for the one we can publish." They also beg writers to "distinguish between magazine copy and book-worthy material, and between private fantasies and worthwhile literature."

"Many editors have great compassion for writers," says Bloch. "We understand the emotional commitment they put into their work. I've seen editors really despondent over having to reject a manuscript. The blow to the writer is intense. We're hurting people all the time. We've also had authors who have taken as long as twelve years to deliver a book and other writers who can't bring themselves to finish a book at all because of fear of rejection. The only way to be successful is to accept rejection; it's the mark of the pro."

Most publishers agree that rejections must be short and general. When they try the detailed personal letter describing why a manuscript is rejected, back comes a long reply from the writer, either reviling the publisher for stupidity or begging for a chance to rewrite and submit again. Writers are upset when they receive form rejection slips, but they go crazy when they get one of those "you almost made it" responses from a publisher. Bantam's Bloch says that on occasion he will do a personal letter to someone who comes close. "But the writer must understand that's the end of it. If we want a rewrite, we'll ask for it."

One of those rare publishers who doesn't mind phone calls from writers is Melvin Powers of Wilshire Books (North Hollywood). "I can tell if an idea is right for us," says Powers, who also admits that he doesn't tell writers the truth when he rejects. "The author is sensitive about the material and will not agree with or appreciate the criticism. My publishing house is open to writers, but they should have some horse sense about their work, get help from teachers, and not be babes in the woods about contracts."

Andrew Ettinger, editorial director of Harlequin Books West, describes the "guilt and frustration that goes with the editor's badge." He says, "Some of the writers really get to me. They send pathetic hard luck stories along with their manuscripts and we feel awful about having to reject them." Harlequin editor Grippo has made it her personal crusade to tell writers there are a variety of reasons for rejections that have nothing to do with the quality of their work. "It could be timing, distribution problems, too costly to print, the wrong publisher."

Tarcher admits, "Sometimes we just don't realize the potential in a book, or have had a bad breakfast that morning. Many bestsellers were rejected by smart editors. Perhaps our reactions have heavy elements of the unconscious. I may reject because I am simply not interested in the subject. And, of course, publishers choose books on a commercial basis. They may think, 'This is not good, but my God, will it sell!' "

Sloan says, "I feel sad when I look at a manuscript and it's terrible. I think, what a waste of time. On the other hand, who knows, maybe it's therapy, good for the writer to get it out of his or her system. We should all be publishing fewer books, but then the result would be fewer published authors."

"Much of what we publish," says Jean-Louis Brindamour of Strawberry Hill Press (San Francisco), "is rejected by larger publishing houses—frequently, we feel, because they don't have as much foresight as we do." He also admitted that although he is not actively seeking manuscripts, he will look at anything that comes in "because one never knows what may be in the process of creation."

Writers (published or rejected) are often confused at the apparently crass behavior of publishing people, and Tarcher attempts to explain. "Life is complex," he says, "and the publishing business is more complex than life. Authors tend to focus entirely on their own books and believe they've written a book that will sell a million copies. I talk with my authors and explain we are working in a crowded market— 40,000 books published a year, 425,000 titles currently available. I understand how an author who has put in years on a book is driven to the point of wanting to kill if the publisher doesn't do his job correctly. But publishers are human too. We lose control over a book that passes through so many hands from concept to placement in the bookstores."

"When a horrendous mistake occurs," continues Tarcher, "let us say in the printing of a book, the author is undoubtedly running around screaming, 'My publisher killed me!' No, actually we died together. Publishers and authors have in some cases badly failed each other. So you see, for every writer cursing a publisher, there's a publisher cursing a writer."

Reflecting the dream of every publisher, Tarcher says, "I still wake up each morning thinking maybe that book I've been waiting for all week, all month, all my life, will come into the office today."

THE WRITERS' TURN

Up to this point we've discussed the ways you get started in the writing business. We've talked about the need for establishing realistic goals. We've discussed the business end of the profession and those essentials all writers must learn if they're to effectively run the obstacle course and survive basic training. We've made the point—repeatedly—that too many fledgling writers merely sit down at a typewriter one day and start pecking away without the slightest notion of what makes for a salable article or book. We've tried to stress that writing is a craft with rules and guidelines to direct you and keep you on track.

In all fairness, however, it must be said that we've brought you only to the point where most newcomers to the business start to flounder, suffer a few setbacks, then fall by the wayside—never to put pen to paper again, except to sign Christmas cards or business letters. We've just gotten you started—charged your battery of will power, as it were.

The problem now—at that point where many potentially fine writers fail—is how to stick with your work and keep your writing electrolytes bubbling. There have been untold numbers of instances involving first-sale writers (lucky with their initial try in the marketplace) who never sold that second or third article. They gave up, drained of hope and energy, completely demoralized, cursing an unseen coterie of villains made up of editors, publishers, agents, and other writers.

There have been far fewer instances where less talented, but driven writers stuck to their desks and finally labored through what agent Donald MacCampbell calls "the labyrinths of the literary marketplace."

What's the difference between the two types? What keeps one writer going despite a ream of rejection slips—while another folds in frustration? What recharges one freelancer's battery and sustains his effort—while another's will power gives out and he sells his typewriter for a mess of pottage?

The fact is, you'll get almost as many answers as the number of writers you talk with. None of us quite agree, except on one key issue: the necessity of coming up with those particular disciplines (or tricks) that keep *you* witing. Dr. Peale says you must think positively. Dale Carnegie made a fortune with his winning-friends-and-influencing-people routine, and Dr. Wayne W. Dyer recommends knowng *Your Erroneous Zones*. (All how-to books, by the way, and each one a bestseller by a writer who has not been singled out as a distinguished literary talent!)

Just as you do by doing, and start by starting, you keep going by keeping going. Trite? Sure, and so are the theories behind the three books I've just cited. But they worked for the three writers—and over the years they've obviously worked for millions of people.

Most of us stick with our work through sheer force of discipline—and because we like to eat. Most of us struggle, curse, perspire, pray a little and rewrite a lot. . .and require gallons of coffee and singular effort to sit there and keep ourselves at work. No writer ever made it as a freelancer *without* vigorous self-discipline.

Here's ASJA officer Evelyn Kaye, who came to this country from England (where she was a reporter for the *Manchester Guardian* and the Reuters News Agency), and her theories on momentum.

THE WRITER'S DISCIPLINE
by Evelyn Kaye

When you first start out as a freelance writer, you may have a couple of editorial contacts, perhaps an assignment, and you're ready to go out and look for more work for the future. How do you keep that first enthusiastic impetus going through the weeks and months and years ahead? What's the best way to discipline yourself to make sure that ideas and proposals are sent out, and that projects are written on time? Is there a secret to sticking to it despite the rejections, the delays, the schemes that fall through, and the frustrations of dealing with magazines, editors, and publishers who move as frequently as traveling circuses?

From my years of freelancing and from talking with scores of other writers, I can tell you that there is no one answer. Every writer finds an individual system to keep the typewriter clacking; if it works, use it. So here are some of the methods that have worked for me, plus some ideas from other writers who've shared their experiences.

What spurs me on each day are the habits I acquired in my years as a reporter at a busy news agency. Every day I came in for my shift—and no matter if it was nine in the morning, two in the afternoon, or eleven at night, I was expected to check, research, interview, reread, and rewrite my work for publication. The setting was far from ideal; in those 1960s days, there were clacking teletype machines continually operating, phones ringing, people walking round, papers dumped on my desk "for immediate attention," a rickety manual typewriter, and an overheated atmosphere. But despite everything, I wrote news stories, feature articles, and article series, and went to interviews, news conferences, and meetings.

What I do is convince myself that being a freelancer is an extension of those full-time days. Instead of having an editor snarling at me in the morning waiting for my copy, I set my own deadlines. It is harder to begin each day without the informal friendliness of a newsroom—but the tools of the trade are just the same. Here's my desk, typewriter, paper, telephone, and files. Surely, I tell myself, I can work just as efficiently in this quieter, less harried atmosphere as I did in the craziness of the news agency.

There are internal and external aids to help me along the way—because keeping yourself going is always tough. If you've ever worked anywhere at a full-time job you know the essential part is to get there each morning and then get down to work. If you've done that, you can transfer those skills to coping as a freelance writer.

I accept that writing is my work, a daily job, a regular commitment of my time and energy on which I spend the major portion of my working day. It is for me a nine-to-five job, with weekends off, although the hours are a little more flexible. However, if something comes up that will take a chunk of time out of that working day, I will turn it down—because I am working. I will pick up the dry cleaning only on my lunch hour; I will take the books back to the library if I need to go there for research; I will not volunteer to help with the town beautification committee, which meets in the mornings.

I've found that for me this stern approach is the best way to make sure that I sit down at my typewriter or desk and keep on working. Sure, there are exceptions—days when I juggle other things and find myself writing in the evening. And of course there are interruptions that can't be avoided. But I try to avoid losing any of those precious hours during the day when I should be working, and commit the time I once spent writing pages for the news agency to writing pages of material I am going to sell myself.

Some writers feel they need to wait for "inspiration" until they sit down and write. I have never been part of that school. My empathy is with the writer who said that he liked to be sitting at his desk every day so that should inspiration strike him suddenly he would be ready for it.

Support Systems

To cope daily on your own as a writer, you need some moral and physical support. First you need:

Somewhere to Write

My first desk was in a closet-sized room off the hallway of our apartment. But it was a major step. For the first time I did not have to keep clearing my papers off the dining room table; I was settled in a permanent place. Having my own place to work where I can leave my notes and papers is an essential for me. The better organized the area, the easier it is to get going. Some writers say they can write anywhere, but most professional writers set up the most efficient offices they can. Some use card indexes for material; others use charts for research; most have a filing system for ideas and clippings; many have extensive lists of contacts and resource people. The most recent—and expensive—innovation is the computer word processor, which many successful writers now use. Yet two top writers both told me they are still tapping away on their portable manual typewriters because they "don't like the hum of the electric ones."

Again, it's what works for you. But if you are on your own, you will find that a filing system, contact lists, a good library research connection, and access to a copying machine will make the daily swing of writing much simpler to begin.

One writer of a regular column in a major women's magazine said that her breakthrough was renting office space instead of trying to work out of the house. "It was the only way I could really get going" she admitted, "and it's made a real difference."

Scheduling

When you've organized your work space, you have to fill the time you're there. My schedule used to be fixed for me; it began when my children left for school at 8:15 a.m. and ended when they rushed through the door at 3 p.m., disrupting the peaceful house. That kind of deadline is often very effective. Now that they're older and my time is more flexible, I sometimes find it harder to get started without the 3 p.m. threat. But it's essential that you set definite hours with time off, breaks, and endings.

Schedule your working time when you know you're at your best. One writer I know likes to work from about 4 p.m. to midnight, and requests "no morning phone calls." Another has found her most productive time is from dawn to noon—so she's at her desk by six o'clock. And another always prefers to work in the evenings and through the night—which can put a strain on a marriage. Pick your time—and stay with it.

Be realistic about what you can achieve. It takes more than a day to write a bestselling novel or a world-shattering biography. Successful freelance writers are there for days, weeks, months, and years completing their work. Sometimes you can work day and night to finish a piece, and be worn out afterwards. But I've learned that after a certain point I am not working constructively and will have to tear up what I write when I reread it later. For me, intense work for three or four hours is best, followed by a break, and then another uninterrupted session. Other writers work straight through a project and then take a break. Some writers only work for an hour or two at the same project and then turn to another. If you are working full-time at writing on your own, you have to find out when you can work best, and use those hours for your projects.

Personal Nudges

Sometimes it's the little things that keep you going.

Put your phone answering service or machine on so you won't be distracted by phone calls and stop working. Somehow knowing that no phone call can reach you makes you start.

Keep a stack of bills in front of you to remind you why it is you are sitting there.

Shake up your daily routine sometimes. If you always come to your desk after a shower and coffee, come in one morning as soon as you get up. Then when you've done some work, take a shower and come back refreshed to start again.

Always leave your work with a page unfinished, so when you come back you'll have something to start with.

There are always those days when it's really hard to get going, when the Energy Inertia Syndrome seems to have jammed your actions with cotton candy. Try the following short-term methods for unsticking the block.

Time-tests

Persuade yourself that if you work for half an hour, which is only thirty minutes, you will at least have made a start. Then, if you can face it, you might do another half hour. Somehow, once you start and the half hour has passed, you realize that another half hour won't be too hard, and by then you're well on your way. I don't know why the first ten minutes are always the hardest.

Bribes

These work for me—but maybe I'm susceptible to promises, promises. Try telling yourself that if you manage to finish this article/section/page/outline, you'll be allowed to go and get the mail waiting outside. Or that you'll be allowed to have a coffee break. Or—this is one of my summer favorites—you'll be able to sit in the sun for half an hour. Or if you finish a certain amount of work, you will be allowed to make a phone call to a friend. Sounds a little crazy—but if it works, use it.

Lists

Make a list of exactly what needs to be done, e.g., "rewrite introduction, retype quotations, insert additional research." Make it even more detailed if you like—"insert material on page 3, add paragraphs on page 5." The point is to break down what lies waiting to be done into smaller units. Then start with the first item on the list. That should only take a few minutes. Cross it off the list. And move on. Once you've seen what needs to be done in detail, it spurs you on to do the rest.

In general, list-making in a notebook or on scraps of paper can be a great asset in planning what needs to be done. I have a workbook in which there is a weekly list of projects and activities I'm supposed to do, and a long-term list of projects over a period of weeks and sometimes months. The key point of a list is priorities. Take a red pen and number each point in order of importance. Here's where you will be able to see what you have to do. "Finish article for Monday deadline" should have a big "1" beside it, while "Call Sally for meeting" can be given a "5." If things don't get done, you move them to the next week's list.

If you find you're not getting *anything* done, give up the list. This is probably not the system for you.

Dealing with Rejection

One of the most draining parts of being a freelance writer is coping with the constant rejection. Because of course you have to face rejection; if all the ideas, proposals, and articles you suggested came through you'd be too busy to do them all, right?

In nearly ten years of freelancing, I have never learned to love rejection. I do not love those polite letters assuring me that it's a great idea but they can't use it because they already have a piece in the works on the same topic. I do not love those form notes thanking me for thinking of them and urging me to try again. I do not love my book proposals thudding through the mail with photocopied letters from publishers who feel it's "not quite right" for them. I do not love phone calls from editors saying "Sorry—not for us." And I particularly do not love the belated call after they have said yes, to say that the editor has left or that the idea is not going to work out or that the magazine is folding.

So I have learned that even though I have had articles published in major magazines and three nonfiction books to my credit, I am still not good at loving rejection. I overreact, and take it personally. I go into a deep, depressed state reliving the most unhappy moments of my writing career and sink into a "how-did-I-ever-imagine-I-could-be-a-writer" soliloquy.

Should any of these symptons afflict you, let me tell you how to survive. First, admit you're miserable. Yes, they should have taken your work and published it. But they didn't.

One wise writer said "Read the letter they sent you and remember that it means what it says. That's all." There's no need to read between every line and convince yourself that you are rejected forever. If they say "We already have a piece on this topic," chances are they already have a piece on this topic. And if they say, "Try us again" they probably mean "Send in a few more ideas." That's all.

When you are still smarting from the first pain of the rejection, it's hard to be alone. I've found that one of the supports a writers' group (like ASJA) can provide is an understanding ear in times of crisis. A phone call to a fellow writer may bring moral support and the comforting word "They did that to me, too," or "They're always terrible to work with." After the first pain subsides, look at the rejected piece again, and decide if it can be fixed, or if it is perfectly fine. Then send it out somewhere else right away. Or if you have doubts about its salability, put together some other ideas and send them back to the first editor. Or try and see him or her to talk over the other ideas you have.

Sad to say, after several acceptances the pain of rejection is only more keen. When a magazine that had accepted several pieces suddenly said, "No," it was twice as painful as the twenty times my would-be novel has come back from publishers, rejected. I don't know why it hurts me more—but it does.

Unfortunately, the only cure for rejection is acceptance, and it's hard to be accepted 100 percent of the time.

Recharging Yourself

Occasionally you'll find yourself sitting at your desk, your lists empty, your papers clear, your phone silent, and a great void where ideas used to flow. What you need now is a prod, a catalyst, a nibble of bait to get you moving.

File-flipping

If you're a freelancer, you are keeping files of clippings, notes, ideas, comments, and quotations on those subjects that interest you and you want to write about. Now is the time to take out your files and look through them. You'll find that great idea you thought of in the middle of another assignment that you can follow up on; or the newspaper item that will work beautifully as a magazine idea; or the set of statistics you kept because they were so intriguing and you meant to investigate. If you've been keeping good files, you should find half a dozen ideas waiting for you.

Writer's Market

On two occasions when I was stuck I've sold ideas by looking through *Writer's Market*. Once I found a TV magazine I hadn't heard of, called for a sample copy, and sold an idea over the phone! The second time, I was reminded of a magazine I had not thought of for an unsold piece I had done before, and wrote to them and sold them the idea. There's a mine of golden information about magazines you might not have thought of for your special knowledge and all kinds of thoughts and possibilities come to mind as you read through.

Library-leafing

Going to the library to look through the ideas in the magazines index is often helpful in spurring ideas for new topics. Or simply looking through the magazines on display for article topics you might not have considered for your specialty.

Out-of-town Papers

Whenever I travel I buy as many local newspapers and magazines as I can—because there's certain to be some good ideas that I can use when I go home. If you're not traveling, you can still buy out-of-town papers at some newsstands, or subscribe for a while if you'd like to ensure an ongoing supply of fresh viewpoints. A browse through the New Hampshire or New Mexico or New Brunswick papers—assuming you don't live in any of those places—can start off a whole new chain of thinking and get you back to your typewriter again.

Try the Phone Book

I often look through the Yellow Pages of telephone books. Once I found a new contact for a book I was writing listed under my book subject! Other times ideas for articles come from some of the headings and listings that reflect what services and products people are offering and buying.

Talk to People

Writers are notoriously isolated and alone. But in order to get ideas, to find out what is happening in the real world, to hear different viewpoints, you have to mix with and listen to the everyday experiences of *nonwriters*. Talk to people in lines, at restaurants, on buses. Attend conferences on subjects that interest you. Go to meetings of groups that pique your curiosity. Listen to what is being discussed, what makes people react, what topics excite them. Ideas often come from a chance comment, a remark tossed out casually, an unexpected reaction—but you should be there to hear it, and rush back to your typewriter, refired to go back to work.

Getting up each day knowing that it's just you and your writing against the world can be a little overwhelming. It's rather like starting out on a tightrope, hoping that your skills and techniques will get you safely to the other side. You only have to keep your head, keep cool, and keep your balance. And if you don't make it this time, you can always try again. Just put a clean piece of paper into the typewriter and you're on your way.

That's how Evelyn Kaye manages her writing disciplines. Now let's look at how another ASJA member has mastered writing habits conducive to steady productivity. Isobel Silden doesn't write from midnight to dawn as Henry Miller used to work, but, like the rest of us, has formed her own methods through a combination of necessity plus trial and error. Read for yourself what works for Silden.

DISCIPLINE YOURSELF
by Isobel Silden

Among the uninitiated, there exists the somewhat fey and wholly unreasonable impression that because the freelance writer works at home, the freelance writer isn't REALLY working. It's okay to drop in. It's okay to call in midday for a prolonged, chatty conversation. Anything goes, 'cause you're at home.

Right? Totally wrong!

You know you're working, hard. Now, you must convince your immediate world of that fact.

Here's how I do it.

Unless I'm expecting someone, I simply don't answer my doorbell. My office is in the front of the house, so I can see who is approaching. I have been known to crawl on hands and knees into the back of the house, so the visitor can't see me through the window.

It's good exercise.

Sometimes I'm trapped: I'm typing and it can be heard through the windows. With ice in my voice, I say through the door—never open it, you're lost if you do—"I'm working, and I can't be disturbed. Sorry. Call me later."

Have I lost friends doing this? Well, yes. Once. But she was a crashing bore, and I'd never wanted to pursue the friendship anyway. Most people say they respect my discipline and understand completely.

I handle phone calls the same way, saying either that I'm expecting an important call (I'm ALWAYS expecting an important call; isn't every freelancer?), or "I'm working on a story point and I don't want to interrupt my trend of thought. Let me call you after five."

And that works, too. Even people who don't work nine to five jobs understand my not wanting to be interrupted.

"Do you work every day?" is one of the more inane questions put to me by my more inane acquaintances. Not friends, heaven forbid. The answer is, "Well, yes, that's how I earn my living. Don't YOU work every day?" That shuts 'em up. I make it very clear to people that I start work at nine every morning and I quit at five or six and sometimes seven, when the job is done. I also work weekends when necessary. And that leads me, with a nifty transition, into self-discipline.

There is another wonderful, but inaccurate, theory among beginning freelancers that your time is your own and you can work when you feel like it.

Well, of course you can, if your creditors are willing to wait until you feel like paying your bills, if your stomach is willing to wait until you earn enough money to feed it.

Freelancing is a business like any other. But unlike most, you have no one to account to but yourself. And if you're not a tough boss, your business could go belly-up in short order.

My boss, me, gives an hour for lunch every day, unless I'm wildly rushed on deadline for an article. Then my boss allows time for a cup of soup and it's back to the typewriter. Finish up the work on time, make your deadline, and maybe you can have Monday afternoon off to sit in the sun. I make deals with myself.

Forget sleeping until noon. Forget lunch with the old gang. *Don't* forget a round of tennis or golf, or time for a walk or run. You don't have to be a sloth; you've got to stay in shape.

When I started freelancing, it was after years of working in an office. I knew about discipline: I'd worked from nine until six. So it was quite automatic for me to set up a system. I was *so* disciplined that I couldn't go to work unless I took my purse with me! I'd been accustomed to seeing it sitting on my desk all those years. It had to be on the table next to my typewriter, so the creative juices could flow without distraction.

It's not easy for a married woman to embark on a freelancing career if she's working at home, and most of us do. I was married at the time I began freelancing, and my then-husband came and went at odd hours. He was quite capable of fixing his own lunch if he came home at noon, and he'd been doing it all those years I'd been working in an office. Now, however, I was home, and he'd think nothing of coming into my office and asking me to fix him a sandwich!

"I'm working," I'd protest, but it didn't do any good.

"You're here, so fix me a sandwich," he'd ask and this good, subservient ninny would. I won't say this was the cause of the divorce, but it didn't add to my everlasting joy.

It should be clearly understood among family members that just because Mom is at home typing away does not mean she is available to drop everything and revert back to being housemaid, cook, messenger, chauffeur, seamstress, financial adviser, etc. Research all the housewives-mothers who've made it typing in the kitchen and flaunt their success at your family. Maybe then they'll get off your case.

Seriously, this discipline thing must be enforced upon you and everyone around you.

One freelance writer friend keeps the answering machine on all day so she won't be tempted to answer the telephone. At five o'clock she hears who phoned and returns the calls. To be sure, she has missed some business calls that way and couldn't talk to the people until next day, but she simply explains she was out on an interview, and no one objects.

Another friend has found it impossible to work at home. The baby cries. His wife talks on the phone. Neighbors come around. So he went out and rented himself a tiny one-room office. Into it he moved his desk, chair, typewriter, and supplies. That's all. No pictures. No phone. No couch. Nothing to distract him. And in he goes every morning. He comes out for a while at lunch and returns to work until the end of the day.

"I purposely picked an inside office so I wouldn't be tempted to go out for a walk on a nice day. This way, I never know if it's raining. There's no window, there are no interruptions, no distractions."

It wouldn't work for everyone, but it's great for him. He's happy, he's satisfied, and most important, he's earning a good living.

Another friend confided she was strongly tempted to strangle her son one afternoon when he barged into her home office while she was wrestling with a tricky plot turn on her newest novel.

"I didn't hear the typewriter, so I didn't think you were working," the youngster said.

"Doesn't thinking count?" his irate mother snarled.

Her solution? Next time she and her husband checked into a hotel, she "liberated" the *Do Not Disturb* sign. It now hangs on her office doorknob, and when she doesn't want to be bothered, the entire family can tell at a glance.

If she's just doing busy work like filing, she flips the sign or leaves the door open. It's worked wonders for her blood pressure.

We freelancers are a delicate breed. We must live with rejection and creativity does not always flow like water from the faucet. So we must remain firmly disciplined in all areas of our work. Determine your own work schedule. Start at nine and continue through the day, as I do. It works best for me. Or start at noon and quit at eight or nine in the evening, if you prefer.

But establish a routine and try not to vary it. Of course, there will be times when you must go out to interview a subject, times when you have to transcribe tapes or do the filing. But you're working within the routine you have established, and the time will eventually come when, if you're not working, something will feel amiss, awry. "What is wrong with this picture?" You will have upset your routine, and may feel faintly edgy.

That's why it's difficult for me to go on vacation. Without my typewriter at my fingertips, I feel incomplete.

And what a good feeling it is to be reunited with it, typing away, fulfilling my destiny.

I wish you the same joy of accomplishment and realization.

Writing Habits

Neither Evelyn Kaye nor Isobel Silden would insist that her method will work for you. As time passes you'll find yourself developing a set of devices that you'll use almost daily to keep yourself at the typewriter or word processor. Here are a few that have worked for other professionals I've talked with:

1. Try to write at the same time every day. Routine is habit-forming, and good habits will increase your output.

2. Dress comfortably, and write in surroundings where you function best. As obvious as these things may seem, they're nonetheless important to uninterrupted work.

3. Fix a minimum word goal to write each day. Whether it's 500 or 1,500 words a day, most professional writers set some such rate for themselves. You'll soon find your own comfortable rate through experience and practice.

4. If you're stuck in the middle of a piece or a book chapter, break for a time. Do some filing or check your references on another idea you've been toying with. Do some market research on those magazines you've intended to try. By then you may see your way past the problem area and out of the temporary rut.

5. On the other hand, if you're in full creative swing and the thoughts and sentences are flowing easily, avoid stopping for that cup of coffee or to verify a particular fact. Fix your coffee later and while you're drinking it, check that fact.

6. Get through a rough first draft as quickly as possible. It may not be too pretty, perhaps it won't be all that well organized, but after it's

on paper, rewriting can be relatively easy *and* rewarding. Some writers disagree—they despise rewriting—but I've found it takes less resolution than getting started on that dreaded first draft.

7. *Never wait for the muse.* If you wait until you feel like writing, the competition will usually get there first with your unique idea. We all have individual cycles of productivity (I'm writing this at 4:30 a.m., for example). Find yours and use these periods 100 percent. You can take a nap later.

All these methods, including those discussed by Kaye and Silden, work for the individual involved. It doesn't matter how zany or bizarre yours happen to be. If they work for you, they're good. Nor does it matter what your field of writing is or if you're young, old, thin, fat, freelancing part- or full-time. The sum and substance of the matter—of sticking to your work—is to get yourself into a groove, form a routine for writing. And then stick to it with the dedication of a Dominican monk.

One thing is certain: no one can do it for you. You must do it yourself, in your own way and in your special time. Your chances for success in this business are just as good as the next person's—and those chances are within yourself.

THE WAYS OF WRITERS

No chapter on the writing life would be complete without a discussion of habits of writers—as opposed to writing habits. As agent Donald MacCampbell observes, "More than most craftsmen, writers possess a rare capacity for messing up their lives." Alcohol, in particular has wrecked more than one promising writing career. Hemingway once noted that after a session of writing you are as empty as when you have made love; what Hemingway did not say is that the writer shouldn't fill that void with booze (as he too often did). This doesn't mean you must be a teetotaler in order to write. It simply means there's a world of difference in writers who drink and drinkers who rarely write. As Brendan Gill says in *Here at the New Yorker*, "In this country more than in any other that I know of, the relationship between writers and alcohol is a curiously close one. . . . Among the dead, we have only to think of Faulkner, Hemingway, Fitzgerald, Lardner, Marquand, Sinclair Lewis, O'Hara, Crane, Edward Arlington Robinson, Wallace Stevens, O'Neill, Philip Barry, Millay, Dorothy Parker, Hammett, Roethke, Robert Benchley, and Berryman. Among the living , the list is equally long. . . ."

I like what Erica Jong—who admits to an occasional glass of wine—says about writing and drinking: "Drinking is a useful way *not* to write, hence its popularity among writers. In my own case, I actually prefer writing to drinking. It is absolutely impossible to do both simultaneously." Also, James F. Fixx, author of *The Complete Book of Running:* "When a good writer is also a big drinker, I suspect he's good in spite of it, not because of it. I used to try occasionally to write after a few drinks. I couldn't do it. Now I never even try."

I make no judgment on the matter other than to say that anything—booze, sex, eating Twinkies—that interferes with your work to the extent that your writing is wooden, your talent diminished, is a shameful waste. I'm not prepared to go quite as far as Shakespeare, who wrote in Sonnet 129: "The expense of spirit in a waste of shame is lust in action." But the Bard's insights are *never* to be summarily ignored.

THE ROAD AHEAD

It seems to many beginners that the most successful writers— those at the very top, whose names we all know and whose work we've read—must lead charmed lives. What astonishing luck to have bestselling books, motion picture adaptations, appearances on "The Tonight Show"! It's hard to imagine a Russell Baker or a Joan Didion as a beginner, facing piling rejection slips and hounding creditors. But every writer's career began at the beginning.

Here are excerpts from a keynote speech at one of the ASJA's annual Nonfiction Writers Conferences, where the speaker accepted the first ASJA Excellence Award for Nonfiction for a book titled *Roots*. It was during a twenty-year stint in the U.S. Coast Guard that Alex Haley realized that he wanted, more than anything in the world, to become a freelance writer. That realization took him to assignments from magazines such as *Reader's Digest* and *Playboy* to *The Autobiography of Malcolm X* in 1965 and, eleven years later, to *Roots*.

ON BECOMING A WRITER
by Alex Haley

On Odds and Obstacles

"I have heard—and I think it probably is true—that of every thousand people who set out saying they would like to write professionally, probably one will actually succeed in becoming a full-time freelance writer. The reason the odds are so overwhelming is that there are so many obstacles that knock off so many people along the way. It's no discredit to those people. It's just that the obstacles are of a nature to try the very soul of a human being. The thing of being rejected over and over and over, year in and year out, is something that will test everything in you, and then some.

"I would take the stuff I'd written, pick a magazine, pluck some editor's name from the masthead, and mail them out. And it came to be that as faithfully as I sent them out with the self-addressed, stamped envelope, they would come back in the self-addressed, stamped envelope. I grew to expect that they would come back; when I mailed each one out, I knew it was coming back. I was almost fatalistic about it. Every single story came back with a rejection—a printed rejection. Generally, at the time, they were, 'Thank you for thinking of us.' The *Reader's Digest* had a classic one: 'This does not quite jell for us.' "

On First Thrills

"After about *five years* of those consistent printed rejections, one day the familiar self-addressed, stamped envelope returned with my manuscript, with my printed rejection slip, but on that printed rejection slip, someone had penciled the words, 'Nice try!' I'll never forget it. Something in that story had prompted somebody to read it and to say that. I have since had lots of pretty exciting things happen, but I can't think of a single one that of itself excited me more than those two words at that particular time, under those circumstances.

"My first sale was to the old *This Week* magazine. It was a little piece about amusing things that had happened in the U.S. Coast Guard, and I got one hundred dollars for it. I just stood there and wept, it was so unbelievable."

On Career Planning

"Reflect upon various professions. When people finish high school and decide, as many have, that they want to be a nurse, a doctor, an architect, or whatever, most of those things have some kind of time tag affixed to them. You know that if you wish to be, say, a teacher, you are going to invest at least four years of hard effort following high school, to learn the things necessary to get a teaching degree. If it's a surgeon you want to be, you're talking about anywhere from ten to twelve years. And so on with almost all professions. But with writing, it's nebulous. I think most people who think about writing have a very hazy idea about the time and amount of work that's going to be involved. I can't remember a single young, aspiring writer I've met from whom I got the impression that they really were prepared to work five, eight, ten years to achieve this; most of them seem to have the impression that it's something quick—maybe six months, or two years. Now the hard, realistic fact is that it is at least as difficult to become a surgeon as it is to become a writer, and vice versa. Hardly anyone who is sucessful at writing has come to be so without at least a decade of hard, hard work and going through the rejection slips, the psychic putdowns, and all the rest of it."

On Hitting Bottom

"My low point has now become a symbol for me. I was living in Greenwich Village; it was soon after I got out of the service. I was at that stage that I'm sure many of you have experienced: you want to write, and you have told friends of yours that you want to write, and your friends say to you, 'Yeah? Jeez, that's fine. But why don't you get a job?' Well, that was consistently being said to me. I owed everybody I knew. I was scared. One morning a friend of mine who was in the civil service called and very excitedly told me a job was available as a public-information specialist. It paid six thousand dollars a year, and I could have it—but I had to take it before noon, because it had to be opened to the public at one o'clock. I said to him the first thing that came into my head: 'No, I'm sorry. I just want to keep trying to make it.' And he banged the phone down—because I owed him, too.

"That afternoon, I went walking around this little one room that I had at 92 Grove Street, near Sheridan Square, in the basement, taking a kind of psychic inventory. What the hell had I done? I had just turned down six thousand dollars a year, in the condition I was in. I was looking around at little things—everything I had was in that one room—and I looked in the cabinet where I had food, supposedly. All that was in there were two cans of sardines—marked two for twenty-one cents, so you know how long ago that was. And I had eighteen cents in cash. I thought, well, this was it—and I also thought, from here there's nowhere to go but up. I dropped the sardines and the nickel, dime, and three pennies into a sack, twisted the neck, and dropped it into a box.

"It stayed in there for about six years. And then, when I sold my first piece to the *Saturday Evening Post,* I took out the cans of sardines and the nickel, dime, and three pennies and had them mounted. Against green velvet. Under glass. I have them now; they're on the wall—in Beverly Hills.

"What those things represent is the central thing that I, or any of these writers who have grown older and have sold, would tell you: the idea of hanging in there when you don't know, when there's no way to know. If you don't hang in there, you may as well never have begun. It was a kind of special feeling for me when on one side of the sardines I put up the announcement of the nine Emmys my book had won in television, and on the other side, the Pulitzer Prize. I'm glad I hung in there."

On Requisites

"I suppose the best advice I could give to aspiring writers is that you must ask yourself, 'Do I really want to do this thing? If I do, am I willing to pay the price?' One must be willing to pay that price, psychically as well as physically—to endure whatever comes, in the sense of rejections, putdowns, feelings of worthlessness, bad times, and so forth. George Plimpton [a prior speaker] said something about suicide, in connection with Ernest Hemingway. I know I've thought about suicide behind rejection slips. You're entitled to thirty minutes of suicidal thoughts—and then you get up and you go again. There's all this talk that in order to be a writer one has to have this great talent. I think talent, as such, is very overrated. The big requisite, above everything else and far above talent, is that one must have innately, or must develop, a really extraordinary sense of self-discipline. You have to be able to make yourself sit down day in, day out, night in, night out, at that machine—or with your pencil, or whatever you write with—and stay with it. Otherwise, things just won't happen for you."

On Choices

"If it does happen for you, I think it's the greatest thing that *can* happen. I have to say that with all the tough things that have happened, and the good things that are happening now, if I had my pick of anything in the world that I could be—if I could just push a button and *be* it—there is nothing in the world that I would rather be than what I am right now: a writer."

DIMPLES AND WARTS

If it seems to you that we've bent over backward to present the dark clouds hovering over the freelancer's life, you're right. The would-be writers who flinch at the mention of commercial aspects of this business—word rates, categories of articles or books, manufactured bestsellers, peddling your book—won't make it. They like the idea of being writers but refuse to accept the crass marketing element. They reject the notion that writers are craftspeople engaged in what Hal Borland so aptly calls "the plain uninspired job of putting word after word, sentence after sentence, in what adds up to a structure of meaning." It would be unfair, as many rainbow-splashed books about writing are, to not present the warts along with the dimples. Our job is not to indulge the few dilettantes but to be of help to the many who have something that begs to be said in magazine article or book form—but aren't quite sure how to say it or to whom it should be sent once it's said.

But there *are* dimples on the face of freelance writing. It's a rugged way of life, sure, but it has its merits. ASJA writer-lecturer Ronald Gross, founder of Writers in the Public Interest, who has done much to encourage young freelancers in their work, lists these positive points:

1. We can generate and act on our own ideas.
2. We can use our time and energy to suit our personal style and rhythms.
3. We get continuing credit, exposure, and recognition for our work.
4. We can cut down or eliminate activities and contracts we find distasteful or unproductive.
5. We save the several hours each day most salaried people spend in travel, meetings, office socializing, etc.
6. We set our own priorities.
7. We can take a flyer—go for the big jackpot.
8. We can get paid for the same work more than once.
9. We can use our freedom to plug into events, people, occasions, and activities that pay off in money and pleasure.
10. We benefit and expand our horizons through constant exposure to new fields.
11. We are constantly meeting new, significant people through contacts on diverse assignments.
12. We enjoy the sense of our life's work developing along lines we have shaped ourselves.

Yes, writing can be exciting for those who stick it out and retain their competitive edge. To them, great or not so great, the mail carrier's coming is an event of genuine interest. But, acceptance or rejection, these writers are never bored.

In fact, in few other professions can a person say with knowing gratitude, "I won this success myself." For as Stanley Vestal says in *Professional Writing* (Macmillan, 1938), "Luck and influence will not write books or plays or stories, nor will the public long pay hard money for inferior work. Indeed, writing is one of the few professions left in which it is still possible to be really independent, self-sufficient, and successful, too."

One outstanding ASJA professional whose career offers beginning writers a combination of rare and satisfying accomplishments and rewards to shoot for is Vance Packard, author of bestsellers galore. His books, all nonfiction landmarks, include *Animal IQ, The Hidden Persuaders, The Status Seekers, The Waste Makers*, and *The Naked Society*. The following piece demonstrates that the nonfiction writer's is a priveleged calling.

WRITERS AS EXPLORERS
by Vance Packard

In the last quarter of a century, there has been a great upsurge in the number of professional persuaders. There are literally hundreds of thousands of skilled people spending their time selling a particular viewpoint as cleverly as they can. Even in the government there are tens of thousands involved in this type of effort (e.g., lobbyists, spokespersons for special interest groups).

The challenge for the public is to try to see through the assertions and strategies of persuasion and arrive at the truth. This is one place where the nonfiction writer can and does serve a very important function. By sifting through all the various claims and uncovering the methods used to color the facts, and by trying to state the situation as honestly as possible in the light of the most valid knowledge available, the writer-reporter best serves the general public.

In my own role, I see myself primarily as an explorer plumbing for the truth in situations where there is great upheaval and uncertainty in people's lives.

Throughout my professional life, all forty-five years of it, I've been an investigative reporter—first as a newspaperman, then a magazine writer, and finally as a book author. But irrespective of where I've hung my writer's hat, I've been an explorer looking into situations that intrigued me, seemed to be of public interest, and deserved to be brought into public light. Many of the situations I have focused on were those that primarily involved efforts to influence or manipulate people's behavior.

Whatever the writer's focus, I think there is nothing more gratifying than being a social explorer. This is especially true if you can choose your area of inquiry, work at your own pace, and dig into the subject until you are satisfied that you have something of value to say.

Actually there are two aspects to such exploration. Not all nonfiction writers have the time to assay an issue at great length. However, they can assume an important role by chipping away near the surface long enough to establish that a significant problem exists, and to alert the public to whatever they do find. Others who have the time can make an in-depth probe; they find out and put together the pieces and lay a new picture out before the public.

Despite any drawbacks to this sort of total immersion, I would not have it any other way. I am satisfied with my own work to the extent that I can offer readers insights on what is happening in their world—a sense of revelation about events around them that they did not understand before.

Often my explorations get me into areas almost wholly new to me. For example, in my recent book, *The People Shapers,* I had to educate myself in several disciplines unfamiliar to me— genetics, human reproductive biology, operant conditioning, brain physiology, gerontology. I realized I didn't know a thing about these specialized subjects, but I felt I had to understand them to describe the scope of people-shaping that is occurring. I had to educate myself before I could even start pulling together a picture that made sense to me. And that's a major reason why it took five years to finish.

There is another role that many nonfiction writers have chosen to fill. That is to be a persuader as well as an enlightener. Many writers, especially in the last decade or so, have become advocates, and that is certainly an accepted role today. But it's just not my bag. My mental bent and training are those of the observer, and I simply try to call the shots as I see them. Often people ask me if I'm a pessimist or an optimist. But I'm neither: simply an observer. This frequently disappoints the readers who would prefer to have me put on the mantle of a crusader in relation to some of the developments I've reported in my books. This was especially true regarding all the razzle-dazzle going on to hoodwink consumers. But the simple fact is that in writing about washing machines that fell apart, for instance, it was not the machines themselves that interested me, but how people could be influenced to act irrationally by certain persuasion techniques.

Thus I see my goal as laying the facts out in full and truthful array. If others choose to grasp the implication of that information and use it as a springboard for advocacy, fine. Frequently, the writer chooses to become involved in the issue personally, and one of the more recent theories on the function of the nonfiction writer hinges on that point: namely, that the writer should have an emotional stake in whatever topic is explored. A few years ago a leading New York book reviewer said that he would no longer take a book seriously if its author did not significantly involve himself in the presentation. In other words, he called for the Norman Mailer type of reporting, with great emphasis on feeling and sensations and personal dramatization. This was rather hard on writers like myself whose entire training has prompted them to be objective bystanders. The line between fiction and nonfiction was pretty thin for a while. And it's becoming less distinguishable all the time.

In retrospect, I still prefer the role of the observer. In today's world, it is increasingly difficult for the average person to understand what is going on. The smaller the globe becomes in the jet-age sense, the more fragmented, highly technological and highly sophisticated it tends to be in terms of issues and conflict. In this I see the role of the objective reporter as increasingly important, in order to try to give society some confidence in what it sees and what it decides to believe. This can best be achieved by rendering information that is both authentic and balanced.

Does writing magazine articles and books to sell sound demanding, now that you've been exposed to the basics? Well, it *is* demanding, but each day that passes sees new writers, young and old, giving the craft a try. And many of these same writers are discovering that fresh, well-structured writing that informs and entertains usually finds an editor eager to buy. They are at once pleased and surprised to find that those willing to take the necessary steps of sensible preparation are most welcome in the ranks of freelance writers.

Chapter Six

SPECIALIZATION —IS IT FOR YOU?

Today, most freelancers will tell you that specialization—achieving "expert" status in a specialty area such as health, sports, or the environment—is one of the surest ways of getting into print. The unrivaled heyday of the big general magazine is history; gone are the old family periodicals such as *American, Collier's,* and *Liberty.* In their place we have the *American Rifleman, TV Guide,* and *Money* magazine. Modern readers have turned to magazines for trends and information about their special interests.

Still, many freelancers working today absolutely refuse to specialize. They call themselves "generalists" and prefer to take what one writer calls "the shotgun approach" (writing for several entirely different markets). In this connection, Bergen Evans wrote, "There are great pressures toward specialization in modern life. I beg you—the student writer—to resist them." Evans thought two guides should determine the novice writer's focus area: the writer's own interest and the promise of the subject.

Both approaches—generalizing or specializing—have their pluses and minuses. No subjects, after all, are in themselves either good or bad. Quality writing depends on the depth of your interest in a particular subject and what you can do with it.

To present the pros and cons of whether to specialize in a given field or to diversify your efforts, we've asked five ASJA writers to discuss the matter. Two say specialize; two opt for the versatility of the generalist. One, Norman Schreiber, tells you why he prefers to work the middle of the road—by writing about different subject areas while still pursuing some specialties. It's no paradox that there's much truth in these differing opinions. That's what makes horse races—and writing.

The ability to turn out good articles and books on diverse topics and subjects is one test of the professional craftsperson. But most of us have lately seen the dollars-and-sense need for earning expert status in at least one or two special-interest areas.

Specializing is yet one more decision for you, the writer, but it's also another privilege, one that permits you to dig deeply into whatever subject might interest you or in which you have a special expertise. It also enables you to share your knowledge, insights, and findings with your own special audience.

Moreover, as you read what our panel of observers has to say, consider that in recent years the specialized publications, on the whole, are increasing their readerships much faster than the mass-circulation magazines—and at considerably less cost. Why? In John Fischer's view, "The reason is that our society, in its growing complexity, needs more and more educated people to keep it running. As our universities turn them out, they also produce, inevitably, a growing public that is dissatisifed with the bland banalities of the mass media." (*The Stupidity Problem: and Other Harassments*, Harper and Row, 1964).

One fact is certain as magazine and book publishers respond to change: readers have narrowed the focus of what they want to read about, or have become part of special-interest groups. For every general magazine that went out of business in the 1950s and 1960s several new specialty magazines appeared. From *Ms.* to *Mother Earth News*, from *International Wildlife* to *Inc.*, the vitality and growth of specialized publications are indisputable and likely to continue in coming years.

IN FAVOR OF SPECIALIZATION
by Julie Candler

A freelance writer without a speciality is like the individual who plays chess against an expert. The game is so easy for its champions that they sometimes visit local chess clubs and play up to eight opponents simultaneously. A specialist can move from one board to the next, quickly and effortlessly making the right moves while mentally juggling all eight games. Each club player, meanwhile, is agonizing over the next move of a knight or pawn.

If you're a general writer, you're like the individual chess player pitted against the champion. But instead of playing only one expert, you may be competing against a number of others who specialize. You must match their skills or you lose. No matter what subject you query an editor about, you may be rejected in favor of the specialist. If *you* were an editor assigning a story on medical care or home improvements, wouldn't you choose the writer who covers the subject full-time? It's a good argument for becoming an expert in one specific field.

Another benefit is the security specialization offers if you work hard, because expertise usually leads to rapid repeat sales with magazines of similar interests. There are fewer high-paying publications in today's market and more and more specialty magazines paying $250 to $300. It's a matter of arithmetic. To write for $300 markets and still pay your bills, you have to write more articles. Therefore, there's seldom time to do extensive research on every article.

Imagine the hours it takes a non-expert to research and write an in-depth article on nuclear waste, or the stock market, or how to prepare an income tax return. You might spend days getting the facts and interviewing authorities. So, to get paid for the time you have invested, you need to write other versions of your article and sell them to several different publications. Thus, without making a conscious decision, you would begin to be a specialist in that field—and if your output were great enough, more secure financially.

Inventory Yourself

If you're thinking about specializing, ask these six questions about your qualifications and work requirements.

1. Is there a subject that really interests and excites me? Do I want to read, hear, and see everything possible about it? Do I find myself turning private conversations into interviews to get others' ideas about my special field? Do I eavesdrop at pubs and cocktail parties to get information? (If so, your chances of success are greater since curiosity is essential for any writer.)

2. Am I good at keeping files? ASJA member Jack Harrison Pollack, biographer of Earl Warren, says, "Never throw anything away. It's incredible how things keep cropping up." You need to be a clip-and-filer. (I sometimes use the "free-association" system of filing; the trouble is that when I want to retrieve a clipping from my files, it may take me two days to freely associate with it again. Use a method that enables you to find your clippings fast.)

3. Do I enjoy research? (It helps to have the investigative inclinations of a Woodward or Bernstein. If you like to attend conferences, read newsletters, and go to lectures, you'll stay ahead of new trends and developments in your field.)

4. Am I creative? (You need ingenuity to keep coming up with fresh, salable articles or book angles on the same basic subject.)

5. Am I a businessperson? (You have to be well-organized to keep the queries going out and assignments coming in. To keep enough money in the bank to tide yourself over in dry spells, you need to be a magician.)

6. Am I a skillful enough writer to make my subject understandable to any reading audience? If I'm writing about the space age, can I make it both engaging and comprehensible for a general audience? Can I explain technological advances to readers of scientific publications? (Your skill and ability to write clearly is your most important requirement.)

To get started, learn good research techniques. Do what Alvin Toffler, author of *The Third Wave* and *Future Shock,* recommends: "Get your nose out of books and get out and talk to people."

At first it's wise to ask experts to check your work. The background knowledge in your field will come after you've invested many lengthy days. Talk with these authorities and listen to what they have to say. Then, read any books or articles they may have written on the subject. Be sure to write for the best known, most widely read publications you can. For example, an article in the Sunday *New York Times Magazine* can give you priceless exposure. And as your reputation as an expert grows, accept all invitations to speak to groups and appear on radio or TV. It all helps to interest people in reading your articles and books.

Start Where You Are

My own speciality just happened, because I live in Motown. People from Los Angeles talk movies; New Yorkers get wrapped up in fashion and finance, plays, and publishing. Detroiters live and breathe cars. I was especially interested because my father had been a car dealer.

When I became a working wife and mother, it was at an ad agency with—naturally—an automotive account. I began writing about cars. After that I spent five years on a newspaper, then switched to freelance writing and public relations. One of my first assignments was a monthly column called "Woman at the Wheel" for *Motor News* (now *Michigan Living*), Michigan's AAA publication. It paid the huge sum of $30 per column. (The fee has improved a lot since then.)

Eventually, I sent the tearsheets to *Woman's Day* when I learned they were considering an automotive column. They were interested enough to assign articles on a month-to-month basis. For eighteen years I wrote twelve articles per year for *Woman's Day.* My contract was renewed annually. It assured me of at least one monthly sale to a major magazine. It was my financial mainstay.

The column had been appearing for two years when an editor wrote, "It occurs to us that the material in your columns would make a good book. If interested, contact us." The book that resulted, *Woman at the Wheel*, led to numerous radio and television appearances and newspaper interviews. The recognition made it easier to get assignments from other editors. (However, under my contract with *Woman's Day*, I was restricted from writing for other women's magazines.)

Nevertheless, it was only three years ago that I felt courageous enough to drop the public relations work and become a full-time freelance writer. Since then, I have had more time to develop new markets for my work: *Advertising Age*, Volkswagen's *Small World*, United Airlines' *Mainliner*, *Ford Times*, Ward's *Auto World*, *Scouting*, *Michigan Living*, and *Michigan Business*. Most of the articles are about automobiles, but some are on related subjects like camping, travel, or the business of marketing cars to women. I'm also a regular contributor to the automotive publication *Jobber/Retailer*.

Specialization Spinoffs

If you elect to specialize, you may find still other opportunities resulting from it. You could get an assignment to write a textbook, perhaps based on one of your books. There may be invitations to lecture or to teach. (You can tape your lectures and that may give you the basis for another book.)

Keep in mind that nice things often happen if you choose a subject that merits your complete interest and enthusiasm, or a cause that inspires your dedication. "Writing on something you have a commitment to leads to financial gain," says ASJA member and author Ronald Gross, director of Writers in the Public Interest. "Once you are established, gratifying assignments come your way without your having to hustle."

If you've worried about getting in a rut, don't forget that if a subject begins to bore you, you can always divorce yourself from it and try something new. I remember the recommendation of Murray Teigh Bloom, author of *The 13th Man*, speaking at a conference held by ASJA. "At least once every five years," he told us, "play a wild card. . .something in an area you have had nothing to do with. . .an attempt to break out of a pattern. It's good for your psychic health, the equivalent of a hundred sweepstakes tickets."

As for the future, Bloom predicts more competition from, of all people, specialists. "Freelancing in the eighties," he says, "won't be remotely close to what it was in the fifties. We will have a peculiar kind of competition . . . from this enormous body of Ph.D.'s without jobs, some of whom can write. Lawyers also will be descending on us, some who decided they hated law school. Many of them are would-be writers. There is no entry-level certification. There is literally nothing. Anyone can get into this business." He adds that magazine rates are getting worse and admits, "I don't know the answer."

Well, the answer is to be a pro. "Being a professional writer," says ASJA past president Terry Morris, "is writing an article as quickly as possible because you can't afford to put too much time into it, but still writing it professionally. You must never elect to do a shoddy job."

Be better than the college professor, lawyer, or Ph.D. who can write. Or the M.D. who wants a byline in a magazine as well as on a prescription pad. Those people are specialists first and writers second.

If you're a professional writer first and a scholar and authority second, you and your typewriter can outclass the specialist who isn't a pro. You'll have a profitable and delightful time while doing it and enjoy a solid reputation as well.

THE JOY OF *NOT* SPECIALIZING
by Alan D. Haas

When I was a young lad growing up in New York City, like other kids I frequently spent my after-school hours playing stickball, schoolyard touch football, and playground softball. Unlike other kids, I also spent a great many afternoons in the local library reading the classics—Tolstoy, Dickens, Balzac, et al.

Like other kids, I often cut classes to go to the Paramount theater to hear Benny Goodman, Tommy Dorsey, and Glenn Miller. Unlike other kids, I attended the Metropolitan Opera (the old house on Thirty-ninth Street), standing in the back of the orchestra for $2, delighting in performances of *Traviata*, *Aida*, and *Boheme*.

Like other kids, I agonized over algebra, used crib notes for French and Latin exams, and messed up lab experiments in science class. Unlike other kids I became a devotee of ballet and modern dance, going to see Martha Graham, Jośe Limon, and the City Center Ballet. (I never told anyone about my interest in dance—I would have been ostracized, without a doubt.)

I also should mention that the thing I enjoyed most at school was writing English compositions and term papers, something most of my contemporaries detested.

By the time I got to college, I was given a sports scholarship as a left-handed pitcher on the baseball team, while most of my extracurricular activity was concerned with the arts, politics, and current affairs.

On the one hand, I was a political science major, head of the history club, a member of the student council and editor of the school newspaper. On the other hand, I was an ardent fan of the New York Giants' teams (baseball and football). The day Bobby Thomson hit that famous home run to win a pennant and beat out the Brooklyn Dodgers was one of the happiest of my life—as was the day I was able to acquire a complete set of *Encyclopaedia Britannica*.

Writers Can Be Jacks-of-All-Trades

When I realized my prospects for becoming a major league baseball player were slim indeed, I opted to be a journalist, a career that seemed to offer a chance to learn about everything without being a master of anything. It turned out to be the right choice.

After a few years of holding down jobs with *Newsweek*, a business paper, a trade journal, and editing a small-town newspaper in New Jersey, I was again restless. At one time or other I was writing exclusively about textiles, or about shipping and foreign trade, or about the china and glass industry, none of which interested me particularly.

So I resigned from the nine-to-five world and became a freelancer, not realizing in my blind ignorance that only about 300 persons in the entire U.S. could earn a living this way. Again, however, it was the right choice.

I could write about anything I wanted and if it was good enough it would sell. I taught myself photography by acquiring two Rolliflex cameras, since at the time photojournalism was the vogue.

After a year or two of experimentation, I found that magazine and newspaper editors liked my writing and were actually willing to pay for what I had been doing for free in English class. It was an astonishing revelation. I could be true to myself and also earn a decent—if not glorious—living.

No Pigeonholes, Please

But problems began to develop. I discovered that if I did a nice piece on parent-child relationships, for instance, editors right away wanted to pigeonhole me as a writer about family life. If I did a photo essay on the life of alley cats, I was categorized as an animal photographer. (Most editors keep a little card file—so-and-so does well with celebrities, what's-his-name does excellent political "think" pieces, photographer X does pretty still lifes and portraits, etc.) There was a payoff, if one became, say, an expert on taxes. But I didn't want to write about taxes all the time, and anyway, most of the jobs would come up only once a year.

So I made it my business to develop a diversified list of clients. I wrote for travel magazines, auto magazines, in-flights, health and medical publications, Sunday supplements, science books, and more.

Of course I didn't know anything about any of these subjects when I started out, but I did know how to use the library. By consulting the *Readers' Guide to Periodical Literature* I could find out what had been written on any topic in the past few years, and with diligent reading of half a dozen articles I could become an overnight expert on anything.

The formula for magazine and newspaper articles on most any subject is pretty much standardized. You need a few good anecdotes, some comments from experts in the field, perhaps a couple of pertinent statistics from government or private research sources. The rest was just a matter of good organization and clear, logical exposition of a theme that threads through the story and *voilà*—you have a 2,500-word piece that any editor would like to see come across the desk.

Oh, yes, you have to keep up—peruse the *New York Times*, the newsweeklies, some of the better consumer monthlies, the source books and so on. But I was always interested in everything anyway, so this wasn't a chore but a pleasure. Editors had to rethink and put me in a new classification: good general feature writer on matters of topical interest.

I don't want to commit the cardinal sin of generalizing too much. There are those who do prefer to be slotted as an expert on education or pop psychology or spectator sports or whatever; for them, that's the best way to go. But not for me. I am by nature eclectic and I choose to do what comes naturally to me. Any established writer will tell you that you have to have a deep and abiding interest in whatever field you select in order to succeed.

What is the difference between an amateur and a professional? A professional writes what sells, and what sells is what that writer knows best and does best. That's the golden rule. There are no others.

Allow Me to Generalize

I also found that being a nonspecialist was good business. When photojournalism died I wasn't devastated like so many others. If you focus on theatrical interviews you have eliminated ninety percent or more of all the markets in the U.S. And what happens if a couple of your client magazines go out of business, or the editor who likes your stuff leaves or gets fired? You are out in the cold, and you can't suddenly shift gears and get assignments to write about electronics or space exploration.

If I were asked for advice, I would tell the new writer starting out to leave most of the specialized pieces to professors of engineering or literature or biology. They are much better equipped for that job anyhow. What an editor wants from a freelancer is an idea that neither that editor nor anyone else has thought of, and to do that you have to be versatile; a halfback who knows how to hit the right hole in the line; wherever it opens up. There are literally thousands of magazines about chess or skiing or auto racing, but very few pay anything much. The better-paying, large-circulation magazines need writers who can switch gears and write about the "hot topic" of the moment.

Well, that's about it. You'll have to excuse me now—I am getting ready to write a piece about video games, so I'm going to go to an arcade and play *Pac-Man* for a few hours. After that, I'll be into home computers, the single parent or whatever else is new and upcoming—subjects only a nonspecialist can afford to dabble in.

SPECIALIZATION: THE PLEASURES AND PITFALLS
by Roberta Roesch

A specialty is like a second self—a constant alter ego. So it's vital to choose one carefully unless, as happened in my case, a specialty chooses *you*.

Many of us intuitively gravitate toward specialties, and when this happens, move in fast and make the most of it. It's good insurance to write about things that interest you—about subjects you both enjoy and understand.

I began writing as a generalist, and still consider myself primarily a generalist. But specialties provide extra dividends and complement other projects, so I'm grateful that during my career I've had a few specialties. One has been writing about women and work, and that's the example I'll use here. I started as a magazine editor. But when my children came along, I decided to stay at home and use every moment I could find to get a start as a freelance writer. During that time my mentor—although she didn't know it—was a woman named Anne Heywood who wrote a syndicated column on women's job potential. I was ripe for this advice, and as I followed Heywood's column and listened to her on talk shows I grew increasingly interested in women's potential and began to write articles in this field.

Specialty Writing—Start Small

The articles I sold were small ones with checks to match. But I saved all my clips as they came in and put them together as impressively as I could in a portfolio. Alone, they were insignificant. But together they made a package, and when I read in the *New York Times* that Anne Heywood had died, I gathered my courage and portfolio of clips and went to King Features Syndicate to apply for her job. It was the old story of being at the right corner with the right thing at the right time, and no one was more surprised than I that I was picked for the job. I suddenly had a specialty.

I got into this specialty in the early sixties, when even *The Feminine Mystique* had yet to emerge on the scene. Since only a handful of writers then were exploring women and work, this specialty served me well for many years.

As it took me out among people for interviews and research, it was a stimulating change from the "aloneness" of being a writer. It opened a great many doors for me, and I found that along with helping develop a writing career, writing on specialized subjects can fill your files with material you can tailor to fit many markets and spin off in many directions.

Specialization Pays

For me this means that—along with writing a syndicated newspaper column—I could also use my specialty for magazine columns and articles, lectures, job seminars, workshops, and panel discussions; corporate and public relations work; radio and TV interviews; and nonfiction books. I quickly learned that one thing feeds another and specialists can collect many checks using the same basic research for a variety of paying projects.

Once I'd picked up this practical fact and sent out article queries and book proposals (I also made program presentations to department stores, shopping malls, women's centers, colleges, etc.), I fell into the habit of making absolutely sure that whenever I interviewed *anyone* for *anything* at all, I obtained enough background material, quotes, anecdotes, and research sources for one or more magazine articles or features; human-interest stories for books; and illustrative material for lectures. This is like money in the bank. For an example of how it works, I once interviewed Helga Volpe and Wini Atkinson, two New Jersey women who'd launched an unusual business venture called "Wild Wieners." They provided glamorized hot dog carts with different types of plain and fancy weiners and sauces for parties—both children's and adult's. It was a unique idea that proved successful and the article discussed not only the concept but the two women's philosophy of business partnership.

My one and only interview with Helga Volpe and Wini Atkinson was for my newspaper column. But during the interview I asked enough questions and collected enough additional information that ultimately I included material from that interview in several magazine pieces, a session of lectures on starting a business, and a chapter in a book.

Take a Look at Books

If you want to write a book on your specialty, remember that it's almost impossible to market books when a subject becomes so overdone that everyone is writing about it. If you wait until that happens editors and sales personnel will feel that your book—regardless of its merit— will never find a sizable enough readership to earn a significant profit. So check the current *Books in Print* at your local library to see if your chosen specialty area is already overworked. (The *Subject Guide* volumes are best for this purpose.)

As you check *Books in Print,* keep in mind that even though a few books are out on the subject, if you can come up with a new, fresh treatment you may still have a chance at publication. You cannot overlook the importance of slanting subject material.

And as you look toward book publication it makes good business sense to aim your specialized writing at a well-defined audience. For example, whenever I think of a job book I must first ask myself: Will it be a book for women starting out? Will it be a book for middle managers? Will it be a book for blue collar workers? Most of all for a book sale, you need to think through your specialty well enough to come up with an out-of-the-ordinary handle that is either very timely or that hasn't been done before.

During the recession economy of the late seventies I felt that, despite women's rights and the progress women had made, too many were giving up too soon because of employment setbacks and endless job hunts. I decided the time was ripe—and so did an editor—to collect one hundred of my newspaper columns and package them under the title *There's Always A Right Job For Every Woman.*

All the research was in my files because of my specialty, and when the book was published it led to magazine spin-offs and excerpts, a lucrative writing and speaking assignment for a major New York corporation, and a chance to serve on a national advisory committee for women's opportunities.

Occasionally your specialty can result in a book project first. Then you can spin off in reverse on lectures, articles and features. For instance, while looking for book ideas in *Subject Guide to Books in Print*, I noted there wasn't a single book on weekend job opportunities. The topic seemed like a good one, so I wrote a proposal for *Jobs for Weekends*, and after that book was published I did several newspaper columns and features from the research I'd done for the book. Later I used my backlog of material to sell two articles to *Glamour*, one to *Mademoiselle*, and one to *Family Weekly*. In addition, I developed a program on alternative ways to make money and lectured on the subject.

A Specialty Just for You

Because of my experience, I believe, as noted, that an excellent way to determine whether specialization is for you is to discover on some fine day that a specialty is choosing you. But if, instead, you go specialty-shopping and choose one for yourself, try to select a subject that everyone—and everyone's brother and sister—isn't writing about. If you merely copy somebody else you will be one of many. Your market will be overcrowded, and your rewards won't be great. In addition, ask and answer the following six questions:

1. Do I care about the subject a great deal? *Why* do I care about it?
2. Do readers care about it? Do they need information on it?
3. Does the specialty match a timely and important trend? Will the trend have a long life, or is it just a passing fad?
4. Similarly, can I maintain my interest in and enthusiasm for the subject long enough to do a good writing job?
5. Can I take this subject in many directions and do a number of spin-offs?
6. Does this specialty provide enough variety potential for me to make it financially worthwhile?

Obviously, it's important to analyze markets for your specialty and gear it to as many as you can. Some specialties are more limited than others. But happily, in my own case, my specialty of writing about women and work had few limitations. It gradually spread out to the whole panorama of people's jobs and careers. Also, along with writing for the women's market, it lent itself to sales to the following markets: club and fraternal, business and finance, child care and parental guidance, consumer service and business opportunities, education, general interest, health, hobby and craft, retirement, and young adults. Add newspapers and weekly magazine sections and know why I feel lucky to have had widespread market capability in one of my specializations.

As you hit more and more markets your specialty is bound to grow. But the only way to insure this is to stay in tune with the times and keep ahead of trends. A treatment that was great when you started may become obsolete with the years—and if you're not up to the minute you'll be obsolete, too. To cite a personal example again, when I began writing about women and work my emphasis was always on how to break in and get a good start. Today that approach is dated, because most women are working and the thing that interests them most now is how to handle the problems they face in their working lives. A specialist who doesn't keep pace has no place in the market today.

Stay Up-to-Date

Once you pair yourself with a specialty, research endlessly. Keep in touch with people in your specialty and get on all kinds of mailing lists so you'll stay on top of what's current in the field. If your work lends itself to lectures, devise one basic speech, then personalize your beginnings and endings to fit each speaking engagement.

To get in line for assignments and jobs in many spin-off markets, develop a good portfolio in which you mount copies of your specialized writing on plastic-covered sheets. Your offerings may be small at first, but gradually you'll have a track record—and photocopied articles—to show editors and other employers who hand out work in your field.

The financial range of specialties varies with the one you choose, of course. The specialty I've discussed here has afforded a wide range of payment through the years—from a low $100 for a mini-feature (300 to 500 words) to substantial four-figure checks for major magazine articles. Book profits are always variable, and newspaper work pays most when syndicated. Syndication, however, is a difficult market to crack.

Along with their financial potential, specialties have emotional rewards. They're a wonderful way to touch people's lives, and I psych myself up when I'm down financially by reading the mail. For example:

"I always read your features because your stories of people make me aware of the fields I'm interested in knowing about. On my own, I never feel free to approach people in these fields and ask them how they got there. Because it seems too intimate, I'm too timid to ask these personal questions. But people are greedy to hear the answers and learn how other people got started. And every tidbit of information that you give helps because, sometimes, just a hint in the right direction can really start the wheels rolling."

"I have just finished reading your book. It has been so encouraging to me. I thank you for sharing these inspiring stories. I think the most important lesson I learned from your book is that I am in charge of my life. I can accomplish my goals no matter what obstacles are in my path. Because of my husband's work we move about every three years. In some ways, I know this could be a serious impediment to my career, but I am learning to view it as a means of acquiring a variety of job experiences. I believe that in the long run the many different jobs will be an asset to me in the goals I've set for myself. Thank you for helping me with these goals."

Despite these pleasures—and others—there are pitfalls in specialization too, and the one to be most aware of is the tendency to get typecast. Because this danger abounds, I believe in being a generalist *first* and a specialist as an *extra*—and if you have interests in several fields, specialize in more than one. This is a good idea since a second pitfall is the fact that specialities get saturated; pioneer specialists in any field are followed by imitators. Moreover, interest—both the writer's and reader's—can wane, so when that day comes it's time to move on to a specialty with a new focus.

But as you take on new challenges you'll find job assignments will continue to come from any specialties you've had. Your old specialist self will keep popping up even as you gravitate toward a new writing self and when it does, make the most of it.

THERE'S STILL A NICHE FOR THE GENERALIST
by Martin Abramson

"What do you know about art?" the editor asked me over the phone.

"Very little," I answered candidly.

"What do you know about art as a medium of investment, in preference to investments in stocks, CDs, or real estate?"

"Very little," I answered again.

"We'd like to run an article on the subject. You can handle it, can't you?"

"Yes, it sounds interesting."

"Well, go ahead and do it."

Now why in the world would the editor of a major magazine hand out an assignment to a writer who confesses he knows almost nothing about the subject at hand? The answer is that the editor knew me as a competent generalist with the versatility to produce an article on almost any subject that would make lively reading and that also would not be honeycombed with errors. If my image in the editor's office were that of a writer who concentrated only on microwave cooking, caribou hunting, or middle-aged depression, he would not have handed me this assignment—nor would he be inclined to look with favor on ideas I might present outside my declared specialty.

As long as editors remain willing to let me write about subjects diverse as art as an investment, the sport of cricket, the blessings of plastic surgery, the delights of Caribbean travel, and the sordid lives of heroin pushers, I intend to cling to my niche as a generalist against the weighted opinion of so many writers that specialization is the way to go.

General Advantages

A specialist may be wedded to a field that has slipped into a fallow period, a specialty that's simply not forthcoming with new developments to write about. The specialist is then stuck on "hold," whereas the generalist can simply jump over to another field.

Another reason for opting for the generalist way of life is that you are guaranteed freedom from ennui. Can you imagine how insufferably boring it must be to write about nothing else but animal husbandry or prison conditions? Even a subject as deliciously exciting as sex can get dull if you must spend all your time counting and analyzing orgasms. Inevitably, the writer who becomes bored will also bore his or her readers.

We generalists never get bored because we can leave the field of art or money management before it becomes a drag and charge our professional batteries by flitting off to the world of space exploration or, say, co-ed dorms. The generalist doesn't tarry so long in one arena that he or she becomes as stale as yesterday's rye bread. Generalists also rate high socially. As ASJA member Neal Ashby, an old friend and fellow generalist, points out, "Generalists are the most interesting people to be with because their horizons are boundless and they never get stuck in a rut." The specialist who talks endlessly about the minutiae of a particular specialty will put everybody within earshot to sleep.

Be Versatile

The work of a magazine generalist is a natural progression for anyone with a newspaper background. As a newspaper reporter, I had to write about a murder trial one day, a strike at a garment factory the next, and Miss America's arrival in town the day following. I had to become an instant expert on a new phase of human activity almost every day, then translate the expertise into hard copy in time to make deadline. You follow the same pattern for magazine articles and nonfiction books, although you must add more depth and perspective (i.e., do more research and interview experts with varying opinions) than is required for a newspaper feature.

How do you develop "instant expertise"? First, you should be an avid reader so that you spot new trends and angles in a variety of fields. Then you find a real expert, or a combination of experts, in the field you are cultivating for the nonce and extract their knowledge through detailed and well-prepared questions. Your questioning and your interviewing should include (a) a note of apology and (b) a note of flattery. The apology is by way of stating that you are new to this area and have a lot to learn. The flattery includes apprising your source that you have been told that he—or she—is such an outstanding authority that a public service will be performed by the communication of his— or her— views and expertise to a public waiting with bated breath for this information. Your role, you explain, is that of the communicator acting as go-between between those on Mount Olympus and the little people below. As you develop interviewing savvy you will learn when (and how) to diplomatically direct your source away from an endless ramble into off-the-track details and back onto the main track of the major developments that will interest your readers.

The Big Question

You will also never forget to ask, at one point or another, "What's new about this?" or "What's different?" or "What's so unusual?" When your editor sees your copy, he or she will want to read what's new, what's different from what we've heard before.

The generalist who depends on only one expert to develop instant expertise risks being mouse-trapped into selling an individual point of view. The best way to navigate this hazard is to check what one expert tells you with what you can glean from other experts, or thoroughly reliable trade sources. Then use your professional judgment to decide what points of view need watering down.

The good generalist must be not only a sharp interviewer, but a keen observer. If you are writing about how whales live in captivity, go out to the aquarium and observe the whales (after you've finished your office interviews with the whale-keepers), take notes on all the idiosyncracies of cetacean behavior—and again, do not be bashful about asking questions and more questions about anything that confuses you. The extra question you ask when you are exploring new terrain may help you avoid the error that will bring down the wrath of nit-pickers. Another cautionary tactic used by the seasoned generalist is to check all the technical points in your copy with your expert source *before* you send in the article. This is not an invitation to censorship or to prior approval of everything you write, but insurance that you have not garbled your facts.

When you have finished your article and are ready to go traipsing down another avenue of journalistic activity, do not kiss your expert source a final goodbye. Make sure to send copies of your article when it's published, and hang on to his or her phone number. The expert, who has been helpful to you once, will be helpful again when in the future you want to do another article in this field. In time, you will accumulate many phone numbers in many fields.

For all I've said about the way generalists can sustain themselves, neophytes may have trouble getting articles accepted if editors don't know them as pros who can deliver on a variety of subjects. This problem could be resolved in one of two ways: (1) Come up with an idea so scintillating that the editor will tell you to go to it or at least give it a try, no matter what his or her doubt; or (2) Attach yourself to the professional in the field for an "as told to" article. This makes you a specialist by adoption. Do the same in another field and you'll be a specialist by adoption in spades. Then use the published articles to convince editors you can do all sorts of good pieces with the third-person approach.

CYRANO WAS RIGHT
by Norman Schreiber

The agonizing decision as to whether one should be a specialist or generalist is one of life's funnier questions. After all, the mass of writers lead lives of quiet specialization.

A generalist is one whose repertoire includes articles that cover a range of topics. Each piece, however, has very specific subject matter and can be considered specialized. In other words, scratch a generalist and you will find a closet specialist. On the other hand, most avowed specialists tend to be human beings. On a private, and perhaps even a professional level, they display an interest in a great many topics. How then can you be a specialist when you're really a generalist at heart?

In order to get your black belt in specialty writing, take what I call the Cyrano tour. One of Cyrano de Bergerac's ingenious schemes for going to the moon involved a magnet. The idea was to toss a magnet into the air, let it attract you upward, and then toss it again. Each succeeding toss takes you higher.

Instead of traveling from earth to moon you will move from neo-novice to sophomore to *specialist*. You will have two very interesting magnets—snowballing knowledge and specialized magazines, including trade publications. When we generalists wish to appear authoritative, we find an expert to interview. (This might be called gilt by association.) The same reasoning works when we want to be seen as specialists: we find a setting that lends us authority. If your photography article appears in *Popular Photography* you are *de facto* a specialist. If the same article appears in *Southern Living* you are only possibly a specialist.

How could a mere babe, a tyro, a tenderfoot possibly write for specialized magazines? They have their regular contributors who know so much and have all those wonderful contacts and always get taken out for lunch.

Well, let me share one of the most important of the 89,236 major rules of freelancing I have been privileged to learn. Everything starts with research, and research is what takes you from what you know to what you don't know. Let's rejoice in the simplistic view that everything is related, one way or another to everything else. Take what you know and apply it to the field you wish to enter. Be a *neo-novice*. Wear the badge proudly. This works even if—nay, particularly if—what you know is left-fieldsville compared to the material currently being printed in that field.

If you are a teacher you may not be qualified to write about computer theory or the top ten primo programming tips. You can, however, assess computers in the classroom or the ten biggest errors in educational software. If you are a dancer, you may not be accepted as a medical whiz or travel maven. But you will have a respectful audience if you write about the care and feeding of the leg or a grand tour of the world's leading ballet troupes. Furthermore, if you are cursed with a business background, you are extremely valuable to trade publications in any field you wish to enter. You may know little about fashion, medicine, or music, but you may know a heck of a lot about marketing, distribution, sales, or what it takes to run a retail store. That background lends you a certain authority that makes editors salivate. They have to please their audience of professionals and businesspeople who need good, useful information.

You have another tool to bring to your new field. In what type of articles do you excel? I'm not asking about subject matter, I'm talking tone, structure, and format. For example, I'm good at describing people and events. I'm also good at doing roundups (a roundup is a piece about a collection of people or items, all of which share some common characteristic). On the other hand, my entire career contains only one trend piece. (This is an article that declares some great theory or truth, amply supported by current examples. It is popular among writers who cover the arts.)

Your arsenal of journalisic strengths includes the methods you have developed to research, organize, and communicate. Probably, these strengths already have helped you when encountering new subject matters; they can do no less with new specialties.

Of course, placing an article in a specialized magazine does not a specialist make. The feat *does* make it possible to place a second, third, and fourth article in that specialized magazine. Where will you get your second idea for the magazine? You have three choices. You can reach into that same part of your background that helped you score with the first piece. Or you may devise an idea that comes from some useful and timely scrap of knowledge picked up while researching the first piece. What is the third choice? It is a synthesis of the first two. Previous knowledge plus discovery can join to form a new idea. You're still working from what you know—it's just that now you know more. You're a sophomore. A wondrous thing happens in this period. You begin to learn the specialty's jargon—that secret tongue only the true believers are allowed to speak. You may not use the jargon in your articles, but you'll know what people are meaning. You'll have a little list of sources—people willing to give you information and background. You'll have a sense of leading personalities, companies, institutions. You'll find yourself in a conversation with Someone Who Knows More Than You and you'll have the delicious experience of holding your own. Furthermore, you might find the Someone Who Knows appreciating the insights you can contribute. Great day in the morning! You have a point of view. You are a specialist.

This will be verified in a very interesting way. You will find that when you go to other publications and call yourself a specialist and cite your contributions to *Specialty Monthly* you will be taken seriously. And why not? Your credits and background all point to one truth: you are a specialist and still a generalist at heart. You may not be the world's greatest authority or even a working journeyman in the field. Still you will speak with the authority that comes from knowledge. You might write a great article about brain surgery, but don't worry, it won't inspire me to ask you to do a little lobe job on my gray matter.

As a matter of fact, being a specialist has little to do with maintaining mountains of knowledge. It has to do with the outside world's perception of you and your acceptance of that perception. Don't reach for your proverbs. Being a *successful* specialist has an awful lot to do with knowledge. Fortunately, it generally takes a while to succeed. That's another good reason to be a generalist at heart, even when you're a specialist.

"In the whirling universe of communications, a great celestial system spins spectacularly but unseen and unknown. It is the brilliant and ever-expanding phenomenon of specialized publications. Formed of giant galaxies, shining constellations, and splendid single stars, it influences all our lives and we see it every day but remain ignorant of its powerful and persuasive spell."

—James L.C. Ford
Magazines for Millions: The Story
of Specialized Publications

PART TWO

THE NEW WORLD OF NONFICTION

George Moore held that to have suffered and to have known the beautiful are the two requirements for successful writing. The point is well taken: successful writers, fiction or nonfiction, literary or commercial, must have done something, seen something, felt something in their lives worth recording. This, of course, presupposes an intense interest in the world around us, for the world is the writer's province.

The dazzling achievements of science and technology in the last century have only broadened that province. Discoveries and "breakthroughs"—in aerospace, chemistry, biology, energy, conservation, physics—in short, every field of science, are meat for the writer hungry to understand—and explain—the world.

A similar knowledge explosion has occurred in the areas of which the average person is more aware: business-finance, consumerism, food-nutrition, medicine, psychology, home and garden—the areas that affect every aspect of our daily lives. No matter what your interest, there's an audience—and a magazine and a book publisher sensitive to that interest.

We're all familiar with perhaps half a dozen specialized publications, but few are aware they belong to a family with over 22,000 members. We grew up with *Humpty Dumpty* or *Jack and Jill,* graduated to *American Girl* or *Boys' Life.* Then suddenly we were reading *Popular Science* or *Seventeen.* As adults, our jobs brought us in contact with, say, *Iron Age* or *Editor & Publisher,* and our hobbies led to *Rudder* or *Horse and Horseman.* As parents and homeowners, we subscribed to *Family Health* and the *Old House Journal.*

All these are specialized publications. But they're representatives of those few in the mass-circulation spotlight. Thousands of lesser-known, specialized publications serve to entertain, inform, and enlighten men and women in every hour of every day, companions in every activity.

The specialized markets take a back seat to none. They have millions upon millions of readers, and often are more stable and enduring than the huge mass-circulation general giants. Specialized magazines—offering sparkling stories, dazzling photos, fun and fact—have an estimated aggregate single-issue circulation of over a billion, and are produced by a dedicated army of some one hundred thousand professionals.

For beginners as well as veteran freelancers, the continuing swing to specialization has brought ever-brighter writing prospects. Breaking into print has become easier for experts in a given field. The specialized publishing fields are among the most secure today in that ever-desired (but seemingly impossible) world of publishing staff job possibilities. Specialization, often the key to fast repeat sales for newcomers, can be a sure way to develop a solid reputation as a dependable writer.

Moreover, there is a shortage of professional talent available to interested, hungry editors in many fields. Journalism schools are presently advising students to specialize. And when a new writer surfaces who proves his/her competence and reliability, that writer is quickly told, "We have work for you!"

Hal Borland says it best in *How To Write and Sell Non-Fiction:* "There was a time when one man's curiosity could encompass most of the world and a large part of mankind's significant activity. That day is long past. The writer of today must have specialized knowledge and background in some field, and even within one field it is often necessary to specialize. Our general knowledge has broadened to a point where no one can contain it all. Of the science writers today, no more than a handful can write adequately about medicine, psychiatry, nuclear physics, chemistry, and astronomy and show the essential basic understanding of all those fields. In the field of social science alone, we have specialists in crime, in politics, in education, in labor relations, in the rehabilitation of the handicapped. Even the sports writer becomes a specialist—in football, or baseball, or golf, or tennis."

Chances are you already have a specialty without realizing it. Make a list of the areas of expertise you feel you'd like to share with others and perhaps try expressing in words. What are your interests, hobbies, special talents—things you do better than most? Maybe you're a math whiz with a particular interest in data processing. Or an outdoor type with hunting and fishing skills. It doesn't matter: you can convert your talent into cash by becoming recognized as an authority in a particular writing field. All you need is curiosity, competence in a specific area, the determination to turn your know-how into interesting and intelligible words—and a sensible career plan. Another plus is that after you have a few specialty sales under your belt, and your byline is familiar in a given field, editors will think of you when needs arise. When you have produced specialty pieces for several different magazines, you will have the credentials to approach a general-interest magazine as something of an expert yourself; you should also by this time have a solid network of contacts with some of the established experts in your field. In time, you can branch out into related specialties.

Keep this in mind when reading the following chapters on specific fields of interest. Consider carefully the field(s) in which you might wish to write. You may become a writer for or about business, children, gardening, travel, nutrition, or medicine.

Most of these fields of specialization are *subject* areas—religion, sports, hobby-craft; three are *focus* areas of particular interest: women's markets; children's and young people's markets; and trade, company and professional journals. We'd like to stress that the beginner can get a good start by writing for these focus areas on topics that fall within the other specialties. For example, women's markets publish articles concerning medicine/health, consumerism, food and nutrition, travel and leisure, psychology and psychiatry, home and garden, and more.

As you move into Part II, I'd like to offer a message brought to my attention by the late Beatrice Schapper, a longtime ASJA member, and best expressed by Goethe's couplet:

> Whatever you do, or dream you can, begin it!
> Boldness has genius, power and magic in it.

Chapter Seven

WRITING SCIENCE AND HIGH TECH

Ninety percent of all scientists who have ever lived are alive and working today. No wonder scientific discoveries are a fact of life. Today we can jet across the country faster than our grandparents could travel from one town to the next. With a flip of a switch, we watch events as they happen halfway around the world, and think nothing of photos taken by orbiting satellites—we see them on the nightly news. Ever more compact data storing and manipulating devices have revolutionized our lives, in wristwatches and video games, electronic data banks and home computers.

Science writers Emerson Clarke and Vernon Root say that in the decade of the 1950s our technical and scientific knowledge doubled; in the 1970s it doubled again, and in the '80s and beyond, it will multiply three or four times more. Researchers at Bell Laboratories estimate that there is more information in one weekday edition of the *New York Times* than a person in the sixteenth century processed in an entire lifetime.

These quantum advances have also been described by Clarke and Root as "beginning to look like a spinning flywheel that's being spun faster, ever faster." Some authorities believe that unless that momentum is brought under control, our civilization, like the Clarke-Root flywheel, "may soon exceed its cohesive limits and fly to pieces."

Evidence of this is everywhere. Consider the by-products of modern technology alone—from auto exhausts to industrial and nuclear wastes. Acid rains shower our crops and our cities; rivers are now channels of pollution; and refuse is generated at a rate that could fill the Grand Canyon by the year 2000!

We need to turn the forces of science and high tech full circle, to try and solve the problems of earlier uncontrolled "progress." To do this, scientists and engineers must not only seek new knowledge and create new developments, they must narrow the communications gap between themselves and society. And this is where technical and science writers enter the picture.

Writers are the "bridgers." They write the articles and books that explain scientific and high-tech developments to a concerned and interested public. But not everyone can understand these complex subjects well enough to both portray them accurately and bring them to life. Writers in this field must be comfortable working with technical data, and have a knowledge of the physical world.

A distinction is usually made between technical and science writers in terms of their audience. Technical writing, *per se*, is writing about science and engineering for a technically trained audience, and is consequently more difficult for the average person to understand. Science writing, on the other hand, is writing about the same subjects for both a professional and a lay audience. For you, me, and the rest of the general public, it must be entertaining as well as technically correct.

Both categories of freelance writers develop a solid specialty and a reputation only after years of experience in their fields. And each field, as you will see, offers a variety of subject material and opportunity.

WRITING SCIENCE:
YOU ARE WHAT YOU KNOW
by Jack Fincher

More than any other specialty in nonfiction, I suspect, writing science appeals to those of us who like to think of ourselves as lifetime students—lollygagging around in a free global university with our books and typewriters, burdened by no earthly obligation to get a degree now or later, at liberty to pick and choose what appeals to us more or less at will, events and the marketplace permitting. In other words, if you don't have a consuming, informal, ultimately dilettantish urge to know how things work and tell about it—mundane things and exotic things, big things and little things, momentous things and trivial things, *all* things—you would be wise to try something else. Interviewing movie stars, perhaps.

Which is not to say that you should avoid science writing if your primary interest is people. A healthy appreciation of humanity won't hold you back. As I tell students, in any field of writing you don't have to *like* people; as a lifelong member of the club *homo sapiens*, however, you do have to find them compelling. Scientists, after all, are people first and scientists afterward—an eternal verity you ignore at your story's peril, especially during interviews. For that matter, people are on balance the most fascinating "things" in the world, their inner workings its most engrossing mystery. And scientists, by and large, are among the most interesting people I know. (As compared, say, to most professional athletes.)

No, I only mean that to be satisfied with the demands and rewards of writing science, you had best be the kind of writer who is turned on by the new, the novel, and the complex, even when it appears in the old, the familiar, and the seemingly uncomplicated. The kind who doesn't mind getting your brain stretched a bit in the process of putting down on paper, in 3,000 crisply understandable words or less, a new discovery, a new problem, or an old problem newly tackled in the sciences, whether those sciences be—monumental misnomer—"soft" (social) or "hard" (physical).

The kind of writer, in brief, who is more interested in the *meaning* of a person's achievement than in the person *or* the achievement; who prefers to write from the head instead of the heart; who brings to every story not a bleeding sensibility but an inquiring mind. By its very nature, that kind of insatiably curious mentality is usually a few cuts above and beyond the dese-dem-and-dose school of police reporting, but you needn't have a Ph.D. to play. Too much of an academic pedigree, in fact, can get in the way of translating what's needed by general audiences. (Technical writing is another matter. There, the more formal or hands-on expertise, the better.)

For example, I've had five years of college here and abroad—but not one semester of high school chemistry or physics and only the most basic algebra and geometry. I learned what chemistry I required from writing about the brain, physics from writing about space travel, math from writing about computers. I tend to forget much of it as soon as I've used it, anyway. I could never pass a first-year chemistry exam, but I've learned a thing or two about neuropeptides that few Ph.D.s outside a relatively narrow field of human physiology have even dreamed of. (If I could only remember them, sometimes, at parties, I do. Then my wife Claire has to rush in and rescue the glassy-eyed listener before pedantic overkill occurs. This after-hours danger awaiting those around the science writer too much taken with his latest story is best expressed by the anecdote James Thurber told about the little girl who brought back a library book she had been given for a class report and announced that it contained "more about penguins than I want to know." Thurber might have added, but didn't, that the librarian probably went on to write science for the *New York Times*.)

I have been writing about science and/or medicine off and on for over twenty-five years now, and what drew me to it initially is just as true and (I trust) as tempting today: the sure knowledge that this is one specialty where, as a given, you know a hell of a lot more about the story you just wrote or suggested than your editor does—*and your editor knows it*. Hence, you're customarily given unusual latitude to express yourself with—generally—only minimum interference in the form of gratuitous cutting, superfluous rewriting, and the last-minute inclusion of an editor's crippling preconceptions.

(This doesn't apply to the few national magazines devoted to science or equipped with science departments, of course. Editors there often know enough to be dangerous. But again, by definition, what you're writing about is probably new enough that even *they* are willing to be instructed. Indeed, if they are good at their jobs, they expect to be.)

In short, you are pretty much on your own—with all the responsibility for reliability, accuracy, and readability that the heady independence of flying solo entails. With the possible exception of sports (which I still write for comic relief), no other writing specialty allows you such freedom of simile, metaphor, and analogy—or, correspondingly, more room to fail and fall into the murky and the fatuous, even as you think you're being your most lucid and brilliant.

Be warned: you are up there high without a net. A lot of editors recall who won the 1926 World Series and can name the three best left-handed tennis players on earth. Few know what a quark is or what GIGO means. (GIGO is computer talk, and means "garbage in, garbage out.") If you write about these things, you had better know this and a lot more about each than your readers—because a lot of them will write your editor a letter if you're even marginally, subtly in the wrong.

So much for caveats. You want to be a science writer? Onward.

How do I get started? To paraphrase Voltaire (I think), so you want to write science, do you; very well, then, write science. But first, if you haven't gotten into the habit already, read it. Read—and emulate—the best. Read Lewis Thomas, Paul Pietsch, Richard Restak, Fuller Torrey, the late Loren Eiseley—anomalies all, scientists who can *write*. Read also the likes of Alvin Toffler, Michael Gold, Terry Dunkel, Albert Rosenfeld, and Maya Pines—writers who can write science. Stylistically, you will then be stealing only from the best. For if you read only the best, you can't keep from it, actually.

Where do I start? You don't have to live near a major research center or a nationally known medical teaching facility, but it helps. Indeed, writing science in a small town without ready access to those who make scientific breakthroughs (i.e., get the big government and corporate grants) can be hazardous to your economic health—unless you already have the professional reputation that would impel a major magazine, newspaper or book publisher to send you there at its expense, in which case you can stop reading this right now and get back to work.

Whom do I *not* start with? Attempting to crash the major science freelance markets at the top isn't recommended. Book publishers won't talk to you (unless you've got the bona fides, exclusive entree, or a dynamite idea all your own so devastating they *have* to deal with you, which means marry you off with someone identifiable and credentialed). High-paying mgazines open to freelance science writing are comparatively few: *Omni, Science 83* (which will become *Science 84* in that year, *Science 85* the year after that, and so on), *Smithsonian, Audubon, Reader's Digest,* sometimes *Playboy* (sexual or futuristic material).

Or—if it has a strong medical or social interest—such women's magazines as *McCall's, Ladies' Home Journal* and *Family Circle.* The competition is fierce, sales limited; with rare exceptions, over-the-transom submissions are a waste of time, energy, and postage. Smaller (i.e., lesser-paying) publications are a mite more accessible, but again, personal contact and introductions carry the day. Most magazines remotely worth your trouble are headquartered in New York City, so if you live far away and want to make contact, write them first for an appointment and come prepared to lay siege to several if you want the trip to pay for itself.

Whom *do* I start with? Assuming you're just starting out in the business or are willing to take the pay cut that a cross-over in specialties may cost you, consider getting into science writing by going to work for a university news bureau or corporate public relations department that offers opportunities to cover or promote, either in-house or out, the research and/or development of science, medicine, and technology. Both the experience you get and the contacts you make can be invaluable—not just in the mechanics of writing science, but in getting to know scientists. From there, you can better make the jump to a good-sized newspaper and the daily writing to deadline that can sharpen both your word skills and your sense of what makes a good story and how to go after it.

Where do I get my ideas? If you're freelance, from newspapers, usually. Rarely, unless you work in or around an institution, do good science stories come to you by word of mouth. Subscribe to the nearest major newspaper of any stature. In my area, for instance, the *San Francisco Chronicle* can be bought on the same day, which gives me access not only to a couple of first-rate newspaper science writers—David Perlman and Charles Pettit—but to the Times-Post Service and the wire services. Perlman/Pettit and company are full-time science writers, which means they not only respect their field and their craft, they also have a longer-term perspective of what's going on in the world of science at large and where new developments in their geographic area fit, as well as how they should be weighted. Both are too busy at what they do to sell elsewhere, generally, so I look upon them as my early warning system as to what's happening in my area (the Pacific coast) that I should pay attention to. The Times-Post service is not as professional in science but its editors do have an idea what's important, so it's another (if somewhat more porous) early warning system. Wire services—AP, UPI—are like blips on a radar screen. What they report may bear looking at, but never trust them to assess a science story's true value or to report it with great reliability. And, for that matter, never, *never* attempt to sell a story idea to a national client purely on the basis of what you read in the newspaper. Always follow up with a phone call or two to the principal sources to make sure the story is as advertised.

Here's a tip: some major universities and research institutions—in my area, Stanford, Salk Institute, Rand Corporation—mail regular news releases and such to credentialed science writers if requested. Once you have published credits you're proud of, you can send photocopied tearsheets to these outfits together with a letter requesting you be added to their mailing list. Although these releases seldom pay off in stories, they provide a backup check on the papers, which can still miss a trick or two now and then. After years of skimming unproductive releases from major medical centers, I recently ran across one that yielded twelve pages in *Science 82*—a story updating two decades of development in a field of wide medical interest (premature babies) that, because it failed to contain any one new development, elicited no interest at all from San Francisco bay area newspapers.

And don't ignore television, particularly documentaries. The day of TV snobbery on the part of print media is, or should be, past. Because the better documentary shows—"Nova," for instance—scale their stuff down to an even lower common denominator of audience than magazines, and because they attempt to be all-inclusive in a one-shot treatment, a good TV documentary may contain a half-dozen pieces of related research, each of which could make a major story in a national magazine. Heresy to say so, maybe, but true.

How do I sell a story idea? In science, as in other fields open to the freelance specialist, stories are usually sold in advance, with a written "suggestion"—a narrative outline of the idea written in the style you propose to use, any length from a paragraph to a page or two, in the form of a letter or story synopsis, depending on what the publication wants and how well you and the editor know each other. If you've worked with an editor before, sometimes you can "pre-sell" your ideas with a personal phone call, which has the advantage of saving you the trouble of writing a suggestion to the magazine's specification if they've already made a conflicting assignment. Usually the editor, even if interested, will want the idea in writing anyway, because most magazines today assign by—or make a pretense of assigning by—committee. But if you're on a cordial telephone basis with an editor, it never hurts to sound the magazine out for its current attitudes, approaches, enthusiasms, etc.

Once I've got the assignment, how do I proceed? One of the nicest things about writing science today is that the age-old image of the cloistered eccentric working in an ivory tower oblivious to—and suspicious of—the outside world is largely a myth. And for a very good reason: money—which is to say, research backing. Most science worth writing about takes enormous funding. That funding comes either from the government, from foundations, or from private sources such as corporations—all of which are eager to justify with publicity (tasteful publicity, of course) both their participation and the results (when positive). Therefore, if reasonably qualified, you will be welcomed with open arms.

Most universities, institutes, and corporations that conduct (or fund) significant research retain public relations people whose job is to bridge the gap between their science researchers and the press. Fortunately for you, their caliber is usually high. It never hurts to phone the scientist directly with your request for story materials and an interview; you may get them. But if the scientist's employer runs a tight ship, you will probably be referred to someone in public relations. Don't be dismayed. As I said, given the nature of what they are pushing, most are quality people who can genuinely help with a story. In addition to sending you background material to better help you to know the scientist and his or her work, and prepare yourself for an effective interview, the PR people will often have important tips on the scientist's personality, professional crotchets, and how best to approach him or her. Look upon the PR person as your ally, unless you have reason to suspect otherwise. After all, you are all in this together with the same end in mind: the best possible story on a new development.

Once I've gotten the go-ahead, what? You're a lifetime student, don't forget, so *do your homework.* Don't be content with what the scientist or the institution sends you. Go to the library and check *Reader's Guide* for what has been published in the last five years on the subject. Get copies of all of it. Make notes on what you do and don't understand. Distill from those notes a set of questions. Never, *never* go to see topflight scientists unprepared. Their time is valuable, and they won't hesitate to let you know if you've obviously not done your homework.

How do I interview a scientist? Like porcupines make love: carefully. By that I mean come prepared, having read everything about the subject and the scientist that you can—within reason. Clearly, if you're writing a $1,000 magazine story of 2,500 words, you can't be expected to read four technical books on the subject. But make sure you have read what the scientist and the PR office have sent you, plus what has been deemed important enough to have made the national magazines in the last five years. Science is an ongoing continuum: what your interviewee has done usually fits into the big picture somewhere; it rarely stands alone. Knowing how it fits will both flatter your scientist and persuade him or her you are serious and at least interested, if not too knowledgeable.

Anything different about interviewing them? Not really, but there are a couple of points I think should be stressed. For one thing, even if a scientist is an exalted Nobel Prize winner, don't forget that by consenting to see you he or she is not just doing you a favor, but satisfying his or her need to acquire greater public recognition. Think of the interview as a contract. The scientist has agreed to take the time and trouble to be as lucid and communicative as possible; you in turn have agreed for your own purposes to help him or her do that. And you do it only by putting aside your own natural awe—and often embarrassment at knowing so little—to be honest in the crucial question of whether he or she is succeeding at getting the material across. In short, *never fake understanding*. It may make the interview go more smoothly, but in the end you will have betrayed both your own calling and the scientist's efforts to communicate clearly. And remember, the truth will out—to mutual mortification—in what you write.

Admittedly, there is a delicate balance here. As a former *Life* magazine science staffer, I subscribe to the old Henry Luce dictum that it is essential to ask the dumb question. By that I mean, and I feel sure Harry Luce meant, too, asking the obvious question that yields the unobvious answer. But to that I would add, it is equally essential that the dumb question issue from a state of preparedness. You have read all that you can profitably digest on the subject, you have ruled out a lot of useless dumb questions, but after reflection there still seems to be something simple you have failed to grasp. Or the scientist has just said something he or she clearly thinks is self-evident but that puzzles the holy hell out of you. Backtrack. Ask. It may be stupid, it may be obvious—you can't win 'em all—but if it isn't obvious to you, get an answer. The scientist has that obligation. You don't do him or her—or yourself or your story or the scientist's employer—a service by nodding and smiling vapidly or quickly moving on to the next question to "save time." For sure as you do, you will have to get back later by telephone for clarification—and that *will* take time he or she hadn't planned on.

Won't I seem like an idiot? Won't that hurt the interview? Maybe. That's a risk you run. But remember what you're there for. You're not an undergraduate trying to hype your marks in classroom discussion, and you're not a graduate student trying to impress your professor. The caliber of your story is the only grade you stand to get. For that matter, frequently and surprisingly, the scientist too may discover—or may already know and *you* will discover—that the simple question contains the seeds of a real dilemma or breakthrough concept that goes to the roots of the science. I've seen this lead to an exhilarating exchange and exciting discoveries for both. Static, predigested interviews thus injected with the obvious can explode into vivid life that leaves both of you, as with any two reasonably intelligent people talking, enriched and rewarded—and your story enhanced immeasurably as a consequence.

One tip, though, about attitude: simple, dumb questions should stem from an earnest, nakedly open desire to know the answer. They should never be used in the spirit of flip ice-breakers. Show the remotest pride in your breezy ignorance and you slam a door. Nobody, certainly not a Nobel Prize winner, wants his or her work or person made light of. As with all interviewing, use your own good judgment about dealing with your subject. Scientists *are* human beings, remember. They have insecurities, jealousies, rivalries, resentment over being passed over, etc., just like anybody else, and these cannot help but inform their behavior and responses during an interview. But the better prepared you are, the more homework you've done, the more your attention will be freed to deal with their humanity.

Should I bother with a tape recorder? Opinions vary, but I think so. In something as complex as science, I think tape is important. Have it transcribed, annotate it to the materials you've been given, work from the whole package to construct your story. Tapes, I'm convinced, are imperative for several reasons. For one, they will convince the scientist you intend to quote accurately. Your interviewee may ask for a transcript; provide it. The scientist may go over some of the answers and improve them.

For another thing, having a tape going—while it doesn't prevent you from taking an occasional note on the direction it's going—will enable you to *think* about what is being answered, which in turn will free you to modify or shape your questions accordingly. It also helps you really *hear* what is being said. After a quarter century of doing it both ways, I'm increasingly convinced that *something* gets lost—the question, the answer, provocative nuances—if you're so busy doing one thing you neglect the other.

What about letting the scientist or the staff see my story draft? Isn't this violating a cardinal tenet of my profession, not to mention looking for trouble? Others will disagree, but I've come to the conclusion that there is nothing I write that cannot be improved by the friendly, conscientious intercession of those I write about. After all, I think, it is an implicit part of the contract, time and circumstances permitting. This is the *scientist's* story as well as *yours*. It belongs to both of you, and both of you have an interest in making it the best you can. (Interviewing a Mafia don obviously carries its own set of ground rules, and they differ.) I cannot remember a time when a scientist has hopelessly fouled up or delayed a story sent for comments and corrections. More often than not, scientists and staff will be be impressed (or overwhelmed) by your industry—or won't have the time to screw it up in major league fashion, anyway. After all, they have their own jobs, their own time-consuming commitments. On balance, I think the gains outweigh the losses. Having the courage (yes, the courage, come on, be honest) to share your work builds trust, minimizes errors, and creates a good feeling that will carry over into future stories. Think of the converse: if you refuse to show your story on ethical grounds and it turns out to contain disastrous errors, you have probably lost a source for good.

Any thoughts on how to organize a science story? With clips, tapes, and brochures it sounds like a bigger job than usual. It is. A good interview should last at least two hours and produce thirty to forty pages of typescript. (The ratio of gold to dross and wheat to chaff usually depends on whether the scientist is a lecturer/teacher. If so, his or her thoughts are often well-organized and systematic. If not, *you* will have to organize them.) Adding past stories and handouts may give you a tidy pile of documentation an inch or more thick.

Do not despair. Read everything through. Underline key points and quotes in pencil. Think about everything. Set down on a blank tablet a "laundry list" of the points you wish to make, in any order they come to mind, then go back and order them sequentially in terms of which seems most naturally to follow the other. Take each of them, one after another, and write under each the further points and ideas that spring to mind in connection with it. Reread everything at least one more time to make sure you haven't overlooked anything important. Take the various points and sub-points and write them down again, inserting a bunch of numbers and letters to designate their varying weights and relationships and—*voilà!* You've got a working outline.

Remember Ernie Havermann's dictum: no magazine story should deal with more than the ten major points a reader can remember. Take those points and key each to a different color, then underline all the lines you have already made, section by section. Jot in the margins of your typescript or photocopy a phrase that fixes its meaning in relation to the section in question ("discovery of chemical," "history of research leading to it," "possible future applications," etc.).

Sometimes, if the subject is particularly intricate and the story or research especially long, I go back and either retype this distillation—so as to see the trees as well as the forest—separating each section and putting it in the order it will be written about. Or I take a ruler and transparent tape and cut and paste slivers, paragraphs, part-pages and pages into the order in which I wish to write it, folding in pages of handouts, other published stories, and the interview typescript as called for.

Agreed, like sharpening pencils or going to the mailbox, this procedure can be abused and overdone. It can become not only an excuse for not writing but a substitute for writing. Yet anything that ultimately helps you become familiar with your material and its internal relationships is never lost time. And curiously, I find that the more time I spend in this tedious organizational exercise, the less time I have to spend writing.

This will eliminate or minimize the need to rewrite, right? Minimize, maybe; eliminate, no. Writing is still writing and research is still research. Organizing your materials will help organize your thoughts. But for me, anyway, the first crack at the typewriter is seldom acceptable. Maybe you're lucky; maybe you're different. (Robert Heinlein and I once had a knock-down, drag-out debate about this.) But in nonfiction, in science writing, I've always felt that there is nothing I write that cannot be helped by my own editing and that of others.

Any last thoughts? About those metaphors, similes, and analogies. Absolutely indispensable to making science spring alive and clear to the general reader, I agree, but beware of the notion that they can save you from having to do the supremely hard work of thinking clearly and writing to communicate that. I used to think that even the most abstruse idea could be conveyed in a simple analogy if only I could find it. Alas, this is pursuing the Holy Grail; the world, and science, are not always simple. Sure, simplify where possible, but more important, clarify where not. Above all, beware the glittering image that ends by dazzling the vision instead of enhancing it. Some principles have good and simple analogies by their very natures; some just do not. Put another way, the pump is a near-perfect analogy for the heart (in a limited sense) because the heart, after all, *is* a pump. Just as the lungs are bellows. But I'd be careful about likening the nervous system to, say, an electronic pinball machine. You may think you're communicating, your analogy may be admirably lucid in its own terms, but you can still end up conveying nothing of the science you intended—or worse, distorting it irreparably.

In sum, learn to be wary of those turns of phrase that strike you as pure gold because you had to labor so hard to mine them. As Faulkner said in a similar context, "Kill your darlings." If you don't, your editor will. Or should.

And oh yes, enjoy. If you don't, write something else. Write something else anyway. For it's fatal to your pocketbook to be, as actors find, typecast. Science markets are limited. Establish your reputation if you wish, but never hesitate to step outside science and write other things—the farther removed, the better.

RANDOM THOUGHTS ON SCIENCE AND TECHNOLOGY WRITING
by George deLucenay Leon

Ask any ten writers why they chose that particular career and you'll get ten answers. They all have different reasons for what they're doing. Some write for hoped-for fame, others for the money, and still others for the same reason they might have chosen psychiatry, acting, or brain surgery—it's what they wanted to do. All this boils down to saying that I can tell only my own reasons. So excuse a lot of "I" and "me"; I cannot pretend to be able to explore the souls of other writers.

As to my reasons—you see how quickly the personal pronoun comes in—I graduated as an electrical engineer. When I came away with the diploma certifying that I took all the required courses plus a few more, I suddenly realized I did not want to be a practicing engineer. Furthermore, at that time, there were many more engineers than there were jobs.

However, many technical magazines had advertising sales positions open. My technical background helped me understand the jargon used in advertisements and articles so I could be convincing as to why potential clients should advertise.

It was only a short jump to filling the pages with my own writing rather than the clients' ads. And no doubt my engineering background helped. Nevertheless, I often wrote articles that resulted more from research than previous knowledge.

At the same time, I became interested in high fidelity. Reading books and magazines dedicated to hi-fi helped me understand what electronics was all about. From that research I eventually wrote hundreds of articles, three books, and quite a few pamphlets and sales manuals.

Later, working as an editor for a McGraw-Hill electronics magazine, I gained valuable insights as to what was useful in a submitted manuscript and what was plain dross. I found the single greatest fault—and the reason for turning down many manuscripts—was that writers hadn't taken the trouble to study my magazine. We didn't print business news, so why send me an article about Joe Glutch becoming president of YZX Electronics? Another reason many manuscripts failed to see the light of printed day was that they extolled the benefits of a supposedly new concept or product when it was really an old, tired idea.

"Many are called, but few are chosen." Remember that when trying to sell an article to a specialized publication. An editor receives scores of articles, outlines, and queries each month, but may publish only a dozen articles per issue. They are the ones that are meaty, well-written, show thorough research, and above all, that promise to be of interest to readers. Editors are no better than the last issue. They must please their readers or risk losing their jobs. They must choose what they think is best for their publications. Their choices may seem arbitrary; but, as a writer, you have to accept that as a way of life.

Put yourself in the editor's place. If he or she runs a publication whose editorial stance is antinuclear, then he or she cannot consider a story written for a nuclear plant designer. It's an obvious point and while *you* wouldn't do anything as stupid as that, I've seen some pieces that came close. So approach with care. Think before you go ahead.

Before submitting anything, even before starting to write, you should study several issues of the magazine you want to sell to. What is their style? How long are the articles generally? Are photos used? Color or black and white?

PLACING AN ARTICLE

One day you say to yourself, "There's a company that makes widgets. I also read in the newspaper that they received a patent on a new type of widget." Ask yourself, "Is there a story in that?"

Quite possibly there is. How to go about it? Is there a magazine specializing in the field of widgets? Go to the library. Get a copy of *Standard Rate and Data* on business publications. Let's say that widgets are important components in drilling for oil.

Look up "Oil" in *Standard Rate*. There are several such magazines listed. Study the publisher's editorial statement for each. In one case it reads, "*Pipeline News* is edited for companies involved in distribution, drilling equipment, and pipeline transportation." That looks good. The personnel are listed in the next paragraph. The managing editor is Robert Smith. If you have a recent copy of *Standard Rate*—it comes out every month—the information is up to date. The address and phone number of the publication are listed. Above all, you now know that the magazine is read by pumping engineers and drilling engineers. Since these are the people who buy and use widgets, you're on the right track.

You now go to the Universal Widget Company and find out from the promotion director, advertising manager, or even the president if they want to publicize their new product. Let's say they do and they would like you to write an article.

In writing for industrial magazines, there are two roads open to you: one is to be paid by the manufacturer; the other is to be recompensed by the magazine (we'll deal with that option later). The promotion manager will pay you if you can place a piece in *Pipeline News*. You'll have to place the article yourself, particularly if you're not well established. Later, when you have many writing credits, you can refuse that particular chore.

The first step, before querying the magazine, is to do some preliminary research. To get your article off the ground you must interview the designer of the new widget. Why is it different? What made it possible to get a patent on it? Is it smaller, lighter, cheaper, longer-lasting?

Find from the sales manager what their sales forecast happens to be. You have, or should have, studied widgets when you were at the library. You may have picked up some buzz words—terms currently used in the oil industry. How does the widget fit into the system? The widget company or the library is certain to have back issues of *Pipeline News*. Read them—thoroughly.

Armed with your newfound knowledge, you write or call Robert Smith, the editor. I usually telephone; a long-distance call is impressive. Here's what my conversation might be like:

"I have an assignment from the Universal Widget Company to do an article on their latest product. It is so unusual that they were just granted Patent #123,456,789. The new widget is expected to be on the market in six months. And I don't have to tell you about the importance of widgets in the drilling business. This model is guaranteed to last 40 percent longer and will be 30 percent cheaper than any competitive product. It's an exciting story and one that every reader of your magazine will want to know about. I can provide you with photos and a 2,000-word article."

You noticed I quoted the actual percentages, the actual patent number. Don't give generalities. Be specific. Show the editor you know what you're going to be writing about. Above all, be enthusiastic. If you aren't, why should the editor be?

Whenever I can, I try to show the editor I'm familiar with the magazine. For example, I might mention that my article would have the same general characteristics as one about drill bits in the January issue—and the editor won't take it amiss if you say what a fine piece you thought such-and-such an article was.

So Robert Smith says, "Sounds good. Send me an outline." I find about two pages is usually sufficient for an outline. It should cover pretty much what you told the editor on the telephone. Mention what the proposed length of the article will be and mention whom you will be quoting. Hit only with the salient facts. And stress the dramatic elements. They always exist. Find them. You might add that you can obtain color photos for the cover.

Again, careful study of the magazine can bear fruit. Are the cover shots just of equipment? Or people? Your cover photo, if it is to be considered, must match the general style of the publication. Whether you take your own photographs, or get your photo from the company that manufactures the equipment, it must match previous covers in overall style and form—and color. (A black-and-white photo won't do if the magazine always runs four-color covers.)

Next, let your contact person at the Universal Widget Company look over your outline. He or she can make valuable suggestions and help you avoid mistakes. After all, they know more about their business than you can learn in a few hours of conversation. Get whomever you're seeing to become involved. Demonstrate the article's value to the company, show how they can benefit from the piece, appeal to their vanity by explaining that company personnel will be quoted in the story.

A few days after you think Smith received your outline, follow it up with a telephone call. Did he get it? Did he like it? If the answers are "Yes," you're ready to run. Will he consider giving you the cover?

Write—I stress the word, *write*—to Universal Widgets stating what you are going to do and recapitulating their agreement with you as to payment, including extra money for photos if you are supplying them. The biggest disagreements come from oral arrangements. Anyone can misunderstand, so get it in writing.

Once the article is written to your satisfaction—using your outline to make certain you've covered every point—show it to your contact at Universal. Accept his or her suggestions unless they go counter to what the editor told you. Otherwise, be grateful for suggestions. (You may have to rewrite.)

All of the above is based on the first option I mentioned: getting paid by the company or its public relations agency. The second option is payment from the magazine. The course taken by you as a writer is about the same, except that on your call to the editor you must make him or her understand that *the magazine* is to pay you. If the editor agrees, send a confirming letter in which you repeat his or her instructions and the points you intend to cover. Also confirm the deadline for filing the story and use of photos, if any. Your letter will state that you will not undertake a similar story for a competitive magazine.

However, you do have another outlet to serve the research you've done. Sell to a different market entirely. Let's say the widget is made of a special steel alloy. An article could go into a steel production magazine. Again, *Standard Rate and Data* is your source. Occasionally, just occasionally, you might run a certain story in a consumer magazine if an appropriate "hook" (or angle) can be found that makes the story of interest to the average consumer (e.g., how widgets are used in six different time-saving home appliances).

Freelance Technical Writing Through Ad Agencies

I do much of my work for ad agencies and public relations agencies whose clients include manufacturers of a new steel, an addition to an aircraft, or a new integrated circuit for a computer. Many agencies cannot afford a full-time writer for such clients. If you can prove your work is satisfactory and that you are not a prima donna (you can take criticism), then you may be of value to the agency. Remember that the client is always right! He or she pays the bills and so has the last word. That doesn't mean you cannot express an opinion when you feel you are right. But if the client—the agency or *its* client—is obdurate, either accept the suggested changes or refuse the assignment.

The real professional accepts criticisms, even changes, by the client and by the editor. Sometimes they don't seem to make much sense, but then, much of life is nonsensical. Take the criticism in stride—all the way to the bank. If you've done your best you can hold your head up high. You can learn from changes made in your article. I know I do, frequently.

The Science Writer's Library

A few final words. The local library is fine, depending upon how complete its reference material happens to be. But you should have a small reference library of your own. There are books every writer should own. Along with the usual writer's reference books—a dictionary, a thesaurus, a few of the standard style books—you'll need reference books specific to your field. Since I write on electronics, I have a recently issued dictionary of electronics, plus glossaries of terms used in telecommunications and an encyclopedia of computer words.

Each industry has its own reference literature. Use the periodical listing in your library or your local bookstore to find what's current. Buy what you can.

If all of the above confuses you, remember that you don't need to know anything about a subject to write about it. I happen to be an engineer, but I write in many disciplines in which I have had little or no background. Once, when I did a piece on cryogenics, I had to look up the word in the dictionary. When I saw the manufacturer who made the pipes that carried gas that was super-cooled into a liquid, I asked him questions; I didn't try to hide my ignorance. I read all the manuals they had printed. I got an idea who used it, how they used the product.

Whatever type of technical writing you plan to do, your education must never stop. Science moves on and so must you. You will end up learning more than you can use. That's what makes you an expert.

WRITING ABOUT SCIENCE . . . WHATEVER THAT IS!
by Marvin Grosswirth

According to people who are supposed to know about such things, the excruciating pain of a kidney-stone attack is roughly equivalent to that of childbirth. And I believe it.

It was a kidney stone—or, to be more precise, a couple of mites of gravel—that drove me to writing about science.

When I first appeared on the examining table of Louis J. Rosenfeld, M.D., a prominent (one's personal physicians are always prominent) New York urologist, I had already written several magazine articles and a couple of books for a small, new, struggling publisher. I had also decided that writing for a living was what I wanted to do. I was not being terribly successful at it, but with the support and encouragement of my patient and understanding wife, who had the added attribute of a decent income, I felt fairly confident that I would make it. After all, I had started early in 1970 and my writing income was doubling each year. I calculated that at that rate, I would reach break-even by around 1975. (It turned out to be a fairly accurate prediction. Unfortunately, my writing income no longer doubles each year, but it is a fairly decent living.)

Such notions, however, were hardly predominant in my mind on that day in 1972 as I sat in pain and embarrassment—the latter caused by the totally inadequate hospital gown—on the examining table in Dr. Rosenfeld's office. Elizabeth, his wife, assistant, and X-ray technician, attempted small talk to distract me as we waited for the doctor to finish with another patient and render his diagnosis.

"What kind of work do you do?" she began.

"Writer," I croaked.

"Oh, really? What do you write about?"

"Whatever they pay me to write about."

(Pause.) "I wish Louie would write a book."

Why is it, I silently moaned, that whenever someone learns that I'm a writer, he or she insists on telling me about a bestseller begging to be written?

"I wish he'd write a book about vasectomy,"she continued, following with a short, brilliant dissertation on the merits and benefits of this surgical procedure, as far as both mankind in general and men in particular were concerned. By the time she was finished, she had convinced me: a book about vasectomy might be a good idea, at that.

When I left Dr. Rosenfeld's office half an hour later, feeling considerably better because he had told me I wasn't dying, he and I had a gentleman's agreement to collaborate .on a book about vasectomy. Prentice-Hall published *The Truth About Vasectomy*, by Louis J. Rosenfeld, M.D., and Marvin Grosswirth, the following year. The book, unfortunately, was not a success, possibly because five or six other publishers had similar ideas and had beaten us to the punch. Nevertheless, my career as a science writer was launched.

At about that time, the *Saturday Review* was undergoing one of its many incarnations and was now appearing as four magazines, one of which was called the *Saturday Review of Science*. Frank Kendig was the new editor. I was introduced to Frank, who was intrigued by the idea of a story about vasectomy. My first major article appeared as a cover story, but Frank had, in the meantime, moved over to *Science Digest*. Needless to say, I followed him with three article queries, all of which he accepted. In the meantime, Frank and the publisher had developed a difference of opinion, so while the assignments were confirmed by Kendig, it was to Dick Teresi that my articles were submitted.

That was the beginning of a five-year relationship with *Science Digest*, during which I averaged an article a month until the magazine changed its editor, its format, and its style. I have also since written a health-and-medicine column and articles on science for a variety of science-for-the-layperson publications, inflight magazines, semi-technical journals, and women's magazines. Obviously every writer's approach is highly personal and individual, but here are my thoughts on the subject.

"SCIENCE WRITING" VS. "WRITING ABOUT SCIENCE"

To begin with—and, to me, most important—I am not a "science writer." I am a writer who frequently writes about scientific subjects. This is not a mere semantic nicety. I define a science writer as someone who writes exclusively about science and has a scientific background. My background in science consists of some general courses in junior and senior high school, a little high school biology, and a year of physics at CCNY at night (all but forgotten except for the Ds I received as final grades in both semesters and my gratitude that they weren't Fs).

Whenever I interview an expert, I always begin by explaining that I am writing for an intelligent audience that is both interested in, and essentially ignorant of, science. I further explain that I am eminently qualified to do so because that description fits me. I advise the expert that, while I have done some homework on the subject, I will be asking questions about things that seem basic and simple—even simplistic— to him or her. During the interview, I ask the expert to spell words that are unfamiliar to me. After the interview, I have sometimes called back to get a word that did not come through clearly on my tape. Yes, I use a tape recorder all the time: not only does it keep me from having to hastily scribble notes, but I have never been accused—even wrongly—of misquoting anyone.

Homework

"Homework" consists of boning up on the subject of the article. There are several ways to do that. First, check your own references. You should have access to a good encyclopedia, even if it's in the public library. You should probably invest in your own copy of a good science dictionary, a good medical dictionary, and a copy of *Asimov's Guide to Science*, by, obviously, Isaac Asimov (Basic Books). Also, don't overlook your unabridged dictionary, which defines, succinctly and clearly, far more scientific terms than you might imagine.

When you set up your interview with an expert, ask him or her to send you any background material that he or she considers useful. You'll probably wind up with copies of the expert's own papers, much of which will be incomprehensible, but they will, at worst, familiarize you with the terminology and at best provide some information on which to build your questions.

In the likely event that you are not the first to write about the subject in question, check the *Reader's Guide to Periodical Literature* and the *Reader's Guide to Scientific Literature* at the local library and seek out the previously published articles. Your librarian can help you with other listings, such as the *Index Medicus*. Given the rapidity with which scientific developments occur these days, it is probably a waste of time to bother with articles more than two years old, unless you need historical material.

Don't hesitate to ask your subject(s) for sources of additional information. One of my most successful articles was based on the theory of an oceanographic chemist that the oceans can safely be used for dumping wastes. At the conclusion of the interview, I asked him to name his strongest opponent. He gave me not one but two names. I interviewed both by telephone for a solid, well-balanced piece that gave both sides of the argument from the viewpoints of acknowledged experts in the field.

"But Is It Science?"

After Frank Kendig left *Science Digest*, he became the first executive editor of a dramatic new magazine, *Omni*, which is considered by many to be the progenitor of the rash of "pop" science magazines that have appeared in recent years. It was in that capacity that he said, at a meeting of the American Society of Journalists and Authors: "Any article can be a science article." That is, perhaps, something of an overstatement. Still, it's easy to see how an article about, say, a new tire, could be written as a "how-to" piece for a general publication, a product evaluation for an automotive magazine, and a technical treatise for the appropriate journal.

Frank's comment made me smile, because it reminded me of an incident which had occurred several years earlier. The ASJA conducts a writers' conference every year with a variety of specialty workshops. During one of the workshops on science writing, about two-thirds into the session an intense young man asked: "How do you define science?" Everyone groaned. The answer, if you have any sense, is that you don't. Someone once asked David Ben-Gurion how he defined a Jew. He said: "If you think you're a Jew, and everyone else thinks you're a Jew, then you're a Jew." That's not a bad rule to apply to "science": if you think it's science, your editor thinks it's science, and your readers think it's science, then it's science.

The dictionary (specifically, the paperbound edition of the *Oxford American Dictionary*, published by Avon) defines science as "a branch of knowledge requiring systematic study and method, especially one of those dealing with substances, animal and vegetable life, and natural laws. . . ." There are, however, other definitions that working editors and writers go by, and they can be as confusing and nonspecific as the dictionary one. For example, some people consider themselves medical writers. Others consider themselves health-and-personal-care writers. But since health and personal care are part of medical science, why not health-and-medicine writers? And did you catch that "medical science" in the last sentence? Why not, then, health/medicine/science? Why not, indeed. As I said, if you think it's science, and your editor . . . etc., etc.

That word "science" gets kicked around a lot—as in "computer science," which purists might claim is not science at all, but "technology." Someone (I wish I could remember who, so that I could give proper credit) once gave me an excellent rule of thumb to go by: in general, "science" is considered to be the investigation of new principles, phenomena, and the like, while "technology" is the application of those innovations. That's a handy distinction to keep in mind for your own mental tranquility, but from the standpoint of a working writer, it may be unnecessary, because just as many editors use "health/medicine/science" as one word, another group, just as large, uses "science-and-technology" as one word. That's good enough for me, especially when it comes to getting work.

Once more, with feeling: If you think it's science, and your editor thinks it's science, then it's science.

THE WRITER AND THE READER

By now, you know enough about writing to understand the importance of establishing a communication link between you and your reader, so there's not much point in belaboring the subject here. Since this is essentially about my personal approach to writing about science, I'll simply review, quickly, some of the rules that govern my work.

1. I take nothing for granted. I never assume the reader already knows the meaning of certain terms, abbreviations, or acronyms, or is familiar with the names of people I mention or quote. I study the publication I'm writing for to determine the level of knowledge the reader is likely to have. When I write about computers for *Datamation* (probably the computer industry's leading trade journal), I don't have to explain the difference between a microcomputer and a mainframe. When I write for the *Journal of Commerce*, I do. I try to keep such explanations brief, unless they are what the article itself is about. For example: "A mainframe is a large, centralized computer, usually accessible through a number of terminals placed at various locations throughout the company or organization. A microcomputer is a small, desk-top computer, frequently referred to as a 'personal' computer."

2. I'm careful to avoid being patronizing or condescending. It's easy to assume an air of superiority, bordering on arrogance, when writing about highly technical stuff. Phrases like "as everyone knows" or "it is common knowledge by now" are not only offensive; they're inaccurate. If it's common knowledge, why am I writing about it?

3. I avoid burdening the reader with too many unneeded details that are likely to be boring. A prominent genetic engineering researcher explained to me, in exquisite detail, how a molecule is separated from a DNA specimen. It took him twenty minutes to describe it, and another fifteen to define the terms he rattled off that I had never heard before. In the finished article, I simply told the reader that the molecule is separated through a series of intricate procedures. (Had I written the article for an audience of scientists, the procedure, rather than what it was expected to accomplish, probably would have been the focal point and would have been given step by step.)

4. Whenever possible, I try to let the reader know what it all means to him or her. Almost every story is about something that affects our lives, either directly or indirectly. The reader has both the right and the desire to know about that.

5. I always find writing about science/technology fascinating and exciting, because doing the research gives me a sense of discovery. I try to let the reader share and experience the feeling.

THE MARKET

People who want to write about science usually begin by trying to sell story ideas to science magazines. Of course, that's an important and valid market, but it's by no means exclusive. Virtually every magazine being published is a market for a scientifically oriented article. Health and medicine, consumer electronics, computers and sociology, innovations in transportation, new forms of entertainment and education—these are only a minuscule sampling of the areas that relate to science.

After all, if you think it's science, and your editor thinks it's science . . .

WRITING SCIENCE BOOKS FOR YOUNG PEOPLE
by Peter R. Limburg

Like many science popularizers, I wasn't a science major in college. Not that I had no interest in science—I had wanted to become a chemist—but flunking out of freshman math took care of that. So I majored in international relations.

At any rate, after college, a deadly job as a bank trainee, a stint in the Army, and graduate school, I found myself in a temporary job with an encyclopedia publisher. This stretched into something semipermanent, and I became an editorial assistant, working under the geography editor.

Eventually I left for another job (virtually the only way to get a raise back in the late 1950s) working on a picture atlas. Following that, thanks to my encyclopedia experience, I was put to work on *The Harper. Encyclopedia of Science*. This brought me into the scientific fold, where I labored mightily at translating abstruse scientese into something comprehensible to the educated layman. I also worked at adding substance to public relations puffery.

In the process, I found I had a knack for presenting scientific and technological information in a clear and understandable way, and that I actually enjoyed it. (One of the joys of being a writer—or an editor—is that you're always learning something new.) My next job was helping put together *The New Book of Knowledge (NBK)*, a set written for children and for which I still have a good deal of affection. And which I still use on occasion for basic information for my own writing.

On the *NBK* I became departmental editor for Products and Industries, a category that essentially embraced the articles that neither the science editor nor the social studies editor cared for. However, there were many fascinating topics, such as the petroleum industry, iron and steel production, various types of engines and so on. Needless to say, I learned a great deal in this job and sharpened my writing skills by adapting scientific and technical material to a fifth-grade reading level. I also had a boss who was tough to please. I was always pleasantly surprised when she thought I'd done a good job.

A former teacher, this woman was keenly aware that young readers, although they may know what the words mean, lack the background to fully understand what the writer or editor is talking about; therefore it's the responsibility of the writer or editor to provide that background and to lay the information out as clearly and simply as possible. She also insisted that the ideas be presented in a logical sequence. These were invaluable lessons, and I have found they apply with equal force to material written for adult readers.

When the *NBK* was completed and the staff phased out, my boss encouraged me to try doing a book for Franklin Watts, another firm in the Grolier complex, since Mr. Watts himself was very enthusiastic about everything connected with the *NBK*. I submitted several ideas for books, all based on subjects I had become familiar with in my work, and he suggested I try the topic of engines. I did, and, after much editorial delay, the book was published. It won a commendation from the American Association for the Advancement of Science (AAAS), and of course I was thrilled at such recognition for my first book. (Alas, sales languished for lack of promotion, and my literary firstborn eventually went out of print without earning back its extremely modest advance.)

By the time *The First Book of Engines* was published, I was two jobs further on. A colleague who had also written a children's book said, "You ought to get in touch with my agent."

I did, and the result was another book assignment based on one of a series of ideas I submitted. Again, the subject was one from my past experience at the *NBK*. I subsequently did several more books for this house. It may be of interest that the initial book was placed there because my agent and the juvenile editor were good friends. (As you can see, it helps to have contacts in the business; previous experience works to your advantage, too.)

At the end of 1970 I went freelance, a decision I have never regretted, although it brought some lean times with it. However, eventually I was fortunate enough to make a connection with the General Books Division of *Reader's Digest* (RDGB), which has been a pretty steady source of work. The people there are a really nice bunch, and they take great care with the books they create. In addition to my assignments writing segments and book chapters for RDGB, I have had occasional assignments for other clients (one came via an editor at RDGB, the rest mainly through my own contacts). I have combined freelance assignments with writing my own books. This has generally worked well, although the pressure of deadlines has sometimes meant that I've had to postpone work on my own material in order to meet a freelance commitment (such as magazine articles or the Reader's Digest chapters), or that I've had to turn down a freelance assignment to make time for my own book.

Deciding to Write for Children

I started writing for children and young adults for several reasons. First, I already knew how to do it when I gathered the courage to try something on my own, rather than simply rewriting other people's material. Second, at that time (mid-1960s) juvenile publishing still enjoyed its traditional position: a stable, ongoing market in which a conscientious author could expect modest but steady profits for years and years on every title. Third, there was a voracious demand for informational books for young people, thanks to the shock administered to American society by the Soviet Union's launching the first artificial satellite and to Title II of the National Defense Act. No one could foresee that the Vietnam war would shortly plunge educational publishing into a depression. And who could have predicted how profound—at times seemingly irrecoverable—that depression would turn out to be?

I would caution anyone thinking of writing informational books for young people that both topics and content of books are controlled by school curricula. Over ninety percent of all books designated as juveniles are purchased by schools and libraries. And while it is not unreasonable that the market calls the tune, it can be extremely frustrating.

Through experience, I learned that I didn't like writing books for the lowest elementary grades. There are too many curriculum-related restrictions—not so much on language if it's explained in context, but on concepts. To me, it's like trying to write with someone's hand clamped over my mouth. "Oh, no, they don't get this until fourth grade," was typical of the sort of mentality I often had to contend with. Usually I lost, since the publisher had all the guns. I find writing for the fifth grade and up far more congenial; indeed, for me, the higher the grade level, the easier the writing becomes.

But to turn out a decent informational book for any reading level, you first learn enough about the topic to give a knowledgeable presentation. Then you boil down this acquired knowledge so it can be understood by the intended audience. The less boiling down and simplification required, the easier the writer's task. To be sure, it *is* a challenge to present scientific concepts for little kids, but I found the challenge palled after the first few times. [Editor's note: A number of writers prefer the absolute simplification of primary grades curriculum.]

A challenge of a different sort is reader preference. Kids always seem to like adventure stories and sports bios, so these books generally do well. The young reader who wants to find out about diesel engines or flintlock rifles, in contrast, comes along less frequently. Therefore most science books have a limited market, as school boards, teachers, and librarians place a lower priority on purchasing them.

WHAT TO WRITE ABOUT

Where do I get my ideas? As you may have gathered, many of my ideas stem from previous work; others come from things I read in newspapers or magazines. Some excellent ideas have been suggested by my wife. Some have been assigned to me by editors with whom I have already dealt.

Once or twice, pure serendipity has played a part, as in my book, *Watch Out, It's Poison Ivy!* In that case, I dropped in on an editor to discuss ideas and found her horribly swollen and in severe discomfort. A city-bred person, she had recently moved to the country and contracted a horrendous case of poison ivy while pulling up weeds and brush at the end of her garden. "Lee," I said, "why not do a book on poison ivy?" She agreed on the spot. That book led to a follow-up on poisonous plants.

One book does not always lead so directly to another but I have found that once an editor has learned to trust you for conscientious, craftsmanlike work, more assignments are forthcoming. I cannot say that I have consciously tailored my ideas to a particular market; rather, I propose what interests me and send the proposal around to various publishers. I think that this results in a better book—at least it does where I am concerned.

I have heard that other authors make exhaustive market surveys, studying *Books in Print*, school syllabi, and publishers' catalogs, determining where the gaps are and then working up proposals, but I find this approach too discouraging and tedious. Once the proposal is accepted and the manuscript in progress, I take my cues from the editor, since the editor presumably knows the market.

I don't think any serious writer should supinely accept everything the editor says, however. Editors are human, and they are often wrong. Often, too, they are unfamiliar with the subject matter. I'd guess that perhaps ten to twenty percent of the changes they suggest are improvements, a like number disasters, and the balance don't really make very much difference one way or another. In general, I've found that if I explain to an editor the reasons why I want to present a certain concept in a certain way, she or he will go along.

A great deal depends on luck. Does an editor feel there is a "need" (translation: a market opening) for the idea you have proposed? Has this topic not been covered in, say, the last five years? Can the editor sell your proposal to the marketing committee at the publishing house? What shape are the schools' library budgets in?

Distressing things have happened in publishing since I took the plunge, due largely to conglomerate takeovers of publishing firms. Sad to say, their conglomerate executives are completely ignorant of the mechanics of publishing and expect books to be turned out like washing machines. Editors at one house I used to deal with are now forced to reduce advances and royalties to authors, and to try to compel authors to accept further reduced royalties on reprints. As a consequence, they now must deal almost entirely with first-time authors for whom the satisfaction of seeing their names in print is reward enough. These editors tell me most of the material that comes in now is so bad that they have to rewrite it completely.

DEADLINES AND RESEARCH

For my own self-respect, I try to turn in a well-written manuscript with a minimum of interlinear inserts and penciled corrections. Neatness is always appreciated by the editors who work on manuscripts. Punctuality in meeting deadlines is also appreciated (as a former editor, I know how much). I have sinned in this respect myself, but always let the editor know when I am running late. Courtesy makes for good working relationships.

Setting a deadline is a problem to begin with. On my more ambitious books, such as *Farming the Waters*, I've found that the research has taken much longer than anticipated. This is because one topic leads to another and I must get all the facts. Then, putting it all together often takes more time than I'd expected. When an editor asks me, "When can you get the manuscript in?" I always say, "I honestly don't know, and I don't want to give you a phony deadline that I can't meet." But since the editor has to have *some* kind of framework for the production schedule, we usually compromise on a tentative deadline.

Research is actually the fun part of a book for me. The hard part is translating this acquired knowledge to paper. When I began freelancing, my idea of research was to go down to the public library and take out some good books on the subject, photocopying whatever I couldn't take with me. (This limited idea of research was due to the training of my first job, where the management was so incredibly penny-pinching that the editors weren't even permitted to make a phone call query to a local contributor.) Later, however, I sometimes found that the information I needed wasn't available in books, and that I had to go out and talk to people.

It turned out that these personal experiences invariably produced better books. A case in point was my book *Chickens, Chickens, Chickens,* for which I visited the Perdue experimental farm in Maryland, talked with distinguished poultry scientists at Cornell, and visited Rutgers University for insights into yet other aspects of the chicken industry. Similarly, my books on oceanography and oceanographic institutions (*Oceanographic Institution* and *Science Studies the Sea*) and on aquaculture (*Farming the Waters*) would have been impossible without visits to schools of oceanography or marine science and to aquacultural installations.

I will never forget my first sight of trout eggs by the thousands on their incubation trays, nor how the trout went into a feeding frenzy at chow time. The great concrete "ponds" in which trout are raised in Idaho's "Magic Valley" were another unforgettable sight. (Seeing the mighty springs that gushed from the wall of the Snake River Canyon was a completely unexpected fringe benefit of the trip.) Then there was my visit to the Lummi Indian oyster hatchery on Puget Sound, where the director took me out on the tribal oyster flats and fed me freshly picked oysters.

PROPOSALS, ADVANCES, AND MAKING A LIVING

Keeping track of manuscripts may be a problem for journalists who have a number in circulation concurrently. With books, I seldom have more than one proposal out at a time, and that isn't hard to keep track of. A copy of a cover letter for each proposal tells me at a glance when the proposal was submitted, and when it's time (usually after four to six weeks) to nudge the editor. This is one of the situations in which an agent comes in handy.

Royalties and advances depend to a large extent on how much leverage you have with your publisher, and this, in turn, depends on what the publisher thinks your book will earn. If the publisher thinks your book will clear $10,000, it is unrealistic to demand a $5,000 advance. Try to find out at negotiation time what your publisher thinks the market will be, then get the best advance you can. This is, after all, the only money you can be sure of seeing.

Unfortunately, publishers have a 90-day grace period after the dates on which they are supposed to send you your statements, and they all use them to the full. Some even delay beyond that point, unless you or your agent call them to account. And royalty checks are often drawn on banks in out-of-the-way places, so it takes an extra ten days to two weeks before the check clears—thus giving the publisher use of those funds at the author's expense.

Can you make a living writing children's books? In my experience, no. I know of only one writer who is a full-time writer of juveniles, and he is not only extremely disciplined and prolific but also an excellent salesman for his own ideas. One other I know ekes out his juvenile earnings by ghostwriting adult books for popular authors. I myself inherited money that covered some of my expenses, and freelancing covered the rest. Most of my writer friends write strictly as a sideline and hold regular jobs to make ends meet. Often these jobs are in publishing or teaching. And some are homemakers whose children are old enough to be in school and out from underfoot at least part of the day.

If this assessment of the juvenile nonfiction market sounds discouraging, it is at least realistic. There are other reasons for writing than becoming the next Irving Wallace. One is the intellectual stimulus; you're always making new decisions. Another is the satisfaction of having accomplished something worthwhile. Some call it ego gratification, but under any name it's legitimate and important. You get the feeling of having made a contribution to knowledge, and of having brought pleasure as well as information to some young person somewhere. And there is always the outside chance that one of your books will be a moneymaker.

WRITING ABOUT SPACE FLIGHT
by Louis Alexander

A few days before the next space shuttle flight blasts off, a diverse group of men and women will gather at Kennedy Space Center in central Florida and at Johnson Space Center near Houston, Texas. A handful check in at Marshall Space Flight Center in northern Alabama and at Edwards Air Force Base in southern California. Reporters, broadcasters, photographers, technicians—all will come to cover one of the most dramatic and longest-running stories in twentieth-century science writing: space flight.

Three thousand media people were accredited to cover John Glenn's epochal three orbits around the earth in 1962, and three thousand to cover the first moon landing in 1969. Nowadays a space shuttle flight draws a few hundred. But that includes the reporters who will reach millions of listeners and viewers through the ABC, CBS, and NBC television networks, Mutual and Westinghouse radio, the BBC, stations in Japan, and stations served by EBU (the European Broadcast Union). It includes writers for Associated Press and United Press International, dozens of major newspapers here and abroad, magazine writers and freelance photographers—not to mention a sprinkling of reporters and radio newscasters from the astronauts' home towns, plus dozens of technical experts writing for engineers, scientists, and technologists in the sciences and professions.

You are writing about space flight when you report which astronauts NASA has just assigned to the next space flight. You are reporting space flight when you interview astronauts about how they became interested in the first place, and about how their families manage their uncommon daily lives. You're covering space flight when you report what happened today at the Johnson, Kennedy, or Marshall Space Centers or en route. You're reporting space flight when you spread the word about what new purchases NASA has opened bidding for.

You're also writing about space flight when you track down in tedious detail the exact description of what delayed the countdown for several hours—then explain it in popular words of no more than two syllables; and when you digest hours of action and conversation into a dozen inches of fast-moving, easy-to-understand newspaper copy, or ninety seconds of radio news. Or when you flip through a hundred pages of data, then cautiously work through portions of it to come up with an important, exclusive explanation that has eluded other reporters. And when you report the emotions that an astronaut and his or her family are going through. And even when you let your imagination roam through the "What if . . .?" areas of life and relate them to everyday people until you visualize an exciting way to combine the facts of space flight with their potential impact upon events and families—some real but many fresh from your imagination (e.g., "a weekend on the moon for under $1,000").

WHAT SPACE WRITING ENTAILS

Writing about space flight is a matter of boning up constantly on the technical and scientific activities at the space centers and assembly plants, and astronauts' and researchers' scheduled activities, and then turning out in layman's language a relatively simple illustration of their significance. (You really score when you come up with a description that fidgety, precise scientists accept as "adequate.")

It's a matter of talking shop with those news sources you have time for, and gradually learning enough about space flight to keep up your end of the conversation. Out of such chats come an understanding of how each person functions in each job, and a list of people who will trust you to satisfactorily explain their specialties to the general public.

You have to stop regarding astronauts as demigods, yet retain your respect for them as real people in the questions you ask (e.g., "Aren't you ever afraid?").

You have to accept data processing for what it is. That begins when you discover that the same scientists who treat the computer as a real person ("The computer told us that . . .") also joke about "GIGO," which means "garbage in, garbage out." Data-processing results are only as good as the data that go into the computer, and the program that processes—or "massages"—those data.

You have to earn the respect of scientists and engineers, and bring them gradually to respect your journalism. Many an engineer is wont to say, "I don't want to answer your questions because you won't understand"; "My work is so technical that reporters never get it right"; or "Read my last technical paper, and then I may be willing to give you an appointment to answer your questions."

You earn their respect by asking intelligent questions, and by writing articles and stories that correctly report the events and information, even if you have to fight the editor or news director to retain your way of stating things because it will more closely approximate the scientific, medical, and technological terminology.

BUILDING A SPACE FLIGHT BACKGROUND

How in the world do you acquire all this information? How can you ever expect to feel at ease interviewing these experts—much less make *them* feel at ease answering your questions? How are you going to break through the upbeat, optimistic, "team player" attitudes of astronauts and top officialdom—and should you try, in the expectation that the real story, their real attitudes, are different underneath?

Most of the reporters who now cover space flight for general audiences came out of college with liberal arts degrees, a minimum of psychology and sociology, and a distaste for things mathematical or business—but gradually learned science writing.

Books explaining the principles of space flight are widely available. Pamphlets—published by contractors about the things they make and do for space flight—are even better, for they teach you a little at a time and make a special effort to keep it simple.

You need to know some basics of physics, chemistry, biology, and meteorology. Reading these primers will help you understand when you get into discussions of what happens in space: the orbital dynamics, thermal and conductivity properties of metals in a near-vacuum where temperatures change suddenly from around 270 degrees (Fahrenheit) in direct sunshine to -250 degrees in adjacent shade. You will be able to discuss the hazards of manned space flight—where the body would explode in a vacuum (if it doesn't freeze or boil first) unless blanketed with pressure equal to at least a third of the earth's atmosphere—for instance, pure oxygen in the cabin of the spacecraft and the safety of a space suit (more usefully called a pressure suit).

Many of your readers and listeners know no more than you do; so, for your first efforts, you should include those explanations for them. That was the content of one of my first stories on space flight, a five-part series for the North American Newspaper Alliance (now Independent News Alliance) in about sixty newspapers, explaining in ordinary language those technical basics that had to be accomplished, or overcome, to enable mankind to escape the earth's gravity and go into orbit, or land on the moon and Mars.

Information for the Asking

NASA mails press releases to people who have a serious interest in what's going on. They prune the list during periods of retrenchment and expand it during periods of great activity. NASA's educational branch has an extensive collection of books and booklets that are usually yours for the asking but sometimes for the purchase.

NASA also periodically conducts press briefings in advance of each new program and each flight. Long before the first space shuttle flight, the media were invited to briefings on how the shuttle operates, its advantages (and disadvantages), and how a typical mission would be staged. The experts then conducted a question-and-answer session with reporters.

Not long before each flight, NASA conducts briefings on the upcoming flight plan, the scientific experiments, other special activities, and any new equipment that will fly for the first time—such as the pressure suit that two mission specialist/astronauts were to test on the fifth space mission, STS-5. Tapes and transcripts of the presentations are available on request (transcripts are not always immediately available).

Manufacturers likewise conduct briefings and offer press kits to accredited members of the media. These contain information about their equipment—ranging from a thick, loose-leaf reference book about the orbiter itself to a pamphlet about one system and a single sheet about some small item. The press kits contain pictures, and usually biographies, of key people, together with names and phone numbers of contact people with additional information. The key manufacturers and providers of services generally send a knowledgeable representative (or several) to the news centers at Kennedy and Johnson, where they're available to answer your questions (although some reporters joke half-seriously that if anything goes wrong with a company's equipment it may take a while to locate that press representative).

NASA provides a news center for media people who write for accreditation on their newspaper, magazine, or broadcast station letterhead and have it signed by the editor or news director. Accreditation for freelancers is a little more difficult, but NASA generally approves a media badge for a writer who describes to them the specific project he or she is working on, assuming it's a project that requires being in the news center.

The countdown is piped into the news center over a public address system and closed-circuit television. A public information officer, who has trained with Mission Control teams and is familiar with the conditions the flight director and controllers work under, runs the system. While the flight is in orbit, conversations between the crew and Mission Control—so-called air-to-ground—are broadcast in the news center via the public address system. Transcripts of the air-to-ground conversations gradually arrive at the news center, page by page, until literally hundreds of pages of word-for-word reports are available to the press.

At the end of each shift in the control center, generally eight to ten hours, the flight director conducts a press briefing. Often he brings one or two of the controllers who were involved in the major events during that shift. Tapes and transcripts of these briefings are available a few hours later.

NASA does a lot to make the writer's job easy—and accurate. And so do the manufacturers and providers of special services. Notices of changes in the crew's flight activities are also broadcast into the news center and later distributed there in print. Reporters also get the exact data from the launching, the advance timetable for special events, the schedule for television broadcasts from space, and the eventual landing time.

THE EVOLUTION OF SPACE REPORTING

When space flight began in the 1960s, reporters would crowd around the flight and mission directors for information. They crowded within a few dozen yards of Pad Number 5 to watch and describe the lift-offs. Soon the Kennedy Space Center (then Cape Canaveral) built bleachers for the press, and a clear viewing area for photographers at a safe distance from larger rocket launchings off Pad 14. (By the time the Apollo-Saturn missions began at Pad 39, the safe distance was a full three miles and reporters brought binoculars.) The bleachers are covered from the Florida sun (unlike the VIP bleachers, which are an equal distance from the pad) and have electrical connections, phone outlets, and broadcast feeds connected right into the public address system carrying the countdown. Reporters can plug in their tape recorders and networks can plug in their feeds directly to their affiliate stations.

The pay phones behind the bleachers have special adapters so that tape can be played directly into newsrooms throughout the country. The concession stand has soft drinks and sandwiches—never enough and none too tasty—to help reporters, broadcasters, and photographers survive the long waits and delays of countdown while technicians are making quick fixes out on the pad.

When the Johnson Space Center control room was built twenty years ago, there were two small press viewing rooms directly behind the flight controllers. But NASA was touchy about what might happen during an emergency and refused to admit the press—even though the rest of the viewing room seated eighty-some VIPs. The press made do with what it considered second-hand coverage through the NASA information officer handling the camera that focused around the control room; that officer could also change which voices to feed into the public address system.

NASA did a good job. But the reporters weren't absolutely sure nothing was being concealed from the cameras or kept off the closed-circuit voice network to the news center. They believed—and repeatedly said so to every official within earshot—that if the press couldn't see for itself and hear for itself, it would be possible to cover up a tragedy by denying First Amendment press freedom.

The brewing storm burst in 1966, during the Gemini 8 mission. Shortly after Neil Armstrong and Dave Scott had performed the first docking in the history of space flight, plugging their two-man capsule into an Agena rocket, something went seriously wrong. The Gemini Control public information officer reported in a weak, uncertain voice over the public address system that Gemini had undocked from the Agena. More reports would follow . . .

As junior reporter in Houston for the ABC network, I was on duty while others dined and celebrated the docking. The voice I heard wasn't the one expected, and Gemini was not scheduled to undock for several hours, so I alerted ABC immediately. (I believe I was three minutes ahead of AP, UPI, and the other broadcast networks; a "beat" like that is one of the satisfactions that competitive reporters live for.)

NASA resolutely refused to let the press hear the air-to-ground conversations between Mission Control and the astronauts. The press might "misunderstand" the sounds, NASA said, which everybody assumed meant frantic voices, voices of urgency, voices of doom. During the entire emergency the press was allowed to hear only the voice of Gemini Control, one of the NASA's own, delivering the commentary— much like the announcer at football and baseball games. But events in space were a lot more significant and controversial than a close call at home plate: millions of people all over the world were concerned.

The networks followed the story live. In the wee morning hours across America, the spacecraft dropped safely into the Pacific Ocean; a few hours after that, a destroyer hove alongside and rescued the astronauts. Newspaper headlines screamed the report of the rescue the next morning.

But it was not until about noon of that day, after NASA had time to reassure itself about everything, that they released all the tapes of the air-to-ground conversations. That's when the press discovered exactly how it was with the astronauts: Armstrong and Scott reported that their spacecraft suddenly began whirling round and round, out of control. One thruster valve was stuck in the open position, pouring propellant into that motor only, which caused the nearly weightless spacecraft to revolve faster and faster. The spinning increased to a dizzying one revolution per second, and although the astronauts undocked from their Agena target, the spinning did not stop.

Fortunately, the spinning did stop when the whole thruster system ran out of fuel; the astronauts finally got the spacecraft under control again. But they had been drawing fuel from their alternate supply (every manned spacecraft system has a backup). They would have to return to earth immediately.

What impressed the listening reporters and broadcasters was how calmly and professionally the astronauts reported conditions, despite great stress. Each listener realized it would have been wonderful if he could have reported that professionalism to the public while it was happening instead of having to speculate on the possibility of frenzy and panic. By the time we heard it as it really was, the story took second place to news of greater immediacy; the truth of the situation had to wait for magazine reports.

It wasn't till the eve of the Apollo 13 mission four years later that the new chief of public information at Houston, Brian Duff, persuaded officials that NASA had more to gain than lose by opening direct access to the control room. Public interest had been declining after that first landing on the moon in 1969, and Congress was questioning NASA budgets more closely. Broadening the media's access to the news would help both NASA and the press.

Duff arranged for one print reporter and one broadcast reporter to represent the entire press pool during periods of several hours each. (I had the privilege of becoming the first print reporter during the countdown and launch.) Sitting in that eyewitness booth with the dials and switches enabling them to tune in to various conversations in Mission Control, reporters could see and hear for themselves what was going on, regardless of what the voice of Apollo Control was reporting to the news center. The observers were obligated to write reports of what happened during their stays—which NASA reproduced at once—and also to answer questions from the press pool.

The new policy of openness got a severe test almost immediately. Fifty-five hours after launch, when Apollo 13 was 150,000 miles from earth, Mission Control heard Jim Lovell say, "Houston, we've got a problem." A flask of compressed oxygen had exploded; the electricity supply was dangerously low.

NASA stood by its new policy. This time, pool observers were escorted into the viewing booths and reported first-hand what Mission Control was hearing and doing, together with how calmly the controllers were coping with their jobs. Most members of the press (and many NASA officials as well) believe everyone benefited from the confidence and accuracy of the reporting.

A Typical Launch—for a Reporter

For every single mission the most exciting experience is the blast-off. (Once I overheard another reporter say to his editor, "After the first time, you think it's gonna be boring. But the blast-off is always a tremendous thrill!") Illuminated all night by floodlights, the space shuttle has been standing on the launching pad. Launch time will come soon after sunrise, while crosswinds and clouds are at their least. Public and press anticipation has been building up throughout the countdown.

As photographers peer across the lagoon toward the pad where small plumes of smoke trail from two or three escape valves, everyone listens to the voice of Shuttle Control over the public address system throughout the press bleachers, the individual "shacks" of the wire services, the networks, and other major news agencies.

During the last few minutes the voice keeps up a continuous flow of countdown information until—how soon it seems!—it's counting in unison with the controllers: "ten . . . nine . . . eight . . . we have ignition!"—everyone sees a rolling, rapidly spreading, cottony ball of smoke pushed by fires bright as hell's blast furnace—". . . three . . . two . . . one . . ."—and the hundreds of thousands of tons rise, seemingly slowly, yet so rapidly that the tail has passed the top of the service tower almost in the blinking of the eye that registered the flames of ignition. In no more than two or three breathless minutes the shuttle, huge tanks and all, has shrunk to a bright dot in the sky and then disappeared. Some of the press continue to watch on the closed-circuit television monitors as NASA telescopic cameras follow it. Others start typing their latest stories.

As soon as the tail of the entire package passes the top of the launch-pad tower, control of the mission passes to the Houston center. Some reporters, especially the magazine writers, forgo the brief excitement at Kennedy to follow the hours and days of the mission at Johnson Space Center. Others rush from the bleachers to the airport at Orlando and reach Houston in time to attend the second change-of-shift briefing. Some leapfrog Houston and go on to southern California for the landing at Edwards Air Force Base. A few have been following events over closed circuits at NASA centers at Huntsville, Alabama and Washington, D.C.; they stay where they are.

At Kennedy, the writers have talked with experts about pre-launch and launch. At Huntsville, they have talked with experts about rocketry and some of the international payloads; at Washington, with the top officialdom whose influence upon Congress and the budget are most direct; at Houston, with the experts on astronaut training, flight planning, and Mission Control itself; and at Edwards, with the experts in charge of landing and post-landing activities. For photographers, the only exciting visuals occur at Kennedy and Edwards; elsewhere there are only mug shots, training devices, briefings, and copies of pictures rushed from Kennedy or Edwards.

Midnight across America is midday across Asia. Europe awakens not long after the United States goes to sleep. Around the world a broadcaster somewhere is getting ready to go on the air. Somewhere around the world, deadline is approaching for newspapers in some nation, some state. Someone is always preparing a story in the news center.

Most of the hours writers spend during each mission are routine. They read the transcripts and review their notes. As they digest the technical information, they decide what will be of most interest to *their* individual audiences. They calculate how to explain things clearly and briefly—and that is as big a job as choosing what to report out of the massive amount of information they receive. (I sometimes feel that I'm a translator.)

After the astronauts land the shuttle at Edwards, the top officials join in a post-landing press conference with the flight director, linked by closed-circuit voice and TV so they can answer questions from reporters everywhere on the circuit.

TV, radio, and daily newspapers close out their final stories and depart the news centers. But the magazine writers, the special news services, and some freelancers remain for another day—some for several days. They wrap up their special interests and depart. Or they linger until they can attend the press conference at which the astronauts report their experiences. That's when the people-minded writers finally observe the astronauts' reactions and get answers to some personal questions. Then, also, the biggest bundle of pictures is distributed to the media that have signed up for them. However, this may be ten days or two weeks after the landing; some writers leave promptly after the landing and return for the astronauts' reports.

WHAT TO REPORT

Magazine readers' interests vary widely, from wanting to know how the computer systems are working to how the astronauts' families feel. Some popular magazines want their readers to understand the importance of what is happening, and others want to sensationalize crises, big and little. Many trade journals want reports on the electronics, the cryogenics, the thermodynamics, the flight trajectories, and the astronauts' biomedical responses.

One freelancer came to Houston just to size up the nutritional aspects of the astronauts' diet versus the physiological conditions they faced during space flight. A few magazines analyze the economics, while scientific and technological magazines report the significance of events and results for the future of each discipline and each industry.

Magazine writers discuss the technical details and the meanings of events with information officers for NASA and representatives of McDonnell-Douglas, Rockwell, TRW, the Department of Defense, the Canadian government, and many other companies and scientific agencies. (Defense is in charge of emergency recoveries by ships and planes around the world, and NASA pays for their services—just as Defense pays NASA for carrying an occasional, always secret, payload into orbit aboard the shuttle.) For those magazine writers, NASA arranges interviews with the most knowledgeable and responsible official available. NASA would prefer that magazine writers interview during periods when a shuttle is not aloft, when officials are under less stress. But most book and magazines writers have no desire to finance any more travel and hotel expense than is absolutely necessary to get a good story. For the writers, it's a rare opportunity to put together a well-rounded story in a single location, because so many knowledgeable people have converged on the Johnson Space Center.

THE FUTURE OF SPACE REPORTING

Shuttle missions are lifting off increasingly frequently. During 1982 the test flights blasted into orbit about three to four months apart, but the arrival of the second shuttle, the Challenger, doubled the NASA fleet and shortened intervals between operational, commercial missions during 1983. By the time the fleet grows to four spacecraft— no later than 1985—NASA expects to launch operational flights every two weeks. Commercial and scientific organizations have many satellites for long-distance phone connections, television and radio network circuits, and data-processing relays that they'll pay NASA to launch, and pallets containing many research projects are waiting to get into orbit. Scientists are waiting with increasing impatience for these projects to be completed, and many readers will want details.

A scientific satellite currently in orbit isn't working, and NASA expects to send astronauts to repair it or replace the useless "black box" with one that works. There's a space telescope to be placed in orbit from the shuttle. And by 1987, McDonnell-Douglas wants to unload from one or more orbiting shuttles a space factory of its own that will provide raw materials of a scarce pharmaceutical compound for sale to hospitals and individuals. Other companies have plans for products that require better welding or more perfect roundness than they can get in production within the earth's gravity and atmosphere. A space-age surprise is that carrying out some of this work in orbit, and paying NASA for the use of the space shuttle, will be cheaper than carrying it out on earth.

The French are offering manufacturers and scientific agencies the technical advantages of launchings closer to the equator, atop Ariane rockets; those launchings may cost less than the American space shuttle, even though the Americans' costs are reduced because the shuttle is available for multiple flights up to a hundred. The Soviets have been planning a space station larger and longer-lasting than their Salyut and the American Skylab; they *have* been exchanging data from their space researches, believe it or not, with the West (although scientists this side of the Iron Curtain remain cautious about the extent of Soviet cooperation). But that means there are magazine stories and books about Soviet space activities. And in addition, NASA's former chief astronaut Deke Slayton is flight director for an experimental *commercial* skylab launch—part of the commercial competition with government for the profits they believe they can make providing space launches for those who'll pay.

Besides the manned space flights, many things are happening in unmanned satellites and space probes. There are a variety of scientific, technological, business, and even personal matters for writers to write about. Pioneer is on its way beyond the super-distant planet Pluto to probe the vast reaches of the galaxy; no one really knows how far it may go, how long it will send back information, or what—or *whom*—Pioneer may encounter out there.

Landsat is collecting and recording data about earth itself that farmers, geologists, and scientists can use. Weather reconnaissance satellites are making weather forecasts more reliable and reporting hurricanes' and typhoons' every movement. Defense satellites are—well, only Defense knows and Defense does not want to tell, although some sources are willing and eager to leak information to the press.

Space flight has brought about progress in many branches of science. There are also news and feature articles to be written about projects that have taken a back seat to budget cuts—stories about what experts think is being lost or gained or postponed.

FINDING YOUR CORNER OF THE FIELD

Many editors underestimate the popularity of space and space flight stories among their readers, listeners, and viewers. This reduces your competition, as a freelancer, against the salaried staffers; the field is a little more open, though you'll have to sell your work harder or smarter—or both. Among the evidence to support your case, you may wish to point out that, in reading about space flights, huge numbers of science fiction buffs have the jump on readers of other kinds of literature—thanks to Arthur Clarke, Robert Heinlein, Ray Bradbury, Isaac Asimov, and other writers—and are eager for hard news of space exploration.

Explainers, too, are popular with the public, from astonomer Carl Sagan to that darling of would-be space colonists, Gerald O'Neill of "The High Frontier." And it was the attraction of a special televison series on science that kept the venerable Walter Cronkite from full retirement.

Among essayists and commentators who've brought their interests in space flight to fruition have been Tom Wolfe (*The Right Stuff*) and Norman Mailer (*Of a Fire on the Moon*). Many other fine writers less known to the general reading public include James Oberg (*Red Star in Orbit*, about Soviet space endeavors) and Bill Shelton (*Stowaway to the Moon*). And still other knowledgeable space writers, hardly known outside their special audiences or their magazine articles, work to expand the frontiers of reader understanding.

Among all this diversity of interests, for all the interests of the millions of readers in this country and abroad, there's room for *you* and *your* special interests in space. As for mine, besides covering the missions and writing astronaut profiles, I'm working on a series of books that will present manned space flight as adventure/history.

Begin getting acquainted now with whatever you don't know, wherever your chief interests lie. Join those of us writing in this intriguing field—one that is expanding almost as fast as the discoveries from the probes, the satellites, and the manned spacecraft flights. Fill some editorial space with *your* writings about outer space.

WRITING ABOUT HOME ELECTRONICS
by Ivan B. Berger

I didn't start out to be a specialist writer; I didn't start out to be a writer at all. It happened largely because I'd accidentally gotten the right education for it.

I wrote poetry in elementary and high school, but that doesn't count. I started college as a physics major; I didn't become an English major till my second calculus course. That combination gave me a good background for what I do now, which requires a mixture of technical and literary sensibilities.

It also left me the problem of how to squeeze a career out of my major. I considered teaching (which I've never yet tried) and writing ad copy (which took me five years to get into and about five more to leave). And I got interested in high fidelity.

The trouble was that I couldn't fully understand the hi-fi catalogs, nor could I find a book that properly explained them. I thought perhaps I'd write that book, someday (I haven't yet), and started taking notes on it. Meanwhile, I left school, got a job, and my notetaking slowed to a crawl.

About a year after I left college, a friend spotted an ad in *Saturday Review:* "NEEDED. For national magazine. Someone who knows high fidelity from consoles to components. Write Box xxx . . . " I applied, pointing out that I knew both home and broadcast consoles (courtesy of my college radio station, WYBC), and that I also knew the sound of live music well from ushering in my college concert hall. I took my application letter through eight drafts on paper, and many more in my head. A month or so later, I was asked to write my first article, for *Saturday Review.* I wrote for them for sixteen years.

Shortly thereafter, I met Larry Klein, then an editor at *Electronics Illustrated.* I wrote an article for him at *EI.* When he moved to *Hi-Fi Stereo Review,* I wrote one for him there, too. (I wrote for *that* magazine for eighteen years, till I joined the staff of its competitor, *Audio*.) Other opportunities gradually came my way, in part because I introduced myself to every editor I met. By the time I'd been writing for a year, I had enough in print to allow myself the treat of looking up my works in the *Readers' Guide to Periodical Literature*.

Somewhere in the middle, I finally got a chance to write ad copy for a hi-fi account. The good part of advertising, I found, was being paid well to write well. The bad part was having to write only what a lot of other people, some of them very insecure about it, told me to. I kept writing articles on the side about hi-fi and my other hobby, photography.

In the sixties, writing about high-tech hobbies like these meant limited markets, but at least there was little competition. At one time, I was contributing to all three major hi-fi magazines at once, using a different name in each—the editors all knew what I was doing, but wanted their readers to think I was theirs exclusively.

Only specialized magazines like these and magazines with a strong music angle (like *Saturday Review*) ran articles on audio. High fidelity still had limited appeal to the man on the street—and an even more limited appeal to editors, who tend to be more artistically than technically inclined. Nonetheless, I made a few good sales, including reprints in some major newspapers, and regular contributions to *Esquire*.

By the mid-sixties, I had written perhaps a quarter million words (including ad copy) and had been published in more than forty periodicals, mostly U.S. but some abroad (including one in Flemish). And because of recessionary belt-tightening at my ad agency, I was out of a job.

Learning from My Mistakes

For two years, I simultaneously looked for a new job and supported myself through freelance ad and article writing. I did miserably, because of three mistakes.

One was to waste too much time looking for a job. Freelancing—if you're going to make a good living—is a very full-time occupation; in a recession, it gets even harder because it takes more time to find work. Lose a few hours a day on job interviews and waiting for them, and you can easily wind up having to work all night, never sleeping.

My second mistake was to let ad agencies waste too much of my time. Ad people love to call meetings—the larger the merrier (although the more people present, the less gets done). They love to have freelancers sit in to swell the ranks. But the ad people are being paid for that time. Freelancers aren't—unless they specifically charge for it, and say so in advance. I eventually learned to limit meetings in advance to an hour or two per job, and charge portal-to-portal time (like a plumber) for meetings beyond the minimum. This doesn't so much earn me more as save me time.

I also learned to probe for the real deadlines when I got an agency assignment. Agencies love phony deadlines—a two-day rush for you to do it, three weeks for them to look it over before giving it back to you to revise. If you're free the next few days, then do it. But if not, don't panic and take the job instead of sleep; instead, state from the outset you can't make their deadline. Better than half the time (especially if they know your work), they'll give you a new deadline you can live with. Other times, they'll probably ask you to recommend someone else to handle the job. Do it; if you're good, they'll call you first next time (if you're too busy to work for them, you must be good, right?). But try not to recommend someone who's phenomenally better!

My third mistake was not to watch my receivables closely enough. I got dependent on one agency client who practically monopolized my work, then hung me up for several thousand dollars over several months. I remember one week when I earned eight hundred dollars (probably to be paid in 90 days) while trying to get through the week on just ten dollars cash.

Eventually, I got a staff job with another of my agency clients, then left when I got a chance to be an editor at *Popular Mechanics*. I worked there for five years as electronics and photography editor, then left to become senior editor at *Popular Electronics*.

That job lasted two years. Then I took a temporary job as an ad copywriter again, under an account executive renowned for being hard to work with. After two weeks of him, I calculated how much it would cost me to quit and write freelance articles (about $10,000 per year), and decided that it would be worth it. I gave six weeks' notice, though: the money was too good to drop before I'd built up a little backlog, and good enough that if I'd stayed longer I might have gotten hooked.

This was possible only because the market for my specialty had changed. Home electronics was booming. Editors now had two reasons to cover it—their readers were interested, and there were advertisers out there with big money to spend in magazines whose coverage seemed to prove that their readers cared. Magazines that had not done so now covered electronics seriously.

I missed the boat on some of these by not being persuasive or persistent enough. For example, I queried *Playboy* five or six times over the years when they barely touched hi-fi, then gave up just about the time they decided it was worth their while. That's one of the dangers of a specialty—sometimes you can see what's going to be hot before your markets can. So don't give up too soon.

Had I written better query letters, I might have convinced them it was worth their while sooner. While I've written advertising, I hate advertising myself; that keeps me from writing query letters or answers to personnel ads as well as I write articles. I've almost never gotten into a new magazine by cold-canvassing it.

Occasionally, I sell to a new market because I've met an editor somewhere. As I become better known in my specialties, I am often recommended to editors who seek articles in my field—which makes me even more well known. Being a specialist gets me many such recommendations—but none, of course, for articles outside my specialties.

Those specialties keep changing with the times, too. As the home electronics market broadened to include video and home computers, I began writing about them. This proved a lifesaver. The big boom in audio has slowed, and few but the specialist magazines now cover it. Video and computers are fresh and exciting, though, and editors want articles about them—even when they don't expect ad dollars to ensue. If my only specialty were audio, I'd have starved as a freelancer.

The new excitement in electronics has one side effect. Now that there's real money to be made, and the possibility of more general exposure, the topic attracts better writers. It's no longer enough to be technically accurate, or even accurate and lucid; today, you must be interesting, too.

The field will probably continue growing and changing, at least for the next two or three decades. Electronics will be integral to all our lives until something's developed to replace it. So all readers will need guidance on what the new gadgets will do for them and how to buy them; many readers will want to learn how the new developments work.

SURVIVING AS A SPECIALIST

Specializing narrows your competition, and narrows but focuses your opportunities. As a specialist, you may spend less time writing for high-paying general publications than for specialty publications that pay less but buy more.

You'll also be able to use your time efficiently. Once you have researched a topic for one article, you're prepared to write on that topic again. Once you've researched a dozen on that topic, you're all set to go on writing about it, with deepening insight, for years—provided you can wring more than one idea from it.

For example, suppose you want to write about what's new in TV sets. As it stands, that could interest *TV Guide*, *Popular Science*, and *Video*, to name three obvious possibilities. (Beware of the obvious: all three have regular contributors or staffers who'd be likely to cover that.) Concentrate on how the new sets' features enhance cable viewing, and you have a piece for magazines that go to cable viewers. Build the story around the direct picture inputs found on more and more such sets, and you have a piece for the computer magazines on "How the New TV Sets Double as Computer Displays." (With a trade angle, you could sell that to the computer retail magazines, too. For example, how a retailer sold a carload of new sets with a 72-hour Sale-a-Thon.) For *Money* or *Changing Times*, try "The New TV Sets—Worth Trading in Your Old Ones For?" or "How to Buy the Best in This Year's New TVs"—and so on.

You have to be imaginative in thinking up new angles. While I was writing this article, I got four requests for articles on the importance of computer software. If I couldn't give each one a different slant and feel, I'd quickly get a reputation for self-plagiarism.

Specialization helps, here, by letting you see the different possibilities in a general topic. You also have a head start on the generalist assigned to the same topic, because you get to know who's who and what's what, which can cut your research time immensely. (The generalist, however, may bring a fresher—if sometimes naive—viewpoint to the subject.)

If you specialize, keep as much information as you can on tap. Libraries are invaluable, because they give you background in depth. But the information in books is inevitably a little stale, at least for a fast-moving subject. So I also keep extensive files. As I read articles on topics I may later write on, I clip and file them.

This takes more time than simply filing the magazines they came from. But it also takes less space—and lets you spend your time filing when things are slow, not searching frantically for something when you're right on deadline. People with better visual memories tend to keep their magazines intact, remembering that the piece they want was in a given magazine, a given year.

Book, PR, and Advertising Markets

In the long run, writing books can pay off better than articles, although that's a gamble—the books may not sell. In the short run, articles pay better than books. I've tended to overemphasize the article side, and have only two books (one co-authored) to my credit as yet. I know other writers in my field who make far more than I by writing books, living on continued royalties from prior books while writing the next. Getting the time to write those prior books has been my problem.

Your specialized knowledge can also pay off in PR and advertising markets. Unless you have a real flair (and, preferably, some experience at advertising copy), you may not get much opportunity to write actual advertisements. But ad agencies frequently farm out catalogs and brochures that their in-house writers may lack both the knowledge and humility to handle. PR agencies frequently need help, too, either because a given product takes more technical knowledge than their in-house writers have, or because a client is introducing so many new products at once that there aren't enough people in the agency to write it all. Manufacturers sometimes need writing, too, such as instruction books and sales training manuals. I've written all of the above, not to mention technical papers and speeches.

Specialization also leads to full-time job opportunities, as well as giving you something to fall back (or even forward) on when jobs end. Most of the freelancers in my field either have been or will be editors, just as I've been both.

Bear this in mind, as well as the fact that writers who share a specialty also tend to share one another's company a lot. That makes it easier to get on one another's nerves—and it's important that you don't. Sooner or later, either you or your colleagues will be editors to whom you'll have to sell, or you'll be an editor trying to get articles from them. Either way, being on good terms helps both of you.

LABORING IN THE VINEYARDS OF TECHNOLOGY
by David A. Anderton

I woke on my birthday, a May Monday, and knew that I did not want to ride the damned bus into New York one more time. By the time I arrived at the office, I had decided. My doctor examined me on Tuesday; Thursday I got the favorable results, and Friday I walked into my editor's office and quit. I had nothing in mind, no clients waiting, no client to take with me. Further, I had a wife, two sons—one about to enter college—and a house in Ridgewood, New Jersey, which was not exactly a low-cost district. But I had a rebuilt 1919 model Remington Noiseless typewriter and unshakable confidence that I was a better writer about aeronautical subjects than anybody else in the United States, if not the world.

To give substance to that claim, I had graduated from college with a degree in aeronautical engineering and, as a designer of aircraft and missiles for two top aerospace companies, had risen to project engineer. I had written about aviation for more than twenty years, first infrequently as a freelancer, and then full-time on McGraw-Hill's *Aviation Week & Space Technology* (*AW&ST*). During the years with *AW&ST*, I produced probably two million words of copy. It was copy that had to be written against the pressures of two deadlines each week; it dealt almost exclusively with complex technical subjects, written in language that top executives could understand; and it had to be accurate. That job had been my journalism school, my writers' workshops, my personal teacher. I had learned to write fast and accurately. And that's what I had when I determined to make it on my own.

Since 1963, I have been a full-time freelance writer and photographer specializing in the broad reaches of aerospace technology. My rates, and my total income, have climbed continually. I enjoy the luxury of being able to refuse work, and to choose the best of two or more offered assignments. I work at home, in a separate office wing, and I lunch with my wife, listen to my jazz records, look out the window at the green lawn and growing garden, and in general enjoy life a lot more than if I were still commuting to the big green building on Forty-second Street.

Paying My Dues

But it was not always so good. From May through December that first year, I grossed $700. That was 1963, a year in which $700 was definitely below the poverty level. My first son was accepted into college in 1964. Ridgewood had not lowered its taxes. It was time to look at what I was doing wrong. So I did what I should have done before leaving McGraw-Hill (although if I *had* done it then, I might not have left, and I'd be dead now instead of healthy, wealthy, and wise).

I made a market survey. I discovered it was useless to try to survive by writing about aviation for magazines, because airplane magazines—not to put too fine a point on it—were, and remain, cheap. Aviation is full of egotists (you noticed?) who are so sublimely happy to get a prominent byline that they will trade that sacred symbol for a hundred dollars. Further, aviation is full of twenty-five-year-old writers who recreate fifty-year-old events as if they had been there, vigorously rewriting all the clippings they can collect on Lindbergh's flight, or on a balloon ascension at an 1890 country fair. They all have other jobs, live at home, and use their article earnings to buy parts for another radio-controlled model, or another hour or so of flight time in a Cessna 152. Fine, and good for them. But not good for me.

I then made a careful study of earned income for 1963. That $700 had come from one source: the Curtiss-Wright Corporation, whose public relations director was a sympathetic guy who knew when a writer needed a job. For him, I prepared a series of background press releases (for the trade) on the fabrication of thin-walled steel casings for huge solid-propellant rocket motors. I also wrote a general press release and a detailed technical memo on the construction. It all required a single visit to the C-W plant about ten miles from my home, and two or three days of writing. My fee was promptly paid, and the releases and the backgrounders were used and widely reprinted—verbatim, in some cases, under another writer's byline, which gives you a clue about ethics in aviation writing. [Editor's note: Similar ethics prevail in some other fields.]

Getting Smart

Hole E. Cow, I thought, *there* is the way to make money. There must be other corporations that need this sort of thing. What I did well—what I had been doing for thirteen years on *AW&ST*—was to explain complex subjects in simpler language tailored for a specific audience. I wrote about steel rocket motor casings, or active radar guidance, or turbojet combustion, or the aerodynamics of a supersonic transport, and I explained them so that people understood them.

And that—writing about the complexities of aeronautical research and technology—is what I have been doing for the better part of the past two decades.

But I write infrequently for magazines, and the aviation books I do are labors of love, because I am an airplane nut. I write professionally for business and government, and this anecdote explains exactly why. The late, legendary Willy Sutton once was asked by an interviewer why he concentrated his considerable talents only on robbing banks. Willy gave the reporter a look reserved for the abysmally dumb. "Because," explained Willy carefully, "that's where the money is."

I write for corporations and the United States Government, because that's where the money is. Further, that's where there is minimum annoyance. The clients know what they want, and often have prepared a definitive and comprehensive work statement. They pay on time, and well. They honor deals made with executives who have been promoted, demoted, resigned, or retired since your original contacts with them.

I have heard and read countless gripes by writers against publications and editors, ranging from delayed payment through questionable ethics to downright dishonesty. I have yet to hear similar complaints against either industry or government. If you *had* to find some example, you probably could. I can think of one government agency, whose initials are NASA, that could speed its paperwork.

They want your work yesterday, but are unwilling to be invoiced before tomorrow.

I've had a couple of experiences when the material I wrote was never used. It wasn't my fault, happily; the requirements had changed. If my client had been one of the better magazines, I would have received a "kill" fee, a portion of the original agreed-upon price as a sop for the work done. In both cases, my invoice was paid in full. Businesspeople know when business has been done.

A Variety of Assignments

Over the years I've written advertising copy, brochures, direct-mail sales letters, educational booklets, passenger comfort and safety literature for business aircraft, speeches for managers and executives, corporate histories, a guide to a museum, newsletters, exhibit scripts, sales literature, marketing promotion, research memorandums, and probably some other things I can't think of right now. That list may impress you, but its real purpose is to indicate the wealth of varied assignments available in industry and government if you work seriously at the job—by making personal contacts, by sending letters and queries to companies, by using the phone.

Some of my most exciting assignments have come from the National Aeronautics and Space Administration. By the law that established NASA, the agency is required to make a major effort in public education. That means publications and that, in turn, means assignments. For NASA, I've written educational publications on both the Apollo 11 and Apollo 17 lunar exploration voyages—the first and the last of those milestone missions. I've also written most of the recent publications on aeronautical research and technology, including a fifty- and an updated, sixty-year research history of the first NASA aeronautical laboratory, the Langley Research Center. In the course of NASA work, I have traveled to research centers all over the United States, watched an Apollo launch, sat in Mission Control, and spent fascinating hours interviewing the top scientists and engineers associated with developments in aerospace technology.

A very special side benefit is that I continually update my knowledge by such visits; the information I get goes directly into publications, but also adds to my memory bank and comes in handy time after time in other assignments.

Recently, I had the assignment of a lifetime for an aviation enthusiast: write a new guide for the National Air and Space Museum (NASM). I love that museum; I can spend hours there, looking at the exhibits, studying the history of flight. But with that assignment not only could I go and visit the exhibits, I was *paid* to go and visit the exhibits.

NASA had to cut back its publication program when the Reagan Administration came to Washington, and I felt that maybe writing about aeronautical research and technology was going to become a lost art. While I was trying to plan what else to do in order to take up the slack in my schedule and finances, I was asked to write by a designer of museum exhibits. The reference had come from the NASM, for which I was grateful, and it brought me into an entirely new sphere of work that I never had dreamed existed.

Industrial and museum exhibits are developed by specialist companies; I don't suppose there are too many of them. But almost every exhibit requires some words to go along with it. If not labels or text, those words will be in an outline or a detailed script describing the exhibit and its theme and its development, so that the designers have guidelines to follow. With no past experience whatsoever, I became a writer of museum exhibit scripts.

TWENTY-ONE TIPS FOR SUCCESS

Relating my own experiences and excitements is of little value unless you can draw some useful conclusions from them. Here are some I've put together that combine conclusions with advice and experience.

1. To deal with business and government, act like a businessperson. Get a conservative letterhead; leave off the rainbows and smiling faces. Bill promptly—either at the completion of the work or on the first of the month. Don't be afraid to send a 30-day reminder if you haven't been paid by the end of the month.

2. Industry and government like fixed-price bids for work, and they'll want the same from you. That's tough, because a lot of the work they want is open-ended. Early in your relationship, establish what you furnish: a first draft, or a draft with one rewrite, for a fixed sum. State on your bid that work above that level will require additional compensation at the rate of $X per hour or day. After you have worked for a company for a while, and you have an easy and fairly informal working relationship, you can probably change to quoting daily or hourly rates, and they'll go along with it. "They" is industry, and only some of industry at that. Government won't.

3. Try to arrange a retainer with one or more clients, guaranteeing them time in return for a guaranteed monthly amount. Retainers are a solid foundation for a freelance life, and they certainly ease the perennial cash flow problems.

4. Remember that the customer is buying your experience as well as your service. Both are worth money. Whenever I encounter resistance to my rates, I tell a story I read somewhere about a power company with a rough-running turbine. They called in a specialist in turbines, who looked, listened, and then took a small leather mallet from his tool case and tapped the main bearing twice. The noise and vibration stopped. When his bill arrived, it was for $1,000, and the company was outraged. An explanation and a detailed breakdown were demanded. By return mail, the invoice came back: "For hitting turbine bearing twice with mallet, $10. For knowing where to hit, $990." It works every time.

5. If anybody complains about the rates you charge and compares them to what public relations personnel earn, remind him or her that they do not have to contribute to your pension, your medical insurance, your overhead, the cost of your typewriter, desk, office space, heat, light, paper, etc. They'll get the point.

6. Expect to lose some. I once wrote four drafts of a proposed corporate brochure during a period of several months (I wasn't that slow; the president of the company was always away and was the slowest reviewer I've ever encountered). At the end, the president said, "I don't think you quite grasp the points I'm trying to make." And that was that. Sequel: apparently nobody else did, either. I was not the first—or the last—writer to work with that president on that project. It has yet to see the light of day.

7. Never write a speech for an executive who will not spend time with you. It will be a lousy speech, it will be drafted and redrafted many times, and nobody will be happy with the final result.

8. Remember that every manager knows he or she can write better than you, and would, if he or she could only find the time. So allow the manager to make changes in your copy, to insert prized phrases and paragraphs, and to insist on the current buzz words. Then thank him or her for the contributions, and subtly, gently, and carefully excise them as much as possible. There are degrees to which this can be done, and you have to develop a sense, through experience, of how far you can train these managers, most of whom are atrocious writers who communicate in a jargon known only to themselves and God.

9. Expect the last-minute high-pressure assignment. "The boss just told me he has to have a speech by tomorrow night for the annual convention of the Outer Hebrides Wool-Gatherers and Weavers. Ya

gotta help me!" And there you are in the driver's seat. If you know that the crisis is real, and the crunch has arrived, quote your most outrageous price. Double, even triple, your going rate. That lends seriousness to the crisis, and it also ensures that they may not bother you again with this kind of nonsense. The boss has known for six months he had to give that speech, and his public relations people never got around to writing it, that's all. They'll find the money. By the way, quote double-time for weekends and holiday work. The unions get it, and you should too.

10. Be prepared for the Great Change in Plans. This is a last-minute executive whim that effectively throws out everything you've done to that point, and completely redirects the work. Start over, trying to smile, but don't throw away what you've already completed. Nine times out of ten, the plans will change several times more and end up fairly close to the original.

11. Every company has at least one person whose life story would make a fascinating book, and he or she will tell you so as soon as it is known that you are a writer-in-temporary-residence. Avoid those people like the plague; their lives are of interest to themselves, perhaps to three other people, but not to any larger audience. I know one professional writer who is embroiled in writing a two-volume biography of an aging pilot simply because he never learned how to refuse.

12. If you're an exceptionally fast writer, never tell the customer. Don't overdo it in the other direction, either. But estimate the time that you think a job will take and add a cushion for corporate or government indecision, review procedures, and unforeseen delays.

13. Don't bluff. Your customer will know more about the subject than you do, regardless of how smart you are and how long you have been writing about it. If you are asked for work that you feel uncomfortable with, say so up front and avoid a lot of trouble later.

14. Keep educating yourself in the technology you're working in. Subscribe to the magazines, talk to people, use your time at the company and the government agency to search out their current publications in your field of interest, and articles written about the companies or the executives.

15. Look for the internal spinoff opportunity. A speech for a top executive to be presented to a relatively small audience might be the basis for an excellent article ghosted under the executive's name for

one of the trade publications. Or suggest that it be edited—by you, of course—for wider distribution throughout the company by newsletter, company newspaper, or direct mailings.

16. Submerge—nay, drown—your ego. Most of what you write will be credited to somebody else, especially if it is a brilliant piece of work or a speech. You have to decide whether you want a byline or the money. If the former, write for the op-ed pages of your local paper; if the latter, come on along!

17. Freelance working conditions being what they are, we tend to accept every assignment offered, because we never really know if and when the one after that will come along. That leads to a very crowded schedule, and to working your buns off. It's useless advice, and I don't always follow it myself, but try it: turn down some work so there is time to relax.

18. Deliver clean copy, on time. That has to be the first rule for any professional writer, working in any environment. You'd be astonished at the appearance of some manuscripts; I know, because I've been asked to review aeronautical manuscripts.

19. Productivity is what counts. Get the most capable typewriter or word processor you can afford, learn to write rapidly and accurately, and make it run hot. Have a telephone answering service or a machine that will do that chore for you, and use it. Paper, ribbons, lift-off tape, and other supplies are cheap; use them lavishly. You can't save money that way. I have long since relegated my 1919 Remington Noiseless to my private museum of collectibles. It has been replaced by, in rapid sequence, a rented IBM Executive, a purchased IBM Selectric I, an IBM Selectric II, an IBM Model 75, a Qyx/Exxon Level 4-D Intelligent Typewriter and, even as I write, an order for an Exxon 510 word processor. The last three machines have been bought about one year apart. Productivity begets prosperity.

20. Develop your own rules. Mine work for me; you need a set to work for you. If some of these can help, I'm delighted.

21. I thought it might go without saying, but I'd better say it anyway. You have to have some specialty, and you need some expertise in that specialty. You've read how I acquired mine, and all the unemployed engineers and scientists reading this are excellent candidates for a similar experience. It is far easier for an engineer to learn to write, and in plain English, than it is for a writer to learn engineering and write computer programs.

I want to exit with a simple lesson, but an especially valuable one for those who want to labor in the vineyards of technology. When I first joined the staff of *Aviation Week*, I was assigned some subjects that included reports on technology issued by the National Advisory Committee for Aeronautics, NASA's predecessor agency. While trying to translate one report from Engineerspeak into English, I received the first, and only, lesson I ever had in writing. My mentor was Irving Stone, senior editor on the magazine staff and a beloved friend. He escorted me to a window that overlooked Forty-second Street. Twenty-one stories down, we could see a man standing on the corner of Forty-second and Eighth Avenue, reading one of the tabloid dailies. "Write it for him," Irv said. Four words; the distilled philosophy of Irv's lifetime of expository writing. It was the best advice I ever received. And since then, I've been trying to write for the guy on the corner who reads the tabloid. If I can explain the wake vortex phenomenon to him, or show him why it's important to add winglets to big wings, or to droop the leading edges of a training aircraft, I've reached my goal.

And besides all that satisfaction, I've been able to hang around airplanes and the marvelous people who design and build and test them, and I've been paid well to do all that. Harold Robbins never had it better.

Additional Resources

Aviation/Space Writers Association, Cliffwood Rd., Chester, NJ 07930. Gives annual awards for writing, public relations, public affairs officers, company communications, visual communications, and helicopter heroism. Publications include a newsletter, a *Manual*, and two books.

Aerospace Industries Association of America, 1725 De Sales St. NW, Washington, DC 20036. Maintains statistical, historical and other information relative to the industry. Offers aid in arranging interviews, statistics, brochures and pamphlets, placement on mailing list, newsletter. Publications include an annual report and *Aerospace* (quarterly).

American Association for the Advancement of Science, 1776 Massachusetts Ave. NW, Washington, DC 20036. Offers statistics, brochures, pamphlets, placement on mailing list, and frequent press releases. Publications include *Science*, a magazine free to members or available by subscription.

American Institute of Physics, 335 E. 45th St., New York, NY 10017. Offers aid in arranging interviews, annual reports, brochures and pamphlets, computerized information searches, library facilities, photos, placement on mailing lists, press kits, research assistance, statistics. Runs newsrooms and news conferences for scientific meetings; administers science writing awards. Publications include primary physics journals, press releases, radio and TV reports, annual booklet *Physics News in 19--*.

American National Metric Council, 5410 Grosvenor Lane, Bethesda, MD 20814. Answers questions and provides information on metric issues. Publications include monthly newsletter on metric usage in various industries, editorial guide for correct use of metric measurements, history of measurement in U.S., consumer guides.

Council for the Advancement of Science Writing, 618 N. Elmwood, Oak Park, IL 60302. Holds annual briefings on new horizons in science. Has established training programs in science, medical reporting for journalists, and a program to place experienced writers in residency at scientific facilities. Presents Nate Hazeltine Fellowships in Science Writing. Publishes *A Guide to Careers in Science Writing*.

Engineering Index, 345 E. 47th St., New York, NY 10017. International publisher of multidisciplinary engineering information, covering agriculture and engineering, food technology, technical data. Offers bibliographies, brochures, newsletter.

Electronic Industries Association, 2001 Eye St. NW, Washington, DC 20006. Provides consumer education and career guidance. Offers annual reports, biographies, brochures and pamphlets, photos, press kits, and statistics. Publications index available, free on request. Publications include *Trade Directory and Membership List, Audio Industry Consumer Study, Market Data Book*, various standards and regulations.

ERK Clearinghouse on Science, Mathematics, and Environmental Education, 1200 Chambers Rd., 3rd Floor, Columbus, OH 43212. Offers information searches and packets, publications list, consultant services, bulletins, newsletters.

Library of Congress, Science and Technology Division, 10 First St. SE, Washington, DC 20540. Offers brochures and pamphlets, computerized information searches, library facilities (3 million books, 60,000 journals, 3 million technical reports), telephone reference services. Publications include *LC Science Tracer Bullets,* an informal series of literature guides designed to help a reader locate published materials.

National Academy of Sciences, 2101 Constitution Ave. NW, Washington, DC 20418. Private membership group which helps arrange interviews; provides annual reports to members of the working press (including freelance writers with assignments).

National Association of Science Writers, P.O. Box 294, Greenlawn, NY 11740. Writers and editors engaged in the preparation and interpretation of science news for the public. Presents awards; sponsors competitions. Publishes *Guide to Careers in Science Writing, Handbook for Press Arrangements at Scientific Meetings,* and a newsletter.

National Bureau of Standards, Department of Commerce, Washington, DC 20234. Provides analytical and technical information covering health/medicine (related to physical and measurement standards), industry, product information, science, and technical data. Offers aid in arranging interviews, annual reports, bibliographies, biographies, brochures and pamphlets, information searches, placement on mailing list, photos, and press kits. *NBS List of Publications* describes the bureau's periodicals, NBS interagency reports, publications catalogs, and other items.

National Geographic Society, 17th and M St. NW, Washington, DC 20036. Offers information searches, photos, press kits. Publications available.

National Science Foundation, 1800 G St. NW, Washington, DC 20550. Offers aid in arranging interviews, annual reports, bibliographies, statistics, brochures and pamphlets, placement on mailing list, newsletter, press kits. Publications available.

National Technical Information Service, 5285 Port Royal Rd., Springfield, VA 22181. Provides information about technological innovations; helps locate reports via on-line computer search service. Abstracts new research reports in twenty-six different newsletters. Information (some available on magnetic tape) covers science, technology, social sciences, administration, and more.

Scientists' Institute for Public Information, Media Resource Service, 355 Lexington Ave., New York, NY 10017. Offers aid in arranging interviews, informational newsletters, placement on mailing lists. Publications include *SIPIscope* (bimonthly newsletter).

Society for the Encouragement of Research and Invention, 100 Summit Ave., Box 412, Summit, NJ 07901. Provides advisory, how-to, referral, and technical information on any field of science and technology. Offers aid in arranging interviews, brochures and pamphlets, informational newsletter, library facilities. Publications include quarterly bulletin.

Chapter Eight

WRITING ABOUT THE ENVIRONMENT AND ENERGY

John Muir has been credited with the statement that one tug at a single thing in nature finds it attached to everything else in the world. Unless you've been living on Mars, you know that, for more than a century, the tugging and tampering with the natural system has accelerated alarmingly.

Noel Brown, United Nations Environment Program director in New York, said recently, "The earth's resources are being destroyed at a terrifying rate and the human race must do something about it. We must make people concerned not only with conservation, but with the future of the planet."

Energy and environment are closely and controversially related; they're really two sides of the same coin. Environment is the natural state—fast disappearing—and energy is one of the prime reasons we exploit the environment. The critical function and concern of freelance writers in the field is to ensure that the reading public is provided with factual information. They must not only sound the alarm, as Michael Frome did in his excellent book *Battle for the Wilderness*, but report environmental and ecological triumphs. Perhaps most important, they should provide ideas for effective action through the media, political channels, and local organizing.

Man is an important figure in ecology. He may be only one species among the million and a half inhabiting this planet, but he is a most dangerous one, daily upsetting delicate relationships that took millions of years to develop and which he doesn't really understand. One ecologist said, "Nature is not more complicated than we think—it is more complicated than we *can* think."

Yet, in spite of such pessimism, or awe at the supreme mystery of being, the goal of those who would write in this field is to help us understand that the spaceship earth, with its limited supply of land, water, air, and food, and its fragile natural balances, must support the six billion persons expected to live within its closed system in the year 2000. Writers must necessarily report on every aspect of this universal problem for environmental and energy markets.

In this chapter, three of the country's outstanding environmental writers present their views about freelancing in this specialized field—chronicling editorial potholes as well as opportunities. Each has a reputation for balanced reporting, for fully and fairly representing what he has learned in an industry where objectivity often takes a back seat to pretension and self-interest, of the personal or institutional variety.

Would-be and present freelancers will profit themselves—and the rest of us—by contemplating what they have to say.

ABC'S OF WRITING ABOUT NATURE AND THE OUTDOORS
by Edward R. Ricciuti

Gracefully, the slim Oriental woman bent down and scratched the large leopard's belly. She had other pets, too: a Great Dane padded about, its heavy collar studded with spikes, and across the room, coiled on a cushion, was a big python that was perhaps eighteen feet long.

I was in the headquarters of an international animal dealer based in Bangkok, Thailand. My hostess was reputed to be a major trafficker in wildlife—including endangered species in which trade is prohibited. Her hair hung below her waist, and she wore a high-necked black dress slit to the thigh. No wonder United States Customs agents working on animal smuggling cases called her the "Dragon Lady," after the comic strip character from "Terry and Pirates."

I hoped she would not divine my real purpose for visiting her backstreet compound. I was not, as I claimed, really a buyer of rare birds, but investigating animal smuggling for *Audubon* magazine. If I were discovered, I suspected—the suspicion was later supported by people who knew the lady—I would be in serious trouble, perhaps the worst kind.

Since 1971, when I started out as a full-time freelance writer, I have covered many stories similar to the one described above. I've had plenty of excitement in various corners of the world, if not as much financial reward as I might have wished (although I've been able to support a wife and three children). While I can and do write about other topics, I specialize in nature, conservation, and outdoor sports such as hunting, fishing, and diving.

A LIFELONG LOVE

As a child I had an abiding interest in nature and wildlife. I kept a journal of wildlife observations and maintained a small home zoo of frogs, turtles, and similar critters. I read all I could find on natural history while still in elementary grades, so my background in the subject goes back pretty far. And the habit of keeping nature notes has served me well as a freelancer.

My childhood interest in natural history gradually broadened to include other areas of science, although wildlife continued to hold the most excitement. But as a communications major at the University of Notre Dame, I thought of science as nothing more than an avocation. After graduation I joined the staff of a New Jersey newspaper and worked as a general-assignment reporter eventually covering courts, crime, and investigative stories.

One of these concerned foreign "drug pirates" who stole antibiotic cultures from American pharmaceutical companies, hoping to reproduce them. To cover the long-running story, I had to learn about the science and technology of antibiotic production. This opened up more science stories for me. Then the newspaper enrolled me in an on-the-job training program for new science writers sponsored by the Council for the Advancement of Science Writing.

Further Education

After two years' trying, I was accepted as a Sloan-Rockefeller Advanced Science Writing Fellow at Columbia University. This full fellowship enabled me to study various sciences for a year and equipped me as a specialist. While a Fellow, I also worked part-time in the American Museum of Natural History public relations department. After completing the fellowship, I landed a job as associate editor at *Science World*, a magazine for high school students published by Scholastic Magazines. While at *Science World*—a job that involved writing and editing—I attempted my first freelance writing. Many major magazines—more than I care to remember—rejected my ideas, but I was able to sell articles to drugstore trade magazines for a few cents a word.

I left *Science World* after two years to become a curator at the New York Zoological Society, which operated the Bronx Zoo, New York Aquarium, Osborn Laboratories of Marine Sciences, a research station in Trinidad, and conservation and research programs in countries around the world. My responsibilities included editing and publishing the Society's popular magazine, *Animal Kingdom*, plus all other publications, popular and scientific. My office also handled public relations and advertising, the library, photographic services, and community relations.

As a curator of the Society I gained broad exposure to the natural world on field trips and expeditions. I traveled to such places as the Everglades and Okefenokee Swamp, helped transport whales from Hudson Bay to the aquarium, tagged sharks, and dived for laboratory specimens.

The experiences I underwent in my Society position enabled me to freelance more extensively on a part-time basis. My old employer, *Science World*, gave me many assignments, and several newspaper syndicates purchased my articles. Still, I could not crack the major magazines.

A Little Help from My Friends

A break came when a former *Science World* colleague became an editor at Harper and Row. She encouraged me to write a children's book based on the whale-catching expedition to Hudson Bay. This book described capturing belugas, or white whales, and was well received; it is still selling today. Once the whale book was completed I began another, describing through a simple story why most wild animals do not make good pets.

Meanwhile, I had decided to try full-time freelancing. For a year I prepared, saving vacation time, and lining up book and magazine assignments. I resigned as curator when I felt I had enough resources and assignments to last a year, by the end of which I figured I'd know my prospects over the long haul.

Again, my connections helped. Part of my job at the Society was to promote conservation by appearing on various radio and television programs. I had been appearing as an animal handler on a television program, "Patchwork Family." Hearing that I was leaving the Society, the show's producer asked me to continue as a cast member on about four programs a month. This provided a regular, though unimpressive, income. The Society also took me on as a consultant for three months, which worked out as a day or two a week and guaranteed more income.

But I still hadn't cracked the major magazine markets. Finally, I asked the literary agency that handled my books to help me with magazines. I wrote a query based on observations I had made in Puerto Rico of the nearly extinct Puerto Rican parrot; my agent sold it to *Audubon*. On my own, I lacked the confidence to approach *Audubon*— or any other major market—and was astonished when my query was accepted. (There is a lesson here: don't be afraid to try the big ones.) It made me feel for the first time like a truly professional freelancer and added immeasurably to my track record.

EXPERIENCE PAYS OFF

Audubon liked my article and gave me more assignments. Gradually, I began to sell to other magazines, such as *National Wildlife*. The wildlife and conservation expertise I had gained at the Society was immensely helpful—but then, so were the boyhood and subsequent years of nature reading.

My first adult book, *Killers of the Seas* (Walker and Company), was based largely on experiences I'd had while a curator—diving with whales, catching sharks, and collecting sundry other fishes. While my own experiences provided the foundation for the book, I added information from interviews with marine biologists, historical accounts, and the scientific literature. (The book, by the way, has been translated into Italian, German, and Russian.)

At this point I realized that to fully exploit my chosen field, I needed exposure to wildlife in many parts of the world. I really couldn't afford to go on my own, but I did anyway. The better portion of two book advances paid for trips to Poland, western Europe, and East Africa, but these were the last major travels I have paid for. Since then my magazine and consulting assignments have regularly included travel expenses.

There's More to This Than Money

Not all magazines, however, have the resources to pay for travel. Nor, in fact, do fees for articles involving considerable travel to faraway places always fully compensate for the time expended. But the long-term benefits are great. Assignments to such exotic locales as the Cameroons, Hong Kong, or Peru net not only money, but experience that further builds your expertise and credibility—and that will show in books and articles for years to come.

One way of increasing compensation for jobs requiring substantial travel and research is to spin off other assignments from them. A magazine may send you to Tanzania, for example, to do a story on lions; while there, you may be able to write a piece about ostriches for another magazine. If you do, however, remember that your allegiance and responsibility are first and foremost to the magazine that's picking up the tab. It is unethical—and you'll eventually be caught if you attempt it—to bill the sponsoring publication for expenses incurred while researching a spinoff piece.

As for payment, the most I have received for an article is $6,000. I have written for as low as $25, and for all sums between the two extremes. I consider payment to be only one of the reasons for writing articles: time spent on the piece, quality of the magazine (and whether it may some day pay more), experience from research, and simply whether I am interested in the subject also play a role in my decision to take an assignment. Once accepted, however, it's only sensible that the assignment be done well whatever the fee. Quality builds reputations and sells writers. If your name is on it, the article had better be good.

One Good Thing Leads to Another

As a rule most of my books are based on personal experience or work. I have received no advances or royalties sufficient to undertake books on subjects that require vast amounts of research in unfamiliar territory or do not afford material for spinoff articles. As many other writers do, however, I continue to hope for the will-o'-the-wisp big strike.

Books and solid articles may lead to worthwhile consulting jobs, which in turn provide information and experience for more books and articles. For instance, my writings on marine life resulted in a job for the architect of the new National Aquarium at Baltimore: my assignment was to develop the theme for the aquarium and its exhibits and then to write the exhibit text. Wildlife conservation writing led to a consultancy for the International Union for the Conservation of Nature and Natural Resources, a group based near Geneva, Switzerland, which has considerable interest in conservation of developing lands. I was to help put together a sourcebook in language understandable to bureaucrats, politicians, and other nonbiologists—especially from the Third World—describing the need for genetic diversity. This assignment afforded considerable foreign travel and contact with noted scientists and gave me immensely valuable experience.

I have compiled a checklist for success in this specialty (beyond what's common to all freelancers). They are as follows.

- Be a good investigator—a detective, if you will. A background as a general-assignment and investigative reporter will help in this respect.
- Be able to work under unfamiliar conditions without backup. Typically, you should be able to show up at an airport in a strange country in the middle of the night and, though unable to speak the language, find a hotel and within a day make contacts to help you with your story.
- Appreciate peoples of diverse backgrounds and cultures and get along with them.
- Be street-wise, especially if working on a story that might be sensitive to the government or powerful people of the country you are visiting. On occasion, you may investigate some dicey situations—ivory smuggling, for instance. Always be circumspect and cautious. Anticipate uncomfortable situations. Remember that the rules may be different from back home. (By way of example, I was investigating a South American conservation issue when a prominent and powerful individual with a vested interest in the controversy implied to me that one of his political opponents, who had been traveling to the interior

with me, was smuggling drugs. Charges of drug smuggling in that particular country had landed many Americans in the worst of prisons, where they often waited months or years for trial. Each time I returned to my hotel room, I checked my luggage on the outside chance that someone had planted something illicit there.)

- Understand law-enforcement agents and agencies and be able to work with them. Again, a background as a newspaper journalist helps here.

- Don't panic in scary situations. Coming around the corner of a tent in the dark and suddenly finding yourself nose to nose with a Cape buffalo is potentially disastrous, but by calmly backing away all ends well.

- Be in relatively good shape, with some outdoor skills. Being a certified SCUBA diver, for instance, has given me access to stories that otherwise would have been denied me. Being in shape from workouts at the gym helped me negotiate trails in the thin air of the high Andes within a few hours of arriving there and without need for much acclimation. Knowing some self-defense isn't a bad idea either.

- Have a strong stomach. Food and water are sometimes less than desirable in the back country.

- Your depth of knowledge and accuracy must rival that of the scientist. When you are writing about animal behavior, for instance, your research observations must be as solid as a field biologist's. Your writing must demonstrate a deep understanding of the natural world. Good editors in this field quickly pick out writers who are naive; so do scientists, who are less than ready to help unsophisticated journalists. The greater your attention to nuances, details, and accuracy, the more assistance you will get.

At this stage of the game, I get many article assignments from editors who know me. Or sometimes editors I've worked with for a long time ask me for a list of ideas, then select those they like. On the other hand, each time I approach a new magazine or editor I must sell myself all over again. After selling two pieces to *Outdoor Life*, for example, I still had to write and rewrite a query three times to get approval for my third idea.

Don't Overspecialize

For long-term survival as a freelancer, it's important to continually explore new areas where you can build a reputation. Remember the dinosaurs: they were overspecialized and couldn't cope with a changing environment. The same thing can happen to writers who confine their specialty within bounds that are too narrow.

A few years ago, for instance, I decided to expand into fishing and hunting and other outdoor activities—a natural outgrowth of my nature writings. I have been an avid hunter and fisherman for years and sought to combine my knowledge of these sports with wildlife biology. It was to some extent like starting all over again—first with small markets, then slowly moving on to those that paid more. I got a great boost by joining the Outdoor Writers Association of America, which opened doors to editors and information sources in the outdoor field.

It was important to build a track record as an outdoor sports writer. I wrote short articles on fishing for newspaper syndicates, and got into the pages of *Outdoor Life*—not by writing specifically on hunting or fishing but on nature. I edited a series of how-to-fish books by a small regional publisher, and wrote two of them. Pay was minimal but it added credentials and built recognition. In addition, I wrote reports for a big-game hunters' newsletter.

Slowly, I have added this new subspecialty and expect to become as versatile in outdoor sports writing as in my other subjects. And even as my writing in this new area progresses I have started to explore another avenue—outdoor radio. My first venture was a regular fishing program on a small local station, which taught me the ropes.

If my experience demonstrates anything, it is that unless you can enter the world of the freelance nature and outdoor writer with an unusual splash, you should build slowly, carefully, and purposefully, always looking for new avenues to explore and never getting so comfortable you are left at the curb. You need to carry on a continuing program of self-education, learning more about your subject and keeping abreast of new developments. This was dramatized for me a few years ago when I wrote a brief article on porcupines that mentioned the way the fisher, a big weasel, was said to attack and overturn a porcupine to kill and eat it. I described the technique, which had long been reported in the scientific literature; later I learned from a North Carolina biologist that new observations prove this to be incorrect. Had I checked the most recent scientific literature on porcupines or fishers, I wouldn't have made a mistake for all to read.

Despite the excitement, I still face a problem common to freelance writers—earning enough to live on. There have been good years, but lean ones as well. Books have bombed. Projects that were supposed to be completed and paid for in a year have taken two or three because of glitches out of my control. I haven't earned as a freelancer what I might have with a regular job, but we have survived. And that's important because I truly enjoy my work. Even though at times it can be financially difficult, I'll be happy as long as I can continue in this field.

STAKE YOUR CLAIM TO A PERFECT ASSIGNMENT
by Howard Peacock

This is about how a few elementary lessons in freelance marketing helped me land the Perfect Assignment. Correction—it was *almost* perfect; even a "flawless" Navajo rug contains at least one error or missed stitch. The assignment combined writing about my favorite topics, photographing my favorite scenes and subjects, and working with my favorite kinds of folks. All my expenses were covered and I was paid my top daily rate within two to three weeks after billing my client. What more could a word-wrangler ask?

As it happened, my background helped land this assignment. I grew up three miles from the Spindletop oil field, where in 1901 the Lucas Gusher rocketed America and the world into the Age of Liquid Petroleum; three blocks from the baseball park in Beaumont, Texas, where Hank Greenberg, Schoolboy Rowe, and a dozen other diamond greats dazzled minor-league crowds before moving on to the majors and baseball immortality; and the distance required to demolish a triple-dip ice cream cone before reaching the Big Thicket, a forested wonderland known to scientists as the biological crossroads of North America. It seemed natural to start keeping notes on ballplayers, oil patch people, and Big Thicket critters about as soon as I could print words on a Big Chief tablet with a Jumbo Pencil. After high school I wrote baseball for the afternoon daily, then edited a Navy weekly newspaper during World War II. I've been freelancing part- and full-time ever since.

A while back I outlined a fantasy called the "Perfect Assignment." I wanted to write a journal of the four seasons in the Big Thicket. I also wanted to tell the story of an oil well from start to finish. And, somehow, folklore had to be involved; I relish the traditions of pioneers and their descendants who still hold to many of the old ways. The three elements seemed disconnected, a journalistic Mulligan stew, but so what? I pinned that memo to the wall. A couple of days later, I added: "All expenses paid and a handsome fee." The next day I tacked on another stipulation: "The whole thing becomes a big, beautiful book."

I'm not going to tell you that this fantasy came totally true. But a few months later, a peculiar sequence of events began clicking into place.

It started one evening while I was drowsing over a newsletter of the Big Thicket Association, a small but intensely dedicated volunteer group who marshalled a national fight to save parts of the Big Thicket wilderness before it disappeared forever into the maw of Progress. After a fifty-year battle with absentee commercial interests, the Association's efforts climaxed when, in 1974, a parcel totaling 84,550 acres of the Big Thicket was declared America's first National Preserve. (I'd been an officer of the Association during the final years of that fight, and served a hitch as president.)

On this particular evening, I scanned boldface cap headings over gray blocks of type: PINE FARMS . . . MINERAL EXPLORATION . . . BEECH CREEK TRAIL . . . I was just about ready to drop the newsletter on my snoozing lapcat when a phrase popped out at me. "The first full-fledged test of the new procedures," it began. I refocused my eyes and read the entire item headed MINERAL EXPLORATION. Then I practically bolted for my typewriter.

The gist of it was that a major oil company held license to drill a deep well in the Big Thicket National Preserve. My research determined that it was the *first* well ever drilled in a National Preserve. Moreover, it would bore below one of America's most delicately balanced and complex environments: nine major ecosystems, with their widely diverse flora, dovetail in the Big Thicket, an environmental phenomenon that occurs nowhere else in North America and perhaps in no other locale of comparable size in the world. The company would be drilling under special regulations imposed by the National Park Service to protect the area's ecosystems.

Next day, I fired off a proposal to the public relations director of the company, a subsidiary of Atlantic Richfield, which I knew to be one of the nation's most enlightened and progressive corporations on matters of environmental concern.

"Your company will be drilling an oil well in the Big Thicket, which is among America's most sensitive environments," I began. "As a former president of the Big Thicket Association, and as a writer and photographer of nature and oil industry articles, I have a special awareness of the problems in this situation."

I suggested telling the story of this unprecedented operation through a journal encompassing the work at the well site and the natural phenomena of flora and fauna in the immediate area, plus appropriate local folklore. I also proposed extensive color photography for documentation, as well as possible publication.

I attached tearsheets of my work and a credits-and-credentials list, which included a quote from a letter by a Time, Inc. vice president: "Let me repeat what I have said over the phone: I think you did a wonderful job and—miracle of miracles—you delivered it on time." I hoped that quote would strengthen my proposal.

Nothing happened for a few weeks. Then a phone call came from the PR director of ARCO. "Your proposal is unusual," he began. "I've talked to several of our officers about it. We're interested. Can you come to Dallas for some additional discussion?"

I met with the manager of environmental operations, the PR director, and two engineers who were developing the drilling plans for the W.T. Carter Wildcat No. 1, the official name of the well. (A "wildcat," in oil lingo, is a well drilled in an area previously unexplored for oil and gas.) The questions and answers lasted two hours, covering such topics as the company's integrity in environmental concerns, its operating policies, the particular ecosystem at the drilling site, and my familiarity with tight holes. (A "tight hole" is a well where all data about depth, core samplings, and other vital facts remain secret to protect the drilling firm's investment. In this case that investment ran to many millions of dollars.) At stake also was my credibility as a naturalist and my long-held personal conviction that we need both sanctuaries of unspoiled nature, such as the Big Thicket National Preserve, and new energy resources—and that we can have both. But old enmities must go. Each new situation must be approached in a constructive spirit of solution-seeking—a spirit that recognizes the validity of both the environmentalists' and energy-producers' positions, and utilizes the goodwill of both parties.

"There are some positive elements in this exchange," commented Bob Jirsa, the PR director, ending the session. "We'll be in touch."

A week later I got the go-ahead. Either party could cancel the agreement with ten days' notice. No one was sure how the project would work out. My job was to visit the well site from time to time, observe, interview, take photographs, and write about what I found from the vantage point of a Big Thicket naturalist. If the project proved worthwhile and the W.T. Carter Wildcat became an "elephant"—a super oil or gas strike—we could talk about the possibility of a book to commemorate this first-ever operation. No promises, of course, but we'd talk. A book! Wow!

The writing and photography went beautifully, but the good stuff didn't stop there. Spinoffs developed. One was a feature story about a geologist working on the Carter Wildcat who raised racehorses in his spare time. The man thrived on high risks at work and at play. The story brought $600. I was also hired to lead a field trip in the Big Thicket for the ARCO Speakers Bureau, resulting not only in a day's fee for guide service but also material for a magazine feature on an exceptional team of corporate employees, ranging from fieldhands and secretaries to high-level executives. A valuable bonus to the entire project was getting to know and work with a new bunch of interesting oil patch people—ARCO's scientists, drilling bosses, rig men, and an imaginative and highly professional public relations staff.

When it ended several months later, the Perfect Assignment

proved to be an elementary course in freelance marketing and production, covering a half-dozen basic lessons. Here they are:

1. *Stake your claim.* Establish your field of expertise, which is
   what editors buy, early on. What do you most enjoy reading
   about and writing about—birds? bugs? landforms? drilling
   tools? a particular region? home applications of energy?
   dowsing for oil? overnight oil millionaires? Whatever, that's
   probably your basic field. It will deliver subspecialties and,
   eventually, one or two more main fields. My own choice of
   the Big Thicket and the oil patch as specialties spring from
   childhood interests. Years of first-hand experiences, nonstop reading, and consorting with naturalists and oilmen reinforced my early choices. My writing got a boost when I
   broke into newspaper work on the sports desk, doing baseball stories and mixing with the game's picturesque characters.

2. *Draw a bead on your target.* What kind of assignment do you
   crave, deep down? Write it out. Write exactly what you want
   to cover in a single Great Assignment. No idle essay, this.
   You're steering your subconscious mind toward a terrific
   goal. It may veer and backfire along the way, but it knows
   precisely where you want to go and it's committed to that target. Stay in your field, of course. If your specialty is alligators,
   don't specify a two-months' cruise with Dolly Parton or Tom
   Selleck as a food and music critic.

3. *Feel Pavlovian.* Tell your brain to always and forever be on the
   alert for story possibilities, no matter what you're looking at,
   hearing, or reading. Train the brain to ring your bell when the
   right phrase crops up. My good times with the Carter Wildcat
   project began with a few dull words in an obscure newsletter.
   On my wall now is a list of sixty-nine more story ideas, half of
   them resulting from the Pavlovian reflex of recognizing viable topics as they simply passed my way, the other half coming from completed assignments. More about that in a
   minute.

4. *Solve a problem.* You can sell words and pictures about energy
   and the environment as long as you can solve problems for
   people who wield checkbooks. That includes editors, PR
   managers, agency directors, and other heroic figures in the
   jungle of freelance journalism. "Filling needs" is another way
   of saying solving problems. An editor's problem is always
   finding superior stories on topics vital to the interests of his or
   her readers. Help that editor! The same principle applies to
   project proposals. A major problem in the Carter Wildcat case

was the credibility of the oil industry. Could a major oil company drill a well in an exquisitely delicate ecosystem—a declared national treasure—without disrupting it? My proposal said: we will see; we'll document the answer in words and photographs. The basic lesson is: try to empathize with the decisionmaker to solve a particular problem, to fill an editorial need.

5. *Do it right*. The finest editor I know, or know of, is Downs Matthews of *Exxon USA*. He has won more national and international awards than Exxon can afford to build walls for. (Almost.) Matthews is a warm-hearted friend, but a cool, thoroughly professional editor, and a cold, needle-fanged critic.

   "What you've given me here," he once began a phone call after I had delivered an assignment, "is not a feature article, but umpteen pages of blankety-blank notes!" I quickly turned the conversation to the positive channels of a rewrite with smoother transitions.

   One trait that marks Matthews as a superb editor is his practice of giving detailed guidelines to writers. I've done a passel of stories for *Exxon USA*, averaging one hit on about every nine brilliant queries, and always the acceptance letter includes the major points that Matthews wants covered in the research and in the article. It's important to have that kind of understanding with an editor, at least orally but preferably in writing. I received similar aid from the ARCO people. Lesson: if guidelines don't come automatically, ask for them. They help you do the story right.

6. *Old stories never die. They just need plucking*. Every finished and published article on energy and the environment I've ever seen contains at least one seed for another story or sale. Here are a few examples. My pamphlet on a stretch of arid sandylands in the Big Thicket led to a contract for a book for Little, Brown and Company. A story on the Big Thicket in *Texas Highways* led to a yarn about Spindletop, another story about folk medicine, and five current assignments. *Gulf States* magazine bought a story on endangered species, then one on hurricanes; both were spawned by a tale of the Big Thicket. (Please note how one specialty, the Big Thicket, usually kicks off the process.) A story on the East Texas Oil Field got reprinted, for a nice fee, in a midwestern magazine that also bought reprint rights to an article on America's independent oil operators; both were originally done for *Exxon USA*. The W. T. Carter Wildcat project grew partly out of my portfolio of

274 COMPLETE GUIDE TO WRITING NONFICTION

> nature and oil patch stories. Lesson: examine every complet-
> ed story for a fresh connection. It's there. The official theme
> song for freelancers should be: "Oh, the head bone's connect-
> ed to the neck bone, an' the neck bone's connected to the
> shoulder bone, an'. . ."

I wish I could tell you here that my gorgeous oversized book on the
W.T. Carter Wildcat No. 1 will be out any day now, so get your coffee
table ready. Fact is, there won't be any book. The project came to an
abrupt halt: the Carter Wildcat was a dry hole. It cost ARCO millions of
dollars. When I got a call one day and heard the downbeat voice say,
"We're going to have to plug the hole," I knew I'd come to trail's end.
Some of my best work and pictures will probably never see print. For
my client, about the only positive thing emerging from that 20,000-
foot-deep hole was an unprecedented commendation by the National
Park Service for environmental care and cooperation under super-
tough conditions.

That's where my Pavlov bell bonged again.

I'm happy to report that at this writing I'm working on an assignment to produce a slide program, tentatively entitled "ARCO's Big
Thicket Challenge," relating how a stringent new set of environmental
rules and red tape were met and mastered.

Somehow, some way, I hope to work a baseball story into the
script. Right now, I don't see how. But it's summertime again in the Big
Thicket, and freckled kids are stirring up dust in the cleared fields, sliding into dried cow-pies masquerading as bases, and learning how heroes and bums are born. At many a rig, the drilling boss's trailer
resounds with the whoops and groans of big-league drama on TV or radio, competing with the clang and whump of pipe-tripping. I suddenly
miss writing about baseball.

Obviously it's time to devise a new Perfect Assignment. The ingredients for this one start with the wildflowers of this region. One estimate on flowering species runs to 1,000; let's say I want to do a
photographic essay on about 500 showy species. The next element is
the oil patch. How about a day in the life of a rookie roustabout on an
offshore drilling rig? Fine. Somehow, we're gonna also work baseball
into this assignment. Finally, folklore. Lemme see. Just across the state
line, across the Sabine River into Louisiana, is Cajun country—mother
lode of folklore. We're gonna liven up this assignment with boogie
fiddlin'—a Cajun specialty—and honkytonk dancin' styles. Then
there's all those Cajun recipes—crawfish pie, a whole cultural cuisine
based on Evangeline hot peppers! . . .

Hold it! Something clicked. Baseball. Cajun country. Of course—
Guidry, RON GUIDRY! Fireballing ace southpaw of the New York Yankees! Favorite son of wild-eyed whooping Cajun sports fans! We

gonna work Ron Guidry into this assignment like a *fais-do-do,* a Cajun shindig, so to speak. We gonna track back to Ron's boyhood. Where's the sandlot where he learned to play "scratch up" baseball? Who coached him? Does he come back home in winter? Are there any young Guidrys on the sandlots of Evangeline country today—kids who can throw a baseball like a bolt of lightning? Kids named maybe Clotieaux . . .Thibodeaux. . .Fontenot. Sonofagun, we gonna have fun on the bayou!

Muse on, *couzon,* I tell myself. Of such dreams are Perfect Assignments built. Try it. You can do as well or better!

ENVIRONMENTAL WRITERS WANTED—BRAVE, BOLD, DETERMINED
by Michael Frome

In 1980, I received a letter from Lucy P., writing to tell me about herself and to ask my advice on whether, and how, to make a career in environmental writing. On the face of it, Lucy appeared qualified, at least qualified to ask. She had graduated from the University of Tennessee in 1978 with a major in environmental studies. For the past six months she had worked as a reporter for a daily newspaper, with occasional chances to cover environmental events and issues. Her letter was well composed and neatly typed—which in itself is something these days.

Lucy posed these questions: "What general advice would you have for someone in my position? Are there trade journals or other sources where job opportunities in science or environmental writing might be included? From your experience, do you think there is a demand right now for people who can write well about environmental concerns?"

I could sum it up simply for Lucy, or for Luke, or John, or anyone searching for guidance and a beginning in what might be called the "environmental field." Demand, nay; need and challenge for anyone tough enough, yea, verily.

But the choice is not simple. My own life has taught me that writing independently about the environment —setting down what I really want to say, what I feel must be said—is about as easy as earning a living by farming. It can be done, but you have to rise early in the morning and labor in the fields until the sun goes down. There is said to be lots of money in turning out racy novels, for those who can and care to, but a letter published in the May 1980 newsletter of the American Society of Journalists and Authors reveals the lot of choosing other themes. Jamie Maxtone Graham, a Scottish writer, explained his resignation from that organization:

"I came into the Society as a reformed farmer. Today I regard myself as a reformed writer, and I look back without much regret on half a lifetime spent in two callings where the producer is, most of the time, had for a mug.

"In farming, the grain merchant and the meat packer name the price of the product, which has no relationship to the cost of producing it. In the writing trade, the editor and publisher name the price—for a type of product whose supply always exceeds demand."

So Mr. Graham decided to better invest his $65 annual dues in half a dozen bottles of Scotch. His report is offered not to discourage, but to caution that writing—especially on the environment—is for the brave, bold, and determined.

A DEMANDING AND CONTROVERSIAL FIELD

My dream and goal are to encourage hopeful young (and old) writers, committed to principle, to take up the cudgels. The environment, or "energy and the environment," is a field filled with mystery and adventure, awaiting and demanding literary and journalistic exploration and exposition. Recent decades have produced some marvelous environmental writers—including Rachel Carson, Aldo Leopold, Richard Neuberger, Bernard DeVoto, Sigurd Olson, Wallace Stegner, Paul Brooks, and William O. Douglas, all heroic personalities—but we need many more to bring out the facts and stir the public consciousness.

Energy and the environment bear prominently on community health and prosperity, broad public policy, national security, and world peace. Wars have been waged to secure and protect supplies of raw materials. Strong nations have declined because they dissipated their storehouses of natural resources. So history is written.

Nevertheless, only occasionally have energy and the environment become popular themes before the public eye. Only intermittently have they been covered extensively in the media or given freelance writers a market for articles and books.

But the environment makes for classics. Early in this century, Theodore Roosevelt led what has been called "the first conservation wave," which established national parks, forests, and wildlife refuges. In 1910, Gifford Pinchot, Roosevelt's closest adviser on conservation during his time as President, became embroiled in a celebrated controversy with Interior Secretary Richard A. Ballinger (an appointee of Roosevelt's predecessor, William Howard Taft). The immediate issue focused on extensive coal lands in Alaska, claimed under public-land laws and about to be sold to a Wall Street syndicate. Pinchot's dramatic charges of fraudulence were picked up by reformers, muckrakers, and an alert press. His dismissal from the government by President Taft led to Roosevelt's return to politics and his 1912 third-party campaign.

The Teapot Dome scandal in the 1920s became another landmark in energy and the environment: the case in which Harding's luckless Secretary of the Interior, Albert B. Fall, went to jail for bribery after secretly issuing leases to federal oil fields in Wyoming. For every such episode that comes to light, however, it frightens me to contemplate how many must go unreported and unprobed.

In our own time, environmental protection became a popular cause during the Kennedy and Johnson administrations. Interior Secretary Stewart L. Udall became the apostle of the "third wave" (the second wave having been the Franklin D. Roosevelt period). He authored an influential book, *The Quiet Crisis*, with literary assistance from Wallace Stegner, Alvin Josephy, and others. It was published in the early '60s, the same period as *Silent Spring*, an epochal work by Rachel Carson, a government biologist who soared far above and beyond the levels of bureaucracy. Udall did much good, setting up new national parks and working with Lady Bird Johnson in promoting what they called "natural beauty"—but he did plenty of political conniving, too, which came to light later in a book called *The Rockefellers*, by Peter Collier and David Horowitz, published in 1976.

But perhaps Udall was not so much to blame; for, as he once reflected, on becoming Secretary of the Interior, he found that a hundred or more reporters were covering the Pentagon—while not one was assigned full-time to Interior. There was little watching, probing, or prodding; public relations were neatly packaged by government agencies.

Americans are exposed daily, nightly, weekly, and monthly to bland fare and sanitized entertainment, complete with lush color pages and zoom-zoom television. The writer who wants to buck the trend faces a tough road. There are easier ways to succeed in this profession than writing meaningfully about the environment, but this topic offers certain other rewards. Satisfaction comes from providing access to viewpoints that otherwise might be shut out, and influencing public policy toward public good—as opposed to the dominant force of powerful, self-serving interests. As one reader wrote me after my dismissal from *Field & Stream:* "History books are records of events and the doings of individuals who didn't go with the flow."

Media—Mostly Mass Merchandising

The main purpose of television is to sell things—most of which people don't need. Programs are designed to keep people entertained between commercials. News broadcasters and commentators now resemble actors, and the bigger the audience, the more they must restrain their thoughts and words.

Real-estate scandals and polluted atmospheric conditions are everywhere—but newspapers that expose them are few. The *Washington Post* brought the Watergate scandal to light—yet it frequently promotes the cause of builders and boomers while treating concerned citizen groups as "kooks" at best and ignoring local environmental issues as if they didn't exist.

Newspapers and wire services cover "stories." If one nation invades another and kills many people, that becomes a story. If black people erupt in urban ghettos and burn enough buildings, that becomes a story. Tragedies like Love Canal and Three Mile Island are the rare environmental episodes that do make stories. Members and supporters of the Clamshell Alliance at Seabrook, New Hampshire, produced a story too big to ignore—yet the media treated it as a confrontation rather than a nuclear warning. The pall of smoke that hangs over the country, the poisons in soil and water, the vanishing open space, soaring overpopulation, disappearance of species—these threats to the future of the nation, the human race, even the planet, are not considered sufficiently vivid by most in the media to constitute much of an ongoing story.

When reporters—and most freelance writers—do cover environmental matters, they proceed to the main source of news: the public relations person—who knows how to provide the statistics, the human interest, the good quotations, and the sense of expertise and authority that make a story, all the while serving the interests of those who can afford to pay for PR. It may be the mayor, plant manager, national park superintendent, or the utility company president. The PR man in *The China Syndrome* was drawn from life, as were the words of his boss in ordering him to cover up the nuclear leak: "Take care of the press—that's what you're paid to do!"

China Syndrome is an environmental document of powerful dimensions. Jane Fonda's "boss" at the TV station didn't want her to get involved in the nuclear-plant controversy, but to stick to her knitting as a well-coiffed doll covering entertaining features such as the tiger's birthday at the zoo. Fonda's character, however, insisted on following her reporter's nose on the course that led her and Jack Lemmon (plant foreman), against life-threatening odds, to evoke the truth.

I think of *China Syndrome* as a contemporary classic in the same sense as *Silent Spring*. Actress Jane Fonda and writer Rachel Carson demonstrate the opportunity and challenge awaiting hopefuls like Lucy P. There is so much to be done and damn few who are doing it. Lots of bodies rattle around and draw paychecks, writing what the market dictates. There are good people who largely have been institutional-ized. The movers and shakers are scant.

EXPERIENCE IS THE BEST EDUCATION

I hadn't planned on being an environmental writer, but wouldn't want to be any other kind. It strikes me that a writer has the right and responsibility to probe any avenues in which he or she feels that inves-tigation and exposition may serve the public good. Over the years I've been challenged because I lack a technical background in forestry and wildlife management; yet professional training in a given field is not a requirement for critical, objective, useful examination. To the contrary, the writer brings to research broader values than a professional bred on syndromes and formulas of specialized training.

Think for a moment of some of those who came along through ex-perience and experiment. Mark Twain had a fourth- or fifth-grade edu-cation, yet drew from life and real people to open new horizons in literature. John Muir left the University of Wisconsin for what he called the University of the Wilderness, living more outdoors than in, per-ceiving the landscape in terms of both poetry and science, and conceiv-ing the movement for preservation.

Years ago I visited Benton MacKaye, a forester, planner, and au-thor best known for his pioneering concept of the Appalachian Trail, the renowned mountaintop footpath that extends from Maine to Geor-gia. Our conversation touched on Lewis Mumford, MacKaye's long-time friend, who had written such books as *Technics and Civilization*, *The Culture of Cities*, *The Condition of Man*, *The Conduct of Man*, and *The City in History*. I voiced the assumption that Mumford had been trained as an architect or a planner. "No," MacKaye corrected, "he started the same as you—as a journalist, a newspaperman."

Mumford turned curiosity and practicality into influential creativi-ty. Practical experience is imperative. A university degree is like a li-cense for employment, rather than a testament of knowledge and skills gained. If you attend a graduate school of journalism, the underlying objective will be employment in newspaper work, television, public re-lations, or advertising, preferably where the money is good. Likewise, those in schools of forestry and wildlife management generally look ahead to jobs in federal and state agencies and in the timber industry. It is one thing to train as a professional by defined rules and rote and then be devoured by the system; it's quite another to learn from life a way that enables one to serve society usefully, to challenge the system so that it may sustain and renew itself.

I recall the fervor of youth in the period leading to Earth Day of

1970. Young people were rocking the boat as it had not been rocked before. Even the staid American Association for the Advancement of Science felt compelled to allow students to participate at its annual meeting. The students proceeded to criticize the "misuse of science and technology" which has brought about pollution and a mode of production based on waste; they charged that science is controlled by the federal government and big corporations. But their elders were largely unmoved. As one official retorted, "The AAAS has been concerned about this before these kids got into high school."

Perhaps so, but galloping environmental decay bespeaks the need of something new and different from the recital of accomplishments by an older generation that has failed. What we need today is a revolution of thought to sweep the world and to question the old ideas and institutions of medicine, religion, science, communications. In our country the challenge demands a critical examination of old national goals measured in sheer economics and of traditional personal goals. To find one's place in the search for new social standards, to participate in shaping an order based on humanism and naturalism—that may not be the best job opportunity economically, but those who succeed find their own rewards.

That is what *The Feminine Mystique* is about, and *Roots*, and *Silent Spring*, and environmental writing. Career achievement in the truly creative, constructive sense doesn't come easy; and the career itself may be more the result of accident than design, as I can readily attest.

Getting into Environment Through a Side Door

Following World War II, I returned to Washington, D.C. as a young reporter at the *Post* (where I had worked as a copy boy before the war). I did well there and was eager to get ahead—so eager that I jumped at an opportunity elsewhere. It proved to be a mistake; within a year I was back in Washington, working in public relations for the American Automobile Association. I recall one evening, at Constitution Hall, meeting Katherine Graham, the daughter of the *Post* publisher and later the queen bee herself. She asked what I was doing; when I explained, she snickered about what a letdown it must be from the *Post*.

There was much in what she said, of course, but every bit of experience, plus or minus, adds to a writer's storehouse of knowledge. While at AAA, my specialty was the field of travel. I learned a lot about this country, first hand, and met many editors. Around Washington, I followed the activities of government agencies and Congressional committees. The AAA assigned me to develop an anti-billboard legislative and publicity program to protect roadsides from blight. I also issued materials decrying and trying to close down those tacky roadside zoos. I became interested in national parks, whose popularity was soaring beyond adequate staffing or protection. Happily, I was not involved in promotion of freeway construction.

During my ten years with AAA, I developed an expertise in the travel field. Editors and writers would call about trends and article ideas. *Holiday* magazine sent an editor to consult me about how best to structure a proposed series of offbeat motor tours. And shortly thereafter the magazine inquired whether my employer would allow me to write the first two or three articles as models of the series (which AAA permitted, providing it was mentioned and the articles were written on my own time). Then *Woman's Day* asked me to do a piece on travel planning. As these avenues opened, I yearned to write under my own name rather than on behalf of a trade association.

Travel writing was the track that led me into the environment. Once on my own, I contributed articles to the same editors with whom I had worked before, principally at *Holiday*, *Woman's Day*, *Parade*, and *Changing Times*. A friend steered me to Doubleday, for which I wrote two travel guides. Always in these materials I would emphasize activities in national parks, national forests, and the outdoors.

Hitting the "Big Time"

Thus I was "discovered" by Clint Davis, the PR director of the Forest Service. Even since the days of its first chief, Gifford Pinchot—a forester, but also an ingenious PR man—that agency had recognized the value of the media in shaping public policy. During the 1940s and '50s, Forest Service personnel had aided historian Bernard DeVoto with research and background information for his brilliant columns for *Harper's* that blew the steam out of attempted land grabs in the West. With DeVoto's passing, Davis evidently reckoned I might prove a fitting replacement. He invited me on a pack trip in the Bridger Wilderness of Wyoming and from there to explore national forests in Idaho. The experience changed my life; I felt indeed that I was following the paths of DeVoto and Richard L. Neuberger, freelance writer and U.S. Senator from Oregon—both of whom I admired immensely.

I wrote *Whose Woods These Are—The Story of the National Forests*, for Doubleday, which led editors there to assign me to write *Strangers in High Places—The Story of the Great Smoky Mountains*. Coward McCann asked me to write two juveniles: one about Virginia (where I lived), the other called *The Varmints—Our Unwanted Wildlife*. I became a columnist for the first time, offering my own opinion on conservation and natural resource politics in *American Forests*, the monthly magazine of the American Forestry Association.

In 1966 the editors of *Holiday* noted the natural beauty movement and asked me for a major piece analyzing it, in Washington and across the country. I observed the President in a bill-signing at the White House; interviewed Cabinet members, Senators, Congressmen, industry and conservation leaders; visited the Grand Canyon and redwoods. It was a great writing exercise; the editors twice returned what I considered finished manuscripts with pointed questions, forcing me to learn more about my subject. The feature that emerged, "The Politics of Conservation," dealt with public desire to meet the onrushing environmental crisis and the inadequate, sugar-coated response of politicians and public officials. I've been writing the same theme, with variations, ever since.

In early 1977, soon after that article appeared, I received a letter from Clare Conley, a man I had never met, who was editor of *Field & Stream*. "Why don't you write such articles for us?" he asked. It struck me as a welcome opportunity to reach a large and important audience of hunters and fishermen, who should be concerned with the environment as much as any group in America.

Following publication of two articles, I was appointed conservation editor of *Field & Stream*. As a contributing editor, I was provided with a base of operation, an income and expense account, a regular monthly feature, and latitude to pursue other activities. From my first column, which appeared in the issue of June, 1968, I would contribute seventy-five monthly columns and twelve major features until publication of my last column in November, 1974.

During my tenure I covered a lot of American territory. I wrote about the effects of logging on wildlife, drainage of waterfowl breeding areas of the northern prairies, the threat of dams at Hells Canyon on the Oregon-Idaho border, the Cross-Florida Barge Canal, and environmental issues in Alaska. I interviewed, and came to know personally, key figures in Washington; investigated eagle killings in Wyoming; defended professional game biologists in Oklahoma; called for a change of leadership in the National Park Service. As conservation editor of *Field & Stream*, I addressed state wildlife federations, chapters of Trout Unlimited, the national Izaak Walton League convention, the Sierra Club Wilderness conference, and various university audiences.

The magazine tackled critical issues and challenged special economic interests without fear or favor. One of my proudest achievements was to edit a special section in the June, 1970 issue commemorating the magazine's seventy-fifth anniversary. "A Symposium on the Shape of Tomorrow" opened with a surprisingly perceptive statement by President Nixon (prepared by some thoughtful White House writer) and featured provocative articles by distinguished educators and scientists, including Barry Commoner, Paul Ehrlich, and Eugene P. Odum.

Field & Stream hit the political issues, too. In autumn pre-election issues of 1968, 1970, and 1972, we published a special feature, "Rate Your Candidate," showing readers how to evaluate Congressmen and Congressional candidates on crucial environmental concerns. The 1972 article rated the performance of every member of the House and Senate, stirring complaints from those with low grades (including the Republican leader of the House, Gerald R. Ford).

Whistleblowing Invites Censure

However, anyone who dishes it out must prepare to take it as well. Freedom of expression is more a goal than a given. Thomas Jefferson recognized the constant effort required, when he wrote:

"No experiment can be more interesting than that we are now trying, and which we trust will end in establishing that man may be governed by reason and truth. Our first objective should therefore be to leave open all avenues of truth. The most effective hitherto found is the freedom of the press. It is, therefore, the first shut up by those who fear the investigation of their action."

In 1971, the executive vice-president of the American Forestry Association, William E. Towell, directed the editor of *American Forests*, James B. Craig, to censor my column of independent commentary. As Towell wrote in his directive: "Frome, in the future, is not to write critically about the U.S. Forest Service, the forestry industry, the profession or about controversial forestry issues."

I had become disturbed about management practices in the national forests and the liaison between industry and the Forest Service, and felt compelled to express these concerns through my column. Despite the domination of its board by representatives of industry and the Forest Service, the American Forestry Association presumed to be a membership organization, serving the public interest. Though invited to remain as long as I ducked the issues, I couldn't take the censorship and was fired.

"Mike tells it 'like it is,' not necessarily like we'd like to think it is," wrote Interior Secretary Walter J. Hickel in my behalf, as the affair became public. "This independent viewpoint and the willingness to face the naked truth of issues before us has been one of the strong appeals of *American Forests*."

The dismissal from that magazine taught me a great deal: I could stand up and take it, I could survive, and I must continue to call the shots as I see them—to demonstrate that it can be done. And, after all, I still had *Field & Stream* (where one of my colleagues, Dick Starnes, wrote a tribute, "How the Clearcutters Tried to Gag Mike Frome").

But changes were taking place there, too. CBS, which had lately acquired *Field & Stream,* shuffled management at the top. Conley was fired, replaced by Jack Samson. I was directed to write in generalities without naming names. Yet that is precisely the point—the naming of names, the assessment of responsibility for actions affecting the environment and quality of life, is the fulfillment of free expression through Jefferson's "open avenues of truth."

Early in 1974 I sent a memo to Samson regarding plans for another pre-election "Rate Your Candidate" feature, but he ruled it out completely. "I feel this is definitely not the year of the environment," he replied. "The energy crisis has caused a backlash I don't want to subject *Field & Stream* to at this time."

I should have recognized that my days were numbered. In October 1974 I received a letter of dismissal, as bland as the magazine was destined to become. Samson gave no reason except that the management wanted "a modification in the editorial approach."

Environmentalism at *Field and Stream,* once I was gone, would be expressed in affirmative answers to such headline questions as "Oil and Water: Can They Mix?" An editorial by Samson sounded to me like an Exxon annual report: "Our nation has its energy problems, and the welfare of 100 million depends on us working with our vital industries to see that the environment is protected, not upon those forcing those industries to come to a complete halt . . . . We are in a serious recession now. But stop all development of resources in the name of preservation only and we answer to several million unemployed."

There were many speculations as to why I lost my job. One of the most telling was reported in an article about my dismissal in *Time* magazine, November 4, 1974: "Rhode Island Senator John Pastore was cited [in my 1972 "Rate Your Candidate" article] as 'marginal'—a particular concern to CBS. Pastore chairs the Subcommittee on Communication, with jurisdiction over broadcasting regulations. His committee hearings are often an ordeal for the networks, and broadcast executives are always fearful of restrictive legislation. Clare Dean Conley, then *Stream*'s editor, recalls: 'We got vibes from CBS that they didn't want trouble with Pastore. The word was 'Do what you have to do, but take it easy.' That Frome refused to do, with the result that he lost his biggest platform."

Many individuals and organizations protested my dismissal. The American Society of Journalists and Authors led a heroic effort in my defense, for which I will always be grateful.

"Frome has raised the consciousness of millions of readers from bag limits and such to the real question of what's happening to our resources and what can be done to protect them," Joe B. Browder, Director of the Environmental Policy Center, was quoted in the *Time* article. "The true outdoor people are the key to the environmental problem because they know something of how the real earth operates," a *Field & Stream* reader wrote to me. "You have been one of the few with access to this group who have been making strenuous efforts to alert these people to the 'shadows of coming events.' I will miss your column."

THE DIFFICULT PATH OF "REAL" NEWS

Truth-telling is critical in journalism. It forces a political, social, and economic system to continually examine and upgrade itself. The following statements regarding my dismissal reflect how difficult this can be:

Representative Silvio Conte, as quoted in the *Congressional Record*, December 13, 1974, said: "Mike Frome was fired because he created too much heat in the kitchen for the media barons at the Columbia Broadcasting System, which is *Field & Stream's* corporate parent. Because he occasionally dared to attack those politicians who control legislation and committees important to CBS, Mike Frome was censored, censured—and finally dismissed."

Tom Bell, in a front-page editorial in *High Country News*: "The hypocrisy of our system could never be better illustrated than in the case of Mike Frome. We tout our system as being one of freedom for the individual, and we particularly tout our freedom of speech and expression. His experiences give the lie to just how much freedom we really do have."

Peter Harnik, director of Environmental Action, in a letter to CBS Chairman William S. Paley: "Michael Frome's dismissal lends credence to the growing popular conception that the media today exists more to mollify the public than to educate. And it bolsters the feeling that the last place people should turn to for 'real' news and analysis is the major networks and magazines."

Rather than feel discouraged, I was uplifted by the support I received. Truth-telling must and will prevail. "Knowledge will forever govern ignorance," as James Madison wrote, "and a people who mean to be their own governors must arm themselves with the power that knowledge gives." What greater goal could a journalist set for himself? What finer reputation could he earn than as one who arms the people with the power that knowledge gives?

I think of Henry David Thoreau—the rich inspiration in his writings, the independence of his life. In 1849 he refused to pay his taxes. It was his way of protesting the unjust U.S. war against Mexico. For his act of civil disobedience, he was jailed. Ralph Waldo Emerson, his close friend, wanted to pay his taxes for him, but Thoreau refused. The frustrated Emerson came to the prison to visit Thoreau. "Henry," he demanded, "what are you doing in there?" To which Thoreau calmly replied, "What are *you* doing out there?" But then, Thoreau followed a simple creed: "The only obligation which I have a right to assume is to do at any time what I think right." Thoreau spoke for us all who want our words to rise above the mediocre. How in the world can I say anything less?

Free Speech Exchanged for Caution

It grieves me that able editors aren't free to grant freedom to their authors. In 1977 I wrote about national parks for *Mainliner*, the United Airlines magazine. After it appeared, I received a nice note from Fred R. Smith, editorial director of East/West Network (which publishes the magazine for the airline): "A few short things were cut for space and we elided the discussion of the redwoods as United didn't want to be involved in that controversy. Otherwise, I think you will agree it is a great picture issue."

In 1982, to cite another example, the editorial director at Du Pont called to ask me to write an article on the Delaware River for their external house organ. I was then author-in-residence at the Pinchot Institute for Conservation Studies at Milford, Pennsylvania, in the Delaware Valley, and was very interested in the subject. The article was to describe the improvement in water quality in the river over the course of recent years. I would gladly do it, I advised, providing I could make my own investigation and determination. But that, I was told, wasn't the point of the story: Du Pont's experts had already made the judgment on water quality and the writer was expected to interview and record the statements of company-chosen authorities. Clearly it was best I bow out at the beginning.

Publications of national environmental organizations appear as likely markets, but they have their own sacred cows and shibboleths. "I, for one, continue to be grateful that environmentalists have such an outspoken ally," wrote Les Line, editor of the highly successful, slick *Audubon* magazine, in 1972. Yet in the next paragraph: "At breakfast the other day, you proposed a critique of the National Park Service for *Audubon*. Before we go further, Mike, can you sketch for me what you plan to cover and say? One thing we cannot do is get involved in personalities. And because of the sensitiveness of the subject, the article would have to be approved by both [the vice-president and president of National Audubon]."

The Sierra Club magazine is another attractive publication. In 1977 I was assigned to write a memorial tribute to one of my grass-roots heroes, Guy M. Brandborg, an old Montana populist and two-fisted crusader for conservation and sound forestry practice. When the article appeared, the editor sent me a little *billet doux:* "It has been somewhat edited and, as you can see, somewhat revised, too." With the gutsy stuff eliminated, is what they meant.

I don't mean to sound discouraging, or discouraged—if I were I'd be doing something else. But my philosophy is to let truth hang out and consequences follow, whatever they may be. Environmental writing, as I have sought to practice it, demands a strong stomach and high principle. There are opportunities and there will be more of them. Ronald Reagan and James G. Watt have made the environment an important topic again; I don't see how it can diminish.

ALTERNATIVE AVENUES FOR ENVIRONMENTAL ISSUES

"People have to know what other avenues, if any, are open to outspoken environmental writers such as you," wrote Donald McDonald, editor of *The Center Magazine,* early in 1975; "what other recriminatory actions have been taken against other writers who 'name names'; the degree to which writers self-censor their own work, anticipate trouble and sanitize their writing to the point of banality; the connections between Congressmen and special business interests (mining, lumbering, etc.), and the mass-media with its cross-ownership of interests."

His letter led to an assignment to write an article, which appeared under the title, "Freedom of the Press—For Those Who Own One." It didn't pay very much, but it did appear in print. Despite *The Center's* small circulation, it was widely read and reprinted in the *Congressional Record.* And it led to another assignment for the same magazine, about whistleblowers in the federal government, which I prepared with the aid of a grant from the Fund for Investigative Journalism.

The Center Magazine ceased publication, alas, but there will always be other outlets. When one door closes, another opens. The next outlet may not be as large or as well-paying as the last, but you never know where it may lead. After *Field & Stream,* I became a columnist for *Defenders of Wildlife.* (The editor called me after reading the *Time* article and said, "You can write anything you want—as long as you don't get us sued for libel.") My series on "The Un-Greening of the National Parks," which won the ASJA Mort Weisinger Award for the best magazine feature of the year, appeared in *Travel Agent* magazine, of all places, and later was reprinted in *National Parks* and in a book, *National Parks in Crisis.*

For five years I wrote a weekly column ("Environmental Trails") for the *Los Angeles Times,* and loved it while it lasted. When I moved west to Idaho in 1982, the publisher of *Western Outdoors*, Burt Twilegar, invited me to become environmental editor and columnist; I accepted forthwith. It was wonderful to have the chance to communicate once again with the audience of hunters and fishermen. It renewed my faith and confidence in the American system, considering that Burt knew all about the old controversy at *Field & Stream*. When someone wrote a letter to *Western Outdoors* complaining about my continued publication in *Defenders of Wildlife*, Twilegar responded: "We'll judge Michael Frome on what he writes for *this* magazine."

INGENUITY UNCOVERS UNEXPLORED ISSUES

The truth is the field of energy and the environment is wide open, with a thousand freelance articles and a thousand books waiting to be written. But they take imagination, initiative and desire. Rachel Carson had been recognized in a small way before *Silent Spring*, but that was a book she *had* to write and which her editors at Houghton Mifflin could not resist.

My observation is that creative book editors are eager to review environmental manuscripts of merit, but there must be something special and different about each one to earn its way in a harsh marketplace. But then, how can anything of significance be dashed off in short order? Collier and Horowitz gave three years of their lives in detailed research and writing of *The Rockefellers*. In their case, a supportive and sympathetic editor at Holt, Rinehart encouraged them to keep going and helped to obtain an additional advance.

There *are* sources of financial backing. The Fund for Investigative Journalism, of Washington, D.C. (mentioned earlier), is designed "to increase public knowledge about the concealed, obscure or complex aspects of matters significantly affecting the public." It awards grants to writers "to enable them to probe abuses of authority or the malfunctioning of institutions and systems which harm the public." *High Country News*, a regional environmental biweekly headquartered at Lander, Wyoming, maintains a research foundation to provide small sums to energetic, promising writers.

In 1939, Kenneth Crawford, a respected Washington correspondent, authored a book called *The Pressure Boys: The Inside Story of Lobbying in the United States*. In one chapter he referred to the syndrome of "Greeleyism." It was, he wrote, "the policy of lumbermen leading the Forest Service by the hand." It was named for William B. Greeley, a Chief of the Forest Service in the 1920s who had led that agency away from the bold course charted by its founder, Gifford Pinchot, and who, on retirement, became an industry lobbyist. Crawford wrote of how the liaison between a federal bureau and industry was manifested through the American Forestry Association.

Much has been written about the "military-industrial complex," but precious little to update Crawford and show the connection between resource and environmental agencies and the industries they ostensibly regulate. Some of it came out in the scandal that shook the Environmental Protection Agency during the Reagan administration, but was there more to it? What was the full scope of promises and arrangements? What does it bode for the present and future of the country and for the democratic process?

Such raw materials for environmental writing have barely been tapped. Neither has the real nature of the energy "crisis" and its solution. A principal challenge of our time involves energy, that is true. Americans have been led to believe that we desperately require the exploration and exploitation of new energy sources, but isn't it possible the crisis actually derives from overconsumption and waste? Industries and government leaders bespeak the need of accelerated development to provide jobs and feed the growth spiral, but might not depletion of resources undermine opportunity for employment and the national welfare?

The people are not informed because most channels of information are controlled by forces that feed on overconsumption and waste. That only makes the challenge more inviting. I can't give Lucy P. all the answers in her quest for a career—she must find them for herself. When she, or someone like her, asks for my advice, I can say as follows: Set aside fear and apprehension and chart your destiny. Don't wait for it to come to you but shape your own future writing about the environment, if that's what you want. You may not prove to be another Rachel Carson, but then again you may. That's not really as important as making some positive contribution to society in your chosen field.

It works; from my own life I know it works. That I have uncensored outlets open to my writing, and that I should have a place to lecture at the University of Idaho (as I did earlier at the University of Vermont), give me faith in myself and in the American system. The only trouble with democracy is that we take it for granted. Writers—and professors, too—should be leaders in free expression, rather than finding one reason or another for playing it safe.

I feel imbued with hope. I follow and commend the course of William Lloyd Garrison, who wrote: "I am in earnest. I will not equivocate. I will not excuse. I will not retreat a single inch. And I will be heard." What better example and advice can I provide to the aspiring writer on the environment or on any theme? We are the human machinery that stimulates and sustains the democratic system.

Additional Resources

American Museum of Science & Energy, 300 S. Tulane Ave., Oak Ridge, TN 37830. Exhibitions in science and alternative energy areas. Operated for the United States Department of Energy (DOE) by Science Applications, Inc.; provides advisory, historical, and interpretative information. Photos also available. Free catalog or brochure available on request.

American Petroleum Institute, 2101 L St. NW, Washington, DC 20037. Provides analytical, bibliographical, historical, referral, technical, and trade information covering energy, particularly petroleum. Offers B&W glossy photos pertaining to petroleum for noncommercial, non-advertising use *only*.

American Solar Energy Society, Inc., 110 W. 34th St., New York, NY 10001. Provides advisory, bibliographical, referral, and technical information. Offers annual reports, informational newsletters, placement on mailing lists. Offers published materials with technical details of ongoing research and development in every aspect of solar energy. Conferences present technical materials and provide industry with opportunities to expose new developments and products.

Central Abstracting & Indexing Service, American Petroleum Institute, 156 William St., New York, NY 10038. Monitors technical journals and business-news publications of importance to the petroleum industry to call attention to pertinent new developments. Provides bibliographical and trade information covering petroleum and alternative energy technology, and petroleum-related business news. Offers information searches.

Department of Energy, Office of Public Affairs, 1000 Independence Ave. SW, Washington, DC 20585. A clearinghouse for policy statements issued by the department office. Answers public and private inquiries and helps educate the public about energy topics. Provides walk-in service for Department of Energy publications. Offers information of a general nature related to energy matters.

Department of the Interior, Interior Bldg., Washington, DC 20240. The nation's principal conservation agency, with responsibilities for energy, water, fish, wildlife, mineral, land, park and recreational resources, and Indian and territorial affairs. Provides information covering all concerns of the Department of the Interior.

Environmental Action Coalition, 417 Lafayette St., New York, NY 10003. Provides interpretative, referral, and technical information on a wide variety of environmental topics. Most information covers solid waste and hazardous/toxic wastes, urban forestry, water-related issues. Information on teaching environmental topics a specialty. Offers aid in arranging interviews, statistics, brochures and pamphlets, placement on mailing list, newsletter, press releases. Publications include *Cycle* (membership newsletter) and *Echo* (children's newsletter).

Environmental Action, Inc., 1346 Connecticut Ave. NW, #741, Washington, DC 20036. Provides comprehensive information on pollution and energy issues, plus a full range of other environmental issues: housing, military spending and the nuclear freeze; what's happening in the environmental movement; what members can do as citizen activists. Offers annual reports, brochures and pamphlets, computerized information searches, informational newsletters, placement on mailing lists, press kits, research assistance. Publications include *Environmental Action* magazine.

Environmental Defense Fund, 444 Park Ave. S., 9th Floor, New York, NY 10016. Provides comprehensive information on ecology, water quality, air pollution, health effects of toxic chemicals, species extinction and protection, utility company investment analyses (alternative energy sources), and more. Offers aid in arranging interviews, annual reports, brochures and pamphlets, informational newsletters, press kits. Publications include *EDF Letter* (newsletter which describes EDF activities) and numerous others on toxic chemicals, utility and investment studies.

Environmental Protection Agency, 401 M St. NW, Rm. 2404, Headquarters Library, Washington, DC 20460. Offers pamphlets and brochures; maintains library. Publications include popular booklets and leaflets on water and air pollution, solid waste management, radiation and pesticides control, noise abatement and control.

Forest Service, U.S. Department of Agriculture, Box 2417, Washington, DC 20013. Provides advisory, factual, historical, and referral information on forestry, forest resources, national forests. Offers informational reference services, news releases.

Independent Petroleum Association of America, 1101 16th St. NW, Washington, DC 20036. Represents 7,000 independent producers of domestic crude oil and natural gas. Provides trade information on crude oil and natural gas—economics, industry, and energy. Offers aid in arranging interviews, statistics, brochures and pamphlets. Publications include *Petroleum Independent* (bimonthly magazine) and *The Oil Producing Industry in Your State.*

National Audubon Society, 950 Third Ave., New York, NY 10022. Provides historical, interpretative, referral, and technical information on endangered species, land preservation, pollution, natural history. Offers brochures and pamphlets, library facilities, placement on mailing lists. Publications include *From Outrage to Action* (history), *Selling the Bugs Out* (wise use of pesticides), fact sheets.

Resource Policy Institute, 1346 Connecticut Ave. NW #217, Washington, DC 20036. Provides advisory, how-to, referral, and technical information on energy, environment, materials technology, and policy, including hazardous waste, conservation, etc. Offers research assistance. Publications include *The Waste Watchers, Toxic Substances: Decisions and Values,* and others.

Sierra Club, 530 Bush St., San Francisco, CA 94108. Provides referrals to issue experts within the club; printed materials on club history, policy, and programs. Publications include *Sierra* (bimonthly) and *National News Report* (biweekly).

Technical Information Project, Inc., 1346 Connecticut Ave. NW, Washington, DC 20036. Provides comprehensive information on hazardous and nonhazardous waste management, energy conservation, recycling, technology assessment, emergency planning, other related energy/environment fields. Offers brochures and pamphlets, placement on mailing lists, research assistance, telephone reference services.

Izaak Walton League of America, Inc., 1800 N. Kent St., Suite 806, Arlington, VA 22209. Provides analytical and interpretative information covering public lands, air and water pollution, acid rain, wetlands, soil conservation, wildlife management. Offers publications and interviews with staff experts on major conservation issues.

World Information Service on Energy, 1346 Connecticut Ave. NW, Rm. 533, Washington, DC 20036. An international news service which provides information and networking to grassroots antinuclear and safe energy groups around the world. Provides information on nuclear energy, appropriate energy, uranium mining, movement tactics. Offers brochures and pamphlets, informational newsletters, placement on mailing lists. Publications include *News Communique* (weekly), *Bulletin* (monthly), *Keep It in the Ground* (newsletter).

Chapter Nine

WRITING ABOUT MEDICINE AND HEALTH

In few areas has the knowledge explosion been more evident than in the fields of health and medicine. Research scientists, physicians, surgeons, pharmaceutical chemists have made great strides, uncovering better ways to help us cope with the omnipresent fact of human illness and ultimate mortality.

The fruits of their daily labors are mind-boggling: vaccines which virtually eliminate heretofore fatal diseases; the science of genetics; transplants for many parts of the human body—even artificial organs; biofeedback; do-it-yourself and preventive medicine; medical spin-offs from space research; improved childbirth techniques; even dying patients restored to life. Not only are people living longer, but those beyond middle age are experiencing a much-improved quality of life. We have, indeed, traveled some distance since the French chemist Marcelin Berthelot wrote in 1901, "The world has no more mystery for us."

But medical progress is so rapid that it's increasingly difficult for those involved, not to mention the average reader, to keep up with developments in the field. The writer-specialist who freelances in medicine and health chronicles the advances and discoveries taking place every day in the laboratories, hospitals, and research centers of the world. These writers share in a very special way mankind's ongoing battle against disease, pain, suffering, and premature death. Their work in investigating and reporting what's happening in medicine allows us to learn the latest thinking on how best we can guard that indispensable asset, our own health.

According to a 1982 Gallup poll of what's important to Americans, "being in good physical health" ranks second only to "having a good family life." They believe, like Ralph Waldo Emerson, "the first wealth is health." Thus nearly every publication is a potential market for an appropriate—that is, slanted for their audience—health or medical piece. The directory, *Magazine for Libraries*, lists more than two hundred markets—some health-specific, many general interest—that use medicine and health articles, everything from *AMA Journal* to *Working Woman*, from *Weight Watcher's Magazine* to *New Republic*. And virtually every major book publisher will take a look at a solidly researched nonfiction book dealing with health. After all, who is not fascinated by the workings—and nonworkings—of their own bodies?

As noted in the following pages by Patrick McGrady, there is a noticeable trend in this field toward collaboration—more professionals are working with freelance writers—for both books and magazine articles.

Here, then, is our forum of ASJA freelancers, each a recognized writer of both articles and books in the medicine and health fields. As Ruth Winter says, "A doctor may help one or a hundred patients, but a meticulous and informative medical writer may help thousands."

THE MAKING OF A MEDICAL WRITER
by Dodi Schultz

Going into medicine as a profession is difficult. You must plod through stuffy science courses in college, then endure four more years of schooling—plus up to seven or eight years of postgraduate study, depending on the specialty you choose. After all that, you must work long hours and assume responsibility for the health and even the survival of others. Should you inadvertently fail in that responsibility, you may be rewarded with a malpractice suit and the prospect of losing your reputation, worldly goods, and the opportunity ever again to earn a living in your profession.

Writing about medicine, on the other hand, is easy. You don't need a medical degree or, in fact, any other degree. You get to read fascinating medical journals, but nobody quizzes you on their content. You get to interview people on the front lines of medical research, which gives you a glimpse into the future. You get to interview the people who worry about the patients, but you don't have to do any of that worrying. You get to look over the shoulders—and into the minds—of those involved in the day-to-day complexities which constitute medical care. You get to understand a myriad of medical problems, from both the patients' and the doctors' viewpoint, without having to suffer those problems yourself.

You also get to do a lot of extracurricular work, such as answering phone calls from friends who ask you to explain what their physicians have said and to assure them that the prescribed medication makes sense. And then you get to hear your spouse threaten to turn you in for practicing without a license.

And you also enjoy a special edge in the highly competitive world of freelance journalism.

THE SPECIALTY ADVANTAGE

Every freelance writer faces the inevitable round of idea submissions to editors, with the inevitable rejections and the occasional acceptance/assignment. Yes, even established writers' ideas are at times rejected. (And it *still* hurts.) Suffice it to say that as you gain writing experience, you're far less likely to get the "not for us" turndown and far more apt to be told that the idea is perfect for the magazine but something very much like it is already in the works.

But the specialized writer will endure fewer rejections. At some point (never, of course, as soon as you'd like), you will begin to receive calls and letters from editors who have a thought for an article and would like to know if you are interested in writing it. In short, you have become known as an expert in your subject area. Editors have learned that you understand that area, can dig up experts, and can understand the technical jargon—which, in this case, means you can translate from "medicalese" into words ordinary people can understand.

Of my last ten article assignments, I originated the ideas for just three; in the other seven instances, the editors came to me.

There is an additional, subtle advantage in medical writing. It has to do with the fact that editors are not just editors; they are people, even as you and I. They may or may not own cars or computers. They may or may not be interested in gardening, or boating, or jogging, or interior decoration. But they get colds and toothaches; they stub their toes and wrench their backs; they have friends and relatives with the entire range of medical problems. And, as they are aware, so do their readers. That means any medical topic short of exotic tropical diseases is likely to interest most editors. (And if their readers are wont to travel to exotic tropical climes, anything goes.)

So how do you acquire this expertise? Where to begin?

A State of Mind

Don't begin at all if you're not truly intrigued by the questions and curious about the answers. All nonfiction writing involves continual learning and we are, in a sense, perennial students, except that the learning proceeds at our own pace, rather than in a formal academic program. Whether you're going to write about food, finance, photography, or medicine—that curiosity, that urge to know more, must be present.

I do what I do because I'm fascinated by how antibiotics attack bacteria, why some people get cancer and some don't, what makes the body turn against itself to trigger the disorders called autoimmune disease. Doubtless such interests seem unduly morbid to some—but then I can't fathom some writers' preoccupation with the innards of computers, the intrigues among celebrities, or the ins and outs of the stock market.

I had little opportunity to pursue my medical interests during a number of years in advertising and publicity and four as a staff writer/editor at Dell's (now defunct) women's service magazines—where I wrote about fashion, cooking, and how to do your hair, but also managed to grab for myself any stories with the slightest medical slant, from pregnancy to dandruff.

That was nearly two decades ago. I finally went off on my own after my husband and I decided we could afford a six months' trial of not knowing when the checks would arrive. Naturally, I took whatever came along and continued to write fashion, cooking and how-to-do-your-hair copy, as well as industrial advertising copy and articles on topics as diverse as seashell collecting, starting a mail-order business, and community organization. My first big *specialty* break was a story for *Ladies' Home Journal*. I was assigned to interview Dr. Arnold Friedman, a world-famous neurologist then associated with Columbia University and an internationally acclaimed authority on the subject of headaches. My assignment was to explain the causes of and treatments for headaches to *Journal* readers.

I knew, at that point, next to nothing about headaches. My interview subject knew just about everything and had published many discourses in medical journals, as well as medical-school texts. When I called Dr. Friedman's office to arrange for the interview, I asked to be sent whatever reprints or other pieces of literature were available. While I was waiting for it to arrive, I spent some time at the library of the New York Academy of Medicine, perusing not only current literature but also—in the library's rare book room—ancient texts detailing the history and folklore of headache treatment, since I had discovered that was a special interest of Dr. Friedman. I took notes as I studied and jotted down questions.

Dr. Friedman was a bit intimidating on our first encounter. Although I later learned that he is a warm, genial man with a keen sense of humor, my first impression was that of a brusque, no-nonsense professor more accustomed to demanding answers than dispensing them, and someone with whom I had best keep on my toes. But I'd done my homework well. I knew I'd passed a major hurdle when one response was a thoughtful, "That is a very good question." (I was to find, in many other interviews with many other physicians, that this is a heartening sign.)

And, as luck would have it, I had—or thought I had—noticed something. I phrased it hesitantly: "I may be wrong, but it seems to me there's a discrepancy between two of these pieces of literature. In this journal article you say . . . but that appears to be contradicted in this proof of the chapter you're writing for the neurology text." He frowned and said sharply, "Let me see that." I waited for what seemed like ten years but was probably no more than ten seconds. Finally, he nodded. The proof contained a typographical error that he'd missed, and I'd caught.

I wrote the article. It was accepted and appeared in the *Journal* in late 1970. The following year, I received a call from Dr. Friedman. He and a psychiatrist colleague had a manuscript, a draft of a book for lay-persons on the subject of headaches—but they had concluded that somehow, it was not quite right. Would I look at it, with an eye to reorganization and rewrite? To make a long story short, *The Headache Book*, by Arnold P. Friedman, M.D. and Shervert H. Frazier, Jr., M.D., with Dodi Schultz, was published by Dodd, Mead & Company in 1973.

HOMEWORK, AND MORE HOMEWORK

I said earlier that the medical writer is in large part a translator. To be a translator, you must understand the language you're translating. Don't expect overnight fluency. Do expect to consult a dictionary frequently. It is helpful, in this regard, to own the latest edition of *Stedman's Medical Dictionary* and/or *Dorland's Illustrated Medical Dictionary.*

It's also helpful to be familiar with trends and events in the world of medicine, and it is not enough to read the *New York Times* and the "Medicine" section of *Time* magazine. They are in the same business you are in.

Medicine consists of some two dozen specialties, many with multiple subspecialties; each of these has its own journal(s). If you were to read all of them regularly, you would have no time for writing, let alone eating or sleeping. Nor is it necessary to do so. Any major developments in dermatology, radiology, ophthalmology and the other specialties are bound to make the general medical publications as well.

Probably the best sources of original material, because they are our nation's most prestigious, are the *Journal of the American Medical Association (JAMA)* and the *New England Journal of Medicine;* any serious medical writer should, I think, subscribe to both. For straight news, add the weekly tabloid *Medical Tribune* and/or the biweekly magazine *Medical World News.* For an overseas viewpoint, the British *Lancet* (distributed in the United States by Little, Brown) is helpful. For data on new drugs and other therapies, the biweekly *Medical Letter* is invaluable. These are for starters; there are many other publications you will learn about as you write in the field.

All of the above are available at a good medical library; but your own subscriptions—although the costs are geared to physicians', not writers', incomes—are more convenient because you can clip and file articles for reference. (I have six two-drawer file cabinets filled with such material.) You *should*, however, have access to a good medical library. There are times when you'll need to delve more deeply into a narrow topic, and you'll want to consult the specialty journals and medical texts. Do this *before* you seek out real, live people.

A few years back, I received a call from a child psychiatrist, an old friend. "You're a journalist," he began, "and there's something I need to know." He had embarked on an effort to publicize the tragedy of child abuse in his community and to explain how it might be prevented by early intervention. The local newspaper had sent a reporter to elicit his views. During the interview, my friend found himself saying, "As Kempe has pointed out. . ." The reporter interrupted with "Who?" My friend repeated the name and was again interrupted, this time with, "How do you spell that?" My friend patiently explained that he was referring to Dr. C. Henry Kempe, a pioneer investigator and writer in the field, who had coined the phrase "battered child syndrome." Had the reporter not read anything by Kempe before setting up the interview? "No," she replied, "I wanted to keep an open mind."

"Now my question to you," said my friend after relating this incident, "is this: is that the way professional journalists work?"

No, it is not. An open mind is something we should all maintain; ignorance is something else. Aside from your looking like something of an ass, it is plainly insulting to expect your interviewee to do your homework for you. It is fine to ask a gynecologist to spell out her diagnostic criteria for primary dysmenorrhea; it is not fine to ask her to define the term, or to explain the menstrual cycle, or give you an anatomy lesson on the female reproductive organs. It is acceptable to seek a cardiologist's views on optimal postinfarction therapy for heart-attack patients; it is not acceptable to ask him to explain the process of coronary artery disease. Those basics are part of your homework.

FROM THE HORSE'S MOUTH

While the homework is essential, what brings your story to life, and makes it unique, is people. None of the boning-up can replace insights, voiced only to you and never before published, that result from interviewing. Your in-person presence is sometimes needed; I could not have written nearly as vivid a story about anorexia nervosa, the self-starvation disease, as I did for *Viva* in 1977, if I had not actually met its gaunt young victims. I would have written less forcefully on the need for motorcyclists to wear helmets—in a book on accident prevention and emergency care—had I not spent time with my co-author in Bellevue Hospital's emergency room, where I saw the shattered body of a cyclist whose brain remained intact only because of a helmet. And sometimes, physicians insist on talking face to face.

But interviewing can often be done by telephone. What you frequently want are facts, opinions, and answers to questions, not—unless your interviewee *is* your subject—a look at his or her clothing, office, or lifestyle.

Most interviewees, I've found, are extremely helpful and even eager to suggest *other* sources. For one 1982 article for *McCall's*, for example, my first call was to a National Institutes of Health investigator who had published a report on pertinent research in a medical journal. From there came a string of referrals to physicians ranging from upstate New York to southern California.

On another story, a 1981 piece for *Parents* called "Safety On Wheels," I first tapped the United States Consumer Product Safety Commission in Washington, D.C. and the American Academy of Pediatrics in Evanston, Illinois, which I knew had a committee on child safety. The federal commission suggested I speak with the Bicycle Manufacturers Association which, it turned out, had developed a helpful set of purchasing guidelines for parents. The bicycle manufacturers' spokesman, in return, suggested two other sources I hadn't known existed: the Bicycle Federation, which provides information to educators and has ideas on how bike riding should be taught; and the League of American Wheelmen, a one-hundred-year-old national organization of biking enthusiasts.

Questions and Answers

When talking about youngsters riding bicycles safely, you're not going to find much disagreement. One source may be more in favor of formal safety courses than others. But all will endorse the fundamentals—buy the right size bike, teach kids the rules of the road, and so on. On other subjects, that's not always so; there may be sharply differing views.

In some such instances, one or another will clearly be in the right, and your readers should not be left hanging. ("Despite Dr. X's widely publicized theory that daily doses of vinegar will cure arthritis, reputable rheumatologists warn against relying on such unproven remedies.") But in others, you may find that established authorities are in genuine disagreement.

For a 1983 *Self* article, for instance, I was assigned to look into the role of the trace metal zinc in optimum health and in deficiency disorders. A number of researchers had correlated marked zinc deficiency with conditions ranging from dwarfism to sensory disturbances, and I cited these. But an important question was: How concerned should the average, healthy person be? Are most folks getting enough zinc? The answer turned out to be that the experts disagree. I stated that in so many words and quoted three eminent authorities, who said, essentially: don't worry; worry a little; worry a lot because millions of Americans are zinc-deficient.

Granted, this did not offer readers any pat guidelines on which to rely. But when equally knowledgeable and reputable sources diverge, it's the journalist's reponsibility not to reach conclusions but to report that divergence. It also seems to me that the latter shows more respect for readers.

In a situation where research tells you disagreement looms large, should you stir the controversy by inviting adversary comment? Yes, I think so. Asking Dr. A, "What do you think of Dr. B's hypothesis?" will make the situation clearer to you, since Dr. A may provide illuminating details. And, whether or not your finished piece quotes Dr. A, it will enable you to more clearly spell out the nature of the debate. Of course, if Dr. A's criticism includes an allegation of, say, bumbling error on Dr. B's part, you are obliged—if you are going to cite that criticism—to seek out Dr. B's side of the story.

BOOKS: SHARING THE LOAD

In books, as in articles, opinion and fact must be clearly labeled. But there's a difference. Generally speaking, a magazine article by a nonphysician will examine all aspects of a medical controversy. A book, however, can take a far narrower point of view, with no need to elicit opposing opinions. That is especially true if you have a physician collaborator, because of his or her professional judgment in medical matters.

I'd published a few books before I got the idea for my first in-depth tome on a medical topic. Good idea, said the publisher to whom my then-agent presented the proposal, but find an M.D.; we want medical authority behind this book so readers will know they're getting real expertise. I found the physician, and *The Mothers' Medical Encyclopedia*, by Virginia E. Pomeranz, M.D. and yours truly, was published in 1972. (A revised and expanded edition, retitled *The Mothers' and Fathers' Medical Encyclopedia*, appeared five years later.)

I have now collaborated with six different physicians on a total of eight books, and I've contracted for three others. Of the eleven books, only two were my ideas. Of the other nine, six ideas originated with the physicians and three with the publishers. (Of the latter, one asked for a new edition of a published book; one came up with the thought, found the physicians, then sought a writer; the third brought me the premise and left me to turn up an appropriate co-author.) As with magazine articles, word of your expertise gets around.

Collaboration on health/medicine books has a couple of advantages beyond the selling power of that "M.D." on the cover. One is a shift of responsibility—not for the writing, which is almost wholly yours, but for medical matters per se; if there are goofs, it's your co-author's fault. The other is that author publicity is almost always solely the physician's chore. Radio and TV talk-show hosts want to hear the eye doctor, not you, explain how to cope with cataracts and answer listeners' or viewers' questions about contact lenses. (Some writers who enjoy being interviewed on talk shows—which I do not—would consider this a distinct *dis*advantage.)

The Bottom Line

At the beginning, I briefly encapsuled the major fascinations and minor aggravations of medical writing. For the sake of completeness, I must add one of each.

There is frequently a minor drawback during the early months, or even years, of pursuing this occupation: susceptibility to each and every ailment treated in an article or book, from common, garden-variety ills to rare afflictions which cannot be contracted except by spending months in a mosquito-infested tropical jungle. You get over this eventually. In the meantime, you can assure yourself that you have an extremely creative imagination.

The other facet of medical writing involves one of the most rewarding experiences a writer can have: the reader's letter expressing gratitude for the hope you have offered a child with cancer, or the reassurance you have offered a depressed chronic-illness victim, or the timely warning which has sent a diabetic to seek treatment. It doesn't happen often; in this as in every field, complaints and questions outnumber compliments.

But when it happens, it is truly a joy, because it confirms your very existence as a writer. And that makes everything worthwhile.

A Postscript

I want to add a point-of-view note on the matter of markets for medical-writing expertise. Many of my fellow contributors to this book have doubtless sung the praises—and hailed the profits—of purveying one's services to purchasers other than publishers. There *are* such possibilities in the health/medical area.

I have, for example, occasionally ghostwritten material (e.g., speeches to be delivered to medical groups) for physicians. I would not hesitate to write for a voluntary hospital, a university, or similar institution. But despite a number of opportunities, I have deliberately shunned one area which a number of writers have found extremely lucrative: I do *no* work for pharmaceutical (or medical-equipment) manufacturers or their advertising or public relations agencies. The reason is simply that I want to avoid even the *appearance* of a conflict of interests.

A number of colleagues with whom I have discussed this question see no problem. One said, "I'm totally independent. The fact that I've written a news release for a drug company, or its PR agency, has nothing to do with how I describe the firm's products in an article or book. I've been paid to write that release, period." Another would draw a line between strictly promotional product-related copy and other copy: "I don't do material touting the advantages, say, of a new vaccine against pneumonia. But I have no hesitation about writing the backgrounder that goes in the kit."

(To explain the terms in that last sentence: Often, when a new medication or other treatment is announced, writers and editors are handed or sent not only a news release but a package known as a *press kit*. The kit is typically a folder containing a number of items, variously including a straight news release, photograph(s) of the product, information on the company, data on distinguished researchers involved in product development, quotes from prominent physicians who have confirmed the efficacy of the product in independent studies, medical journal reprints of reports of such studies, and, often, a *backgrounder*. A backgrounder is provided to give writers and editors some peg on which to hang the story. In the case of pneumonia vaccine, it might detail the various infectious agents causing pneumonia, describe symptoms of the illness, trace the history of pneumonia treatment, and single out those segments of the population for whom pneumonia poses the most serious threat. It does not push, and typically does not even mention, the product. It is "clean.")

I happen to think my colleagues are practicing a bit of convenient rationalization and ignoring a certain reality. I question neither the integrity of the first writer nor the sincerity of the second. I do, however, wonder how these individuals might be viewed by those who don't know them as well as I do. It seems to me that readers have a right to assume that we are completely disinterested and impartial, specifically, that we derive *no* part of our income from commercial interests. I think our editors are also entitled to that assumption. (I would, incidentally, apply this to other topics as well. Just as I don't take on jobs for Ciba-Geigy or Sterling Drug, I would like to know as a reader that I'm not getting money-management advice from someone in the pay of Shearson/American Express, or a searching analysis of comparative auto performance from a writer who turns out news releases for General Motors.)

I believe, in short, that our *internal* vow of independence is not enough. *Appearances* count, too. And, like Caesar's wife, we must be above suspicion.

SPECIALTY: HEALTH AND MEDICINE
by Barbara Goodheart

Surely health and medicine are among the most interesting and rewarding specialties for today's freelance writer. The fact that a medical writer's work may influence the health and happiness of countless people was recently underscored in the 1982 Mort Weisinger Award competition, in which three of the four final selections dealt with medical topics. [Editor's note: The Mort Weisinger Award, given in memory of a late ASJA president and founding member of the Society, singles out distinguished magazine-article writing by a Society member.)

You can become an expert in several medical areas and cover them for both consumer and specialty markets. Also, one of the hottest areas today is medical education. Advertising firms and pharmaceutical companies look for writers to provide continuing medical-education programs for physicians and nurses and to supply monographs, texts, tests, and audiovisual scripts for pharmaceutical salespeople.

Have You Got What It Takes?

What qualifications does a medical writer need? Although my bachelor's degree in biology is extremely helpful, many excellent writers in the field studied English literature, journalism, or even engineering in college. A medical writer does need a good basic education and a willingness to research a subject thoroughly.

Equally important is something I can best describe as an almost intuitive feel for what is *solid* versus what's *trendy* in medicine. The writer who is carried away by Dr. X's new cure which no one else in the medical community endorses should try writing in another field. A medical writer also must be able to relate to physicians and to see them realistically—not as demigods, nor as people just out to make a buck. Many writers lose lucrative assignments because they cannot conduct interviews without belittling or antagonizing physicians.

Coming Up with Ideas

The following are good sources:

- Experts you're working with on other assignments. A virologist I was interviewing for a *Lady's Circle* article on the common cold gave me a very early lead on the German measles vaccine, then being developed. After an advance go-ahead from *Today's Health*, I stayed on top of the story until it was published the month the vaccine was released to the public.
- Medical conventions. (Consult your newspaper's listing of upcoming conventions in your city.) Visit the press room at the convention and read the press releases. The public relations staff will arrange interviews, and you can visit sessions if you wish.
- Newspapers, consumer magazines, medical publications such as *Medical World News, Medical Tribune*, and specialty journals. To save time, simply toss your clippings into a cardboard box. (I learned this wonderful trick from ASJA member Elliott McCleary, and it has saved me countless hours of filing.) When you're looking for a query idea, go through your box of clips and see what gels. While doing this one day, I found several clips that suggested an article on annual checkups. I queried *Family Weekly*, fleshed out the idea, and sold the story. (Medical clips become old fast. When the box is full, throw away the bottom half of the pile.)

Gathering Information

If you're researching a topic, your local research librarian may be able to order scientific papers and books for you; this varies from state to state. Or, to use the medical library at the nearest medical school, present your credentials to the head librarian and ask for permission. (If you're a beginner, your local librarian may be able to provide you with a pass.) Look for information on your topic in the *Index Medicus*.

Alternatively, some librarians will do a Medline search for you, usually for a fee.

Modern technology provides us with research tools at our fingertips. Through my word-processing/communications system, I can dial Dialog and immediately access Medline, the Magazine Index, the Newspaper Index, or dozens of other data bases. I scan pertinent abstracts right on my screen or order printouts to be sent by first class mail the same evening. You can really impress an editor or client who calls with a question when you say, "I'll call you back in five minutes," and when you do, rattle off all kinds of up-to-the-minute information! This is one of the many benefits of word-processing systems with communications capabilities.

Sometimes you can save time and money by hiring a graduate student to do research. Some master's or doctorate candidates work for reasonable fees, turn up information quickly, and are a tremendous help in emergencies. I once needed information and graphics on the smoking habits of various international populations with data organized by country, sex, and age. I called my researcher and two days later received copies of about sixty pages of text and tables from a variety of publications. The bill wasn't much more than I would have spent on transportation and lunch, and I saved almost a full working day.

If you're starting a long-term project and want to invest in a few textbooks, you'll usually find a medical bookstore near the medical library. In addition to special books for your project, you'll probably need such basic texts as the annual *Physicians' Desk Reference (PDR)*, the *Merck Manual*, a medical dictionary, *Guyton's Textbook of Medical Physiology*, and *Manual for Authors & Editors* (a stylebook prepared by the American Medical Association).

Finding Subject-Matter Experts

The public information office at a medical school or teaching hospital can usually put you in touch with an appropriate expert. Many major teaching hospitals publish a directory with a detailed listing of experts by subject; it's a good idea to keep several of these on your library shelf. Experts you've worked with on previous projects may be able to provide information on your current assignment or recommend an appropriate source for interviewing.

Organizing Research Materials

Once you've completed your research, you can save time if you organize before starting to write. I use a system similar to one described by ASJA member Robert Gannon in *A Treasury of Tips for Writers.* I put my notes, reprints, and articles in a pile. Then I plan my article or book chapter, jotting each major topic heading on a 3x5-inch index card—for example, "lead," "nuts and bolts paragraph," "history lead-in," "end," etc. (Using index cards rather than legal-size paper simplifies reorganization and expansion.) I then begin reading or rereading my references. When I come to a section I want to use, I mark the reference and note the volume and page on an index card. After I've finished, I write each section, referring to the indicated references. The index cards serve as my permanent record of reference sources.

Fact Checking

To verify accuracy, I send my sources two copies of the manuscript sections in which they're quoted along with a paragraph or two preceding and following the section to indicate context. If the topic is a sensitive one, I may send the entire article to an expert. In either case, I ask the expert to sign and return one copy or to call me collect within a week if there are any questions or comments. I also mention that unless I hear, I'll assume the manuscript is accurate. (After publication, I send my sources a copy of the magazine along with a thank-you note.)

Working with Corporate Clients

When you're accustomed to working with magazine or book editors, it's difficult at first to answer a corporate client's (e.g., pharmaceutical house's or medical equipment manufacturer's) query, "How much do you charge?"

First, decide on an appropriate daily rate. Don't make it too low. Daily rates of $250 or $300 are not unusual for experienced medical writers with good track records, and many go higher; beginning writers should charge at least $100 to $150 per day. Remember, you're paying overhead and Social Security, and you don't get the fringe benefits staff writers do. Nor do you usually get a byline or future rights. The full-time freelance equivalent of a $30,000 gross salary is about $37.50 per productive hour, or $262.50 for a seven-hour writing day. Of course you probably won't make that much starting out, but it's a goal to shoot for.

Next, estimate how many days a project will take. This is often difficult. I've underestimated many times over the years, and I've learned to ask key questions:

- "How many meetings must I attend?" Clients can "meeting"

you to death! If a client specifies one day, include that in the estimate—but add that any additional meetings will be billed at the daily rate.

- Does the client provide all references? If not, fees for library time and computer searches should be included in the quote or, by agreement, billed separately.
- Does the project require internal referencing (references numbered in the body of the manuscript and keyed at articles' end)? Must the references be highlighted and returned to the client? More time, more money.
- What about rewrites? If you're a highly experienced professional, one rewrite should be included and additional rewrites billed. If you're a beginner, you may have to do additional drafts without extra pay. Rewrites resulting from the client's changes in the project's content or scope should always be billed.
- "Who makes the final editorial decision?" The ideal situation is that a physician or a subject-matter expert not associated with the drug company has editorial control. The worst situation is when no one appears to have decision-making power. Beware! Your draft may be returned to you with diverse written comments from a variety of anonymous people, but without a final decision. More hassle, more time, much more money!
- "How quickly do you pay? Is there advance payment?" A company should either pay within two or three weeks of the invoice date or provide up-front money. Some do both.
- "What is the maximum number of pages for this project?" Some companies deliberately understate the number of pages, hoping to pay less. Protect yourself by specifying additional payment if the content specified by the client requires additional pages.
- "When is the deadline?" A tight deadline is worth more money, and the client should pay for messenger service or express mail.

After you have the answers to these questions, you'll find it easier to estimate how many pages you can produce per day. Then multiply days needed by your daily rate to determine your fee for the project.

On accepting an assignment, read the contract carefully and have your attorney check it if you have questions. If the company doesn't use contracts, you can protect yourself by drafting a letter of agreement based on the ASJA form (see Appendix).

Using a Logbook

Only by keeping a record of your working time can you determine your actual earnings so as to set realistic fees in the future. (I keep careful track, which is why I rarely write magazine articles these days; the pay per hour is very low.) I record my time for every project, specifying meetings, background work, research, first-draft writing, revision, and hand-holding (e.g., keeping the client happy). I try to get more than one project out of any assignment involving heavy research and background work. When I finish a project I compare the actual hours spent and total income with my original estimate. Sometimes I make a killing; somtimes I take a bath. But thanks to my logbook, my estimates are getting more realistic.

Marketing

To make certain I'm doing enough promotion to keep getting assignments, I also note in my logbook the time I spend making and maintaining contacts. It's essential to keep clients and editors thinking about you from time to time while you're busy with other projects. You can do this by sending a brief note or an updated résumé, phoning every few months, or taking the client or editor to lunch occasionally. Unless you do this, you're likely to find yourself with nothing to do after you finish a project. But if you market yourself effectively and provide your editors and clients with accurate, well-written material, you'll stay busy and make a good living in medical writing.

PRESCRIPTION FOR HEALTH AND MEDICAL WRITING
by Ruth Winter

Why are you qualified to write about a health or medical subject? Who would want to read what you wrote?

If you can answer those two questions satisfactorily, your chances of selling articles and books to health-related markets are probably better than in any other specialty. Nothing interests readers more than their own well-being.

You do not need a medical degree or a Ph.D. in science to write about health and medicine, although such qualifications certainly help. You do, however, have to be a careful researcher, a patient interviewer, and a reporter who can recognize and shape a good story.

Why should anyone care about what you write? The answer is— and it is the key to all successful writing—they *don't* care unless it affects them directly. Today, most people are flooded with information from many sources. It is very difficult to get and keep their attention with descriptions of startling advances in cell biology or in space technology unless you can convince them that such findings affect them personally. That's the job of the health and medical writer.

Best-Selling Subjects

What subjects are the most popular?

The truth is that what readers most want to know concerns common diseases that affect them now or might in the future—cancer, arthritis, heart disease, and emotional ills.

A committee judging an annual science writers' award for the American Heart Association declined to give the prize one year. They felt none of the articles submitted "presented any new information and that by now, everyone knows the heart is a 'fist-sized' organ."

I venture to say that not everyone does know the heart is a fist-sized organ, although science writers certainly do. The point was that no one was creative enough to come up with fresh material about a subject of universal interest.

What else can be written about heart disease? Who would read it? Everyone who has had a heart attack, or who feels he or she may have a heart attack, or who loves someone suffering from cardiovascular disease will read every word on the subject. They can never get enough information—if only to check on the recommendations of their doctors. Since heart disease is the number one killer in the United States, you can see what a potential market it is.

I don't mean that all you have to do is rush out and write an article about heart disease or cancer and it will sell immediately. There is a lot of competition among medical writers, and some not only write well but have "M.D." after their names. But editors are always looking for fresh angles and new developments in health and medicine.

To Market, To Market

Let's say you've identified a really good story. Where do you think you can sell it?

First, let's take the toughest market—newspaper syndication. The syndication field today makes political campaigns look like sugar and spice. But for some reason, medical writers all dream of having a syndicated column. Almost every newspaper and magazine has its own medical columnist. The news services pick up stories from local papers and send them out nationally, often without additional pay to the writer and at little cost to the subscribing media. Or the news wires and feature syndicates may pay medical writers a small flat fee for an article or column and then send it out in a package with articles on politics, beauty, money, and other subjects.

Columnists fortunate enough to have their columns sold on an individual basis get a royalty. Newspapers pay according to circulation, a few dollars per week. The columnist splits the income, usually fifty-fifty, with the syndicate. If you're being syndicated to a lot of big newspapers, the money adds up nicely. But how many big papers need columns? If a newspaper takes your column, it has to drop someone else's. Finally, syndicates receive an average of one hundred column ideas per week, stacking the odds against you.

Nevertheless, this doesn't mean it can't be done. I did it. If you come up with the right idea at the right time, you may do it too.

The same thing applies to the magazine field. The top markets—and by that I mean the big women's and men's magazines—are hard to crack. They pay several thousand dollars for a major article. Naturally, most health and medical writers would like to write for them instead of the magazines that pay twenty-five dollars or give free copies to contributors. But since there are few big magazines left and lots of medical writers, you can imagine the competition. Again, that doesn't mean it can't be done.

Most of the news magazines are staff-written. The smaller, "intellectual" magazines are also hard to crack becasue you're competing with professors who have to "publish or perish" and the famous who want to keep their names before the "right" public. But there is a good market in the special-interest magazines (such as inflight and fraternal publications) which pay a few hundred dollars for an article.

With regard to books, be sure your subject is not only of lasting interest to the public but to you. It takes at least nine months to produce a book and you may lose interest in the topic after living with it for a while. Also, the information on scientific subjects may be out of date by the time it is published. Unfortunately, the books that sell best to the consumer market are often trendy books that describe easy cures or way-out, do-it-yourself treatments. There are, however, books on basic subjects such as breast feeding, easing a child's visit to the hospital, and diabetes, that don't make the best-seller lists but do sell steadily for years. Assume, however, that a solid, scientifically sound book provides more satisfaction in the doing than in the dollars.

If you are determined to be a health and medical writer, here's my prescription based on more than thirty years in the field:

• Look for a good story nearby. Your local hospital, nearby medical school, or branch offices of national health groups can provide you with leads. Among the easier stories to sell are those about "a child in jeopardy" or the "brave sufferer" who overcame dangerous illness or who succumbed after a valiant fight. Are there innovative techniques or new treatment methods being used by scientists near you? Newspapers and newsletters often provide leads.

• Don't take "No" for an answer. If you believe a researcher has information for a good story, be persistent. Doctors and other scientists are often busy, and insensitive to writers' deadlines. They may return your calls three months later. If, however, they are reluctant to reveal what they are doing, point out that the public has a right to know, since so much of their work is supported by public funds.

• Be wary of the overeager. At one time, doctors and scientists were publicity shy. Now, some have hired public relations firms. Just because someone has an advanced degree doesn't mean he or she is reliable. Always check with others in the same field to put a research claim in perspective.

• Be prepared. Study as much about the subject as you can *before* your first interview. Every institution has a public relations representative today. Ask that person for background materials, published papers, and biographies of the researchers in advance, if possible. Look up material in your library. Check *Readers' Guide To Periodical Literature* and the *New York Times Index* to track down other articles on the same subject. If you find the material very difficult to understand, go into the children's library section. Often there is a book on the subject written in simple terms. You'll find everything from computers to DNA on the shelves there.

• Use a tape recorder. In today's litigious society, should a researcher decide to deny something he or she said, you can say, "I have it on tape." Furthermore, when dealing with a difficult subject, you may miss a lot during the interview, and by listening to the tape several times, you can make sure that everything is accurate and understandable.

• Don't be afraid to ask for explanations. Most researchers are eager to explain the significance of their work and to make sure you understand the project.

• Translate. It is your job as a writer to interpret in English what scientists are doing and to point out the significance of their work. Most researchers have a tendency to overqualify everything they say so you have to make an effort to keep the material simple and to the point.

• Have a basic library. Keep a good medical dictionary on hand. I like *Stedman's* (Williams and Wilkins). Also vital are *The Merck Manual of Diagnosis and Therapy* (Merck Sharp and Dohme Laboratories) and the *Physicians' Desk Reference* (Medical Economics Company), which gives the generic and trade names of drugs, their uses and side effects. You should also subscribe to journals. The basic ones are: the *Journal of the American Medical Association*, the *New England Journal of Medicine*, and *Science*. Subscribe also to those on specialties interesting you most.

• Be responsible. You must be careful when describing advances, particularly concerning cancer or degenerative diseases. In dramatizing your story, don't give false hope. It's cruel.

• Be accurate. You can't be held responsible for the mistakes of editors, headline writers, or others handling your story once it is out of your hands, but you must check and recheck your facts. In other areas of reporting, editors frown on writers' submitting manuscripts to sources for a fact check because it slows things down. I try to read my articles to sources over the phone. I tell them they may cite errors in fact but that the writing is my own. Almost all make some changes, some of them nitpicking. It is up to you to decide if the alterations are legitimate. (Even doctors are fallible. The *American Medical News* described a case in which a patient was being treated for a painful right ear and the physician prescribed a combination antibiotic and local anesthetic. In writing the prescription, the physician left out the period after the "R"—the abbreviation for *right*. The person administering the medication interpreted the directions as "rear" and the patient received three doses of ear drops in his rectum before the error was discovered.)

Health and medical writing is the area in which the most *new* news is being made. There are only so many ways to commit a murder or run a political campaign, but scientists are constantly making discoveries about something that interests all of us—our bodies. The fields of immunology and endocrinology are bursting with new information about how we live and respond to our environment.

If you want to write a newspaper column, magazine article, or book about a medical subject, do it even if your chances of selling it are a million to one. Pick a subject of wide interest. Do solid research. Make the significance clear, and have persistence and a thick skin. You have to really want to do it and believe that eventually you will do it. No one can discourage a real writer, and that's healthy for the world.

HOW THE PROFESSIONAL WRITES FOR MEDICINE/HEALTH MARKETS
by Morris A. Wessel, M.D.

The first thing I do whenever I consider writing an article is to clarify why the subject is important. This is a difficult and time-consuming process.

I sometimes ponder for weeks trying to decide which health problem I will tackle: I reflect on ideas and possible topics in the shower, when shaving, before going to sleep at night, early in the morning before arising, or while walking my dog. Indeed, my dog is probably the best-educated canine in pediatrics in the United States. The only problem is that she's never critical. She likes what I say, regardless of subject or the quality of my English. Nevertheless, talking aloud helps me get a handle on what I want to say before I write. This stream-of-consciousness process, as Ardis Whitman emphasizes (*A Treasury of Tips for Writers*, Writer's Digest Books), sooner or later leads to finding the focus for a piece.

DEVELOPING AN ARTICLE IDEA

Take the common problem of infants suffering inexplicable periods of irritability, fussiness, or crying that often develop into agonizing and inconsolable moments of screaming, known as *colic*. These babies draw up their knees against a distended abdomen as they suffer severe cramps. Expulsion of gas through the rectum is common. The babies act hungry, but feeding usually offers no relief, and often makes the condition worse. A day consists of a few quiet hours, usually in the morning, then the babies become increasingly restless and begin screaming. This often continues late into the evening or past midnight. They finally go to sleep, only to begin the distressing cycle of discomfort again the next day.

Colic severely distresses not only infants, but their parents, particularly new parents, who feel inadequate, helpless, and angry. They spend hours without sleep, attempting to comfort the infant. More than one parent has wished the baby had never been born. Others (I am often told years later) consider leaving the baby on their pediatrician's doorstep! (I myself remember thirty years ago taking many a car ride in the evening with my infant son after discovering that driving on the Wilbur Cross Parkway was an effective way of comforting him. Gasoline was cheaper in those days.)

As I listened to parents, observed babies, and read studies of infants done at the Mayo Clinic and Yale Medical School, I began to comprehend how these babies were temperamentally and physiologically unique. I thought that by writing a short article on how these babies differed from easier-to-care-for infants, I would help reduce parents' frustration and discouragement. I had observed in my own practice, as well as in the data from the infant studies, that most colicky babies spontaneously become cured at eight to ten weeks of age. Relief was in sight in due time. I talked to the editor of *Parents* magazine, and she agreed to consider a manuscript on infant colic.

I then began to translate the medical terminology describing colicky behavior into lay terms. After hours of research, I concluded that these infants were *highly sensitive*. They reacted just like other babies, only more so! External stimuli, like noises and tension in the family, and internal stimuli like gas pains or stomachache—slightly disturbing to most babies—caused intense discomfort for colicky babies.

When these babies were happy and enjoying life, however, they seemed to put more of themselves into joyousness. They laughed more quickly than noncolicky babies, smiled from ear to ear, and beamed and cooed when played with. They overreacted in a positive way as well as negative.

"Is Your Baby a Sparkler?" appeared in the February 1963 issue of *Parents*. I received hundreds of letters from *both* medical and lay readers expressing appreciation for an understandable description of why some babies are colicky. That article was my first success as a *popular* writer. I learned that common everyday pediatric problems are of interest to editors and readers. I have been writing ever since.

ANSWER FREQUENTLY ASKED QUESTIONS

Let me cite another example. There are certain seasons—mid-May when grasses begin to bloom; mid-August when ragweed appears; September when school opens—when I am deluged with phone calls and visits from parents. The complaints go like this: "My six-year-old has been coughing for weeks . . . My toddler has had a cold for six weeks . . . Ever since school started my children have been coughing . . . He is full of pep, but he coughs constantly . . . He did this last year at the same time too. He's all choked up . . . His eyes are red . . . He rubs his nose all the time and this drives me crazy . . . Now my husband is coughing . . . I'm a little congested too . . . I don't think it is serious . . . but it seems so endless . . . Do you think it could be an allergy, or is it just the increase in colds that happens whenever school opens? . . . I have hay fever in the spring and my husband used to have asthma as a child . . ."

The symptoms are normally caused by either an allergic reaction to molds and pollens in the air, or the heightened incidence of colds in any community due to children's increased contact with each other after vacation from school. Frequently both factors are involved.

As I listened to parents, I sensed that the basic problem was not whether the symptoms were allergic in origin, or whether I could suggest any medication, but rather how could they be certain that these symptoms didn't represent bronchitis, tonsillitis, pneumonia, or cystic fibrosis. Parents seek consultation to make certain they are not overlooking a serious condition that might lead to complications if un-treated. They seek reassurance that it is safe to let their children run around, in spite of the coughing and sneezing.

I decided to query an editor with an article idea on how to differen-tiate sneezes and coughs due to allergy or viral infection from more se-rious conditions. The articles editor of *Ladies' Home Journal* responded positively, and the piece appeared in that magazine in February 1982.

More Idea Sources

Another stimulus for me is to recognize the "spirit of the times." For example, I published "A Death in the Family—the Impact on Chil-dren" in the *Journal of the American Medical Association* in 1975, and re-ceived many requests for reprints.

The response to this article and the increasing professional and lay discussions of death, dying, and bereavement represent a determined effort to offer help to families when a loved one dies. Erna Furman's *A Child's Parent Dies* (Yale Press, 1975) emphasized that bereaved chil-dren were likely to be ignored, sometimes to the point of neglect. This is wrong. It is unfair. Children need the same consideration—that is, honest discussion, nurturing, and comforting in their sadness at the time of the loss of someone they love and who loved them—as do adults. Parents and others caring for children should concentrate on comforting a child in his sadness, rather than trying to prevent a child from being sad. A child's loss is very real and he/she has reason and need to be sad.

I concluded that the widespread discussion of this formerly taboo subject suggested a vast reading audience, and I sold an article on chil-dren's bereavement to *Ladies' Home Journal*.

GETTING DOWN TO WORK

The formulation of an idea and an approach for an article is the first step; the query is the second step; an acceptance (or a tentative go-ahead) is the third step. Once the idea is sold, the hard work begins. Only after hours in the library spent reading what the textbooks and professional journals say about the subject, and more hours thinking about how this fits into my experience, am I ready to write. What re-sults is a synthesis of my professional experience and observations with what others have said about the topic.

My next step is to write a lead sentence and then make a detailed outline. Some fortunate writers are able to prepare a rough draft at this stage without the benefit of an outline. I cannot do this. I need to draw up a careful plan in order to avoid repetition.

In order to succeed in writing, it's important to keep writing. Early in my career, seeing a published piece in a local daily or weekly newspaper or in magazines once distributed with diapers made me feel I was "getting there." It motivated me to continue writing, despite many rejected manuscripts. However, over the years I began to receive acceptances, so that currently many of my queries result in assignments.

CUT, REVISE, AND EDIT

Doctors—and I am no exception—tend to use too many words to say nothing. The secret to good writing, as William Zinsser stresses in *On Writing Well* (Harper and Row, 1976), is to strip every sentence down to its sparsest components. I find that I need to read my manuscript many times. I lay it aside for a few days, then review it. No matter how many times I read a manuscript (even after it's published!).I always find words that clutter the meaning. Eliminate every extra adverb, double negative, and if possible, every passive verb. I keep asking, "What am I trying to say?" Reading aloud often makes poor phrasing and awkwardness obvious. If it isn't absolutely clear to me, then it won't be clear to anyone else.

Professionals often develop jargon. The psychoanalytic literature is a case in point. Suffering over a death and mourning are universal experiences. The psychoanalysts talk about "decathexing." *Cathexis* means the concentration of one's emotional energy and attachment on a person or subject. And *decathexis* means ending one's attachment to a person or subject. How much simpler to talk about "the process of letting go," what we all must do when a loved one dies.

A writer who may not be an expert, but who researches a subject thoroughly, often unwittingly adopts professional jargon. The writing becomes obtuse and complex. This is regrettable, since the material then loses its appeal for editors and readers.

Be aware of style. Every writer has one *and* so does every publication. Peruse back issues before you send a query, or seek an appointment with an editor.

AN AIR OF AUTHORITY

Medical journals prefer crisp, well-documented statements with many references to previously published articles by experts in the field. Writing for lay magazines is different. You must write with an authoritative air conveying that you know your subject. This does not mean using a lot of technical terms or jargon. It means just the opposite. It is important to keep one's prose nontechnical.

Gaining this authoritative tone comes in many ways. The best, of course, is that gained from years of clinical experience as a professional. However, writers can gain this aura in other ways. It results from spending many hours in a library, reading what experts say about a particular subject. Talking with specialists in the field also helps. After being steeped in the subject for several weeks or months, the writer feels comfortable about the subject. This is communicated to the reader.

After years of working with children, adolescents, and parents, I'm convinced it's possible to do this. Don't talk down to a reader. Just use simple, clear prose and resort frequently to *Roget's Thesaurus* or a dictionary to find just the right word to convey a complex message simply.

I find it helpful when reading newspaper articles, particularly on the Op-Ed pages, to ask why one article reads easily and interests me while another bores me. What is it about the writer's style that makes his or her work so understandable and readable? Tom Wicker, Anthony Lewis, Leonard Silk, and James Reston (all of the *New York Times*) are masters at expository writing. They eliminate extra words, avoid technical terms, and thus increase the readability of their columns for everyone.

It is hard work to write. But it is rewarding, particularly when the finished article is helpful to others. That is my goal, after all, both in the practice of pediatrics and in writing.

WRITING FOR THE HEALTH AND FITNESS MARKETS
by Kathryn Lance

Anyone who knew me when I was growing up would probably be surprised to learn that I make my living as a health and fitness writer. In grade school, I was always the last person chosen for sports teams. In high school and college, I did my best to avoid gym classes and, when trapped, took such noneffort-requiring subjects as billiards and posture. Until shortly before my thirtieth birthday I had no interest in, or knowledge of, anything even remotely related to care of the body. Sports, exercise, healthy diet—what were these compared to reading books and writing in my secret journal? As far as I was concerned, my body was simply a handy carrying case for my brain. I simply assumed my health would take care of itself. My grandparents were in their eighties and I figured I would live to a ripe old age even though I did smoke, was overweight, and didn't exercise.

But when I was twenty-nine, I discovered I had high blood pressure. For the first time, my own mortality became a reality for me. Despite my dislike of exercise and calorie counting, I realized I wasn't going to write the Great American Novel if I died of a stroke or heart attack by age thirty-five. Neither did I want to become dependent for life on the drugs which control blood pressure, which I had heard have the side effects of lethargy and depression. From my reading I had learned just enough about fitness to know that exercise was supposed to lower blood pressure in some cases. Though I imagined it an arduous task, and was certain I'd hate it, I started jogging.

Becoming a True Believer

Now, this all happened in 1973, long before the current running boom. After a few weeks of jogging, I felt physically good, my blood pressure went down and, eventually, my body underwent a complete transformation. With the zeal of a true convert, I began buttonholing acquaintances and friends—to tell them about the miracles of jogging. And I began to read about exercise, diet, and fitness. But except for *Aerobics* by Ken Cooper, I could find little in the libraries and bookstores about my current passion. It's hard to believe now, but there was practically nothing then available about jogging. I wanted to know more. I discussed the topic endlessly with everyone I met, especially fellow joggers. And then one day the answer came to me: if there were no books on the market about jogging, I would write one.

I go on at length about this because I want to stress that, in order to become a successful writer in any field, but particularly one that is somewhat technical, as mine is, you should be extremely interested in the subject. You don't have to be a fanatic, as I was, but it helps.

FIND A NEED . . .

The second lesson I gained from my early experience is what I call Lance's freelance rule—at least it's the way I always start when I'm writing about a specialized subject. Once interested in a given field, your next step is to find a lack of information somewhere within the field—and to supply that information. Furthermore, as I discovered and you can too, one interest leads to others. Although I started out writing about running, my research taught me a lot about general health and fitness, so that I began writing on other topics as well.

But back to my first book, on running. As a beginning runner and a *woman* I experienced psychological and physical difficulties. I got cat-calls from men, had trouble finding running shoes to fit, and because of my lack of athletic experience, didn't really know *how* to run. What was I supposed to do with my arms? Should I run on my toes or flat-footed? I soon realized from talking to other people that a lot of wom-en, particularly my age, would have the same types of problems.

I decided to direct the book at them. I would tell them how to get started, what to wear, how to stick with it, and how to avoid all the has-sles specific to women. In short, I would answer for my readers the questions I had faced as a beginning woman runner. My goal, apart from writing my own book, was to convert other people to running. Although I didn't know it at the time, I had just followed the third rule for successful freelancing: decide who your audience is, and limit the topic accordingly.

Getting Started

In my naiveté as an article writer, I thought I would just sit down, write the book, then try to sell it. Luckily, a friend suggested I first do a proposal to show to an agent friend of his. I had no idea how to write a proposal, so I went to the library and looked through back copies of *Writer's Digest* until I found a how-to for writing a proposal. Following the article's guidelines, I wrote a short sample chapter and then a de-tailed chapter outline, listing everything I had discovered or still wanted to know about running.

It turned out the agent was most impressed by my enthusiasm. The sample chapter, to be the first in the book, read as if I were doing what I actually *had* been doing for months—talking to another woman, trying to persuade her to start jogging. "This makes me want to take up jogging myself," the agent said. "Let's send it out and see what hap-pens."

The first two publishers rejected the proposal. One pointed out, "This might make an interesting magazine article, but nobody would want to read a whole book about running." The third publisher, Bobbs-Merrill, bought the proposal with a modest advance. In my continuing naiveté, I agreed to write the book in four months. (I had a full-time job at the time!) That brings me to another of Lance's rules: If you have any say in the matter, ask for as long a deadline as possible. You can get a piece in early, but you can't always control delays due to research and writing difficulties.

READ, RESEARCH, AND WRITE

And then the real work began. I started with a lot of enthusiasm but not a lot of knowledge. My first step was research. I read everything I could find on fitness and running. I read physiology textbooks to find out how muscles work and the physical benefits of exercise. I chose my reading in the same way I do now, the "scattershot" approach: I looked through any books or magazines I came across.

Rather than doing preliminary research to find out what existed, I took what I could find and let one book lead me to another. I have been told by other writers that this is a most unscientific approach, but it has always worked for me, and has often led me to other interests. In fact, it was this initial reading that led me to my next major interest, weight training.

I wanted the book to be both useful and accurate, so I arranged through the local Road Runners Club for a doctor interested in running to read my manuscript for accuracy, with the fitness director of a local YMCA to serve as my consultant. I also prepared a questionnaire for women runners and distributed it at races. I read the hundred or so completed questionnaires and conducted in-depth interviews with two dozen of the women. Knowing nothing about interviewing technique, I simply asked the women about the things I was most interested in, letting one question lead to another.

After assembling the research in categories which corresponded to chapter divisions, I began to write and rewrite. I sent the manuscript out, only to see it come back again and again, from the doctor, from my consultant, from my editor. The deadline was approaching and I worked longer and longer hours, eventually taking a leave of absence from my job (to which I never returned full-time).

My editor urged me to include more anecdotes, and I found the questionnaires valuable for this. At the time, for example, there was little written in medical or popular literature about the effects of exercise on pregnant women. Through my interviews, I found several women who had run during pregnancy and was able to get anecdotal advice for pregnant women considering running.

As I wrote I kept in mind that my goal was not to snow readers with my erudition, but to persuade them to begin running. The vast majority of material I collected never went into the book, but in some mysterious way it made the book more authoritative and served me later on when I began to write about other fitness topics.

Running for Health and Beauty was published in 1977. As a first book, it was not extensively promoted, but it dealt with an idea whose time had come (*see a need and fill it*) and sold quite well by word of mouth. Including a subsequent paperback edition, the book eventually sold over half a million copies.

An Expert Is Born

As a result of the book's success, and because of the growing interest in fitness, I began receiving requests to write articles about running for various magazines. At the same time, I became interested in weight training because of the reading I had done on the physiology of fitness. This led to my second book, *Getting Strong,* a woman's guide to weight training. I proceeded with this book in much the same way as the first. I began by trying to lift weights, and discovered there was virtually no literature on the subject for women. So I read everything I could find on weight training, interviewed experts, and arranged for a team of physiologists to serve as my consultants. Also, with their help, I devised a weight-training program and tested it (complete with questionnaire) on dozens of women.

By the time I finished *Getting Strong* I knew about as much about the field of exercise and exercise physiology as any layman could. I had also compiled a list of consultants and files on just about every aspect of the fitness field. And I continued to write magazine articles when requested, learning more each time.

My interest in fitness led me to an interest in general health improvement, so I began to study nutrition. Since each of my books featured a section on exercise as an aid in losing weight, I began getting requests to write diet articles. Subsequently, I read widely in the field of weight loss, interviewed experts, and built up a new set of files.

Throughout the years, I have not much changed the techniques I learned for the first book. Magazine articles are shorter, of course, and there isn't time to do the exhaustive "scattershot" research I do for books. But I use a similar method. I read as much as time allows and interview as many people as possible. I still aim my writing at women much like myself, and though I am now quite knowledgeable, I try never to talk down to my readers, but to share with them what I have learned. I imagine them as I was—not knowing much about the subject but curious to learn.

A HEALTHY MARKET

The fitness and health field is growing and changing, with new magazines appearing every day. In addition, the traditional—primarily women's—magazines still use a great deal of material. Publishers are always open to new books in the field. I must emphasize the "new."

Admittedly, the competition is keener now than when I started, but if you are thinking of writing for this field, I would advise you to begin as I did: start with a strong interest in at least some aspect of that field. Read as much as you can about the subject, and talk to experts. Depending on your particular interest, you can find experts by calling local colleges, gyms, and hospitals. Your family doctor may be a valuable resource—my gynecologist always sets aside time during the regular examination to answer questions related to my work. As long as you give proper credit, most people will be happy to help you with a project (you may have to pay a small fee from time to time, but it's worth it for the air of authority). Writing for this field is not easy; much research will be technical and tedious, but all of it is important. Even if you never tell your readers what is happening on a cellular level during muscle movement (and you almost certainly won't!), you yourself need to have a pretty good idea of how muscles work when discussing exercise. Read and talk to people; find out what the trends are. Keep looking for that one area you are especially interested in, that nobody has yet written about to your satisfaction. Discover that "need," and then fill it. And good luck!

TIPS FOR MEDICAL WRITERS
by Gloria Hochman

Twelve years ago, an editor asked me to write an article on new developments in family therapy. My research revealed that family therapy was being used to cure victims of anorexia nervosa, the illness where people—mainly young women—starve themselves to become thin. (This now well-known illness had not yet been written about in the popular press.)

My editor was intrigued by the subject, delighted with the story I wrote, and immediately assigned me to another medical piece. This time it was about lupus, another little-known disease that, like anorexia nervosa, affects a disproportionate number of young women. A third medical assignment followed, and before I understood how it happened, I was a medical writer.

Since that time, medicine and science have become my specialties, although approximately 35 percent of my work focuses on other subjects, usually social issues.

The principles of effective medical writing, I have found, are not much different from those of other kinds of writing. Of course, each writer develops techniques that work for him or her.

Following are some techniques that work for me.

- Begin work at the library. Before I interview my first expert, I spend a lot of time, first at the general library, then at the medical library, to become familiar with my subject. In this way, I learn the jargon and am in a better position to speak intelligently with my sources.

- Prepare questions for interviews in advance. This saves time, prevents important issues from getting lost, and helps determine the direction of the story. It is important, however, not to be rigid but to permit the interview to go where your source takes it. He or she may make comments you had not anticipated and that are important to develop. So, even though you've prepared your interview questions beforehand, it is essential that you listen carefully to what the interviewee is saying.

- Keep files on topics that interest you and that you may want to write about in the future. (I date every clipping and file it by subject.)

- Keep a file on every person you interview for an article, with name, title, address, and telephone number. Not only is this information often necessary for editors, but it also gives you easy access to people you want to interview in the future.

- I tape all of my interviews. This ensures that quotes will be accurate and prevents a source from saying, "I never said that." This is especially important in medical reporting.

- Don't take shortcuts. If one source gives you information that contradicts that given you by another source, go back and check with your first source to get a reaction.

- Make friends with the librarians in the libraries you use most. When they know you, they can be extremely helpful in making research easier. I often drop notes to librarians who have been especially helpful, together with copies of the finished articles (which they might otherwise never see) to thank them for their help.

- Cultivate your source's secretary. It is often the secretary who determines if and when your calls go through. Tell the secretary why you are calling and what your story is about.

- Send thank-you notes to sources who have given you a lot of interview time, and be sure to send them copies of the published articles.

- When you are speaking with an expert on your subject, ask who else you should be talking to for your story. This can save a lot of time determining excellent sources.

- When you are doing a telephone interview, set it up in advance. It is unlikely that a source will be available for a forty-five minute conversation when you first call. Give the source the courtesy of setting up a mutually convenient time and indicate how much time will be needed.

• I usually check direct quotes with my sources. There are writers who do not, but in medical writing, I want to do this to ensure accuracy.

• Don't assume anything. Even if you see a person's name printed on a convention program, do not assume that it is spelled correctly or that the title is correct. Check with the source.

In trying to stress the importance of accuracy, one of my editors once said, "Do you think your mother loves you? Check it out."

YOUR SECRET FOR GETTING THROUGH TO DOCTORS
by Howard R. Lewis

A suburban family physician I'll call Arthur Delaney receives about fifty promotional, advertising, and educational pieces in his mail each day. He points to his wastebasket and says, "Most of them go in there, unread."

Why?

"They're *useless!*"

The typical physician is that pragmatic about anything you write for him. As Dr. Delaney puts it: "If you can't do something for me or my patients, forget it. I'm too busy to bother with you."

Small wonder. The average physician feels overburdened by his or her practice. Art Delaney, for example, gets up before 7:00 a.m. By 8:00 a.m. he's at the first of two hospitals, seeing patients and attending to other hospital-related responsibilities. He also tries to fit in quick consultations with other doctors and take care of activities he performs for his community and medical society.

He's often late for his first office appointment, scheduled for 1:00 p.m. He runs late the rest of the day, slowed down further by drop-ins, phone calls, protracted visits, and unexpected problems. He's rarely out of the office before 6:00 p.m. He then returns to the hospitals to check his patients again.

On top of this, he has an avalanche of paperwork and a stack of unread journals. He's often preoccupied with one or two tough cases, and perhaps with emotional encounters with patients and families. He's constantly mindful of the threat of malpractice litigation. In addition, he has a wife, children, and other private interests that deserve more time.

"If I get home before 8 o'clock I'm lucky," he reflects. "And you want to waste my time?"

BREAKING THE BUSYNESS BARRIER

After twenty-five years in medical writing and marketing, I'm well aware that competing for a physician's attention is *the* major problem for any medically oriented communicator. This is true whether you're reporting a research finding or delivering a commercial message. It's true whether you're writing an article, ad, brochure, press release, script, speech, or package insert. Furthermore, the physicians you generally most want to reach—those who see the most patients, prescribe the most drugs, buy the most equipment—are likely to be the hardest to contact because of the busyness barrier.

Too often, I've seen imaginative, four-color mailings thrown away—the literature doesn't even get to the physician's desk—because the secretary senses they'd only waste the doctor's time. One equipment manufacturer kept having that experience, and asked me to critique his mailings. I reported, "You're telling the doctor what you want him to hear rather than what he wants to know." We improved customer response considerably by redrafting the brochure and titling it *Making the Best Use of Your Office ECG.*

SOLUTION: SERVICE COPY

I've found that the best way to reach doctors is to offer them "service copy," information that is directly applicable. A scientific report, for example, should specify how the physician can apply it to his or her practice. An ad or other promotional piece should not only carry the company's message but also provide genuinely helpful advice.

Service copy stands the best chance of getting past the physician's secretary, who has usually been told to pass on only material the doctor is likely to find important. And service copy has the greatest likelihood of capturing the physician's attention, because the information can be applied to his or her practice.

Service copy commands the highest readership in medical publications. Get a good feel for service copy by glancing through the editorial contents of *Medical Economics* and *Patient Care,* two of the most widely read periodicals in medicine.

Medical Economics, which deals with physicians' personal as well as professional business affairs, was medicine's first how-to publication. A recent issue includes articles such as "How the Pension Pros Are Battling Inflation," "Six Low-Cost Gadgets That Conserve Energy," "Plan Ahead—Just In Case You Have to Fire an Associate," and "When Two Offices Are Better Than One."

Patient Care was started by *Medical Economics* staff members who saw the potential of offering doctors a similar practical approach in clinical matters. Contents of a recent issue included "When Memory Problems Are Treatable," "What to Do About Scalp Inflammation," and "Home Care for Myocardial Infarction?"

You get the idea. But how do you make it work? *And* how do you serve the interests of your specific product or service? Here are some tips I offer my writer-clients:

1. Make "you-tilitarianism" your watchword. Before taking a second look at anything they're asked to read, physicians are wont to ask, "What's in this for me?" Therefore, whenever possible, talk directly to *"you"* (the doctor-reader) and give information *"you"* can use.

Physicians generally like being addressed directly. This is often merely a matter of repackaging information. I was helping a malpractice insurance company develop an information program for physicians. The company had prepared a brochure titled *Medical Records: The Doctor's Best Friend.* Though full of helpful information, its use of the third person (referring to "the doctor" or "the physician") made it dull reading.

The doctor would be more likely to apply the information to himself or herself (the company's goal) if the brochure were retitled "Medical Records: *Your* Best Friend in Court," and if third-person references were changed into the second-person "you" form. Compare the difference in readability between these two ways of saying the same thing:

Third person: Physicians should be alert to the need for distinguishing between what the patient tells the doctor and what the doctor discovers himself.

Second person: Distinguish between what a patient tells you and what you discover yourself.

Don't worry about using imperatives (instructions like "distinguish" and "don't worry"). If your advice is good, doctors won't be offended.

Like other readers, physicians enjoy reading warm, colloquial prose. Listen to doctors talking to each other. Their speech is easygoing "Americanese" mixed with medical terminology for precision. Capture that in your copy and the physician-reader gets the feeling of conferring with a kindred spirit.

Write as if you were sending the doctor a personal letter. Emphasize practical advice. The busy physician is more likely to give your message a thorough reading if he or she senses it contains needed help.

Adopt a service-oriented attitude. You'll ordinarily know more about your product and its general field than the physician does. The more effort you spend actually helping, in sincerely saying, "I want to aid you in solving a problem," the more the doctor will welcome and act on your message, rather than resist and ignore it.

2. Recognize the physician's priorities. Patient care is of paramount interest to the physician in private practice. It's the meat and potatoes of life, the measure of his or her humanitarianism and scientific skills. Also of prime interest is a concomitant of patient care: avoiding mistakes that may injure the patient (and land the doctor in court—you cannot overestimate the fear physicians have of legal trouble).

Also high-ranking in physicians' priorities is the desire for more free time. Tell a physician how to be more efficient, how to get home earlier, and you'll almost certainly get that doctor's attention. Far behind in most physicians' priorities are goals such as increased earnings, reduction in size of practice, and greater specialization.

News generally has high readership among doctors, who are trained to seek the latest information. So consider playing up the most current development, preferably in the form "Here's news you can use." Sometimes you merely need to give a new slant to an old feature of your product. One major tranquilizer is effective for the treatment of hyperactive children. A fresh emphasis on that use gives the quality of news.

Many doctors worry and feel harassed. The immediate future is of great interest to them, and brief items are extremely popular with doctors. While I was an editor at one journal I helped develop a "What's Ahead" department, which is made up of a number of telegram-like forecasts. Its readership is so high that it's now placed in the back of the book to help pull readers through the entire issue.

3. Aim with a rifle, not a shotgun. Once you've established your basic message, it will pay to direct it at specific audiences (as determined by the advertiser). There will be extra printing costs for individualizing mail pieces, but that expenditure will probably be more than offset by the number of bull's-eyes you hit.

It's a layman's fallacy to lump all doctors together. There's as much difference between a neurologist and a gastroenterologist as there is between an electrician and a plumber. The more on-target you are to the characteristics of your reader-physician's specialty, the more the doctor will feel "They're talking to *me!*" And the more likely you are to elicit interest.

Besides targeting doctors based on specialty, you can direct information to them based on prescription preferences. Drawing on survey data widely available from medical marketing companies, you can direct mailings to doctors who prescribe, for example, Alphazine over Betazine. Similarly, you can get data on the tendencies of individual physicians to try new, promising drugs in their practices. The marketer of a new drug (or other product) would probably get the best responses from self-described "Innovator," "Early Adopter" and "Early Majority" physicians. What if your product has been on the market for some time? Then, with messages pointing up your history of proved success, you might do well appealing to physicians who call themselves "Late Majority" or "Traditionalist."

Before you send out any literature, though, have it reviewed by members—the more the better—of your target audience. With judicious questioning you'll be able to get closer and closer to the interests and experiences of the physicians you want to reach, so as to better tailor your copy. You're almost certain to be surprised. They occupy so special a world that few laypersons can deduce what's on physicians' minds.

Equally important, your reviewers will help you avoid inaccuracies. Anyone who's ever done medical writing knows that even the most apparently simple statement is fraught with traps. Doctors are only too aware of the catastrophes that can result from errors, and they're likely to make confetti of your words and reputation if they spot mistakes.

4. Understate and substantiate. Physicians are justifiably skeptical of puffery. In making decisions, especially on clinical matters, they have an extraordinary inclination toward the specific and concrete. Within the limits of readability, you're better off telling too much than too little.

Where was your product used? By whom? How? On what kind of patients, and how many of them? With what effect? Assume the physician-reader thinks you're lying, and try to prove you're telling the truth.

Skeptical physicians ask, "Who says so?" before they read, much less trust, a report. As much as possible, make use of the hierarchy of medical validity. At the top are the major medical schools and journals; if you can provide a copy of an article from a prestigious journal which documents the effectiveness of your product, you have a mail piece worth its weight in gold. Also held in high esteem are other established medical channels. A physician may throw away most of the mail, but is almost sure to open any envelope from his or her medical society or professional association. (Many of these groups will include new product flyers, brochures or announcements in their routine mailings.)

5. Pack in product-use details. By showing doctors *how* your product can be used, product-use details not only contribute to your message's service quality, but make your message more believable.

For a clinical product you need to explain how various categories of patients—children, the aged, pregnant women, as well as the debilitated of different types—should be treated. If you make these essential distinctions, you'll help get your product used.

Also, place your product in its proper context, even if it means mentioning your competitors. In clinical matters, physicians think in terms of systems, of syndromes, of whole categories of drugs and other remedies. In a doctor's eyes, your product does not stand alone but must be considered in the context of patient care and in relation to other products performing similar functions. Even for nonclinical products and services, your sales appeal will be greater if you follow the pattern of medical logic—which requires information for purposes of comparison.

Advertisers usually insist on sending, or at least offering, a free trial of their product or service. Physicians are used to getting pharmaceutical samples, if only as a way of proceeding cautiously in trying a product. Samples can lift your offering from the mere printed word—which the skeptical doctor tends to mistrust—to personal experience, on which he or she tends to rely.

How do you get these assignments? Send samples of your work to advertising agencies and public relations firms that handle health-related accounts. And don't forget the large number of physicians who need writers to help them draft articles, reports, and speeches. You can reach doctors through classified ads, medical publications, and via bulletin boards in doctors' lounges in hospitals. A good headline for your ad: Ghostwriter Available.

To land these assignments, your best presentation is an article you've had published. Good medical writers are in relatively short supply, so if you can show a published article in any respected medical publication, you have a head start in securing assignments.

ON HOW I BECAME A MEDICAL WRITER
by Suzanne Loebl

If anyone had ever told me that one day I would earn my keep as a medical writer, I would have laughed. Though composition—whether in German, French, English, or Dutch—was probably my best subject, and I wrote lots of letters people loved receiving, I never paid much attention to these skills. So when the time came to think of making a living, I studied chemistry.

I worked in chemistry until I had children, knowing full well that some day I would either have to earn an advanced academic degree or do something else.

That "something else" started out as a need to make money. At the time, I took stock of everything I had ever learned: languages; typing, because my father had said all girls need to learn how to type so that they can make a living; and chemistry, so that I could take over a small family business. This medley qualified me to be a freelance scientific translator and abstractor of medical articles.

It was a good analysis of the situation, and the best decision of my life. There was always plenty of work I could do at home and the work paid rather well, but, more important, I wrote reams.

Learning—On and Off the Job

I worked for Esso Petroleum part-time at home for three-and-a-half years. The job mostly involved doing abstracts of interest to those woking in the petroleum industry. Some of the articles were simple to abstract, others were very complex and involved. My editor in those days was a Mr. Zarember, whom I saw but once during all those years, but I will be forever grateful for the accuracy that the job taught me, his excellent editing, and the writing speed I acquired (I had to produce roughly two abstracts per hour).

When the Esso job ended, I firmly resolved never to go back to the laboratory. By then I realized I knew much more science than most journalists, and much more journalism than most chemists.

I next registered for a couple of writing courses at the New School in New York. That year the science-writing course was taught by the editor-in-chief of Grolier Press. I continued to do my abstracts and translations, but also completed the imaginative assignments given by the instructor, who'd decided I had a special ability to write science for children.

Before the year was over, I had started on a juvenile science book, *Fighting the Unseen: The Story of Viruses*. It took me a whole year to write that book, and I enjoyed the experience immensely. My two children, by then five and seven, were mobilized as junior editors. I still thought that I would make a living as a technical writer, but I realized that I enjoyed writing from scratch much more than translating endless articles done by others.

When the manuscript was nearly finished, my teacher suggested I send it to some publishers. I didn't have much faith that it would be bought, but it was certainly worth the postage. Imagine my surprise when Abelard and Schuman bought the book. The advance was only $300, but who cared.

That was the beginning. *Fighting the Unseen* came out in 1968. Abelard and Schuman bought my second book and, almost simultaneously, I was selected as a fellow in the Advanced Science Writing program at the Graduate School of Journalism of Columbia University.

Writing as a Career

I discovered, at Columbia and elsewhere, that a writer can use his or her skills in many different ways. We all probably have some ambitions difficult to fulfill, like writing the Great American Novel, the Definitive Biography of so-and-so, or our own personal philosophy. Some writers are lucky and fulfill their ambitions. Most of us settle for writing some things for money, some for glory, and some because we feel that they must be said.

Some of us have public relations jobs (I was science editor of the Arthritis Foundation for six years, writing releases and newsletters and running newsrooms). Some writers work for banks, hospitals, the food industry, pharmaceutical houses, etc. Many writers are fine teachers.

I have found that writing begets writing, and that it is better, especially in the beginning, to *also* write material that will get published (e.g., ad copy, public relations, newsletters, etc.) than to write only book proposals and articles that have a good chance of being rejected—not necessarily because they are bad, but for many reasons, including capricious ones.

It Goes with the Territory

Frances Schwartz, my first editor, gave me one of many valuable lessons early in my career. She said, "If you want to be in this business, you cannot afford to be too touchy." Indeed, most professional writers still receive more rejections than acceptances, and all have to worry about such things as whether the book will be publicized or reviewed, whether it will be in the bookstores, and whether people will still be interested in the book by the time it comes out.

I am a full-time freelance writer now, supporting myself at an acceptable rate. I write mostly books and, mostly, I like it. I work very hard—more so than I did when I had a nine-to-five job. The freedom of being self-employed is an illusion, as I told an envious friend of mine—a teacher with two solid months' vacation—who asked me whether I "work or just write."

I am also lonely. I miss the chitchat and social life that comes with an office. I have to make a great deal of effort to get enough exercise, and I belong to a number of committees just because I am a gregarious person.

Yet despite rejections and other concerns, my readers make this up-and-down business worthwhile. When a reader tells me my book really helped him or her to understand why they couldn't have a baby—or even better, that it helped them to have one—I am very satisfied.

I do many different things: writing textbooks, a very few articles, trade books, how-to books, press releases, drug launches, and patient-education materials. Recently, I completed my first film, *New Developments in the Drug Industry.* As this is being a written, I am teaching an advanced writing course at the Polytechnic Institute of New York.

I probably will be a medical writer for the rest of my life, but who knows. I might still write that Great American Novel that will still be read long after I am in the blue yonder.

MEDICAL WRITING AND THE MEDICAL COLLABORATION SUBSPECIALTY
by Patrick M. McGrady Jr.

My father, Pat McGrady Sr., was science editor of the American Cancer Society for over a quarter of a century. It was a job that he carved out for himself with great precision. All the ACS wanted was some kind of public relations that would keep them out of hot water and inspire contributions, but he decided to give them both more and less. He declined to do puffery, but gave them total coverage of the interesting research done on cancer. And he traveled anywhere in the world to get the story.

A headstrong Irishman from Anaconda, Montana, who was endowed with a good mind and a withering charm, my father made the job his own. He refused to kowtow to the powers-that-be at the ACS, and waged running battles to protect his fiefdom over the length of his tenure. He honestly scorned power and money, and showed the influence that could be imposed with two fingers working a staccato on a Smith-Corona and a set of highball glasses, ice cubes, and an unlimited supply of Jack Daniels for the science writers.

He was a newsman. I mean that as his father before him believed in the Eucharist and daily communion, Pat McGrady Sr. believed in the *news.* The world offered no higher calling, take it from him, than covering the news accurately, succinctly, and stylishly. He did not actually *force* his three sons into the news business, but neither could he imagine what else three "over-educated" (Yale, Yale, and Harvard) sons might work at to stave off starvation.

He was proudest of his exploits as a newsman: in phoning in to the

AP office the correct verdict on the Lindbergh kidnapping trial (following the notorious erroneous report by another reporter that went round the world), his coverage of the *Morro Castle* disaster, the outbreak of the Manchurian War, the rise of Hitler to power in the thirties (for *Esquire*), and on and on.

So he made his job for the ACS a newsman's job, covering basic cancer research. He enriched the data banks of the professionals he glorified by giving them tidbits he'd picked up everywhere. His title was not public relations man or press officer but "science editor"—which was most befitting the responsibility, the respectability, and the integrity he brought to the job.

He got the physicians and researchers together with one another and with the press. The end result was a welter of widely published, beautifully done, accurate pieces from his typewriter, but carrying a little editing and the bylines of the famous science writers.

There was a year-round flow of cancer stories, but it became torrential just before the little old ladies began making their can-waving pitch door-to-door in April. I think he was never adequately credited for the role he played in boosting the ACS annual collection from the piddling amounts it got in the '40s to the nearly $200 million it gets today.

It was he who initiated the idea of the now famous ACS Science Writers Seminar, which began as a traveling circus to the various research centers, and evolved into a major scientific conference in pleasant places in Arizona and Florida, fueled by the presence of the nation's top researchers, its best medical writers, and its finest whiskey.

A Family Tradition

My father did his job so well that it was dispiriting for me to contemplate swimming in the pool he crowded. I resolved that, whatever else I did in life, I would *never* become a newspaperman or *God forbid!* a medical writer. With a degree in international relations from Yale and fluency in French, Russian, German, and Yiddish, I planned to join the Foreign Service, or maybe the CIA.

On that sunny June day in 1954 in New Haven when I got my B.A. and new fountain pen from the folks, I was faced with the predicament of what to do with them. There was no money for further study, and one look at the CIA and Foreign Service spooks was enough to convince me I didn't want a job at either place.

Clearly, I would *have* to work. My father didn't want to push anything, but if I *did* want to earn some money, I might call some old friends of his to see if they could make an introduction or two. Science writer Delos Smith at United Press. Sam Blackman at the Associated Press in New York. Clifton Daniels at the *New York Times*. As it turned out, I needed and used them all.

I quit the copy-boy job on the *Times* after three weeks of carrying more coffee than copy. I got fired from UP after a couple of months in Boston and Albany. (As comrade Jack Sack, the famous writer who was doing pieces for the *New Yorker* while covering the legislature in Albany for us, put it, "Maybe it would help if you learned how to write better.")

I lost the trust of the Minneapolis AP bureau chief when I began correcting *his* "A Wire" copy one Sunday morning when we were alone in the office. Hadn't he said: "Nobody-around-here's copy is sacred, Pat, so if you see something wrong, you just go ahead and put it in shape"? Yes, but he had also said: "You guys from Back East probably think we're slow and stupid out here, and you'll learn soon enough to suppress that arrogance," or words to that effect.

The point is that you don't monkey with the bureau chief's copy, even if he invites you to. He wrote scary memos. He'd sit there, mud dripping from his boots onto his desk, coonskin hat warming his slippery scalp and neck, pounding out edicts, ukases, rules, punishments, and faint praise. I was fired on the twenty-ninth day of my fifth month with the firm—a day shy of seniority. The chief told me that, had I played my cards right—come into the bureau 20 minutes early and stayed 20 minutes late each day, not mangled perfectly adequate copy from another staffer—why, within four or five years, I could have become, with a break or two, bureau chief in Fargo, North Dakota!

Cognizance of what success in Minneapolis would have brought me made this otherwise unhappy separation more bearable.

I next signed on with the *Chicago Sun-Times*—a job that was sheer joy, working with real people in the greatest, most competitive newspaper town in America, getting one good break after another: using my Russian to interview Soviet Foreign Minister Vyacheslav P. Molotov en route to San Francisco for the tenth anniversary of the United Nations; working as assistant night city editor covering crime, manhunts, fires; everything. The job, of course, came through another of my father's contacts, science writer Bob Kleckner. It was a landmark—the first writing job I didn't get fired from.

LEARNING THE CRAFT

Whatever I may have thought about newspapering, I did learn to write better. I think it vital for every medical writer to learn the craft of writing from good writers as early as possible.

I always advise young writers to spend at least a couple years on the staffs of several publications to learn journalism. You need the harbor of a steady paycheck, and above all, a good editor to show you how *not* to write. Far better to have your atrocities excised by a tough editor who will give you a piece of his mind than to have the corrections take the form of multiple rejection slips, with no explanations.

The topical expertise will come with exposure to doctors and medical literature, and it can happen at any time. But skill at assembling words, sentences, and paragraphs should be acquired soon in a writer's career, or it may never be acquired.

A Secure Specialty

The market's demands can be a powerful force in determining professional directions. I have two friends whose first love is show business; one lives in Manhattan and the other in Hollywood. My Manhattanite friend is a producer of plays; my Hollywood friend produces television shows. When there is no call for their entertainment productions, both men make a living as their father taught them to do—by selling carpets. Both hate carpets. But the fact is that there are *always* people who need linoleum or pile rugs.

A good medical writer need never go unemployed. Readers are fascinated with the world of medicine and medical research, and articles and books on these subjects abound. A freelancer's lot is one of insecurity, but the medical specialty is a great way to reduce the insecurity quotient.

An Indirect Route to Medical Writing

Medical writing, as I said, was the one area I resolved to stay clear of. After five years in broadcasting, and writing a book for the Fund for the Republic (*Television Critics in a Free Society*, 1959), I got a terrific job: Moscow bureau chief for *Newsweek*. After six months, the KGB decided that they did not want this Russian-speaking correspondent in the country any longer, and the CIA people at the American Embassy were greatly relieved by this decision. Both intelligence agencies prevailed upon the magazine to fire me for my various indiscretions. ("Using personal conversations with embassy personnel as the basis for news stories," ran a confidential memo from the local CIA officer to the State Department.)

The natural thing, it seemed to me, would be to write a book about my adventures in Moscow. I outlined one and sent it to a wonderful literary agent named Gunther Stuhlmann. A former editor of Berlin's *Der*

Monat and editor of the diaries of Anais Nin, Gunther was a terrific boost for a young author who had only a foundation-subsidized book to his credit. Gunther had energy and optimism. He forwarded only laudatory editorial rejections and made me feel like a pro.

One day he said: "Ellis Amburn at Coward-McCann likes your proposal but doesn't think any book on Russia will sell now. He'll give you a $6000 advance to do a book on rejuvenation, though."

I said thanks, but no thanks. I still had foreign correspondence in mind for the day that the Russians lifted my *persona non grata* status. But six months later, as my dollars shrank to pennies, I asked Gunther if the Amburn offer was still good. It was. I found an article on rejuvenation in an old *Encyclopedia Britannica* and a good piece in *True* by a buddy, Geoffrey Bocca. [Editor's Note: Geoffrey Bocca, a former ASJA member, died as this book was going to press.] I wrote up an outline in one night, submitted it the next day, and had a contract within two weeks.

My father's reaction was curious. This book was a mistake. How could anyone write a serious book on "rejuvenation," since there was no such thing? The publisher's advance would never see me through the project. Moreover, I'd never finish it. And was I aware that he had been planning a book on aging? And since he would do that book one day, I could not use his files on the subject.

A Little Help From My Friends

If he would not help with the book directly, he had helped indirectly. Our dinner conversations over the past two decades had had a distinct medical tinge. Our guests were physicians and biologists and physiologists. And he had patiently explained about ATP, DNA, hormones and enzymes, tumor markers, chemotherapy, and the like. So, at the very least, my Yale biology course was buttressed by a medical sensibility. It really helped.

I also had the newsman's effrontery to believe that I could master any technical subject with a dictionary and an encyclopedia and by merely asking the experts to clarify the hard parts. But what I did not know when I began was that I would need a mentor—a medical professional to guide me through the mazes I would explore in the eighteen months it took me to research and write *The Youth Doctors: The Beautiful People and the Doctors Who Try to Keep Them That Way.*

I was lucky to find him early on, at the Third International Gerontological Congress in Vienna in the fall of 1966. He was a true Renaissance Englishman, an anarchist, a poet, a novelist, a journalist, a physician, whose concerns embraced the whole of medicine but who was primarily interested in sex and aging. His name was Alex Comfort.

Alex performed his uncompensated role of mentor superbly: pointing out the pros from the phonies, the promising research from the quackery, and yes, clarifying the hard parts. I'd invite him to dinner and switch on my tape recorder the moment he crossed the doorsill. I'm forever grateful for the insights he gave me on the substance of good medicine and sound doctoring.

A Specialty Writer Emerges

The Youth Doctors put me on the map. It sold only 15,000 copies in hardcover and another 200,000 in its Ace paperback edition. But we sold countless serializations in *Ladies' Home Journal, Vogue, True* (the *good* old *True*, that is), *Esquire, Coronet, Status,* and a slew of foreign magazines and newspapers. Furthermore, we sold rights to Japan, Germany, France, Italy and England. *Book World* named it one of the one hundred best books of 1968 and asked me to review books on science and medicine on an irregular basis. I had not only written a good book, I had acquired a specialty. I received an unending flood of article requests from magazine editors.

The book's success got me a good advance from Macmillan on my next book, *The Love Doctors* ($34,000); some lucrative ghosting jobs; and, pretty much by natural evolution, a subspecialty of medical collaboration.

TWO HEADS ARE BETTER THAN ONE

There are advantages to medical collaborations that you should consider. You need no particular genius, except a talent for organizing the work of an exceptional professional. This way, you—talented writer with a typewriter or computer and nothing earthshaking to say— can make an enormous amount of money by helping a somewhat inarticulate, somewhat confused professional bring his or her important message to the reading public.

What did I learn from turning a literary collaboration into a bestseller? The most important advice I can give, I think, is to stick to substance in choosing your collaborators and topics. There is a difference between substance and wishful thinking, but many writers never learn the difference, never discipline themselves to turn down that fast buck for the schlock project that will imprison them for a year or two and not sell well because they really didn't like it in the first place. Make the most of your time. Too many writers waste their time on assignments, notions, projects that are peripheral at best and colossally unexciting to the reading public.

The substance I had going for me with *The Pritikin Program for Diet and Exercise* was a health heretic of admirable genius, a situation crying for redress, and a provable point. The heretic, of course, was Pritikin; the situation was a nation victimized by junk food. And the provable point was that serious heart conditions and other degenerative diseases could be improved or prevented by this diet-and-exercise program.

Before the Beginning

But the first decision I had to make was whether I wanted to do anything at all with Pritikin. I had never heard of the man till Paul Glenn, a philanthropist friend of mine, asked me to try the diet, visit Pritikin in Santa Barbara, and give him some publicity. Could I, he asked, get him into the *New York Times*, the *National Enquirer*, or somewhere?

Paul is not a professional enthusiast, and his good judgment had been demonstrated time and again on Wall Street. His personal fortune was large enough for him to go into semiretirement and fund pet medical research projects (such as the Jarvik artificial heart and the American Aging Association) through his Glenn Medical Foundation.

When Paul Glenn or E.F. Hutton talks, McGrady listens.

Any writer whose name is before the public and does as much radio and TV as I do gets scores of requests for professional collaboration every year. The question is: Which will be worthwhile, and which will merely waste your time? If you can't make a sound decision on which project to tackle, you'll waste your time with pleasant but dull people doing nonessential, unexciting work. And you may never get a crack at writing the kind of book that millions of people will buy.

What you definitely *don't* want is a professional who has made a mint of money in his practice and is now eager for a book as a vehicle for an ego trip. Even a *worst*-seller can serve *him* well and make *him* money by expanding his practice. But it won't make *you* money. You will spend a year or so organizing his thoughts and achievements; putting his rambling, incoherent musings into English; giving him a free ride on the tube; and multiplying his six- or seven-figure annual income. And he won't necessarily care if the books aren't in the stores, if the jacket didn't turn out right, or if Berkeley or Bantam declined your publisher's invitation to join in the reprint auction. You've put him on the map and given him a literary tool for income enhancement—*his* income enhancement. And you are out in the cold, still flogging articles, sending out outlines for three or four books to dozens of publishers, and wondering how you're going to pay last month's rent.

So, picking your professional and your subject are the first major decisions you face. Flunk that, and you are out of the ballgame.

THE COLLABORATION CONTRACT

I am always asked: What kind of arrangement should there be between the writer and professional in a collaboration? There is no standard arrangement. And like everything from marriage to buying a house or waging war, the power you bring to the collaboration will be important in determining who gets what.

What *is* important is that you *get it all down on paper* beforehand, including the minutest details of the collaboration: who gets what when; what happens when one partner defaults; whether you get to write the sequels; your respective jacket credits; copyright ownership; the fee (if any) for writing and researching the outline; who pays expenses. I always stipulate that my collaborator foot the bill for transcriptions of our interviews and submit all research in typewritten form (no inspired midnight calls).

It is true that many authors simply split fifty-fifty with collaborators. I won't do that any more. It isn't fair to a veteran author who will help increase his collaborator's nonliterary income by making the collaborator famous. It isn't fair to the writer who has to spend weeks or months developing a selling outline for a publisher—and then wait weeks or months till a contract is drawn up and an advance is paid.

I now charge up to $50,000 for writing an outline. Yes, *just for the outline.* Because I am almost certain I can sell it to a publisher and because I am committing myself totally to the project for a couple of years, during which the publisher's advance may not keep me in the style to which I've been accustomed.

Fifty thousand dollars is a mere ten patients for a Nathan Pritikin, or a dozen face lifts for some plastic surgeons, or a half dozen patients for a cancer specialist. But it's *my* blood, sweat, tears, and time. I also take a greater-than-50-percent share of all royalties across the board—meaning book club rights, serializations, all reprint sales, paperback, the works. And so far, I have not had an unhappy collaborator.

COLLABORATOR QUALIFICATIONS

So what do you look for in a collaborator? You want someone obsessed with his or her subject, almost to the exclusion of everything else. That is Nathan Pritikin. When a old acquaintance of mine, Gloria Swanson, called him during one of our work sessions in Santa Barbara one day, they chatted for half an hour or so. After the call, he turned to me and said, "This woman said her name was Swanson or something. *Gloria* Swanson. Wonder who she is?"

Perfect. Here was a man who had made money on some electronic patents and spent the last thirty years studying nutrition and virtually nothing else. He obviously didn't go to movies, never got drunk, didn't gamble, never womanized, and couldn't tell you the difference between Anaconda and Spit-in-the-Ocean if his life depended on it. Fortunately for me.

Nathan Pritikin's life was his work. And his nutritional theories were nothing but sheer heresy. His diet was a 180-degree turnaround from every popular diet in the world. Most diets produced weight loss with high-fat, high-protein foods. He did it with carbohydrates, traditionally scorned because they give you an appetite.

It's been about eight years since Paul Glenn paid my way from New York to visit this then unknown nutritionist in Santa Barbara and to see if I could give him a few lines of publicity. And in those years, all of the studies I, as a medical writer, have come across, bear out the theories of this unbearably skinny, intolerably healthy, sixtyish inventor become nutrition guru to millions.

After my visit to Pritikin's artery farm in southern California, I wrote an article for *Woman's Day*. The article was well read on Madison Avenue. Seven publishers began bidding for the rights to a book on the diet. Two won: Grosset and Dunlap for hardcover, Bantam for paperback. Together, they paid a six-figure advance for the book.

Life's Little Mysteries

Why would so many people pay $15 or even $3.95 for a book that does little more than to tell them to eat food as it's grown? For that, in a nutshell, is the whole diet. Vegetables, whole grains, and fruit. Nothing more.

Why should people want to buy a book that tells them that two cigarettes a day are enough to deprive them of an adequate oxygen supply? That told them, before Harvard, that coffee could shorten their lives eight ways? That told the nutrition sophisticates that they could kill themselves with too much protein? That banished all your favorite foods—not just for a quick weight-loss period of two or three weeks—but forever? Meaning no more potato chips, sizzling steaks, peanut butter, gravies, Roquefort dressings, Big Macs, Twinkies, Arbys, Kentucky Fried Chicken, or even sugar in your pink lemonade?

I still wonder why, myself.

Yet by the time our book was being sold to the jobbers, the book was already a bestseller. It stayed on the *New York Times* list for a full 52 weeks. To date, we've sold just shy of 400,000 copies in hardcover and there are another two million paperback copies in print. It was a *Literary Guild* selection and has been serialized in countless newspapers and magazines. Our royalties are well over the million mark.

Many authors believe that you have to have loads of media advertising to sell a book. Our experience proves that you don't. We had a couple of small ads in a few papers. The book sold by word of mouth almost exclusively. People who tried it and found that—with nothing more than the foods we recommended and long, vigorous daily walks—you could, in a matter of days, dramatically lower blood pressure, lose up to a pound a day, feel 20 years younger, do without an hour or two of sleep nightly, lose pain from your arthritis, stop taking oral insulin, and not have to shell out $30,000 for that triple-coronary-bypass operation.

Secrets of Success

I was given a free hand in putting the book together. And that is important. I was able to put every good idea I could think of into this book. There are many authors who think in terms of series of books. This idea will go into the first book, and that one will be saved for a follow-up book. I do not work this way. My feeling is that the competition is so severe, one does well to give every book its very best shot—loading it with a maximum charge—both in terms of substance and creative form.

And for the first time in my career, on the advice of a Romanian friend who said he couldn't understand all the big words I used in previous books, I kept the writing in the Pritikin book as simple as possible. Much of the book was a simple question-and-answer format. I also insisted, however, that Pritikin himself write a section for doctors in that marvelous, confounding, and annoying prescription-pad jargon that doctors use—in order that he be taken seriously by them. The combination proved successful. While we got some flak from the medical profession at first, doctors are now our very best friends. In fact, several thousand of them correspond with Pritikin's Longevity Center in Santa Monica.

MAKING IGNORANCE PAY

A writer, alone among professionals, has the luxury of being able to consider his or her research as an educational enterprise. In uncoverings of facts and anecdotes and ambience related to the subject, the writer can, as no expert can, impart to the reader the thrill and flavor of first encounter. He or she can, further, by playing surrogate for the innocent reader, simplify the material.

I was blessed with colossal ignorance about nutrition. I maintain, quite seriously, that innocence—blind, obstinate ignorance that we writers are notorious for—can be a very valuable asset in writing any nonfiction book. If, that is, you are really dumb enough not to know what your collaborator-expert is saying and rude enough to insist that he spell it all out for you in kindergarten language. If you can do that, your chances of writing something clear and understandable for a few million people may not be bad at all.

Additional Resources

American Academy of Family Physicians, 1740 W. 92nd St., Kansas City, MO 64114. Provides information on health care delivery. Offers aid in arranging interviews, annual reports, biographies, brochures and pamphlets, informational newsletters, photos, placement on mailing lists, press kits, statistics. Publications include *AAFP Reporter* and *American Family Physician*.

American Cancer Society, Inc., Four W. 35th St., New York, NY 10001. Provides advisory and referral information on cancer, plus programs in research, education, and service to the cancer patient.

American Dental Association, 211 E. Chicago Ave., Chicago, IL 60611. Provides historical, referral, technical, and trade information on all dental topics.

American Holistic Health Sciences Association, 1766 Cumberland, Suite 208, St. Charles, IL 60174. Provides information on self-responsibility for health, nutrition, natural health methods, unconventional medicine. Publications include informational newsletters, over 100 books and tapes on alternative/holistic health subjects, and *Alternative Health-Subjects Schools* (annual directory).

American Hospital Association, 840 N. Lake Shore Dr., Chicago, IL 60611. Offers aid in arranging interviews, bibliographies, statistics, brochures and pamphlets, placement on mailing list, newsletter, press kits, press releases. Publications include *AHA Guide to Health Care, AHA Hospital Books, Hospital Week.*

American Medical Association, 535 N. Dearborn St., Chicago, IL

60610. Provides advisory, interpretative and referral information on medicine, health care, and science. Offers statistics, brochures and pamphlets, clipping services, library searches, placement on mailing list, newsletter. Publications list available.

American Medical Writers Association, 5272 River Rd., Suite 370, Bethesda, MD 20016. Publishes a newsletter, the quarterly *Journal of Medical Communications*, an annual membership directory, and a *Freelance Directory*. Bestows awards for medical books and films.

Centers for Disease Control, 1600 Clifton Rd. NE, Atlanta, GA 30333. Provides advisory and technical information on prevention of disease and injury. Offers reference and background materials, photographs on communicable diseases and their subjects, placement on mailing list. Publications include the *Morbidity and Mortality Weekly Report* and *Surveillance Reports*.

Dental Library, University of Southern California, Norris Dental Society Center, Los Angeles, CA 90007. Provides advisory, bibliographical, historical, how-to, and referral information primarily on dental medicine. Offers bibliographies and information searches. Access to MEDLINE and other computer-generated bibliographies is available through the dental library at a minimal fee.

MEDLINE Data Base, National Library of Medicine, 8600 Rockville Pike, Bethesda, MD 20209. Data base containing 500,000 references to recently-published articles in health science. MEDLINE is accessible at about 2,000 medical schools, hospitals, and government agencies. Provides bibliographical information on health sciences; offers information searches. Publications include an informational brochure.

National Center for Health Services Research, OASH, PHS, Department of Health and Human Services, 3700 East-West Hwy., Hyattsville, MD 20782. Supports research; offers brochures and pamphlets, and placement on mailing list. Publications list available.

National Institutes of Health, Division of Research Resources, Bethesda, MD 20014. Offers aid in arranging interviews, statistics, brochures and pamphlets, photos. Publications include *Division of Research Resources: Meeting the Research Resource Needs of the Biomedical Sciences*.

National Kidney Foundation, 2 Park Ave., New York, NY 10016. Offers aid in arranging interviews, annual reports, bibliographies, brochures and pamphlets, placement on mailing list, statistics, quarterly newsletter.

National League for Nursing, 10 Columbus Circle, New York, NY 10019. Provides information on nursing education, practice, and manpower, plus nursing-related, health care issues. Offers aid in arranging interviews, annual reports, statistics, brochures and pamphlets, placement on mailing list. Hundreds of publications dealing with a variety of subjects; publications catalog available.

National Library of Medicine, 8600 Rockville Pike, Bethesda, MD 20209. Medical library offers B&W and color photos on the history of medicine (portraits, scenes and pictures of institutions); photos are not related to current personalities, events, or medical science.

National Society for Medical Research, 1029 Vermont Ave. NW, Suite 700, Washington, DC 20005. Provides information on animals used in biomedical and behavioral research. Offers annual reports, monthly bulletin, news service, journalism award, special publications, data bank, exhibits, brochures and pamphlets, placement on mailing list, newsletter, press kits. Operates a news service for the media, describing benefits of animal experimentation. Publications include several booklets and brochures; write for the publications list.

Chapter Ten

WRITING PSYCHOLOGY

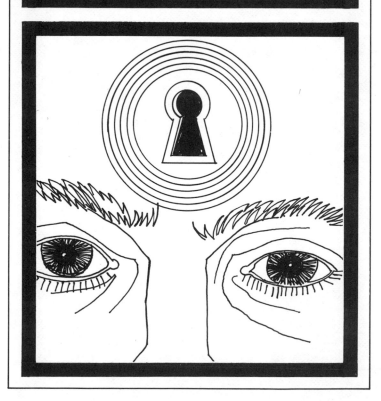

In these stressful times, awareness of emotional-physical interactions is a must for anyone who would stay in control of his or her life. Psychology writers strive to help readers lead richer, more satisfying lives by helping them understand and *change* destructive mental and behavioral patterns. Their articles and books suggest ways to improve interpersonal relationships, communicate more effectively, and offer alternatives when life's problems seem overwhelming. They also help readers recognize when they need to seek professional help.

Specialists in this field are an important link between practitioners and the general public; they communicate the latest scientific thinking regarding the mind, emotions, and mental health—psychosomatic factors in cancer and heart disease, the origins of creativity, psychological effects of urban living, and new findings on the hemispheres of the brain, for example. And although the self-help movement encompasses everything from how to be more attractive to how to do your own taxes, a big chunk of it is devoted to psychological topics—everything from coping with rebellious adolescents to mourning the death of a parent, from managing stress to improving your marriage, from minimizing sibling rivalry to preparing for retirement, from how to quit smoking to how to *enjoy* commitments.

Literature has always been concerned with "the dark nights of the soul," and this area of specialization puts a writer's natural introspection to good use, examining as it does the nature of the psyche, the nature of being, and the human condition. Psychological writing often draws upon the writer's own ruminations and observations about human nature and human interactions—and reader attention is guaranteed, because the magic "you" is built right into the subject.

Markets for psychological writing range from the broadest of general-circulation publications to specialized scholarly journals. Read on to discover the challenges and opportunities that await those who chart the interior frontier—specialists in psychology and psychiatry.

PSYCHOLOGY AND PSYCHIATRY:
A WEALTH OF IDEAS
by Cima Star

People constantly ask me how I got into writing about psychology and psychiatry. They are generally more subtle than they were during the years I lived in Italy, when the question was often put, "How could a pretty little thing like you be doing such serious work?" and accompanied by a salacious pat on the arm. My answer then was to draw myself up to my full five feet three inches and reply, "Because, *signore,* I am a *doctoressa!"*

That shut them up, slowed down the hands, and occasionally even resulted in an intelligent conversation. The statement was also *true,* because in Italy in those days, anyone who had attended any sort of college was considered a "doctor."

Though the question is likely to be more diplomatically phrased today, it still remains something of a mystery to most nonwriters how someone who is "just a writer" can explain the intricacies of any of the sciences.

My college major was psychology and that answer seems to satisfy people. That I simply fell into writing, however, is perhaps even more accurate, because my earliest reporting had nothing to do with psychology, but with fashion and the celluloid world of "Hollywood on the Tiber" in Rome.

The truest of the truths about my penchant for the field, about my passion for probing the whys and wherefores of people's lives, probably stems from my isolated life as an only child on a farm in California's San Gabriel Valley. Despite the environment, I never evinced the faintest interest in the flora and fauna of farm life. My world was the printed page, my temple the town library. Then there was a radio show called "Grand Central Station . . . Crossroads of a Thousand Lives." All week, I would wait eagerly for ten o'clock Saturday morning, when the show was broadcast. And I would dream of one day arriving in New York via Grand Central Station and learning about those thousands of lives, probing those lives, dissecting and analyzing and recreating those lives. I was going to grow up and live in a garret in New York City and spend hours in Grand Central Station watching people, then go home to my garret and write about them.

I did just that, more or less, although I quickly tired of garrets.

Psychology was my college major not because I wanted to specialize, but simply because it interested me. Formally studying the mechanics of journalism never crossed my mind. I had apprenticed on high school newspapers and yearbooks and had done part-time work for weekly journals. I had read Ben Hecht and knew that the way to become a writer and journalist was to get a job and write and report. Besides, I had spent my high school years immersed in Freud, Jung, Plato, and Aristotle.

Be Fascinated

Basically, the surest way to succeed in the specialty of psychology or psychiatry is to love either so much, to be so fascinated, that you dedicate yourself to the field and to knowing its practitioners, whether you intend to write or not.

Resources and research material in the field are so abundant that you could spend a lifetime burrowing into the treasures of new ideas and research, and never have time to write a word. The periodicals department of almost any library carries at least half a dozen professional journals. Hundreds of journals are received by major research libraries at universities. Most hospitals and medical schools have psychiatric departments; most universities have psychology departments. The professionals in these fields are, for the most part, friendly and eager to help you. Many of them are also anxious to get publicity, because their public images can be as vital to their careers as the work they do. As a group, they tend to be more literate and witty than most, which makes them delightfully quotable.

Just the other day, I was researching an article on adulterous wives for *Boston* magazine and called a local psychologist for his comments. "If infancy is good for infants, adultery is good for adults," he quipped before settling into an invaluable discussion of the psychology of adultery.

A psychiatrist not only gave me another marvelous quote— "People like to think of morality as what they do with their orifices"— but in so doing, provided the slant for the article.

The press office of the American Psychiatric Association boasts a staff that is infinitely patient and helpful to writers. Pick your topic and call them, and they will direct you to professionals.

ATTEND MEETINGS AND CONFERENCES

The APA holds an annual meeting at which nearly ten thousand psychiatrists meet to present the latest findings in their field. Any writer or reporter may cover this meeting, and it is a candy store of article ideas. In fact, I doubt that any writer could come close to absorbing all the ideas available in any *one* day at the meeting.

Many universities, hospitals, and community health organizations sponsor conferences and seminars throughout the United States on psychiatric and psychological topics. Writers flock to these, for they offer ideas, interview possibilities, and usually plenty of camaraderie and good conversation to boot. Even one good story idea may net several articles.

For example, some years ago I attended the annual psychoanalytic conferences at Adelphi University on Long Island, New York. That year, the themes were violence and aggression. One of the speakers talked about the psychopathic personality, the person who appears to have no superego, no conscience, no guilt. I interviewed a number of professionals at the conference on their findings on psychopaths, and sold a series of articles to a feature syndicate on the psychoanalytic view of violent crime. Then, starting with a single interview with the same speaker who had touched briefly on sexual psychopathy, I began work on a piece which eventually sold to *Cosmopolitan* as "The Cruel Lover," the charming psychopath so many single women encounter sooner or later. I did a general piece on the psychopathic personality for another magazine, then later sold that to several European markets. I have since done several spinoff pieces on various aspects of psychopathy, and have used much of the background material gleaned that one day in dozens of other related articles.

Resources Are Everywhere

The major pharmaceutical houses, such as Ciba and Roche, manufacturing psychogenic drugs, are another invaluable and willing resource. Write to the press office of any and they will send you reams of material, not only on their products and how and why they work, but research studies on the conditions—anxiety, depression, psychoses of all kinds—which they alleviate.

If you have a penchant for the dramatic, you will find it aplenty in psychology and psychiatry. Pick any recent murder case reported in your local newspaper. Call ten professionals in the field. Ask them their opinion of the defendant's sanity. You will probably get no fewer than ten different opinions. You'll probably do better to draw your conclusions from the opinions of lawyers, but the "psychs" will give your article plenty of controversy, pathos, and lively opinions.

GETTING PUBLISHED

How do you break into the field? The easiest way is the obvious: pick a topic that interests you, find an original slant for it, do some research on the topic and on the potential markets, then write a query to an editor.

For instance, a number of years ago I became fascinated by what happened to the wives of corporate executives transferred to Europe. I suspect the situation has since changed, but fifteen years ago the move to a foreign country was often a powerfully traumatic event in the lives of these women. They tended to be young, with small children, inexperienced, and totally devoted to husbands who were totally devoted to their careers. The move abroad was bewildering and frightening to many, more than a few of whom became agoraphobic. Others simply withdrew into themselves. Some, however, flourished like tulips brought from the wintry basement into the springtime sun. I wondered what the difference was, and how we, as an American community in Europe, could help these women to grow and gain from the experience rather than to retreat and wither.

I queried the editor of the Paris edition of the *New York Herald Tribune* and got the assignment. I interviewed psychologists and psychiatrists, clergymen and embassy personnel, and most of all, young American wives. The story made the back page of the paper, which was the best showcase an English language writer in Europe could get.

That story was the beginning of several years as a featured columnist for the *Trib*. The story gave me a lot of personal satisfaction, too, for it was instrumental in the founding of support services for American wives abroad. Corporations became more aware and more supportive of the wives of their upwardly mobile executives. And the story became part of a larger article which was later syndicated in the United States.

The Pros and Cons

As in all things, there are pluses and minuses to this field. The biggest minus is the competition. Not only are there hundreds of competent writers out there vying for space in the market, there are also hundreds of psychologists, psychiatrists, psychoanalysts, social workers, and lay therapists—many of them fine writers—trying to get bylines in the same publications. Worse yet, a lot of these professionals are so desperate for publication that they will work for paltry sums or nothing as long as they get a byline. This does little to raise fees paid to writers who are in the business to earn a living.

On the plus side, the market is almost limitless. We are a nation of people endlessly fascinated by the psyche; as a society we are almost hypochondriacal in our devotion to mental health in all its mysterious aspects. *Writer's Market* lists nearly twenty publications in the health field, all of which buy articles on varying aspects of psychology and psychiatry. The women's magazines rely heavily on such articles. The "Living" or "Women's" pages of your daily newspaper run articles, often freelanced, almost every day on some aspect of psychology or psychiatry. The men's, business, fraternal, and company magazines are also constant purchasers of psychologically oriented material.

Hospitals, universities, health centers, and drug companies often use freelancers to write brochures, training manuals, or other materials. Psychologists and psychiatrists themselves often look for writers to either collaborate with them on writing projects or ghostwrite their material. [Editor's note: You can get such jobs by making personal calls, phone calls, mailing résumés, or knowing someone . . . who perhaps knows someone.]

A reputation as a specialist in this field can also net you unexpected rewards. Celebrity interviews are among the toughest assignments to get for freelance writers who aren't part of a magazine's regular stable of contributors. But if you have an idea for a celebrity piece with a sharp psychological twist, and you have a good reputation as a specialist in your field, you will often get the assignment the day the editor receives your query. An example of this is a profile I did of Anthony Quinn for the *New York Times* "Special Features." I knew a little about Quinn's disadvantaged childhood and adolescence in Los Angeles, and I knew that after many years' residence in Rome, he was returning to the United States to settle down in his hometown. I drew a good case for his powerful drive to prove himself through an appearance of arrogance, to justify his life by coming home a hero. I wrote the query and got the assignment.

Another advantage of the field lies in its very nature. The subject matter lends itself to the best kind of writing. Ideally, every article you write should be lively, dramatic, and satisfying to the reader. Like the short story, the article should begin by tantalizing, move into a richly tapestried middle, and close with an emotionally compelling dénouement.

In many fields, this is difficult. I can tell you from experience that it is tough to write an exciting article for an engineering magazine on the construction of a new multimillion-dollar complex. But when writing about a new treatment for depression, for example, your material is the stuff of high drama. You have men, women, and children suffering the most painful and potentially fatal of emotional illnesses. Your heroes— doctors, therapists—are the knights in shining armor. You have human lives saved, resurrected, delivered into the summer sun from the despairing winter of depression. There is no way you can write a boring story!

WRITING ABOUT PSYCHOLOGY FOR THE GENERAL READER
by Elizabeth Friar Williams, M.S.

I became interested in psychology as a result of having grown up an upper-middle-class girl in Buffalo, New York. The connection, I realize, may not seem immediately apparent to everyone, so let me explain. In Buffalo, in the nineteen thirties and forties, people didn't have sexual relations at all, not even if—maybe especially if—they were married; they never expressed anger with loud voices or bad language; they never earned a salary that could be mentioned in dollars and cents; no one hated or even felt ambivalent toward family members; no one had emotional problems or went to a psychiatrist or counselor of any kind; or got divorced; or fired. *To speak of.*

I noticed, however, that my parents were different at home and in public and the fatal thought struck me that perhaps *everybody* was! That meant they had secrets, and these secrets became irresistible to me. I made it my business to inquire of adults who came to the house whether they *really* liked their spouses and children, how much money they earned, with whom they were *really* in love, whether their maid left because of an illegitimate pregnancy, what *really* happened to Aunt Sarah who was said to be working in New York, and whether Uncle Bob had never married because he was *really* waiting for me to grow up, as he promised. I was admonished regularly by my horrified father to "stop asking personal questions," but I couldn't. I felt profoundly that my life depended on my knowing the truth about people. Looking back, I think I sensed that my sanity depended on it: it was crucial for me to know what reality was in a society of hypocrisy, lies, and secrets. It became not only impossible for me to lie about myself, but my mission to tell ignorant others the truths rather than the "official" stories and myths.

A Career in Psychology

The motivation to find the truth prompted me during adolescence to read psychological literature and as an adult to become a psychotherapist. This way I would learn people's secrets and help them at the same time. The motivation to tell others the truth compels me to write for the general public. I believe psychologists and other scientists should write not only for each other but for laymen, who could benefit greatly. Let me give an example from psychology. Studies have shown repeatedly that certain patients get better in therapy regardless of the therapist's orientation. They also indicate that for many patients, group psychotherapy is as effective as individual therapy. But there is a big difference in the fees charged for different treatments.

Psychoanalysts in metropolitan areas charge from $80 to $125 per 45-minute session. A counselor calling herself a "feminist therapist," on the other hand, may charge as little as $5 per session. While there are great differences in the price of the therapeutic hour, there may be little or no difference in the outcome of treatments and surprisingly, there may be little difference in technique in spite of what therapists say they do in the treatment! You are still working with a patient who has specific problems, specific "client style," and specific resistances. No matter what the therapist's training, he or she still has to address himself or herself to this particular patient, must attempt to reach *this* person, and the treatment offered has to be flexible enough to do that. If it takes a Gestalt-therapy technique ("be the lump in your throat") to disgorge the emotion a patient is trying to "swallow," a psychoanalyst is just as likely to try it as a Gestalt therapist, but the price may be a lot higher. This is the kind of thing I think the public should know about but doesn't. I see it as my business to tell them as much as it's my business to be a professional therapist.

I am a feminist therapist, one who is interested in how socialization as a female prevents women from feeling good about themselves, from pursuing goals other than family-related ones, and how such socialization predisposes women to a variety of psychological and physical troubles that are not neurotic in the old sense of the word but are an almost inevitable response to growing up female in our society.

I began writing to share these issues with the reading public. I felt it was very important for men and women to understand how their culture was distressing and limiting both sexes. I felt that if people knew this, they would be helped at least to see that there was nothing "wrong" with women that propelled so many of them to therapists, but that there was (and is) plenty wrong with the rules by which we encourage women to feel blameworthy, inferior, dependent, and depressed.

I felt a great sense of vocation in writing *Notes of a Feminist Therapist* for the general public. The response to the book encouraged me— many, many women wrote me to say it made a big difference in their lives. So I began to write for women's magazines. Usually I write something that expresses a somewhat unconventional or unstereotyped point of view. For example, I wrote an article for *Cosmopolitan* called "How to Survive *His* Depression!" which cautioned women to "not be his nurse—you've got needs too."

Sometimes I feel strongly enough about an issue to write an article without having an assignment—for example, "When Dieting Is Bad for You," on absurd and self-destructive obsession with slimness and diets which can lead to a devastating and often fatal disease, anorexia nervosa. I was and am appalled that although magazines occasionally run articles warning against anorexia, they almost never refuse an article that deals with yet another way to starve oneself! Out of my passionate conviction about this I wrote an article called "Dieting May Be Bad for You," which my wonderful agent, Helen Brann, sent around and around in the days when she handled articles. Nobody took it for about a year. Then one day Julia Kagan, a feminist who was then articles editor at *McCall's*, saw it and liked it very much. Interestingly enough, the problem she had with it was the title. In order to make it less radical it had to be called "When Dieting Is Bad For You."

SUBJECTIVE VS. OBJECTIVE WRITING

My experience as a feminist writer has shown me that it's not necessary to compromise principles for the national media. This should be of interest to those social scientists who believe their sophistication or radicalism might not be shared by the general reader. But if you, as the writer, know who your readers are and can empathize with their anxieties about social change, you can present your point of view in a non-threatening manner. Do this by using lots of case material, which people enjoy reading anyway. When you present the human side— real people's feelings and lives—of your story, most readers can identify with something about themselves, thus allaying anxieties about your message. Not all topics are controversial, of course, and not all stories require the writer to take a position. Often an objective reportorial stance is needed to let readers make their own judgments.

Psychology Is a Science

Although psychology is a *science*, it is often not treated as one by nonprofessionals.

For example, when the American Psychological Association held its 1982 meeting in Washington, D.C., the lead story about the convention in the *Washington Post* and in national newsmagazines was about a jellybean experiment purporting to show that a person's character could be ascertained by his or her choice of jellybean colors! This story made headlines in newspapers around the country. Ignored were the convention's many papers on prevention of nuclear warfare, attitudes toward the aging, educational studies, and a thousand other topics.

The convention had even featured a symposium called "Presenting Psychology to the Public," which included a *Washington Post* science writer as a panelist!

This is an enormous problem for psychologists, who should be taken seriously as scientists. Important and serious issues studied by psychologists do not reach the public often enough in thoughtful and accurate presentations. What do reach the public are articles and trade books contributing to the American Pipe Dream: using a particular formula, you can become thin enough, affluent enough, orgasmic enough, mentally healthy enough, truly *ad nauseam*, to "become the person you always wanted to be." These formulas are not usually questioned as they should be by writers publicizing them.

KNOW YOUR SUBJECT

A responsible psychology writer should be familiar with the research methodology of the behavioral sciences. If that means taking some graduate courses, then do it. A psychology writer ought to be familiar enough with names that show up frequently in the literature to know individual biases and reputations in the field. If your source thinks that all homosexuals are sick people, then you had best report this along with the source's research results on homosexuals. A responsible psychology writer should know what types of questions to ask about an experiment report. Who were the controls? Who were the subjects—demographically, racially, sexually—and how many were there? Has the study been replicated? What were the results? What do the experimenters describe as possible sources of error? How do the experimenters feel about the results' being extrapolated beyond the subjects tested? All this information is in an original research report if published in a reputable journal.

One other point: the less-than-professional psychology writer will often pass on stories from other newspapers or magazines because something has, just through repetition, become a "hot" topic, such as "the new chastity" was a few years ago. That was somebody's idea, but an idea isn't a fact, and informal chats over the telephone with therapists are no substitute for research done in the library or city health department.

The Topnotch Psychology Writer

Two excellent models for the aspiring psychology writer are Carol Tavris and Morton Hunt. Tavris, a Ph.D. social psychologist, is a researcher and freelance writer on psychology. She also frequently reviews "pop psychology" books and does a superb job of applying stringent criticism of the author's method of inquiry, the author's credentials (i.e., his or her suitability to engage in the data collection he or she claims to have employed), the social significance of the results, and so forth. She is aware of the social context in which research takes place and can evaluate someone's work from a position of awareness of the society, its values, prejudices, frivolities, and so on. She is aware of other psychologists' work in the area under discussion. She is a pleasure to read and has integrity as both a reporter and critic.

ASJA member Morton Hunt is a distinguished and scholarly journalist who is not a professional social scientist, but could be. He is aware of the significant work done in psychology, particularly recently in cognitive and social psychology. He is more familiar with the professional literature than many psychologists. He has met many of the more important figures in contemporary psychology and knows exactly to whom he should go for the most accurate and current background data. Although he may call a friend for information, his *friend* is likely to be the president of an American Psychological Association division or someone else with an established professional reputation—not the therapist around the corner, who may have little to offer beyond an opinion.

The Professional as Freelancer

If you are a psychologist or psychotherapist seeking to break into freelance writing, I suggest you start with a book for the general reader. Getting into the magazine market is difficult because of competition from so many excellent, well-known writers.

Nonetheless, here's how a friend of mine cracked the periodicals market: a distinguished social psychologist, a professor whose name is known to most graduate students and social psychologists in this country, my friend wanted to place an article on nuclear proliferation with the *New York Times Magazine*. He felt he had something to tell the general public about conflict resolution, his major research area for thirty-five years. But no matter how distinguished his academic reputation, his name meant nothing to the *Times* editor. Knowing this would be the case, he asked a friend—a famous freelance writer who had written often for the *Times*—to write him a letter of introduction. The writer did this, and it resulted in an article assignment on nuclear conflict resolution.

A warning about writing for magazines: editors are very alert to psychotherapists who want to promote their treatment methods by writing articles, and they are not likely to be fooled by the public relations article in disguised form. Most articles are supposed to be objective. Be aware that if you want to discuss, say, agoraphobia, it should be as a psychological disturbance for which there have been many different treatments, some more successful than others, and many different practitioners of each kind of treatment. Criticisms or limitations of the various treatments should be covered, including criticisms of the treatment you prefer!

Writing for the general public requires that the writer be genuinely interested in and respectful of everybody involved: the subjects and the readers. Readers want to hear about people, not theories. They want to know how your idea or the ideas of others will affect their lives. They want an answer to the question, "So what?" If you can't describe the relevance of your point for ordinary people, or if you don't want to, or don't respect their curiosity, or skepticism, then you shouldn't be trying to write for the public. The public wants to be informed and, to my way of thinking, that's the best possible goal of psychology writing: to inform people of what's going on in the field that can help or harm them in very specific and well-defined ways.

I have described writing about psychology from the perspective of a writer who is both a scientist and a person with a political point of view not shared by all. The objectivity required by the best science writing may seem to deny the possibility of expressing the writer's opinions simultaneously. My own experience indicates that this can be achieved if you are open and aboveboard about your own biases and commitments, and are careful to include others' viewpoints where objectivity warrants it.

WRITING OF LOVE AND HATE
by Lucy Freeman

Why specialize in psychology and psychiatry—the mental health field? Because this era of specialization can be lucrative, the subject is newsworthy, and it is *also* exciting, challenging, and stimulating to seek answers to questions on human behavior, answers that deal with the emotions of love and hate.

I didn't begin my career, however, in this fascinating field. I started off as a general news reporter. After about six years in the city room of the *New York Times*, I started to feel bored with interviewing visiting celebrities and reporting on politicians' speeches, the Easter parades, the circus, and those odd features such as poodles giving parties at society homes to raise money for settlement houses.

Returning from an out-of-town assignment one January, my train ground to a dead stop. The conductor informed us the snow was so deep on the tracks, and there were so many stalled trains ahead, we might stay in that secluded spot for hours.

What was I to do? I had read all the magazines and the mystery purchased to while away the ride. I searched through my luggage for an answer. A large, unlined white pad I used for notes stared up at me. I had torn off a few pages for the conference stories, thrown them away after filing. Well, what was I waiting for? What did I usually do to escape boredom, ennui, rage?

I usually wrote only on assignment, when someone told me what to do—echo of a mother's firm voice in childhood. The city editor had been a substitute mother. And in the last few years, he had been supplemented by another mother—a psychoanalyst.

I had seen the psychoanalyst ostensibly to relieve an acute "sinus" condition for which doctors could find no physical cause. The sinus cleared up after talking to the psychoanalyst and having a good cry for the first time in my adult life. The release of tears somehow freed my stuffed nose. By then I realized I had conflicts too deep for tears alone, so I kept seeing the analyst. Slowly, I was losing the anxiety that had compulsively driven me to achieve, to compete.

As the train sat in the silence of the snowbanks, a small voice within asked: "Why don't you write a magazine article, for which you would get paid, telling what you are getting out of therapy? No one's done this from the patient's point of view."

I wrote the first four words, the title: "View From the Couch." Then slowly the pencil started moving across the white pages. By the time I had written about five thousand words, the train had started again. I didn't realize it, but I was on my way from general news to a specialized beat on the paper, magazine articles, books and, later, a television movie and a play that all had to do in one way or another with mental health.

COME UP WITH NEW IDEAS

That first magazine article was published in *Mercury*, thanks to a writer friend who introduced me to the editor. "It's a new idea," he said, "the patient having her say about analysis."

After the article appeared I had another new idea, which I proposed to the city editor: "You've got a reporter specializing in ship news, another in real estate, another in radio. Don't you think the study of human behavior is worth a specialty?"

The editor stared at me, then said, "Take it, it's yours." Thus the *Times* got a new specialty.

My first book—*Fight Against Fears*—was a spinoff of that original magazine article. From then on I was strictly a specialist, writing nothing but articles and books on psychology-related topics.

I was lucky. The book became a bestseller. I met a man who loved the book, also said he loved me; he persuaded me to give up my job on the *Times*, move to Chicago where he worked in the health field, and marry him. My analyst was ending the analysis, my father had just died, my mother was moving to Florida, and I thought, Why not try Chicago? I left the *Times*, tears in my eyes as I cleaned out my desk, but with a feeling of relief that I would now escape the daily deadline which always hung over my head like a fourth-estate sword of Damocles.

The marriage lasted a rocky two years. I started a second analysis in Chicago and kept writing: articles on mental health for the Chicago newspapers, a book about Michael Reese Hospital, another about a Chicago murderer. When my analyst died suddenly, I returned to New York. I kept writing books, one after another, until I found I'd written fifty-three, a number with psychoanalysts, psychiatrists, and psychologists as co-authors, including Dr. Karl Menninger, whom I had known from newspaper days. It had been an editor's idea that I go to Topeka and dig through Dr. Menninger's files for unpublished letters and manuscripts, get him to update his views on topical psychiatric subjects, and then we'd have a new book, which was called *Sparks*. (Over his and my objection; I rarely win a battle with an editor over a title—you have to fight hard, and they always say, "It's not commercial, it doesn't tell what the book's about.")

PREPARE TO RESEARCH

I found the research of newspaper days stood me in good stead for magazine articles and books. For a newspaper story I attended a convention and listened to or read, if there was a copy for the press room, experts' speeches. Once in a while someone sent me an article from a professional journal that yielded a special feature (nowadays it's more common for specialist reporters to have complimentary subscriptions to the journals).

The same sources can be used for magazine articles *and* books. Attend conventions for psychoanalysts, psychiatrists, psychologists, or social workers. If a convention paper interests you, contact the author to ask about collaboration.

BE CAUTIOUS IN SELECTING EXPERTS

In the mental health field you have a variety of experts willing to be quoted in magazine articles or who want to collaborate on books. Some are competent and others are not, for there are therapists of all persuasions. Freud's prediction that psychoanalysis in America would become "distorted" and "diluted" has come true.

The mental health field requires a sense of ethics on the writer's part. You are dealing with the delicate matter of people's emotional health. There are many unqualified therapists, not only the poorly trained but the charlatans, and the writer owes it to readers to present only the views of the most qualified. In this field, as in life, the adage "Let the buyer beware" still holds.

The Collaboration

In the specialty of mental health, where the writer usually isn't the expert, you often work with a co-author who is an expert. This has its advantages and disadvantages. It depends of course on the co-author. Most of mine have proved thoughtful, considerate, and hard-working, carrying their share of the work in order to earn their share of the profits, usually a fifty-fifty split. Sometimes the writer may want a higher percentage if he or she does most of the work, or may want to keep the entire first part of the advance and let the expert have the second. In rare cases, the professional will let the writer keep the whole advance, or ask for an equal sum from the first royalties. This, of course, is risky for the expert since there is no guarantee the book will earn back the advance.

It is amusing how some experts are apt to forget they had a writer. One of my nonpsychology books, titled *All The Way*, was the biography of jockey Ted Atkinson. Ted appeared on the Ed Sullivan show to promote his book. He called the next morning and said in an apologetic tone, "I didn't mention you as co-author because I thought my name was enough to sell a book about racing." I thought of the perfect retort a week later: "I don't mind at all, Ted, that you claim full credit for writing the book if you'll just say I rode the horse."

Some professionals insist their names come first on the jacket. Writers usually produce enough single credit books not to begrudge a co-author first billing, especially if the co-author is the expert.

IDEAS ARE THE KEY

Sometimes ideas come in unexpectedly from left field. A phone call from an editor or your agent, or a would-be co-author, results in a successful book. On the other hand, an idea you are sold on falls on its face and dies of exhaustion after being rejected by a dozen editors. But never give up on those ideas about which you have conviction. Times change, editors change, and you may be able to sell it in a few years.

Sometimes anger will stimulate a book idea. Not so long ago I got an assignment from a scholarly magazine to do an article on "Freud and Women." The editor, a woman, then refused to print what I had written, saying it was not academic enough for her audience. I was furious because, in giving the assignment, she had asked me to write for the average reader. Not long after, an editor asked what I would like to write a book about—yes, sometimes they do! I thought, then said, "Freud and the women in his life and how he felt about women." The editor said, "Sounds good to me. Write a summary." I smiled, said, "I just happen to have a 5,000-word summary at home." I wrote the book *Freud and Women*, with Dr. Herbert A. Strean, a psychoanalyst. I must send a copy of it to that magazine editor, come to think of it, if I can refrain from writing an appropriate inscription.

One book often leads to another, as one article leads to another. Research uncovers fascinating ideas that can result in books when expanded. My book *Freud and Women*, for example, led to a biography of Anna Freud, with Dr. Hendrik Ruitenbeek. The doctor had done extensive research on her, had an embryonic manuscript, and was seeking a co-author.

Book editors, whom I know better than magazine editors, vary in personality and in the control they keep over a book. Some want to see it as you write it; others wait until the manuscript is completed. Some accept your point of view; others want theirs inserted. Most are thoughtful, helpful, and fair.

You Can Have More than One Readership

Within the specialty of mental health there are two audiences for books. You can write for the professional audience or for the lay audience. I have never written for the professional, but there are writers who find it financially rewarding. Their audience is the growing field known as "the mental health professional," which includes social workers and psychiatric nurses, as well as psychoanalysts, psychiatrists, and psychologists.

You can also write on subjects outside our specialty. I have done a book, as mentioned, with a jockey; one with Tennessee Williams' mother who wanted to tell of *her* dramatic life; and a children's book. It is fun at times to go afield; you feel refreshed when you return to your specialty.

OPPORTUNITIES ABOUND

In mental health, the markets are many: magazine articles, books, columns, documentary films. And you never know what the spinoff may be. My book *Betrayal*, the true story of a young woman who won a lawsuit against a psychiatrist for using sex as therapy, became a two-hour television film on NBC starring Rip Torn and Leslie Anne Warren. *The Story of Anna O.*, my biography of psychiatric patient Bertha Pappenheim, has just been optioned for a movie. Such options are nice but should be viewed as unexpected surprises. In this case, my book led to an article in the *New York Times Magazine* on the 100th anniversary of Pappenheim's birth, being commemorated by a two-day panel discussion on what her case had contributed to the understanding of human behavior.

You'll find that once you've written a book on mental health, you'll be in demand by the experts who cannot write. You, in turn, have to become expert in deciding which of their ideas may be commercial and which will prove a waste of your time.

The door today is wide open in this specialty. We are only a half-step out of the jungle in tackling the emotional troubles of the world's inhabitants. There is plenty of new exploration to be written about: understanding the aggression drive; how hostility affects the sexual drive; understanding of stages of our emotional development; what leads someone to become a murderer, a suicide, or a schizophrenic; the early relationship between mother and child, with many studies showing how this affects later life; how our emotional state affects our bodies, causing many psychosomatic illnesses.

As you write about all this, there is an extra dividend. You learn about yourself. This is one specialty in which you are doubly rewarded: you earn money *and* you gain self-knowledge as you do your research and write. How can you help but like what you do? Your pleasure will show in your writing and in your day-to-day living.

ALL IN THE FAMILY
by Claire Berman

"Write about something you know," said Professor John Koewenhowen back when I was a student in his *Writing the Journal* class. The place was Barnard College. The time, the fifties. I commuted to the campus on 116th Street from my home in Brooklyn five days a week, and so I began to write a series of subway studies—observations of the people I saw every day.

Like an artist without a sketchpad, I sometimes felt uncomfortable about staring at a passenger. The object of my gaze squirmed or returned my stare, in which case *I* squirmed. What right had I to invade the privacy of others? "You're a writer. That gives you all the license you need to study people," said the late John Cheever, who taught the Barnard seminar in short-story writing.

Over the years, I have produced a good deal of writing about what I know *and* taken advantage of a writer's license to study people so as to understand how they order their lives. In the process, I have developed a specialty writing about children and families.

But not for a while. In the beginning, with a Bachelor of Arts degree, a major in English, I wondered how I was going to make any kind of living. After a few false starts, I became an editorial assistant at a major general-interest magazine and, although I still did not make a living (women editorial assistants in those days were well groomed and poorly paid, while young men became assistant editors), I did begin to learn how to handle a magazine article.

I did not, however, get much opportunity to write. The attitude at the magazine was that good editors were hard to find, but writers were a dime a dozen. I became a good editor. (That dividing line has blurred and I now note many editors writing for their magazines. Ironically, as a freelance writer, I'm not pleased about this development.) I was finally allowed to write two or three articles, which appeared beneath my byline—oh happy day!

At this point, I retired to take care of my child. I then spent a lot of time on a bench in the Eighty-third Street playground in Riverside Park, where I found myself observing other people and their children. And there were afternoons in Central Park and at the American Museum of Natural History, and story hours at the libraries.

As more and more parents began to desert the park bench for suburban backyards, and after my one child became children, friends and relatives became worried about our family's welfare. "Sure, the city works for *you*," they would say, "but aren't you sacrificing the children for your own comfort?"

FIND A NEED . . . AND FILL IT

I grew tired of answering that question. I was enjoying the city more *because* of the places and programs I'd discovered with the children. The pediatrician said my children were thriving. Sacrificing the children, indeed!

Clearly there was a need for a book to point out the richness of city life for people with children. Experts' advice would be included. For example, in one chapter the many music schools would be listed, with explanations of various teaching methods (Suzuki, Orff, Dalcroze) and their theories about the appropriate ages for beginning lessons on different instruments. Each chapter would be treated similarly.

I wrote an outline of what the proposed book would contain, chapter by chapter, and the reason it was sorely needed. I remember modestly describing the book as "one that would do for city parents, and those who visited with children, what Dr. Spock did for child care." A friend from my magazine-publishing days suggested an agent and in short order the outline was sold to a publisher.

I've not made so easy a sale since. The publication of *A Great City for Kids* was significant in many ways. The first, and most obvious, is that it got me back to writing. Second, by becoming an author on the subject, I was not only a parent; I'd taken the step toward becoming an "authority" and was invited to give lectures and appear on local radio and television talk shows. I had also built my own expertise on a personal interest in a subject, which I then followed up by interviewing authorities in the field. That is a technique I rely on to this day.

One Thing Leads to Another

Two chapters of the book were picked up by *New York*, and I eventually became a contributing editor to the magazine and wrote a column called "Children." I also contributed pieces on other issues, notably consumer affairs. The good part of this association was that I could assume (rightly, as it turned out) that whatever interested me would be of interest to our readers, for I was one of them. When I considered buying a used piano, for example, I would wangle an assignment on how to buy a used piano. After receiving an obscene phone call, I could write about how to handle unwanted callers. And when I came across a pack of stray dogs on the city streets one afternoon, I could turn that into material for an article too.

About this time, I became interested in the subject of adoption. The way this came about illustrates the unplanned manner in which an area of expertise is sometimes developed.

IDEAS FROM EVERYDAY EXPERIENCES

My husband and I were having dinner in a Chinese restaurant when he spotted an old acquaintance waiting with his wife for a table. We asked them to join us. During the course of dinner, the couple told us about themselves, including (and in great detail) their desire to adopt a child, and the difficulties they were encountering. I returned home determined to learn more about adoption.

A visit to the library—a good place to begin any research project—

turned up a few books on the subject. Most were written for a professional audience. The one good book for general readership was outdated. It dealt with infant adoption, whereas our dinner companions had indicated that there now were far fewer adoptable infants than applicants to adopt them. The professional literature (mostly articles in scholarly journals) confirmed this. There were, in fact, hundreds of youngsters waiting for families, I learned, but they were children whose special emotional, physical, or intellectual needs required special efforts in their behalf. Many were members of minority groups, or they came as a "package"—three or more brothers and sisters per family. "Special-needs children" is the general term for these types of children.

Families interested in adoption could be helped by knowing about the different kinds of children, the challenges and rewards experienced by parents who had adopted a mentally retarded child, for example, or a teenager whose turbulent life history they might never understand. I developed an outline explaining the general topic, the need for a book, and of how I proposed to handle the information, including chapter contents. I decided to interview adoptive families as well as those individuals working in the field or conducting and writing scholarly surveys. This way, I hoped to bring the experience to life for my readers.

Research, Research, and More Research

After a contract with a publisher was signed, and well before I began to conduct interviews, I read everything I could get my hands on, and attended every adoption conference or meeting I could find.

I cannot overemphasize the importance to a nonfiction writer of doing good research. Only after you've acquired a reasonable understanding of the material can you hope to conduct an intelligent interview. Sharp questions elicit detailed responses. Conversely, the source who does not respect an interviewer is likely to tell him or her little of substance. (I remember once when I interviewed an orthodontist in connection with an article on corrective dentistry for adults. The doctor expressed surprise. "I hadn't anticipated such tough questions," he said. "You've really looked into this. I'll have to give you more time than we planned on." We arranged a second meeting, at which time the doctor was extremely helpful. There is no shortcut to doing your homework.)

The book that resulted from all the homework on adoption was *We Take This Child: A Candid Look at Modern Adoption*. It was dedicated to the little boy adopted by the couple we talked to in the Chinese restaurant.

Getting to the Source

A few words about interviewing may be helpful. I'm often asked, "How do you find your subjects?" It's a good idea to start by contacting friends and acquaintances. Few experiences are unique. Someone is bound to know somebody else who has dealt with the situation you're researching. And that person will have a friend.

To obtain geographic distribution, try to get a list of organizations (e.g., *Encyclopedia of Associations*) across the country that deal with your topic, and they'll lead you to their members. People like to be given the opportunity to tell their stories. If they've been well listened to, chances are that you'll be told about a friend whom "you really ought to meet." I never cease to be amazed by the way one good interview leads to another.

You've spoken to enough people when you begin to hear the same things over and over again, when you can anticipate what the answers to your questions will be. It's then time to write.

THERE'S MORE TO THIS THAN MONEY

People often ask about a book, "Was it successful?" It is easy to respond in the affirmative if you can point to impressive sales, first-serial rights picked up by one major magazine (or several), serialization in the newspapers, reprint rights bought by a paperback publisher, a main selection by the book clubs, and adaptation for a major motion picture.

That didn't happen to the book on adoption. We sold a few rights; I appeared on several talk shows. But success can be measured in other ways. When the book showed up in the office of an editor at the *Times*, she was reminded of the work I'd done for *New York* and called me in to ask if I'd serve as guest columnist of the paper's "Parent/Child" column while the regular columnist was on vacation.

At about this time, I received a phone call from the director of the North American Center on Adoption, a project of the Child Welfare League of America (whose fine library I had used when I began my research). She'd read the book, liked it, and asked if we could meet. We could and did. As a result, and as this is being written, I am in my sixth year as Director of Public Education of the Center, where I originated and edit a national quarterly, *Adoption Report*. I work at the League part-time, which has allowed me to continue to write as a freelancer. It's no surprise that many assignments that have come my way have to do with adoption, including lectures and consultant work for several television programs. And there's been time to do other books.

Making It as a Stepparent also set up a specialty, this one focusing on the changing family. The issue is current, so I've found additional opportunities to write about it in magazines as varied as *Town and Country* and *Sourcebook,* distributed to high school seniors. I've also written a public affairs pamphlet on remarriage, and a children's book, *"What Am I Doing in a Stepfamily?"*

SPECIALIZE, BUT DON'T SET LIMITS

If you establish a specialty, you will find opportunities to work in a number of different markets. The important point to keep in mind is that you must continue to be knowledgeable about what's going on in your field.

Specialization need not mean exclusivity. I've written about kidnapping, career changes, advertising, education and business. For a time, I was regarded by one major newspaper as an expert on animals—simply because I wrote an article for them on the fecal matter left by dogs all over the city. (It was the newspaper editor who changed the word I used to "fecal matter.")

Specialization does mean that editors may think of you when a particular topic comes up in editorial meetings. (Then again, they may not. So it's up to you to remind them, every once in a while, that you exist.) You run the risk, of course, of being categorized according to your specialty. *You* know that you're capable of writing on a variety of subjects, and you may even have the clips to prove it, but you may not be given the chance. (You may even be thought of under different categories at different markets. For a while, I was the family person at *New York* and the business specialist at a major airline magazine, and I could not cross the line with either client.)

There is another problem, one that the children-and-families writer sometimes faces. You may find yourself competing for printed space and air time with the very psychiatrists and psychologists you have interviewed. You will notice that bylines in popular magazines are, more and more, accompanied by the M.D. or Ph.D. When an acquisitions editor presents a book proposal to the sales force at a publishing house for consideration (and, increasingly, the sales force's evaluation of a book's potential success is critical to the decision whether to offer the writer a contract), one of the questions the staff will raise concerns promotion. Talk show producers like to schedule appearances by the experts ("I advise my patients to . . . ") or by someone who's able and willing to describe a personal experience ("Following my divorce, I . . . "). If this is the case in the area in which you'd like to specialize, you may want to get that degree.

THE WHY OF PSYCHIATRIC WRITING
by Flora Rheta Schreiber

As an undergraduate and graduate student at Columbia University, I took many courses in psychology, but I did not major in that subject. I majored in English, theatre, and speech. At that time I could not have known that, as a writer of magazine articles, syndicated columns, and books, my major themes would derive from psychology and psychiatry and that I would be known as a psychiatric writer.

The transition from my academic specialities was, actually, quite natural. You cannot be steeped in the motivations of Hamlet or Oedipus Rex, Hedda Gabler or Tom Jones without having taken a plunge into the wellsprings of human behavior, the main concern of psychological and psychiatric writings.

Writers are drawn to this field by temperament and a special approach to life. Essentially their concern is less with the world around them than with the inner self; less with *what* people do than with *why* they do it. It is not today's newspaper headline that is the subject of a psychiatric article. The subject emerges from the forces in human beings from which these headlines result. In this sense, a psychiatric writer is most concerned with anonymous people whose stories are rooted in significant human motivation and behavior. In psychiatric subjects, the writer must be willing to explore the abnormal as well as the normal, the delusional along with the real. This kind of writer must have sensitively attuned perceptions, compassion, and an analytical mind.

BECOMING A SPECIALIST

Having chosen this field, the writer must establish close contacts with those who treat the mentally ill, are concerned with mental health, and who do basic research in the field. These practitioners include M.D.'s who specialize in psychiatry and psychoanalysis, lay psychoanalysts, clinical psychologists, and psychiatric social workers. The writer needs access to case histories, to new research, and to psychological and psychiatric conferences and symposia. Papers delivered at the meetings of the American Psychiatric Association, the American Psychological Association, the Academy of Psychoanalysis, the New York Center for Psychoanalysis, and a variety of other organizations are frequently used as source material for articles and books.

The psychiatric writer will also find it helpful to consult various abstracts of current research, such as are issued by the United States

Department of Health and Human Services in Washington, D.C., and the National Institute of Mental Health in Bethesda, Maryland. Also helpful are popular psychological magazines like *Psychology Today*, specialty magazines like *Science Digest* and *Scientific American* that sometimes feature articles about psychological and psychiatric subjects, and scholarly publications such as the *Journal of the American Academy of Psychoanalysis, the American Journal of Psychiatry*, and the *American Journal of Psychoanalysis*, written for psychiatrists and psychoanalysts.

COLLABORATE WITH THE PROFESSIONALS

In my own career, I have developed a working relationship with many psychiatrists and psychoanalysts and have published articles about their patients or their research in a variety of consumer magazines, including *Good Housekeeping, Cosmopolitan, Ladies' Home Journal, Redbook, Family Circle, Family Weekly, Woman's Day, Modern Maturity*, and *Science Digest*. My profiles of political figures—every president from Truman through Nixon and members of their families—have been strongly psychological. This has been especially true of my numerous articles about Lyndon and Lady Bird Johnson and of my *Good Housekeeping* article entitled "My Son, Richard Nixon," by Hannah Milhous Nixon as told to me.

My access to new psychiatric research became especially strong after Melvin Herman, executive director of the National Association of Private Psychiatric Hospitals, and I became psychiatry co-editors of *Science Digest*.

With the late Stuart Long I wrote a syndicated column, "Syndrome, U.S.A.," which approached politics in psychiatric terms. He was the expert in politics, I in psychiatry, and together we took a behavioral look at current events.

My association with Dr. Murray Bowen, a family psychotherapist, led to my writing a series of articles. "The Tragedy of Emotional Divorce," which was published in *Cosmopolitan* and won a Family Service Association award, dealt with the emotional distance between a husband and wife in an emotionally disturbed family. This article was followed, in the same magazine, by one entitled "Family Therapy," which concerned a family Dr. Bowen had treated. As spinoffs, I wrote articles about "sick" families for *Family Weekly* and *Science Digest*.

To write these pieces, I studied Dr. Bowen's records, read collateral books on the subject, and spent some forty hours interviewing him. As a writer, my task was to translate psychiatric concepts into language understandable to the layperson, and to tell a dramatic story with characters that would come to life on the printed page.

My association with Dr. Cornelia Wilbur led to my writing "I Was Raising a Homosexual Child" for *Cosmopolitan*. The article tells a mother's story of discovering the first signs of homosexuality in her preadolescent son, a patient of Dr. Wilbur. The article was bylined by a pseudonymous mother as told to me.

On the day the article reached the newsstands Dr. Wilbur telephoned me and said, "Now I have something really good for you to write." In her office a few days later she asked me to write a book about a patient named Sybil. The girl was suffering from the rare illness of multiple personality and was the first multiple personality to be psychoanalyzed. I asked whether the patient's personalities had been integrated. The answer was no. I replied that until she was, there could be no book, for to be effective the story had to have not only a beginning and a middle, but also an end.

"Wouldn't you like to meet Sybil anyway?" Dr. Wilbur asked.

"Who wouldn't?" I replied.

On an autumn evening in 1962, Dr. Wilbur and I had dinner with Sybil at a restaurant on New York City's Madison Avenue. Sybil seemed constrained and remote. But there was an affinity between us that became evident when we talked about the poetry of Emily Dickinson. While I was still in college I had written an article about Emily's poetry, a psychograph as I called it, that was published in *Poet Lore* magazine.

I did not commit myself to writing a book about Sybil, but she and I became friends. She frequently visited my apartment and often told me about what took place in the analytic sessions. Sybil developed a particularly close relationship with my mother, who became the antithesis for her of her sadistic, schizophrenic mother.

Sybil was integrated into one person after I had known her and her other selves for three years. I then began formal research for the book. The confidences I shared with Sybil and Dr. Wilbur and my direct contacts with the other selves had to be supplemented by a systematized approach to the case as a whole and to Sybil's entire life. I read widely in the medical literature about *grande hystérie* with multiple personalities, the formal name for Sybil's illness, and I discussed the general aspects of the case with various psychiatrists in addition to Dr. Wilbur. I talked with people who had known Sybil in her midwestern hometown and in New York City. I physically followed the routes Sybil had taken during some of her adventures as her alternating selves.

To obtain a coherent story, I had to explore all documents connected with Sybil's 11-year psychoanalysis. These included Dr. Wilbur's daily notes in the course of 2,354 office sessions, Sybil's essays—written as part of the treatment procedure—and taped recordings of the analytic sessions. I also studied Sybil's diaries (kept from adolescence through the first year of analysis), letters, family and hospital records, and newspapers and records of Sybil's hometown during the years that her family lived there.

It took seven years.

I prepared a presentation which was sent to every publisher in New York City—and unanimously rejected. One editor of a major house said he would give me a contract if I agreed to reduce the number of selves from sixteen to four. He said that readers couldn't follow the activities of sixteen, and the book in that form would be unwieldy. I replied that, since I had not created the sixteen, I was powerless to eliminate twelve of them.

Fortunately, an old friend of mine, associated with Cowles Books, sold the company on the book. (Cowles was sold to the Henry Regnery Company, which ultimately published *Sybil*.)

The rest is publishing history. Four days after publication in May 1973, *Sybil* made the bestseller list. It remained a national bestseller for over six months and was several times in the number one position. The same was true for the paperback edition, published by Warner Books in May 1974. The book was published in sixteen foreign countries and was a bestseller in several of these countries. To date, Warner has published six million copies and released a new edition in November, 1982. A main selection of the Psychology Today Book Club, a featured alternate of the Literary Guild, and the recipient of a Medical Writers award, *Sybil* was also a four-hour TV drama produced by Lorimar. Since the initial production, the drama has been frequently repeated not only on NBC, the network on which it was originally aired, but on other networks and local stations. A motion picture based on the television drama has been shown throughout the world.

After *Sybil*, I looked for another psychological and psychiatric subject and found it in Joseph Kallinger. Simon and Schuster published *The Shoemaker: The Anatomy of a Psychopath* in 1983.

People in Pennsylvania, New Jersey, Maryland, New York, and Connecticut will remember Joseph Kallinger as a thirty-eight-year-old Philadelphia shoemaker who, with his thirteen-year-old son Michael, went on a seven-week crime spree in late 1974 and early 1975. The surface story as reported in the media told little; my book, which approaches crime psychologically and is essentially an exploration of madness, probes the unknown story. It is the first internal look at a man who kills because of his psychosis—a psychotic killer, as opposed to the sociopathic killers whom Truman Capote presented in *In Cold Blood*.

Through many thousands of hours of conversation over a six-year period, I traced with Kallinger the origin and the development both of his psychosis and his crimes. I traced the genesis of murder from child abuse and from a specific childhood incident that became the origin of both a psychosis and of the crimes that were inseparable from the psychosis.

The data were further interpreted by the late Dr. Silvano Arieti, a world-renowned psychiatrist and leading authority on schizophrenia, who twice examined Kallinger as a private patient and studied my book and Kallinger's total psychiatric record. Dr. Arieti had examined the Boston Strangler but could not find in him any connection between his crimes and a psychosis. In the case of Joseph Kallinger, however, Dr. Arieti maintained that the crimes and the psychosis were one and that without the psychosis the crimes would not have taken place.

The case of Joseph Kallinger has become a landmark in psychiatry. The *Journal of the Academy of Psychoanalysis* published the article Dr. Arieti and I wrote about Kallinger. In addition, I was invited to deliver a paper about this unique and arresting case at the May 1982 conference of the Academy of Psychoanalysis.

As I've noted, to specialize in psychological and psychiatric subjects you must be willing to explore the abnormal as well as the normal, the delusional along with the real. Above all, you must not be judgmental in a narrow, moralistic sense. Before passing judgment, you must discover *why* the subject does what he or she does and must see the subject in light of that *why*.

Why should you become a psychiatric writer? The field offers infinite fascination and challenge. The rewards in this sense are great. Economically, your rewards are similar to those in any other field of writing. You will get the going rate in consumer magazines. Books in the field, as in any other, are a gamble. The time invested in a book is inevitably long and the risks therefore are great. But the end, both in terms of social contribution and monetary success, can—and often does—justify the means.

Additional Resources

Alcohol, Drug Abuse and Mental Health Administration, National Clearinghouse for Alcohol, National Clearinghouse for Drug Abuse, National Clearinghouse for Mental Health, 5600 Fishers Lane, Rockville, MD 20857. Provides support for research, and technical assistance for communication and prevention activity. Offers brochures and pamphlets, newsletter, placement on mailing list, press kits, photos. Three publication lists available—one each on alcohol, drug abuse, mental health.

American Association for Marriage and Family Therapy, 924 W. Ninth, Upland, CA 91786. Has thirteen accredited training centers throughout the U.S.; provides a national marriage and family therapy referral-service from its national office. Publications include a bimonthly newspaper and a quarterly journal.

American Psychiatric Association, 1400 K St. NW, Washington, DC 20005. Provides comprehensive information on psychiatric care, psychiatric insurance, mental illnesses. Offers aid in arranging interviews, bibliographies, biographies, statistics, brochures and pamphlets, placement on mailing list. Typically available each year are more than four hundred individual papers on a wide range of topics, plus intermittent news releases regarding new studies published in the APA journals. Write for publications list.

American Psychotherapy Association, P.O. Box 2436, West Palm Beach, FL 33402. Compiles statistics; sponsors competitions. Maintains library and biographical archives, plus Board of Examiners in Psychotherapy to evaluate training, experience, and professional excellence of individuals. Bestows awards to individuals and associations making outstanding contributions to the profession.

Association for Advancement of Behavior Therapy, 420 Lexington Ave., New York, NY 10170. Provides referral information on populations, settings, techniques, treatments, and special areas of interest in behavior therapy. Offers aid in arranging interviews, brochures and pamphlets, telephone reference services. Publications list available.

Association of Existential Psychology and Psychiatry, 40 E. 89th St., New York, NY 10028. Offers journal, newsletter, publications list.

Association of Psychiatric Outpatient Centers of America, Psychological Clinic, Box 6142, University, AL 35486. Conducts research; provides consultative services; holds regional symposia. Publishes newsletter, journal, dissertations, monographs, proceedings of annual meeting.

Center for Responsive Psychology, Brooklyn College, Brooklyn, NY 11210. Provides comprehensive information covering social psychology, law, and related fields. Offers brochures and pamphlets, informational newsletter, placement on mailing lists, research assistance, statistics, telephone reference services, expert witnesses, and research-related services. Publications include *Social Action and the Law* (quarterly newsmagazine), and relevant articles and reprints.

Foundation for Better Living, Box 183, 201 E. 87th St., New York, NY 10028. Conducts discussion groups, seminars, and classes for clergymen, psychologists, psychiatrists, teachers, parents, and lay people; sponsors lectures. Publishes *Journal for Better Living* (semiannual); compiles bibliographies.

Group for the Advancement of Psychiatry, % Jack Weinberg, M.D., Illinois State Psychiatric Institute, 1601 W. Taylor St., Chicago, IL 60612. Publishes extensive group of reports on such subjects as school desegregation, use of nuclear energy, religion, psychiatry in the armed forces, mental retardation, cross-cultural communication, medical uses of hypnosis, and the college experience. Publications are available only from the Publications Office of the Group for the Advancement of Psychiatry, 30 E. 29th St., New York, NY 10016.

Institute for Social Research, 426 Thompson St., Ann Arbor, MI 48104. Provides information on survey methodology, economics, journalism, politics, urban planning, education, psychology, sociology, organizational studies, use of time, and more. Offers aid in arranging interviews, informational newsletters, library facilities and archives, placement on mailing lists, research assistance, telephone reference services. Publications include newsletter (quarterly), *Economic Outlook USA* (quarterly), and other research reports and surveys.

Institute for Research in Hypnosis & Psychotherapy, 10 W. 66th St., New York, NY 10023. Provides comprehensive information on mental health, hypnotherapy, hypnoanalysis, hypnosis research, and hypnosis-psychosomatics. Offers aid in arranging interviews, annual reports, biographies, brochures and pamphlets, informational newsletters, library facilities, placement on mailing lists, research assistance, statistics. Library contains numerous reprints, books, tape recordings, biographical archives.

National Psychological Association for Psychoanalysis, 150 W. 13th St., New York, NY 10011. Professional society for practicing psychoanalysts. Offers information and private referral service for the public. Maintains library; publishes *News and Reviews* (quarterly), *The Psychoanalytic Review* (quarterly), *Bulletin* (annual).

The Psychology Society, 100 Beekman St., New York, NY 10038. Provides information on social and marital relationships, prison reform, and more. Offers aid in arranging interviews and aid in securing specific data.

Chapter Eleven

WRITING RELIGION

The words *religion writing* may conjure up visions of solemn treatises and flaming evangelical missives.

A great deal of religion writing *is* intended to teach, proselytize, or inspire the reader. And a great many writers take satisfaction in shining some spiritual light on their readers' lives. But this area of specialization is much much more. Religion writing can also mean a hard-hitting interview with a controversial religious leader, an exposé of a mind-controlling, larcenous cult, a human-interest feature on a tent revival or a Shinto purification rite. The possibilities are as diverse as religion itself. In fact, writing in this field is not defined by subject so much as by *slant*—it's intended for people who share common beliefs, whose lives embrace a certain ethic. And the line between religion and secular writing blurs in the inspirational article, which is intended to uplift and enlighten the varied readers of general publications.

Religion publications are the biggest market for religion writing. These have had a strong and steady influence throughout the history of magazine journalism in the United States since *American Magazine* was edited by the Rev. William Smith in 1757. As James L.C. Ford notes in *Magazines for Millions*, "Mainly the religious magazine has been the voice of conviction and faith, often a particularized denominational faith, but seldom only a still, small voice."

Professor Ford estimates there are more than 1,700 religion magazines existing today, and notes that "tiny indeed is the religious group which does not possess and publish at least one."

The many types of religion publications include denominational magazines and periodicals; general magazines; magazines for women, men, children, young people, or families. There are also theological journals, trade publications, regional publications, and house organs.

Beyond magazines, there are new and growing challenges for writers. There's a constant demand for newsletter writers and editors, for radio and television programs, and for motion pictures. The field is wide open and thriving. Electronic technology is increasing the religion writer's opportunities each and every day with such innovations as video cassettes for home playback units. Cable is sending more religious television programming into the nation's homes. At present, more new TV channels are being considered by the Federal Communications Commission, ditto for religious broadcasting (radio) networks.

The growing market for religion books is evidenced by the 5,000-plus new titles that appear annually in member stores of the Christian Booksellers Association. The Jewish publishing world is enjoying similar growth. Among well-known magazines edited or published by or for American Jews (and, in some cases, the general reader) are *Commentary, American Judaism, National Jewish Monthly,* and *Hadassah* (official publication of the Women's Zionist Organization of America). Jewish juvenile publications include *Young Judaean* and *World Over.* Foreign book markets are also expanding; new domestic ones are opening.

Elaine Wright Colvin, co-editor of *The Religious Writers Marketplace* (a guide to more than 1,500 publishers and publications in the religion field), says, "The wide-reaching religious market is open to the serious freelancer who is willing to study, work, and pursue his craft with diligence." She adds, ". . . every editor is looking for that freelancer who has something to say and can communicate it in a lively manner to his eager audience."

Religion writing is a good place for beginners to break in, and though the pay may not be as much as for other writing specialties, the breadth and diversity of the booming religion market is enough to warm the cockles of any freelancer's heart.

WRITING FOR RELIGION MARKETS
by Richard Quebedeaux

In the not-too-distant past, most of the noteworthy religion books and magazine articles were written by professional theologians and ministers. Today, however, even bestsellers in religion are authored, as well as read, by lay people. The religion media as a whole have gained visibility among the American public, as witnessed by the rise to national prominence of celebrity television evangelists and the "electronic church" in the late 1970s. The field of religion—mainly Christian—writing has been growing, flourishing and, some would say, exploding during the same period. More markets for books and articles and more writers in the field emerge each year, at a time when sales of religion publications exceed $600 million annually. To help the increasing numbers of those entering this expanding literary market, there are now more than 30 national Christian writers' conferences held every year, and many more regionally. These have been supplemented by the formation in unprecedented numbers of local Christian writers' groups across the United States, and by the introduction of correspondence courses on professional religion writing.

In these pages I intend first to describe and analyze the current market for religion publications. Second, I'll relate my experiences as a professional writer on Christianity—how I chose the field, how I developed a continuing interest in it, and why I made it my primary freelance writing business.

RELIGION PUBLISHERS AND READERS

The present market for religion publications ranges from children's stories and Sunday school curricula to highly technical theological monographs and social-scientific studies, sermons to popular psychology, how-to books on church growth to Christian sex manuals. No matter how scholarly, esoteric, or controversial the subject, there is probably at least one religion publisher who will consider it.

Periodicals—from academic journals to breezy popular monthlies—make up a large and many-faceted segment of the religion market. These include many newsletters and small magazines geared to the particular needs and interests of religion writers themselves. Denominational magazines, published for both laity and ministers, take on special importance as well because virtually every Christian denomination has at least one journal for clergy and one for lay readers. Some of these have very impressive circulation figures. A number of more general, interdenominational magazines are also significant. Among them are popular evangelical monthlies like the *Christian Herald* (200,000) and *Moody Monthly* (325,000), and ministers' journals such as *Christianity Today* (185,000) for evangelicals and the *Christian Century* (33,000) for an ecumenical audience. In addition, there are religion periodicals focusing on women, men, families, youth, children, scholars, booksellers, poets, and other special-interest groups. Virtually all these publications accept proposals and completed manuscripts from qualified freelancers sympathetic to the magazine's editorial stance—an *extremely* important requirement—and understanding of the interests of its readership.

At this point, it should be said that religion periodicals, like their secular counterparts, most often have staff writers (although a few rely chiefly on voluntary help). Also, about one hundred secular dailies hire full-time religion reporters, as do the major news agencies. In addition, a variety of syndicates distribute religion columns and other features by leading personalities such as Billy Graham and Andrew Greeley. Opportunities in religion writing abound, not only for freelancers, but also for staff writers and reporters—positions that often allow freelancing on the side.

When it comes to religion book publishing, the spectrum of offerings is as wide as that in the magazine market. But some book topics are *far* more popular and salable than others. For instance, among Catholics there has been a major resurgence of interest in prayer, mysticism, and "spiritual renewal" since the 1970s. Books on these subjects have sold extraordinarily well. Among Protestants—who represent a broader religious market—the pecking order of favorite topics looks something like this:

1. Marriage and the family
2. Self-help for Christian living
3. "Bible prophecy" (e.g., the Second Coming of Christ)
4. Devotional and inspirational works, including fiction
5. Popular psychology
6. Personal experience and celebrity conversion stories, declining in popularity
7. Pastors' helps
8. Contemporary social issues
9. Academic Bible studies and commentaries
10. Church growth (how to make it happen)

There are other "hot" subjects as well, such as an increasing interest in the classic fiction of C.S. Lewis and the Inklings (including Dorothy Sayers and J.R.R. Tolkien). Within Protestant and Catholic academic circles, the major focus of attention since the 1970s has been Latin American "liberation theology," an indigenous integration of classical Christian doctrines and spirituality with an essentially Marxian analysis of society. European and North American theological scholarship has dealt frequently with issues such as feminism, racial equality, and homosexuality, coming to them from positions as diverse as conservative evangelicalism, Protestant ecumenism, and Marxist Christianity. Outside Christianity, an example of a successful book is Rabbi Harold S. Kushner's *When Bad Things Happen to Good People*.

Such is the religion book market in America today. But it must always be remembered that each new generation of religious believers emerges and matures with new interests and concerns for the market to meet. The experiences and convictions that sold books in the 1960s are very different from those successfully in print since the 1970s. Religion writers who stay informed and aware of developments will never have to worry about markets for their work, however secular society generally becomes. Religious needs and aspirations aren't likely to vanish in the foreseeable future. In fact, writers can look forward to additional media markets in coming years, including video discs, new and more sophisticated Christian television stations, Christian and Jewish cable networks, textbooks for the growing number of private Christian schools, and a rapidly changing and expanding Christian music industry. All of this constitutes the *good* news about writing for religion markets. But there is *bad* news, too, and not a little of it!

The Realities of the Marketplace

The bad news for religion writers involves the nature of the genre's readership and the restrictions that readership imposes on writers. It is also to be found in the paltry remuneration freelance magazine writers, with few exceptions, can expect.

Eighty percent of all religion books sold in the United States are bought by women, most of whom are conservative Christians. These readers most often buy their books in the "Bible bookstores" of the Christian Booksellers Association (CBA), an umbrella organization serving more than twenty-seven hundred member stores nationwide. Only the most popular religion titles are generally found in secular bookstores. (For an excellent analysis of the current market for publications on religion, see William Gentz, ed., *Writing to Inspire* [Writer's Digest Books, 1982].)

And who, exactly, *are* the Christian women, children, and men who constitute this market? The majority of adult readers have a high-school education and are not culturally elite. When they buy religion publications, they choose magazines and books with broad popular appeal among their fellow Christians, written in a simple fashion to help them meet their everyday problems. They expect three basic things from their reading: entertainment, consolation, and encouragement. And by and large, they will not read books or articles with which they don't agree (not unlike most other readers).

Religion writers who hope to be successful must gear their topics and treatment to the interests of the typical religion book buyer in this country today—a wife and homemaker, aged twenty-five to forty, with a high school education or less and two children. This reader's primary concerns are her husband's success and the stability of their family, issues that create a great deal of anxiety for her. Thus, today's religion bestseller is usually "experience-oriented, life-centered, and Bible-based," as one leading Christian marketing executive put it. Recent bestselling titles include Tim and Beverly La Haye's *The Act of Marriage* (a sex manual for the born-again), Marjorie Decker's *The Christian Mother Goose Book*, Anne Ortlund's *Children Are Wet Cement*, Frances Hunter's *God's Answer to Fat, Lose It*, and Hal Lindsey's *The 1980s: Countdown to Armageddon*. (Lindsey was named by the *New York Times* as the bestselling author of the 1970s, with sales of over fifteen million dollars alone for his book *The Late Great Planet Earth*.)

Because of the *kind* of religion books typically published and the secular media's lack of interest in religion, it is rare for review organs like the *New York Times Book Review* or the *New York Review of Books* to critique religion books. Major book clubs like The Literary Guild and Book-of-the-Month Club virtually ignore religion titles. Religion writers must write primarily for believers and expect to see reviews of their books only in the religion media.

Most periodicals and book publishers that accept religion topics from freelancers are listed in *Writer's Market*, with the major exception of scholarly journals. Those may be inspected in theological seminary libraries. Two often overlooked, but important, publishers of academic religion titles are Scholars Press (Chico, California), affiliated with the American Academy of Religion, and The Edwin Mellen Press (Lewiston, New York). Both specialize in academic monographs, theses, and series with very limited popular appeal. To save money, neither publisher sets type. Authors submit manuscripts exactly as they want them to appear in print. Sold by mail order alone, most books do not see a first printing of more than five hundred copies. Nonetheless, the quality and stature of both houses are gradually approaching that of leading university presses. It's more difficult to publish scholarly religion through university presses; many are backlogged three years or more.

Despite the overriding anti-intellectual and noncontroversial character of popular religion books and magazines today, a writer *can* get scholarly and controversial works published *somewhere*. But the financial rewards for even the most groundbreaking academic articles and books in all fields are negligible. The only secure incomes are earned by religion staff writers on secular newspapers and periodicals, and their religion counterparts, whose pay at the beginner and midcareer levels is roughly commensurate with that of other professional writers. Salaries of religion writers attached to media staffs range from $10,000 to $50,000. A few top journalists earn close to the higher figure, but most do well to reach $25,000. The same can be said of religion book editors. The astronomical earnings so common in secular entertainment and sports industries are confined mainly to successful television evangelists.

When it comes to freelancers, they have a much more difficult time. Many religion periodicals pay *nothing* for articles or reviews. The rest, as even a cursory reading of *Writer's Market* will reveal, pay less, sometimes far less, than comparable journals in other fields. And there are hardly *any* religion magazines offering more than two hundred dollars for a lead article. Advances on royalties for religion books are better, but they, too, are less likely to equal the five-figure sums comparable secular titles might command. And not many religion authors command advances of more than a few thousand dollars per book. Practically speaking, freelance writers cannot usually make a decent living writing for the religion media alone—unless they achieve success with a religion bestseller such as authors Hal Lindsey, Marjorie Holmes, and Dr. James Dobson have done.

ETHICS AND ACCURACY— TELLING THE *WHOLE* STORY

At this point, a few words should be said about something all too often forgotten when writing for religion markets—the writer's *ethical* obligations. Religion is an important matter for most Americans. It comprises the believer's highest values and aspirations, and thus warrants a degree of *respect* often lacking in secular reporters' prose. This widespread lack of respect, empathy, and compassion for religious believers—from the New Christian Right to the "cults"—has largely been the consequence of two weaknesses in the field of religion journalism that need to be remedied.

First, many journalists and writers are quick to pass judgment on a religion or its leader, although they have never had personal interaction with any of the group's faithful members. Instead, their writing is based on the negative stories of former members, be they Moonies or Mormons or fundamentalists. Any writer seeking truth has an obligation to gather evidence from both sides of an issue before making an evaluation. Too many religion writers refuse to attend services and other activities of the groups they critique and, therefore, can have *no* understanding of how the church, cult, or religion sees *itself*. Sociologists call the attempt of outside investigators to gain firsthand experience of groups they study "participant observation"—a practice that should be *mandatory* for all religion journalists and authors. In a democratic and pluralistic society, in which every religion—however unpopular it might be with the majority—has equal protection under the law, we must learn to understand those whose beliefs seem peculiar to us. No one can be more helpful in this task than authors and journalists willing to be painfully objective and walk in another person's shoes *before* writing.

Second (and this is like unto the first weakness), many religion journalists and other writers simply don't have enough "book knowledge" to handle their specialization well. Professional theologians still argue that a seminary education, which most writers lack, is the only solution. I suggest, however, that the writer educate himself about religion in America—the trends, the tensions, the personalities—by reading several important books. All these works, whatever the personal convictions of the authors—from liberal to fundamentalist—take a scholarly critical approach to even their own traditions, and treat others with uncommon respect. They also direct the reader to other significant sources dealing with the same and related issues by providing ample documentation and bibliographies. These books have attained the status of standards in the field and will not lose their overall value even when technically out-of-date.

First among them is Winthrop S. Hudson's *Religion in America,* third edition (Scribners, 1981), the best scholarly and readable history of religion in the United States currently available. This highly objective work surveys and touches at least a little of virtually everyone and everything important in that history, from the beginning to the present day. Hudson should be supplemented by Deane William Ferm's *Contemporary American Theologies* (Seabury Press, 1981), which discusses the present spectrum of theological thinking—from Latin American liberation theology to evangelical theology—in much greater depth and with even more objectivity. Ferm, however, omits two significant contemporary religious groupings in his survey—fundamentalism and the cults (or "new religious movements," as scholars prefer to call them)—which must be read about elsewhere. These groupings are treated most interestingly and helpfully in Jerry Falwell's *The Fundamentalist Phenomenon* (Doubleday, 1981) and David G. Bromley and Anson Shupe's *Strange Gods: The Great American Cult Scare* (Beacon Press, 1981). Falwell's book, written mainly by two professors at his Liberty Baptist College and Seminary, is—despite the rhetoric and apologetic—a valuable historical and contemporary assessment of fundamentalism by (amazingly) self-critical insiders. Shupe and Bromley are objective sociologists who, in *Strange Gods,* completely demystify the cults, all of which have been subjected to gross misrepresentations by the popular media. Reading this book will shock many journalists and other writers who have heard the "cult story" only from the most vehement detractors.

Finally, two of my own books will help both secular and religion writers understand the contemporary "born-again" movement, of which fundamentalism and some of the cults are only two segments. *The Worldly Evangelicals* (Harper and Row, 1978) focuses on modern evangelicalism—a middle-of-the-road stance between fundamentalism and liberalism—and surveys almost all of the major individuals and organizations within the movement, locating them, their beliefs and behavior, in relationship to each other and to the wider culture. In *By What Authority: The Rise of Personality Cults in American Christianity* (Harper and Row, 1982), I trace the historical origins and rise of "celebrity leaders" (and the authority they wield) in modern American religion, from Billy Sunday and Aimee Semple McPherson to Oral Roberts, Pat Boone, and Jimmy Carter. This book is especially valuable for writers because it evaluates—in greater depth than in this essay—the kinds of written and electronic media offerings "popular" in today's religion market.

No critical reader can be expected to agree with all the data and perspectives put forward by the aforementioned authors. But reading them, and gaining firsthand experience of the churches and movements discussed, will make it possible for journalists and other writers on religion to fulfill their high calling in more knowledgeable and charitable ways than they have most often done in the past.

A PERSONAL JOURNEY

My story is not typical of many in the profession. I never wanted to be a writer and didn't consciously prepare for this career until *after* my first book was published. I didn't choose the freelance writing profession at all. It chose me.

My intense religious background had a major effect on the studies I chose in college and the degrees I eventually took, with the result that I gradually settled on religion itself—church history, to be exact—as my specialty, and pursued it through ten years of postgraduate education, including seminary. My goal was to teach. I had deep convictions about the revolutionary potential of Christianity, born out of reaction to my fundamentalist upbringing, and I wanted to share those feelings with students who were at that place, too. But I didn't want to write. Sure, I knew I'd *have* to "publish or perish" as a professor, but I never intended to write more than was absolutely necessary. Quite frankly, writing had always been a burden for me; only once in my entire undergraduate and graduate career can I remember a paper marked "well-written."

But things changed dramatically in 1971 while I was researching my doctoral thesis in Berkeley. I met a retired theologian who was also the founder of a well-known religion magazine. We discussed for three hours my passion at the time, the young born-again Christians—onetime "Jesus freaks"—who were becoming politically and socially radical without discarding their evangelical roots. My new friend had never heard of "radical" born-again Christians—they were rare in 1971—and he invited me to write an article on these young evangelicals for his journal. It was published at the end of the year, and I received my fifty-dollar honorarium.

I liked the article, but, more importantly, so did an editor at Harper

and Row, who invited me to propose a book on the same theme—
which I did without hesitation. Although writing had previously been
a chore, the popular *and* academic prestige of Harper and Row and the
advance they offered (which I needed desperately) motivated me to
complete the manuscript within the time span allowed by my contract
(publishers *always* appreciate on-time submissions, and rarely get
them). *The Young Evangelicals* was published in 1974, and, lucky for me
as a writer, the book's title became the catchphrase of a new generation
of younger, more liberal, and born-again intellectuals and activists
who gained widespread media visibility later in the decade. (Jimmy
Carter, for example, was a prime example of this kind of evangelical
Christian.) Like the movement it heralded, *The Young Evangelicals* also
became well known and was extensively reviewed in the religion media.

The success of my first book—much more evident in rave reviews
than in sales—enabled me to sell my unfinished Ph.D. thesis to a trade
publisher. It was published as a book in 1976, and, by that time, I had
begun to consider myself a professional freelance writer. With the academic job crunch, only beginning to be felt at the time, I was happy to
have another career option. Furthermore, I did manage to earn a marginal living—it reached $12,000 annually at one point—on writing
alone, and, gradually, was able to supplement this up-and-down income with lecture and consultant fees. In the years following my second book, I wrote three more and thereupon became a leading
authority on evangelical Christianity in America—thus fulfilling my
ambition to become a recognized scholar, but in a different way than I
had expected.

THE IMPORTANCE OF DISCIPLINE

I became a writer only with a great deal of struggling and suffering, although this may not be apparent from what I have said. To manage the production of six books in less than ten years, it was necessary
to cultivate a regular discipline for writing from the beginning.

I compose a complete working outline of the book before starting
to write. As I research, I fit relevant articles and books to be used as
sources into the relevant topic within the outline. Because I live in a
university community where library holdings in contemporary religion are excellent, I don't usually write "note cards" during research.
Rather, I merely indicate the work and its location (in a library or in my
notes) with the intention of reading it fully and using it only when my
composition itself has reached that stage.

When the bulk of research has been finished, I set a date on which to begin the writing itself—and I *don't* flinch about this. From that point on, until completion, I write no fewer than three double-spaced pages per day, six days a week. I do the initial composition in longhand after breakfast, and type the product (with that all-important first revision) after lunch, finishing for the day no later than 3:00 p.m. Built into this system, moreover, are rewards I give myself at each juncture—from good meals and regular "r & r" to an extra day off at the completion of each chapter.

Five Cs for Success

Although I had to come up with this discipline quickly in order to finish my first book on time, it stuck and has worked extremely well for me since then. But I have also developed a specific method for producing ideas and finished prose that enables me to write with a great deal of confidence. This method might be called "the 5 Cs of successful non-fiction writing." I offer these because they deal with areas prospective writers are most likely to struggle with.

First, the primary issue is **content.** Does it need to be written, and am *I* the one to write it? Getting good and salable ideas is the hardest part of writing for religion markets today, because so much is being published and the religion scene can change completely in just a few years.

Second, **clarity.** Very simply (and this is often overlooked by writers), can the market I'm writing for understand my work? Too many academic theologians and other specialists write for no one but themselves and a few colleagues who are able to understand their technical, "in-house" jargon, and are interested enough to wade through it. Likewise, many popular religion writers use theological lingo that outsiders couldn't relate to even *if* they were so inclined (e.g., "rapture," "dispensation," "discipling," and "the last days," to name a few).

Third, **conciseness** is important. Readers today are increasingly less willing to read long books, especially those that could have been written just as well in half the number of pages.

Fourth, there is the matter—again, often forgotten—of **coherence.** Does the work hold together in theme and development from beginning to end? Is it logically integrated, consistent, and intelligible *as a whole* rather than merely as the sum of its parts? Many journalists write brilliant short pieces but cannot write a two-hundred-page book on one single topic. Let no one be fooled; authors of books and journalists are often a breed apart at this point.

Fifth and finally, **conviction.** Do I have the willingness to write what I believe is true and needed, whatever the cost? Even more than politics, religion always has an unsettling, if not earthshaking, effect when it challenges the status quo. Here freelance writers can come out on top, however, because only successful freelancers without institutional affiliation have the freedom to write *exactly* as they see fit. No one hired them, and no one can fire them!

It is this freedom of expression that has been my greatest joy as a professional writer, and it never ceases to motivate me to go even further than I have gone in the past. I am a controversialist—born and bred that way—but where would I be without the books that gave me a forum to do what I knew had to be done? My success as a freelancer has made the career I once never considered a source of deep personal fulfillment.

THE GOD BEAT
by Charles Austin

All writers want to touch the hearts of their readers, to reach them in a special way. Whether they write novels or news stories, whether they specialize in information or inspiration, writers strive to relate something meaningful so that life can be better, more interesting, or more satisfying.

When the subject is faith, spirituality, moral values, or even unbelief, there is almost inevitable contact with the reader. A reader may agree or disagree; the writing may provoke inspiration or anger; but the contact with the writer is instant, because these are the topics that go directly into our souls.

Professional religion writers do not believe the unsubstantiated but widespread rumors of the decline of American churches. Churches are changing rapidly, of course, but that only makes them more interesting to write about.

Despite all the talk of our "secular age," statistics prove without a doubt that religion is a significant part of our society. Slightly more than 42 percent of the American population worship at a church or synagogue almost every week, according to the Gallup Poll. That means millions of people give religion an important place in their lives.

As a newspaper reporter and freelancer, I've written about national politics, lifestyles, municipal government, and the arts. But the response to my articles on religion is always more intense, more personal, and more gratifying. Religion writers know that people out there are reading and that they care about what they read. We know people have passionate feelings about faith. They are the people we write about. They are our readers.

VARIATIONS ON THE GOD BEAT

Religion writers fall into two general categories—those who write about religion for the secular press and those who write for the religious press. Most of us in the field have done both.

I've made a good living as a religion writer and have tried most of the variations of the profession. My first sale was a religion story sold to a local weekly newspaper. (Secular newspapers that buy freelance pieces often like good features about churches in their area.)

At another point in my life, writing for church-related publications was a profitable sideline, supplementing my income. (Nearly every American religious body publishes magazines and newspapers, and many have their own publishing houses for books and church school materials. Most depend heavily on freelancers.)

I was once a full-time staff writer for an agency specializing in religion news. Later, I joined the staff of a church-related news service and wrote articles and features that were syndicated to the religion and secular press. Then, as a general assignment reporter for a daily newspaper, I made religion my mini-beat and was able to offer the paper something they would not have had without me.

While every beat has a certain routine, nearly twenty years of writing about religion has convinced me that there are no limits to what a religion writer can explore. Religion today is a wide-open field. I've written articles about scientists and their faith, politics and the churches, and international affairs. I've covered evangelism rallies and interviewed leaders of controversial sects. Working for the church press, I've filed copy from Dar es Salaam, Vienna, Rio de Janeiro, Rome, and East Berlin.

The professional religion writer can do many different things, from basic journalism to scholarly research. Few fields of writing offer as much flexibility or variety.

The Journalist

If you are basically a journalist, as I am, you can have the satisfaction of translating the ideas and activities of religious figures into stories that will inform readers, who may or may not be actively religious. This kind of reporting is immensely gratifying. I once listened for several hours while a prominent Dutch Roman Catholic theologian talked of developments in his church. Other reporters at the press luncheon laid down their pens and fidgeted, but I was taking notes furiously because it was clear to me that people should hear what this man had to say.

A general assignment reporter who attends a church convention or other meeting is apt to see only the obvious, most dramatic story. A good religion writer understands the theology and the church politics behind any new development, and the story will contain a more useful perspective for the reader.

I'm also convinced that a writer who specializes in religion journalism wins a fair amount of job security by covering relatively uncrowded turf. A recent survey showed that the majority of the nation's editors are not as "religious" as the population in general. Therefore a good editor will value a religion writer who can provide access and interpretation to that part of society.

The Inspiration Writer

Basic reporting is only one outlet for religion writers. Some choose another aspect of the profession—they write to inspire. Thousands of inspirational books and articles are published each year, many of them by writers of deep faith who consider their writing a "ministry" to others, whether they do it full-time or through occasional articles for a devotional periodical.

Stories about people of strong faith, articles that lead the reader through spiritual reflections on daily problems, books that explore the intricacies of belief, prayer, or scripture are constantly in demand.

In this kind of writing an author turns to his or her own deep emotions, not bound by the conventions of regular journalism. Many inspirational books become bestsellers or are syndicated in newspapers and magazines. There are other rewards as well. Each year, I write a short series of Bible meditations for a very small inspirational publication. They don't pay very much, but every year I receive several letters from people who say they are grateful for my words because the short devotional helped them with a spiritual problem.

The market for inspirational writing is one of the broadest of the religion publishing field. Stop at several local churches and look at the variety of magazines they provide to their members. Look at the shelves of inspirational books at a bookstore, and you'll see how many publishers want writing that gives people a spiritual lift.

But this kind of writing is harder than it first seems to the "inspired" author. Because it is such a competitive field, the work must be exceedingly well done. Being "moved by God" and possessing a missionary or evangelical spirit will not get you published in many places. Your mountain-top experience may be another person's boring manuscript. Sometimes the writer of inspirational articles has to work hard to sublimate personal spiritual passion. What editors want to read is a manuscript that will help others gain insights into their problems, not marvel at your zeal or peace of mind.

Educational Materials

If you're looking for steady work as a freelance writer or editor in the field of religion, you will want to consider educational writing. Churches are constantly updating their Sunday school materials, and they want a constant flow of new courses on contemporary issues or Bible studies aimed at special age groups. I don't know a single professional religion writer who has not written Sunday school courses, study booklets, or filmstrips for several denominations. Those who plan Sunday school curricula often will get a theologian and an education specialist together to develop a course, and then dump their copy into the lap of a professional writer for polishing.

Besides being a good source of income for the writer, the research you do for this type of writing nearly always leads to ideas for other articles and, sometimes, books. You are already getting paid for the work and are able to make extended use of information you gather.

GETTING INTO THE GOD BEAT

Breaking into the world of religion writing is very much like entering any of the other specialized markets.

Modern religion writers are, first of all, professional writers. The editorial skills they need are the same as those required of a sportswriter or political reporter. In some newsrooms around the country, the God beat is still looked down upon and considered training ground for the new kid or a pasture for the soon-to-be-retired old guy. But that view is fading rapidly, and the better newspapers now recognize that religion is a field requiring special skills and a well-developed sense of how and why people believe.

Nor is the religion press today a playground for amateurs. Most denominations invest considerable funds in their magazines and other publications. Anyone who thinks a religion magazine is easy to write for, and takes short cuts in research, writing, or marketing manuscripts will collect a lot of rejection slips.

Who Does It?

Who writes about religion?

In the secular press, the religion writers are an especially diverse lot. Most of us began as general assignment reporters and have covered a variety of beats. Some of us have graduate degrees in theology, a few were once ministers. Formal theological education is a help but not an absolute necessity. The dean of American religion writers, George

Cornell of the Associated Press, has been on the beat for so long that he knows more theology than many bishops. Some of us are actively involved in our own churches; others are not.

Specific preparation is an asset if you want to write for the religion press. You need a thorough knowledge of the church for which you are writing. When I was running a news service for several Lutheran denominations, a freelancer sent me a nicely written inspirational feature on how important praying the rosary had been for her. Perhaps the writer didn't know that form of piety was not practiced by Lutherans, or maybe she was trying to win Lutherans over to Catholicism. In either case, the approach was unprofessional and I rejected the manuscript.

You don't have to pass judgment on points of doctrine when you write for the religion press. You don't even have to agree with all the doctrines of those for whom you write. But you do have to understand them, because they are important to your readers. It's also necessary to keep an open mind about doctrine if you want to gain broad experience in writing about religion. Unless you take a staff position on a denominational magazine, or severely limit your markets, you will be writing for people of varied beliefs. The readers of *Eternity*, an evangelical Christian magazine, view the Bible differently from the people who read *New World Outlook*, a Methodist mission magazine.

Your own religious views may be neither evangelical nor Methodist, but to write for those publications, you must be sensitive to their doctrines.

Does It Pay?

A quick glance at *Writer's Market* will let the prospective religion writer in on the unpleasant side of the field. Many of the markets do not pay very much.

You will find magazines offering from fifty to two hundred dollars for articles, a rate that both frustrates and angers the professional writer. But there are ways in which the professional religion writer can improve his or her situation.

First, recognize that most editors are not stupid or miserly and are often willing to pay for quality work. I've been paid double their standard rate by some editors because they know they can depend on me and value my knowledge of the field. Before you reach this point, however, you have to establish a track record. That may mean, unfortunately, taking some of those unprofessional rates for professional work.

The book market, particularly the inspirational market, is more lucrative, and advances and royalties from publishers are generally comparable to those given by secular publishers.

Payment for writing educational curricula varies, depending on the publisher and the type of work. One publisher may pay $800 for a study guide on a contemporary issue; another could offer several thousand dollars to a writer who prepares a year-long church school course.

Today, most churches like to have seasoned professionals on their denominational magazines or in their communications offices, so they try to offer competitive salaries for their writers and editors. They won't match the pay of topflight magazines, of course, but the competent religion writer on a good denominational magazine can earn a professional income.

WHAT DO YOU WRITE?

The religion freelancer will quickly learn what all other freelancers know about marketing: an editor likes what an editor likes, and often an editor cannot tell you what the editor likes until a neatly typed, polished manuscript is on the desk. Sometimes an article idea that looked like a cover story to an editor in May will be a back-of-the-book story by June or a rejection slip by July. Uncertainties go with the freelance life.

But the professional writer can learn to make educated guesses about the markets, and, in some ways, that process is easier for the religion writer.

Certain facts are obvious. Baptist magazines like articles about Baptists. Inspirational publications want stories about prayer, meditation, and spirituality. General-interest denominational magazines need articles appealing to the whole family and news about what that part of the church is doing.

When you study the church magazines, you will notice that they serve different purposes. Some are primarily news magazines; others stress feature articles. Others focus on specific topics such as evangelism or missions. Some like articles about a local church; others prefer more cosmic treatment of a current issue.

Here are some types of articles that appear in religion publications.

The personality profile. All churches like to shine spotlights on members who are doing unusual, worthwhile, or interesting things as part of their religious commitment. Sometimes people connect their beliefs to their profession in fascinating ways. I've heard of a computer programmer who sets up bookkeeping systems for Catholic parishes, and I know of a fireman who was just ordained a Baptist minister.

The lively local church. When a congregation meets adversity and triumphs, or brings a creative solution to a local problem, it's a story for that church's denominational magazine.

The think piece. What are religious thinkers saying about contemporary issues? Newspapers are full of issues with ethical or spiritual dimensions. Readers of church publications like to know what their theologians have to say on such matters.

Straight news. When the North Carolina Baptist convention holds its annual meeting, that's worth an article for the church's news service, general magazines or local newspapers. If it discusses changing values in American family life, you are on your way to another article. (Incidentally, most denominations have news services, and these could be potential markets for hard news stories about churches in your area.)

The personal experience. People like to know how others cope with emotional or spiritual problems. If your faith has helped you through a crisis, you may be able to help others by sharing your experience.

The unusual event. The emphasis here is "unusual." Potluck suppers are not unusual. Fiftieth anniversaries are not very unusual. A church with a husband-and-wife team of pastors *is* unusual.

Some church magazines also print book and movie reviews, recipes, question-and-answer features, puzzles, photo essays, or children's stories. To know what is possible, you have to study the markets carefully.

After explaining your idea and qualifications to an editor in a query or phone call, you should take another close look at the magazine you are writing for. Do they like anecdotal leads? Are there lots of quotes in the feature? Is the style formal or personal? This is the time to consider the doctrinal and ethical teachings of the faith that publishes the magazine. One magazine might not appreciate a reference to a minister's pouring himself a gin and tonic at the end of a day; another would like that insight into how the clergyman relaxes.

Of course, as a professional writing in a competitive field, you should submit a neatly typed manuscript using the standard format and enclosing a return envelope and postage. If you have queried an editor, a cover letter will remind him that he is expecting your piece.

I feel that unless you have a formal theological education or experience in professional church work, your ticket into the other areas of religion writing will be your clip file of articles in church-related magazines or a long list of credits for religious articles published in the secular press.

Once you have that ticket, you can think about books (turning a personal profile into an inspirational biography), educational materials (taking a contemporary topic and preparing a study guide for church school students), and other outlets.

More Opportunities

There are many ways a professional religion writer can add to his or her income beside magazine articles, news stories, educational materials, and books. Here are some of them, the result of a brainstorming session involving a few freelancers:

Newsletters. Offer your editorial skills to local churches that publish parish newsletters.

Reports. Denominations and interreligion agencies often hire outside writers to prepare reports, brochures, or other materials. Sometimes these jobs go to public relations firms, but your credits as someone knowledgeable about religion should get you the job.

Histories. When churches and synagogues pass landmark years—fifty, seventy-five, one hundred—they often produce a history as part of the celebration. It may be the kind of job too big for the dedicated volunteer to handle. As a professional writer, you can offer them a historical book in which they can take pride.

Press relations. For conventions, anniversaries, dedications, and other special events, churches and synagogues often need news releases and other written materials. Be careful, however, to avoid a conflict of interest here. You can't accept a fee from a church to handle its public relations and then ask an editor to pay you for an article about that church. That's unprofessional and dishonest.

Conferences. A religion writer interprets religion to the press; and sometimes that same writer can interpret the press to the religion establishment. I've spoken on churches and the media at numerous meetings of pastors, church officials, and others. My goal is to help the church people understand the media and develop a wholesome relationship with the press. That makes my job easier.

DANGERS AND DEMONS

"Is religion writing safe?" was the title of a talk I once gave to some journalism students. While you probably won't incur the wrath of organized crime, there are some professional and spiritual pitfalls.

Many people go into the field because they are deeply religious and see their work as responding to a divine call. God does indeed call writers. That's how we got the scriptures, right? But all religion writing is not preaching or evangelism. If you choose to write because you want to communicate your faith and inspire others, fine. There are markets for your work. But in the broader fields of religion journalism you must be objective, and many times you will have to repress your desire to preach or tell the world your version of the truth. I think it helps to recall the most significant theological question of all: "Has it ever occurred to you that you may be wrong?"

Sometimes those of us who cover religion for the secular press think the work can be dangerous to our faith. The religion writer cannot afford to hold to a romantic view of the church and its leaders. Professionally, we must see the church as just another institution in society and the men and women who run it as fair targets for investigation and scrutiny. If we pulled our punches, we would be less than professional. To keep from becoming cynical, we find ways to revitalize our own spirituality, if that is important to our lives.

Two demons—sentimentality and cynicism—constantly lurk around the typewriter of the religion writer. The demon of sentimentality encourages us to write syrupy stories that lack depth although they may temporarily warm hearts. The demon of cynicism chuckles when we exploit an event, belittle religious feelings, or sensationalize a story just to make a buck or because we know that approach will get an editor's approval.

I once wrote a long article about a controversial sect for an evangelical Christian magazine. My intent was to report accurately, and I knew my readers would not be sympathetic to the subject. After the article was printed I got a number of letters, and two of them convinced me that this was one of the best pieces I had written up to that time. One said in effect, "Thank you for exposing that satanic cult!" Another letter, from a member of the sect, said, "I am grateful for your fair, balanced presentation of our doctrines." I had succeeded in making my report accurate and objective, and our readers drew their own conclusions.

To write about religion and make contact with your readers—and that is, after all, the goal of all writers—you need to show respect for things of the spirit, and be sensitive to your readers' feelings about their faith. Good editors, and there are many of them in the religion press, will recognize that respect and sensitivity; and they will buy your manuscripts.

SHARING THE GOOD NEWS
by Karen O'Connor

I jumped into my car that chilly September evening and sped away from the curb as fast as I could—relieved to be away from the house, the kids, the dishes, and the endless diapers. All I wanted was some time to shop—alone. "I deserve it," I told myself defensively, as I swung into the crowded parking lot. Little did I know then that God had other plans for me that night—plans that would alter my life for all time.

Are you interested? Do you want to know more? I hope so. Because the above paragraph is the lead for my recent personal experience article, "A Night to Remember." And my intention as a writer for the religion markets is to share, discuss, and illustrate some discovery I've made about the process of living—in this case the miracles I've experienced through an unexpected friendship with a severely handicapped mother of two small children, a friendship that began that night in the parking lot of a neighborhood shopping mall.

Like all my writing for the religion markets, this piece came directly out of my experience. Articles of this type are called *personal experience* and/or *inspirational*. The two are closely related, and most of my writing has elements of both.

What I like best about this kind of piece is that I never have to go further than my own life to find plenty of material. I get paid to do it. And so can you.

The purpose of personal experience/inspirationals is quite simple—to *inspire!* Not preach, dictate, or judge. In fact, editors are on guard for the tacked-on moral, the sermon in disguise, and the amateur psychiatrist's approach to people's problems. Editors of religion publications want articles, not epistles, deliberations, or ivory-tower dissertations.

I have not always known the difference. In the early days of my career, I had lofty ideas about how I could inspire the readers of the highly regarded Catholic periodical, *St. Anthony Messenger.* My first article was inspiring, all right. Father Harrington, the editor, was so moved he returned the manuscript within twenty-four hours with a polite note stating that he preferred his readers to be uplifted, not talked down to.

The letter was a most valuable writing lesson. Thanks to his direct and encouraging remarks, I revised the piece (twice more, no less) and he bought it. More important, in his letter of acceptance he thanked me for being a "patient and careful writer." I got the message. People want to be led by the hand, not beaten up with a bat—or a Bible.

My experience with *St. Anthony Messenger* is a prime example of one of the most attractive aspects of the religion market—editors. Generally speaking, they are thorough, friendly, and impeccably ethical. I have always been treated with warmth and respect, and I frequently receive short personal notes even on a rejection slip. The editor of *Purpose* magazine thanked me recently for sharing with him my insight about the healing power of forgiveness. And Kenneth Holland of *These*

Times expressed his joy that my brother and I had resolved a difficulty between us, something I had written about in my article, "Peace at Any Price—What's the Cost?" He said it held his interest from beginning to end, and although he couldn't use it just then, he felt it deserved to be published. Encouraged, I sent it out again, and within two weeks sold it to *Unity.*

There are friendly, approachable editors in other markets, of course, but it is often the exception rather than the rule. In the religion markets, however, I have found this respect and support to *be* the rule.

And the encouragement I receive always comes back to my readers, because when I am inspired and appreciated by editors, my writing reflects it. Then everyone wins—readers, writers, and editors.

LABORERS OF LOVE

Editors of religion publications are aware that most people do not discover their spiritual selves in the silence of meditation. In fact, most of us find our way in the busy throng of life itself. As writers for this market, we must be sensitive to that fact and give people what they most want—a friendly and gentle nudge toward a more abundant expression of life.

A strong, sensitive message in the hands of a caring writer is important to this mission, and editors know it. That is why they are always on the lookout for talented newcomers, as well as the veteran professional. Although unpublished writers are welcome, standards are no less exacting than for other specialty markets. No slipshod piece dashed off over morning coffee will do.

These high standards work in favor of the writer. They make the religion market an excellent training ground for the beginner and a stable and steady source of work for the professional. It is one of the few specialties that is truly open to anyone who is committed to the craft of writing and the quality of life. Credits here are not nearly as important as having something worthwhile to say and then saying it well.

Steve Lawhead, former editor of the Christian youth publication *Campus Life,* said in a recent magazine piece that editors of religion publications are looking for articles of 1,000 to 2,500 words written in a bright, casual tone. "This casual tone," said Lawhead, "is somewhat deceptive; it requires tighter writing with more attention to detail than perhaps a more 'sophisticated' style." And it consists of simple language. Short words and sentences. Action verbs. Adjectives and adverbs kept to a minimum. "Today's editors," he added, "prefer their theology in small doses and wrapped in human terms—something the guy next door can relate to."

Although religion markets purchase and publish a wide variety of material, including humor and hard-hitting commentaries on contemporary issues, personal experience and inspirationals are among the most popular. They will always be in demand. Why? Because first and foremost they're about people. And according to magazine surveys and letters to editors, what people want to read about most is people.

Building Upon Rock

Although the subject matter of such articles is familiar and the research generally uncomplicated, they are not usually as simple to write as they are to read. It's easy to be fooled by the somewhat breezy, conversational tone, the warm and friendly approach, or the poised and polished style. But you can be certain that any truly moving inspirational article, no matter how freely it flows from your typewriter, rests on a solid foundation of certainty and skill.

"Evergreens," as these articles are sometimes called because of their year-round appeal, offer plenty of fresh illustrations, lively anecdotes, and enough quotes and dialogue to keep them people-centered. Even an intense, dramatic personal-experience piece includes a variety of emotions and examples as it builds to a strong crescendo, then descends to a smooth and satisfying conclusion.

Readers want to know that it is possible to transform the pain and disappointment of life into joy and fulfillment. Many, in fact, are desperate for a guiding hand to lead them across the bridge from despair to the Divine. Your shared experience, your voice, your article, may be just what they are looking for at that moment. Something you write could be the catalyst for a profound change in the lives of hundreds of thousands of people.

At first, this may sound like a heavy and frightening responsibility for a writer. Viewed from another angle, however, it's a great privilege to have this opportunity to touch so many people so intimately. And there is no one right way to do it. Spiritual movement takes many forms. You may reach readers with a chuckle, a tear, a sigh, even a deep belly laugh. In fact, laughter and enlightenment go together!

As long as you share yourself fully and express the truth as you experience it in your life, people will respond to what you have to say, and out of that, discover what's true for them.

BY THEIR FRUITS YOU WILL KNOW THEM

Reading, studying, and analyzing the kind of articles you wish to write and the magazines you wish to write for is one of the most important basic "rules" to follow. In fact, I can't stress it enough. By doing just that, I sold my first piece in this field, unsolicited, to *Marriage & Family Living*. I received a prompt reply and payment, and a few months later opened the mail to discover the article as the cover story for the magazine's October 1973 issue.

You do not have to be a member of the denomination you wish to write for. It is essential to become familiar with the basic philosophy of those denominations, however, and to know something about their tenets and taboos.

Editors are not shy about voicing these requirements. In *Writer's Market*, for example, Thomas Witherspoon of *Unity* magazine says he wants "inspirational articles, metaphysical in nature, about individuals who are using Christian principles in their living." The editor of the *Baptist Herald*, on the other hand, says, "We want articles of general religious interest. . . . We hold a rather conservative religious line." If you're not certain about the metaphysical or conservative approach, read the publication.

Father Harrington of *St. Anthony Messenger* shares this tip with prospective contributors: "The freelancer should ask why his/her proposed article would be appropriate for us, rather than for *Redbook* or *Saturday Evening Post*." Good point! Why indeed?

How *is* your article for the religion market different from those in the secular magazines? It's a question each of us needs to ask *before* we begin writing.

I wrote a piece called "The Healing Power of Forgiveness" on the spiritual and emotional turmoil I experienced over the woman involved with my former husband during our marriage. Why didn't I send it to *Ladies' Home Journal* or *Redbook*? Because it focused on my spiritual transformation. Leaving out that important discovery in order to fit the secular market would rob the piece of its integrity. It *belonged* in the religion market. And that's where it sold.

Scope, a magazine for Lutheran women, paid for it two weeks after submission. In seeking an appropriate market I checked *Writer's Market*, where the editor of this publication spelled out her needs clearly: "We want articles that tell how faith has affected, or can influence, the lives of women or their families." My article fit this description. As a result, everybody won!

RECEIVING YOUR REWARD

Generally speaking, you can expect to earn from $50 to $300, occasionally more, for an article in the religion field. Although it is important to be paid for our work (after all, we are in business as well as art), religion writing profits the writer in many other ways. I have earned most in experience, friendship, and guidance. And the valuable training I've received by writing and marketing month after month has helped me to expand my talents in all areas of writing and teaching.

Many religion publications are receptive to simultaneous submissions, as long as the readership and circulation of the markets do not conflict with one another. Therefore, you can increase your income and reach a wider audience by selling a piece several times—to the Methodists, Catholics, Lutherans and so on, an opportunity generally not available in other fields.

For example, you might sell first rights for a thousand-word personal experience piece for one hundred dollars. Then after publication, sell it five or six or ten times more as a reprint for twenty-five to sixty dollars apiece. From one writing you've earned several times the original fee and reached several hundred thousand readers as well.

If you submit simultaneously the first time out, individual payments may be smaller, since the rights are not exclusive, but again, you can still bring in several fees totaling $300 or $400 dollars for one article. And in the case of inspirationals, I feel well paid at that amount, since my articles rarely require in-depth research and I can often write one in a few hours' time.

If you submit your work to editors who accept simultaneous submissions, you should identify your work as such. The phrase *Simultaneous Submission* or *SS* in the upper right-hand corner of the manuscript is sufficient. Then add a line saying, "Exclusive rights in your denomination." You will be reassuring editors that if they buy the piece for their Methodist or Catholic audience, they will not suddenly discover it in a competitive magazine.

Because the style and actual treatment of this type of article are so individual, most editors prefer to see the completed manuscript. Some, however, want queries so they can determine whether the topic and timing fit in with their plans for future issues. I generally send the complete manuscript if it's a thousand words or fewer. I query for anything over that and for seasonal pieces, since special issues are often planned eight to twelve months ahead.

To be sure of the various requirements—rates, rights, queries, and type of articles wanted (and they do differ from one publication to another)—it's best to check *Writer's Market* before mailing your manuscript. It's also very helpful to send for the writers' guidelines and a sample copy of the magazines you are aiming for. Most editors will send you a free copy. Since their budgets are generally small, however, it's courteous to include return postage with your request.

PEARLS OF GREAT PRICE

Ideas, like precious gems, sometimes need a bit of polishing to bring out their sparkle. Alert writers know this and waste no time choosing and polishing the gems they find in overheard conversations, plays and television programs, newspaper articles, travel, or family life. They know from their own lives that shared experiences inspire people and often touch their faith and awaken spirituality.

Recognizing and developing these ideas is not as difficult as it may seem. An exercise that works well for me whenever the well goes dry is to make a list of five or ten people, organizations, events, or experiences that have contributed to my life in some way. You might try it. For example, your neighborhood dry cleaner might have shared some bit of wisdom about his grandson that inspired you, or your experience in the church choir has opened you up to prayer through music, or your father has taught you a lifelong lesson about friendship.

From there, start playing with titles. See how many spring from the experiences on your list. Get them down as fast as you can. Don't stop to think about whether or not they're good or bad. Just write!

From that list, choose one or more and begin writing whatever comes to mind about that topic. After a couple of pages of random thoughts, look for a point or recurring theme in the notes. See how you might arrange and expand it to be shared with other people.

If you still feel stuck, look at the idea from the reader's point of view. If you picked up an article on your chosen subject, what would you want to get from it? Answer that and you're on your way. For me, it works every time. During the past months I've come up with these:

Article Title/Idea	Source
1. "Ten Ways to Keep Spiritually Fit"	My daily run and aerobic dance class
2. "Turn Your Prayer into a Song"	Conversation about music and meditation
3. "Ears to Hear . . . Eyes to See"	The Parables of Jesus
4. "What Can I Do For You Today, God?"	A friend's shared insight about her relationship with God
5. "The Best Gift of All— Yourself"	A local speaking engagement

Another article resulted from a phone conversation I had with my daughter during her stay in France. I hung up the receiver, damp-eyed and filled with tender memories of my little girl, now a woman, and the very special friendship we have shared over the years.

I sat down at my desk and let my thoughts and feelings spill onto the page. From these ramblings I sorted and separated my moods and memories, thoughts and feelings, and came up with the following lead:

I remember clearly the day I sent my oldest daughter off to kindergarten. She's twenty years old this year, yet that moment is as fresh as our recent phone conversation.

I held her little hand firmly in mine. Part of me wanted to scoot her through the door with a big smile and a kiss. Another part wished I could turn back home and put off this milestone a little longer. I also remember being a bit jealous of her pretty teacher and all the new friends she'd have in no time. Would I ever be as important to her again as I had been those first five years?

I titled it "The Special Joy of Friendship," and then developed the idea by enlarging on the theme—parents are a child's first friends—to include friendship with oneself, with family, with other people, and how the experience of friendship can enrich and enliven our relationship with God and life itself.

SOWING THE SEEDS

After choosing an experience and jotting down some thoughts and anecdotes you want to include, you might find it useful to follow a proven format for writing a creative article. Naturally, you'll want to add your own special seasonings as you become more comfortable with your ability, just as the experienced cook brings variations to a time-tested recipe. But basic ingredients, a proper blend, and appropriate timing are as important to a satisfying inspirational as they are to a mouth-watering apple pie. And on days when your writing just won't fall into place, you can always return to that proven recipe and start from scratch.

Majorie Holmes, long-time professional writer of inspirationals and author of *Writing the Creative Article*, discusses in her book an ancient yet effective format for this kind of article: "The anecdote-and-discussion form of creative article is probably the most *natural* form of human discourse," she says. "It is also one of the most ancient.

"The Bible is filled with examples of truth vividly demonstrated through incidents in the lives of people. The effective use of this form is particularly apparent in the New Testament, where we find Christ teaching and preaching in parables. He would first state his premise and then prove its validity by means of a story to which his listeners could relate." And he chose subject matter common to their experiences—fishing, farming, family life—so they could apply his teachings in their everyday lives.

Today's audience is no different in that respect. Listen to any conversation about human relationships and you'll see how it follows a similar format. People love to discuss their views, then illustrate a particular point with an example from their own lives. Personal experience and inspirationals are that simple—a conversation with your reader about a shared human emotion, polished and illustrated in human terms for the written page.

Make Straight the Path

One thing to watch for on your path to publication is overdramatization. It's easy to be swept away by memory and emotion, particularly in this specialized field, to forget that our first job as writers is to communicate effectively.

To be clear and effective communicators, however, we must learn to be efficient, to economize on words as much as possible. You can become a master editor of your own work by approaching it as a gardener might inspect a flower bed. Read and examine it carefully, then prune all the dead twigs and weeds—words, phrases, or paragraphs—that smack of sentimentality, self-pity, or self-righteousness. People are inspired when we share the bouquet of life, but are quickly put off if we boast.

Editors know the difference. As one editor stated firmly, "We do not want preachy articles." There again is the reminder common to all denominational markets. Inspire, inform, influence—but leave the preaching to the pulpit!

What they're also saying is that in writing this highly personal kind of article, we must keep the audience in mind. In other words, what might work as an entry in a diary or journal does not necessarily make an article. Readers look for the following:

- a strong, eye-catching lead using an illustrative anecdote
- a statement of your theme within the first few paragraphs
- additional illustrations to enlarge the theme
- smooth transitions linking one anecdote to another
- a few suggestions, if appropriate, so they can apply your discovery or insight to their lives
- a sound and satisfying concluding paragraph or statement that reemphasizes the theme.

Even if the ending is not "happy," it can still be satisfying if it provides personal insight, spiritual realization, and honest human emotion.

More than anything, people who read personal experience and inspirational articles want to identify with what you have to say. They want to know they are not alone on the spiritual path, that other people share similar experiences, and that deep within, each of us has what we need to make it back to our Father's House.

As writers for the religion market, we have the joy and privilege of providing that spiritual support. The more we share from our hearts, without pomp and sentiment, the greater our gift.

WRITING FOR THE RELIGIOUS PRESS
by Antoinette Bosco

As I was preparing this article, an editor called to ask if I would do a piece for the magazine's October issue under a working title of "What Has Happened to Halloween?"

She wanted me to talk about how the celebration of Halloween had gone from the religious "All Hallow E'en," to its heyday as "trick or treat," to where it is now—a source of danger, drawing out perverted people to play sick tricks on children.

"Get me some comments from psychologists to try to get an explanation for why Halloween is turning into a horror story," she said, giving me a deadline.

Would you have guessed such an assignment came from a religious publication? If so, then you are already aware that the majority of the publications under the umbrella of the religious press have substance and are professional.

The religious press today is looking for information, not piety; for reality, not Pollyanna; for inspiration, not poetic ramblings.

The person who called me was Ila Stabile, long-time editor of *Marriage and Family Living*, published at Abbey Press, founded by the Benedictine monks, in St. Meinrad, Indiana.

"There's a decided resurgence of religious interest," she said. "And for our magazine, we see our development continuing in two areas. One is to maintain an emphasis that is very much ecumenical, broadening our base in terms of information so as to reach out to more people. Another is to seek out more articles that deal with secular issues and trends, but with a religious emphasis. To do this, we're starting with themes, focusing on something very current. We owe our readers more meat," she said.

In every story they see, Stabile added, they ask, "Is this about *to-day*—or could it just as well be about last year? The religious press has to make sure it's *today*."

One other point made by this editor is that for the religious press to flourish, it has to emulate some of the modern design and marketing trends that make secular publications attractive. "We have to know what sells and what gets the attention of readers," she said, adding that the "Madison Avenue flavor" has helped reshape the look and presentation of the content of many religious publications.

RELIGION WRITING—YESTERDAY AND TODAY

Anyone trying to break into the religious press today should consider Stabile's words. Her message is clearly that writing religious copy is not easy, simple, or anything goes. It is, instead, a highly specialized, evolving field.

The word *religion* comes from the Latin, originally meaning the bond between man and the gods. Later, religion came to be seen as man's recognition that there is a controlling, superhuman power entitled to be obeyed, revered, and worshipped. The relationship between man and that controlling power—God—is, however, worked out on earth. Thus, while one's sights are on heaven, one's feet are on the ground, here on earth, and the challenge is to learn how to live and make sense out of life, achieving harmony with the Divine Order.

The goal of the religious press, then, is to help readers meet that challenge—at the same time reinforcing what it means to be a believer in a spiritual tradition or dogma. Its approach is generally to tell a story from the perspective of what it means to be human, moral, and ethical.

But readers still are ordinary people who are going to choose how they'll spend their time. They may pick up a religious publication because they're searching for something not in the secular press, but they also want to be informed, inspired and, depending on the publication, reinforced or challenged in their beliefs. This means that rule number one in writing for the religious press is that preaching is not the way to get any written message across.

When I started writing nearly thirty years ago, it was the "party lines" of the church denominations the magazines represented.

Writers didn't have much luck submitting articles that posed uncomfortable questions. I remember, for example, being unable to place two articles in Catholic magazines in 1956, even though I had over fifty others published in the religious press that same year. One was titled "Let's Bring the Collection Up to Date." It resulted in some funny rejection slips bearing evasive comments that while this was an important area of reform, it was a "pastoral," not a layman's, problem. Ten years later, after the Second Vatican Council, almost every subject was a layman's problem. The change was well reflected in the Catholic press.

The other article was a reflective piece on the necessity of young mothers' keeping up with their education and interests while they raise young children, to avoid becoming too stagnant to pick up and move into their own interests later on. I called it "Prepare Now for Forty." The theme, stale today, didn't make the Catholic press, because this idea was too threatening to motherhood in an era when the birth control question was kept locked in a box.

Today, the popular religious press has lost much of this timidity, and the writer no longer works within clearly defined dogmatic boundaries. There is a new freedom evident in the articles published, which is a reflection of what is hapening in Christianity, Judaism, and all the religious denominations and sects. A writer focusing on the religious press needs to know the houses of worship—where they have changed and where they have remained the same—and know them well.

Two main areas of change have been the blossoming of social consciousness and ecumenicalism, which is the move towards de-insulating the religious denominations from one another so that understanding, and ultimately unity, may be achieved.

These developments have caused phenomenal changes both in the churches and in the religious press.

WHAT YOU NEED TO SUCCEED

What does this mean for the writer? You've got to be not only skilled in your craft, excellent in your presentation, but also "with it"— right on top of daily developments in religion.

Some of the most important qualifications needed by a would-be writer for the religious press today are:

You have to have a good knowledge of theology. How familiar are names like Robert McAfee Brown, Harvey Cox, Karl Rahner, Hans Küng, Malcolm Boyd, Alexander Schmeman, Marc Tannenbaum? What are these thinkers saying today that is making an impact on theology and on spiritual living?

You have to have a background broad enough to make you sensitive to the crucial areas of social concern. The churches have left their too-long-comfortable places of hiding from the needs of the world. The rat-infested slums of the inner city, the color line in suburbia, drug addicts, unwed mothers, alcoholics, migrant farm workers, the old, the lonely—these are all the concern of the churches, but manifested in new ways. To take a specific example: the churches have traveled the bridge from delivering a sermon on the needs of the aged, to getting involved in the infighting for a retirement community, or increased welfare benefits, or community merchandise discounts, or housing tax breaks. These are the kind of real social-action stories the religious press writer seeks out today.

You have to understand what an authentic morality is for this generation. Topics are discussed in the religious press now that a few years ago were either taboo or were handled in sermon-terms. These include homosexuality, divorce and remarriage, abortion, a just-war theory, extramarital sex and living arrangements. The writer needs to do much reading, interviewing, and analyzing in order to make valid, intelligent observations about morality in modern situations if he or she expects to interest an editor enough to buy an article.

You have to be willing to work long and hard at research. No religious publication editor is interested in unsubstantiated opinions, sloppy facts, or tumble-type rewrites from newspaper clippings. Research is a must. Photos are more important than ever, too, since pictures whet a reader's interest more quickly than copy alone.

The Marketplace

If you plan to break into the religious press you must know your market. Religious publications cannot be characterized as being "all the same." In fact, they are more characterized by their differences. The approach to writing an article for the Catholic press is vastly different from writing for evangelical publications. And writing for a Catholic family magazine, like *Marriage & Family Living,* is different from writing for a "think" one, like *Commonweal,* or a "party-line" one, like *Liguorian.* You must have some knowledge of the basic tenets of any denomination publishing a magazine to which you'd like to sell.

The bible for the religious press—as for other publication categories—is *Writer's Market,* which spells out what each magazine and book publisher is seeking. Once you identify the magazines you would like to sell to, study them.

Query letters are the best way to approach an editor in the religious press. Enclose a sample of your writing if you are new to the publication.

Except for specific proselytizing magazines, the subject matter covered in the religious press is broad. Local newspapers are still a good source for story ideas. Look at today's headlines, from major to minor ones, and ask how the events of our times affect the way we live our lives; the questions you ask yourself can be a good starting point for an article. You must not, however, sit down and offer your opinions, but rather do solid interviews with experts and/or the people involved.

I'll share another personal example. About a dozen years ago, the subject of marriage was making news because the older marriage was in trouble. Divorce had started to escalate, and everyone pointed to the lack of communication as the culprit. Someone contacted me about a new idea being introduced into this country from the Spanish Christian Family Movement. It was a weekend for married couples called Marriage Encounter. The weekend incorporated many techniques, all designed to open communication between the couple, and reports were that this was having phenomenal success in Spain.

Marriage is always a natural for the religious press, because it is the foundation of family life. Here I not only had the subject of marriage, but the factor of communication, with a success message saying this new idea was working.

I wrote several articles on this, including one, after about two years when some disillusionment was setting in, called "The Pros and Cons of Marriage Encounter." It was carried in a diocesan Catholic newspaper and generated well over one hundred letters.

Armed with these letters, I proposed a book and got an immediate contract with Abbey Press. My book, *Marriage Encounter: A Rediscovery of Love*, was published in January 1973, the first book on the subject.

For the past eight years I have been writing a syndicated column for the National Catholic News Service in Washington, under the general title of "The Bottom Line," carried in up to twenty-five Catholic diocesan weekly newspapers. My readers are men, women, clergy, laity, young, old, living in states from Maine to California. I have a carton of letters received from them over the years. The subjects that have stirred the most response have been loneliness, depression, Reaganomics, older children leaving home, homosexuality, single parenting, spirituality, and aging.

But I want to point out that although a column is something like writer's utopia, allowing you to express your thoughts, feelings, and expertise on subjects of your choice, I still weighted these columns with information as well as opinion. For example, a column on the need for older citizens to demand respectful treatment was told through an interview with a septuagenarian who was author of a book called *Elders in Rebellion*. Homosexuality was a tale of Dignity, a Catholic group for gays. Reaganomics was a report on my trip to Washington for the September 19, 1981, Solidarity Day.

GETTING STARTED

People always ask, "How did you get started?" Actually, I began with an ideal. In 1945, as a seventeen-year-old freshman in a Catholic college, I heard Father James Keller, founder of the Christophers, speak at one of our weekly assembly meetings. He challenged us to "change the world," and one of the ways he suggested to accomplish this was writing. I was a pre-med student, but medical school fell through (mainly because I was female and poor) and I married. I decided a few years later to become a writer as I raised my family.

The advice then, as now, was "write about what you know." We had adopted a fifteen-year-old boy, taking him straight out of a country slum and off the welfare rolls of an upstate New York town. I thought this would be a good story with which to start. I wrote the story and sent it, along with a letter about how I wanted to start writing for Catholic publications, to *Sign* magazine. I got it back with a curt rejection note saying briefly, bluntly, devastatingly, and oh so honestly, "Professional writing requires much practice."

About ten years later I sold that piece, rewritten, to *Marriage* magazine. It was titled "The Son We Chose." By then I had practiced much and had sold much, but still I had accumulated the proverbial cartons of rejection slips, enough to paper the walls, as they say.

After that first rejection, I began another story. We'd had a rough experience trying to rent an apartment because we had a baby and a fifteen-year-old. No one wanted us. This had forced us to borrow money for a house, which fortunately had an apartment in it to rent. Because of our experience with "no children" rentals, I ran an ad for this apartment for rent with the condition "must have children." The ad caught the attention of the newspaper's editorial department, made the front page, and I was given an orchid by the city for my social concern.

This was the story I next wrote and sent to a magazine called the *Voice of Saint Jude* (now *U.S. Catholic*). The editor liked it, but sent it back for some rewriting. He also needed photos. What he liked about the piece, he said, was that it covered several issues: a social problem, prejudice against children in housing (this was 1953), the idealism of a young couple, a creative idea, and a community response.

Those ingredients still sell a story to the religious press. Naturally, seeing my story in print was a great way to get hooked on writing. I also learned early that editors of religious publications are exceptionally warm and human and most helpful in working with you if your work has possibilities.

If you are new at writing and seriously thinking about writing for the religious press, I suggest that you begin by selecting a group of magazines that appeal to you, that carry articles you feel are comparable to ones that you could, or would like to, write. Then choose a subject, do some preliminary research on it, select your theme and approach, and query the editor.

Some recent subjects I have written on have been "Families for

Prayer," an organized plan for family communication and spirituality, developed by the group founded by Father Patrick Peyton, who popularized the motto "The family that prays together, stays together"; "Single Parenting Your Child Through Adolescence"; "What Happens to Marriage When a Child Dies"; and a newspaper feature on how the Catholic school-closing syndrome has peaked and is now going into reverse.

A point I cannot overstate is that your article must be researched, outlined, and written professionally. The religious press is a specialized market requiring a high level of quality writing, research, and analytical skills, all used to tell your story with human sensitivity. Even if you are producing an inspirational piece coming from your inner depths, this requires practical hard work.

Research is done through your interviews with the people directly involved. Background information can be found in libraries. Most importantly, never hesitate to call official sources such as chancery offices, bishops, and national headquarters, like the United States Catholic Conference in Washington or the Protestant Council of Churches on Riverside Drive in Manhattan.

GOD IS GOOD COPY

God is good copy today. He—and sometimes, she—has become a popular subject even for major secular publications, because readers have discovered that God is a controversial figure. And, as we all know, controversy is a pastime dear to the hearts of the American public.

You find warring camps—the traditionalists against the progressives; the campaigners for jazz bands and liturgical dance against the more sentimental who want to stick to the celestial organ; the socially avant-garde who want the clergymen in a picket line (and would as soon have this be clergywomen) against the wary who get nervous when men of the cloth step down from the pulpit.

Spirituality also seems to be making a comeback. For example, a television news broadcast on the NBC *Today Show* reported on a breakfast prayer group meeting weekly, composed of—surprise—Wall Street stockbrokers, analysts, and corporate heads. I read this first, by the way, in the *Wall Street Journal*. I believe this means that religious writing is a ripe field for both beginners and professionals, because a new wave of interest in religion has arrived.

The religious press is a working, vital press, making new and challenging demands of its writers. You can find your stories in the secular press, from your community, and from your personal life.

All it takes is the hard work to tell those stories. But the doors here open readily to the writer who respects the field enough to produce quality work, and they are friendly doors.

WRITING THE RELIGIOUS ARTICLE
by Ardis Whitman

Come back with me to the year 1979, to the end of a rewarding day in Los Angeles.

I have been here two days as part of a nationwide research trip for an article I am writing for the *Reader's Digest*. The first day was full of problems. I had been unable to locate a minister I wanted very much to talk to; and, after an afternoon at one of America's most famous churches, I was up most of the night trying to balance, in my notes, the remarkable achievements of the church against a troubling vein of bombast and commercialism.

But today has been better. I was able to reach the minister of a black congregation in town, a gentle, gifted human being whose academic honors—including a Fulbright scholarship—are as great as the warmth of his heart. We had a long, late breakfast together and I felt a deep understanding of what he and his church have been trying to do.

Then I went to an appointment at a seminary some distance from the city, and here I talked for hours with a professor who has been doing extensive studies of the churches in this area; while eating my lunch on the patio outside the seminary dining room, I fell into a provocative exchange with both students and teachers, encountering some who were hopeful for the church and some who were deeply pessimistic.

On the way back to Los Angeles on the bus I met an agnostic young man, and we happily sharpened our wits on each other. Now, in my room at midnight, with two full tapes and a bulging notebook before me, I am trying to weave together the day's enormous input, to think through this small segment of a vast subject.

THE HUMAN DRAMA

Writing the religion article is often like that—rewarding and frustrating, confusing and satisfying, always overwhelming and sometimes very dramatic. Some may think of writing religion articles as a safe and placid occupation. Nothing could be further from the truth. Religion—in the last few decades especially—is a battlefield, an eruption of conflicting ideas, a demonstration of what it means to be human.

Looking back through the years of reporting, I remember a tide of running Yale students pouring through the streets of New Haven in an effort to get the best seats to hear the allegedly heretical Bishop James Pike talk about theology. I remember ministers of churches in the South fired almost on the spot for trying to bring blacks into white congregrations. I remember interviews with clergymen who espoused the astonishing "God is dead" theology. I remember a long session with a self-labeled "hustler" from Harlem whom I met while he was expounding his view of the Bible in a nearby church.

Perhaps it is because, from childhood on, I have seen the drama of religion, that I came early to the writing of religion articles. In fact, the first article I ever had published, decades ago, was a religious one. It was about a minister's last sermon before retiring, and it sold to a tiny magazine that *would* have paid me ten dollars if it had not gone bankrupt immediately after obtaining my article!

In spite of this inauspicious start, I have come back to such writing again and again through the years, although I don't write religion articles exclusively. Rather, I think of my field as simply the human being, in childhood and adolescence, in love and out of it, in joy and sorrow, in anger and hope. I write about religion simply because it is a part—I think a major part—of human experience.

My own background leads to it naturally. I am a minister's daughter. Years ago, in the small town in Nova Scotia where I was born, life in the parsonage was definitely more interesting and, it seemed to me, more significant than it was anywhere else in town.

Obviously such a background helps in writing religion articles. Indeed, religion writing almost *requires* personal experience. I suppose a purely "hard news" piece might be written without it, but I'm not even sure of that. Reporting on religion is not like covering a stock-car race or a fashion show. It is a complex, sensitive, intricate subject; and whether you write a profile of one person or a piece about millions, it is a very individual and human one.

Of course you need not be a minister's child to acquire such experience, but you should get it from somewhere. Personal experience warms the article, helps the reader to identify, gives the writer a familiarity with the people and places needed for the backing of authority, and, above all, supplies ample anecdotes. At the very least, a would-be religion writer needs a keen interest in the subject, a curiosity about the place of religion in human life, and a concern about the direction of religion in our times.

A CRITICAL EYE

But a word of warning: don't confine your experience to piety and orthodoxy. A critical eye is absolutely necessary in any religion reporting and useful even in inspirational pieces. In particular, you need to see with something of a merciless view the frequent inadequacies of churches, their human failure to carry out the central core of their mission, and their rising and falling fortunes.

It is helpful if you have gone through the stages of belief and unbelief. You should also be able to entertain points of view other than your own, even though that may be the point of view you are presenting. Without this broad-mindedness you may fall into the first deadly sin of the religion writer—you may be preachy. And, in a reportorial piece, you will lack integrity and objectivity. (Parenthetically, you are free to write articles with a point of view antagonistic to religion, but it must be said that the market for them is very narrow indeed.)

Personal experience is important, but another kind of knowledge is equally so. Unless you are going to be writing purely personal-experience pieces, a wide and sophisticated knowledge of the *field* of religion is essential. Ignorance in this area is widespread—presumably among writers as among the rest of the population—and religious authorities are very touchy about it.

Therefore, anyone who plans to do religion reporting will need at least some knowledge of the great religion classics: William James's *Varieties of Religious Experience,* St. Augustine's *Confessions,* Jung's *Modern Man In Search of a Soul,* to name several. You will need also a considerable knowledge of churches and denominations within the body of Christianity, as well as of the broad spectrum of other religious faiths that have flourished in this country. You will need a thorough understanding of the issues over which church and society are caught in dialogue. For example, there has recently been much turmoil in the news about biblical fundamentalism, born-again Christians, the Moral Majority and so forth. To write about this successfully, you will need far more sources than the news stories. Such background is even more necessary in writing the politics-religion piece, such as an article on religion and civil rights, or on liberation theology.

Most of all, you need a sense of religion in context, not how you see it by itself but how you see it in relation to individual and social crises. Altogether, the amount of knowledge needed makes it a weighty subject for anyone to choose. But if it is not easy, it *is* tremendously rewarding, exposing you to fascinating personalities and adding much growth and understanding to your life.

SOURCES OF INSPIRATION

Still ready to try? OK. *Now where do you get the ideas for your articles?* They are all around you. You go to church, find the service uninspiring and think, "I'd like to write about what worship *should* be like." You find that women still hold subordinate positions in most churches and yet remain the backbone—numerically, at least—of the church, and you'd like to explore that. You are about to do something your faith says is wrong. Arguing it out for yourself, you grow curious about what religion has to do with the code of ethics we live by, and you want to find answers. You go to a charismatic church service, or a storefront church in a ghetto, or the meeting of a rebellious faction of a denomination, or a Buddhist gathering, and decide you'd like to report it. You read that the government is wrestling with where and when religious groups should pay taxes, and you'd like to find out more. You have— or remember—a religious experience of your own and you want to tell about it.

Or you hear or read an arresting comment and it starts you thinking. Once, while I was lazily half-reading, half-listening to the television, I heard a girl on a discussion program say angrily, "What can the church give me that I can't get better somewhere else?" Her words stayed with me and became the motif—and the lead—for a piece I did for *Woman's Day* called "Why I Still Want the Church."

Where could you sell these or other religious articles? Honesty compels me to say that, for the moment, in the popular, secular press, there seems to be less interest in religious subjects—and, indeed, in serious subjects in general—than there was in the revolutionary sixties and the spiritually minded seventies.

The sixties was a golden age for serious writers. Even the mass publications felt free to explore the big issues that assail and nurture human beings. It was in that decade that writing about religion became a major part of my experience. Religious reportorial articles were in demand as the ferment of the time made religion news. I remember a day when, in amazement and delight, I received a request from the editor of *Redbook* for a piece on how we think about God in our time.

During that period, I wrote a series of religion articles for *Redbook* and *McCall's* under such titles as "What Christians Share with Jews," "What Young Protestants Really Believe," "The Rebellion of the Young Priests," "The View from the Pulpit"—a huge survey piece, "The Children of Interfaith Marriage," and "The Churches and Sex," to name several.

In the early seventies, there was a flurry of interest in meditation—the geography of the spirit—and I wrote a semireligious piece for the *Reader's Digest* called "The Art of Meditation." It blossomed into a book.

It would be harder to publish these articles today in the popular press. But I am sure the change is momentary and brought about largely by our present concentration on economic survival. In general, the latter part of the twentieth century has given rise to a considerable interest in religious subjects of all kinds.

MARKETS—TEMPORAL AND SPIRITUAL

First, the religion magazines and newspapers. There are legions of them, ranging from the house organs of the smallest sects to the prestigious giants like the *Christian Century, Christianity and Crisis, Christianity Today, National Jewish Monthly, Commonweal, Christian Science Monitor,* the *Hadassah Newsletter,* and so on. Some of these are quite unsophisticated; others are prodigiously knowledgeable and sometimes scholarly. Very few of them appear on the newsstands, but they can be found in libraries—especially seminary libraries—and in the places of worship of the respective faiths. They are listed in the *Writer's Market* and similar publications found at almost any library.

It must be said that pay is very small, since funding is restricted. In a list of such markets, I found religion magazines that paid as low as $10! It climbs from there to $200 or $300 or, in one case, $400.

Some scholarly religion magazines are difficult to get into because the writer needs to be a scholar himself. But others—in what one might call the middle rank—are comparatively easy to write for and a good market for the beginner. But be sure to see *at least* one copy of the magazine you are approaching. You need to find out if it is conservative or liberal and what causes it supports. Ask yourself in what areas you and its editors agree, and where you differ. Is it worth it to you to try to get around what may, in the end, amount to a violation of your own beliefs? How long are their articles? What is the style of writing they are happiest with?

A second place to sell is still the secular press. As noted before, the market here is not as open as it was. Still, I doubt there is any magazine in this field that would not at times welcome a good religion article. *McCall's,* for example, published a short but very important survey of American opinion on life after death, a popular subject in recent years. Then, too, most magazines still feature religious pieces at Hanukkah-Christmas and Passover-Easter and often find it hard to get them. Such articles, of course, should be in the editor's hands at least six months before the holiday season.

Altogether, the market is less easy to describe than it was in the sixties and early seventies. In general, there seem to be fewer reportorial pieces, but more inspirational and personal-experience ones.

In recent years I have written a good many religious pieces for the *Reader's Digest*—always a good market for religion articles—some reportorial, some inspirational, many a little of both. They have titles such as "We Need New Ways to Pray," "Six Special Powers of Prayer," "Four Remarkable Churches," and "This, Too, Is Worship."

There are some unexpected markets, too. Through the years, *Playboy* has published an occasional piece on a religious topic, although the slant and flavor are unique and should be studied carefully. There are also magazines that buy religion pieces associated with their own special interests. Travel magazines, for example, may be interested in stories of shrines, celebrated churches, retreat places, or exotic religions in faraway countries. Or a parents' magazine may be open to a piece on, say, how you have taught your child religion.

Finally, there is the scholarly market, which includes some of the top religion magazines. But it is a very difficult field for the freelancer because it almost of necessity requires that you be an authority in the field.

Since the pendulum constantly swings, the best advice is to go to the library, the newsstand, and the *Readers' Guide to Periodical Literature* to see which magazines are buying now in this field.

About pay. Fees for religious writing *in the popular press* are, of course, comparable to those for writing in any other field. The major popular magazines pay in four figures. Once I got $7,500 for a religion survey piece that took an unusual amount of time. Probably $2,500 would be nearer the average, although the beginner would likely get less, possibly considerably less.

The big problem for the beginner is the assignment. Reportorial articles on religion, as on other subjects, should not be attempted without assignment. (For one thing, where else will you get the money for traveling?) Assignments are truly hard for the beginner to get. But personal experience and inspirational articles and profile pieces of some remarkable person you've met are not as restricted. They sometimes make it without prior arrangement if sufficiently moving, and they can be the entering wedge for reportorial articles later.

SOURCES OF INFORMATION

Let us say now that you've come far enough to get that first assigned piece. *Where do you go for the information you need?* Here, at least, there is cheerful news. Information is readily available. If they feel they are dealing with a serious writer, most religion authorities are gracious about being interviewed; and the literature is, of course, voluminous. It is not the difficulty of getting information that will daunt you but the flood of data available.

Where do you start? First, as I said earlier, with your own experience. But it is necessary that that experience be *available* to you. Hence the value of a daybook or a journal in which you preserve your thoughts, experiences, and inspirations.

Beyond your personal experience, get acquainted with the resources of your locality. Go to a bar mitzvah, a Billy Graham crusade, or a charismatic service. Discover a young minister in a nearby small town who has taken courageous stands in support of the civil rights of Hispanics. Visit a local church that is a center for the arts and artists. Every house of worship is a learning place. Churches and synagogues today are rich in inventiveness, and even a small congregation in a small town may be trying new ways of expressing its faith. Read the religious page in your local newspaper and in that of the nearest big city. Read the local news attentively. Not only ideas but research material and anecdotes turn up in every newspaper, religious and news magazines, and on television.

File and keep names of people—obscure or famous—in whose lives there have been great religious happenings. Read profiles of people of great faith and spirituality. Keep a running book of quotations. And, of course, the library is crammed with books on various aspects of religion. You will need to own or borrow Leo Rosten's *Guide and Almanac of Religions in America*. A new book, the *World Christian Encyclopedia*, promises to be a source of vast information. And, of course, in time, if you're going to continue to write religion articles, you will want to put together your own religion library.

And then there are special *places* to go for information. Look under Religious Organizations in the Yellow Pages to see what is available to you locally. If you want to know what is new and exciting in this field, keep in touch with the Religious News Service. Subscribing to it is expensive but, with permission, the serious writer may read in the RNS files or look for their material in a subscribing library such as that of the National Conference of Christians and Jews in New York, or in seminary and university libraries elsewhere.

Moreover, all or most of the polling organizations do a great many religious surveys. To contact them: The Gallup Poll, 53 Bank Street, Princeton, New Jersey 08540; The Roper Poll, The Roper Organization, Inc., 205 East Forty-second Street, New York, New York 10017; Louis Harris and Associates, 630 Fifth Avenue, New York, New York 10020. You can also contact the National Council of Churches, the World Council of Churches, the National Conference of Christians and Jews, and the Institute of Religion and Health in New York. [Editor's note:

For the addresses of these and other sources of information, see Additional Resources at the end of this chapter.]

The All-Important Interview

And you will, of course, need to *interview*. This is a whole subject in itself, especially in this field where the opportunities of talking with knowledgeable people are so vast and, as I said before, fairly easy to arrange. I can remember a brusque brush-off only once. (You will have trouble getting interviews only if you don't have an assignment.)

How do you find these people? Excellent knowledgeable authorities are available to talk to at the organizations previously mentioned, many of them quartered at the Interchurch Center at 475 Riverside Drive, New York, New York 10115. And the *New York Times* and news magazines will keep you abreast of many authorities in the field. For example, in the 1960s, Bishop Pike's controversial views were banner headlines and so, one time, was the fact that he would be in New Haven, thirty miles from me. So I called him and made sure of an interview.

With experience, your list will swell. Remember, though, that important religion authorities and controversial figures are on the go. You will need ingenuity and patience to reach them. Once, pursuing Saul Alinsky, the courageous, controversial Jewish sociologist who fought for civil rights in the 1960s (often working closely with religious organizations), I rushed to New York for an appointment with him. I arrived to find that he was cancelling it because he had an unexpected funeral to attend and, immediately afterward, had to be in Syracuse for demonstrations.

After apologizing, he said abruptly, "Why don't you come to Syracuse?" I hurried off to *Redbook* (where I had the article assignment) to get some extra money, arrived in Syracuse almost as soon as he did, and settled in for a good long interview.

I once learned that a priest I needed to talk to was at that moment studying in the New York Public Library and found him there—a bit of a problem since I had no idea what he looked like and the place seemed full of researching priests.

But interviewing *should not be confined to authorities*. Everyone has something to say about religion, and some of it is very interesting. Besides, you cannot be reporting accurately unless you know what the man—and woman—on the street is thinking.

Interesting laymen are always around at religious conferences. Newspapers also turn up provocative people. For example, I once read the story of a Staten Island couple who had an ingenious interfaith marriage. I filed it, remembered it when an editor asked me to do an article on such marriages, called the couple, and spent a wonderful evening with them and their children.

Some interviews—with both authorities and laymen—happen spontaneously and you must be ready for them. Once, on a plane, I glanced at my neighbor and found I was sitting next to Martin Luther King! We had three hours and I got more from this at-ease conversation than I did from a formal interview later on. On another occasion, during the racial crisis of the sixties, I chanced to sit between a Methodist woman from South Carolina and a Methodist man from Long Island. With a little guidance, it was easy to get an intriguing argument started, and I sat back happily and listened.

Talk to people wherever they are. During the 1965 civil rights demonstrations in Selma, Alabama, I went through Harlem with a tape recorder questioning passersby on the street and turning up poignant answers. And recently, in a luxurious restaurant in Kentucky, a man leaned across from a nearby table and—to my astonishment—asked if I were a born-again Christian. I challenged the meaning of the phrase; people at other tables joined in and there was a provocative discussion.

Sometimes these spontaneous responses are important enough to provoke a whole new train of thought. For example, a sensitive young Catholic I met on a train told me religion was difficult for his generation. "We'll have to start over again from within ourselves," he said. It is a sentence that has been in my thinking on religion articles ever since. I remember, too, another young man at a religious conference who said—when I asked him what disturbed him most in his church— "Why, nothing. I wouldn't go if it did." That complacent, don't-look-under-the-surface remark has also sparked intriguing questions.

As must be clear by now, the big problem is that the research and the interviews snowball so fast it is almost impossible to pare them down into an article. In this field, there is scarcely ever a disappointing interview, and it is always horrifying to think how much must be left out.

Of course, the rules for interviewing on *any* subject apply here. Never go to an arranged interview without some knowledge of what this man or woman thinks and publicly says. Be clear what it is that you want to know. This doesn't mean that you'll need a list of elaborately prepared questions. But you *will* need to have in mind a few really pungent ones.

Establish rapport as soon as possible. If time allows, roam about a bit in the beginning, not only to establish your own knowledgeability but to probe for the areas in which your interviewee really sparkles— the areas in which he or she has had the richest experience.

You need to have in hand what you want to *ask;* but don't make up your mind in advance what you want your interviewee to *tell* you. In fact, an open mind is never more necessary than in an interview. Though not a conservative, I was once nearly moved to tears when a very conservative minister I was interviewing tried to prove his point by reciting from his Bible with much eloquence and love. The understanding I felt helped me in writing the article.

WRITING FROM A COMPLEX WEAVE

Finally, how do you *write* the piece? How do you most effectively present what you have found and experienced?

First, even in a reportorial piece, what is needed is a complex weave of your own thinking, your own experience, and your journalistic discoveries. At least, that is what is best for the kind of writing I do.

For example, when I wrote the article called "We Need New Ways to Pray" for the *Reader's Digest,* I used the following lead:

From the beginning of recorded history, prayer has been man's ultimate resort in time of trouble, his response to guilt and the need for forgiveness; his way of expressing what is deepest and best in himself. Yet today—even among religious people—prayer seems to be on the decline.

I went on to *report* the reasons for saying so and summed that up with the following:

Like all worship, prayer must start from the condition of the man who prays, and be relevant to what he is. . . .What kind of prayer then makes sense today?

In the rest of the piece, I attempted to answer that question with my own thinking and with both personal experience and the experience of others.

Use moving anecdotes and definitions where needed. Whether or not you are going to include definitions in the piece, define your terms in advance so that you know, for your own sake, what you are really thinking. Ask yourself: "What do I really mean when I say *religion?* When I say *the Church?* When I mention *salvation* or *ritual?*" Be aware of the dangers of using loosely such words and phrases as *evangelicals, fundamentalists, Protestantism, Jews believe, Catholics believe.* Today, the Judaeo-Christian faiths take their followers in so many directions that generalizations about churches and religious believers are much more dangerous than they used to be.

Be careful, too, not to preach from your momentarily superior pulpit. Share and search along with the reader, admitting your own problems of faith.

Writing the religion article is not easy. Breaking into the religion market with in-depth pieces takes much time. But it is deeply rewarding. Through the years of writing these pieces, I have grown a good deal, spiritually and emotionally.

The world-famous cellist, Pablo Casals, was once asked what legacy he wanted to leave to the world. "It is always the same," he said, "the lesson of never underestimating life." It is easy to remember that lesson when you are writing the religion article, for the depths and heights of life are always around you.

WRITE WHAT YOU KNOW AND BELIEVE IN ITS WORTH
by George Devine

Most of you have seen the play or movie version of *I Remember Mama*. The story concludes with the success of a daughter who had wanted desperately to become a published author, but faced rejection after rejection. What seemed to turn the tide was Mama, who took it upon herself to solicit, then repeat to her daughter, the advice of a famous writer: *write what you know*. This was what the young lady in the case had not realized, and this was why she wasted time preparing manuscripts about exotic topics and faraway places of which she had no knowledge. When she did sell her first story, for a sum of money and of a readership greater than she had dreamed, it was because she had written of Mama—her love and appreciation for her—and her remembrances of intimate experiences that were sad, happy, funny, and universal.

Write what you know. The principle has always been sound. It was followed by the prophet Amos, who used the imagery of a shepherd to explain the word of Yahweh to the people of Israel. The same principle is followed with success by newspapers and broadcast media which employ gourmets to write about food and athletes to write about sports. The implication is simple but profound: someone who has an interest in a subject is the logical person to tell the story. Technique is important, surely, but first there must be the enthusiasm, or at least knowledge, sufficient to motivate the storyteller to tell the story in a clear, interesting, and complete manner.

Like the young woman in *I Remember Mama*, aspiring writers have no need to go to faraway places for which the mind must reach beyond reason. It is not even necessary to go to journalism school. It *is* necessary to *write what you know*, and to do so with interest, clarity, accuracy, and conviction.

GETTING INTO PRINT

I came to understand these principles when I sold my first article to a magazine. At the risk of appearing to tell old war stories, I feel this is one worth relating. I was studying at Marquette University for a Master of Arts in theology, with plans to enter the teaching profession. Marquette had a well-respected journalism school then (still does), and I lived next door to the old J-school on North Thirteenth Street in Milwaukee. One of my friends was a graduate student in journalism whose professor had assigned him to write a feature article geared to a specific magazine market of the student's choosing. My friend elected to write about the wave of young Catholic laypeople, such as myself, who were studying theology in the early 1960s and entering a professional field previously limited to members of the clergy and religious orders. My journalist friend chose me as an interview subject. As our conversations progressed, I learned that the story was being written for *America* magazine, although it would not actually be submitted. Also, I realized that his dogged pursuit of the story still left gaps in both information and style. Finally, I was aware that the old *Voice of Saint Jude* magazine, published by the Claretian Fathers in Chicago, was being modernized into *U.S. Catholic*, which would be hungry for good nonfiction copy of a timely nature. I helped my friend repair his manuscript and sell it to *U.S. Catholic*, and we shared the byline and fee. After a decade of writing as an amateur for school publications in a student capacity, I had turned pro.

In later years I would sell my master's thesis to the same house, Claretian Publications. Instead of "Israel: The People of the Exodus/ Covenant," it became *Why Read the Old Testament?*, with eight printings from 1966 through 1978 and a Spanish translation (*¿Por qué debemos leer el Antiguo Testamento?*) in 1972 (ten years later, still one of their bestsellers!). To the same Claretians, I sold a follow-up story on "The New Theologians" (1965); the update was "The New Theologians Revisited," in *U.S. Catholic* (1969). Meanwhile, the former story had been reprinted in *Catholic Digest* (1965). The spinoffs from my first story sale were good, but not over yet. Convinced that layfolk had been invited into Catholic theological schools and then found themselves frustrated in a limited job market, I wanted to expose that ironic situation. The *National Catholic Reporter* had run a story on this and was not ready for another; *The Critic* would have been a good market, but did not agree that the story was significant; "establishment" Catholic periodicals like *America* refused to touch it; *Commonweal* was not interested. But I believed in the story and kept developing it, hoping someone would help me tell it. It appeared October 31, 1971, in "The Week in Review" in the *New York Times,* and became the first of many pieces I sold to the Good Gray Lady of Forty-third Street, for either that section, the book review, the real estate department, or the "Op-ed" page. Like the budding author in *I Remember Mama,* I wrote what I knew, believed in what I wrote, and kept searching for a market that would publish what I had written.

The same "stick-to-it" attitude in *writing what you know* paid off with a secular piece I wrote for *California Living,* the widely read Sunday magazine of the San Francisco *Examiner.* I had sold them an article on my old neighborhood in 1978 ("Growing Up in the Fog"), after several tries at lesser local markets, and felt inspired to do more writing for them—nostalgia with regional emphasis, a staple in their diet. My story on oldtime radio in the Bay Area was rejected in 1979, and since the magazine didn't want to hold onto it, I resubmitted it and it was rejected again. In 1980 and 1981 I tried it again, but they had no need for it and didn't want to tie it up, despite my protestations that they could keep it. In 1982 the fifth submission (or fourth *re*submission) succeeded. It was *not* a matter of revising the manuscript at all, but rather of redirecting the editors' attention to it from time to time.

Seven Suggestions

In sum, *writing what you know and believing in what you write* will help you to have your material published, providing you follow certain practical suggestions:

1. *Become an expert in your chosen field(s).*

No one feels more satisfaction than the person who knows what he is talking about. This could be you as you write your article; or, it could be someone who writes a letter to the editor, correcting an error in a published article you have written. If it is the latter, your material will lose value and your chances of being published in the future diminish. If it is the former, editors and readers will respect you as an authoritative source they will want to read again.

2. *Don't be afraid to shoot for the top.*

If you don't aim for top markets in your field(s), you may bypass instant success—and future spinoffs. Your favorite magazine (or newspaper, or television series, or whatever) as a reader should be your favorite as a writer. After all, people who read a certain source begin to write in a manner influenced by it and appropriate to it. If you don't make your first-choice market, try to find out why. Sometimes the market source itself will tell you. Most of the time, however, you must figure out why your material doesn't sell. You may have chosen a market saturated with recent material on your topic, or one that doesn't use freelance material, or one that doesn't read material not submitted by agents, or any number of other reasons. This leads to the next principle.

3. *Learn the market, and know alternative markets.*

Some years ago I learned, when not writing on assignment, to write material for a series of markets, with the most likely first, less likely afterwards, and least likely last. I sometimes made the mistake of trying lesser markets first, since I considered them better shots at a "quick sale," and I had guessed incorrectly (afraid to "shoot for the top"). But writers should have alternate routes in mind. In addition to developing the kind of hands-on, intimate knowledge of the market that comes with professional knowledge and experience accumulated over the years, a freelancer can use sources like *Writer's Market, Writer's Handbook* and others that will provide an overview of specific markets by topic, type, region, etc. Also very useful are the internal publications and meetings of professional societies.

4. *Become a professional.*

This means more than getting paid for writing. It means developing a *professional attitude.* One key element of great value here is membership in appropriate professional organizations such as the ASJA, Society of Professional Journalists/Sigma Delta Chi, and the like. In addition to receiving market news and enjoying the company of other writers, such groups help you sharpen your skills and renew your enthusiasm. Many professional organizations allow only established writers to become members, but standards are not so exclusive as to shut out all but the authors of bestsellers and the winners of Pulitzers, although you may find yourself rubbing elbows with such from time to time. Once your publication record qualifies you for membership in one or more of these organizations, you owe it to yourself and to your profession to participate.

5. *Don't assume only agents can sell manuscripts.*

Many agents deal only with established writers, and one must *become* established by selling one's own material first. Also, many agents will market books but not articles, so even then you will be on your own. Learn how to approach editors directly and sell them on your stuff. Remember: your material must be right for the market, and you must believe in it.

6. *Don't be afraid to ask questions.*

Some editors see potential in writers who are willing to take suggestions. If your material's rejection puzzles you, try to find reasons before automatically bouncing it out to another market. You may learn a lot!

7. *Don't be afraid to do an occasional "freebie."*

Writing for free sounds like a curious mixture of charity and scabbing. On a regular basis, it is unprofessional, unproductive, and weakens the position of all writers, including yourself. On an *occasional* basis, it may benefit you to write an article for which you are not paid, or for which you are paid less than your professional peers generally accept as fair. Every professional writer, I believe, began writing freebies for a school paper or magazine. For me, this led to a paying job covering the same area—California professional sports—for Fan Publications (*Giants Journal, Angel Country, Warrior Gold, Oakland A's Newspaper*). And my writing at below-market rates for the editorial page of the archdiocesan newspaper in Newark, New Jersey, doubtless helped me develop the ability to sell similar material at the going rate to the "Op-ed" page of the *New York Times*. Most of the time, we must stick to our professional guns when it comes to payment. But once in a while, there is a trade-off, and sometimes we pay into the fund of common knowledge by writing material without monetary payment.

Additional Resources

Academy of Religion and Psychical Research, 326 Tunxis Ave., Bloomfield, CT 06002. Encourages dialogue, idea exchange, and cooperation between clergy, academics in philosophy and religion, and the researchers and scientists in parapsychology and related fields. Conducts conferences and seminars. Maintains library of 6,000 volumes. Publishes *Journal of Religion and Psychical Research* (quarterly).

American Jewish Committee, % Institute of Human Relations, 165 E. 56th St., New York, NY 10022. Conducts program of education and human relations, maintains library. Publishes journals, books, reprints, articles, bibliographies, and more.

Associated Church Press, P.O. Box 306, 321 James, Geneva, IL 60134. Sponsors editorial workshops, research in Christian journalism, and national awards program for excellence in content, makeup, and typography. Publishes directory of member publications, including information on editors, and circulation frequency of publication.

B'Nai B'Rith International, 1640 Rhode Island Ave. NW, Washington, DC 20036. Provides religious, cultural, civic, and social programs for teenagers and the Jewish students and faculty of some 350 college campuses. Bestows awards for outstanding humanitarian services. Maintains museum and speakers bureau. Conducts studies on important Jewish issues, published on a timely basis. Publishes *International Jewish Monthly*, and Judaism Pamphlet Series.

Buddhist Vihara Society, 5017 16th St. NW, Washington, DC 20011. Operates a bookstore and mail-order service, holds discussions; provides lecturers, conducts classes on Buddhism and meditation for adults and children; organizes celebrations on days of special Buddhist significance. Publishes *Washington Buddhist* (quarterly newsletter), brochures, and a devotional handbook.

Catholic Press Association, 119 N. Park Ave., Rockville Centre, NY 11570. Maintains 33 committees, including Catholic Press Directory, Catholic Press Month, Journalism Awards, Postal Rates, Special Awards. Sponsors research programs and specialized education. Maintains placement service. Publishes the *Catholic Journalist* (monthly), and bulletins.

Evangelical Press Association, % Gary Warner, P.O. Box 4550, Overland Park, KS 66205. Maintains placement service, bestows awards. Publications include *E.P. News Service* (weekly), and *Liaison* (bimonthly).

National Conference of Christians and Jews, 43 W. 57th St., New York, NY 10019. Offers programming in the areas of adults, youth, community relations, the administration of justice, equal opportunity in industry, intercreedal relations, education. Provides a religious news service; arranges training programs and workshops in human relations. Presents national and regional Humanitarian Awards and National Mass Media Awards. Sponsors Brotherhood Week. Publishes a quarterly newsletter and an annual report.

National Council of Churches of Christ in the U.S.A., 475 Riverside Dr., New York, NY 10115. Programs include global literacy teaching with Christian literature; publishing Sunday School educational material; coordinating and assisting church work in worldwide medical missions programs; supplying food, clothing and shelter worldwide;

coordinating refugee placement in U.S. communities; providing leadership training in religious education, pastoral care, higher education, criminal justice, religious liberty, ecumenical action. Publishes *Chronicles* (quarterly) and *Yearbook of American and Canadian Churches.*

National Spiritual Assembly of the Baha'is of the U.S., 112 Linden Ave., Wilmette, IL 60091. Promotes: elimination of prejudice; economic justice based upon spiritual principles; independent investigation of truth; international auxiliary language; equality of men and women; world government for maintenance of lasting peace. Baha'i literature has been translated into 630 languages and dialects. Publishes *American Baha'i* (monthly), *Baha'i News* (monthly), and *World Order Magazine* (semiannual).

Religion Newswriters Association, % Ben Kaufman, Cincinnati Enquirer, 617 Vine St., Cincinnati, OH 45202. Religion news editor and reporters on secular daily and weekly newspapers, news services, and newsmagazines. Presents Supple, Schachern, and Cassels Memorial awards annually. Publishes bimonthly *News Letter.*

Religious News Service, 43 W. 57th St., New York, NY 10019. Disseminates news of interest to the entire religious constituency. Provides daily news reports, features, photo service. Affiliated with National Conference of Christians and Jews.

World Council of Churches, 150, Route de Ferney, CH-1211 Geneva 20, Switzerland. Conducts wide range of programs of witness, service, unity, and renewal throughout the world. Maintains Ecumenical Institute, and educational center with graduate seminar, near Geneva, Switzerland. Conducts extensive refugee and resettlement program. Maintains library in Geneva dealing with Christian unity, church history, theology. Publications include *Ecumenical Press Service* (biweekly), *One World* (monthly), *Exchange* (bimonthly), and *Ecumenical Review* (quarterly).

[Editor's Note: Virtually all major religions—and denominations—have a news and information services division that provides assistance to writers and the media.]

Chapter Twelve

WRITING FOR WOMEN'S MARKETS

If you think women's magazines focus exclusively on the three Cs of homemaking—cooking, cleaning, and children—think again. Women are half of the human race, with all the concerns of men, and some unique ones of their own; they're interested in everything from career advancement to stepparenting, needlework to money management. Markets in this field are as varied as *Family Circle* and *Cosmopolitan*, *Woman's Day* and *Playgirl*, *Mademoiselle* and *Ms.*, *Hadassah* and *Harper's Bazaar*.

The number of publications for women continues to grow at an amazing rate, each designed to appeal to a particular, well-defined readership. For example, in recent years there has been a rash of start-ups aimed at the millions of women pouring into the work force. Some of these include *Savvy, Working Woman,* and McCall's *Working Mother.* In fact, there's a publication for just about any women's interest group you might mention: *Graduate Women, Modern Bride, Women's Sports, Farm Wife News.*

Writes Elaine Fantle Shimberg (contributor to these pages and author of *How to Be a Successful Housewife/Writer*) in the June 1983 issue of *Writer's Digest:* "For the writer, the women's market is exciting for the very reason it can be troublesome. It's fluid. It changes like the sand bar at the beach, shifting ever so slightly even as you watch it. Woman's basic interests—self, family, husband/lover, work, and community—probably won't change all that much. But the world she moves in does change. Forecasting these changes, recording today, and anticipating tomorrow is what makes the women's market fascinating. If you follow one magazine through a period of years, you'll find it's a microcosm of women's history. With determination, dedication, and discipline, you can be part of it."

The women's "slicks" are among the highest-paying markets on the newsstand, so arm yourself for heavy competition. Read the magazines and study them carefully before you query, since each addresses a particular audience in a different way, even though the article subject categories in many cases may appear to be the same: lifestyle, workplace problems, beauty, child care, marriage, and so on. In fact, this is an area of specialization that encompasses nearly every other area discussed in this book: medicine and health, psychology, travel and leisure, business and finance, consumerism, hobby-craft, food and nutrition, home and garden, environment and energy, religion and sports.

Writing requirements for the large consumer and service magazines in the women's field are rigid and inflexible. What's more, many of the editors tend to favor established writers. But even these editors admit that the need for nurturing new talent remains strong and constant, and they are always open to writers with new ideas. Some men who have never been able to sell to the women's magazines maintain that editors show preferential treatment to women writers. But when a byline appears in these periodicals, it has less to do with gender than with that elusive commodity we call *talent*.

What sell are well-researched, sprightly written articles with a strong, fresh, and newsworthy women's angle. These are the solid, unchangeable facts of the matter, and the writer's sex has little or nothing to do with it. (Except, of course, in those obvious first-person experience pieces where a man is automatically disqualified. Even then he might do an as-told-to piece on a specific topic—and sometimes, a women's magazine may welcome a man's viewpoint on a topic such as child care or divorce.)

Don't forget books—readership surveys indicate that book buyers are predominantly female. Thus publishers are always on the lookout for how-to books aimed at women readers, with an emphasis on self-help, self-improvement, practical guidance, ideas for stretching money, improving relationships, advancing a career, or looking attractive.

Like any other specialized field of writing, be it articles or books, the road to publication in the women's markets is open to everyone, if—and only if—they come equipped with realistic ideas, specific new themes, and top-quality writing directed to the right audience. Read on for instruction on how to write for and sell to this vibrant and dynamic segment of today's writing market.

WRITING ARTICLES AND BOOKS FOR THE WOMEN'S MARKET
by Elaine Fantle Shimberg

If you haven't read a women's magazine in the past ten years, this may not be the market for you. As any couturier can tell you, yesterday's fashions seldom sell.

Today's woman is not her grandmother or mother; her interests and concerns are different and her books and magazines reflect these differences. Not only must you be aware of these ever-constant changes, but you must understand how to write to them according to the specializations within the market itself. Each women's-interest magazine differs from the others; each has a specific type of reader and although there is, of course, some cross-over, the writer who ignores these variations will have no success writing for the women's market.

THE WOMEN'S MARKET . . .

There is no one role model for this market. Women today have many more options than they had twenty, ten, or even five years ago. Magazines have sprung up to satisfy interests generated by these options. Women today are lawyers, advertising executives, truck drivers, teachers, homemakers, mechanics; and the list grows. The typical "women's market" is greatly diversified.

There are specialized magazines such as *Bluegrass Women, Women in Business, Ladycom,* and *Farm Wife News.* There are the general magazines, the so-called "Seven Sisters": *McCall's, Good Housekeeping, Redbook, Ladies' Home Journal, Woman's Day, Family Circle,* and *Better Homes and Gardens.* There are others such as *Glamour, Self, Women's Sports, Vogue, Ms., Working Mother,* and *Savvy.*

There is overlap in the readership of these magazines. A woman—married or single, homemaker or employee—may read several that cover her various interests. Women, like men, do not fall neatly into tight little compartments. Their reading habits often make their magazine-subscription lists quite eclectic; their library shelves reveal their varied interests.

From Sheila Gibbons, editor of *Ladycom:* "Women today want more depth in their magazines. They're better educated, more aware. Women's magazines have always offered more pragmatic information than men's. Men tend to read more for escape and entertainment. We're getting more articles on finances, sexual and emotional health, and the role of fathers within a family setting."

Basically, however, most women's magazines act as a sounding board for feelings, exploring the concerns and interests of today's woman.

"Women have complicated lives," says Sondra Forsyth Enos, executive editor of *Ladies' Home Journal.* "We have health problems unlike those of men. We have less time for our friends. Women are at a time in their lives when they want help with concerns they would have shared with another woman. It's back-fence conversation, woman-to-woman, all the things that touch a woman's life. The women's magazine acts as the formal extension of our sisterly lines."

Books for women are no different. They help women play "catch-up" in a world where the rules, and even the *games,* change as they are being played. With few role models to emulate, women turn to "women's-interest" sections of bookstores to learn how to make, manage, and enjoy time, money, friends, and good health. Books written especially for women become the mentors men find in the flesh.

. . . and How to Write for It

Probably the best way to get ideas for this market is to become an unabashed eavesdropper. It's a habit that is improper and rude—and extremely handy for a writer.

By listening to conversations, you learn what people are worrying about, what makes them laugh or cry, what makes them curious and/or indignant. People are basically self-interested. Women want to know "How to Communicate When *You're* the Boss," "How to Put Mystery in Your Marriage," "Low-Calorie Brown-Bagging in the Executive Lunchroom," "Can Babies and Board Rooms Mix?" and "How to Keep Up Without Giving Out."

All these titles are ideas for articles that speak to a woman's concerns. Write to her; use the "you" key on your typewriter. Get the reader involved, and you'll find yourself getting more acceptances than rejections.

Carry a notebook with you. Begin writing down article ideas from conversational bits you overhear. It can be women's conversations, what men say about the women in their lives (or those they would *like* to have in their lives), or what children have to say. Be alert to news reports of happenings that you can personalize for women readers, *specific* women readers of a particular magazine.

Being mothers can make many readers interested in a certain book or article. Those of us with families tend to be filled with guilt of one sort or another: Are we feeding our children properly? How can we encourage our kids without doing too much for them? What should we do about our teenagers and the family car, or about alcohol and other drugs? Most of us wonder if we could be better parents. Tell us how we can and we'll probably read your article or buy your book.

I began writing for this market through self-interest. Our five children were aged eight and under. Through my writing I was able to express and share my frustrations, fears, and joys of parenthood. One of my first articles, "How to Run Away from Home," was totally based on my advice to myself about taking a day off from child care. Apparently, this need wasn't unique to me, as *Baby Talk* magazine published it for their readers.

My first book, *How to Be a Successful Housewife/Writer,* also came from personal experience, as well as from listening to the complaints of most of my female writing friends. We were all struggling to find time for our writing. We traded the brief moments of pleasure that came with publication for hours of guilt for "denying" our families our constant attention. We apologized for staying away from club meetings and teas when everyone knew we weren't "really working," just sitting at home with our typewriters.

It wasn't until I overheard a male writer say *he* had no trouble working at home that my ideas began to germinate. *He* kept regular writing hours, letting his wife answer the phone and keep the kids from underfoot; *he* stayed with a chapter until it was done or dinner was ready, whichever came first.

I organized my thoughts, drew up a proposed outline, and sent my query to a publisher of self-help books for writers. The year was 1972. My stamped, self-addressed envelope came back with a letter from the then-editor: "I don't see how the problems of a woman writer are any different from a man's."

The years passed. As I continued to juggle raising our five children and pursuing my freelance writing, I remained convinced there *was* a difference. It was advantageous for a writer to have a loyal and loving wife at hand to smooth the way. I had none. Nor did any of the women writers I heard muttering about their frustrations. In 1978, I sent an almost identical query back to the same publisher. This time the editors were more attuned to the fact that women who tried to write from their homes had problems not faced by male writers. The proposal was accepted and a year later my book was published.

The point of this example is that you must know your potential reader and know that she can identify with your topic. You must be determined, continuing to develop and market an idea you believe in even if it takes months or even years to discover an editor who shares your belief. Your writing must speak to the reader as you would a friend, neither talking down nor speaking over her head. You must "connect," making her feel that by reading your book or article you have either entertained her, made her understand and thus cope with her life better, or shown her a new way to do something that is significant to her.

YOUR OWN UNIQUE PERSPECTIVE

Obviously, there are not too many totally original ideas. Many articles and books deal with ways to lose weight, save money, find happiness, or prevent problems. It is how well we, as writers, tell those stories, how much of our uniqueness we inject, how skillfully we bring the reader into our work, that makes one article differ from another on the same subject. You need a "gimmick," a special slant that makes your story shine, dazzling the editor and blinding him or her to the others piled like snowdrifts high on the desk.

In a writing class I have taught, I demonstrate this individuality among writers with a simple exercise. I ask the class to write a few paragraphs detailing how to change a light bulb. It's a task we all do. Probably no one ever had to show us how. It's simple, basic, and *should* be explained similarly by most people. Yet when a class of prospective writers reads its work aloud, everyone is amazed. Some of the paragraphs are funny; others are filled with technical detail—how to check the wattage, which way to turn the bulb, how to set a ladder so you don't slip. Each writer used a different style of writing to explain. That's what made each paragraph unique and what made some superior to others.

In many of my women's articles, I use personal experience as a base. That, along with other case histories, helps to put emotion into the articles and to answer the all-important question, "Who cares?" But you seldom can rely on personal experience alone. Your article needs the support of experts, other case histories, and research data.

When my oldest child was about two and a half, she climbed to the top of a dresser, pried the cap of a bottle of baby aspirin off with her teeth, and ingested the contents of the bottle. After she had her stomach pumped and was out of danger (and I was out of shock), I realized this could happen to any family. Perhaps my experience could serve as a warning. I used it as the lead for an article, one that I sold in different forms, three times.

The first time was to a local newspaper. My story was supported by information from local pediatricians, the Poison Control Center, and other parents who had shared my experience.

When I decided to "go national," I rewrote the article for *Essence*, a monthly magazine for black women. For this article, I used national statistics and quotes from experts throughout the United States. (This is known as getting "geographic spread.") I wrote specifically to the readership of this magazine.

When I decided to take my idea abroad, I rewrote it, slanted it to a British market, used statistics gathered by the British Medical Association, and switched my Americanisms to expressions common in the United Kingdom. The article sold to *Mother* magazine, a British publication.

In each of these cases, I knew my reader, knew her concerns, could picture her reading my article, and wrote to answer her unasked question, "What does this mean to me?"

Be Specific

Whenever you write, be specific. Don't talk in general terms about displaced homemakers trying to develop job skills; interview some. Get to know these women as people. Tell their individual stories. Make statistics human. Personalize—give us actual names if you can. Describe the woman you're talking about so the reader can visualize her. When we read a general news story, we shake our head. When it's personalized, it shakes our hearts.

Try to get more background, do more interviews, and absorb more data than you can possibly use. (Don't research forever, however. At some point, you must write the story.) When you have an excess of material, you have more freedom in your writing; you can select the best quote from a handful of psychologists, rather than using one you're stuck with because it's all you have.

Be Accurate

Never think you can write down to this market. If you don't respect women and their needs, find another specialty.

Take pride in your accuracy. You'll find that most magazines in this field have staff members whose responsibility it is to contact your experts to see if you've quoted them accurately. These people probably will ask you for addresses and phone numbers of everyone mentioned in your article, so be prepared. Keep notes and stay organized. Don't try to bluff your way through. If you don't have the information, the editor may think you've made it up—and will refuse to publish your work.

I often contact the interviewees myself and read what I've quoted, just to be certain it's accurate. With medically oriented articles, I have at least one and preferably two physicians proof my work.

Most editors are overworked—overwhelmed with queries and manuscripts. If given the choice between buying an article from a careless writer or one who is known to check his or her facts, which would *you* pick?

STUDY THE MARKETS

Most magazines are targeted to a specific audience, and publishers spend a great deal of money to learn all they can about their readers. Though you might have the most terrific idea in the world, editors won't buy it if they don't think it will appeal to their particular readers.

Take time to look up each magazine's needs in reference books like *Writer's Market*. Read the magazine to get a feel for what is being published. Study the ads. Visualize the typical reader. How old is she? Does she work outside the home? Does she have children? If so, how many? How old are the kids? How much education does your prospective reader have? What are her needs? Her fears? Her stress points? Understand her, write for her and to her.

Rebecca Greer, articles editor of *Woman's Day*, once said that her magazine looked for articles dealing with the five Ms—marriage, medicine, motherhood, money, and modern living. Actually, this is a pretty good list for many of the women's magazines. But you must understand their individual differences; each has its own specific set of requirements.

For example: *Woman's Day* is a service magazine, showing the reader how to improve her life; *McCall's* deals largely with emotions and relationships; *Ladies' Home Journal* uses documentaries of real life drama; *Good Housekeeping* likes personal-experience stories that inform and entertain active women; *Glamour* speaks to the college-educated woman aged eighteen to thirty-four, and deals with relationships; *Family Circle* uses people stories dealing with the problem-solving aspects of family life.

Remember the importance of age difference in the readers of these magazines. The average age of the *Redbook* reader is in the twenties; with the *McCall's* reader, it's the mid to late thirties. That means the ages of their children vary. Their parents are different in age as well. The problems and needs of these two groups are not the same. Keep this in mind as you plan your article.

I purposely have kept the requirements general when speaking of any of the women's markets. Their needs are subject to change; new developments are treated in the monthly writers' magazines such as *The Writer* and *Writer's Digest*, and can also be detected by reading the magazines. The following suggestions, however, are true for all the periodicals, from the "Seven Sisters" who pay the most, down to the magazine with the smallest freelance budget. My list includes:

- Study the market; *read* the magazines you want to write for. Don't forget the "smaller" markets. My article on how to give fun but inexpensive parties was published in a regional edition of *Woman's Day*. It paid less, but it was good exposure. Markets like *Ladycom*, *Lady's Circle*, and *Bride's* may not pay the most, but they can become steady markets once you know their needs.
- List the subjects covered in the past few issues of a particular magazine. Do you see any similarities? Any trends?
- Analyze the articles. What is the typical length? Are they writ-

ten objectively or subjectively? How are they slanted?

- Are photos included with the article? If so, how many? Who is in them? Are they in color or black and white? Can you furnish pictures? (If so, be sure to include that fact in your query.)
- Trim your idea down to size. Make sure you can tell your idea in one sentence; make it concise so you don't wander away from the point. (If you're writing about giving inexpensive parties, don't let time-saving tips creep in.) On the other hand, be sure you have enough material to sustain an article.
- Be realistic in your approach. Remember that most of us don't want to hear about Superwoman. We're Wonder Woman with tarnished bracelets. Let us know that the heroine forgets to thaw anything out for dinner, that she's got a pimple on her chin and stubble on her legs. Then, even though she lands the handsome prince and the major account for her firm, we can still identify with her.
- Don't feel you have to be in New York to write for these markets. If you live in Yankton, South Dakota or Parrott, Georgia, you may have an idea those big-city folks haven't thought of.
- Remember that the women's movement has affected most women in some way, however subtle. Women *are* changed. Your writing must reflect this heightened consciousness.

Sure-Fire Topics

Most of us are attracted by self-help books and articles. This probably is because we are filled with self-doubt and insecurities. Make us feel fat, guilty, or vulnerable unless we read your work. Tell us how to be better employees, wives, mothers, daughters, athletes, cooks . . . the list is endless. We want to improve ourselves but we want to escape as well. Make us laugh—and cry. Make us care. Stir us to action.

Adapt to Change

The range of material for this market is endless—but it is ever-changing. You must stay alert; you must continually update your information. Otherwise, you'll find yourself left behind in the freelancing rat race.

A *Ladies' Home Journal* article in the March 1950 issue told of an editor's comment fifty years earlier: "The rush of women into offices and stores has ended," he said. "Most women have shown themselves to be naturally incompetent in business." His prediction for the twentieth century: "Practically all working girls back in the home."

In 1955, that magazine's columnist, Clifford R. Adams, Ph.D., wrote about skills necessary for being a good wife. "Unless she would rather quit her job than slight her duties as wife and homemaker, she is better qualified for business than marriage." He added, "The happy wife adapts her moods to her husband's. . . ."

Yes, times do change, and the writer must adapt to these changes if he or she is to be successful in the women's market.

Susan B. Anthony said, "Modern invention has banished the spinning wheel, and the same law of progress makes the woman of to-day a different woman from her grandmother."

Stay abreast of this progress. You'll find success not only in this field but in others as well. My writing has led me into giving speeches and seminars on time management, working out of the home, writing, and two-career marriages; into writing a newspaper column; into being a co-hostess on a television talk show; and most satisfying of all, has introduced me to interesting women I might never have met had I not begun writing for the women's market.

Think of the women's market as a vast one, for it is. You'll find possible women's markets listed under such headings as *child care, confession, business, religion,* and *sports.*

What is a woman? I answered that in *How to Be a Successful House-wife/Writer.* "We all have many facets, like a stained-glass window, with the sections reflecting differently depending on the day and the angle of the sun. I am a symbiotic blend, each part dependent on the other for nourishment."

Feed those many faces of Eve and you'll find writing for the women's market very satisfying—and very profitable as well.

WHAT DO WOMEN'S MAGAZINES WANT?
by Pamela Bayless

If Freud were alive today to pose his classic question, "What do women want?" he might be directed to a nearby magazine emporium to leaf through the myriad of publications loosely labeled "women's magazines."

The founder of psychoanalysis would no doubt be astonished at the collage of tastes and concerns, problems and ambitions, desires and dreams of contemporary American women of all ages and races, marital and economic status, that is chronicled in the pages of these varied journals.

Freud would also be dazed by the panoply of topics and products to be found there. But he would be most dumbfounded to see sexuality treated in a straightforward manner, from technique and health-related concerns to pleasure and psychological barriers. For nothing is off limits today, not even the traditional male preoccupations with sex, money, and power. Nearly every woman today can find a magazine that speaks to her and reflects her interests. Contemporary women's magazines are evolving closely after the women they aim to please, shifting their editorial focus frequently to incorporate new trends and sometimes altering their demographics as their readership advances in age. *Seventeen*, for example, hopes to keep its adolescent audience well into their twenties. *Glamour* has escorted entire generations it took to college campuses into first careers, from first date to first divorce. As the youth market of yore marches toward midlife, women's magazines are finding new ways to address changing concerns.

No women's magazine today has remained untouched by the major changes affecting women's status that characterized the 1970s. All have responded to these far-reaching social and economic shifts. *Ms.* was once the only magazine to chronicle the women's movement and subsequent changes in status. Now it has mothered a number of spinoffs for special segments of women's interests and inspired a feminist tone in traditional publications as well. New magazines such as *Working Mother*, instructing a largely single-parent readership in the balancing act, and *Savvy*, the magazine for executive women, would have been unthinkable in the 1960s for the small number of readers they might have attracted then.

Not only the new magazines, but the old standbys as well, are keeping pace with these changes. The "Seven Sisters"—*Better Homes and Gardens, Family Circle, Good Housekeeping, Ladies' Home Journal, McCall's, Redbook,* and *Woman's Day*—have always focused on the homemaker. None has abandoned the home context, yet most have widened it to encompass the increasing numbers of their readers in the world of work outside the home. Some magazines remain general; others have become more trendy than traditional. But none is untouched by the wider interests of today's women.

The "younger sisters," including *Cosmopolitan, Glamour, Mademoiselle,* and *Self,* still incorporate fashion and traditional concerns of younger women. Articles on relationships are increasingly sophisticated, however, and pieces on the workplace recognize that many readers now actively pursue careers rather than work only out of necessity or until Mr. Right comes along. The traditional fashion magazines, on the other hand—*Harper's Bazaar, Town and Country, Vogue*—have greatly enlarged their vistas, with feature material on topics from investments and health to careers and the arts.

New titles reflect a variety of new interests, with a narrowed focus on some particular phase of the women's market. *Bride's* has been joined by *Playgirl, Slimmer,* and *Women's Sports,* to name but a few examples.

THE KEY TO MARKETING STRATEGY

With the new magazines on the market and the greatly expanded horizons of the old guard, writers today can find an appropriate publication for nearly any kind of article they wish to sell to a women's audience. The key lies in finding the right magazine and then learning the language it speaks—the tone, the focus, and the subject of an article itself must fit the publication's style.

The real trick, one that often separates the novice writer from the professional, is marketing strategy. And to know and recognize your market, there is no substitute for *research.* Your proposal, no matter how exciting, won't stand a chance if it goes to the wrong place.

Your research can take several forms. Your regular reading of a particular magazine may familiarize you with its style and contents so that you sense when your idea would stand a fair chance. Regular browsing on newsstands can give a good overview of women's magazines through covers and tables of contents. *Writer's Market* also offers a concise view of the article needs of a number of women's publications. But nothing substitutes for a session in your library periodical room, methodically studying and jotting notes on articles in a year's back issues of your target publication.

Only after you're familiar with current titles will you know that *Savvy* won't want your hamburger-stretcher recipes, or that *Woman's Day* probably won't publish your survey of MBA programs.

Don't assume that because you were once a regular reader of a magazine that you still know the market. *Working Woman,* which several years ago appealed to secretaries who wanted articles on expanded career opportunities, revamped itself in 1981 as "the *Business Week* for women." Today's middle-management reader is already very involved in a career, and that *raison d'être* pervades even the articles on vacations and leisure. *Redbook* in early 1982 decided to change the tone of its service-oriented pieces from an authoritative to a peer point of view, becoming more informal, even humorous. The magazine's look changed as well, with a new cover and different format.

A change in graphics and appearance, from the cover to the content, may signal a magazine's shift in editorial focus. A new self-image can cue not only its readers to a fresh approach; alert authors will take notice of such changes in identity as well.

The Reader Profile

Other subtle clues about a magazine's readership can be found in the advertising pages. Editors and publishers are closely keying content to a well-defined *reader profile,* and the advertisers who buy space in those pages hope to reach the woman of a certain age group, level of education, salary, and "disposable income." For example, a magazine advertising Pampers and featuring clip-out grocery coupons is obviously targeting a reader whose major concerns differ from those who are potential buyers of Guccis and Cadillac Sevilles.

Some magazines readily furnish writers with their reader profiles if requested. The profile may be incorporated into a set of writers' guidelines, which provide useful information on what the publication seeks in freelance material. That's the surest way to angle your story to the right woman.

Keeping current with demographic and social trends affecting women's lives will put you a step ahead as well. Magazine editors are always eyeing those statistics carefully, and need writers who can help them adapt their editorial content.

Some of the women's magazines claim to publish "anything of interest to women," but a careful observer will soon realize that what would appeal to *Mademoiselle* readers might not make it into the pages of *Ms.,* and vice versa. However, there is a striking similarity among the articles favored by many women's magazines; high on most subject lists these days are articles on health, fitness, sexuality, relationships, money, and coping with everything from late motherhood to juggling job and family responsibilities.

What makes the difference, however, is the focus of the article. Is it to be aimed at the aged eighteen-to-thirty-four career-minded set or the broader, nineteen-to-fifty-nine age range made up of both homemakers and office workers? The tone is important as well—each magazine speaks to its readers with a unique voice, heavy on advice or purposely nonjudgmental. So your style should be geared to the women reading a specific magazine.

An article on money management might be written in several ways. For example, *Family Circle* would want a heavy "service" orientation instructing its young to middle-aged readers with family incomes generally under $20,000 how to apply a savings strategy to their lives. But if for *Self,* your article would also have a strong "how-to" focus, what editor-in-chief Phyllis Star Wilson calls "accessibility," so the practical reader can take your idea and act on it.

But your personal finance article would take on an altogether different focus for *Working Woman,* whose readers are largely executives and professionals. "We are not a magazine for beginners," says articles editor Julia Kagan. "Our readers know what a CD and a money market fund are. The market is very sophisticated."

Likewise, the cultural dynamics of our time, from a zooming divorce rate to single-parent families, two-career couples to an increasingly aging population, are of concern to all women's magazines, which aim to help their readers understand and cope. Yet you would write about living alone in very different veins to the young *Cosmopolitan* reader and to a "displaced homemaker" reading *McCall's*.

If you've researched a given publication well, you'll have an idea of the general tone. Is the writing short, concise, snappy? Or is there a more philosophical, eloquent bent, like the sort of piece you'd like to write? Is the reader addressed as "you"? Is she referred to as a "girl" or a "woman"? Most magazines try for a consistent, familiar tone.

Savvy seeks a sophisticated style of writing in all articles. But for *Essence*, the full-service magazine for black women, editor Audrey Edwards stresses a chatty, personal, and warm quality, since she seeks to build a sense of community among readers. "The magazine is somewhat like a family," she explains. "We sometimes address readers as 'we' or 'sisters.' "

Mademoiselle looks for writing that is "interesting, provocative, stimulating, and exciting," says editor Amy Levin. "We care about style. There is nothing new to be said about meeting a man, but what is written needs to be exciting to read. We like unusual writing—we want the writer to have her own style and feel free to use it."

Also, Levin adds, she values honesty and directness. "No euphemisms on sex," she says. "We take a very contemporary point of view which speaks to our readers and doesn't alienate them." A majority of magazine editors would agree.

FINDING THE RIGHT SUBJECT

With the wide range of subject matter in women's magazines, you should have no trouble finding a subject. You may have to look no further than your own personal experience.

While traveling in South America, I came across a newspaper account of an outrageous incident in a Brazilian girls' school. I wrote on it for the *Ms.* "Gazette" section. In a fit of pique when my bank raised its fees on checking accounts, I did some research to find a cheaper alternative and turned it into "Bargain Checking: How to Shop for It" for *Self*.

My first-hand knowledge of a career area paid off as well. As a fund-raising writer for a nonprofit organization, I was assigned by *Working Woman* to do a survey piece on fund-raising as a career option for women and drew on my professional acquaintances as sources. Keeping an ear to the ground for stories told by friends or acquaintances can pay off too. I broke into *Working Woman* with a profile of a friend in Ford's pilot program to train women in car sales.

Be aware that a piece you write for another publication may, with a woman's angle or focus, be reworked as the basis for a women's magazine article. My research for a *Venture* cover story on people who'd become millionaires when their companies went public turned up the names of very few women. But I tracked down some of those rare and wealthy women entrepreneurs and derived an article for *Working Woman*.

Not for Women Only

Male writers have something very special to offer the women's magazines—their own perspective. Of course, all categories of articles are open to men, from money to medicine to decorating. But with the current emphasis on relationships, the male viewpoint is especially intriguing to female readers. Some magazines, such as *Savvy* and *Glamour*, feature regular opinion columns written by men. Articles on diverse topics such as fathering, paternity leave, the male point of view on divorce or couple counseling, impotence—the list of possibilities is limitless.

Whether you are male or female, your own life experience is a bottomless well of story ideas for women's publications. A health problem you've conquered through self-treatment or surgery very likely holds universal interest, as well as an off-the-beaten-track vacation you've taken. Some magazines have special first-person sections open to outside contributors; *Redbook*'s "Young Mother's Story" is one.

And whether your special interest is sports or sociology, there may be a place in a number of magazines for such a story. Even those whose sole focus was fashion have now expanded into many areas. Never assume a magazine uses only one subject line, for they are constantly broadening their horizons.

Political pieces may now be placed in various publications. While *Ms.*, with its ideology of something-for-every-feminist from lesbians to "free" children, may seem the one place for a political viewpoint, *McCall's* can be as well—one story dealt with children's nuclear nightmares. *Redbook* published an interview with Helen Caldicott of Physicians for Social Responsibility after the Three Mile Island accident. Numerous publications took a stand for the Equal Rights Amendment and keep a constant watch on legislation affecting women.

Book reviews and fiction have a place in various women's magazines. Topics on women's history may find space in *Ms.*, while *Made-*

moiselle is constantly on the lookout for newsworthy original research. Academic studies undertaken on how women handle jealousy, how they fear success, and the chemistry of meeting people have all resulted in successful news or feature articles.

Don't Forget Your Hometown Newspaper

If you want to write women's material but don't quite feel ready for the major magazines, you may have to look no further than the women's "lifestyle" or "family" pages of your local newspaper for a market. Although magazines may be your eventual goal, feature material used by many newspapers is practically indistinguishable from some magazine articles, with the possible exception of length. Newspapers have blank pages to fill every day and must keep a "hopper" full of features.

This is also a good way to build a portfolio. For instance, I first published articles in my hometown newspaper, the *Kansas City Star.* I dispatched from New York pieces about Kansas City natives—an opera singer, performers in *A Chorus Line* and *Best Little Whorehouse in Texas,* media figures and other names in the news. They weren't hard to find—hometowns are often mentioned in *Playbill* and other publications. And the "hometown girl or boy makes good" formula is practically no-fail, if well written and accompanied by a photo.

Your local paper may be able to use food stories, travel articles, or your first-person account of an event or experience. Your objective is to get published and build a portfolio—then you may be able to expand such material eventually for a magazine.

MAKING THE SALE

Now you have a good article idea and you've pinpointed one or more women's magazines that might accept it. How do you go about making the sale?

On most magazines, an articles editor makes the first decision about whether an idea has merit. She may then circulate it to one or more editors for an opinion before making an assignment.

Most articles editors have a stack of such ideas constantly on their desks, so it is rare to find an editor on a major publication who has the time or patience to respond to telephone calls from unknown writers. But more important, since *writing* is what you propose to do, the editor will want to see what you're capable of doing on paper.

You must develop a query letter for your idea, preferably kept to one page to save the editor time (and to avoid the possibility of her misplacing a second sheet). In your well-thought-out and -written query, you will describe your idea and why the readers of *Working Mother* or *Harper's Bazaar* will want to read it. You should summarize the major points or arguments, beginning perhaps with a startling statistic, or a colorful example—something that intrigues the editor to consider your idea. Don't overwrite it; save details for the article itself. If you can provide accompanying photos, do mention that.

How you weave a few paragraphs will be as important as the idea you present, for the letter gives a sense of your style. The query is your chance to prove yourself on paper. Save questions about payment or length until later.

Your query should be accompanied by a couple of well-selected writing samples, clips or tearsheets whenever possible. Select those that show your expertise in the area about which you propose to write, something you've written for another prestigious (and, if possible, competing) publication, or simply something that reveals your thinking process and/or writing at its best. Don't inundate a busy editor with quantity; quality will speak for itself. And don't be overly concerned if you haven't yet published in well-known periodicals; even a good piece from a campus or local paper, or an unpublished sample, can reveal your writing technique or subject expertise. If you have special qualifications or credentials for the subject, mention those in your letter.

You should expect a reply from the magazine, even if only a form letter. After a month has passed, you might want to write or phone to follow up, indicating to the editor's assistant that you would like a reply within two weeks so that you can go on to offer the idea elsewhere. And if the idea is rejected, that's exactly what you'll do; have a list at hand and send the query on to another magazine you've targeted as a possible outlet.

If you get an assignment, a number of magazines will request that a new writer take it "on speculation"—that is, they make no commitment to buy it until they see it. Others may want you to do something short before tackling a major article; some, such as *Ms.*, *Self*, and *Working Woman*, have short "newsletter," "gazette," or "watch" sections that use shorter news items. You can try breaking in by offering a short item in a brief, succinct letter. Other magazines now have "demographic" editions, in essence a special advertising supplement aimed at the higher-income reader; *McCall's* and *Redbook* are two. They are good places for freelance material. *Redbook* "Gold" takes articles on food, beauty care, and financial pieces, such as buying pearls or American antiques.

A few women's magazines don't operate on the standard query-the-articles-editor procedure. At *Ms.* magazine, in an effort to put egalitarian philosophy into practice, your idea must pass a commit-tee—with the result that replies tend to be slow. At *Cosmopolitan*, most story ideas are generated by the editors themselves, filed in looseleaf binders labeled "minor Non-Emotional," etc., and available for a writ-er's perusal by invitation only. *Cosmo* has accepted ideas from freelance queries, but those are the exception to the rule.

Once you have your assignment, expect a contract or confirming letter that specifies your subject, gives a deadline date and rate and terms of payment. Try to get an idea of the range of payments at the magazine, and then negotiate a fair price. If you are less experienced, expect it to be lower than what a regular contributor receives. And then give it your best shot, for once a door has opened, you're well on your way to writing for women's markets.

HOW-TO ARTICLES FOR THE WOMEN'S MAGAZINES by Helen Bottel

If you're adept at "how-to" with heart and a new twist; if you write lucidly, to the point, and with feeling; if you can find a different angle to an old theme; if you've got a hot new diet idea—then you have a good chance for publication in a woman's magazine.

These "liberated" days, it also helps to be female. A successful family relations writer I know has lately sensed reverse discrimination; "If my name were Norma instead of Norman," he comments, "I might make more sales."

While the "Seven Sisters" (*McCall's, Ladies' Home Journal, Woman's Day, Family Circle, Good Housekeeping, Redbook,* and *Better Homes and Garden*) now allow much more frankness, the *basic* subject matter hasn't changed radically in recent years. Emphasis remains on food, fashion, beauty, health, and home management on the (largely) staff-written side. Next come personality pieces, often out of Hollywood or New York. Then there's the freelancer's field, and a good three-fourths of it concerns "how to improve the quality of life for you and/or your loved ones," including such uplifting first-person articles as "Young Mother's Story" (*Redbook*) and "My Problem and How I Solved It" (*Good Housekeeping*).

Women's magazines also buy straight reporting about unusual in-stitutions, groups, or diseases; and they are a challenge because they require much research, considerable investigation, and the opportun-ity to learn. I've always been partial to the assignment that teaches me something new.

HOW-TO FOR HOW-TO'S

How do you write the "how-to"? As with all nonfiction, you start with the *hook*, a slam-bang beginning that catches immediate attention and leads into the *body* of the story. In the body you explain, list procedures, offer proof of their validity via anecdotes and quotes from experts, and instruct readers on how they can apply your ideas to their lives. Then you *close*, and the ending should also pack a wallop, preferably referring back to your initial paragraphs.

Hook, body, close—a simple formula that helps keep a writer on target.

A cardinal rule for magazine articles, the "how-to" in particular, is *avoid unnecessary wandering!* For example, if your title is "Can Self-Hypnosis Change Your Life?" don't distract your audience with a lengthy account of eighteenth-century mesmerism. Your job is to describe self-hypnosis; prove its worth via examples and human-interest items, noting its limitations as well as its advantages; give step-by-step instructions on how it can be achieved; make suggestions on specific ways the practitioner (your reader) will benefit.

Naturally, while you're researching the story you'll amass ten times more material than you need—and you'll be sorely tempted to stuff these fascinating bits of information in somewhere. If you must, do it in the first draft. Then reread and ruthlessly eliminate. No matter how well written, if it doesn't push forward the central theme—and in a "how-to" there must be only one theme—then it's worthless to this particular article. (But you can often use it in the next.)

Another essential rule for the how-to is *announce your intentions fast*, either via anecdote or a more direct approach. Too many writers (I'm one!) spend several hundred words tiptoeing up to the real point of the story. Sure, we feel these lovely phrases of ours set the mood, but editors think differently—and reach for their blue pencils. They understand that a busy magazine reader wants to know up front why she should continue reading, and whether the piece will fit her needs. Although a first-sentence "announcement" isn't imperative, do it soon. Anecdotes make fine hooks—just don't spread them over two or three pages before you get to your main point.

How to Find How-tos

Where do you get ideas for how-tos? Look at your own life. If you've found unique ways to juggle household and family duties with an outside job, share them. If you have a different angle on "beating the blues," shoot off a query. It isn't only in Erma Bombeck-type humor that you can make your hardships work for you. If something is wrong at home or abroad, then your efforts to right it (including advice you've gleaned from experts along the way) may make a good story.

How-to themes also derive from friends' experiences, newspaper items, local television features, and children. Whenever you exclaim, "Hey, that's a terrific idea!" or grouch, "There's got to be a better way!" the seed of a magazine article has been planted.

And if that seed doesn't grow enough to make a full-length story, consider the short-shorts that can earn anywhere from fifty to one thousand dollars, depending on the size of your item and the magazine. Magazines use brief items for a change of pace—also as fillers to intersperse among ads. *Good Housekeeping* likes one-pagers for its regional editions. A quick study of women's magazines will show you where the shorter pieces are welcomed and what types their editors want.

It goes without saying that hopeful writers must research their markets. Each women's magazine concentrates on a different type of woman: What *Cosmopolitan* wants, *Ms.* would probably abhor. A feature about older women wouldn't make *Redbook,* which aims at the under-36 crowd, but it might have a chance at *Good Housekeeping. Woman's World* is for the high-school-educated blue- and pink-collar woman of twenty-five to fifty-five; the *Ladies' Home Journal* is more sophisticated. *Family Circle* and *Woman's Day* like family-oriented material that *Glamour* would shun.

Only one thing do most women's magazines have in common: They're ever-searching for the no-fail, painless, healthy, taste-tempting PERFECT reducing diet, and while each month they claim to have found it, they seem always open to new contenders. If you have the ultimate "how-to-stay-slender" story, written lucidly and with feeling, send it nearly anywhere—you've got a sale!

WRITING A COLUMN FOR WOMEN: TIPS AND TECHNIQUES
by Catherine Lanham Miller

How do you become a columnist for the women's pages of a newspaper?

There is no one road to success. Some have worked long and hard to sell their columns to newspaper editors. And some have stumbled into it.

My skills had been honed by twelve years of writing advertising copy, mostly for women's products, when I left my nine-to-five office job to freelance for women's magazines, trading a weekly paycheck for the thrill of seeing my byline. I gravitated to nonfiction for the mass-circulation publications, the most comfortable transition from my advertising world.

One of my articles developed into a book, *How to Say Yes to Life: A Woman's Guide to Beating the Blahs*. Published by Simon and Schuster in 1971, the book came out about the time the feminist movement was picking up steam. And the philosophy therein was somewhat innovative for its day, stressing that every woman could be happier and have a more fulfilled life by developing her potential.

I soon became recognized as an expert on the subject of helping women live more positively and get more fun out of life. The *Philadelphia Inquirer* serialized the book with great fanfare. I traveled widely to promote the book, lectured extensively in all parts of the country, and created and presented my own seminars. The two-day "Identity" workshops, based on the ideas I had developed in my book, brought in experts to dig into the problems and find possible solutions for women participants.

The *Inquirer* then asked me to expand my thinking into a regular weekly column for their "Living" section. I accepted the challenge as a nice plus and as good promotion for my other projects. It seemed quite natural. I had *stumbled* into being a columnist, and it worked. However, after a year and a half the pressures of other commitments forced me to realize the column was taking too much of my time. So I regretfully said goodbye to the *Inquirer* and continued to write for women's magazines.

In 1980, circumstances suddenly brought me and my family to Carson City, Nevada—new town, new state, new world. My husband and two sons were now fulfilling a dream of their own—operating a family business in a part of the country new to us. But what happens to the transplanted writer, a virtual continent away from East Coast editors, publishers, and agents, with only telephones and less-than-perfect mail service to keep the lifelines open?

I was too much in shock from the uprooting to start any long-term projects immediately, but I knew I had to keep writing or shrivel away.

What does a writer in such a predicament do? This one went to the *Nevada Appeal*, Carson City's daily newspaper, with a circulation of 10,000. Yes, indeed, they would welcome a weekly women's-interest column of the sort I wrote for the *Inquirer*. And, they said, let's call it "Saying *Yes* to Life." (Still on the same old track!)

I thought long and hard before making the final decision. Now I knew what was involved in writing a weekly essay-type column—that it would fracture my time and concentration span, that it would erect an effective roadblock against tackling bigger projects. Knowing myself, I wouldn't be able to toss off a piece of junk each week, but would strive to create a quality product. Was that the best road for me to take?

I decided to go ahead with it for three reasons: 1. To keep myself at the typewriter, forcing myself to think creatively at least once a week. 2. To forge an identity for myself in town. 3. To have a forum for voicing my ideas, and the freedom to say it in my own style.

I knew I couldn't simply replay my former success. I felt a need to think, change, grow, take a new look at my responsibilities to my readers . . . and to myself.

NO MORE "WOMEN'S PAGES"

In the eighties *is* there such a thing as a "women's-interest" column? These days, the interests of men and women intertwine. Men read cooking columns, women read about how to service automobiles, and men read features just as avidly as women.

The trend today is away from "women's" and "society" pages. Now, "activities," "lifestyle," or "family" pages are in. Once it was perceived that men read the hard news, sports pages, business section, and comics, then went striding off to deal with important matters, while the women sat at home clipping recipes. We all know this picture is askew. Today both men and women deal with all facets of life and want to read about those facets in their newspapers.

As a columnist, it is my business to know what's on people's minds, then to tackle the matters I think I can handle. I don't write about science, or politics, or the oil situation in Saudi Arabia; these are not my fields of expertise. My original assignment was to write about subjects close to the hearts of women, and that's my turf. I continue to write about husbands and lovers (or lack of them), homes, jobs, children, in-laws, loneliness, boredom, physical fitness, beauty and grooming, retirement, money management, and leisure time. I do humor, drama, pathos, and nostalgia. I tackle alcoholism, infidelity, displaced homemakers, boring marriages, divorce, and teenage problems. I now realize I'm not writing to middle-aged stay-at-home women. I'm writing to senior citizens, junior high students, human beings of all ages. A woman's column? I don't think so. Instead, a people's column.

FINDING YOUR COLUMN STYLE

To become a successful columnist, it won't do to copy the subject and tone of another columnist's work. You must write a column that is uniquely your own, that blends your interests with your special style as a writer. To develop that column you must first analyze yourself and your abilities to determine what column style is right for you.

My kind of general-commentary weekly feature is perhaps the most difficult to keep going and eats up the most time. Under the umbrella of "Saying *Yes* to Life," I'm trying to accomplish a goal: to give the reader a positive thought, a whiff of fresh air that might make the day a little more enjoyable. I have boundaries that give my column direction and consistency. But it's still 750 words on a different subject every week, a carefully structured piece with a beginning, middle, and end.

If you want to write such a column, you must prepare it with a point of view, a slant that's your very own, and do this without being obnoxiously opinionated. Unlike the journalist who covers a beat, you won't have a network of sources who regularly supply you with nourishment. The column must be dredged up from within yourself. The columnist who follows this route must rely on his or her eyes, ears, intuition, and gut feelings, and must face a constant, unrelenting deadline each week.

What Kind of Column Will You Write?

- Are you a people watcher, with an interest in studying human beings and why they do things? Do you want to motivate, make people laugh, cry, feel? Then maybe a general commentary feature is what you should write.
- Or do you want to write exclusively about your field of expertise? Papers buy columns on travel, astrology, photography, law, money, gardening, consumerism, mental and physical health, political commentary, beauty, child care, cooking, bridge, books, art, music, sports, stamps, coins, and antiques. The list is endless.
- The "what's-going-on-around-town" column is popular in many papers, and is a joy to the paper's management (more advertising! more circulation!) because it mentions local names.

    There are various types: the society kind—who was seen at what party and what they were wearing; the over-the-back-fence kind—"yesterday I met Mary Brown at the bookstore, and she confided to me that . . . "; the type that reports on businesses—new restaurants, shopping malls, services—that would interest the general reader; there's the column that addresses itself to giving recognition to unsung heroes or people who are quietly doing good works.

And then there's the columnist who likes to stir things up and make waves. That columnist will comment, accuse or carry on about local politicians, civic leaders, businessmen, priding himself or herself on hitting nerves, methodically trying to pick fights in print, then sitting back and laughing as the angry mail comes in. Carefully researched, some of these can be helpful in righting wrongs within a community. Often, however, they are sloppily researched, badly written, and a disgrace to the writing profession. In a column of this kind, graceful writing is not as important as good reporting. The item, the scoop, is what gets read, and the more of them the better. Such a column is not written as a seamless structured piece, but a series of quick news flashes.

- The Question-and-Answer column, once it gets going, is probably one of the easier kinds to write because the readers generate the ideas. To do this, you need to qualify as an expert of some kind. "Dear Abby" and "Ann Landers" come to mind, but there are many kinds of such columns and most of the special-interest columns (see above) could be set up in this form.

Use your imagination. Research the town. What might readers like that isn't found in your local paper? How can you use your expertise to fill that need? One rule of thumb worth remembering is "write the kind of column you like to read."

TIPS ON COLUMN WRITING

Here are some of the most-asked questions about writing (and later, selling) a column, with answers from my own experience, from editors, and from other columnists, including members of the ASJA.

Are there special techniques for writing a column? Space is at a premium, newsprint is precious, newspaper readers tend to skim. So you must cut, cut, cut. Otherwise, in the essay type of column, use the same structure you'd use in any thoughtful piece of writing—a grabber opening, a well-thought-out main section, and a summation or surprise ending, or whatever works best to keep your reader with you.

My own style is to try for the conversational, one-to-one approach, as if I were writing my sister. I hope I never sound pedantic or preachy. I try to avoid long, complicated sentences, keeping the copy crisp, tight, readable and lively. And of course, as in any good writing, I try to find a fresh, original way to convey my ideas.

Where do I get my material? Keep your antenna up for thoughts, ideas, and scraps of conversation that could be shaped into a column.

You must be interested in people and what makes them tick. Talk to people, draw them out.

If you've been writing for a while, you may have files of rejected manuscripts, unfinished pieces, thoughts you never developed. Pick the best and use them! And your published work is a gold mine. Although legal restrictions may prevent you from using the material verbatim, who's to say you can't excerpt, update, revise, recycle?

If you're stuck, try leafing through current magazines or browsing through bookshelves—not to steal material, but to jostle your brain for ideas you can develop in your own way. Television can also provide fodder. I got mad at Andy Rooney of "60 Minutes" for a segment he did on women's handbags and wrote a column arguing with him. I try to watch Phil Donahue frequently, to see what's on people's minds.

Whatever presents itself during the course of your day, swirl it around in your head and ask yourself, "Could I use this?"

How far ahead must I work? I know some columnists who wait until the night before their deadline. I couldn't handle that, and usually manage to complete each piece four or five days ahead. Spontaneity, and what's happening now, is what keeps your material fresh. However, it's not a bad idea to have a few columns in reserve for dry spells, a case of flu, or a vacation. And it's certainly wise to keep an ongoing file of ideas so you'll never completely run out of ammunition. My own folder includes untidy notes on backs of envelopes, laundry slips, and matchbook covers.

How do I know to whom I'm talking? Your audience can be difficult to figure, because anybody who reads the paper may dip into it. Use your common sense, study your community, and try not to make obvious mistakes. If the area is heavily industrial, with a large percentage of blue-collar workers, you wouldn't write for the jet-set crowd. If it's a college town, you could get away with somewhat cerebral material. Readers in a farming community might not identify with inner-city problems or lesbian relationships.

In "Saying *Yes* to Life" I try never to write down to my readers. I give them my best writing and don't hesitate to talk about places they've never been, or ideas they may never have thought about before. But I do keep in mind some of my avid readers: the couple who runs the hamburger shop, the cop on the beat, the woman who cleans houses for a living. How can I say this so they will relate to it?

TIPS ON COLUMN SELLING

To many freelancers, writing a column must seem less formidable than selling it. Selling one article can take hard work and professionalism; how much more does it take to sell yourself to an editor as a columnist?

How do I get started? Approach the publisher or editor of your local newspaper, sending a letter outlining your proposal and your expertise. Ask for an appointment, and tell him you'll phone for a confirmed date. Take with you some samples of what you propose to do (maybe five or six columns) and any previously published material. If possible, have in mind a catchy name for your column. If interested, the editor will ask to keep the material to read. (You don't want him to scan it while you're sitting there.) Don't expect an on-the-spot decision; there will probably be a committee meeting before you get a go-ahead.

Should I sign a contract? In launching your new product, you may not be able to get the paper to agree to anything other than "either party may cancel with thirty days' notice." (And, as a beginner, do you really *want* to be tied to a whole year or more? You may get fed up and want to quit.) Many newspaper editors seem to think that a handshake is enough. An exchange of letters outlining your understanding of terms is a good idea.

How many times a week should my column run? Newspaper management will have something to say about that. But only you know how fast you write, how deep the well, how quickly you may be drained. One a week is not unusual. Six a week is superhuman!

What about money? In my judgment, remuneration for freelance columns is generally ridiculous, outrageous, and insulting to a professional writer. (How do *you* like thirty-five cents per column inch?) This situation seems to be general, and fairly inflexible, although I suppose in certain cases, writers manage to work out juicy deals.

Payment is often calculated by the newspaper's circulation. A publisher of an upstate New York paper with a circulation of 10,000 told me, "The most we would pay for a once-a-week column is three dollars." Another source quoted fifty cents per thousand circulation.

You're competing with syndicated columns. An editor will be apt to tell you, "We can get 'Ann Landers' five days a week for five dollars; we buy Jack Anderson's daily feature for six dollars per week." This, of course, is through a syndicate. Ann and Jack can afford these prices because they sell to several hundred newspapers.

To start, price should not be the main consideration. Your aim is to get published. As a beginner, your number one goal is to build your prestige and following. Consider your byline as part payment. Work out the best arrangement you can get, and insist on a reevaluation somewhere up the road.

Don't expect to make a living on your column when you first begin. You must have a salaried job, or an independent income, or other lucrative freelance work, or a spouse who foots the bills. Later it may be possible to increase your income by selling to more than one paper, which brings us to . . .

TIPS ON SYNDICATION

How can I get my column into more than one paper? You've proved to yourself and your editor that you can write a good column and keep it going. You start thinking, "As long as I'm doing all this work, I'd like to spread out to other papers."

What you're telling yourself is that you'd like to syndicate—either through an established organization, or on your own.

Unless you're a superstar, writing a syndicated column can be an underpaid grind, endurable only for the fringe benefits, which are sometimes considerable. Your name becomes known; book ideas may be easier to sell; magazine article assignments may come your way; lecture dates may be offered—all because you're a syndicated columnist.

The syndicate. Syndicates are businesses that specialize in selling the work of writers and artists to newspapers. They usually have a staff of salespeople who call on editors around the country. Backing up syndicate salespeople is a steady stream of printed promotional material. Syndicate and author/artist split the rewards, generally fifty fifty, although some syndicates pay the writer a salary and others buy material outright.

Before you go further, be sure the column you want to syndicate is an *anywhere, anytime* feature. It must be of general interest, with no geographical emphasis. The big syndicates sell to newspapers in all parts of the country and will automatically reject yours if it speaks with a regional accent. (You can self-syndicate on a regional basis, however.)

King Features is probably the largest of the syndicates, but there are many successful ones. To get a complete listing, write for the *Editor and Publisher Syndicate Directory*, care of *Editor and Publisher*, 575 Lexington Avenue, New York, New York 10022. *Writer's Market* (Writer's Digest Books) provides a valuable rundown of syndicates, their current needs, and the names of editors to approach. Additional information is available in *Working Press of The Nation* (National Research Bureau).

Unless you have inside information, deciding which syndicate to approach is like picking a physician out of the Yellow Pages. Only trial and error will prove which is right for you. Don't worry too much about that right now, because getting any syndicate to take your work is difficult for the beginner. Their standards are exacting, even more so in today's economy, with less space available and budgets tight. And the competition is fierce. The giant syndicates get from 200 to 400 proposals a week from people very much like you.

What if you decide to try it anyway?

Set up an appointment with an editor at the syndicate. If going in person is impossible, send a persuasive proposal letter with about six of your best columns (400-800 words). If they've appeared in print, send tearsheets or good photocopies of tearsheets. Remember, you're selling yourself. Make the package neat and professional, and include a self-addressed stamped envelope.

Newspapers who buy your column through a syndicate will likely pay downwards of fifteen dollars per week for six columns a week. (So you can imagine the payments for one a week.) Smaller papers pay less.

If your column is picked up by over one hundred papers of fair-sized circulation, you might earn $400 to $500 per week. The syndicate helps itself to an equal sum for selling your work.

If you sign with a syndicate (a legal contract is very much a part of the process) you should ask for a monthly statement on all subscribing papers and the rates they're paying. When haggling over the contract, you should try for an arrangement that gives a weekly salary or minimum guarantee in addition to the monthly split.

Writers who sign with syndicates are handicapped unless they are backed up with adequate promotion and aggressive selling. No promotion, no new sales, no more cash. The syndicate executives are hardboiled businesspeople, with little sensitivity to writer's block, illness, or family problems. If you sign with them, you produce. And that's that. Of course, they take all the sales hassle off your back, leaving you to concentrate on writing.

Self-syndication. You may not be able to interest a syndicate in your work. Or you may decide you'd rather keep personal control of the column. Well, there's another way to spread your wings, and that's self-syndication.

The marketing of your own column makes you an entrepreneur. Says one woman who has sold her cooking column to some forty papers: "It's a very time-consuming but rewarding experience. You are both the sales force and the creator of the work. You must be geared to wearing different hats." A pair of columnists, specializing in microwave cooking, finally sold to a metropolitan daily. "We were very naive about the newspaper business," one said. "If we had known then how difficult it is to have a weekly column accepted by a newspaper, we would never have attempted it."

If you go this route, no longer are you strictly a writer. Now you are dealing with promotion, artwork, printing, direct selling, billing, and bookkeeping. And above all, clerical work, to keep from sending the same column to the same paper three times in a row.

Here are some suggestions for starting the self-syndication process:

- Get an okay from your base editor. You must keep this important person on your side; you need that "flagship" paper.
- If there are a lot of neighboring towns in your area, you might want to approach papers nearby, thus creating a ripple effect. (But not *too* close. Watch out for overlapping circulation areas.)
- Perhaps you have influential friends in other parts of the country. Ask them to introduce your work to their hometown papers.
- Your hometown paper may belong to a newspaper group, for the trend today seems to be away from independent ownership and toward group management (some loosely, some tightly controlled). If your paper is part of such a group, ask your editor or publisher to recommend your work to the others.
- Branch out to other newspaper groups, getting names and addresses from the *International Yearbook of Editor and Publisher* at your library. (Warning: Newspaper editors tend to job-hop; thus the directory cannot be strictly up-to-date. If you can handle the expense, dial the newspaper for the correct name.)
- If you have a regional preference, you could approach dailies in your favorite state. (Caution: Although your first thought may be to hit the largest city in the state, the big-city paper may insist on exclusivity, barring you from surrounding smaller towns. You might be better off financially to concentrate on peripheral areas.)

However you plan to spread out, you must have the right tools to sell your product. Accept the fact that you must spend some money to assemble a compact, eye-pleasing piece of promotion to mail or leave with editors. Here's one way you might do it:

- Use an inexpensive cardboard folder to contain the various sheets.
- Write a cover letter and have it printed on the best-looking letterhead stationery. Make your copy crisp and confined to one page. For easy reading, divide into subheads, such as *what do I write about? . . . what's different about this column? . . . what's my background? . . . what are the mechanics of buying this column? . . . why should your newspaper buy this column?* The letter should be a real piece of advertising promotion.
- Include a letter of recommendation from your current editor.

- Choose samples of your column. Because tearsheets are messy and inclined to turn yellow, have them photocopied.
- If you have received complimentary letters from readers, excerpt some of the best quotes and photocopy them.
- Include a rate sheet, listing prices for your column.
- Slip in a self-addressed, stamped return postcard to make it easy for the editor to say yes.

So you launch your first mailing, sending your material cold to a complete stranger, a busy editor or publisher who is coping with newsprint shortages, unemployment in his community, falling circulation, and lack of advertising. Two or three weeks pass, and you don't hear from him. Has he tossed your beautiful material into the wastebasket, or is it still on his desk? The only way to know is to phone him. He may be curt and uninterested. But more than likely he'll be courteous. If he says no, he'll probably explain it's because of budget difficulties, or because he's already using a column similar to yours.

Or maybe you get a taker. Hurray, you're in business! By all means, send a friendly little note saying how much you'll enjoy being in that particular paper. Clear up details of the transaction: how and when you'll bill him, how you'll handle the mailing of the columns. (Easiest for you is to mail in manuscript form, perhaps a month's supply at a time.) Offer a glossy photo for use with the headline.

Once you have a few new papers in your stable, you may want to put together a simple mailing piece trumpeting your increase in circulation. (Or that may be the time to take your already successful column to the big syndicates.)

Little by little, inch by painful inch, you find yourself to be a syndicated columnist.

WHAT'S IT LIKE TO BE A COLUMNIST?

The decision to tackle a column and make it pay in terms of satisfaction and monetary reward is not one to be made lightly. It should not be regarded as a little sideline, to dabble in when there's nothing else to do. You should approach it as a commitment that will take a number of working hours each week. And accept the fact that it will occupy your thoughts in the shower, driving down the road, when preparing dinner, or enduring a sleepless night.

Being a Columnist—Debits

- The low pay. I know I would be paid better for my time if I were doing magazine articles, books, or business writing (brochures, ads, sales letters, newsletters).

- The dissipation of impact by writing too many things on too many subjects. If all this effort were being expended on one subject, rather than a weekly smorgasbord, I could produce a book that might get me on the bestseller list. I have just filed my 150th column within a three-year period. 150×750 words $=$ 112,500 words. *That's a fat book!* (Of course, if any publisher becomes interested in doing a collection of my columns, I'm ready.)
- The headlines that appear over my column. If I were to write them, I'd spend a lot of time making sure they were just right. Instead they are written by newspaper copyeditors, who produce headlines to fit the space available to them. Such editors grind out one head after another, under crushing deadline pressure. The hastily concocted results often do more harm than good.
- Typographical errors. I deliver my freshly typed, error-free manuscript promptly, and never see it again until the paper is dropped on my doorstep. The typos I often find in my stories cause me great pain, and sometimes embarrassment. Newspaper readers tend to believe these mistakes are the fault of the writer, and some of them make me look stupid and uninformed. Why all the boo-boos? Pure human error. Despite the marvels of the computer age, somebody must type my copy into a word-processing terminal. And if that somebody has a hangover or a cold, there's a possibility of hitting a wrong key or omitting a whole line. It's the editor's responsibility to correct any mistakes in the proofed copy. What if that editor is being pressured by the corner office, or having a fight with a spouse? Typos in my column!
- Late-night telephone calls. Although newspaper policy frowns on giving out home phone numbers, somehow they get mine. And they call—to tell me how much they enjoyed yesterday's piece, or to argue about some point I've made. I like feedback from readers, but why can't these calls be made during the day?
- The always-there-ness of a constant weekly deadline, the never being able to goof off completely. It's like being a schoolkid with perpetual homework, and guilt gnaws at me if I'm not working.
- The worry about running out of juice. What if sometime the well goes dry?
- The here today, gone tomorrow aspect of my work. A magazine is on the newsstand for a week or month. A book has a

much longer life. But the daily newspaper—today's treasure, tomorrow's trash. In our community, many people heat their homes with woodburning stoves. On winter mornings, I look out over the valley and see smoke curling from hundreds of chimneys. On Thursdays, I regard the scene sorrowfully: "There goes last night's column starting fires all over town."

Being a Columnist—Rewards

- The byline and photo, proclaiming to the world that you are a person with something to say.
- Freedom to write in your own style, without having to stick to anyone's rigid rules. I enjoy trying different imaginative ways of expressing a point of view. I can talk to my great-grandfather's picture, interview a dog, compare myself to a fairytale character, or write a letter to a house—all of which I have done. I do this while always trying to improve the rhythm of words and phrases; improvising in my own special way but always getting back to the basic theme at the end; sticking strictly within what I consider to be the boundaries of good taste; never revealing identities if there's the slightest question; trying never to hurt anyone.
- Knowing that when you have something important to say, you'll see it in print quickly.
- Your column provides entrée to just about anyone you want to meet.
- The pleasure of developing ongoing relationships with readers. A column is short enough that most people read it all, and if you've done your job you'll get your point across. Readers get to feel they know you intimately, even though they may never have set eyes on you. Having a lot of friends around town is nice.
- The possibility of generating interest in your other activities without sacrificing integrity. (I'm not doing that at the moment, but I might someday.) A physician writes a medical column and gets many new patients. A nurseryman writes a little gardening column and customers flock from miles around. A community-minded columnist singlehandedly gets the town behind an important new project.
- The recognition that, by your good writing, you're stimulating readers, getting them to stretch their minds. With my own column, the goal is to get my readers to *feel* something—to laugh, or cry, or get angry, or say, "I know how that is, I've been there," or to decide, "I'm going to do something about

that." It's a powerful stimulus, knowing you have that kind of clout.

The late beloved sports columnist Red Smith summed it all up in his usual style: "Writing a column is easy. All you have to do is open a vein and bleed it out!"

ROAD MAP
TO THE WOMEN'S MAGAZINES
by Bonnie Remsberg

A frequent, favorite topic at writers' conferences is "What Do the Women's Magazines Want?" In more than twenty years of writing for the women's magazines, I have found that there is a simple way to answer that question. Every month, the editors of the women's magazines give you a guide to what they want. They publish a magazine. What it contains is what they want.

That may sound too simplistic. Would-be writers often press for the mysterious, arcane secrets that enable some of us to sell regularly to the major magazines for women and leave others in the "slush pile," that dreaded heap of hundreds of manuscripts, each stained with tears and hope, that comes into every magazine office every month. I wish there were such a secret, and that I, and I alone, knew it. I wish I were that smart. I wish it were that easy.

I'm not. It isn't. I got started writing for the women's magazines exactly the same way everybody else does. I read the magazines until I felt I had overdosed on carrot-cake recipes and ten-day diets, until I could tie a scarf a hundred and one different ways, until I could personally make twenty-two toys out of egg cartons.

It helped that I was a reader of the women's magazines, in the literal sense, because I *did* want to know how to tie a scarf and make a toy. But when I say *read* the magazines, I mean it in the same way your astronomy professor advised you to *read* the night sky. I mean *study.*

When I began writing for magazines, we had a tiny baby and very little money. With the baby sleeping in a stroller, I would stand in a friendly neighborhood drugstore for hours, reading magazines.

The baby is about to graduate from college, and I can now afford to buy the magazines and take them home, but the basic process hasn't changed. To know what the magazines want, I still have to read them. And so do you.

READ BETWEEN THE ARTICLES

Reading *between* the articles may be even more useful than reading the features and fillers themselves. Read the ads especially closely. You know, of course, that advertising salespeople have to know *exactly* who is reading their magazine, in order to know how much they can charge for space and at whom to aim their sales efforts. If you see page after page of ads for nursing bottles and for highchairs in a magazine, you can be pretty sure that magazine has a high proportion of young mamas in its readership. Then you can focus your queries on subjects that interest them. If you see a number of ads for convenience foods, you are looking at a magazine which goes to women who work outside their homes in fairly high proportions. You can probably tell more about your would-be readers from the ads than you can from any writers' guidelines sheet the editor might send you.

You will also, if you read the ads faithfully and meticulously, discover something else that may surprise you. The women's magazines all differ considerably from one another. *Family Circle* is different from *Woman's Day* which is different from *Ladies' Home Journal* which is different from *Good Housekeeping* which is drastically different from *Seventeen*. And so on for each category and genre of magazine.

The wise writer studies these differences carefully until they are ingrained. This does not mean that the same basic idea might not sell at each of those magazines, but it would be handled differently, slanted differently, approached differently in each case. Writers and editors who advise you not to simply send out the same idea or query, wholesale, to a bunch of markets, know what they are talking about. The reason is not that editors don't like to get dog-eared or photocopied material. The reason is that mass-produced ideas don't sell. If an idea is so vague and undefined it can fit anywhere, then it won't be sharply enough focused to *sell* anywhere.

Sit down and talk, face to face, with any editor and he or she will tell you details about the magazines's readers that will astonish you. Magazine editors, and also advertising departments, know how many of their readers work, and at what. They know how many of them smoke, and what. They know how much they make, and how much of it they spend on food, how many children they have, and sometimes (just ask Helen Gurley Brown) what they do in bed.

You can figure this stuff out too. Read the magazine the way you would read a road map. Leave no detail unnoticed. That one tiny detail might tell you something important you should know about the reader. And once you have immersed yourself in these details, once that magazine's readers become as familiar to you as your neighbor, or your mother, or your best friend, then selling to it becomes a matter of simple hard work, of applying the seat of the pants to the seat of the chair and staying there until you get it right.

THE RIGHT ATTITUDE

A journalism professor once told me, "You cannot write with alum in your soul." It took me years to figure out what he was talking about. For a while, I thought he meant bitterness, and I assumed the advice was a cute warning about trying to pour out your own disappointments and frustrations on paper. But after years of writing women's magazine articles, watching others do the same, and listening to the talk of people who wanted to but couldn't, I've come up with a new interpretation. I think what he meant (and I'm absolutely convinced he was right) is that you cannot have contempt for your reader or it won't come out right.

You would be amazed if I told you how many people I have met who talk enviously of selling to women's magazines because of their nice fat checks, but who regard those magazines with scorn. "Of course," one lofty, would-be writer once told me, "I wouldn't *read* those magazines, but I sure would like to sell them a few pieces to pay the rent." Sorry. It won't work.

An editor with that attitude wouldn't last long at a magazine, and neither will you. You don't have to bake your own bread to write for *Family Circle*. You *do* have to realize that warm, loving, intelligent people read the magazine, and that they are deserving of your best, most thoughtful work. Anything else won't sell.

An examination of the mail that comes in response to a well-thought-out article on a particular social issue in any prominent women's magazine you care to name would convince you of this point. By talking down to women, by writing down to women, by *looking* down on women, you do yourself a disservice and damage your chances of surfacing from the mound of query letters.

Which leads me to the overall point to be made by this brief essay. If you have a modicum of writing talent, a typewriter, and enough capital for several sheets of postage stamps, the only other truly important commodity you must possess for success with the women's magazines is *a positive attitude*.

Let me tell you a story. When that same baby, referred to earlier, had just been born, I remember holding her in one arm while I proofread a manuscript with the other. It was an article about girl gangs, written on speculation, for the *Ladies' Home Journal*.

It was rejected.

Twenty-two years later, I flew to England twice to cover an international scoop. The story was the birth of the first American test-tube baby, and it was a cloak-and-dagger operation worthy of the CIA: keeping the story a secret; sweating out the labor pains and the printers' deadlines; smuggling myself and a photographer into the London hospital; writing the story on a borrowed typewriter in a hotel room; flying, manuscript and photos in hand, to New York. If I ever felt like Brenda Starr, that was it.

The story, with cover photo, made a big splash in—of course—the *Ladies' Home Journal.* Can you imagine how I felt walking in to the magazine's office in New York, being hailed as a conquering hero?

In those twenty-two years nothing spectacular had occurred to change me. I hadn't been visited by the talent fairy, or anything else. I had just kept slogging, throwing away the rejection slips and coming back for more.

Now, I don't like rejection any more than you do. I may hate it even worse. But if I hadn't had the memory of that early rejection, I can tell you, the triumph wouldn't have tasted nearly as sweet.

It would also not have been possible. I *learned* a lot from that rejected manuscript (and the others that followed). I learned a lot about interviewing, about construction, about slanting. I learned about vagueness and how it can trip you up. I learned about staying with something until you get it right.

Lots of people don't learn these lessons. Lots of people do. The ones who do sell the articles. You'll see their names again and again.

Sometimes, when I'm doing an interview, after a couple of hours the subject will say, "Well, you should have enough by now for a whole book." This lets me know that person will never write a book.

Things are always harder than you think they are going to be. They always take more time than you think they are going to.

One final thought, on the subject of writing for women's magazines, or anything else for that matter. Sometimes starry-eyed people will say, "Gee, you're a writer. How exciting. You must love to write."

I feel it is necessary to be honest with such deluded souls, so I tell them the truth. "No," I tell them. "I hate to write. It's awful. It's hard work.

"What I like is . . . having written."

Additional Resources

American Association of University Women, 2401 Virginia Ave. NW, Washington, DC 20037. Provides information on women's issues, health, equity, women in government, peace and national security issues. Offers aid in arranging interviews, annual reports, brochures and pamphlets, informational newsletters, press kits. Publications include *The Graduate Woman* (bimonthly) and *Action Alert* (semimonthly).

Child Welfare League of America, Inc., Informational Resource Services, 67 Irving Place, New York, NY 10003. Conducts research; administers special projects such as Permanent Families for Children; publishes a journal and other professional literature; sponsors annual training conferences; provides consultation; maintains a library and information service in New York office and a public affairs office in Washington, DC. Provides information on all aspects of child welfare services. Copies of CWLA's publications list, audiovisual catalog, brochures, and pamphlets are free upon request.

Federation of Organizations for Professional Women, 2000 P St. NW, Suite 403, Washington, DC 20036. Provides information on women scholars, women's rights leaders, sexual harassment, women and psychotherapy, directory of women's organizations, public policy impact on professional women. Publications include *A Woman's Yellow Pages: 570 Organizations Concerned with Women's Issues, Women and Psychotherapy: Consumer Handbook*, and a Sexual Harassment Kit.

Feminist Writers' Guild, P.O. Box 9396, Berkeley, CA 94709. Women writers (published and unpublished) interested in sharing information and experiences. Maintains networking system for members' exchange of specific needs and services. Local chapters organize their own activities, which include writers' retreats, publication of anthologies, workshops, readings. Bestows annual Woman of Promise Award to a previously unpublished writer. Publishes a newsletter and *Words in Our Pocket: The Feminist Writers' Guild Handbook on How to Get Published and Get Paid*.

Home Economics Reading Service, Inc., 1341 G St. NW, Washington, DC 20005. Information available from 1,350 daily metropolitan newspapers on homemaking interests and publicity. Provides advisory and analytical information on food, household equipment, home furnishings, styles.

Homemakers' Equal Rights Association, 48 Rollingwood Dr., Voorhees, NJ 08043. Works to raise the legal and social status of homemakers and to change inequitable laws that govern the married woman. Provides advisory, historical, and interpretative information. Offers brochures and pamphlets, information newsletters, press kits, research assistance, statistics.

International Women's Writing Guild, Box 810, Gracie Station, New York, NY 10028. Sponsors writing conferences and retreats on the east and west coasts. Facilitates manuscript submissions to New York literary agents. Is conducting "a talent bank" pilot project, a job placement effort to place women in writing-related work. Publications include *Network* (six per year), *Writing as an Act of Faith* (monograph), and *The Ethics of Writing: Conflict with Conscience.*

National Center for Family Studies, Clearinghouse on Family Policy & Programs/Clearinghouse on Family Ministries, The Catholic University of America, Washington, DC 20064. Provides bibliographical, how-to, and referral information on family-related subjects. Offers brochures and pamphlets, informational newsletters, research assistance, statistics. Publications include *American Family: National Action Overview* and *American Catholic Family: The Newsletter of National, Diocesan and Parish Family Ministries.*

National League of American Pen Women, 1300 17th St. NW, Washington, DC 20036. Maintains biographical archives and 3,000-volume library. Offers scholarships; conducts seminars; sponsors research programs. Publications include *The Pen Woman* and a quarterly newsletter.

National Organization for Women, 425 13th St. NW, Suite 1048, Washington, DC 20004. Offers aid in arranging interviews, statistics, placement on mailing list, newsletter, photos, press kit. Publications include *NOW Times.*

Wider Opportunities for Women, 1511 K St. SW, Suite 345, Washington, DC 20005. Provides technical assistance, public education, and information related to women's employment. Offers aid in arranging interviews, biographies, statistics, brochures and pamphlets, placement on mailing list, press kits.

Women's Bureau, Department of Labor, 200 Constitution Ave., Washington, DC 20210. Aims to foster and promote women in the work force. Offers statistics, brochures and pamphlets, publications list, technical assistance to organizations.

Women in Communications, Inc., Box 9561, Austin, TX 78766. Provides historical, how-to, and trade information on the communications industry. Offers brochures and pamphlets, placement on mailing list, newsletter, press kits. Publications include professional papers, job and salary survey, careers booklet, and *PRO/COMM, The Professional*

Communicator, a national "magapaper" for members and subscribers ($12/year).

Women in Transition, 112 S. 16th St., 7th Floor, Philadelphia, PA 19102. Provides information on abused women, displaced homemakers, separation and divorce, widowhood, midlife transition, remarriage, marital counseling, career readiness skills, group process skills, single parenting, singlehood, infertility. Publications include *A Facilitator's Guide to Working with Separated and Divorced Women* and *Stepping Out to Work,* a career-readiness curriculum for low-income women.

Working Women's Institute, 593 Park Ave., New York, NY 10021. Provides information on sexual harassment on the job and in education. Offers annual reports, brochures and pamphlets, informational newsletters, library facilities, placement on mailing lists, press kits, research assistance, statistics, telephone reference services. Publications include research reports, brief bank of legal cases, legal publications, reprint service checklist, bibliography, research clearinghouse, legislative checklist.

Chapter Thirteen

WRITING ABOUT FOOD AND NUTRITION

Everyone must eat, so if you think cooking is the spice of life, the writing opportunities—and the challenge—are here for you. Although this market is exacting, it's also voracious—according to a recent *New York Times* survey, cookbooks consistently outsell everything but the Bible.

In addition to the periodicals devoted to epicurean feasts for gourmets, and quick-but-delicious meals for chefs who hold down full-time jobs outside the kitchen, most magazines—general and specialized—use food features which cater to their audiences. Unique party menus and ethnic delights for the upscale slicks, cookery basics for young people, economical and nutritious meals for the women's magazines, campfire cooking for the sportsman, and vegetarian recipes for "new age" publications, are just a few examples.

Many would-be food writers striving to get published have overflowing recipe boxes they're sure could be transformed into a cookbook the world is waiting for. These writers fail to understand the basic differences between a recipe that works for family and friends and one that deserves public attention. It's a long journey from a handful of "good" recipes to getting that collection past the editor and into a published magazine or book. Nowadays it's not enough to be a good cook—with the greater emphasis on low-calorie and healthy diets, you need some technical knowledge, too.

If your interests lie in the field of nutrition, you have your work cut out for you. It's been established that 110 million Americans are overweight; nutritionists are striving mightily to reverse our appalling eating habits. Currently, the norm for an American adult is a blood cholesterol level between 200 and 275 milligrams per deciliter; desirable levels, say officals of the American Heart Association, probably are below 200. In this land of hotdogs, hamburgers, and arteriosclerosis, the popular national diet with its fast foods, fried foods, and junk foods can be changed—it's a matter of public education. That, of course, is where nutrition writers come in.

How, then, do you get started? You do what all freelancers do: discover a need and fill it. The writers whose experiences you are about to read have done just that—from soup to nuts.

WRITING ABOUT FOOD
by Arline Inge

If there is one piece of advice most often handed down to aspiring writers, it is "write what you know." And in these days of special-interest publishing, expertise is everything.

Expertise comes to us from various sources—educational background, recreational interests, professional endeavors, and just plain living. One area in which we all claim first-hand knowledge is food. And food, especially these days, is a fertile area for freelance writers. New cookbooks are needed constantly to keep up with ever-changing styles of cooking, eating, and living. Food magazines are proliferating, and general-interest magazines are finding food sections invaluable in holding reader—and advertiser—interest. Newspapers, of course, must churn out food and restaurant sections to serve both their readers and their supermarket and restaurant advertisers. And all these writing markets (newspapers somewhat less so) are open to freelancers.

START IN THE KITCHEN

With everyone an expert and markets literally gobbling up culinary material, you'd expect the door to success in food writing to be wide open. And it is, but only for those who know the password. That word is *cooking*. Any writer who aspires to substantial and continued success in food writing had better be a cook first and a wordsmith second. Knowing when to turn a pancake brings more points from editors than knowing how to turn a phrase. Magazines and newspapers featuring food are service oriented and bent on sending readers into the kitchen to use the products that appear on their advertising pages. So editors are looking for articles built around recipes—recipes that are inviting and original, that are well constructed and sensible, and that bring satisfying results to readers who try them. Many food magazines, no matter how glossy their graphics or delightful their prose, anxiously add up the number of recipes they give readers in each issue as a measure of success.

Of course, there are other kinds of food writing—restaurant reviewing, travel writing, even straight interviews with food authorities—in which the writer appears to do nothing more than ask a few questions and push the button on the tape recorder. But successful features invariably are the work of writers with the high level of culinary connoisseurship that stems from familiarity with the kitchen. A restaurant reviewer must be able to identify ingredients and cooking methods as well as flavor components of a given dish in order to discuss it in depth. The travel writer, called upon to collect recipes from restaurateurs or private individuals, has to be able to evaluate them as to originality, quality, and adaptability in the home kitchen before turning them in to an editor. And a reporter, of course, must know how to ask the right questions and elaborate upon the answers.

Lucky is the food writer with some of the following elements in his or her background. This check list will help you measure your own chances for success.

Are you (or have you ever been) a:

1. Restaurant cook, chef, or home caterer?
2. Food hobbiest who reads recipes instead of novels in bed?
3. Graduate of a culinary college or cooking or baking school courses (preferably in a number of specialties)?
4. Holder of a degree in food home economics?
5. Professional recipe developer for food companies or ad agencies?
6. Heir to collections of recipes from family or friends?
7. Possessor of an ethnic family cooking background, or have you lived and cooked abroad or in "foody" regions like the southern United States?
8. Expert on nutrition and recipe development in the growing health field?
9. Wine expert with an interest in cooking, able to take advantage of the growing awareness of the interplay of wine and food?

What about literary ability? It helps, of course, to be able to treat your subject with respect and to write informative, entertaining, and literate prose. But even if you lack some of these basics, if you have a knack for angles and a nose for trends—and can get together ten knockout recipes—you'll find that editors will be happy to supply the rest.

COOK UP A SPECIALTY IN FOOD WRITING

Once you've determined that you have the qualifications for success in food, how do you break in? The best way—as is the case in many other writing fields—is to establish yourself as an authority on the subject. Some simple ways are to build a reputation as a great home cook and entertainer, or as a neighborhood caterer. If you are a chef or cooking teacher, that's even better. Armed with credentials, you can easily bring yourself to the attention of local editors. I suggest starting with the local newspaper or city magazine, because the editors will have a local orientation. (One of the simplest ways to arouse the interest of an editor, by the way, is to prepare a sample of the food you plan to query her or him about and send some with your story. It really works!) Once you've built a portfolio of published clippings locally, you are ready to make proposals to editors of regional or national publications and books. (Since book ideas are more difficult to sell—major investments ride on each book venture—I suggest holding back on book proposals until you have built a solid reputation with magazine articles.)

To make an initial query (and basically, the method I outline should work for most magazines), first be certain you have studied your market both for its level of culinary sophistication and level of its readership interest. It's most important to determine whether you are addressing, at one end of the scale, an audience of gourmets willing to spare no expense of time or money to furnish an exquisite table, or, at the other end, working people with families to feed and little spare time or food budget. Audiences can be broken down in countless ways: the bachelor cook, the dieting cook, the party cook, the teen cook, the meal-in-minutes cook, the ethnic cook, and on and on.

Once you've slanted your idea, you are ready to compile your packet. This should consist of a letter that includes a brief summary of your credentials, or a letter plus résumé sheet. There should always be a fistful of clippings or photocopies of your published work that most closely illustrate the article and recipe-writing ability you will bring to the new assignment. The query itself should be concise, but full enough to give the editor a very good idea of how the piece will be focused and developed. Include a list and description of the recipes you plan to use and, if possible, enclose one or two recipes fully worked out. Some editors will merely eyeball them; others will actually try them in their test kitchens as part of their evaluation of the total project.

Time and time again, editors pick up a promising proposal from an unknown, consider it a while, then toss it back into the rejection pile simply because the writer hasn't provided enough information to warrant further investigation. For a first submission, I even advise sending a completed piece on speculation—not in hope of making a sale, since it is difficult to know what subject matter a publication is looking for at any given time (though sales *are* made that way), but because a well-written and -conceived food piece is your best audition for future assignments.

If this appears to characterize food editors as overcautious, or even incompetent to make editorial judgments, let's look at the special problems of the food publishing business. Publications dealing in food are under extreme pressure to ensure the accuracy and validity of their information. A magazine or food section whose recipes resulted in costly and frustrating failures in the reader's kitchen would have as much chance of survival as a TV guide full of schedule errors. Food is expensive, time is precious, and readers know what tastes good. Therefore, in addition to the pencil editing and editorial conference time that is devoted to any magazine manuscript, food editors must test and retest recipes, writing and rewriting instructions to ensure against reader failures. Time wasted on manuscripts that prove faulty in the recipe area is held against writers just as much as illogical writing and unreliable research is. For these reasons—and many others that become clear only when one gets deeper into food and recipe writing—the best food writer is the person who carries spatula in one hand and pencil in the other. And this is a rare and coveted bird. Editors are out there looking for that bird—and they are hungrier, believe it or not, than he or she is.

GET COOKING!
by Helen Worth

Writing about food, wine, and spirits isn't the easiest way to earn a living. But true professionals are few, and there are many avenues open. These include freelance magazine and newspaper feature writing, product reporting for associations, reports and technical papers for corporations, recipe creation and food styling for advertising and public relations agencies, and book publication. Reviews of restaurants and books on food and wine are usually staff-written. Writing successfully in any of these areas can lead to radio and/or television reporting.

Not incidentally, some of the most eminent food and wine writers are men. And the prestigious metropolitan papers for which they write give them considerable power. Consider, for example, the *New York Times* food editor, Craig Claiborne, and the *San Francisco Examiner*'s Harvey Steinman. A man, again—Bob Misch—writes a column on food and wine for the *Women's News Service Syndicate*.

Classics on wine include *Grossman's Guide to Wine, Beers, and Spirits,* by Harold Grossman (Charles Scribner's Sons), and the *Encyclopedia of Wine,* by Frank Schoonmaker (Hastings House). Both books have gone into multiple printings.

Anthony Dias Blue writes regularly on wine and spirits for *Bon Appétit* and reports on those subjects for CBS network radio. Stendahl (a pen name) covers that ground for WNCN, New York City's classical music station. The monetary icing on the cake is earned by performers (an art in itself), like Graham Kerr, who gourmet-gallops marvelously on national television. Not at all incidentally, this, and writing, are rich fields for perks. Samples of food, wine, and cooking equipment come regularly to your door.

Prerequisites for this career are enjoyment and appreciation of food and spirits, an active imagination, and an excellent memory. Add to these a clear, terse—yet lively—writing style. Imagination allows food writers to personalize recipes and to write original and tantalizing leads.

Intensive research provides imagination's wings. Creating and testing recipes are important (and expensive) parts of that research. Culinary skills and kitchen labor with your own pots and pans—the tools of your trade—are imperative for writing about these subjects with intelligence and assurance. Also, you must be able to arrange food and tables artistically.

Look to your library for research in this field. Then build a specialized library by purchasing books you find especially useful. If only one or two recipes in a cookbook intrigue you, or if you find only a few provocative quotes in other works, note these on 3x5-inch index cards.

A shoebox file and master cards for labeling categories will soon grow apace. The categories can include as many headings as you find sensible and convenient. For instance: Soups; Desserts, Frozen; Wines, Varietal; History, Forks, first use of; etc.

Examine basic college textbooks on food, and books dealing with the physics and chemistry of cooking. You don't have to memorize the H_2O-type formulas—these books explain scientific formulae in perfectly good, understandable English. Books dealing with the physics and chemistry of food provide an understanding of cooking—the how, what, why, when, where—an understanding that I call the reasons behind the recipes. They are spelled out in my *Cooking Without Recipes*—a book I needed as an educational adjunct for students of my Helen Worth Cooking School.

Scientific knowledge is invaluable when testing, writing, or editing recipes. For instance, why should all fish and shellfish be cooked at low temperatures? Why does air beaten into egg whites make a soufflé rise? Then there is ongoing nutrition information (which, unfortunately, experts often wryly admit, changes with the daily mail). But knowledge of the latest dictates is an imperative.

Feast on Books

Books on food history, economics, and anthropology also are writing aids. Probably every book you read will lead you to others proving of equal value and interest. Naturally this background reading will not come close to a chair-edge whodunit, but the only way to provide knowledge is to soak it up first.

My college major was English literature and composition. Until I married, I was unaware of my interest in, and love of, cooking. It began, I finally determined, when, as a child, I followed my adored grandmother—a superb cook—around in the kitchen. All unknowing, I had watched and I had learned.

Following my marriage, a literate cornucopia of elegant recipes, *June Platt's Party Cookbook* (Houghton Mifflin), was brought to my attention and started me in my career. I also attribute my career to Mrs. Platt's fastidious and charming writing. I reasoned that if her work was so fascinating, I might find others. And indeed I did!

Led on, I read between thirteen and fifteen books a week. Books on the science of cooking, books on wine and, of course, cookbooks. These last contained so many recipes that sounded delicious, I couldn't resist trying them. I invited friends to enjoy and share the results. Shortly, many of them asked me to teach *them* how to cook, too. The teaching led to my first book, *The Down-on-the-Farm Cookbook*. Incidentally, when I teach, I wonder how I can prefer to write. When I write, I wonder how I can prefer to teach.

In the article, "Recipe for a Cookbook Writer: A Rage to Write/Cook," which I wrote for the *Authors Guild Bulletin*, I said:

Learning about food *can* be continuous, because it is a subject impossible to isolate. Tea influenced American history; cake, French. Psychologists say food equals love. And filled glasses and heaped plates play a part in hospitality and in every celebration.

Anthropology traces cultural patterns through food habits, and with the smallest of giggles, Carême's elaborate *pièces montées* could be considered architecture. As for physiology, the medical profession pays increasing attention to the consequences of diet and nutrition. And, who can forget the mathematical problem beginning: If I have four apples. . . .

Knowledge of food and wine can be gleaned from novels, too. In fact, one published cookbook features the menus and dishes mentioned in the late Rex Stout's "Nero Wolfe" mysteries; another cookbook is devoted to foods described in Dickens's incomparable works.

As far as work habits are concerned, keeping up with reading in the field, testing and creating recipes, and dining in restaurants for research will not leave much time on your hands. So it's probably best to consider your work and your hobby one and the same thing.

The most difficult part of this job for weight watchers involves dining on glorious food and imbibing splendid beverages while still maintaining correct weight and the healthful vigor that indicates that more than lip service is paid the teachings of good nutrition! Otherwise it can be pure joy.

Following is a description of the various options open to you as a freelancer.

WRITING FOR MAGAZINES AND NEWSPAPERS

The top-circulation women's magazines pay handsomely. A few of those that specialize in cooking pay well. (Fortunately for your time and for your eyesight, not many magazines are devoted solely to wine.) To learn what any magazine buys, study several issues to see the kinds of recipes used, the phraseology—e.g.: 1 cup (8 ounces)— and the writing style they favor. To avoid spending a fortune on subscriptions, read magazines you'd like to write for at the library.

As with fashion, there are food fads. These usually are initiated by writers for sophisticated food and wine magazines. They then are picked up by newspaper food editors. Thanks to greater travel since the '40s, more attention has been paid to ethnic recipes in the press. The "new American cuisine," according to Donald Frazier in a story in *Nation's Restaurant News*, emphasizes lightness and intense flavors. In an interview in *U.S. News & World Report*, James Beard, on the other hand, claims that thanks to our native foods, diversity is our kitchen's distinction. "Corn," he notes, "most kinds of beans, various nuts, large strawberries . . . changed the diet of the world."

The subject of dieting, at least since the '30s, is another food-writing perennial. I remember three diets, popular in the '30s, as egregious as those being touted today. There was the *grapefruit diet*, the *banana diet*, and even, have mercy on us all, the *saltine diet*. These and many others are serious sources of dangerous malnutrition.

Suggesting a feature relating to a local event may net you a recipe-story assignment from the editor of your town's newspaper or magazine. For instance, you might be asked to report on the exceptional food served at a church supper, or recipes prepared by the winners of a neighborhood baking contest.

The assignment will be yours only if the editor thinks the idea originated with you and will interest the majority of the paper's readers, because important festivals or food-and-wine events are covered by staff reporters and writers. And much of what they print is taken whole cloth (often even including typographical errors) from public relations releases contributed by corporations and associations glorifying their products. Photos, with terse and lively captions attached, almost always accompany these releases.

Usually public relations stories with recipes and photos are pre-pared by home economists, often on staff. Big and small city newspa-pers fill their food sections with a combination of press releases, syndicated stories and columns, plus original material written by their own food editor and staff, and some freelance features.

When you succeed in placing a story in a local magazine or news-paper, you earn extra money when the feature is sent to additional me-dia. Repeat sales are possible because most require stories exclusive only to their own particular geographical area. Interestingly, the New York Times Syndicate buys only material previously published else-where.

WRITING FOR WINE/SPIRITS PUBLICATIONS

In this sphere, intensive knowledge of your subject is a prerequi-site. Although not easy, it's a pleasurable pursuit, known as palate re-search. Taste-testing wines and/or spirits calls for concentrated application and a keen sense of taste. You must be able to judge and to remember aroma, bouquet, appearance, finish, and body of a host of wines.

That expertise must be combined with an excellent memory for wine names, vintage years, geographical areas where grapes are grown, plus names of chateaus, shippers, and distributors.

Spirits—cognac, liqueurs, etc.—and beer are part and parcel of that knowledge. And the lot presupposes information derived from preliminary and ongoing reading, both past and current.

Articles in these publications feature stories on vineyards as well as interviews with wine growers, distributors, and shippers. Various grape varieties and wines themselves are discussed in separate arti-cles, as are schools that offer wine education.

Features about wine tours are lagniappe for writers. These tours are gratis, include all expenses, and constitute journeys here, there, and everywhere that wine grape varieties are grown.

CORPORATE WRITING

Corporate writing usually pays extremely well. Writing assign-ments can include recipe pamphlets, press releases, plus planting newspaper and magazine stories. If you wish to freelance for associa-tions, corporations, and advertising or public relations agencies, look for them by assiduously following newspaper and magazine advertising columns. Philip Dougherty, for instance, writes an advertising column in the business section of the *New York Times*. Even more information is available in the trade journal *Advertising Age.*

When you read that a corporation or an advertising or public relations agency is taking on a new food or wine account, telephone to find out who will be in charge. In offering your services, write a compelling letter stating your background and your ability to provide provocative marketing ideas that you believe will increase sales. Obviously you will tailor your ideas to the foods and equipment being sold or publicized.

In addition to your own knowledge of the product, you can draw on a variety of sources when writing recipe booklets for corporations, newspaper and/or magazine publicity releases, and scripts for radio or television programs.

I began the lead of a press release to publicize Seagram's convenience-product drink mixes with the following:

It's an educated guess that the first convenience food—hackberry juice—was put together by Peking man some 500,000 years ago. The man (or possibly his lady) pressed small sweet hackberries—a tree fruit—to extract their juice. The drink must have been a seasonal delight.

My educated guess came from *Man's Foods*, by L.B. Jensen (the Garrard Press).

From a mail order catalog I learned that "The 'Manners' fork from the Victoria and Albert Museum is the oldest English silver table fork, dating from 1632. Used for eating pickles by the Rutlands, Manners being their family name. . . ."

This dash of historical information could provide a lead for a silverware product; for relishes; for beef so tender, no knife is needed; or even, if punning is your bent, on table etiquette.

BOOK PUBLICATION

The spate of cookbooks is substantial evidence that by becoming "bibles," they readily and steadily make money. And they fall into many categories. Recipes devoted to different countries cover the world. Some cookbooks feature entertaining, some economy, others speedy preparation. Some deal only with a particular food: the hors d'oeuvre, the pig, the vegetable, the sandwich. The first distinguished book of this genre was M.F.K. Fisher's *Consider The Oyster* (Duell, Sloan and Pearce). Then there are the numbers-game books: cooking for one, for two, for fifty.

You may have written the world's best cookbook. But even if you manage to get it published, it will get short shrift unless you already have an established reputation. Unfortunately, first-book authors do not receive large advances and are accorded little, if any, advertising or publicity.

On the other hand, if you are an experienced writer with food knowledge, you may be asked to ghostwrite a cookbook for a celebrity in the field. Although you will be paid for your work, the celebrity will be designated as the author and your name may not even appear in the book's acknowledgment section.

Self-publication is always an option, but it takes money that comes out of your pocket. Initially there are printing costs. Artwork expenditures include a compelling cover or jacket and any illustrations. And unless your acquaintance numbers in the millions and this multitude guarantees to buy copies of your book, you may be well out of pocket. Advertising constitutes a final and very large expenditure, and another problem lies in finding a distributor for your book.

However, I do know of one happy ending to self-publication. Irma Rombauer submitted her book *The Joy of Cooking* (Bobbs-Merrill) to thirty-two publishers, all of whom rejected her manuscript. Originally, she indignantly published it herself.

Promoting Yourself

The best way to succeed in any field is summed up by the question: Whom do you know? Or, whom do you know who can provide you either with personal or written introductions? With or without this kind of valuable entree, it's up to you to write intriguing letters to persons you believe will profit from the use of your material.

Tell them you have novel sales or public relations ideas and add that you will telephone for an appointment. Wait a week or ten days before doing so. (Even if you live next door, a person-to-person telephone call is the only way to insure that editors or account executives will come to the phone.)

Even the smallest newspapers usually have a food or lifestyle editor. When calling, invite him or her to be your guest at a restaurant or at your home for luncheon or for cocktails. (It is easiest to suggest stories over a bottle of good wine.) The alternative is to include short query ideas with your original letter.

The Villager, a folksy weekly newspaper for Greenwich Village residents, was almost as unsophisticated as my first publicity attempt. It took courage, but I wrote to ask the editor if I could talk to her about my new school. When she acquiesced to an appointment, I sent her a box of homemade, chocolate-frosted, chocolate cake. Both box and I were warmly welcomed. The editor's subsequent piece lauding my work gave me the courage to approach another editor—this time, of a slick magazine that circulated in another nearby Manhattan neighborhood.

I suggested writing a cooking column—they had none—that would include interviews with local celebrities that would feature their favorite recipes. That idea worked, too, and I was on my way to my own national network television program, thanks to a letter I wrote to a talk-show host. I mentioned my school and suggested a demonstration of *crêpes Suzette*. He was delighted with my performance, as was the program's producer. The result: I became hostess of a program, "Shopper's Matinee."

Join food and/or wine societies in your area, even if you dislike organization life. Membership will provide you with contacts and leads for assignments. Some such organizations include the Sommelier Society, *Les Amis du Vin*, and the Wine and Food Society. Home Economists will, of course, find membership in Home Economists in Business eminently helpful. Once your reputation as an authority is secure, try for acceptance in *La Chaîne des Rôtisseurs, Les Amis d'Escoffier*, or the women's arm of the latter organization—*Les Dames d'Escoffier*.

Attending even distant meetings can be worth a tax-deductible journey. But it takes courage, because the name of the game is contacts. Networking is the current term for women helping women, as opposed to the "old boys' network." In any case, whenever, or wherever, you find anyone who might be able to use your work, you must do the courting. So approach and shine.

Although most of these societies usually exist only in large metropolitan areas, smaller towns also may have chapters. If there is no food or wine organization in your area, interest a group of friends in getting together for wine tastings and/or for meals resplendent with epicurean dishes. All of these occasions can provide you with ideas for articles.

RECIPE WRITING

Clarity, simplicity, accuracy, and consistency are prerequisites for recipe writing. And—as you learned at your first-grade teacher's knee—neatness counts.

In reality, there is no new dish; all are simply variations on basic cooking and baking techniques. It's said that you can call a recipe "yours" by changing two ingredients or two of the measurements. If you stick to salt and pepper, you are anthologizing. Your job is to personalize and glamorize recipes—making them vivid and original.

Know, and take advantage of, current trends: speed of preparation, use of convenience products, new food products and equipment, nutrition, health. And don't forget that omnipresent subject—how to lose weight.

Basic Mechanics

1. Type recipes on one side of the page only, double-spaced.
2. List all ingredients in a single column in the order in which they will appear in the method that follows.
3. Do not abbreviate any words.
4. Do not capitalize the letter "t" in a tablespoon measurement to differentiate it from a teaspoon measurement.
5. Except where required for clarity, eliminate the words "a" and "the."
6. To avoid confusion of ingredients, always use the serial comma. For instance: apples, oranges, and sugar and cinnamon. A mixture of sugar and cinnamon in this case is available as a single ingredient. As a further example, a menu illustration could read: soup, fish and chips, salad, and apple pie.

There *have* been writers whose first submissions were accepted. They are to be envied. In the all-too-likely case of a first rejection, either wing your work elsewhere with its stamped, self-addressed envelope; rewrite it; or just tuck it into a file labeled Story Rejects. Then, when you are a sought-after writer, send these stories out again—and this time, look forward to receiving a check for every one!

WRITING FOR FOOD
AND NUTRITION MARKETS
by Beverly Barbour

Writing for the food and nutrition field is booming as it's never boomed before. No more long, dull treatises written by dietitians—today the same information, with recipes, is jazzed up for four basic audiences: the "seductive body" crowd storming the newsstand for *Cosmo;* the "I want to live forever" folks who read *Prevention* and make health food entrepreneurs rich; the "I love to cook" people who subscribe to *Gourmet* or *Bon Appétit;* and the harried "got to feed a family" parents, who clip the sensible recipes in *Good Housekeeping* or *Redbook.*

The advantages of specializing in this field are obvious, because we all love to eat, we all want to maximize the body beautiful, none of us would mind living forever, and everyone wants to make the dollar go further. The food and nutrition market isn't going to die and fade away—these basic needs and interests are here to stay. It's only the approach that changes—constantly.

In the past, the major market for food and nutrition writing was the food and shelter magazines directed to women who stayed home and raised families. Today, most women don't stay home, although many raise families. With their move out of the kitchen, a whole new concept in menu planning and food preparation has emerged: this group needs ideas on how to quickly and economically prepare attractive, nutritious meals that aren't going to gobble up that hard-earned paycheck.

And "they" are not only women: men moved into the kitchen by way of the backyard. In putting on a show with a barbecue grill, they discovered that the ham in the backyard wasn't just on the grill—cooking was *fun*. Then, too, many a man now lives alone who used to have a mom, or a bride, to preside over his alimentary canal. Writing about food and nutrition for men is booming too.

Obviously, you won't provide the same information, or write in the same style, for the swinging single as you will for a trade association booklet, or for a press release on a new product, or for an industry newsletter.

Still, I write for these varied markets and many more. Once the basics are in your brain, or in your files, it isn't difficult to change tone or style.

The basic markets for food writing are public relations and advertising agencies (press releases, booklets, advertisements, new product promotions); book publishers (cookbooks, nutrition books, entertainment how-to's, travel or tour guides with recipes); magazine publishers (articles with recipes or nutritional information, equipment reviews, restaurant reviews); and newspaper publishers (short articles with recipes, directories of food or equipment sources, restaurant reviews, travel/food articles).

But *you must have basic knowledge*. If you're going to write about nutrition, you have to *know* about nutrition—and it's about as controversial a subject as any you could choose right now. Conflicting reports result from various diet and health studies, and every other person appearing on a talk show further confuses the public by promoting his or her own special formula for weight loss or longevity or both. You must read the studies, evaluate the sources and the findings, and (if possible) question the researchers, then attempt to present a balanced picture.

Using Technical Sources

Food and nutrition information maybe gathered from a number of places: public libraries; medical libraries; college and university libraries; the medical press; pharmaceutical trade associations; biochemists; meat, vegetable, and wheat producers, etc.

All libraries will have some periodicals and journals featuring articles on whatever aspect of nutrition you are writing about. Make friends with librarians—they can save you untold hours of research. (Fortunately, a good memory seems to be standard equipment for people who spend their lives sequestered with the printed word.)

Most large food corporations, such as Nabisco Brands or ITT Continental Baking Company, have excellent libraries covering their specific product fields. Often they're willing to let you consult their references. Public relations or consumer relations people can be very helpful in supplying information about the products they distribute. They're anxious to help you present a balanced, accurate story and will direct you to relevant studies and fact sources.

Finding Product Information Sources

Many trade associations finance research regarding their products, and they, in turn, know where the current activity is in their field. They can direct you to people you may wish to interview and will help give you information.

On the other hand, if you are writing a lighter piece, instead of a technical story—say an article about kiwifruit as opposed to one about the effects of diet on cancer—the research will be lighter and easier. And in all probability the paycheck will be heavier.

Your sources for product information might be the Government of New Zealand's Trade Commission (the Kiwifruit Authority of New Zealand), since the kiwifruit originally came from New Zealand, or the public relations agency currently publicizing kiwifruit. You can locate the Trade Commission through the telephone book, or call the country's embassy in Washington, D.C., and work from there.

You can discover the name of a public relations firm publicizing a particular product either from the Trade Commission or from *O'Dwyer's Directory of Public Relations Firms*, which is updated annually and lists accounts handled by various firms. Cross-referenced both by agency names and by their accounts, *O'Dwyer's* is easy to use and available at most libraries—or at any public relations firm where a friend is employed. If you want, you can order a copy for $40 from J.R. O'Dwyer Company, Inc., 271 Madison Avenue, New York, New York 10016.

If the product you're interested in is an American product, check with your state agricultural extension service, or write directly to the Publication Information Office, U.S. Department of Agriculture, Room 507A, Washington, D.C. 20250. You can call (202)447-2791 to determine what's available and the cost, if any. Frequently, you'll be re-

488 COMPLETE GUIDE TO WRITING NONFICTION

ferred to the Superintendent of Documents, together with an item number. And as the Superintendent of Documents' office works only with item numbers, there's no point in contacting them if you have only a subject in mind; contact the Publication Information Office first.

Identify and Interview Authorities

From your reading and research you'll quickly discover who the authorities are in any given field—or at least those persons who are best at getting their names in print. The real authorities are often academics and most of them are very pleasant to work with. They are free with their information, rational in their thinking and their statements, and they don't mind being quoted. In fact, they are often flattered at an interview, relish the attention, and are anxious to set the public straight. They are also generally quite nice about reading your work and making suggestions. On technical subjects, it's good to have several experts do so in case there is a gaping hole somewhere, an error, or you've left yourself open to question.

Researchers all seem to know how to equivocate well. This is very important in a world where any reliable nutritional "truth" can be declared false with the printing of tomorrow's newspaper. You will see many phrases such as, "It appears," "It is assumed," etc. This trick of self-preservation is learned by observation.

Everyone's Favorite—Cookbooks

Every man, woman, and child on the planet earth eats, and that simple daily act makes the person feel he or she is an expert in the food field. Scratch a good cook, and you'll find someone with a cookbook idea filed away in that brain's "futures" file.

It's true almost anyone can gather enough recipes to fill a cookbook (200 to 300 is standard), and many people can invent a simple recipe. But can they get the collection published? Is the book really needed? Would it sell? Is that recipe really going to work for the rest of the world and be judged worthy of the time and money that goes into producing it?

If the answers are "yes," write an outline and seek out a publisher.

FOOLPROOF RECIPES

Recipe "authorities" are not always careful and accurate. Try using the recipe a professional chef gives you sometime, and you may discover he or she has no concept of how a home cook goes about making a dish. Professional chefs don't measure accurately, if they measure at all. Often they don't know themselves exactly how much of anything they put in a recipe, since they're always working against the clock and measure by handfuls and pinches. They also taste their way along—which is fine, but it's hard to taste the printed word.

You will have to take recipes from such sources with a nice big handful of salt and try to control your own blood pressure. Test all recipes; think them through as you read them. Do they seem reasonable; are the proportions feasible; are there directions for pan size, temperature, servings? One trick that I often use is to say to the recipe source, "I can hardly wait to try this one!" The knowledge that you are going to make it and that you'll find it lacking will often spur the giver on to say, "Oh, yes, I forgot to mention the brandy I add at the end." In this way, some other little—or large—omission is often suddenly brought to light.

A good source of tested recipes is the trade association or the public relations firm representing a specific product. For instance, whatever firm has the kiwifruit account probably has someone, somewhere, hard at work developing recipes featuring kiwifruit. Most of these recipes are absolutely reliable—the sources want you to like their product, they want you to buy more of it, and they definitely don't want you thinking the product is no good just because the recipe is no good. Trade association recipes usually work well.

You can also hire a freelance home economist, food consultant, or chef to develop recipes to accompany your writing. Your best source would be to contact someone through your state Home Economics Association: their state directories list freelance home economists, consultants, etc. Many companies use these people rather than running their own test kitchens.

When you are including recipes in an article, keep the publisher's style in mind. Match your recipes to theirs. Do they spell out such words as tablespoon and teaspoon, or do they abbreviate "tbsp." and "tsp.," or do they abbreviate still further and use "T" for tablespoon and "t" for teaspoon?

In every recipe the ingredients should be listed in order of use; when several ingredients are added at the same time you begin the list with the largest quantity. For example: "1 tablespoon cinnamon, ½ teaspoon ginger, ¼ teaspoon mace."

For baked or roasted items, always be certain that you have given the oven temperature and at some point told the reader to preheat the oven. Be sure to tell your reader the length of cooling time, how the pans should be prepared, etc.

Remember that you cannot copyright a recipe; that's why you find slight (one- or two-ingredient or measure) changes as old favorites move from cookbook to cookbook.

Food Photography

Public relations firms, trade associations, or major food companies will often supply photographs for you. Sometimes they will even take photographs especially for your book or story, if the audience is large enough and they are promised credit in the publication.

However, when you do your own photography you will need:

1. A photographer experienced in the art of taking food photographs; this work is different from any other kind of photography and you need a specialist. Note who is getting photo credit in the food magazines, choose a style you like, and track down the person responsible, or go to the Yellow Pages and make a few phone calls.

2. A stylist to choose the china, the glassware, the table linens (or the cutting board, the pots and pans, etc.) and to oversee their use in the photo. He or she will help you decide whether to do a "beauty shot"—a photograph of the finished product looking its very best—or a "process shot"—a photograph of the product in one of its stages of preparation (a sandwich on the cutting board, soup on the stove, etc.).

   If you have the time, and the experience, you can do the styling yourself. The props can often be borrowed, but they must be in scale, must "tell a story" about the dish, etc. In the end, it is always easier to go to a pro. These people are credited in some magazines so looking there can be a source. Or call the test kitchen director for a public relations firm with a lot of food accounts and ask that person to recommend someone to you.

3. A food stylist to actually prepare the food for photographing. This, too, is a secret society for the initiated only, and the practitioners command a lot of money for their skills. It isn't easy to make food that looks lovely and appetizing to the camera, that won't wilt under the lights, and that meets the criteria for "truth."

Your contract with the publisher determines who pays whom— and how much—for preparation, styling, and the photographs.

Your Reference Library

For convenience's sake, you will eventually build up a library of your own. There are three books you *must* have:

- *Composition of Foods.* Handbook No. 8, U.S. Department of Agriculture (Superintendent of Documents, U.S. Government Printing Office, Washington, D.C. 20402). Basic nutrition information, calories count, etc.
- *Larousse Gastronomique,* by Prosper Montagne (Crown Publishers, New York). Describes, gives recipes, and spells out all basic French preparations and foods, plus many from other cuisines.
- *The Joy of Cooking,* by Irma S. Rombauer and Marion Rombauer Becker (Bobbs-Merrill Co., Indianapolis). Covers all the basics of American cookery.

As books are expensive, I seldom buy them retail. I often buy by mail from book discounters at 25 to 35 percent off (they get them "wholesale" and make a small profit on each). I never pass remainder counters without looking to see if a good reference book lies in wait.

Since I review books in a syndicated column, I'm on a number of publishers' review lists. Long ago, I wrote to publishers and sent them copies of my column, so they know I am a "legitimate" reviewer. Now they either automatically send me review copies of their new volumes or send their annual catalog. Then I write and ask for any of the books I want to review. After reviewing, I add some of them to my reference library. (Reviewers are honor-bound to send the publisher two copies of the review they write.)

I also have two legal-sized file drawers filled with nutrition information—booklets, clippings, press releases—and five file drawers filled with food files—primarily recipes—organized under headings: "Appetizers," "Beverages," etc. There are also files with such names as "Coffee" and "Tea." With the recipe files, I don't cross-index, as that would be endlessly time-consuming. I simply know that if I am looking for dessert recipes featuring coffee I check "Coffee," "Beverages," "Desserts," and maybe "Ethnic, French" and "Ethnic, Italian." I might also go to the nutrition files to check "Caffeine" and "Hypertension," depending upon the type of story I was writing.

HOW DO YOU SELL?

The first sale is the hardest—always and forever! What you must do, of course, is identify something that needs to be written about and will sell.

I began writing when I worked as a nutritionist on an Indian reservation and couldn't personally contact enough of the people to have any impact upon their eating patterns. Since the Indian people all read the weekly paper, I asked the editor if he would publish a column featuring recipes utilizing government-donated foods. He said his paper would run it "as space allows."

As the Chippewa have a delightful sense of humor and pride, I tried to write with that in mind. I wrote about how the clever Indians used to cook their soup in hides by adding heated stones to the broth; in the same column I described a nutritious soup anyone could make using the government-donated commodities. The next week I wrote about Indian fry bread, and how to make it and other breads from government-donated flour. And so it went.

The editor, who had originally been a bit reluctant to grant space for recipes, soon urged me to sell the column to other papers. I gathered up my courage and drove to the next county, where on a Saturday afternoon I found the editor out back running his press and sold him my column for 50¢ a week. The next paper paid $1, and so the circulation grew—to 187 newspapers (most of them weeklies).

These columns were later gathered into books. And when you have columns or a book to prove that you know how to put a noun in front of a verb, you can go to another publisher with a bigger and better idea, or to a trade association or a company suggesting a newsletter or brochure.

The real secret of writing for pay in the field of food and nutrition is to find a few holes that need plugging, then to put your ideas forward to plug the holes. It's amazing how much creativity people can have when it comes to marketing what they're capable of producing. Just stir up some ideas and spoon your samples out. Someone will bite!

WRITING FOR THE BOOMING HOLISTIC HEALTH MARKET
by Morton Walker, D.P.M.

Opportunities galore exist in the informational field of holistic health and medicine. There's practically no one in it!

"How's that again?" you might ask. "Aren't there loads of medical journalists supplying complete, correct information about drugs and techniques in texts, speeches, articles, and broadcasts?"

Yes, medical communications specialists provide the popular media with massive doses of medical material to satisfy the appetites of their lay audiences who are endlessly intrigued with affairs of health. They receive input from the five million Americans working as traditionally trained physicians, nurses, pharmacists, hospital personnel, drug industry employees, and allied professionals. *But this is not the health field.* What these mainstream medical professionals do has nothing to do with building health. This army of medical workers is in the disease-treating business.

There is a vast difference between prescriptions, cutting, radiating, and "caring" for the ailing patient on the one hand and guiding him or her back to exuberant, disease-free health on the other. The truth is that no one can be "prescribed" to health. Despite medical public relations efforts and much publicity about new breakthroughs in reversing disorders, there are more degenerative sicknesses and ailments today than ever before.

In my judgment, and in the opinion of others writing in the holistic health field, it's a myth that Americans are healthy. The United States is one of the sickest countries on earth. The degenerative-disease statistics of few other nations are as gruesome as ours. Here are the facts:

- Of those who die in the United States each year, 54.7 percent succumb to heart or vascular disease. Hardening of the arteries is the underlying pathology for six of the ten leading killers of Americans. Arteries harden mainly because of poor nutrition and lack of exercise, according to the holistic physicians belonging to the International Academy of Preventive Medicine.
- Over one billion visits are made to physicians annually in the United States. Another 250 million visits are made to hospital emergency rooms and clinics. This combined medical visitation averages to over five visits per capita per year.
- One person in every American family will have cancer, usually malignant. Current statistics indicate that cancer affects every fourth person and kills every sixth one. The high technology of American society—including everything from chemicals in our air, water, and food, to the stressful pace of modern living—is the suspected cause, says the Cancer Control Society from its national office in Los Angeles.
- Arthritis and rheumatic complaints affect 36 million Americans.
- Over 40 million Americans will spend time in a hospital this year, and this number will grow with time, according to Blue Cross/Blue Shield health insurance companies.
- Nearly 200 million of our citizens suffer from constipation at one time or another during their lives, warns the National Digestive Diseases Education Information Clearinghouse.
- The Linus Pauling Institute of Science and Medicine estimated that we suffered more than 800 million colds during 1981, and the number is anticipated to be greater in the forthcoming years.
- The United States Department of Health and Human Services

states that about $325 billion was spent in 1982 on treating disease, which amounts to $1,200 for each American or $5,000 per family.

- The American Heart Association estimates that 20 million Americans suffer from high blood pressure, a predisposing factor to hardening of the arteries.
- According to the American College of Surgeons, nearly 25 million Americans submit to surgery each year.
- The dental bill for this country is immense because 98.6 percent of its citizens suffer from one or more dental cavities at one time or another during their lives, states the American Dental Association.
- The American Optometric Association acknowledges that defective eyesight affects 60 percent of all Americans. Walking down the street or sitting in a public library, you'll see more people wearing corrective lenses than not.
- Thirty-six million people experience tinnitus or ringing in the ears, which may be a symptom of hardening of the arteries, affirms the American Tinnitus Association.
- Thirty-two million Americans are limited in activities due to chronic disease or disability, says the American Association of Retired Persons.

Similar to the sampling I've listed, the National Center for Health Statistics of the United States Public Health Service publishes volumes of frightening numbers indicating the huge numbers of people functioning at less than optimal health—low level worseness instead of high-level wellness. People are truly in critical condition. They need the type of information made available by magazines and books about orthomolecular nutrition, beneficial diets, total conditioning exercise programs, aerobics, isometrics, isotonics, homeopathy, alternative methods of healing, relaxation techniques, yoga, the ancient forms of body and mind restoration, East/West convergence of lifestyle, food supplementation, food combining, spirituality, magnetic and cosmic healing, herbology, endocrine revitalization, antistress programming, applied and behavioral kinesiology, clinical ecology, natural hygiene, juicing, fasting, fruitology, vegetarianism, integrative medical systems, subtle energies, biofeedback and self-regulation, psychic manipulation, massage, humanistic psychotherapies, naturopathy, chiropractic, osteopathy, natural childbirth, vision therapy, light therapy, art therapy, music therapy, psychophysic approaches, and other holistic dimensions of total health.

All the above comprise the main ingredients of new-age magazines dealing in alternative methods of healing and self-help. The market for quality writing on these subjects is large and expanding. Readers want to know how to take responsibility for their own health.

Merely observing the growing movement toward health—the National Jogging Association points out that 30 million people are jogging every day—indicates how Americans want access to preventive procedures. They are looking for more natural lifestyles and less drug-oriented treatments. Their search—your search, even if you don't yet realize it—is for holistic health and medicine. As a writer for the booming holistic health market, you can prosper by uncovering information on optimal nutrition and alternative methods of healing.

TOPICS FOR THE MARKET

While drug-oriented traditionalists may label holistic health topics "hokum," here are typical examples of the sorts of articles I suggest you should research, query on, and write about for holistic magazine markets:

- Nutrients enabling the reader to have increased mental alertness and brain power, greater physical stamina and vigor, a zest for living, a radiant new complexion and skin tone, an improved figure and appearance, increased potency and sexuality, and more overall strength.
- Techniques of living leading to an ailment-free life, eliminating physician visits, hospitals, and drugs.
- Programs to overcome ailments and illnesses, even "incurable" ones of long standing such as cancer, heart disease, diabetes, kidney disease, glaucoma, cataracts, arthritis, multiple sclerosis, Parkinson's disease, epilepsy, and others.
- Procedures enabling the reader to save several thousand dollars on food, energy, medical, hospital, drug, labor, insurance, and other customary outlays connected with illness.
- Case histories, anecdotes, and testimonials showing how one or more persons overcame common health problems such as:
1. A twenty-year history of acid indigestion that ended in a week because something was taken out of the diet (usually some processed junk food).
2. A diabetic on insulin who got rid of his injections by proper diet maintenance.
3. A hypoglycemic who came back to reality from schizophrenia by being diagnosed correctly and having refined carbohydrates removed from his diet.
4. A twenty-four-year-old severe acne sufferer, whose face looked like the moon with its craters, having her pustules

disappear following a regimen of natural eating.

5. Regular bowel function reestablished in an individual who had not experienced a normal movement for years—how he did it in a short period of time.

6. Breast cancer the size of a lemon, for which physicians advised mastectomy, going away spontaneously from following an alternative metabolic cancer therapy program.

7. How an epileptic of ten years' standing was off his drugs in two weeks, and never suffered another seizure, by taking a natural remedy made from herbs.

8. A twelve-year-old asthmatic victim whose parents sought a holistic physician after spending $10,000 on Establishment medicine and who found relief following holistic medical methods.

Peanuts Are Good Food, Bad Pay

There is, unfortunately, a major stumbling block to earning a good living as a full-time holistic health writer. The new-age and nutritional periodicals don't pay well. Many readers turned writers send in their new discoveries about lifestyle improvements or the secrets of primitive humans to find that magazines like *Let's Live, Bestways,* and *Vegetarian Times* don't pay much. The nonprofessional writer usually is happy just to see his or her idea on the printed page and will accept anything. Also, many health professionals practicing a holistic form of medicine—naturopaths, physicians, osteopaths, homeopaths, herbalists, chiropractors, naprapaths, etc., who build their practices by being in print—don't ask for any payment from the magazine.

This sort of amateur writing often needs a lot of editorial work, of course, and magazine staffs spend time editing practically illiterate articles to make them more readable. In truth, they don't always succeed.

Be forewarned, therefore, that you'll have to face lots of amateurish competition for inadequate financial compensation in the holistic health magazines market.

Even the most widely circulated nutrition magazine in this field, *Prevention*, pays "peanuts"—about $400—for a freelance contribution. Then the magazine annoys you repeatedly by demanding more facts. *Prevention* probably figures it has enough trouble with the Food and Drug Administration without its publishing something that isn't proven by at least two authoritative sources. Consequently, its staff does much of the article research and writing and you'll read the same old nutrition stuff over and over again in its pages. They sometimes reprint their own old articles. It's boring.

Mother Earth News has been noted for courtesy in the editor-writer relationship in the continuing rate survey conducted by the American Society of Journalists and Authors, Inc. for its members. Even so, Mother Earth News is known among professional writers as another cheapie payout with only $400 to $500 for a freelance contribution. Other low levels of payment come from the East/West Journal (averages $250), American Chiropractor (about $200), Bestways ($100), Let's Live ($300), Health Quarterly Plus Two ($150), Health Express ($0), Your Good Health ($150), New Age Journal ($300), Health and Diet Times ($0 to free advertising space), and Whole Life Times ($200). There are probably several more alternative lifestyle magazines to list here, but they come and go so frequently that I've included only those few I'm acquainted with currently.

I have to admit that I started out accepting the small payments of these magazines until I became known. Now, I don't accept low payments. I used their pages as tearsheets to establish credits—the only way to build a healthy income.

Good General-Interest Markets

The best markets for holistic health writing are the tabloids such as the National Enquirer, Star, National Examiner, Globe, and the World Weekly News. Their fees go up to $2,000. I recently received $1,750 against a $400 kill fee from the Star, and $1,000 from the Globe.

Graduating from the tabloids, you move up to the slicks such as Glamour, Harper's Bazaar, Playgirl, Cosmopolitan, Forum, McCall's, and the girlie magazines such as Playboy, Penthouse, Gallery, Hustler, Oui, and Swank. These magazines have been known to accept "far-out" health themes. For example, Gallery paid me $1,000 for a nutrition article published in its August, 1983, issue.

Adhering to the more established medical party line, and therefore unreceptive to holistic health material, are Good Housekeeping, Woman's Day, Esquire, and Reader's Digest. Good Housekeeping, for example, published an article attacking holistic health procedures in its March 1982 issue. Written by Victor Herbert, M.D., J.D., and Stephan Barrett, M.D., this piece said that sixteen different nutrition substances or holistic medical techniques are dangerous to life and pocketbook. When queried by a number of holistic health practitioners and organizations—including the American Academy of Medical Preventics (400 physicians) and the Association for Cardiovascular Therapies—for equal space to answer charges (even as letters to the editors), the Good Housekeeping Institute's director refused. This, despite there being four statements that were, in my view, erroneous in an article of only two published pages. Don't waste your time trying to write for that magazine about holistic health matters.

FINDING STORY IDEAS

Your primary sources for holistic health stories are the doctors who practice this form of medicine. A complete listing of physicians who provide nutritional therapy and other types of alternative healing methods can be found in the appendixes of two books I've written: *The Chelation Answer* (M. Evans, 1982, distributed by E.P. Dutton), and *DMSO: The New Healing Power* (Devine-Adair Publishers, 1983). I give their names, addresses, and telephone numbers. These holistic doctors are a prime source of story ideas. I ask "What are you doing that's new, and works?" Write the doctor nearest you advising of your interest in doing a story about his or her manner of practice. Follow up with a phone call, and arrange for an interview. Take a tape recorder to ensure accuracy of quotations. Transcribe the tape and write the story. Provide the doctor with a copy for editorial changes. You want accuracy so as not to bring down peer review on the doctor's head or an editor's ire on yours.

The rewards of holistic health writing stretch beyond money. Like good nutrition, it is not only helpful, but invaluable, steeped in the intrigue of techniques and the drama of human beings. It has the staying power of service and curiosity. Holism is the medicine of the future, with a growing popularity in the present.

In addition, you personally benefit from learning the many ways to improve your health and extend your life. I do for myself what I write on, and write on what I do for myself. The public benefits even as I'm growing in stamina, strength, potency, attractiveness, vision, and all the other good things that happen when you accept the total holistic approach to living. I follow sexual nutrition, comprising a variety of nutritional aphrodisiac foods (see my book, *Sexual Nutrition*, Coward-McCann, 1983), take vitamins and minerals, faithfully exercise two hours a day, use mind control and meditation, experiment with various modes of fitness equipment, don't smoke or drink alcohol, eat meat less than once a week, have beef only once a month (if that), eliminate refined carbohydrates from my diet, eat higher quantities of complex carbohydrates, and perform good works to uplift my spirit.

In short, I have had far more enjoyment during the past fourteen years from writing about holistic healing than I ever received from practicing podiatric medicine (being a foot doctor) for seventeen years. I didn't savor confinement to a small room, attending a steady procession of bare feet, and the governmental regulation through Medicare and Medicaid. Government and professional association rules were constricting and not creative. Rather than fight my creative nature, I switched to my current profession as full-time freelance medical author and journalist. The change has brought a tremendous boost to my ego and a satisfaction to my psyche. Besides, I make a fine living at it by going beyond the poor payment markets. I've now written for *Self, The Runner, Shape, American Health, Health, Today's Woman, Sports Illustrated,* and other slick magazines that take special articles on optimal nutrition, fitness, and alternative methods of healing.

I have found—as you will—that by taking up medical journalism with a specialty in holistic health, I did not abandon serving others; I only moved onto a larger stage. This is the beauty of the holistic health specialty market. You are helping to heal the masses by bringing them information gleaned in the only way possible: ferreting out facts by going directly to the doctors practicing holistic medicine every day. The following professional associations will be able to refer you directly to holistic doctors:

- American Academy of Nutritional Consultants, 500 Dorian Rd., Westfield, NJ 07090; (201)233-5858
- Society of Biological Psychiatry, Tulane Medical Center, 1415 Tulane Ave., New Orleans, LA 70112; (504)588-5231
- American Academy of Medical Preventics, 6151 West Century Blvd., Suite 1114, Los Angeles, CA 90045; (213)645-5350
- International Academy of Biological Medicine, Inc., P.O. Box 31313, Phoenix, AZ 85046
- International Academy of Metabology, Inc., 1000 East Walnut St., Suite 247, Pasadena CA 91106; (213)795-7772
- Academy of Orthomolecular Psychiatry, 1691 Northern Blvd., Manhasset, NY 11030; (516)627-7260
- American Institute of Homeopathy, 6231 Leesburg Pike, Suite 506, Falls Church, VA 22044; (703)534-4363
- American Chiropractic Association, 2200 Grand Ave., Des Moines, IA 50312; (515)243-1121
- International College of Applied Kinesiology, 542 Michigan Building, Detroit, MI 48226; (313)962-6484
- National Association of Naturopathic Physicians, 609 Sherman Ave., Coeur d'Alene, ID 83814; (208)667-0541

Additional Resources

American Bakers Association, 2020 K St. NW, Suite 850, Washington, DC 20006. Offers aid in arranging interviews, statistics, brochures and pamphlets, placement on mailing list, newsletter, speakers.

American Dietetic Association, 430 N. Michigan Ave., Chicago, IL 60611. Provides bibliographical, technical, professional, and consumer information. Publications catalog available.

American Homebrewers Association, Box 287, Boulder, CO 80306. Provides advisory, bibliographical, historical, how-to, technical, and trade information. Offers informational newsletters, photos, press kits, research assistance, statistics. Publications include *Zymurgy* magazine.

Calorie Control Council, 65 Perimeter Center East, Atlanta, GA 30346. Offers information on dietetic foods and beverages, brochures, pamphlets, statistics.

Council for Responsible Nutrition, 1735 Eye St. NW, Suite 805, Washington, DC 20006. Provides technical and trade information on vitamin/mineral supplements: sales and marketing information, scientific/technical, government relations. Offers aid in arranging interviews, brochures and pamphlets, press kits, statistics.

Food and Nutrition Information Center, USDA, National Agricultural Library Bldg., Room 304, Beltsville, MD 20705. Provides bibliographical, referral, and technical information on human nutrition, nutrition education, food service management, general management. Offers library facilities and telephone reference services.

Frozen Food Action Communication Team, Box 10163, Grand Central Station, New York, NY 10163. Provides analytical, historical, referral, and trade information. Offers brochures and pamphlets, press releases, statistics, telephone reference services. Publications include *Frozen Foods Value and You, Frozen Foods—Microwave Cooking.*

Institute of Food Technologists, 221 N. LaSalle St., Chicago, IL 60601. Provides referral and technical information on nutrition and food safety, processed foods, food additives. Produces both background material and up-to-date status summaries on current scientific topics of food-related concern; maintains trained volunteers who meet regularly with the press. Offers aid in arranging interviews, brochures and pamphlets. Publications include *Food Technology* (monthly, official journal of IFT, free to members), *Journal of Food Science* (bimonthly), *IFT World Directory and Guide* (annual, free to members), career guidance booklets and materials.

International Food Information Service, Lane End House, Shinfield, Reading RG2 9BB, England 0734-883895. Maintains data base of 18,000 abstracts from world literature. Data base information is available as a monthly journal *(Food Science and Technology Abstracts)* and on magnetic tape. Provides advisory, bibliographical, and technical information on food science and technology. Offers bibliographies, information searches, newsletter. Publications include information kit describing service.

National Dairy Council, 6300 N. River Rd., Rosemont, IL 60018. Provides nutrition research and information. Offers statistics, information searches, photos, brochures, pamphlets, placement on mailing list; will arrange interviews. Publications include *Nutrition Source Book.*

National Food Processors Association, 1133 20th St. NW, Washington, DC 30026. Assists those seeking information on food and food processing industry. Publications list available.

National Restaurant Association, One IBM Plaza, Suite 2600, Chicago, IL 60611. Offers annual reports, statistics, press kits; will help arrange interviews. Represents over 125,000 members nationally.

United Fresh Fruit and Vegetable Association, 727 N. Washington St., Alexandria, VA 22311. Provides historical, referral, technical, and trade information on nutrition and consumer-related topics pertaining to fruits and vegetables. Offers brochures, pamphlets and library facilities. Publications include bimonthly magazine and weekly newsletter.

Wine Institute, 165 Post, San Francisco, CA 94108. Provides information, bibliographies, statistics, how-to, information searches, placement on mailing list, photos; arranges interviews. Publications include wine information course.

Chapter Fourteen

WRITING ABOUT HOME AND GARDEN

What is more dear to us than our retreat from the pressure of the world? Our homes, our yards, our balconies, our gardens are our vital link with the earth, an escape from the hectic pace of modern life—the places where we can shape reality in our own image, to our own taste. No wonder that, according to a recent survey by *Folio: The Magazine for Magazine Management*, home service markets ranked fifth in total circulation among consumer markets. The combined circulation of all publications in this market was 21.8 million, or 6.8 percent of all measured consumer magazine circulation—a sizeable market for freelancers.

The big four of the so-called "shelter," or home and garden, magazines are *Better Homes & Gardens, Southern Living, Sunset*, and *House & Garden*. The most venerable home service publication is *House Beautiful*, which was started in 1896 and is still ranked eighth in average circulation with an estimated 843,000 readers monthly. All these magazines have their roots in the soil, as do relative newcomers such as *Organic Gardening, Country Journal*, and *Flower and Garden*. An upstart in the field, *Home*, became one of the hottest major magazines in the country in a little over a year. It appears to have stemmed from what Anatole Broyard calls "the ecology of the harried cosmopolitan soul."

A common feature of these publications is page after page of striking four-color photographs of splendid kitchens, beautiful living rooms, gorgeous bedrooms, and pristine patios. Home plans accompany the decorating interiors, wth emphasis on the latest and most distinctive ideas, not the usual and average (especially in the higher-priced magazines). Reader appeal, as James L.C. Ford noted in *Magazines for Millions*, is based on upward mobility, daydreams, wishful thinking, and escapism—subtly mixed with a soupcon of voyeurism.

The lower-priced magazines in this field feature more practical service articles for the run-of-the-neighborhood reader. To build, buy, or rent? Those are the questions. Also—what kind of heating, how much insurance, are woodstoves practical? *Service* is the key word for those who would write for these magazines. And because readers pay close attention to suggestions and ideas on how to live better materially, the writer must provide facts and expert, detailed advice.

A great deal of what is read in the home service publications is staff-written and produced, but interested new writers who really want to learn the business can get their share of assignments. Opportunities multiply when you consider that, in addition to their regular monthly issues, many of these magazines publish elaborate annuals, specials, guides, and "idea kits."

Garden magazines are primarily how-to-do-it hobby or avocation publications. To write for them, you'd better be up on the latest hybrid, know when and how to prune the peach tree, and be conversant with the compost heap. And, as the writers whose work follows indicate, it helps if you enjoy both the gardening *and* the writing about it.

The home and earth have been the focus of human attention since we left the trees. As long as we continue to care about the comfort and beauty of where we spend most of our free time, the home and garden magazines will ever be close to the heart.

REAPING BUMPER CROPS
FROM GARDEN WRITING
by D.J. Herda

It all began in a little log cabin in West Virginia. Our family was dirt poor, and I had to learn to produce enough food for two adults and thirteen children or starve. I soon learned all there was about growing things. From there, it was but a short step to writing gardening articles and financial independence.

Of course, that makes for an interesting Horatio Alger rags-to-riches tale. But the truth is, I was living in a bedroom suburb outside Chicago when gardening was thrust upon me. I *had* to fill those big brown patches with shrubs, trees, and begonias or risk the wrath of the neighbors, whose yards were already green and lush with growth.

I made a lot of mistakes in those early years of gardening. It seems far more plants died than flourished, which only served to heighten my determination to succeed. After all, no dumb plant was going to get the best of me, no matter how weak its will to survive. True, I was a genuine backwoods banana when it came to understanding the nature of growing things back then. But I was determined to learn.

That determination eventually turned into a bona fide interest, a genuine desire to grow things. I soon found that reading periodicals like *Organic Gardening and Farming* (now simply *Organic Gardening*) and *Horticulture* and talking with successful long-time gardeners armed me with an arsenal of knowledge I had previously lacked. Although I never consciously considered writing for such prestigious publications, I suspect I harbored a subliminal desire to become a good enough gardener to someday qualify me as an expert of sorts. Little did I realize that day was approaching quickly.

Breaking Ground in Garden Writing

In those early days of the garden explosion, the mid-sixties or so, *Organic Gardening* had a reputation for being the *Rolling Stone* of the gardening set. Its articles were well researched and edited and, invariably, as accurate as any in the field. It varied from other publications, though, in that much of the material was reader-originated and -written. Gardeners are notorious for being anything but close-mouthed; once they discover something that works, they're nearly more exuberant about sharing their good garden fortune with others than enjoying the fruits of their labors. And *I* discovered something that works.

I had just ordered several fruit trees by mail. I followed the planting guide carefully and did some auxiliary reading in the various gardening encyclopedias proliferating in my home library. One of the things that intrigued me most was that pruning both roots and top growth was a nearly sure-fire means of maximizing first-year growth and assuring a healthy, hardy tree for coming decades.

I was surprised to find that anything could actually grow faster and taller after being cut back severely. Then I wondered how many other people knew that. When I asked my friends and neighbors if *they* ever pruned their mail-order stock, I found that few people understood the principles behind judicious pruning. What a perfect subject for an article, I thought. And what better magazine to run it than the reader-dominated *Organic Gardening!*

I quickly drafted a short query letter to the editors outlining my recent experiences in pruning fruit trees, as well as my belief that few people knew just how beneficial pruning is. Within a few weeks, I received a response. The editors agreed. I wrote the article, and my first-ever gardening article check arrived in the mail several weeks later. Equally important, the editors suggested I query them on other little-known aspects of gardening. They received tons of queries on topics such as mulching to control weeds and starting melon plants indoors for short-season growing, but very little on such technical topics as pruning.

Getting to the Roots

That early success led to others. Whenever I planted something around the house, I instinctively searched for little-known tips to improve growth or production. Sometimes my sources were technical releases from the county agricultural agent's office, other times general-interest articles in a wide range of periodicals (I researched these in the *Reader's Guide to Periodical Literature* at the public library). Surprisingly, some of the best tips I garnered came right with the plants I ordered via mail, in the form of little planting guides filled with information. Apparently, few people bother reading these guides from cover to cover.

The results of my rooting around for offbeat growing tips were rewarding. My technique soon endeared me not only to the editors of *Organic Gardening*, but to other editors. My first-person, down-home writing style didn't adapt well to some publications—the "ultraslick" magazines, for example—but it nonetheless grew and flourished in a variety of other magazines and newspapers. Before long, I had editors calling *me* for articles on a wide range of gardening subjects: planting bulbs, growing tree-sized plants indoors, protecting plants from insects and diseases, greening up your lawn, producing bumper vegetable crops in small spaces, grafting, and so forth.

Each article I wrote was laced with personal experience, lending an aura of expertise. Each, too, was extensively researched at the public library. It helps in garden writing, just like other fields of writing, to talk with experts—the owners and managers of greenhouses, mail-order seed companies, orchards, and so on. The more you learn, the more knowledgeably you'll be able to write. You needn't possess an agricultural journalism degree to be an expert garden writer, but you must follow every possible lead in researching a story.

DIG DEEP AND YOU WON'T BE DISAPPOINTED

A writer can never know too much about the subject. After receiving a rather straightforward article assignment from *Chicago* magazine for a piece describing the best house-plant stores in the city, I hoofed around to more than forty different shops, talking in detail to anyone who would grant me a few minutes. I learned more about gardening in that month of snooping around for information than in the years of personal experience that preceded it.

And my efforts did not go unrewarded. What began as a simple four-page review ended up as the magazine's cover story, complete with sidebars on caring for house plants, protecting plants from insects and disease, and other mini-topics. The article stretched to fourteen pages, allowing the magazine's advertising representatives to sell plenty of space and turn in a handsome profit for the publisher. In turn, the editors thought very highly of me, which led to further sales. Payment for the article, which was guaranteed at $300, was nearly triple that amount. It doesn't pay to "pad" an article—especially a specialty piece—but it's always wise to do the most complete and professional job possible.

If you're thinking seriously about trying your hand at garden writing, here are some points that may help you break into this specialty field:

• Know your subject well. Whenever possible, experience what you're writing about. If you don't own land or have access to planting space, volunteer your gardening services to friends and neighbors. *Never* mislead either editor or reader into thinking you've experienced something you've actually only researched at the library. That could well backfire, leaving you with egg on your face and one less magazine market to which to sell.

• Add to your personal knowledge through diligent research. There are a number of fine garden encyclopedias and reference books on the market. *Wyman's Gardening Encyclopedia* is one of the most accurate and highly regarded, making it a prime contender for the cornerstone of your gardening library. Also, subscribe to as many gardening magazines as possible, and get on the mailing list of every garden seed company you can find.

• Cover your tracks. Don't promise anybody a rose garden, or you could end up in a thorny bed. Tell your readers how *you* achieve gardening success, but be sure to warn them about potential pitfalls they may encounter in trying to duplicate your success. There are many variables involved in gardening in different parts of the country and from one year to the next.

• Don't overlook local publications that might be interested in gardening articles. Although they seldom pay much and may lack prestige, they nonetheless provide an excellent opportunity to build your reputation . . . *and* your list of garden-writing credits.

• Take plenty of color and black and white photographs of your garden, house plants, and anything else you grow. If you don't already own a camera, buy one and learn how to use it, even if that means enrolling in a photo course or workshop. Often a sharp, colorful photo of your blue-ribbon plants will convince a reluctant editor that you do, indeed, know what you're talking about.

Gardening is a fascinating avocation. Probably more people tend growing, living plants—even if only that potted palm in the living room—than ride bicycles, sail, or raise chickens. That means there's always a need for well-researched, timely, and creative articles on the subject. Garden writing is not a field without competition, but if you know your subject well and persist in producing unique, informative articles, you're nearly guaranteed success.

SELLING THE "SHELTER" MARKET
by John H. Ingersoll

The "shelter" label easily applies to *Better Homes and Gardens, House Beautiful, New Shelter,* and *The Homeowner.* Text and photos rove over every aspect of housing, inside and out: from picking land for a new house to a review of weather vanes to top off the roof ridge; from the best choices among flowering shrubs to new ideas for hanging family portraits. Yet, as a freelancer aiming for this market, you'll quickly discover four truths.

First, the word "shelter," though fairly accurate, falls short of describing the range of material these magazines publish. "What's Happening to Discipline in Our Schools?" for example, a topic many readers would expect to find in *Newsweek,* appeared in *Better Homes and Gardens* recently. Or "Monaco—A Bastion of Great Elegance" might have been a natural for *Signature,* but it appeared in 1982 in *House Beautiful.*

Second, the market for shelter-based magazine articles—remodeling, energy conservation, how-to, gardening, home maintenance—is far wider than the limited group having *home* or some derivation of *home* in the logo. *Redbook* has published special sections on remodeling a house. I did a long piece on saving energy at home for *True,* when it was still being published.

Third, shelter magazines divide loosely into three groups important to the freelancer: high-class, but a poor market; middle- and upper-middle-class, a good to fair market; how-to group, a good to excellent market.

Fourth, and perhaps most attractive to freelancers, is that once you get into this market, opportunities will snowball. A writer friend of mine did a short article on insulating a home, then a pamphlet on the subject for an association, and then a book for a publisher who had seen the pamphlet. He earned a modest fee for the article, and handsome returns on the pamphlet and book.

Let's examine these four truths in detail, beginning with the fourth and working backward. At least four dozen trade and professional publications deal with various aspects of shelter. Many, slanted toward pros and tradespeople, are secondary markets for articles. Reading them will help keep you up-to-date on new techniques, products, and inventions.

For the past two decades, book publishers have been hot on the trail of material that describes steps a reader can take to avoid hiring decorators and architects, or gives advice on working with a pro, or simply presents a houseful of tips on saving maintenance money. A trip to a well-stocked bookstore will reveal shelves packed with guides to housepainting, decorating, carpentry, plumbing, solar energy, remodeling, and the like. Some are remarkably specific: *The Encyclopedia of Hardware*, or *How to Build Your Own Wood Deck*. Others display a title that begins *The Complete Book of . . .* and are quite general.

Finally, writing assignments are handed out occasionally by trade and professional organizations or by agency or producer personnel.

OPPORTUNITIES IN CONSUMER MAGAZINES

Shelter magazines devote most editorial space to the best ideas on decorating, building, remodeling and living in a dwelling. But there's more. *Better Homes and Gardens* carries columns, mostly written by freelancers, on personal money management, health, autos, education, travel, and pets. *House Beautiful* publishes monthly columns by freelancers on beauty, the arts, travel, and pets.

As mentioned before, there are many opportunities for shelter-based articles outside the shelter group. Last year, *Esquire* ran a piece on the educated man's basic tool kit. Several inflight magazines have published freelance articles on residential solar energy and so, recently, have *Omni, Ladies' Home Journal, Working Woman, Smithsonian, Ms., New Yorker*, and *Mother Earth News*. A good home-oriented idea, well put in a query letter, is as likely to command attention at *Playboy* as at *1001 Home Ideas*.

For any freelancer trying this market, the magazines eventually shake down into three general groups. In the topmost group are *Architectural Digest, House and Garden*, and to a somewhat lesser extent, *House Beautiful*. These limited-circulation magazines, directed unabashedly at the wealthy, offer but few opportunities to the freelancer. Says Denise Otis, co-editor of *House and Garden*, "We usually call on specialists in a chosen field—art, for example, or antiques—to write for us. Pure journalists would not find us much of a market."

The second group offers more opportunities for freelance writers—*Better Homes and Gardens, New Shelter, Metropolitan Home, Home*, and *1001 Home Ideas*. Hew to the old maxim of "study the market." While the names sound similar, each has an orientation that would not transfer easily to another magazine in the group. *Better Homes and Gardens* has the largest readership (nearly eight million) and is the mid-America voice for the sound and practical. *New Shelter* is new wave self-help, laced generously with energy conservation advice. *Home* and *Metropolitan Home* strive for an upscale audience, while *1001 Home Ideas* aims a little lower on the economic scale.

The third group represents the best market for freelancers. There are *The Homeowner, Family Handyman,* and the home-based departments of *Popular Mechanics, Popular Science, Mechanix Illustrated,* and *Science and Mechanics.* Fees for articles sold to this group range from fair to quite good (though still some distance from the top fees paid by such periodicals as *McCall's, Playboy,* and *Reader's Digest).* A healthy portion of every magazine is written by freelancers. Editors here are constantly on the lookout for fresh material.

For example, editors at these magazines wouldn't look twice at "How about an article on roof-top solar collectors?" but might respond quickly to "I built a $100 solar collector and I'm saving $250 a year in fuel!" Specific article ideas always pay off faster: not "How to paint the outside of your house," but "Tricks with a paint sprayer that aren't in the book," or "Fear of falling: how to paint a third-story house gable without putting your heart in your mouth."

The story least likely to click in any of the three groups is one tied to a photo sequence of a new house, vacation house, decorating, remodeling, or restoration. With few exceptions, four-color, main-well presentations of house interiors and exteriors are staff-written.

Regional magazines, generally speaking, depend on the freelancers for material. *Sunset* and *Southern Living,* the stars in this field, are exceptions. Both rely heavily on staff-written stories, although there is occasionally some opportunity for outside writers. *Southern Accents,* a regional in the *Architectural Digest* mold, assigns experts for most of their articles.

Much more of a paying prospect are magazines such as *Colorado Homes and Lifestyles, Phoenix Home/Garden, Houston Home and Garden,* and *San Diego Home/Garden.* Fees are fairly good and, as you'd expect, stories must be of interest to the region served by the magazine. A writer living in Houston has an advantage in selling to *Houston Home and Garden,* but a Denver writer could also make a sale if the subject were of sufficient interest to Houston residents. One example: "Reproduction furniture kits you can order by mail" is as valuable to people in Houston as Denver (in fact, anywhere).

On the periphery of the conventional shelter group are magazines demanding technically accurate photojournalistic pieces on narrow specialties. Among them are *Fine Woodworking, Fine Homebuilding, Workbench,* and *Handmade.*

TRADE AND PROFESSIONAL MAGAZINE MARKETS

Represented in this category are magazines that talk directly to the architect, homebuilder, electrician, hardware dealer, plumber, landscape designer—every trade and profession associated with the home. Until its recent demise, *Housing* was a market to me for two or three articles a year, and I currently produce a monthly column for *Roofing, Siding, Insulation*. Fees are somewhat lower than those for consumer magazine articles. While writing for the "trades" doesn't make me wealthy, I find it valuable in an important way. Research for pieces in trade and professional magazines keeps me very much up to date on what's happening, and triggers dozens of story ideas adaptable to consumer magazines.

Keeping up also means subscribing to those magazines most closely related to shelter topics, or making a monthly run to the public library stacks. Some of the better ones include *Interior Design, Architectural Record, Progressive Architecture, Professional Builder, Hardware Age,* and *Professional Remodeling*. From some of these periodicals comes an annual directory issue, listing by category the names of companies producing home-oriented products. These lists are of enormous value when you're asked to produce a survey article on door locks, for example, or home fire extinguishers. Manufacturers will quickly send you background stock photos and releases, if you mention the magazine for which you're writing the survey. It's up to you to sift the facts from the sales pitch.

There are many more markets. As you get involved in shelter writing, the names of relevant trade magazines will turn up in research, at trade shows, or in conversation with people in the field.

The Importance of Graphics

Show-and-tell is far and away the most-used means to communicate a shelter story to readers. While there is opportunity for articles without photos (in the columns of *Better Homes and Gardens,* for example), nearly all material purchased by magazines such as *The Homeowner* requires photos, illustrations, or both.

Although there are ways to skirt the photo issue, you will greatly enhance your chances of making a sale if you are versatile with a 35mm camera. Suppose you're asked to produce a piece on refinishing second-hand furniture. Most manufacturers of paint strippers, paint equipment, and paints/stains have files of how-to photos which you could use. But with your own camera, you can control the sequence of step-by-step photos and limit the shots to a single project (thus more believable to a reader). Plus, most magazines will pay extra for photos. When I produce a story this way, I also find the writing comes more easily—whether I'm photographing my own project or following the course of a pro—probably because I take part in its production. If I shoot a roof repair sequence, for example, the photos trigger my memory about the facts.

Text—Make It Lively

Struggling to get the facts straight on a shelter article, I often write rather dull sentences. I've found the simplest way to overcome this is to get the facts down first. Then I go back, smooth out the rough places, get rid of redundancies, and inject similes or lively anecdotal material. And quotes always help.

For example, in a *Popular Mechanics* piece on maintaining a house furnace, I wrote, "Don't use household oil to lubricate the furnace motor." Very straightforward. Then I added a quote from an expert: " 'That's like pouring varnish into the works,' he said." Or, instead of, "The desk was a mess, badly assembled," try "The desk looked as though it had been pounded together by a chimp wearing boxing gloves" (as I did for a *Family Handyman* article).

Leads tend to be an arrow straight into the subject, or fictionalized. The same shelter magazine often uses both kinds in a single issue. Two pieces I wrote for *Good Ideas* illustrate the point. Straight arrow on the subject of home safety: "Common sense goes a long way toward keeping you whole and safe in your home." Storybook on a review of windows: "A cat curled in sunlight, napping. A child, propped amid pillows, hair a golden halo of backlighting, absorbed totally in *Treasure Island*. Such images come easily to mind with thoughts of a cushioned bay or box window seat."

Or anecdotal on bath remodeling for a *Popular Science* book:

Dwight Mallary ran hot water over his razor and peered into a clear spot on the steamy bath mirror while his wife, Susan, squinted at her hazy reflection and tried to apply eyeliner. They were running late for a dinner important to Dwight's career. Just then, their nine-year-old knocked on the door. "Daddy, I have to go to the bathroom!" Dwight growled his frustration. "Starting tomorrow," he yelled, "we're adding a bath—no matter what it costs us."

EXPERTISE HELPS

Are you an architect, interior designer or builder *and* a writer? Your future ought to be assured. When your writing is rejected, you can turn to designing and building.

Most of us are journalists first. We gravitate to a specialty because we like it, or because we've had *some* experience in that field. For example, I had two years of mechanical engineering in college and apprenticed as a carpenter; in the Army, I built barracks. But I always wanted to write. My career goal and inclinations eventually converged.

Harry Wicks, a seasoned freelancer and now home and shop editor of *Popular Mechanics,* started out as a home builder. There are plenty of similar examples.

But expertise is also an element you absorb as you write. You don't have to know everything there is to know about buying a house to write about house buying. You do need a sharp, inquisitive mind and ability to ask the right questions of people who *do* know how to buy a house. It also helps to have a mind that, as a matter of course, breaks down complicated jobs (building a house) into its simpler forms (mixing concrete for the foundation), in order of appearance (footing, then foundation, then framing, etc.). And you'll find the writing easier if you've experienced some of the work you're describing, and liked doing it.

WORKING THE BOOK PUBLISHING MARKETS

House painting is among the easiest of home maintenance and decorating projects. A person with native intelligence and no prior painting experience should without difficulty be able to take up a paint brush and coat a front door, dining room wall, bedroom ceiling, or tool shed and leave behind barely a flaw. This person would, of course, read and follow instructions on the paint can label.

Incorrect. Or so it would seem by the number of books published each year on house painting. Listed in the latest *Subject Guide to Books in Print* are *thirteen* books on this mundane subject. I have eight in my own library. I guarantee a new volume will be out next year. And the next.

I have to admit that most painting books repeat one another. Each attempts to cover the subject from A to Z. Some limit discussion to indoor or outdoor painting, some to wood finishing or antiquing. But the "new" premise remains. Ten years ago, polyurethane varnish was barely known. Today, it's a "regular."

And there is really no subject so overdone that it can't stand an updated treatment. Systems change. Products and equipment change. New households are formed not only every year but every day. People are looking for help beyond that given on paint can labels. Publishers are looking for writers who can help. If you can bring new light to an old subject or view it freshly, you might very well find a publisher.

For example, no writer has yet produced "When not to paint what," a could-be-valuable collection of *don'ts* in the painting trade: don't paint over shellac, don't paint a wet sliding panel, don't knock out a wasp's nest underneath the eaves if you're standing on a ladder to do it, etc.

The other route is to approach a publisher with a book idea on an up-and-coming subject. After the oil shortage in 1974, the parade of home-energy-conservation books marched out like the graduating classes for the past ten years at West Point.

Either in the works or on the horizon are books on such subjects as backyard hydroelectric power and the coming revolution in solar-generated electricity for each house. Interior space has been and will continue to be covered by writers, but with new slants (e.g., *Living in One Room*, written by two friends of mine, Molly Siple and Jon Naar). Some others that have recently surfaced: *The $50-and-Up Underground House Book, Champagne Decorating on a Beer Budget, How to Buy Solar Heating Without Getting Burnt*, and *Movable Insulation*, a roundup of the very latest energy conservation techniques.

Steer first toward the traditional publishers: Viking; Penguin; Dodd, Mead; Doubleday; McGraw-Hill; etc. Over the long term you should make more money from standard advances and royalties than from publishers offering a flat fee (of which there are a number in the shelter field). There are exceptions, and you ought to compare the promise of an advance/royalty arrangement with the immediate gain of a flat fee if a comparison is presented to you.

I don't know anyone who has amassed a private fortune writing shelter-subject books. But many, such as A.M. Watkins, enjoy a comfortable income from books. Watkins, a long-time ASJA member, has written seven books in this field.

WRITING FOR SHELTER COMPANIES

Jobs for trade and professional organizations and manufacturers are often the most lucrative. Any producer of building materials, furniture, or furnishings is fair game. Associations with memberships in six figures are often on the lookout for writers (the National Association of Home Builders comes to mind). But smaller groups need help, too. Over the years, I've done several brochures for a remodeling organization that recently changed its name to the National Association of the Remodeling Industry.

What kind of writing is needed? Marketing brochures, text for annual reports, scripts for slide shows or video presentations, speeches, and sometimes, whole books. For example, back in 1955, the Stanley Works Company produced with a freelance writer, *How to Work with Tools and Wood*, a 488-page manual that's updated periodically. Well over a million copies have been sold.

Or in 1982, I wrote a single chapter on energy-efficient garage doors for the Wayne Door Company of Mt. Hope, Ohio. The chapter was used in a book on energy conservation produced for the 1982 Knoxville World's Fair. My compensation included expenses for a visit to the Ohio plants and a chance to interview the top executives, plus a fee roughly twice what I normally receive from the highest-paying magazine in this field.

Sounds good, right? Pause, though, before you race to the door of the nearest maker of doors or roof shingles. Companies hand out assignments, as a rule, to seasoned writers, and especially to people they know personally. For example, Stanley picked a writer who had produced a huge how-to encyclopedia for homeowners. When the door company tapped me, I'd been writing on home-related subjects for thirty years.

Shelter might almost be called a sleeper market. Many novice journalists are anxious to break into print with blockbusters on politics, sex, celebrities, making money, or psychology. Writers on shelter subjects are content with their field. They're making a steady, comfortable income, as you'll discover eventually, if you take a step toward shelter.

VEGETABLE GARDENING: MY SPECIALTY BROUGHT ME TO WRITING
by Cynthia B. Driscoll

"I did it! Sold twenty-two articles in my first year of writing. Payment from $50 to $750 an article, including transparencies. I'm really a writer!"

In 1979 when I wrote that, a latent dream had come true. At age 44, because of a recent all-encompassing interest in vegetable gardening, I became a writer. And I'm still incredulous. When I read my words, see my own transparencies published in national magazines, I still thrill, still revel in my lucky life.

Without a specialty, I would not be a writer today.

Always an avid gardener, in 1977 I enrolled in a noncredit course in horticulture at the University of Minnesota, as part of the Master Gardener Program. (Free Master Gardener courses are offered in most states. County agricultural extensions have information on local dates and course descriptions.) In exchange for free tuition, upon completion of the course I became a Minnesota Master Gardener, donating fifty hours a year to my community as a neighborhood representative of the county agricultural extension office.

I quickly became known as the local vegetable lady. I initiated a farmers' market in my tiny town, became a 4-H vegetable garden leader, planned vegetable garden tours, and spoke at garden clubs within a thirty-mile radius of home. I experimented extensively in my own garden, planting new varieties and trying various cultural techniques and first-time-on-the-market products from hybrids to bug remedies.

I enrolled in a few horticulture courses at the University of Wisconsin. After three full quarters, I was truly excited about learning more and more about growing vegetables. My confidence in the field grew, too. And I was gradually building a library and files on garden-related subjects. Almost without my realizing it, my goal became earning my living in the field of horticulture.

My neighbor, a professional home economist and former director of Land O' Lakes Kitchens, was freelancing as a microwave cooking expert. We began to chat about our specialties, sharing ideas and techniques. Her husband is an executive at Webb Publishing Company, and editor of *The Farmer*, so she shared his advice. Often I'd plant a cultivar my neighbor wanted to use in her demonstrations, or give her unusual vegetables to cook by microwave.

I'll never forget that phone call in the fall of 1978 and Mattie's excited voice.

"Webb's purchased a small gardening magazine. Sharon Ross, the new editor, needs writers. Why don't you give her a call?"

Silence.

"Me?"

"Yes, you."

Well, I knew I could write. Anyone with a bachelor's degree from Smith College after who-knows-how-many essay exams had to know how to write. But for a magazine?

Within minutes I had dialed Sharon, and to my complete surprise, she asked me to write a garden planning piece for *The Family Food Garden*.

Hesitating only a moment—I was in the midst of final exams—I agreed. It was the right decision. And after I received a check for $400, I queried Sharon on two more article ideas. Her "yes" confirmed my destiny. I was on my way.

Writing for specialized markets is an easy pathway to getting published. But being a writer requires persistence and all the faith in a field of mustard seeds.

My own writing yielded positive results. Twenty-two manuscripts sold in 1979. Sharon had responded with "go ahead" to seventeen of my ideas. As a matter of fact, in February, March, and May, she published two of my articles per issue.

Meanwhile, my new endeavor led me to the library and on an I-want-to-be-a-writer reading spree. Every book I could find on marketing, magazine article writing, and working writers' methods passed under my eyes and was sifted through my brain. I learned about queries, record keeping, filing systems, reference books, self-discipline, Strunk and White, English language usage, interviewing, editors' preferences, editorial prerogatives, liability, contracts, First North American Serial Rights versus Work-for-Hire Agreements, payment upon acceptance, pay on publication, and neat manuscript packages.

I purchased a camera, a typewriter, and some manuscript-size stiff envelopes. My husband designed stationery with a line drawing of our rural home and garden, as well as my address, phone, and credentials.

In addition to *The Family Food Garden* sales, by March 1979 I had received six "yes, we'll look at your manuscript" replies from eight February queries. Four bought: *Harrowsmith* for $170; *Mother Earth News* for $240; *Organic Gardening* for $200; *Minneapolis/St. Paul* for $500 (after rejections from *Country Journal* and *Twin Cities*). By December *Today's Homes: Plans and Ideas* had bought two $100 stories; *Natural Life* had paid $100 and $50. Although I had not made a living wage, I was one happy beginner and eager to continue.

My first year's enthusiasm for writing as a full-time occupation carried over into the second. And I was lucky it did. Although I worked just as hard, I earned considerably less, selling only nine pieces, three of them to new buyers. Nonetheless, I'd become addicted to this profession. After twenty years of volunteering and nose-wiping, I felt proud, happy, busy, fulfilled. I daydreamed about selling to the big markets, responding daily to editors' calls.

I speculated on new-to-me publications, received files full of rejections, spent time developing snappy queries and techniques for revolving queries among prospects. I developed a 4x6 filing system for information pertinent to my business: queries out, magazines out, manuscripts sold/not paid, manuscripts sold/paid, manuscripts for resale, magazines to work for, magazines wanting complete manuscripts, ideas. My business in a box included a rate schedule to shoot for, transparencies of vegetables, vegetable experiments, and so forth.

Finally, after a full year of organizing, writing, reading, calling, planning, and photographing, editors began to contact me. Whoopee! The first call was from California and was followed by three from North Carolina, New York, and Pennsylvania. And I felt confident enough to demand reasonable rates. No more stories for less than $200 (and that rate suitable for one to two typewritten pages only).

In 1981 a new and very lucrative market brought in dollars galore. Working at $25 per hour writing funding proposals for nonprofit agencies made me even more confident to demand adequate reimbursement for magazine sales.

In just three years I became a writer!

RUNNING YOUR BUSINESS

1. Keep up to date on your specialty by subscribing to professional periodicals. *HortScience* and *The Vegetable Grower* are two I find invaluable.
2. Organize a file system for home reference.
   Markets to write for: include all correspondence and information about each publication such as rates, editor's name, types of articles, number of words, etc.
   Subjects to write about: for me, some of these include fall gardening in the North, tomatoes, cultural techniques, pests, organic gardening helps, and angles for each depending on season, publication, or potential readers.
   Small file box with all essential facts: queries in, queries out, manuscripts in, manuscripts out, manuscripts sold/paid, manuscripts sold/not paid, magazines preferring complete manuscripts, magazines to write for, and ideas.
3. Build a reference library in your specialty: this could include information on history of the subject; current United States Department of Agriculture publications, such as the yearbook; local growing information for newspaper or regional writing; general weather books; pests; soil; specific culture of a vegetable; and so on.
4. Build a writing library: a good dictionary, thesaurus, language usage books (Strunk and White or others), most-used references.
5. Purchase *Writer's Market,* study it and highlight for: number of manuscripts purchased per year; magazine's readership; rights purchased; rates. Keep current on the markets.
6. *Always* read several issues of any magazine before you query. Study for style, depth, and difficulty of concepts. Gear your piece to the readership the *editor* is aiming for. Use quotes, anecdotes, and humor to make the subject interesting. You can be a serious writer and write with a light sense of humor.
7. Be prompt. A "yes, we'd like to see it" letter from an editor deserves an "I'll mail my manuscript by April 15th" from you. Then mail it by April 15th.
8. Package manuscripts and photos neatly, artistically, including SASE, copy of editor's query response, and a very short cover letter, if further explanation is necessary. Any unusual information or quotes I would document in pencil in the margin.

9. Back up all data with research, and be ready to substantiate.
10. Concentrate on selling as well as writing. After a piece is finished, treat it like a business investment—try to get money out of it pronto. Keep the mails busy with queries, manuscripts, and status letters. Never file a rejected manuscript; send it out to a potential purchaser the day it is returned.
11. Let editors know you're interested in the status of your manuscripts. Write status letters two weeks after the editor has promised to contact you. Be businesslike, brief, friendly, and considerate. Expect the same from her or him. Editors who put you off *aren't worth dealing with.* Keep your self-respect and sell faster by withdrawing your manuscript as soon as you sense that you're being "had."
12. Remember that the highest gross sale does not necessarily yield the largest profit. My best sales have been to a small-circulation local suburban newspaper. Two to four times a month, depending on the season, I contracted to mail the editor a gardening piece for $40 plus $5 for each photo. She supplied film. It takes me one hour to write a satisfactory piece; or, I might send a rejected article from another publication. In terms of dollars per hour, sales to this local paper top anything I've done.

The Markets Today

If I were starting a freelance career today, I'd send queries first to **Alternative magazines:**

Harrowsmith, a quality publication that at this writing pays about $200-$300 for garden pieces. My hope is that soon the editors will realize that a lifetime of experience, research, and education is needed to write gardening pieces for them and, therefore, they should pay as much as for their other articles—up to $1,000.

The *Mother Earth News* purchases 150-200 manuscripts per year, so you stand a good chance of selling to them. Easy, quick to deal with. They pay promptly on acceptance, about $100 per published page, including transparencies. You can be collecting interest on *Mother*'s small payments while you correspond again and again with less efficient editors!

Home and garden magazines:

The Family Food Garden, unfortunately for the vegetable writer, has broadened its coverage to include flower gardening, and it's been sold. It's worth a try, however.

Gurney's Gardening News pays upon acceptance and buys 130 manuscripts per year.

Organic Gardening is the big buyer among food gardening publications, purchasing 400-500 manuscripts annually. Until recently, I wouldn't have recommended *Organic Gardening*. However, the managing editor assures me he is sharpening *Organic Gardening*'s style, freshening the layout, *and* paying more.

I'd send my second batch of individually slanted queries to *East West Journal, Family Handyman, Flower and Garden, The Homeowner, Gardens for All News, Country Gentleman, Vegetarian Times, Gemco Courier,* local publications, or general-interest magazines.

With a well-defined angle, home and garden articles are welcomed by general-interest magazine editors. Send clips of published work with your query at least eight months before the article might appear. Gardening is seasonal. A fresh, illustrated vegetable piece appearing just as the buds are bursting stimulates advertisers' sales. Just remember to get your photos a year in advance! Most magazines prefer 64 ASA transparencies or 5"x7" black and white prints.

Finally, believe in yourself. A rejection is *never* a threat to you personally, your abilities or talents. It's simply a statement that now, at this moment in time, an editor does not wish to purchase your piece.

And definitely continue to write. The independent life is a satisfying one. Good luck!

WRITING FOR THE HOME AND GARDEN MARKET, BUT NOT ALWAYS
by Cecile Shapiro

Some are born with specialties, some achieve specialties, and some have specialties thrust upon them. I'm in the last group, and I suspect a great many other freelancers are there with me. I sold my first article because a friend got tired of hearing me detail what was wrong with high school education in general and my current student teaching assignment in particular. "Why don't you write an article instead of telling me about it?" she asked. Write one I did, and since the only magazine I knew of that had a regular section concerned with education—this was 1961—was the *Saturday Review*, I sent my piece to them. In due course, they sent me a check and published the article. I wasn't surprised or even particularly thrilled—I had no idea that mine was a clear case of beginner's luck. But inadvertently, I had hit upon a few

cardinal rules: Write; don't talk about it. Know your subject. Send your
piece to the right market.

The Path to Specialization

But I didn't turn out to be a specialist in education—although I
burned with thousands of words on the subject—because I had not figured out another cardinal rule: Always follow up a successful publishing experience with a query to the same editor on a related subject.
Before you know it, you'll be a specialist, someone most magazine and
book editors value because they like to deal with known qualities.
(Would you let a surgeon perform his or her first operation on you?)

Without the benefit of subsequent experience, I went on teaching
and not writing. Several years later, I returned to college and earned a
graduate degree in English literature, with a specialty in contemporary
fiction. As a student, I chanced to meet the book review editor of the
Saturday Review at a party. After I graduated, my new degree and specialty gave me the courage to call the editor and ask—with a bright
opener like "you may not remember me but"—for a current fiction title
to review. "Sure," she said, and sent a book the next day. (I have no
idea whether my lone published article had a positive influence, but
beginner's luck was still holding.) The moral of the story: Go to parties.
You'll probably have a good time, and you might meet an editor who
can give you a leg up some day.

Soon, I was writing book reviews regularly for the *Saturday Review*,
though "regularly" meant brief reviews of mostly third-string fiction
six to eight times a year. When another editor who had seen my little
polished gems called to ask me to review for his monthly, I began to
feel like a pro. Two accounts! And I got to keep the books!

During this time, I had switched from high school teaching to textbook editing to college teaching. I had more time, so I wrote many
short stories and a few articles, all of which came back so swiftly that I
wondered why everyone always complained about the United States
mail. Yet soon I picked up another account and was busily writing brief
reviews for a third magazine. I not only had a specialty, but a specialty
within a specialty—short, tight reviews of about 250 words. This specialty, however, doesn't really get you anywhere.

Avoiding Overspecialization

To maneuver out of the corner into which I had written myself, I
sent my first query—to *Atlantic*—on a topic dear to my heart. When a
letter arrived from the editor-in-chief himself saying he would be hap-

py to look at the piece when completed, I floated off euphorically to do research. Months later, however, the finished piece was rejected. I was astonished; my "baby" was so brilliant, so perceptive, so filled with a message for which the world was waiting. And I worked so hard on it (a line I learned from my students). I asked another writer, one who was frequently being published (I met him at a party too), if he would read and critique my article. I hoped he would say the piece was great, the editor of the *Atlantic* was out of his mind to reject it, and why didn't I send it to his friend, the editor of *Harper's?* Instead, he told me the thing was boring, wordy, unpublishable. I shipped it off to a university quarterly, where it appeared in the next issue. No one has ever commented on it, aloud or in print. I have often wondered whether anyone read it. And, typically, I was paid in copies of the periodical. Ten, as I recall. I still have some.

This was not a successful maneuver out of the corner, but read with the right attitude, my tale offers several enlightening messages. First, don't be discouraged. There is always someone who will publish your brainchild, even if no money sullies the exchange. Second, don't be intimidated by a famous writer's denigration; maybe he is jealous of your style and wit. Third, don't expect people whose opinion you value—not even your mother—ever to see any of your published work unless you present them with a copy. (That is, unless you write for the *New York Times.* Even if you write only a letter to the *Times* on the most obscure or abstruse subject, you are certain to receive no fewer than a dozen phone calls—nine from relatives, two from friends, and one from someone you can't remember—saying they saw your letter and agree that bus drivers are unnecessarily rude.)

So there I was, still occupying my corner. I'd begun to fear freelancing was not for me when I bumped into an acquaintance, almost literally; he getting out of a down elevator as I was getting into the up. We exchanged greetings and asked each other how things were going in the magazine game. He earned his bread in advertising but, like me, wanted to freelance for a living. I mentioned a piece rejected two or three times that appeared to have no other potential home; he mentioned a new magazine called *House and Garden's Second House Guide* that seemed made to order, the existence of which he had just learned about in the advertising pages of the *New York Times.* An hour in the library to locate the column, a phone call to ask the name of the editor, another hour debating a new title, a couple of minutes typing a fresh title page, and the manuscript was ready to try again. The original title had been something riveting like "How I Spent My Summer Vacation" (I got that from my students too). The new one was supposed to be funny: "Mrs. Shapiro Finds Her Dream House and She Can Hear You Fine Because There Isn't Any Water Running." (It was about an old wreck of a plumbing-free farmhouse we had mortgaged, then spent the summer hammering at in an attempt to make it liveable.) Knowing from experience how family members can respond to unsolicited high spirits, I rushed off to the post office with the manuscript that Friday afternoon before my husband and children could come home and censor me.

Out of the Corner, Into the Markets

You don't have to believe the next part, although it's true. As I was almost out of the door at 9:15 the following Monday morning, on my way to drive one of my daughters someplace she absolutely had to be by nine, the phone rang. "I love your piece!" a bright and cheerful voice sang when I answered. "What piece?" I growled. Eventually I overcame my hostility toward this early-morning cheeriness and my irritation at being delayed long enough to have a fairly reasonable conversation and even to express pleasure at her praise.

The piece I had sent the editor was published, title intact, then the next, and the next, and yet another, each in one of the several *Guides* that *House and Garden* published in those days: *Decorating, Remodeling, Gardens, Kitchens and Baths, American Tradition, Building, Wine and Food.* Articles for the *Guides* were designed to provide information on some aspect of the magazine's title subject in a readable way to an upper-middle-class audience. (Today's *House and Garden* is aimed at an even more affluent segment of the public, and the *Guides* are no longer published.)

One of the articles I wrote for the *Remodeling Guide*, called "Victorian Houses to Live In," outlined the basic nineteenth-century styles of homes and suggested that on the basis of price and construction they were good values for families. Another piece described the search for original paint colors by professionals restoring the interior of an eighteenth-century house and gave readers directions for duplicating the process on their own. About half of each of the *Guides* featured recycled material from the parent *House and Garden;* most of the rest was staff written, with a few pages left for the freelance material. It's my impression that shelter magazines have less interest in freelancers today than when I began writing for them in the early seventies. Even the more general women's magazines tend to use staff people for features on decorating, remodeling, building, architecture, and gardening—not to mention food and cooking, which are almost invariably written in-house. The shelter magazines don't pay freelancers especially well either, so writers keen on specializing in the house and garden market—which includes the fascinating, burgeoning fields of preservation, urban archaeology, city and rural planning—might consider trying for staff positions on newspapers or magazines. Writers with the right background and talent can move on to enviable careers.

After proposing and writing half a dozen or more articles for the *Guides*, I was asked whether I would like to write a column on—you guessed it—books. (So much for getting out of corners, even nicely decorated ones.) The new books assigned, however, were not the latest fiction. They were on decorating, remodeling, building, architecture, gardening, and such. Although it scarcely occurred to me as I read these (mostly beautiful) books that I was boning up on new fields, that was exactly what I was doing. The know-how so painlessly acquired eventually enabled me to write a book on kitchen design and renovation that was selected by five book clubs and went promptly into a second printing.

ALWAYS A GAP TO FILL

Chance can often play a stronger role in your choice of a writing specialty than the most careful planning. Like most workaday writers, I've published articles far afield from my so-called specialties. But the happenstance that allows you to snare a taxi in the rain may also engage you to a subject you'll be wedded to for life. I'd bet that most successful writers take advantage of the gifts of serendipity.

Better Kitchens, for example, was actually my second book. I embarked on my first because an acquaintance who collected and sold prints via mail order noticed a gap in the available literature. No book on the market told collectors how to identify and authenticate original etchings, lithographs, woodcuts, screenprints, and such; no book advised on evaluating prices, or outlined the pros and cons of buying through dealers, print auctions, and publishers; no book suggested the best means of conserving prints. Since I had studied printmaking and was familiar with contemporary prints, she urged me to write a book on the needed information. We collaborated, as it turned out, with the collector-dealer supplying most of the buying and selling material, and with me doing the writing as well as the remaining research, squeezing in a chapter on the history of American prints. After we had completed a couple of chapters and an outline, we sold the book for a respectable advance to Harper and Row. Two years later, it was published in a paperback edition. Clearly, we had identified an area in which a book was needed, then researched and written one that answered the need. The trouble was, several other writers had the same idea within the next year or so; suddenly, there were four books covering more or less the same long-neglected topic. We earned our advance, but not much more.

When You Have a "Pet" Topic

Despite a contract that gave our publisher first option on subsequent work, my proposal for a book on American art was turned down as "too expensive." Art books with extensive color plates are notoriously costly to produce, and neither our agent, nor the next agent we tried, was able to convince any major publisher that our project could be developed profitably. We had nibbles, but on terms that would have cut the illustrations disastrously, distorted the subject, or turned us into long-term indentured servants. We set aside the proposal and, in 1981, went to Yugoslavia, where my husband was a Fulbright visiting professor of fine art at the University of Belgrade for a semester. There we became friends with a delightful couple—a Yugoslav publisher and an English instructor at the University—who invited us to join them at the Motovun (a picturesque hill town near Trieste) for a meeting of publishers from England, Portugal, Germany, Switzerland, Belgium, Japan, the United States, and elsewhere. One of the reasons this group gets together annually is that all of them—some occasionally, others exclusively—publish heavily illustrated, potentially costly books. They cut costs by co-publishing selected titles in several countries and languages. This way, the print runs of color plates can be relatively large, reducing unit cost.

You probably don't need the end of this story spelled out. I am currently at work, with my husband's collaboration, on an ambitious history of twentieth-century American art, to be published by one of the Motovun group.

TRIMMING WORDS TO CUT TIME AND SPACE

We're writing it, and it's proving to be a giant job. Pace is not easy to establish, especially after years of writing concise book reviews and 2,000-word magazine pieces. I bloated several chapters with such a plethora of detail that to continue as copiously would have kept us busy for at least five years and yielded an unpublishable tome of encyclopedic length. We're learning how to cut back, and we aim to produce a work of manageable shape and definitive content in two years. It's challenging, often exciting, and frequently nerve-racking.

It's also fun. And that, I suspect, is the only reason for writers to enter the freelance fray. If you don't enjoy writing, researching, and editing while you're doing it—not later, when, if you're lucky, you may earn praise, money, or on occasion both—why bother? No matter what their specialties, freelancers give up regular paychecks, vacations with pay, perks and privileges from medical insurance to pensions in order to do their thing. Job security is nonexistent and, with few exceptions, most freelancers are unknown to the next new magazine editor or publishing house they approach. Beginners have as much chance of selling their work as the most experienced pro—if it's on the right subject and professionally done. That's part of the lure and the challenge.

By now I'm sure you have worked out the spate of morals issuing from this bit of selective and possibly encouraging autobiography: Don't let your family convince you your jokes are lousy. Always answer the telephone. Never underestmate the role of chance. If you happen to be standing in the right place at the right time, a writing assignment may appear. I'd advise tuning in to ideas and writing opportunities whenever they drift your way.

Then fly with them!

Additional Resources

American Horticultural Society, Mt. Vernon, VA 22121. Membership includes amateur and professional gardeners. Operates free seed exchange service for members. Has established a Plant Sciences Data Center which compiles a computerized inventory of the cultivated plants of North America. Cosponsors two garden symposia each year. Establishing Harold B. Tukey Memorial Library. Publishes the *American Horticulturist* (monthly), handbooks, and directory.

American Wood Council, 1619 Massachusetts Ave. NW, Suite 500, Washington, DC 20036. Promotes the use of wood products in new single-family houses built in metropolitan areas. Offers photos.

Cardinal Industries, 2040 S. Hamilton, Columbus, OH 43227. The nation's largest manufacturer of multifamily dwellings and motels in the United States. Constructs and manages all aspects regarding construction of apartment or motel projects. Offers aid in arranging interviews, annual reports, brochures and pamphlets, placement on mailing list, statistics, newsletter, photos, press kits.

Carpet and Rug Institute, Box 2048, Dalton, GA 30720. Provides advisory, analytical, how-to, referral, and trade information covering economics and history of the industry, and technical data. Offers annual reports, statistics, brochures and pamphlets, press kits. Publications include information to help consumers with carpet purchases and care.

Foundation of the Wall and Ceiling Industry, 25 K St. NE, Washington,

DC 20002. Provides comprehensive information on building codes, asbestos abatement, lien and contract law, estimating, wall and ceiling materials, ASTM and CSI Standards. Offers brochures and pamphlets, informational newsletters, library facilities, photos, placement on mailing lists, research assistance, telephone reference services. Publications include *Construction Dimension* (monthly), *Who's Who in the Wall & Ceiling Industry*, *Buyer's Guide*, and many technical industry bulletins.

Gardens For All, National Association for Gardening, 180 Flynn Ave., Burlington, VT 05401. Provides how-to, technical, and trade information on gardening, how to save money and energy, improving the state of the earth, air, and water, and using natural resources wisely. Offers monthly *Gardens For All News*, brochures, manuals, charts on pests, disease, planting.

Garden Writers Association of America, Inc., 680 Third Ave., New York, NY 12182. Members include newspaper and magazine writers, book authors, broadcasters. Publishes *Garden Writers Bulletin* (bimonthly) and annual membership directory. Its Talent Directory referral service supplies editors with names of writers and photographers, upon request. Gives annual Quill and Trowel Communications Awards in eight categories, plus a $500 GWAA student scholarship. Conducts regional symposia and an annual meeting.

Home Economics Reading Service, Inc., 1341 G St. NW, Washington, DC 20005. Offers information from 1,350 daily metropolitan newspapers on homemaking interests and publicity. Provides advisory and analytical information on food, household equipment, home furnishings, styles.

International Masonry Institute, Market Development Program, 823 15th St. NW, Suite 1001, Washington, DC 20005. Provides advisory, historical, technical, and trade information on loadbearing construction, passive solar, building restoration, fireplaces, architecture, all-weather construction, craftsmanship in construction, masonry materials and more. Offers annual reports, brochures and pamphlets, photos, placement on mailing lists, press kits, statistics. Publications available.

National Association of Home Workshop Writers, 311 Lake Evelyn Dr., West Palm Beach, FL 33411. Exchanges ideas, tips, techniques, and market information through newsletters, and regional and national workshops and meetings. Write for membership requirements and other details of association activity.

National Association of Solar Contractors (NASC), 236 Massachusetts Ave. NE, #610, Washington, DC 20002. Provides advisory, how-to, referral, technical, and trade information on passive/active solar (including design, installation, and servicing of equipment) and all types of renewable energy technology. Offers photos and aid in arranging interviews. Publications include *Solar Energy: An Installer's Guide to Domestic Hot Water*, and *NASC News* (newsletter).

National Garden Bureau, 628 Executive Dr., Willowbrook, IL 60521. Furnishes garden writers with educational materials, how-to and trade information, photos. Makes about four mailings per year to garden writers who request such data.

The National Paint and Coatings Association, 1500 Rhode Island Ave. NW, Washington, DC 20005. Provides advisory, how-to, referral, and technical information on interior and exterior decorating with paint (color trends and selection, special techniques), how-to directions, maintenance and problem-solving advice. Offers brochures and pamphlets, information searches, placement on mailing list, photos, fact sheets on products or techniques, articles for use as background material. All material deals with paint and coatings in generic terms; company and product trade names are never mentioned. Publications list is available.

U.S. Dept. of Agriculture, Office of Public Affairs, Rm. 113-A Administration Bldg. SW, Washington, DC 20250. Provides specific information on any questions, including answers by twenty-four experts on most agricultural and gardening-related subjects.

Vinyl Siding Institute, c/o Summer Rider & Associates, Inc., 355 Lexington Ave., New York, NY 10017. Provides comprehensive information on anything related to the vinyl siding industry. Offers aid in arranging interviews, brochures and pamphlets, photos, placement on mailing lists, press kits, research assistance. Publications include *What Homeowners Want to Know About Solid Vinyl Siding, Cleaning of Vinyl Siding, Rigid Vinyl Siding Application.*

Wallpapers To Go, c/o Russom & Leeper, 350 Pacific Ave., San Francisco, CA 94111. Provides how-to information on decorating with wallcoverings, do-it-yourself tips, wallcovering trends, unusual uses of wallcoverings. Offers brochures and pamphlets, photos, press kits. Publications include *10 Common Mistakes* (in decorating with wallcoverings), *How Many Rolls Do You Need?, Decorating Basics, Wallpapering Crafts, Wallpapering Techniques.*

Chapter Fifteen

WRITING ABOUT HOBBIES AND CRAFTS

Old bottles and books, coins and stamps. Woodworking, model-building, antiques and automobiles, even buttons and bows. No matter what your hobby or craft interest, you can share your enthusiasm and endeavors with millions of other zealots—and make a pretty good buck in the process.

F. A. Rockwell defined an expert as someone who knows no more than you do, but who has it better organized and uses slides. Accordingly, your favorite hobby or craft expertise can be the stuff of which a writing career is made. The field, astonishingly varied and widely represented by all kinds of magazines, is, oddly enough, one that too few freelancers choose. Yet those who have specialized in writing about such activities as the creation of useful and decorative toys, bicycle repair, patchwork quilting, and gem stone collection have fared quite well.

If you're skeptical, just check the current *Writer's Market* and note the number and diversity of publications in the section labeled "Hobby-Craft." The listings usually include more than fifteen pages of magazines geared toward collectors, do-it-yourselfers, and craft-hobbyists. And this doesn't include electronic or radio hobbyists, found under "Science," nor does it cover those publications designed for owners of personal computers, listed in the new "Home Computing" section.

Moreover, many of the large consumer magazines (e.g., *Family Circle, Woman's Day*) are always interested in fresh, lively pieces that deal with utilitarian and/or profitable crafts and hobbies. In addition, many of the science-oriented and electronics magazines are always hungry for "how-to-build-it" articles.

Again, in this field as with other specialty areas, writers must carefully study market listings and individual magazines for the details of article requirements. It can't be repeated too often (since editors say that some freelancers still don't get the word) that only by giving editors what they ask for, in the form that they want, can you stay a jump ahead of your hardworking competitors.

Finally, this is an excellent field for turning magazine articles into appealing book ideas. It's also a good field for writers who might wish to collaborate with a hobbyist or crafts expert who lacks writing ability. In hobby-crafts you can turn a lifelong love affair into a good dollar and an enviable reputation.

WRITING FOR
THE DO-IT-YOURSELF MAGAZINES
by Mort Schultz

So you want to write for the hard-core do-it-yourself magazines? Let's see if you've got what it takes.

Hard-core do-it-yourself? That's telling people how to trouble-shoot and fix cars, how to paint a house, how to fix refrigerators and washing machines, how to build furniture, how to make electronically controlled gadgets—stuff like that.

Those who read the hard-core do-it-yourself magazines aren't looking for entertainment. They want to save money and gain self-satisfaction, so they turn to the do-it-yourself writer to learn how to do things. They want useful information. Successful do-it-yourself writers can make every sentence a fact, yet their writing is both utilitarian *and* interesting.

THE FIRST ESSENTIAL:
FIRST-HAND EXPERIENCE

A basic essential to make it in this field is a willingness to *do* what you're going to write about. Editors of do-it-yourself magazines are sharp. All of them are do-it-yourselfers, so you can't fool them for long. But more important, your published articles could jeopardize the safety and property of your readers if they contain errors. The best way to avoid errors is to first do the job yourself.

For example, telling readers how to repair a toaster if you haven't repaired a toaster is as ludicrous as trying to teach someone to drive if you don't know how. Leaving out an important step or making a factual error could cause the toaster to go blooey. Worse yet, it could give the reader an electric shock that puts him flat on his back.

Don't let me frighten you off. You don't need a degree in engineering to write do-it-yourself articles. Neither do you have to know the subject thoroughly to get the go-ahead from an editor. But once you get the assignment, be prepared to do whatever you're going to write about. You won't last long in this field if you take previously written material, transcribe it into your own words, and peddle it off as yours. Not only is it unethical, you're liable to repeat errors the other writer may have made. Furthermore, editors of do-it-yourself magazines are well acquainted with most previously published articles and books.

Which brings up the point of "freshness." There is seldom a new subject for do-it-yourself magazines. Topics are often repeated, but always with a fresh approach. For this, too, you must rely on experience.

A fresh approach may be a better way you've found to do a particular job. A fresh approach may also be an advancement in technology that affects the way you tackle the same old task. For instance, the advent of computers to control the combustion process in automobile engines opened up a new field that has, to this writing, enabled me to sell ten articles to various do-it-yourself publications.

How did I learn enough about computerized engine control systems to write about them? I spent weeks in Detroit working with engineers at the "Big Three" until I knew as much, if not more, than most mechanics at dealerships.

Are you ready to get started? If so, I'd suggest selecting one area that interests you and becoming an authority by getting hands-on experience. When you're ready, send queries out. Once you've become known as an expert in your particular field, you can always expand your expertise to other areas. For example, I started out twenty-five years ago as an automotive writer. I expanded to home maintenance and repair, then to boating.

THE SECOND ESSENTIAL: WRITING ABILITY

It takes a special kind of writer to prepare do-it-yourself articles. You've either got it or you don't. If you don't, investigate other fields of writing. You can't learn do-it-yourself writing.

What does it take? Being able to write about difficult-to-describe things in simple terms, and writing concisely, yet in detail. Dichotomies? Maybe, but a good do-it-yourself writer can explain complicated procedures in easy-to-understand terms. He or she provides readers with easy-to-follow instructions and instills confidence in readers that they can do things themselves.

At the same time, do-it-yourself writing involves being a slave to detail while conserving magazine space, which is at a premium. Take nothing for granted. If you're telling people how to replace a fan belt in a car, you damn well better tell them to turn off the engine before sticking their noses under the hood.

Silly? Not to me. In 1971, following publication of one of my books for McGraw-Hill, *How to Fix It*, I made a guest appearance on a morning television show in Boston. The topic was how easy it is for women to do many fix-it jobs around the home. For my video example, I decided to demonstrate how to replace a faucet washer.

Well, I went through the whole bit—removing the handle, taping and wrenching off the packing nut, taking out the stem, unscrewing the worn washer, installing the new washer, and reassembling the unit.

Show over, hostess, producer, and a few others slapped me on the back.

"Good show."

Then the associate producer walked over.

"I just took a call from an angry viewer who did what you told her to do," she said. "She now has one very wet bathroom."

I had forgotten to tell viewers to shut off the main water valve. Whoever thought they needed to be told? It was an embarrassing but valuable lesson. As a do-it-yourself writer, you can't take anything for granted.

THE THIRD ESSENTIAL: PHOTOGRAPHY

A topnotch do-it-yourself writer is also a good photographer, so you must be ready to make an educational and financial commitment to photography—educational if you don't know how to take pictures.

Do-it-yourself magazines require that you submit photographs to show readers what you're talking about. Since so much do-it-yourself work calls for the manipulation of small hardware, the best do-it-yourself writers are astute close-up (as well as long-range) photographers.

You can't take do-it-yourself close-up shots with a fixed-lens Polaroid or Kodak Instamatic camera. Photos have to show detail and be well lit, which neither simple camera can do. My basic equipment consists of a Nikon 35mm camera; 50mm conventional focal length and 24mm wide-angle lenses; numbers 1, 2, 3, and 4 close-up lenses; lighting equipment; tripod.

Can't you hire a photographer? Sure, but good ones get big money. You won't make much of a living as a do-it-yourself freelance writer by splitting fees, but it's a way to go if you don't want to be strapped with the high cost of buying photo equipment.

And there's yet another aspect of photography to consider. Shooting film is one thing—getting prints is another. As with hiring a photographer, having someone develop and print for you is expensive. Naturally enough, this could eventually lead to setting up your own darkroom.

In all, you can figure on spending a couple of thousand dollars for your camera and darkroom equipment.

A TYPICAL ASSIGNMENT

To give you an idea of what's involved in writing a do-it-yourself article, let me describe one I did for *Popular Mechanics*. The subject was automobile cooling-system maintenance and repair. It was a two-parter.

The first part dealt with the hands-on things that automobile owners can do themselves: inspecting and replacing hoses, testing a radiator pressure cap with a cooling system tester, removing and testing the thermostat, inspecting the water pump, inspecting and replacing drive belts, inspecting the fan, and pressure-testing the cooling system to find leaks.

How did I research these things? By doing them on several different makes of cars. Why more than one? Because cooling systems differ in some respects. Telling readers with Hondas how to tune up a Chevy cooling system could lead them astray. Research uncovered the differences.

The research for this part of the article took me about four hours. I was able to take photographs at the same time. The second part of the article told the reader what to do about radiator leaks, and how to clean and flush the system and add a fresh cooling agent. This part emphasized that radiator repair often has to be a team effort engaged in by the do-it-yourself automobile owner and the professional radiator repair shop. This led to two days of research.

Part of the time was spent removing a radiator from a car and taking pictures, so I could tell readers the easiest way to do this. The rest of the time—1½ days—was spent in an automotive radiator repair shop repairing radiators. The reason for this was to show and tell readers what's involved, so they could select a reputable shop to do their work.

Totally, this two-part article took me about two weeks to prepare. What could have happened if I had taken shortcuts? Well, in this business, if you make one mistake, the magazine gets letters from irate readers. The editor may forgive you, but you have to answer these letters—and that's unproductive time. If you make one mistake after another, you'll soon be looking for work in another field. It's as simple as that.

You can often get by with "either-or" in some other areas of writing where things are neither black nor white. But when describing a do-it-yourself procedure, there's usually only one way to do it, and that's the right way.

THE HOBBY-CRAFT MARKETS:
SOME RIGHTS TO REMEMBER
by Eugene D. Balsley

It is well known that, when confronted by a woman who asked him to account for an error in his *Dictionary*, the great Dr. Samuel Johnson replied, "Ignorance, madam, pure ignorance." It may be less well known that when young Johnson first came to London, he was confronted by Wilcox, the eminent bookseller. Wilcox lent Johnson five guineas and then asked him, "How do you mean to earn your livelihood in this town?" Johnson answered, "By my literary labors!" Wilcox shook his head in disbelief. "By your literary labors! You had better buy a porter's knot."

The moral and the lesson from history are simple: Johnson, the archetypical freelancer, was able to earn a living at his literary labors without having to work as a porter, and so can you—perhaps not a very good living, but a living. To quote the redoubtable Johnson once more, "No man but a blockhead ever wrote except for money." We shall return to Dr. Johnson again not only because he survived, but because he knew his trade, and the hobby-craft writer can learn from his words.

It is all right to be uninformed about coin collecting, or wallpapering, or macramé. You can write on any and all subjects if you think clearly and ask questions of those informed in the field. Furthermore, if you are interested in writing about hobbies and crafts, you are probably a practitioner: model maker, potter, weaver, photographer, whatever. But to write about your particular activity involves something of a reflexive process; that is, you are going to have to examine what you know how to do from the point of someone who doesn't.

For example, an electronics hobbyist knows not only *how* to solder, but instinctively checks the soldering iron to make sure it's clean and that the point of the iron is filed back into shape from time to time. Your reader will not know this. So in writing about what you can do, you will have to learn from yourself so that you can inform others. So much for *your* skill; what if you're a potter who wants to write about photography?

You should accept as an article of faith that anything worth knowing, and much *not* worth knowing, is written somewhere in a book. Depend upon it, as Samuel Johnson liked to say, there is a book already written that will dispel your ignorance.

You and I know that good writing is a painful and difficult process. It can lead to addiction to cigarettes, alcohol, and caffeine—not to mention churlishness and a never-ending anxiety about money. Therefore you will, perhaps, agree with the late Thomas Mann, who said, "A writer is someone for whom writing is more difficult than for other people."

Take comfort in the fact that most people do not write, either because they do not care to—a luxury you and I cannot afford—or because they have not cultivated the ability to think. But, to a man, to a woman, every living person *believes* he or she could write, "if I only had the time." This totally unfounded belief will be an obstacle to your career and to the amount of money you can make.

Two cases in point. On one occasion I was handed a great bundle of paper, illustrations, notes, and printed matter and given a week to write and deliver a complicated filmscript on cataract surgery. I demurred in my diffident way and was told by my client, "Well, I don't see any problem. It's all there but the words."

If you have done any amount of writing you may laugh at the anecdote, but it will probably be laughter mixed with a sigh and tinged with the shadow of the gallows.

On another occasion I was being plumbed by a chief radiologist in the course of a very undignified and uncomfortable hospital procedure. To pass the time and ease my agony, the doctor and I had a casual conversation. After a quarter of an hour of chatting, the doctor said, "You seem quite intelligent; are you a physician?"

Now a writer, because he or she has frequently endured the painful process of thinking, will agree that a competent writer can handle just about any topic. And handle it well. Given perhaps two weeks and access to a good library, a journeyman writer can become the second- or third-best authority on nearly any topic. If you already are versed in a particular hobby or craft, you enjoy certain advantages. That is to say you can avoid doing some of the research; but you cannot avoid *thinking* about what you want to write. That is why writers sharpen pencils, polish silver, and take the dog for a walk before even considering beginning work. Thinking is burdensome and onerous.

THE WRITER AS READER

If you are a compulsive reader, as many writers are, you will have read widely and with catholic range. This is all grist for the mill; because if you are *really* a reader, you will know at least a little about a lot of things, as well as have the ability to find out more abut an area of interest.

In Boswell's *Life,* Dr. Johnson says, "The greatest part of a writer's time is spent in reading, in order to write; a man will turn over half a library to make one book."

In your reading, and in your work, you will find that in most cases there is *one* reference book that is either the acknowledged authority in the field or, at least, the source you're most comfortable with. Photographers, for example, can consult the fourteen-volume *Kodak Encyclopedia of Practical Photography*. Reader's Digest General Books has many volumes on assorted hobbies and crafts. Visit a hobby shop to see what books they sell or recommend. And above all, go to the public library and consult both major listings like "photography" and clusters of books around "745" in the Dewey classification. Remember the words of H.L. Mencken: "Give me access to a first-rate library for thirty days, and I can become the second-best authority in any field." And depend upon it, there *is* a book that can be your bible and your guide. And by the way, nearly everything published by Reader's Digest General Books in the how-to area is excellent. You can't copy from them, but you can surely learn to write a how-to book.

In the matter of general reference books and dictionaries there is a good deal of dispute. I happen to like the *American Heritage* and the *Shorter Oxford*—although the *Oxford* is designed only for determining the historical origins of English words.

None of this is to say that you should not exploit your strengths. If you are for example, a fairly accomplished practitioner of photography or carpentry, or a picture-framer or potter, that fact will give you some kind of entree to writing assignments in the hobby-craft field. And it will be easier to convince editors and other clients that you are the person for the job.

Editors are, for the most part, human beings like the rest of us. And therefore it's hard to generalize about what they will want to buy from you. But it seems logical that if you can locate *problem* areas in your hobby/craft, then your well-written, logical solution should be most welcome. If you are writing about watch repair and you can tell people how to replace the balance-staff without spilling all the gears and springs on the floor, you should have a successful article.

A *very* good rule in any kind of how-to writing is to give the reader something he or she can do *right now*. Under this rule, an article on working with a particular glaze for pottery wins over a piece on building a $5,000 kiln for firing large quantities of pots. If you know the subject, you can identify the problem areas; if you give the reader a solution that can be put to work at once, you have a winner.

If you are ignorant on the subject, your problem is somewhat more difficult—but not because you can't do the job. If you're a writer, you can write. If you have analogous experience, you can use that to generalize and persuade your client that your can cross over to a related subject. My original training, for example, was in writing and producing nonfiction motion pictures. I was able, after some strenuous talking, to convince a photographic magazine editor that motion pictures were photography.

For the Beginner

If you are just getting started as a hobby-craft writer, learn to write a query letter to an editor. In a query, you outline what you'd like to write on, how long you'd like to make the article, and set down a few of your qualifications. If you wish to appear to be a professional, stretch the truth a *little*. As to what "a little" means: in Cook County, Illinois, where I grew up, there was a shared knowledge among politicians and voters as to the meaning of "honest" graft. At its simplest level, honest graft meant that a good Democrat in need of work was entitled to a job raking leaves in the parks. A contracter who supported the Party (there was only one) ought to get a chance to earn some money building things for the city. But stealing was another matter. And everyone knew the difference.

So, while you may stretch the truth a *little,* do not perjure yourself.

Another thing that will make your queries appear to come from a veteran writer, even if you're not, is to deal with your assignment in terms of so many "words" rather than the more conventional "pages." A standard sheet of typewritten material, double-spaced, consists of about 250 words.

FINDING THE MARKETS

How do you find editors to query?

Look on your coffee table. Which hobby-craft magazines, if any, do you buy or subscribe to? Ask yourself why you get these magazines and what about them interests you. Look on the masthead and pick out a name or a department editor. Send a query.

This is not as hard as it may sound; often, the idea for an article lies right under your nose.

For example, if you are a photographer you *know* that using a tripod is a bother in many situations. You should also know that taking pictures with a tripod supporting your camera makes demonstrably sharper images in just about every case. Set forth the case for *always* using tripods in a short letter of inquiry. Presto! An assignment.

If you practice a hobby or craft, you know where the problem areas lie. Put together something your reader can do right now.

Every hobby or craft has problem areas; seek them out. This is where your ideas are to be found. What is "obvious" to you may be an epiphany to your readers.

You can invest in a directory called *Literary Market Place. LMP* is published annually by R.R. Bowker Company, 1180 Avenue of the Americas, New York, New York 10036. The price, last I heard, was $35;

see if your library doesn't have a copy you can use. The *LMP* has plenty of information about editors, book publishers, and so on.

Another route is to attend writing classes or the Writers' Conference the ASJA sponsors every year. You will learn from the formal sessions, to be sure. But you will also meet your peers and encounter editors. Your fellow writers may offer suggestions, and you have opportunities aplenty to charm editors. You can get a lot of education and make good contacts over a beer or a cup of coffee.

The Going Rates

You will find, or maybe you have already learned, that while a writer's notion of an article on any hobby-craft topic is something that has intrinsic value in and of itself, he is wrong at least some of the time. Because there are publishers who see your work as a sort of filling to be stuck in between the advertisements.

In most cases you will be paid accordingly.

One final *caveat*. There are a few magazines that are "for sale." This means that they will not commission you to write an article unless there is a paid advertisement connected with what you are assigned. If you can afford it, stay away. It cheapens your name and your reputation. There is an old expression in the newspaper business: "Write with your hat on." What it means is that any self-respecting writer should be ready to turn down unsavory or dishonest work and be prepared to leave when under management pressure to compromise. End of lesson.

WRITING FOR HOBBY-CRAFT MARKETS
by Barbara Brabec

In 1965, about the time I left a stimulating office manager's job in Chicago to become a full-time homemaker, the crafts explosion—also known as the "do-it-yourself boom"—was just beginning. A number of craft shops and galleries had opened across the country, and professional craftspeople were finally beginning to get attention from the media and the marketplace.

While the professionals were making money, thousands of hobbyists like me were having a wonderful time making the various projects illustrated in *Creative Crafts*, the leading "how-to" magazine for crafters and one of the few magazine markets for craft writers at that time. (In fact, the 1965 *Writer's Market* listed only fifteen hobby-craft markets, so few they had to be grouped with other periodicals in a section titled "Popular Craft and Science Magazines.")

In sharp contrast is the picture we see today. Still resounding after two decades, the "do-it-yourself-boom" has become part of another "explosion" in America: the cottage-industry/home-business movement, in which many crafts people are involved. Gayle McDowell reported in an article in the September 15, 1982, issue of the craft industry's leading trade journal, *Profitable Crafts Merchandising (PCM)*, "A recent *Crafts* magazine survey indicated more than 60% of the respondents had sold a craft project within the previous year." The kind of hobbyists who read a magazine like *Crafts* are the very ones who sell first on a limited basis and then slowly progress to the part-time home-business stage. In this case, considering the quarter-million readers of the magazine, we're talking about *a lot* of hobbyists trying to get into the home-business industry via crafts.

(According to the number of Schedule C reports attached to personal income tax returns, there are at least ten million home businesses now, and this number is expected to increase sharply in the next ten years. My research in this field suggests that perhaps 40 percent of all home businesses are apt to be connected in some way to the hobby-craft market.)

Just how large is this market? No one knows for sure, but Michael Hartnett, *PCM* editor, estimates that 15 to 20 percent of the population, or as many as 45 million people, are involved in crafts as a hobby. This coincides with figures issued in 1981 by the National Endowment for the Arts, which estimated there were at least 250,000 professional craftspeople who derive income exclusively from their products, and at least 40 million craftspeople in the United States. Obviously, as more consumers become interested in crafts, needlework, and other related hobbies, there will be more editorial coverage on these topics by publishers everywhere—and a continuing need for articles from capable writers.

There is hardly a town or city in America today that does not have some kind of craft shop or annual art and crafts fair/show/bazaar/festival worthy of a writer's attention. In fact, it is estimated that more than six thousand such events are staged annually. The actual number of handcraft shops and galleries (which sell finished crafts, art, and gifts) is unknown, but current directories list more than a thousand buyers who invite contact from craftspeople, and this does not include all those shops in small towns across the nation that sell only the work of local residents. Add to this the more than thirty thousand retailers who sell nothing but craft supplies to hobbyists, and you begin to understand the size and scope of this multibillion-dollar industry.

Consider, too, that professional craftspeople, many of whom began as hobbyists, are now in the media limelight because they produce handcrafted merchandise that offers serious competition for mass-produced items already on the market. Quite a few articles are hung on this "news peg." For example, the competition is so fierce in certain industries, such as the manufacture of hand-sewn garments, toys, dolls, and embroideries, that labor unions are currently fighting to have state laws passed that will seriously curtail, if not put out of business, home-based manufacturers of such items. Articles on this topic are beginning to appear in newspapers and trade publications across the country, and more are needed.

Back in the sixties, craftspeople sold primarily to local craft shops or at fairs; now they're marketing their wares at major gift and trade shows, through national mail-order catalogs, or directly by mail through their own catalogs, as well as through special directory books like *The Goodfellow Catalog of Wonderful Things* (Chilton, 1983). This increased visibility has helped many, but harmed others by gaining the attention of labor unions.

Whereas hobby-craft writers may have been limited in markets and the topics they could write about when the crafts explosion was just beginning, today editors of hundreds of hobby, craft, and consumer periodicals are looking for a variety of material that will satisfy the consumer's growing interest in crafts as a leisure-time pursuit, or as the basis for a part- or full-time home business.

ONE WAY TO GET STARTED

My experience as a writer in the crafts field is unusual, and it all started with a hobby that got out of hand. Once I began to make more things than I could give away, I began to sell, with modest success, at local fairs and in the few craft shops I could find in the Chicago area. I gained actual selling experience that would later prove invaluable to me. At this time, there were only a few special-interest craft periodicals, and my husband suggested maybe we ought to publish one to help beginning craft sellers like me.

With little money and no experience in self-publishing or writing, but with several years of office experience behind me and my usual determination to succeed, I plunged into the job of producing a quarterly magazine. It took me a week to write my first 500-word article, and quite a lot longer to learn how to write copy that would motivate people to send money for a subscription. At that time, I knew nothing about information resources for writers and self-publishers, so I simply learned by doing. I made a lot of mistakes, to be sure.

I had no idea what an editor was supposed to do, but was smart enough to give myself that title and, in time, I figured it out by reading magazines of all kinds. After a while, my readers contributed about half the material, making my writing job a bit easier. Incidentally, I designed each issue and prepared camera-ready art with an IBM Selectric typewriter, a few art aids, and a lot of imagination.

Harry's full-time job prevented him from contributing much to the business, but he did spend more hours as a mail handler than he cares to remember. We mailed thousands of promotional brochures and letters each year to get new subscribers, advertisers, and renewals, plus the quarterly mailing of the magazine itself, which at its peak went to 3,500 readers.

Somehow, *Artisan Crafts* managed not only to survive for five years but to receive high acclaim for its editorial content—interesting when you consider it was written entirely by amateurs. In the years to come, other creative people would similarly start dozens of craft-related magazines, newsletters, and newspapers, strengthening America's communications network for craftspeople.

As a home business, *Artisan Crafts* was never as profitable as Harry and I hoped it would be, but it had other, more important rewards. First, it enabled us to communicate with people in the crafts field, as well as with editors and publishers outside the field—contacts that later proved invaluable to me. The magazine yielded a special bonus for Harry when it channeled him into the production of craft shows for theme parks such as Marriott's Great America and Busch Gardens in Williamsburg, Virginia. The latter sponsored the International Crafts Exposition in 1976 and 1977, and Harry's job was to find forty interesting and unusual craftspeople from America and Europe. This required four trips abroad, and as his secretarial assistant, I got to accompany him on two of those trips, visiting several world capitals, including Moscow. Harry selected and bought merchandise from the foreign craftspeople and figured out how to get everything and everyone to the show on time. During the two-week show, he was the expert who solved the problems and the goodwill ambassador who kept his family of American and foreign craftspeople happy. Harry and I look back on this experience as one of the great adventures of our life—and it never would have happened if we hadn't published the magazine.

Shortly after the magazine ceased publication, I attracted the attention of a publisher who asked me to write the book I would later title *Creative Cash*. (Yes, I know my title is grammatically incorrect, since "cash" can't be "creative"; but I didn't title my book for grammarians, I titled it for *buyers*, who obviously love it.) At this writing, *Creative Cash* is in its third printing with close to 50,000 copies sold, and no end of sales in sight.

The most important thing *Artisan Crafts* did was make me realize I had been a writer all my life, from the time I began to keep a diary as a child. Ironically, I had edited the magazine for five years and written several articles and columns for it before I realized I was actually *writing*. I had always called myself an editor because that sounded more important to me. It was not until I was asked to write a book that I began to think of myself as a writer. Just as suddenly, I realized I knew absolutely nothing about the *craft* of writing, and decided I'd better get busy and do my homework lest I be laughed out of the industry when my book was published.

I began with a visit to the library, a good place for all writers to start. By luck or by chance, the first book I selected was *On Writing Well*, by William Zinsser (Harper and Row), which I have since learned is one of the best books for a beginning writer. I used to think I could not possibly be a writer because I didn't know how to use all those long, difficult-to-pronounce words that some book reviewers and critics seem to think are the mark of good writing. So you can imagine my delight when I read in Zinsser's book that "Clutter is the disease of American writing." His most important message to me was to glean each sentence, remove all unnecessary words, and replace every long word with a shorter one. "Writing improves in direct ratio to the number of things we can keep out of it that shouldn't be there," he stressed.

I read many other books and dozens of back issues of *Writer's Digest* as I was writing my first book, *Creative Cash*. Each time I finished a book or magazine, I'd go back to my manuscript-in-progress and correct the writing mistakes I now realized I was making. Thanks to all the rewriting, I learned a lot about the craft of writing. Except for minor copyediting, *Creative Cash* was published, word for word, exactly as I'd written it.

Shortly before *Creative Cash* was published in late 1979, I was inspired to write a humorous poem based on the idea expressed in the introduction of my book: how one's hobby can literally take over much of the space in one's home. To my amazement, the editor of *Crafts* magazine bought it for $100—my first sale as a freelance writer. This led to a column, "Selling What You Make," also for *Crafts*, which continues today and serves a steadily growing, predominately female audience that is very home-business oriented.

At this point, I saw financial rewards could come from writing on one particular topic and so decided to make crafts marketing my specialty within the already-specialized field of crafts writing. With one column under my belt, I now queried *Creative Crafts* magazine and sold a second column, "The Craft Spotlight," which also continues today. It features creative individuals and their accomplishments as hobbyists or home business owners.

One of my greatest thrills as a new writer was my article sale to

Changing Times, a magazine written largely by in-house editors. A year or so earlier, they'd published an article on how to make money from a hobby, but the resource list at the end of the article was woefully inadequate and out-of-date. I sent a query to the editor, advising that I was a recognized crafts authority who could give him an update on this article and a more comprehensive resource list.

"Turning a Profit on Your Handicraft Hobby" appeared in the October 1979 issue. Although I didn't get a byline, I received $750 for the article—my first big sale as a freelancer. That's when I learned the power of being a "recognized authority." I've been capitalizing on this knowledge ever since.

INCREASING YOUR SALES

You, too, can become a "recognized authority" after you've written a few good articles on one topic. You can become an expert on anything if you set your mind to it. All it takes is time and research, and the ability to absorb and organize information you find. Once you've become an "authority" on a topic, your credit line at the end of articles will reflect this fact, which in turn will make it easier for you to sell additional articles.

To further your research on any topic, always ask for an editor's note at the end of your articles to encourage reader mail. Most editors are happy to do this, and readers are generally responsive when anyone asks them to share information or ideas. I've built a full-time business around this idea, beginning with *Artisan Crafts* and continuing with *Creative Cash*. By including my name and address in the book, and asking readers to share their ideas with me, I've generated mail from thousands of people. These letters, added to my other reader mail, provide "grist for my mill," giving me important foundation material for all my writing.

(An added plus of all this mail is that I've developed a mailing list of more than six thousand known readers of *Creative Cash*, all of whom will receive a special announcement when my second book is ready for sale.)

As a crafts writer, you'll benefit by establishing a communications network similar to mine. Begin by subscribing to selected craft periodicals to connect with interesting craftspeople and influential editors and publishers. Send letters to the editors asking for reader mail that will further your research. To expand your network, make an effort to get acquainted with other writers in this field, connecting with them through writers' magazines and organizations. Far from being a competitor, a fellow crafts writer may be your best ally. I got the contract for

Creative Cash only because a writer friend of mine wasn't interested in doing the book, and recommended my name to the publisher.

As you may have guessed by now, my ulterior motive in writing is always to promote the sale of my book, and the plan works. Few books stay on the shelves of bookstores for more than six months after publication, but *Creative Cash* is still being purchased regularly by major bookstore chains and independent booksellers across the country, proof positive that an author's constant promotion of his or her book can give it a long, profitable life.

My columns and articles generally bear a credit line that mentions my book, and this often brings mail from readers who live in small towns without bookstores. They can't find my book anywhere, and to solve this problem, I began to sell it myself. One thing led to another until I decided that I needed a newsletter in order to communicate with all the people who were writing to me. Thus *Sharing Barbara's Mail* was born in 1981—as of this writing, in its third year of publication, it serves more than one thousand subscribers. The market of my book, newsletter, and related articles continues to expand. A new book is in progress (a general home-business manual and resource directory), and I currently have more ideas for things to write about than I can keep track of. If I chose to be a full-time freelance writer, I could stay busy eight hours a day, seven days a week, writing for hobby, craft, consumer, and trade periodicals. But I prefer to be a newsletter publisher, home-business consultant, and seminar leader. This leaves just enough time to write a limited number of columns and articles, plus a new series of "special reports" I'll be able to sell by mail to craft consumers and home-business owners for years to come.

Now here are a few ideas on topics *you* can write about, along with some guidelines on how to find, and then work with, the lesser-known magazines in the hobby-crafts field. Finally, I'll explain the four basic categories of publications in this field and give you some clues on how to slant articles to each market category.

WHAT CAN I WRITE ABOUT?

Each individual has special talents and know-how in a number of different areas. Begin by analyzing yours. Do you make pottery or do needlework? Are you an avid collector, an antiques buff, or a lover of nostalgia? Are you a whiz at fixing or repairing things? Do you like to refinish furniture?

Do you know interesting, creative people? Do you travel frequently, visiting places others might like to know about (museums, historical restorations, craft villages, etc.)? Have you ever given a workshop, or spoken to a group about your hobby or craft?

Do you have a business background? Know anything about taxes, finance, or legal matters? Ever operated or managed a retail shop or other small business? Taught school? Taught crafts to Boy or Girl Scouts, senior citizens, or the handicapped? Are you a good organizer, promoter, salesperson, or motivating force when it comes to getting things done? Any and all of these ideas, plus the several you've thought about that I haven't, can easily provide the basis for salable articles of interest to many periodicals.

One of the nicest things about the crafts field is that it welcomes newcomers with open arms. Unlike other areas of the publishing world, most of the editors and publishers in this field began as hobbyists, craftspeople, designers, teachers, and so on. Some have journalistic backgrounds, of course, but many successful people in crafts publishing have learned everything on their own, strictly by trial and error. So, when dealing with craft editors, you'll have an easier time of it, as a beginner, than writers in other, more formal fields. And you'll have an even better chance of selling regularly if you're especially knowledgeable about some particular topic.

How do you find all your potential markets, especially the lesser-known, subscription-only periodicals? The current edition of *Writer's Market*—which no self-respecting freelancer would be without—lists sixty magazines in a special "Hobby and Craft Market" category, a dramatic increase from the fifteen listings in the 1965 directory. Included are special-interest publications for collectors of all kinds of things (knives, baskets, books, coins, gems, miniatures, bottles, et al.), plus antiques journals, magazines for model-railroad buffs, needleworkers, handicrafters, fiber artists, woodworkers, and so forth. The editors of these magazines have indicated an interest in a broad range of material, including information and historical articles, interviews, nostalgia, personal opinion, photo features, how-to and technical articles, new-product information, humor and travel pieces, and features on interesting individuals (artists, hobbyists, collectors, craftspeople, shop owners, etc.).

But the publications listed in *Writer's Market* are only the tip of the iceberg when we're talking about periodicals related to the ever-growing field of crafts, needlework, and hobbies, a field I shall hereafter refer to simply as "crafts." When I was researching my book, I turned up more than eighty-five craft periodicals, only fifteen of which I'd seen listed in *Writer's Market*. It would be easy now to come up with twice that many little-known craft magazines, newsletters, and newspapers, many of which actively solicit reader contributions. (The editors would probably solicit material from writers, too, if they knew how to reach them.)

The best way to connect with these little publications is to become a part of the craft community by joining a couple of organizations and subscribing to a couple of the better-known periodicals (see the listing at the end of this article). Established publishers in the crafts field are generous in giving publicity to all new craft publishers because they remember their own humble beginnings and take pleasure in giving a helping hand to newcomers in the field.

UNDERSTANDING YOUR MARKETS

As I see it, periodicals in the hobby-craft field can be divided into four main categories: craft consumer magazines, special-interest craft periodicals, hobby magazines, and trade publications. To successfully sell to any of them, you *must* gain a thorough understanding of the interests and needs of the audiences these publishers serve. Following is a description of each category, with tips on how to write for it.

Craft consumer magazines. A huge, national consumer audience is served by the publishers in this category, as I've already indicated. Magazines like *Crafts, Creative Crafts, Decorating and Craft Ideas,* and *Needlecraft for Today* will be found on most newsstands, and you can connect with other publications in this category by visiting the library and browsing through two reference books: the *Ayer Directory of Publications,* and *Ulrich's International Periodicals Directory.* The first includes newspapers and features an alphabetical index of all periodicals in the book; the second categorizes periodicals by subject matter, particularly helpful if you don't know the names of magazines you need.

Editors of national craft consumer magazines are primarily interested in how-to articles that give step-by-step instructions for specific projects, such as "How to Crochet a Room Divider," or "How to Make a Stained Glass Box." Photographs or line drawings are generally required for such articles. General technique articles are also used by some magazines, such as "Twenty Tips for Decorative Painters," or "How to Work with Ceramic Tile."

Sybil Harp, who edited *Creative Crafts* magazine for many years and is now associate publisher of *Nutshell News,* a magazine for miniaturists, emphasizes that you should consider writing "how-to" articles only if you are "creative enough to produce original craft projects, and able to write technical procedures in a lucid, detailed manner."

In short, before you can tell the average hobbyist how to make something, you must know how to make it yourself. Most of the writers who sell this type of article are, in fact, craft or needlework designers who simply fell into writing when they saw the need. As another editor puts it, "We're looking harder for people who can craft than people who can write."

But there is another possibility. As the editor of *Make It with Leather* indicated in a recent *Writer's Market* listing, even if you're not a leather-crafter, you might work with a leathercrafter to put his or her ideas and projects down on paper, sharing payment for the published article. This idea would work for any craft, in fact, and is particularly suited to writers with a talent for photography.

The most important thing to remember in writing how-to articles is that you must never assume prior knowledge on the part of the reader. Editors always work under the assumption that the reader has never attempted such a project and is totally unfamiliar with the materials and the terminology of the craft, so write accordingly. You might try working with a tape recorder. You (or the person doing the project) should speak into the recorder as the project is being made, noting every step taken, every little problem encountered, and what to do about it. Then use this tape as the basis for a written set of foolproof beginner's instructions.

Project ideas aren't the only things craft consumer magazine editors need, of course. Some magazines are open to new columns, special departments, and articles about annual fairs, craft villages, museums, and so forth. Others offer "guest speaker" spots, or space for personal-opinion pieces, craftsperson profiles and so on. Through consistent reading of the various periodicals in this field, you'll become aware of article possibilities like these. Spend some time at the library skimming back issues of all the consumer craft magazines it carries, and read available market directories and writers' magazines to learn the specific editorial needs of larger magazines which, incidentally, pay very well.

Special-interest craft periodicals. This second category of publications covers a lot of ground, and in this instance, the word "craft" includes all the fiber and needlecraft arts and techniques: macramé, weaving, spinning, needlepoint, embroidery, crochet, knitting, sewing, and so forth. Publications run the gamut from black-and-white to four-color magazines, to an amazing variety of poor to superbly done newsletters and newspapers. Some outstanding periodicals are *Fine Woodworking, Handwoven, Quilter's Newsletter, The Crafts Report, CraftsWoman, Fiberarts, Needlepoint News* and others, most of which are available by subscription only.

Many special-interest periodicals are issued by art and craft organizations, societies, or guilds, but just as many are published by individuals. Some have only a few hundred subscribers while others, *Quilter's Newsletter* for instance, have more than a hundred thousand readers. By and large, these publishers serve the more accomplished, serious hobbyist, home-business owner, and craft professional.

Publications in this category pay less for material than craft consumer magazines, of course, but they offer greater writing opportunities for newcomers. Their editorial needs include everything from how-to projects for beginners to business-oriented articles for professionals, along with humor, interviews, craftsperson profiles, columns, success stories, nostalgia, and personal-opinion essays. And craft publishers always like to publish articles that provide resource lists readers can use to track down additional information about their favorite craft or hobby. For instance, you might write an article about baskets, then close with a list of all the publications, organizations, and related catalogs you can find on this topic.

Again, you *must* read issues of each periodical to understand its editorial needs. Also, obtain writers' guideline sheets if available.

Although professional freelancers are usually unwilling to contribute material for publication on a no-pay basis, beginning writers shouldn't overlook the many craft publications that need material but cannot pay for it, or those that offer token fees at best. As a beginning writer, the national exposure you receive in such publications can often be more valuable than a check, particularly if you're trying to promote yourself as a crafts writer, or if you have anything to sell by mail. As a rule, crafts publishers are more than happy to include the contributor's full name and address and also mention the availability of a brochure or catalog of possible interest to their readers—free advertising, in other words.

What other reason might you have to write for a low-pay/no-pay crafts periodical? If you connect with such a publisher early on, when he or she really needs material, and this publication continues to grow and prosper, you'll be in a great position when payment is finally offered for articles. In the meantime, you'll have gained valuable writing experience, satisfied your need for publication, and possibly developed a loyal following of readers.

When dealing with these small, yet often promising markets, you should remember that many new publishers in this field are amateurs with little or no understanding of the publishing business, not to mention the craft of writing. These are mostly creative, energetic craftspeople, designers, teachers, collectors, mail-order sellers, and other crafts entrepreneurs with some special knowledge or experience in a particular area of the crafts field. Or, to put it another way, these are people who were smart enough to recognize a need, and courageous enough to try to fill it, in spite of their lack of formal training as writers, editors, or publishers.

Understandably, not all of these small publishers survive. A certain percentage of all new periodicals, even those launched by professionals with big money behind them, seem fated to wither and die during their first or second winter. But a surprising number of new crafts periodicals "bloom" in the spring and flower for many years thereafter. Some even yield sister publications with slightly different editorial slants.

Something to remember when dealing with new crafts publishers is that many of them, as publishing novices, won't have the foggiest notion about "first serial rights," or copyright law and your rights as a writer. So make sure you protect yourself by selling to these little publications on a first-rights basis only, and tactfully explain in your query letter exactly what this means: that the publication may use your material only once, after which all rights revert to you. This way, any columns or articles you write for them can someday be revised and resold to larger, better-paying markets. Or, you may decide to self-publish a series of reports or booklets to sell by mail to a particular segment of the crafts consumer market.

Hobby magazines. This market differs sharply from the "how-to" magazines for crafts consumers, though both groups of readers may be called hobbyists. While a craft is often a hobby, a hobby is not always a craft, and therein lies the difference. Consider the hobbyist who collects things, buys and sells antiques, coins, books, or gems, or plays with model trains or lead soldiers. Examples of periodicals in this field would be *American Collector, Antique Monthly, Model Railroader* and so on. The best way to find these markets is by reading listings in writers' directories and magazines, where editorial needs are clearly defined. I have no experience in selling to this market, nor do I know the editors in this field, so that's all I'm going to say about it. I leave it to you to do your own homework in this area.

Trade publications. Magazines in this category include *Profitable Crafts Merchandising, Sew Business, Craft and Art Market*, and *Crafts and Needlework Age/World of Miniatures*, among others. They serve "the industry," which includes manufacturers, wholesalers/distributors, retailers/dealers, publishers, sales representatives, and other businesspeople. Professional craftspeople, and crafts writers in particular, read a variety of trade periodicals to stay abreast of happenings within the industry.

Trade magazines are primarily interested in business-oriented articles that tell their readers how to increase profits, open or expand a shop, deal with the variety of legal and financial details involved in any business, get more mileage out of advertising dollars, and so on. Most of the material in trade magazines is written by in-house editors and by only a few regular freelancers. This is because the average writer simply can't write for this market. As *PCM* editor Mike Hartnett told me, "It is very rare that we find a freelancer who can write well, let alone one who is knowledgeable about the crafts industry."

If you think you're the exception to the rule, first obtain the names and addresses of trade magazines in this field (remember *Ulrich's Direc-*

tory), then request sample copies and writer's guidelines. Don't bother to write, however, unless your letter is typed, preferably on a letterhead. I mention this only because Hartnett told me he receives a surprising number of handwritten query letters. Such letters are ignored because editors figure they'll receive handwritten articles, which they don't want.

KEEP YOUR AUDIENCE IN MIND

To understand the editorial needs of the various market categories I've just described, remember that each audience of readers, though intensely interested in the total crafts picture nationally, has an entirely different attitude about crafts and the marketplace. Always take this into consideration when setting the tone of your articles.

I mentioned earlier the importance of slanting your articles to the needs of each individual publisher. In time, you'll learn to get a lot of mileage out of research on any particular topic, using it as the basis for several articles to be sold to different periodicals in the hobby-craft market. For instance, let's imagine that you've just spent several days researching the general topic of how to get publicity, and now you're ready to write.

1. A crafts consumer or hobby magazine might be interested in an article on how hobbyists can get a feature story published in their local newspaper.

2. A special-interest crafts periodical would be receptive to an article that helps professional craftspeople promote themselves and their work both locally and nationally, or one that tells shop and gallery owners how to get publicity for a special showing of local artists' work.

3. A general consumer magazine might buy tips on how church or community leaders can get publicity for a holiday bazaar or other charitable event, or how a group of individual homeowners can publicize their community garage sale or fund-raising event.

4. A trade publication might buy an article that tells craft retailers how to prepare an effective press release, or one that tells how to use promotional signs in their display windows.

In short, there are many different angles from which to view any given topic, and that's what "slanting" is all about.

I mentioned general consumer magazines in point three, above, and although this group of publications cannot be considered part of the hobby-craft market, it nonetheless offers a good market for certain types of crafts articles, particularly the women's and senior-citizens magazines. Thumb through a few issues on the newsstand, and you'll probably find one or more craft or hobby-related articles in each, including how-to projects, "how-they-did-it" success stories, and how-to-do-it home-business articles. Keep in mind that home businesses are now one of America's greatest underground movements, and many of these people are involved in crafts and hobbies. If my mail is any indication, a growing number of senior citizens and other individuals nearing retirement are particularly interested in learning how to turn hobbies into extra income to supplement Social Security.

I hope by now you have gained new perspective on America's hobby and crafts scene and can see how you might fit into this picture as a writer. As you may have gathered, it takes a certain degree of "craftiness" to be a regularly selling writer in this field. The sooner you learn the tricks of this particular trade, the sooner you'll be selling articles to today's steadily growing hobby-craft market.

Articles are not your only possibility, of course. There are more self-publishers in the crafts field than anyone can keep track of, and you may soon find that you have information that could be published easily in booklet form and sold by mail through inexpensive classified ads in the various craft consumer magazines. Furthermore, once you've come to understand the crafts market, established yourself as a writer in the field, and developed a "craft-networking" communications system, you may find you have all the makings for a good book. The market for crafts books is not as good now as it was a few years ago, but trade publishers will always be interested in books that fill a need in the marketplace.

A Few Last Words of Advice

Now that I've achieved a small degree of fame as a writer in the crafts field, I'll share my secrets of success. First, write about what you know, and pay attention to details. Research your topics carefully, and keep on researching after you've sold an article on any given topic. Someday you'll be able to sell an update to it. Start a file folder for every topic that interests you, and read voraciously with scissors in hand, clipping information for your reference files.

Practice the craft of writing faithfully. Take time to rewrite and rewrite again, as often as necessary; then learn to look at your work objectively, from an editor's point of view. (I do this by putting a finished article aside for several days, then reading it aloud as though I had never seen it.)

Read a variety of books, magazines, and newsletters while also studying the writing techniques of others. Through regular reading you'll develop an instinctive feel for grammar and sentence structure, and your own, individual writing style will gradually emerge. Take time to learn the finer points of spelling, punctuation, and grammar, and don't leave the correcting of your material to editors. Careful writers are rare, and when an editor discovers that *you* care enough to turn in a carefully written manuscript, you'll be remembered.

Take advantage of the wealth of writers' books and magazines available and *heed the advice given therein*. I have gained a thorough self-education in writing, editing, and publishing simply by reading, and you can, too. Above all—and this message should be tattooed on your forehead—*know your market!* Foolish amateurs everywhere insist on writing articles of interest only to them, completely ignoring editorial needs and the clear instructions given in market directories, writers' magazines, and editorial guidelines sheets. Once again, the best way to learn what editors need, and are most likely to buy, is to consistently study the periodicals they edit. To do less is to be unprofessional.

One last thing: Remember that everyone is a beginner at some time, and the degree of success you'll eventually achieve as a writer in this or any other field will be directly related to the amount of time and effort you put into the task. The authors of *$ucceed and Grow Rich Through Persuasion* (Fawcett) put it this way: "All of man's constructive achievements are the result of organized thought directed to definite ends in a positive mental attitude backed by belief."

There's quite a message in that sentence for all of us.

At present, there are no special market lists for crafts writers, except for those occasionally published in writers' magazines and in the annual *Writer's Market* directory. This means you'll have to find your own markets—the lesser-known periodicals, in particular—through a study of available crafts periodicals and through networking with writers, editors, and publishers in the field. Begin this research by requesting information from the following publishers and organizations. Please mention this book and enclose a self-addressed, stamped envelope with your request.

The International Guild of Craft Journalists, Authors and Photographers, 3632 Ashworth North, Seattle, Washington 98103. This is the only organization of its kind, and the best way to get acquainted with other writers in this field. Membership includes a regular *Guild Bulletin*.

The Society of Craft Designers, Box 2176, Newburgh, New York 12550. In spite of its name, this is a valuable organization for writers interested in selling how-to articles and books on the crafts industry. Leading editors and publishers generally attend the Society's annual educational seminar. Membership includes a bimonthly newsletter.

The Crafts Report, 700 Orange Street, Wilmington, Delaware 19801. This newsmonthly of marketing, management, and money for crafts professionals will be of special interest to writers because of its general editorial coverage of the changing crafts scene in America, plus its regular mention of new crafts periodicals, workshops and so on.

Artisan Crafts, Box 398, Libertyville, Illinois 60048. This crafts publisher offers a liaison service for authors and publishers, free to authors who wish to connect with interested book publishers registered with *Artisan Crafts.*

The following books will provide additional, valuable information for crafts writers; both should be available in your library.

Career Opportunities in Crafts—The First Complete Guide for Success as a Crafts Professional, by Elyse Sommer. (Crown, 1977.) Includes an extensive chapter on writing for the crafts field, with several profiles of crafts publishers.

Creative Cash—How to Sell Your Crafts, Needlework, Designs and Know-how, by Barbara Brabec. (First ed., Countryside Books, 1979; second ed., HP Books, 1981.) Has a chapter on writing and self-publishing, plus an extensive resource chapter that includes the addresses of more than one hundred crafts periodicals and organizations.

Additional Resources

Artisan Crafts, P.O. Box 10423, Springfield, MO 65808. Author-Publisher Service (free of charge) assists writers and craft book publishers in getting together with ideas and patterns or designs suitable for publication. Provides telephone consulting service, quick question-and-answer service, cooperative mailings, special reports, information sheets. Newsletter, *Sharing Barbara's Mail.* (For written reply send SASE)

Do-It-Yourself Research Institute, 770 North High School Rd., Indianapolis, IN 46224. Provides trade, industry-related information on size of DIY market, growth trends, activities undertaken, attitudes and lifestyles of DIYers. Offers annual reports, informational newsletters, library facilities, research assistance, statistics, seminars. Publications include seminar materials.

Hobby Industry Association of America, 319 E. 54th St., Elmwood Park, NJ 07407. Organization of manufacturers, wholesalers, retailers, publishers, and allied firms in the hobby industry. Conducts seminars, educational workshops; publishes monthly *Hobby Update*, newsletter, special bulletins.

International Entrepreneurs' Association, 631 Wilshire Bvld., Santa Monica, CA 90401. Provides in-depth information on new and unique small businesses. Information covers business, how-to, and new products. Offers bios, photos, press kits. Publications include magazine and 145 how-to manuals on business.

National Association of Home Workshop Writers, 311 Lake Evelyn Dr., West Palm Beach, FL 33411. Promotes communication among colleagues by sharing information about publishers, marketing conditions, and mutual problems on handling materials.

Chapter Sixteen

WRITING FOR YOUNG PEOPLE

If you think you'd like to specialize in writing for children—be they preschoolers, grade-schoolers, or teenagers—be prepared for change. In recent years, one trend in this field has replaced another almost as swiftly as politicians change their minds. In fact, the modern juvenile and teenage magazines offer a kaleidoscopic editorial mix. Some of the leading magazines give you an idea of the range of categories open to writers: *Highlights for Children, Ranger Rick's Nature Magazine, The Electric Company Magazine, Young Judaean, Cobblestone, Ebony Jr!, Boys' Life, Seventeen, Young Miss,* and *Scholastic Scope.*

Writing for young people takes many forms. It could be the picture book to be read to a toddler or a book on astronomy for high-schoolers. It could be an article explaining rainbows to new readers or sexuality to adolescents. Whatever it is, the special challenge for the writer is to learn—and to remember—how his reader views the world. How much can a child of this age understand? What are his questions, concerns, interests? What is a child's life like today?

Most of all, the writer must respect the child. Writing for young children and teens is not as easy as most new writers think. Many editors of these publications have told me that the material they receive is trite, trivial, or patronizing. If you take a "This is just for kids" attitude, you can soon wallpaper your office with colorful rejection slips.

Many writers for children do both fiction and nonfiction. There is some unavoidable discussion of fiction in these pages but, as Karen O'Connor explains, the techniques for writing fiction and nonfiction for children are pretty much the same. The idea is to tell a good story.

Here are a few don'ts that, if ignored, can guarantee failure:

- Don't write down to the young—they're a lot more sophisticated these days.
- Don't preach or over-moralize—most juvenile magazines are somewhat didactic, it's true, but in their teaching with an eye to sound moral values, they avoid preaching.
- Don't try to write for any of these magazines until you've read several issues of a given publication—know as much as possible about a magazine before submitting material to it.

Other failures among new writers in this field result from not staying up with the times. For example, there are far fewer taboos on editorial content and vocabulary today than in the days of *St. Nicholas* and *Youth's Companion*. The interests, not to mention modes and manners, of readers in this field today are a far cry from those of *American Boy*. Today's children grow up watching realistic, nitty-gritty stories on TV, and there just aren't many themes to which they haven't been exposed.

Another trend, thanks to feminism, has been to avoid sexual stereotyping in children's magazines and books. No longer is "Mommy" the happy homemaker always, while "Daddy" goes off to work every day; no longer do little girls play only with dolls and nurse's kits while the boys play with their cars and cannons.

The book market in this field has also seen considerable change in the last two decades. In uncertain economic times afflicted publishers have been plagued by rising costs of doing business—paper, printing, binding, warehousing, and shipping. And the institutional market for children's books in libraries, both school and public, has been shrinking as a result of budget cuts by local, state, and federal governments.

This affects writers in numerous ways: they must wait longer for reactions to manuscripts; new authors may have a tougher time placing first books; both established pros and newcomers will find that there's a limited call for the book of marginal commercial appeal in today's cautious marketplace.

In the last analysis, however, both publishers and writers in this field are convinced that children of all ages will continue to read magazines and books. And you must actively pursue the new markets along with the old, realizing that only your best efforts are likely to result in that sought-after sale.

It cannot be repeated too often: be a good craftsman—and market intelligently.

THE LITERATURE OF FACT: USING STORYTELLING TECHNIQUES TO MAKE NONFICTION COME ALIVE
by Karen O'Connor

"Come on, honey," Mr. Peters yelled to his wife. But as he stretched out his hand toward her, the driveway opened between them. They faced each other across a gaping hole. Mr. Peters ran to the garage and grabbed an extension cord. He tried to throw it to his wife, but it wouldn't reach. And before he could think what to do next, his house reared like an angry mule and slid toward the sea.

Fact or fiction? A report or a story? Make-believe characters or real-life people? Sometimes it's difficult to tell which is which—at least from a brief excerpt. Why? Because most of today's good books for young people—whether fiction or nonfiction—are alive with picturesque nouns, strong action verbs, plenty of anecdotes, and lively dialogue.

In fact, there are fewer differences between the two than many of us acknowledge. Fiction and nonfiction are simply two branches of the same writing tree. I use story techniques in my nonfiction writing all the time. And I know that many stories and novels involve the same digging, poking, research, and interviewing that nonfiction requires.

For example, in my book, *Nature Runs Wild: True Disaster Stories* (Watts), quoted above, I made a point of including the same "page-turning" elements I had observed in my favorite stories—convincing characters, action, intrigue, drama, and dialogue. Yet, it is nonfiction.

The people I interviewed for my career book, *Working With Horses: A Round-up of Careers* (Dodd, Mead)—a crusty old cowboy, a self-motivated woman owner of a jockey school, and a determined female farrier competing in a formerly all-male profession—each shared stories and experiences that rivaled even the best Western yarn! Again—nonfiction.

And in my recent biography, *Contributions of Women: Literature* (Dillon Press), I used storytelling techniques to recount the lives of five women. However, at no time did I fictionalize any part of their stories; all details are true. In fact, when I began the project, my editor cautioned me against altering the facts in any way. She was very clear about her intention that this book and the others in the series be colorfully written, yet fully accurate.

I enjoyed writing all three books, but I was particularly excited about *Nature Runs Wild*. Unlike the others, it gave me an opportunity to present scientific data and the drama of human interest through the storytelling art. The people, places, quotes, and events of each chapter, from the 1962 avalanche in Peru to the Buffalo blizzard of 1977, are all real.

As raw material in newspapers, magazines, and reports, these same details were dull and dry. I knew that, in order to write a lively and informative book for young people, I had to go beyond the facts. Once again, I used the techniques of storytelling, one of the most effective and dynamic ways to transform straight facts into a spellbinding narrative full of fascinating information.

YOUR CREATIVE PROCESS

"Changing data into information is a creative process," says prolific children's author Jane Yolen in *Writing Books for Children*. It "consists of organizing, distilling, and processing . . . making comparisons and finding commonalities. All these things can be summed up in one word: *recognition.*"

For me, recognition is that exhilarating point of discovery when I suddenly connect a stray fact or a bit of data with something I've experienced. It is this often thrilling element that makes nonfiction writing as creative as writing fiction.

The creative process Yolen talks about is exactly that—a process that you create and polish in your own way and time. It's the result of your individual experience and takes practice and commitment to perfect.

Since we all operate at our own pace, it's best not to use someone else's formula. For a time, you may wish to follow the suggestions here or those of other writers. Then, as you gain more confidence, you'll probably sort through these techniques from time to time, saving some and discarding others, until you have put together a kind of patchwork: each square a shared idea—the whole, something entirely your own.

DISCOVERING AND DEVELOPING IDEAS

The deepest enjoyment of all comes from discovering and developing a marketable idea, then turning the research into something that has meaning, is fun to read, and stretches the boundaries of a young person's imagination.

"Creative thinking," says Rudolf Flesch in *The Art of Readable Writing*, "is just another name for finding new idea-combinations." He suggests that writers draw upon all their ideas, experiences, and memories, then "move them about until you feel the click, the electric spark, the sensation of 'That's it!' "

My most effective ideas have come from my immediate surroundings. Over the years, I've become a kind of snoop, staying alert to the people and events closest to me. I jot down bits of dialogue, names, dates, places, stray facts that intrigue me, snappy titles—whatever catches my imagination and no matter how unrelated they may sound at the time. Then I play with these bits and pieces until something clicks. If an idea takes shape quickly, I continue working with it. If it's slow and frustrating, I put it down and go on to something else.

Abundant resources are all around, so you needn't be concerned about running out of ideas. For example:

Personal experience. Look into your own background, education, and interests. If you've ever worked as a teacher, librarian, scout leader, salesperson, or office worker, as I have, you've probably had many experiences with young people. My first book for the middle grade reader, *How To Make Money* (Watts), sprang directly from my work with children as a Camp Fire leader, mother, and tutor, as did my follow-up book, *Entertaining*.

During the next few years I wrote a tennis dictionary with the help of my tennis-playing son, and our family's interest in horses led me to write the book on careers for horse-lovers.

Friends and acquaintances. Keep your eyes and ears open. People are one of the very best resources for ideas. As Richard Harding Davis said, "The secret of good writing is to say an old thing in a new way or a new thing in an old way." And if you don't, someone else will—at a party, in the dentist's office, at the market, on the tennis court. So be sure to have a pen and pad handy at all times. Then you can get it down before it gets away!

Two educational films and my book *Special Effects* evolved just this way—a conversation between another parent and myself on the sidelines of an ice rink where our sons played hockey. Several contacts for my horse careers book sprang from my friendship with a young student photographer. And the first of many textbook contributions for the Glencoe Publishing Company began after I met and shared my work with the president, the father of one of my daughter's schoolmates.

Research. What you don't live through you can look up—then turn into creative information. That's exactly what I did with *Nature Runs Wild* and the biography of women writers, as well as two educational films and entries for various textbooks.

I also look through the daily newspaper, magazines, and my encyclopedias *intending* to locate topics. It works! A letter in Dear Abby's column, an article in the *Christian Science Monitor,* and a report in the *San Diego Union* all contributed to an idea for a book on animal rights.

Interviews. If you can reach an authority on a particular subject that interests you, so much the better. After receiving a contract from a publisher for *Maybe You Belong In A Zoo!: Zoo and Aquarium Careers* (Dodd, Mead), I contacted the public relations director at the San Diego Zoo. Her assistance was invaluable. She set up at least twenty interviews for me with a variety of zoo personnel: curator, veterinarian, trainer, keeper, restaurant manager, ticket-taker, security guard, horticulturist—even the zoo's animal dentist. In writing *Special Effects: A Guide for Super-8 Filmmakers* (Watts), I interviewed several behind-the-scenes experts at Disney Studios, Paramount, and Universal. It would have been almost impossible to write either book without professional expertise and guidance.

How do you reach experts you need as sources? I usually write a friendly letter introducing myself and the project, then try to follow up with a phone call. If you know someone who has a contact in the field you're interested in, get hold of that person first and find out the best way to proceed. I have found many helpful contacts by just mentioning my current project to a friend, neighbor, or fellow writer.

During the past ten years, I've interviewed hundreds of people, and without exception all were anxious to participate once they knew what I was up to.

I generally set up the interview at the interviewee's convenience, state the approximate time I'll need (usually thirty to sixty minutes), and then prepare for the appointment with a set of specific questions. Although it's best to conduct your meeting in a friendly, conversational way, some basic questions help you stay on target, avoid repetition, lead into colorful and lively personal experiences or anecdotes, and make the most of the time you have.

Too often we tend to minimize our own experience as a source for ideas and contacts. You may know someone who could give you some useful information but you're reluctant to make the call. You may think it's impossible to get an interview unless you're known in the field. Or perhaps you're shy about discussing book plans and ideas with other people.

Actually, talking with people and interviewing experts is one of the easiest and most pleasant ways to expand your writing. People love to share their knowledge and points of view. If you approach them with enthusiasm, confidence, and professionalism, you're bound to come away with many new ideas and a fresh look at some old ones.

ADVENTURE IN WONDERLAND

Writing nonfiction books for young people can be a real adventure. Each new idea takes you down another rabbit hole. During the past three years, for example, I've witnessed surgery on a ten-month-old orangutan, toured the special-effects departments of Disney and Paramount Studios, traveled bumpy back roads with an equine vet, watched meteorologists chart the weather, interviewed one of the last authentic cowboys in the West, and strolled the tree-lined streets of nineteenth-century Amherst via the letters and journals of Emily Dickinson.

Each of these diverse experiences resulted in a book, and each of them at one point was no more than an idea. So if you enjoy digging for bits of information in musty old magazines, tracking down experts, interviewing people at their jobs, poking through letters and journals, and reading and writing until it's the best you can give, then you probably have what it takes to write nonfiction books for young people.

What does that path to publication look like? What steps are involved? How can you get started? There is no exact route. It's a journey each writer must map out for him- or herself. But most children's authors share a few common experiences along the way.

For example, while gathering material for a new book, I find it useful to ask myself two questions—over and over, if necessary. "What does all this mean? And how might it affect the lives of my readers?" The answers were especially useful when I was in the process of selecting anecdotes and biographical data for *Contributions of Women: Literature*.

While writing about Emily Dickinson, for example, I kept my audience of eleven- to fourteen-year-olds in mind and chose one or two incidents of Dickinson's teenage years, which included an excerpt from a letter she wrote at age fifteen to her friend, Abiah Root:

I am growing handsome very fast indeed! I expect I shall be the belle of Amherst when I reach my 17th year. I don't doubt that I shall have perfect crowds of admirers at that age. . . .

It seemed to me that young readers would enjoy finding out that Emily Dickinson, who lived more than a hundred years before their time, was not a stiff Goody Two Shoes hidden away in a dry history text, but a real, live girl who experienced the same dreams and desires as any girl anywhere.

As a writer for young people, it's important to always keep in mind your purpose for writing the book in the first place. It isn't enough to accumulate a great stack of 3x5-inch cards filled with tidy notes. They're important, but they're not enough. To hold the attention of today's lively readers, we need to be as curious and enthusiastic about life as they are. In fact, our books will only be as worthwhile as our willingness to share ourselves and our discoveries.

Young people are not only curious and smart—they're sharp, too. They know the difference between dull, lifeless reporting and the kind of exciting information that only can come from a writer committed to doing whatever it takes to make the best book possible—the kind of book that keeps them turning the pages.

This is also the kind of book editors are looking for. At Follett, for example, the children's book editor wants "to expand nonfiction: feelings, careers, nature, science, and biography for the very young." Messner's editor, on the other hand, is "looking for nonfiction for teens, especially topics that are contemporary and of high interest." And at Holt, Rinehart & Winston, editors are "looking for books with appealing and easily identifiable topics, books kids will be concerned about."

Most children's books are purchased on a royalty basis with advances ranging from $500 to $5000 or more. It is not a field of overnight riches. But the nonfiction book market can be a steady and satisfying source of work and income for the industrious and dedicated children's writer. Although advances are small, the shelf life of a great number of juvenile nonfiction books is good. Many authors continue to receive royalties even several years after publication. As a result, over the long term these books may earn as much or more than a comparable adult book of nonfiction, which often disappears from the stores within six months to a year.

FOLLOW THE YELLOW BRICK ROAD

Whether you write biography, science history, or how-to, you can follow these proven steps on your path to publication. I find them particularly useful on days when I'm stuck for words or when my creative energy has dropped below sea level.

First, clarify your goals. What is the purpose of your book? What is the most useful way to organize it? How can it be of value to your reader? When I'm clear about my goals before I begin, the idea takes shape almost immediately, and the article or book appears to unfold rather than having to be constructed.

While writing *Maybe You Belong In A Zoo!*, I was stuck for days because I had been careless about following this guideline. After interviewing more than twenty people, I thought the material would just fall into place. But it didn't; I had lots of wonderful data and anecdotes, but the book lacked focus and organization.

Finally, I returned to the basics, answered the two questions I discussed earlier, reviewed my material, grouped it logically, added two chapters to tie it all together, and within a few weeks I was ready to polish it up and send it off. I realized later how much time and energy I had lost in trying to build my book without a blueprint.

Approaching an editor with a clear and sound book proposal is also an important part of this first step. Included at the end of this article is a sample of one of mine—a format that has worked well. To make sure I reach the appropriate editor with my book proposals, I rely on *Writer's Market* and the market survey conducted each year by the Society of Children's Book Writers. [Editor's note: See additional resources listed at the end of this chapter.]

You may also find it useful to read and study the various book catalogs. Request your free copy by sending a postcard addressed to the publicity department of any publishing houses that interest you.

Second, commit to the project at hand. My entire writing career transformed when I was asked in a class to look up the meaning of the word *commit*. "To bind or involve [oneself]," said the dictionary. Although I had used this word for years, I had never really made it mine.

Suddenly it was no surprise that my career wasn't moving as quickly as I wanted. I had been too scattered in my approach. I discovered that looking for new ideas wasn't nearly as important as being committed to the ones I already had.

My daughter confronted me with my own lack of commitment two years ago while I was writing *Working With Horses*. I was going through a divorce at the time and my life had all the drama of a soap opera. There were many days when I could hardly face myself, let alone my typewriter. Within four weeks of my deadline I still hadn't written one word. I wanted out!

She reminded me of the principle I had been preaching all her life: *Keep your word.* "Do what you said you'd do, Mom. Even if you never write another book, finish this one. You gave your word."

Her remarks hit me like cold water. She was absolutely right. I would have either results—a published book—or a bunch of reasons why I couldn't finish it. (None of which would interest my publisher or anyone else.) I took a deep breath and got back to work. From the start, the book sold well; received widespread reviews and won second place in the California Press Women's 1981 Communication Contest. I often think of what I'd have missed if I'd given in to my mood.

Third, create an experience for your reader. This point is important to me because it involves the challenge and the fun of writing nonfiction for young people. When putting books and articles together, look for ways to create an opportunity for your readers to have an experience they might not otherwise have.

For example, in *Nature Runs Wild*, they do not simply read a stack of dry seismological data and theory. Instead, they see how science relates to the human experience, how people act during a crisis, how quiet people turn into heroes, how talkative people become scared and shy, and how adults find themselves as much in need of comfort as children. Readers can then compare these experiences with their own and perhaps gain some insight into their lives.

Even in a simple and straightforward how-to book such as *How to Make Money,* young people can relate to Suzy and Bill's Sure-Fire Shopping Service because it creates word pictures that motivate them to set up their own neighborhood businesses. They read for information and entertainment and in the process are inspired to take action.

Jo Carr, author of *Beyond Fact: Nonfiction For Children and Young People* (American Library Association), claims that fine nonfiction writers "make us think deeply" and "make us feel deeply."

Thinking is vital, she feels. We should encourage children to think, to relate one fact to another, to test a familiar idea against a new one, "until at last the child can weave a pattern of increased understanding. What begins as idle curiosity should end as independent thinking."

Moving young people from idle curiosity to independent thinking is the exciting opportunity we have as writers of nonfiction. It is also our privilege to expand their creativity by leading them from the vast outer world of facts into the satisfying inner world of intuition and experience. And the bridge connecting the two is what makes the difference between a factual report and a truly creative work. The sensitive, caring nonfiction writer will not only present his or her particular view of the world, but will go beyond fact and share his or her vision, as well.

WORKING WITH HORSES
A Roundup of Careers

by Karen O'Connor

HOOK
Gain editor's attention with specific facts.

Did you know there are close to 10 million horses in the United States today? More than twice the number of 15 to 20 years ago. As the horse population grows, opportunities to work in the field increase too. According to the American Horse Council, "There is a great need for qualified employees in many areas of the industry." However, since most young people seek only the glamour jobs of rider or trainer, many other good positions go unfilled. For example, work is increasing on breeding farms, at racetracks, and at private training stables. There is also a growing demand for women in the horse business.

SLANT
Competition?
Age group?

Thousands of young horse enthusiasts are anxious to learn about careers in these fascinating and challenging fields. Until now, however, no such book has been published for the middle grade/junior high reader.

VALUE
Purpose of publishing your book.

The real value of this book comes from interviews with top professionals. They offer solid advice and up-to-date career information. They also share personal experiences of the problems and joys in the business. All agree that anyone determined and committed will find the work exciting and satisfying.

FORMAT
What this book
is about.

Proposed Chapter Outline

One —   Your Future in the Horse
         Industry
Two —   So You Want to be a Blacksmith
Three — Racetrack Careers
Four —   Horse Show Occupations
Five —   Training Riding Horses and
         Teaching Young People to Ride
Six —   Training Circus Horses
Seven — Working on a Guest Ranch
Eight — Retail Sales
Nine —   Horse Healers and Helpers
Ten —   Rodeo Riders
Eleven — Breeders
Twelve — More Ways to Learn About
         Working with Horses

Black and white photos shot especially for
this book illustrate each chapter.

MARKET
Sales potential
and shelf life.
IMPORTANT

A leisurely trail ride, the roar of a rodeo, the
grace and beauty of a prize racehorse inspire
and entertain millions each year. As long as
young people continue this love affair with
horses, WORKING WITH HORSES will sell!

THE REWARDS OF WRITING
FOR YOUNG PEOPLE
by Terry Morris

After ten years of freelance writing—chiefly magazine articles for such markets as *McCall's, Redbook, Good Housekeeping,* and *Family Circle*—I had a satisfying and successful career going and thought I could look forward to more of the same. I certainly could never have predicted that my thirteen-year-old son would point me in a wholly new direction.

But that is what happened on January 18, 1961, the day Dr. Thomas Dooley, a medical missionary in Laos, died of cancer at the age of thirty-four. My morning newspaper carried a detailed story about this flamboyant, temperamental Irish-American—a man who made his own rules and drove with single-minded determination toward his goal of saving lives in an area where living conditions were incredibly primitive and witch doctors dispensed medicine. The obituary made interesting reading, but I had heard of Dooley only casually. My reaction was to deplore the loss of such a gifted young man to cancer, then turn the page.

Shortly afterward, my phone rang. The articles editor of *Redbook* was calling to ask if I had read about Dooley's death.

"This is an important story," she said. "We'd like to you to go out to St. Louis and get his mother to work with you on her son's life story."

She indicated that speed was of the essence, since she was sure that other women's magazines would also be interested in the story, and she wanted *Redbook* to have an exclusive, titled "My Son, Tom Dooley." The challenge (and the fee) were exciting, and I agreed to get right on it.

After rereading the obituary closely to obtain leads and contacts to Mrs. Dooley, I got on the phone and was busy talking to Dr. Dooley's most devoted volunteer secretary when my son, Dick, came home from school.

All mothers who try to do their writing at home are familiar with their children's "gotta-talk-to-you-right-away" look, no matter what you are doing or whom you are talking to. Dick was no exception, only this time his usual ebullience was tempered by a certain sadness. I held up a hand to hold him off for a few seconds while I wound up my conversation.

"Thank you very much," I told the secretary. "I'm so grateful for anything you can suggest about reaching Mrs. Dooley."

Ordinarily, Dick's interest in my various assignments was sporadic, depending on whether he felt any involvement with the subject matter, which was rarely the case. Quite understandably. But this time, Dick was full of excitement.

"Did you say Dooley, Mom? You're going to write about *Tom Dooley?*" I described my assignment briefly and his comment was: "Wow! That's fantastic!"

My son reeled off facts about Dooley's life and activities, described the day Dooley addressed the school assembly, and how kids everywhere were into fund-raising "to help Tom in Laos." I gathered that Dooley had become a kind of folk hero to them, sparking their youthful idealism and channeling it into a program of down-to-earth projects under the aegis of the Tom Dooley Foundation.

"An article isn't enough," Dick concluded. "Kids don't read *Redbook*. You ought to write a book, Mom, especially for us."

And that's how, after writing a *Redbook* cover story by Agnes Dooley as told to me, I became the author of a book for young people. Since I had a considerable track record as a writer, and the *Redbook* piece appeared within four months of Dooley's death, I had little difficulty in selling the idea to a book publisher.

The book jacket blurb for *Dr. America: The Story of Tom Dooley* accurately describes what I set out to do:

"Terry Morris has told Tom Dooley's story honestly and excitingly. She has not glossed over his faults nor tried to make him anything but what he was, a man and a doctor who had a job to do. The result is a fast-moving, exciting and fascinating book."

Even some knowledgeable colleagues of mine thought that all I had to do was to rehash the *Redbook* story, scale the vocabulary down to the reading level of ten- to twelve-year olds, and the rest was clear sailing. What they were suggesting reminded me of those early American primitive paintings that depict children as dwarf adults. The little girls wear tight bodices and long, full skirts; the little boys wear starched collars, knee breeches, and buckled shoes; both sexes have puckered brows, pinched lips, and grave, troubled eyes, just like their parents. Well, children are not cut-down adults. Neither are they lame-brains who have to be spoon-fed pureed pap that seeks to cover up or totally deny the seamier sides of the human condition, which even young children are generally bright enough to have observed for themselves.

Dr. America: The Story of Tom Dooley was tailored expressly for my young readers. It was based not only on the material I had garnered from his mother, but also on fresh, in-depth data gathered from his former schoolmasters, boyhood friends, the nuns at St. Mary's Hospital in St. Louis where Tom interned, medical corpsmen who served with him in Vietnam and Laos, students in schools in all parts of America, medical colleagues, volunteer workers. I wanted to project a fully fleshed, many-faceted, complex human being with all his strengths and foibles, his successes and his failures, without either going far beyond or far below my readers' capacity to understand and appreciate the nature of this man and his achievements.

PANNING FOR GOLD

The special challenge of writing for young people is that they demand a book that's exciting to read. You have to rivet their attention in the first paragraph or two. What helps me most are recollections of my own childhood adventures in reading, when all I wanted was a deep chair to curl up in, a juicy apple and a *good* book—one that is, in the language of children's book reports, "a book that caught my interest and held it throughout." That's as good a definition as I have come across.

The key to achieving this kind of young reader response is sifting your material with extreme selectivity before you start writing. You must look for the essential characteristics, the significant details, the revealing incidents when writing for readers of any age, but young people especially will not tolerate having to pan through page after page for gold. They want only the nuggets, not the dust. Not for them are long-winded paragraphs *describing* an action or *explaining* a character trait or *promising* movement in chapters to come. If you have not done the necessary spadework of discarding extraneous detail and selecting and structuring incident and dialogue so that the characters are alive and vital, your young reader will bang the book shut within five or ten minutes and reach for a better one or—horrors—turn on the TV!

Precious Souvenirs

Over and beyond healthy sales and royalty checks, the rewards of writing books for young people are rather special and precious. Among my choicer souvenirs are fan letters from young readers who tear a page out of a loose-leaf notebook and rush to express an opinion. One of these, which rates high marks for candor, reads:

Dear Mrs. Morris, Although I had to read *Dr. America* for a book report, I was really surprised at how much I liked it. I like adventure stories but Tom Dooley's life was so full of adventure, it could just as well be fiction only knowing that a great guy like that really lived made it even better. I'd like to read your next book. Please let me know when it comes out.

P.S. My teacher said that if I write a letter to the author of the book I do a report on and the author answers the letter, I'll get five more points.

I feel that I have really scored as a writer when youngsters tell me how sad or how glad they felt over an incident, or when they become as concerned with a character as this young girl who wrote me:

I kept hoping and hoping that after all those operations, Tom would be cured of cancer even though I knew he did die of it. Why should such a wonderful human being have to die so young when so many really *evil* people go on living to a ripe old age? When I finished *Dr. America* I just started to cry.

Now *that's* reader identification!

Portrait of Humanity

My next book for young people was also, in part, a spinoff from a magazine article assignment, again for *Redbook*. This time editorial interest was focused on American couples who chose to emigrate to Israel, settle on a kibbutz, and raise their children close to the soil in a communal society. The angle was feminist. Were these young wives and mothers truly liberated from traditional domestic duties? Or, as the rather extraordinary title posited, "Can a Young Wife from Baltimore Find Fulfillment Feeding Turkeys on a Farm in Israel?"

What I discovered traveling from kibbutz to kibbutz interviewing American couples has no relevance here except, as you may suspect, that the responses I received were yes, no, and maybe. What has relevance is that the contacts I made and everything I saw, heard, and felt in Israel aroused in me a deep interest in the country.

Since I was there to explore feminist values in Israel, I could think of no better subject than Golda Meir, who within a year of my visit was to become prime minister. Returning home, I began to read everything I could lay my hands on about this redoubtable woman and her involvement in the Zionist cause long before Israel achieved statehood. Here, I thought, was an ideal subject for a biography for young people—history made alive in the person of an enormously productive and vital woman.

Quite unlike Tom Dooley, whose life spanned only thirty-four years, Mrs. Meir was in her early seventies and just reaching the summit of her career. How to do her justice within the sixty thousand words or so generally allotted to books for young people? Her life was so packed with drama, both personal and political, that I had to exercise a relentless selectivity, admitting no material that interfered with the narrative flow and taking great care to capsulize historical events without distorting them.

However, I felt that all the research and planning were merely necessary preliminaries to the great moment when I could meet Mrs. Meir, ask some key questions, and form my own impressions of her personality. Through the good offices of Israeli embassy personnel in New York and Washington, an interview date was set. I left for Israel well beforehand so I could talk to her personal friends and political aides before meeting her.

Waiting in the anteroom of her office in Jerusalem at the appointed hour, I felt dry-mouthed and jittery, even though I had met and written about a president's daughter and a variety of celebrities in show business, sports, and politics. In retrospect, I think my uneasiness stemmed from fear of being disappointed in a woman whom I had come to admire profoundly. All I can say about that hour-and-fifteen-minute interview is that I came away knowing, beyond any shadow of doubt, I had been in the presence of greatness.

I had to celebrate the occasion, even if by myself, and I decided to splurge on a fine meal at the King David Hotel. The Arab who had constituted himself my private taxi driver took me there, and along the way he asked: "You saw Golda? How is she?"

"Marvelous," I said. "A great lady!"

"Golda? She is not great, only like you and me."

I nodded, smiling happily. "You're right. That's what makes her great."

We drove the rest of the way in companionable silence, but in my mind's eye I saw that I had my theme, the cornerstone of the biography. What I would give my young readers was a portrait, not of greatness, but of humanity. And when the waiter at the King David set a glass of red wine before me, I raised it in a toast: "Shalom, Golda!" I murmured, and realized that now I not only had my theme but the title as well.

WHAT DO KIDS WANT TO READ?

You may have heard that young people today are different—more sophisticated, more knowledgeable—than they were in generations past. I disagree. I profoundly believe that what I observe in my garden holds true for the overwhelming majority of children and young teenagers; they need to sink roots into hospitable soil and grow according to their natures. Forcing only weakens the stock; given sunshine and water, they will grow sturdily at their own pace and in their own good time. Today, certainly, many young people are growing up in homes where divorce, alcohol or drug abuse, and sexual promiscuity create impediments to this natural growth process, but generally kids are kids, now as in the past and, happily, always.

My hunch about what young people are like and what they want to read is being confirmed by booksellers all over the country. Ray Walters, who until recently wrote the weekly column "Paperback Talk" in the *New York Times Book Review,* reported that booksellers wished they had something else to offer young people besides "problem" stories and explicit sex. One bookseller was quoted as having asked: "Do you really think the interests of kids today are different than when you and I were kids?"

MORE REWARDS

The enriching experiences of meeting Golda Meir and recreating the astonishing life of Dr. Tom Dooley were rewards in themselves. But there are other rewards that may be more prosaic, yet just as desirable.

On the economic side, although advances on young people's books are generally small (somewhere between $3,000 and $5,000), juvenile titles, unlike adult books, frequently remain in the stores for years. Long-term sales are possible because juvenile books are less faddish.

The *New York Times* recently reported that juvenile books tend to be buried in back corners of bookstores but recently, when the B. Dalton chain clustered some young-adult titles in more prominent positions, it found that sales picked up by nearly 65 percent. Reports from publishers indicate that they "are starting to spend more on advertising, put more authors on tour, and prod sales forces to push juvenile titles more aggressively."

It looks like a good time to come aboard!

ON BEING A (MOSTLY) CHILDREN'S BOOK WRITER
by Barbara Shook Hazen

I didn't set out to be a children's book writer. I got here by happy accident, the way most things seem to happen.

It was the fifties and I was poetry editor of the *Ladies' Home Journal*, in the days when there were such creatures. A friend of mine who also worked there showed her aunt—a vice-president of Golden Books—some of my poems. She liked them—enough to ask me to become an editor. And I did. (Although I didn't write anything in verse again for many years.)

During my three years at Golden, I wrote a few books and edited many more. I worked, learned, fought, and celebrated with artists, authors, layout people, other editors—and myself.

It was an invaluable experience, particularly because it taught me to think visually and to have a feel for the intertwining of art and text. Also, because an editor was responsible for the total book, it gave me an understanding of the process, from idea (discussed at lunch and fought for at an editorial meeting) to manuscript (including revisions, copyediting, and hair-pulling) to layout (checking art for accuracy, fit, and whether it enhanced the text) to finished book (including price, blurb, copyright, captions, instructions, and index, if any). I literally learned on my feet and made mistakes in all the above areas.

I left when my longest work-in-progress, a baby, was imminent. The "baby" now votes, drives a car and goes to college, which tells you how long I've been freelancing.

My freelance career has cut a wide swath, from picture books to adult nonfiction such as the *Dell Encyclopedia of Cats* and *Your Wedding*,

Your Way. I also like nonfiction for "middle-aged" children, approximately eight to thirteen, who are too old for picture books but not quite ready for adult fare.

I still try to think in terms of the total book; I find it more helpful to physically lay a book out than to outline. For a picture book, for instance, I take eight pieces of typewriter paper, cut in half, fold over, staple, and *voilà!*—a very rough thirty-two-page dummy.

I type the text, cut it up, and tape it on the pages. I visualize the illustrations and sometimes write them down in pencil in large balloons. I wish I could sketch, but I can't. Not even decent stick figures. So what is "seen" in the mind's eye has to be translated into words. (**Note:** Many artists and editors don't want to know the author's ideas about illustration. But in setting it up for myself to write, *I* need to know before I write.)

I often write the blurb, or selling copy, first. This helps me define the theme and most important points: what the book is about, where it is headed, and to whom it is directed. When I can't write this relatively easily, it means that idea isn't fully thought out. I may be heading generally in the right direction, but I'm not sure I'm on the right road.

Another writer put it more succinctly: "If you can't define a work in one sentence, you don't have it set—yet."

When working on a longer book, particularly nonfiction, I take the largest sheet of paper I can find and draw paired boxes, about an inch and a half square. I number these like facing book pages, then write in what I intend to write. It never is exactly what I *do* write but it *is* a pattern and helps with proportion and pacing.

Do, Don't Stew

Which brings up my favorite motto regarding anything to do with writing—from technique to discipline (I use the kitchen timer and believe in rewards) to finding a publisher. It was originally said by a friend in reference to child-rearing, but it fits book-raising equally well: "Whatever works."

Another is "Do, don't stew," as thinking about writing is not the same as getting down to the typewriter. (I prefer the typewriter for everything but have several modes of typing, from fast-and-free to "finished," where I watch the keys.)

IDEAS THAT WORK

I find getting ideas easier than executing them. Many a wow-in-the-middle-of-the-night idea simply does not translate into book form.

I also believe that some ideas become beloved for personal reasons, like knickknacks and old sneakers, but don't work on the page. This is particularly true in children's books because there is a tendency to get too involved in your own children or your own remembered childhood.

On the other hand, I am fully convinced that good subjects must have personal relevance. The crux is translating this through words and work into something relatively universal (relatively, because not everyone's universe is the same).

I have gotten my best ideas from eavesdropping, observation, woolgathering, and oddly, after working doghard trying to think through a concept that won't work. Often something else pops up like a crocus and *does* work. It's as if, after a lot of effort, instinct takes over.

I don't believe there are many new subjects, except perhaps in science. The best writing seems to rise out of the subconscious, a shapeless mist seeking a form. In other words, it's been brewing a long time before it's ready to bottle.

I've gotten few viable ideas from my own child, at least not until retrospect. I did write a picture book, *The Many Parts of Me*, out of need when my son Brack was told he had rosy cheeks, only to ask, "What is a cheek?"

But mainly, the mother buttons get in the way of the typewriter keys. The business of being master sergeant, Mom, sandwichmaker and worrier gets in the way of free-flung imagination. It is easier to see someone else's child as inspiration because it's a less cluttered view.

For instance, one muddy March day in New York I was following my neighbor down Lexington Avenue toward the supermarket. She was tugging at her reluctant child, snapping, "Step on it, Andrew." Which he did, into a mud puddle in the gutter, which sprayed thick, sooty brown water over mother, child, and a passerby. She did not find it inspiring or amusing.

I did. Both the scene and the line "Step on it, Andrew" kept burning into my mind so that, when I got home, I typed out the line and pasted it on my "think board."

The next day I played around with the idea, making it wilder and wilder, till it became a "magnificent mud puddle" whose splash, among other things, foiled a robbery, stopped the presses of the *Daily Grind*, and made Andrew a hero, even in his mother's eyes. And *Step On It, Andrew* was published by Atheneum in 1980.

The event triggered the idea. Fantasy took over. That is, I find, something that often happens. But it takes many drafts and directions before a book emerges from the original inspiration and/or event.

Let the Child Take Over

It's important in a book that the child protagonist be the prime mover. The child *makes* things happen and is the hero; any adults are incidental. I seem to take this a step further, which probably demonstrates still-unresolved rebellion, because I relish seeing the child triumph over the adult by being smarter, cleverer, and deeply wiser.

Another for-instance: the idea for *The Gorilla Did It*, which sprang originally from a snip of dialogue half-caught while biking through the park. The gorilla is not only an imaginary playmate but represents the free-wheeling, fun-loving side of humans, the side that both messes up and makes life more loving and laughable. I also wanted the child to "win" in the end by convincing the mother that the gorilla was indeed real, at least to him.

It was only after publication that I realized how deeply imbedded the gorilla was in me, both as a link to my childhood and as a foil to adult responsibilities.

I've also worked with implanted ideas, as when an editor has asked me to do something I wouldn't have on my own. Sometimes this is a story based around a popular character that is hot; other times, it is a subject that fits the editor's book list or personal inclinations.

More than once I have thought "I could never . . .," and then tackled the impossible subject only to find that not only things I expected to think of, but connections I never intended, made the finished result more imaginative in the rendering than was true with more beloved and personal ideas

Whatever the book subject, from pets to names, I like to include touches of humor, oddball facts, and an occasional personal anecdotal example. (One out of the family closet is Aunt Union Forever Shook, whom I used as an example of political naming in *Last, First, Middle and Nick;* the Southern father who named her took a strong stand during the Civil War.)

Surprises happen in the writing, and I think it's good to stretch one's wings. And when asked, to do.

WRITE LOOSE, THEN TIGHTEN

My method of writing would chill the bones of my old English teachers. I do not outline or think all the way through. I simply start to write, even before dummying, which I do after the shape jells somewhat.

When the subject is imaginative or a picture book, I "play" with the idea, loosely and sprawlingly. I don't edit, spell correctly, or prune.

I start loose and pull in. I write down bits of dialogue or phrases that seem to fit in.

I try hard to make myself go, no matter how haphazardly, from beginning to end. Then, after letting it steep in my mind, I take a more judgmental look.

But sometimes there are several more loose drafts and directions between. As long as it hasn't jelled, I can move the words and form around. Maybe I try first person, or third. An animal instead of a real child. A different setting.

At this beginning stage, I might show a manuscript to someone I trust, for advice only; no one is to come to the manuscript with a heavy hammer or blue pencil.

In the middle stage, pacing becomes more important. Usually the beginning needs cutting, the end sharpening. I work on transitions, and finding the best words—everything to make the young reader want to turn the page and want to come back to reread.

In a picture book, I try to make every word count—which is why there may be a hundred pages in the wastebasket for five sent to the publisher. (Knowing which to toss isn't easy, so it's a good idea to keep some of the early drafts. My tendency is still to leave in too much.)

In nonfiction, if the subject is fairly extensive and for an older age group, I type notes on large cards and put them in a file box by subject, so that in a loose way the file, with sections for introduction and ending, *becomes* the first (very rough) draft.

For books for beginning readers, the process is the same as for picture books, except that more emphasis is on repetition and the words are simpler. But not too simple, as I believe in a juicy one thrown in now and then.

The form for any kind of book can best be studied in the bookstore and library. Read everything you can find in your chosen field or genre written for the age group you plan to write for. Everything, that is, that you *like*; there is no point reading the kind of thing you don't want to do.

Ways to Get Unstuck

When stuck, discouraged, or having difficulty starting, copy word for word a page or two from a book of the same ilk—a book that you really like. Do it to measure, line for line, with all the commas and periods. Then crumple and toss the paper away. The act of all that typing gets the juices flowing and provides an outlet for anxiety—and lets you, the writer, then turn to your own thing. (This isn't copying, but rather making a template for the subconscious, a form on which to hang your own words and ideas. It frees rather than fetters imagination.)

I also keep a file called "O.P." (Other People's) in which I stash bits of writing (quotations, excerpts, good beginnings, transitions, and endings) I want to reread and learn from, as well as photocopied pages I love. Pulling out the file is like smelling flowers on a dreary day, with the relished word exciting, and helpful, anew.

Another file is "Words and Phrases," which include a child's wonderful malaprop, a teenager's zesty expression, strong moving verbs, names I find resonant and rich—any of which I may want to use someday in something unthought of yet.

FINDING A PUBLISHER

Finished work in hand doesn't mean finished. The next quandary is where to send the "baby."

I don't have any sure-fire solutions, but I will toss out a few thoughts.

It is impossible to "know" the market exactly in spite of trends. A given editor will like something in spite of the market. Another won't.

I believe that a really excellent and innovative book in just about any field will find a publisher (maybe not the first or even the tenth, but eventually), even in the face of the ups and downs of history, romance, rhyme, readers, and so forth.

I do know that if I try to figure things out too much it hampers creativity. And that I once "found" a publisher by sticking a pin in the *Literary Market Place* (true author's friend that resides in all major libraries and lists current editors at current companies, which also brings up the suggestion that it is better to send to someone, even the wrong someone, than to just-the-company).

Rejection is always hard to take; no one is ever *that* seasoned. But the tendency is to overreact and stash a returned manuscript in the file.

If the rejection is accompanied by a letter with good comments, or "try us again," or suggestions for revision, treasure the positive. No one, these busy days, suggests another go-around unless it's meant. (If you don't want to revise as suggested, that is another thing.) But the editor who bothers, even if he or she didn't buy, is the editor to cultivate, and to try to get to know better.

As to whom to send to in the first place, follow the advice of your local bookstore and/or anyone in the field. A bookstore, even more than the library, shows you what is selling now—and, as companies change, what a particular publisher is coming out with.

Look at the books that are close kin to the kind of thing you are doing. Are they consistently by one publisher, or several? Take notes, learn to know the market, and then send your manuscript out with a prayer and stamped, self-addressed return envelope.

Finding a Voice

I don't think writing is easy, but I think it's well worth it. Why do I? I always wanted to, I suppose, mainly as a way to find my own voice. Writing is also a way of being heard, especially when no one seems to listen.

My first "literary" sale, years ago, when I was in the fifth grade, was a soulful four-line poem to *True Confessions* about the sun and the rain and someday being happy again.

My parents, instead of being delighted, were horrified, because it showed I was becoming more and more like Aunt Union Forever Shook—who also wrote, not at all successfully.

But I kept at it, having also inherited her stubborn streak. Sometimes, still, I hate the act of writing; often I am frustrated by not being able to say what I want the way I want to.

But I increasingly respect and love words. They are friends; they expand my world and give second chances. Writing has helped me know others, and myself, better.

But the best bouquet is to get a letter from a reader who likes what I wrote for the reasons I wrote it. That makes all the weeding and grubwork well worth it.

WRITING FOR YOUNG READERS
by Peggy Mann

Although I didn't realize it at the time, I had my first—and perhaps most valuable—lesson in writing for young readers at age eight. It was a two-word lesson I now apply at once, and throughout, to every book I write for juveniles from beginning reader through young adult.

That summer my parents hired a college student to look after my younger brother and me and our friends. This "nanny" fancied himself a gourmet cook, and one day he sat us all down and described at great length every detail involved in making a strawberry shortcake. We listened in polite (stupefied?) silence until he had finished. Then my four-year-old brother said loudly, "Who cares?"

That is the question. The sitter obviously cared—deeply. But his audience didn't. Nor did he succeed in making us care. Moral: if you wish to write about a subject that concerns you deeply, but that is not a natural for young readers, you've already put up one hurdle for yourself.

This is not to say you should immediately abandon your book idea. After all, one of the most important functions of a writer for children is that of widening the youngsters' horizons. However, if you do choose such a subject, don't expect your intense caring to transmit itself in some magical way to the reader.

Perhaps almost any subject that concerns you deeply can be made interesting to the young reader. The trick is to make him, or her, *care*. (Forgive me, I'm all for feminism, but in this piece I'll omit "hims or hers" and the strange gender *s/he* and revert to the old-fashioned *he, him, his*. But I'll *mean* s/he.)

MAKING THEM CARE

How to avoid that scathing "Who cares?"

One way comes in a sentence I heard from my daughter, then aged ten. I was working on a book called *The Man Who Bought Himself* (the true story of a slave, Peter Still, who did just that). I showed the first chapter to Jenny and she remarked, "I like it because it starts right off."

Start right off—that's also a good aim to keep in mind when writing for adults. Of course, the grown-up reader has more tolerance for the book that begins with a slow unwinding. But for the young reader—whether it's fiction or nonfiction—make very sure that the first paragraphs grab him. After all, you have a lot of competition for his time. That omnipresent television may sit in the same room in which the youngster has settled down with your book. There's the ever-beckoning telephone. Perhaps a baseball game is going on outside.

Be humble. Remember, there's nothing to make the child read past the first few paragraphs. Except you. Your book must not only "start right off"—it must also keep going. A youngster's attention span is shorter than an adult's. Your book can be put down anywhere in midread. However, if you get him involved early, and if you end each chapter on a note of excitement (What's the answer to that question? How will the hero get out of that predicament?), odds are that your reader will keep on turning the pages until he reaches the final one.

A second important precept to keep in mind is this: **Know the age you are writing for.** If the work is fiction, the main characters in that story should be of the same age, or a year or two older. In the only book I've done that was rejected after I wrote it, I forgot this simple point. The subject was one I'd written about extensively for the adult market: the health hazards of marijuana. With the youth-pot epidemic in full swing throughout the country, I wanted to write a book that "had something for everyone" and could reach readers from fifth through twelfth grade. Result: rejection. I had to redo the book completely, aiming this time at fifth- and sixth-graders only. (The result: *Pot—Why Not?*, published by Lothrop, Lee and Shepard.)

A third important guideline is this: **Don't "write down."** As one children's book editor put it: "If your relatives and friends think your story is cute, that is something to worry about. A children's book is not cute." Once you have established your subject, the age group you're aiming at, and some basic approaches that will make that age group care, then—aside from simplifying your language somewhat—forget you're writing a children's book. Just write. If you stand on high and write down to what you imagine to be a child's level the reader will sense this, and will turn off—or perhaps turn on the TV.

If you keep those three concepts in mind, you're well on the way along the road of how to write a children's book.

Books That Help

My own view about children's books is this: there are enough books about little old men and little old ladies and talking dogs and such. I have nothing against such books, and if you want to write in that direction there's surely nothing wrong with it. You'll have a lot of backlist competition, however. (Backlists, of course, are those old standards publishers keep in print because they have built up a following over the years, and when Mama is perusing books in the juvenile section she's likely to say, "Oh, yes, I loved that one when I was Johnny's age." And she'll buy it for him.)

To avoid such subject competition, look for subjects that may be of genuine importance in the child's life.

Although only eleven of the thirty-five books I have written for young readers have been nonfiction, I have used *a nonfiction research approach* for many of these novels. Since other authors in this book will be giving readers a wealth of valuable ideas pertaining to nonfiction research *per se*, and since most of the ideas will be applicable to writers of juvenile as well as adult nonfiction, I thought I might mention the fact that many of these same research techniques can be applied to pure fiction. For some reason, many writers of adult and juvenile fiction seem to feel that the story must derive from their own experience, their own remembered memories, their own subconscious—or from what they have gleaned from being at the edges of other people's lives.

This approach, however, may turn out to be limiting. There is no reason whatever not to use a straightforward nonfiction approach when obtaining (a) the idea for, (b) the background for, (c) in some cases even characters for the juvenile novel.

Regarding point (a): the idea for a book may be derived from such standard nonfiction sources as statistics or interviews. Regarding (b) and (c), this material can be obtained accurately, authentically, and easily by searching out subjects who are *themselves* involved in the problem or situation you wish to write about—and then interviewing them, complete with note-taking and/or tape recorder—just as if you were writing an article or a nonfiction book on the subject.

The following examples will, I hope, illustrate these points.

Selecting a Subject

Upon reading the oft-published statistics about the high rate of divorce, I reasoned that there must be millions of "hurting" children of divorce and decided to write a book on the subject, aimed at readers nine to twelve. But what to say that could be of help to a kid in this shattering situation? To have a book in which Mom and Dad get back together in the end would be fairly phoney and of no help to the child affected by his parents' divorce. In fact, it would only make matters worse—since *his* parents didn't reconcile and remarry.

However, I reasoned, there were two ways in which such a book could be of genuine help to the child of divorce. One: have the young hero feel some of the typical and deep-hidden feelings experienced by the reader. (For example, hating the father for "walking out on Mom and me," even wishing the father dead.) This might serve to relieve the guilt the reader feels when *he* has such thoughts. ("Hey, I'm not the only one who thought that. Joey-in-the-book felt it too!") Expressing this realization to himself is a first step toward expressing it to someone else: a mother, for example, who can help the child deal with what is to him a terrible thought, so evil that it must be kept hidden from everyone.

Another way in which such a book could help, I reasoned, was this: although there would be no happily-ever-after ending, the point could be made that at least Joey was not all alone in his situation. Indeed, at the end of the book he forms a select club of kids who have one thing in common—their parents are divorced. When a youngster reads about a character with the same problems and feelings, he gains insight into himself and is reassured that he is not alone.

Gain Insight Through Interviews

But how to get information and insights for such a book? Since ours is an un-divorced family, I had no personal experience to draw upon. Therefore, I did what I do when I'm writing an article: I interviewed experts. In this case, the experts were not those who got their information second hand (e.g., child psychologists). I interviewed kids whose parents had been divorced. These interviews, it turned out, were not only helpful to me as a writer, but they were helpful to the interviewees as well. If *their* experiences, their pain, could help other kids, it made the personal suffering seem a little more bearable.

Then I interviewed a few adult therapists, who reaffirmed the universality of the responses I'd had from the kids.

And finally (since I'd promised each of my young interviewees complete anonymity), I made up characters and plot for my book based on what I'd learned concerning their feelings and fears. Only in a few instances did I use actual (but nonidentifiable) happenings.

Thus, I used nonfiction techniques to help create a novel.

Although I wrote the book "for" kids of divorce, I kept in mind all the above-mentioned precepts so that it might, I hoped, also appeal to any reader in that age group, including those whose parents are happily married.

My book was called *My Dad Lives in a Downtown Hotel*. It was published by Doubleday, and later in paperback by Scholastic and Avon Books. And, I am happy to say, it did have the effect I'd hoped for. (One letter I received recently was from a mother who wrote: "The teacher phoned me to ask what wonderful thing had happened to Richard. All year he'd sat in class never speaking unless called on. And then only answering in monosyllables. Suddenly, today, he participated. He contributed. He belonged. I told the teacher only one thing had happened to Richard. He'd read *My Dad Lives in a Downtown Hotel*. Then he and I had talked about the book. He opened up about his hidden feelings—for the first time.")

I've gone on at length about *My Dad* because it's a good example of a book that can have a positive impact on young lives. Another book I did of this type was *Twelve Is Too Old* (also for Doubleday), which dealt realistically with the youth-pot scene in junior high and high school.

The subject need not be one that applies directly to everyone. It may describe the circumstances of only a tiny minority of readers, but it should involve each reader as something that could happen to him or to one of his friends. One such book was *There Are Two Kinds of Terrible*, about a boy whose mother dies of cancer. I was asked to write this book by a Doubleday editor whose mother had died when she was a child. "Everyone did everything wrong," she told me. "A book that exposed some of this and which indicated some 'right ways' could be helpful."

"What kid would want to read about *death*?" I asked. But the editor assured me that kids would like such a subject. "One of their highest accolades is, 'It made me cry.' "

So, after research, I wrote the book. I have received countless fan letters that contained those very words of praise: "It made me cry." (Some even noticed that, in the words of one young reader: "Also, there were a lot of places that I had to laugh. I liked that too.")

THE RIGHT IDEA

I first started writing about subjects of genuine concern to young readers when our youngest daughter Betsy was in the second grade. I went along for my annual conference with the teacher and was startled when she asked me, "How do you ever manage in an apartment with two small children and a big dog, a middle-sized dog, and a little dog?"

We had two small children. But no pets at all—not even a turtle. Betsy had fibbed so imaginatively about her dogs that the teacher and everyone else believed her. In talking this over with Betsy, I realized she was justifiably confused. Parents and teachers had praised her for her wonderful imagination. Now she learned from me, for the first time, that fibbing—or, even worse, lying—was wrong. But wasn't fibbing imagination?

I wrote a book for readers in first to third grade to try to clarify this confusing matter: the difference between fibbing (bad) and imagination (good). It was called *The Boy With the Billion Pets* (published by Coward, McCann).

From this experience I learned that in order to discover a subject of real concern to children, it is often necessary to get down on your knees—figuratively speaking—in order to see the world from a youngster's level. What may look like a nothing subject when viewed from the standing height of an adult becomes important when seen through the eyes of a child.

Teachers as Idea Sources

A good source for such subject-ideas is the teacher who deals with children's concerns on a daily and yearly basis. Having had success with the *Billion Pets*, I asked Betsy's third-grade teacher the following question: "If you could have a children's book written on any subject you wanted, what would it be, so far as a real *need* is concerned?"

Without a moment's hesitation she answered, "Every year in every class I run into the same problem. There always seems to be one kid whom all the others turn against. Sometimes for an obvious reason. Sometimes for no reason at all, that I can see. It's too painful and direct to say to a class, 'Why do you all turn against Johnny? How would *you* feel if this were done to you?' That would only make them giggle and turn against Johnny all the more. But if," said the teacher, "I had a story I could read to the children that made them understand what the picked-on child is going through, this could lead to a class discussion on the subject and we'd never need to refer to Johnny at all. We'd be talking about the kid in the book. It could help Johnny a lot."

I wrote *The Twenty-Five Cent Friend* about a child so ostracized that he tried to buy a friend with his allowance. And, according to many letters I've received since, it did improve the situation for many picked-on Johnnys.

Subjects for Nonfiction

I follow the same principles when searching for nonfiction subjects. For example, I've written six biographies. It probably would have been more profitable—bank-statement-wise—to write about popular personalities in sports, rock music, or films. Their stories fully deserve to be written, since young readers want to know about the lives of their immediate and very visible cultural heroes and heroines. However, in my view, youngsters also have a need to become absorbed and involved in lives of great men and women who overcame adversity and who—in that well-worn phrase—made genuine contributions to society. In view of this I chose as biographical subjects the following: (for fifth and sixth graders) *Amelia Earhart: First Lady of Flight; Clara Barton: Battlefield Nurse;* and *Whitney Young, Jr.: Crusader for Equality;* (for junior high students) *Luis Múñoz Marín: The Man Who Re-Made Puerto Rico;* and (for young adults) *Golda: The Life of Israel's Prime Minister* and *Ralph Bunche: UN Peacemaker.*

From letters I received from kids, parents, and teachers, all these books proved profitable in ways more important than dollars and cents.

However, the subject of dollars and cents is one that must be dealt with.

THE GOLDEN EGG?

I understand that some (though perhaps not many) children's book writers do a number of books and then sit back and relax while the royalties roll in year after year. They call their backlog of books their "golden nest egg." I've written over thirty books for young readers. Some have done very well. (Three have made it to TV.) Some do less well. Some are out of print. And royalty checks do come along at regular intervals throughout the year. But never have they accumulated into the golden-egg category. More like a golden grape.

I started writing children's books because I was immersed in a large adult work (*The Last Escape: The Launching of the Largest Secret Rescue Movement of All Time*). This required a tremendous amount of original research. Yet I'd received only a small advance on the book.

Consequently, I had to stop periodically to—as it is pointedly put—make some money. I first achieved this by writing articles, for which I was paid from $1,500 to $3,000 each.

I then discovered that an advance on a children's book would bring just as much. In addition, there was always the chance of making more money via royalties and sale of paperback and other reprint rights. Also, there was the far more important plus to which I have alluded: the satisfaction of sharing positive values with an untold number of young readers.

Therefore, while I was working on *The Last Escape* I stopped writing articles, which I'd regarded as a sure thing, because—unlike magazine fiction—they could be assigned before the piece was written. I took to writing children's books—also a more or less sure thing because, once you have a track record, editors will generally give you a contract on an idea, although some may require a few chapters and an outline. I found that writing a book for grade-school-age readers took about the same amount of time as researching and writing the average magazine article. Consequently, within the twelve-year span it took me to research and write *The Last Escape*, I wrote twenty books for young readers.

To Market, To Market

How about the difficulty of selling juveniles, compared to adult books?

This much may be said: almost all houses that publish children's books will read unsolicited manuscripts (those coming in "over the transom" or without an agent). On the other hand, many houses have let it be known that unsolicited manuscripts written for adults are not welcome—indeed, will not even be read.

Is a children's book thought to be "better' if it comes in from an agent? There are often two piles of manuscripts on an editor's desk: the agents' pile and the unsolicited pile. The agents' pile will be read first. But according to many children's book editors, that is the extent of the advantage an agented manuscript has over the nonagented. It will not receive more favorable consideration; it will only be read more quickly. As to whether it is easier to sell a juvenile than an adult book, in the words of an experienced juvenile editor: "Consider this: far fewer children's books are published each year than adult books—about twenty-five hundred, as compared to many thousands of adult books. From that point of view, more adult manuscripts make it to print. The criteria are no less stringent for juvenile books. The two prime considerations in both areas are excellence and/or marketability."

Speaking of marketability, Miriam Chaikin, a children's book editor for over fifteen years and herself the author of many children's books, puts it like this: "Today, a writer of juvenile books—especially a new writer—must also become something of a 'marketing person.' This means that your query letter (in the case of nonfiction) or your submission of a complete manuscript (in the case of fiction) will have a plus in the editor's mind if you include the following marketing information: Are there any other books on your subject? If so, at what age range are they aimed? When were they published? Are they still in print? How does your book differ from these? These are marketing data that would have to be sought by the editor who is considering your work for publication. If you do the job first, you make things that much easier and speed up consideration of your manuscript."

(You can obtain this information by looking in *Books in Print*, available in most libraries. Books are listed by subject as well as by author and title. Larger libraries have a children's book librarian; you might get helpful marketing information from this source.)

Most children's book editors try to reply to the author within three months of submission. This may seem a long time, and the next obvious question is: "What about simultaneous submission?" As a rule, the answer is no. This practice is frowned upon among children's book editors. They feel that time goes into consideration of a manuscript, and they don't want to spend that time if your book may be accepted first by another publisher.

Sometimes an agent arranges for simultaneous submission for an *adult* book. But this is a carefully orchestrated process in which everyone knows that others are considering the manuscript or proposal at the same time. The manuscript, or author, usually of obvious commercial appeal, goes to the highest bidder. With children's books, on the other hand, most editors will not become involved in a bidding situation or multiple submissions. Indeed, if they know that a manuscript has been submitted simultaneously to other publishers, chances are they will not read it. A children's book editor will usually not even read a photocopied manuscript—unless the author or agent has made it clear that the photocopy should be treated as original and that the manuscript has not been submitted elsewhere at the same time. (Note: A query letter about your manuscript or your idea for a book can be sent to as many publishers as you wish—but even though several express interest, the manuscript itself should be sent to only one at a time.)

Therefore, your manuscript will be considered by only three to six juvenile publishers a year. What is the answer to this? Send it out. Wish it luck. And start on a new book!

WRITING FOR THE YOUNG ADULT
by Sara D. Gilbert

"When you get to be my age," a twelve-year-old told me shortly before my seventh young-adult book was published, "there are a lot of things you want to know, but you really don't feel like asking your parents."

"So where do you find the answers?" I asked, holding my breath.

"Usually, in a book."

Had I known her better, I would have hugged her, tight: my audience! A real, live reader who, to find vital information, goes into a library and takes down one of those books my YA colleagues and I have labored to put on the shelves.

The incident illustrates some basic truths about writing for young people:

• You probably won't get so famous that you will cease to savor encounters with individual "real, live readers." Although there are the Judy Blumes, the Robert Cormiers, and a few other "stars" writing YA material, most of us just sit quietly on library shelves waiting for a "twelve-and-up" to come along. Still, you can enjoy success, a reasonably steady income, and some special satisfactions writing for this age—if you truly understand your audience.

• This age is *not* "juvenile." As my young friend's words show, she and her peers have a sophisticated innocence (or innocent sophistication) that sets them apart from children, teenagers, and adults. It is no accident that publishers and librarians label this market "young adult." These readers *are* adult (think back to when you were twelve, and remember how grown-up *you* felt!); yet they are still young (look back again at that twelve-year-old you, and you'll probably blush at how young you actually were). Although a YA writer shouldn't get too uptight about age ranges or vocabulary lists, the age blend of the audience definitely affects the *style* of writing for this group.

• Because of their stage in life, YA readers do have many questions they "really don't feel like asking their parents," no matter how close the family may be. The bodies and lives of the pre-adolescent and young teen are changing so quickly that they need answers—fast. Also, since the major psychological task of this age is to begin breaking away from parents, it's especially important that they have other *good* sources of information. Finally, they often simply no longer share the tastes or interests (sometimes even the language) of the adults in their lives, and they are looking for material that speaks to them alone. Whether in fiction or fact, books or magazines, writing for young adults needs to focus on their world and touch on those unaskable questions if it is to succeed. These necessities will affect the *content* of your YA work.

• Young-adult readership has perhaps more variety than most audiences; it's not only a matter of taste at this age, but a matter of development and skill, too. My twelve-year-old reader *was* a reader: she was good at it, and turned naturally to books for information and support during what was apparently a normal crisis of adolescence. But, within this age group, you will also find fifteen-year-olds who read at fourth-grade levels yet still want and need entertainment or facts appropriate to their age. You will find kids who "disappear" into books for months on end, and kids whose reading consists of flipping through the pages of a magazine. A street-wise tough and an egghead may be the same age, and although they have totally different tastes and skills, they still need the same information. Some twelve-year-olds have eight-year-old bodies and sixteen-year-old minds, while others have developed with the opposite imbalance. I once went into a panic when an adolescent-medicine specialist told me that people who really need my health book couldn't read—so why didn't I just put together a comic? Then, I realized that I had quite a specific audience: kids who *could* read and who *did* turn to books for help (in my mind, I write to a literate twelve-year-old). Comics with a message are necessary, but I can't do them—perhaps you can. In any case, you do need to choose a segment and write for that audience with which you feel the most comfortable.

PLUSES—AND MINUSES

Although I got into the YA field almost by accident, I've had some success in it because of a seemingly blind sense of the right style, the right contents, and the most comfortable audience. Before trying to analyze that "blind sense" in some fairly useful fashion, let's glance at what we mean by "success"—because writing for young adults does have some special pluses (and minuses).

Pluses: Without meaning to sound idealistically Pollyannaish, I personally get considerable satisfaction out of knowing that my writing does help kids and their families through what can be a rugged period. Also, when you write for this age group, you know you're writing for people who are reading because they want to, and who can be a remarkably receptive and responsive audience. One girl wrote, concerning a recent book of mine, "Thank you for caring." The reader cares, too: hit the right chord, and you can easily impart wisdom or share of yourself.

More pluses:

• In general, YA material, whether books or articles, is shorter than "grownup stuff." Which means you can turn it out in a shorter time and therefore turn out more, or have time for other projects.

• Slightly less expertise is required for YA books than for adult novels or nonfiction. That does *not* mean that you can get away with poor writing or sloppy research, but it does mean that you probably don't have to be, say, a top nuclear physicist (or interview all the top ones) to write about nuclear physics.

• Young adult writing *can* be a way to get started at being published (though note the caveats below). I've found, for instance, that even without a formal background in adolescent development, after a long period of writing *for* this age, I feel comfortable writing *about* it for adults.

• The YA audience is continually revolving, as new generations of "twelve-and-ups" come on the scene each year. While a really hot adult bestseller may make a huge sum at first, it disappears fast unless it's a classic. Books for the YA reader stay around for a long time, because, if they're done well, each year there is a new market for them.

Of course, although there is a trend toward mass-market YAs, meaning big sales for fiction (and some nonfiction), many of the buyers for YAs are still libraries, so although your readership may turn over, your sales may not. And that leads to some of the minuses:

• If you are writing more for big, quick money than for long-term satisfaction, face the fact that YA articles, stories, and books tend to earn smaller fees and advances than projects for adults (but more than is usual for juveniles). If an adult book on nuclear physics gets an advance of $20,000, a YA on the topic will bring $5,000. Young-adult royalties tend to be paid at standard percentage rates, but fewer YA books are sold and they cost less than adult books, so income overall is lower. (But remember that in the time it takes to write one adult book, you can probably write four YAs.)

• Less YA material is published than adult. There are fewer teen magazines and fewer publishers that handle YA material (and those that do have shorter seasonal lists than for their adult books). So to keep on top, you may have to hustle a bit more—pay extra-close attention to trends among kids and in the publishing markets to make a place for yourself and hold on to it.

• The status problem: "Oh, but you just write for kids" is a comment that sets me and my colleagues bristling. The attitude can sometimes create practical problems as well. When I'm setting up research interviews, for instance, I say "I'm writing a book about (whatever) for (whatever publisher)" and wait till after I've gotten in the door to mention that it's a YA book, since many sources feel that informing "just kids" on a subject is a waste of time. Usually, though, the disparagement is only a minor irritation; only when it gets to a point of our being so typecast that we aren't allowed to write for grownups is it a major hurdle.

• Finally, the market and audience can be tricky, and not only for the reasons outlined above. For not only do you have to write to a young audience, you have to *sell* to adults—the parents, librarians, and sometimes the editors—who are almost always filters for the material. Still, there are techniques to get around this problem, and to meet the other challenges posed by the young-adult field.

KNOW YOUR READER

The ancient admonition "Know your market!" is especially important for YA writers, and it means both to understand your reader and to have a feel for the people who buy *for* your reader. You'll want to study the books and magazines written for teens and pre-teens, of course. The YA section of a large library is a good place for books (or the library of a good high school or junior high school, if you can get in), and the shelves of most big newsstands, drugstores, and supermarkets are full of the periodicals you may want to aim for (remember, no matter what their chronological age, your market reads *Seventeen* and the like; older teens read adult magazines).

While you're hanging out (discreetly, of course) in libraries and at newsstands, observe what the kids actually take off the shelves. That can give you a better idea of what they actually want to read than less direct, "expert" advice.

Get to know "your reader" personally. Perhaps you live with one, or teach a bunch. If not, you might volunteer to work with twelve-and-ups in some community organizations. Some background reading on the developmental stage wouldn't hurt either: Gesell, Ginott, Piaget, and Ericson are especially useful, as are some basic developmental psychology textbooks, available in libraries and college bookstores. You'll learn that not only is the YA's body changing rapidly, but the mind and its capabilities are suddenly shifting to "adult" from "child."

Talk with their teachers, their librarians, their counselors—about the kids, about what the kids enjoy reading, and about what the adults think the kids need, want, or should (or shouldn't) have. Remember that, by and large, it's the adults who *buy* the books.

Think back! I dedicated my first YA book, *Fat Free*, to "Fatso"—not someone I knew then, but the me of many years ago. Although, for better or worse, kids are more sophisticated physically and socially than they were when you were that age, if you can remember vividly the feelings, fantasies, and interests you experienced when you were a

YA, you have a good chance of making contact with today's generation.

Respect Your Reader

When you do get to know your reader—whether actually, or by imagining yourself back through time—your style will come naturally, for you will not commit the cardinal sin of writing down to that reader. Instead, feeling an affinity for the reader, you will respect him or her, and that respect will show. I write to my literate twelve-year-old as though I were speaking to an adult, using words and grammar I would use in normal conversation. Some material, for slow readers, does require special vocabulary lists and writer's guidelines, but in most cases you needn't worry about that.

Young-adult readers share with most readers of any age a dislike for the kind of fine writing that shows off a writer's skill more than it gives information or advances a plot. Like most readers, they respond to a personal touch that gets them immediately involved with what they're reading: an anecdote that brings a fact to life; a comment that shows you know that they are special but that they also belong to the human family. And, like almost all of us, they don't want to be preached at. "We might" is almost always better than "you must."

Still, no matter how close you may feel to your reader, you are not a chum. The young adult is reading your material *because* you have already passed through the period that he or she is only just experiencing. Whether in fiction or nonfiction, YAs are looking for answers to questions and solutions to (or escape from) problems that are totally new to them. You're wise, for instance, to stay away from their slang; it will probably be different by the time you're published anyway. Besides, it dates a book, and it dates you.

Consider Your Contents

Content, too, will come fairly easily once you've gotten to know your reader and your market, and once you have an idea of what the kids are likely to be interested in at this age. By and large, where younger children and older teens look for hard facts about the outside world in their nonfiction, the YA tends to be more concerned about personal matters. In fiction, almost anything has appeal—from fantasy through realism to romance. As of this writing (but remember—climates shift) few taboos short of explicit sex, instructions on how to do drugs, or unnecessarily foul language remain in either fiction or non-fiction.

When you are doing your "thinking back," remember that modern young people are developing faster than you probably did—physically and socially—and so at an earlier age are coping with drugs, sex, divorced parents, and concerns about the future. There is nothing that a twelve-and-up mind can't understand, if it's presented clearly.

But, again keep that adult "filter" in mind. Parents pay for most books and leaf through their children's magazines, and even the most open-minded parent is often unwilling to admit that Junior is quite the grownup he actually is. And although librarians (the biggest chunk of the YA market) are certainly not the strait-laced prudes their old image projected, they—and the library boards of schools—need to protect their young clients (and sometimes their own jobs) by selecting material carefully. So if you offend the adults, you may not be able to reach the kids. While you may bridle, as I do, at this sort of passive censorship, you can't ignore it completely and be successful in the YA field. Instead, think positively: "Given what I know about the variability of this age group, how can I best word my material so that the kids will be allowed access to it?"

It may help to remember that a plot based on a socially important issue will help get a controversial novel past a sticky board. In nonfiction, a thorough "further readings" list and good index will sway a dubious librarian.

A Few More Tips

A good editor is essential, I feel, for any writer, and expert editors are perhaps especially important in the YA field, since they are in touch with the shifting moods of both the audience and the marketplace. May you be as lucky in yours as I have been in mine (and I listen to them).

Since community and school libraries make up such a large portion of the YA market, and since library budgets are among the first to be cut in times of tight money, your sales are apt to be tied to the economy more closely than those for adult books. The best way to make money in YA is to keep a steady, overlapping stream of books and articles going. To earn a real living at it, you're wise to diversify. Keep work and contacts going in other areas of the writing business. One nice thing about YA writing is that it does give you time to do just that.

Another nice thing about it: someday you may meet a real live reader, or get a note from one saying, "Thank you for caring."

WRITING FOR—AND ABOUT—TODAY'S TEENAGERS
by Dorothy Siegel

If there's a special trick to writing for young people—or *about* young people—it lies in balancing your material and your own experiences.

I've been a teenager; I am a parent of teenagers. So when writing "about," I blend those two sets of experiences while handling my subject matter. When writing "for," I turn to what can be dredged up from those earlier years, and to my own offspring for their views. (Before becoming the parent of teenagers, I turned to babysitters and neighborhood kids to get a handle on their thoughts and general outlook.)

In the first instance, my readers have been parents who want to learn more about that strange world of adolescence, to understand it better in order to better understand their own children.

For example: *Why* do teens take drugs? How can they be steered away from adolescent drugs? What should parents know about teens' views of the greater world that might lead them to sample dope? Where can they go for help if their own youngsters begin to "use"?

A *Parents* magazine piece of mine dealt with those questions.

Of course, I couldn't do an article on the subject of teens and drugs based on my parental experiences alone, even when it was expanded with family and neighborhood kids' outlooks. ("Mom! Sure, I know about pot-heads—from school. But it's so gross! What a dumb thing to do to your body!" My daughter talks in exclamation points.) So I gave weight to my piece and strengthened it by turning to experts in the field—psychologists, psychiatrists, social workers, and the like.

In this particular case, my editor suggested professional sources. It was up to me to track them down and call or write for an appointment to set up interviews—which, happily, included a group of high schoolers who were themselves fighting drug use, under expert supervision. I could distill their remarks and opinions, adding anecdotal matter gleaned from the youngsters I knew, and shape my piece from this mix. (Whether I quoted professionals or teens, I always checked with them before turning in my final piece to insure there were no misquotes.)

Sometimes a story written for adults can lead to a spinoff for teen readers. For instance, some years back I did an article for *Parents* about summer camps for teens, then a relatively new phenomenon. In this case, I interviewed camp directors and visited one camp, where I talked to campers, counselors, and administrative personnel. The result was a story that informed parents who didn't know about this new alternative to the traditional Camp Wicki-Wacki-Wow scene with its time-honored basket-weaving, pottery, and candle-making activities.

Soon afterward, I reshaped my material into a piece for teen readers of the now-defunct *Compact* magazine.

The *Parents* piece was designed to inform and reassure readers, advising them how to choose a teen summer camp, explaining what it offered and pointing out safety features to consider. Anecdotal comments from staff and campers gave life to my piece, which could otherwise have been a dry recital of "how-to" commentary (how to judge the quality of a camp, its staff, its program).

On the other hand, the *Compact* article was designed to open teen eyes to this new summer-vacation possibility. So I described activities—and again spiced this material with quotes, almost entirely from campers themselves.

It sounds simple—and it is. When writing *about* teens, put yourself in their parents' place. Ask yourself what *you* would want to know about this strange species, the adolescent, and research your subject with that in mind. When writing *for* young people, try to recall what *you* would have wanted to know about the subject when you were that age and—again—dig up your story material with that in mind.

In both instances, it might help to get a handle on things by talking with high school teachers and other professionals who deal with teens regularly. They can give you insights into the workings of young people's minds.

Books That Keep Them Reading

Writing books for young people is slightly different from writing articles. But only slightly. Keep an eye out for what would interest them. And, as always, try to put yourself in their mental set.

Take my book *Winners—Eight Special Young People,* published by Julian Messner in 1978. It was a collection of stories—each chapter really something like a full article—about young people who have overcome serious handicaps. One chapter dealt with a congenitally, profoundly deaf young man who successfully attended college and embarked on a career teaching the deaf. Another chapter told the story of a hemophiliac who, after several setbacks, built a career for himself in a service field. A third chapter was built around the experiences of a young woman, once addicted to hard drugs, who kicked the habit, went on to become a hairdresser, and now spends part of her spare time working with youthful addicts.

Winners seemed to strike a chord with young readers. It appealed to their natural compassion and sensitivity, which was the point. To be successful, nonfiction books for young people should focus on subject matter they can empathize with. Naturally, the writer must have a strong interest in his/her material. (It would have been hard not to have felt that way about my subjects, for their successes were astonishing.)

The subject of my most recent book for young adults. *The Glory Road—The Story of Josh White*, was even more dramatic. Published by Harcourt Brace Jovanovich in 1982, it's the biography of a black folk singer who was a leading figure in the field of modern folk music.

My book covered aspects of White's life that would grab the attention of young people: his years of grinding poverty as a child; his later success as a popular folk singer; his appearance before the House Committee on Un-American Activities, which adversely affected his career; his fighting comeback afterward. I also included scenes of the racial prejudice he had to deal with from his earliest days. I had no doubt young readers would be taken with Josh White the fighter as well as the glamorous figure he later became.

Both these books were based on interviews. With *Winners*, the writing involved drawing on what I learned from my subjects as we talked about their handicaps. My tape recorder was invaluable here. I transcribed the interviews, then cut and expanded in order to bring those very personal experiences to life—as much in the actual words of my subjects as possible.

For *The Glory Road*, I interviewed fifty people who had known White—only three of them in person, the rest by telephone. (I used a special pickup that made it possible to tape the interview on a cassette recorder, thus freeing my hands to make written notes of possible follow-up questions for another occasion. Such pick-ups are available in most radio/electronics supply stores.) But since this was the biography of a man whose background was somewhat hard to piece together, I also had to research the period in which he lived and worked, which made this book more demanding than *Winners*.

When addressing young readers, either in articles or books, I've always written the same way I do for adults. There's never been any question of the "right" vocabulary, because I treat these readers as adults. They resent being patronized; *I* did as a teenager! So it has always been a matter of trying to find subjects that would interest them, and dealing with my material in ways that would keep them reading.

A PERSONAL SUCCESS STORY: WHY IT PAYS TO PERSEVERE
by Walter Oleksy

How did a fifty-three-year-old bachelor think he could write for and about teenagers, even though he had no offspring of his own? The answer is simple. I love young people (except when they're noisy) and love writing for pre-teens and teenagers.

I think I've always wanted to write for kids, but my route to making a living primarily writing books for young people was circuitous. I began writing short stories while still in high school. (They were awful, but I didn't know that.) Afterward, I went out into the real world to work; my jobs included a position with the *Chicago Tribune*—in their garage. This was followed by a stint in their accounting department (although I'm terrible at math). At the same time I attended a no-credit short-story-writing class.

After two and a half years I was ready for college. Experience on the student newspaper at Michigan State led to a summer job for a small Michigan weekly paper and a permanent job after college on an Indiana daily. Then came two years in the Army, and I became managing editor of the weekly paper for the Third Armored Division. When I wasn't writing Army articles I was writing short stories and the beginnings of novels that never got sold.

After the Army I worked for the daily paper in Fort Wayne, Indiana, then came back to Chicago and worked a year for the City News Bureau. An opening came up on the *Tribune* and, about eight years after having worked in its garage as a parts hander-outer for truck mechanics, I was a reporter for the neighborhood section. Almost seven years later yet—after covering police beats and the criminal and federal courts, and after being a general assignment reporter, assistant television editor, city desk rewrite man, and assistant editor of the Sunday magazine—I left. There simply hadn't been enough feature writing to satisfy me.

I hadn't written much on the side while at the *Tribune*. Maybe I was too busy as a reporter to come home at night and write anything else, although the idea still tugged at me.

I became editor of a feature magazine for Goodyear. It was a great job, but didn't fill that creative hole inside me. So at night I wrote short stories that still never sold and parts of books that still never got published.

Three years of editing the Goodyear magazine left me bored. I quit and became editor of a Chicago feature-cultural magazine, *Chicago-Land*. After six months, it folded. I became assistant editor of *Discovery*, the quarterly travel magazine of the Allstate Motor Club, part of Allstate Insurance.

I loved the travel magazine but hated working for a big paternalistic company. During three years there I wrote more and more at night and on weekends. Very little sold, but I was learning. And it gave me the satisfaction I wasn't getting from my job.

TAKING THE PLUNGE

After three years at Allstate, I quit. I'd had enough of working for other people. I would try freelancing. I was about forty and just had me to feed, clothe, and house, so I could chance it.

I started out freelancing making the same mistake most freelancers make: I tried writing short stories and novels. Nothing sold. Finally I had to face reality. To survive, I had to write magazine articles.

So I switched from spending about 75 percent of my time on fiction and 25 percent on articles to the other way around. Soon I was meeting my monthly bills. Not getting ahead, but doing as well as people who "work" for a living. I was able to at least live from month to month.

Occasionally, I would sell an article to *Jack and Jill* or *Humpty Dumpty*. My first sale of a juvenile magazine article was about how kids can start their own neighborhood newspaper! At two cents a word, I got paid about $25, but it was okay. I liked having something in a kids' magazine.

After about a year of freelancing, writing for travel and how-to magazines, selling to various sections of the *Chicago Tribune* (including the Sunday magazine), I sold my first book. I'd sent a query to Parker Publishing Company, part of Prentice-Hall, suggesting a book on how to write and get published. They gave me a contract and a $1,000 advance. Now it's twelve years later and the book, *1,000 Tested Money-Making Markets for Writers*, out of print in hardcover, is still giving me modest semi-annual royalties in paperback.

Then I met a Chicago agent and through him sold *The Old Country Cook Book*, a hardcover containing about 500 recipes from ethnic grandmothers in Chicago. It flopped, overpriced at $13.95 during a recession. Want some remainders for $2 each?

MAKING IT

About then, I was writing pre-teen novels on the side, but none got published. My agent returned one of the novels to me and said, "It doesn't have a chance." He didn't even want to send it out.

What the heck, I thought. I'll send it around on my own. So I did. Out went *If I'm Lost, How Come I Found You?*, a novel about an orphan, Quacky, looking for a father. He goes to live with his old Aunt Maggie who is in the slammer for shoplifting because she can't live on her Social Security. She leaves a note telling him not to let anybody else stay at her house unless he charging them rent. When two bank robbers choose her house to hide out in, Quacky lets them stay—charging them rent. It becomes a madhouse with people coming and going, and Quacky winds up getting a father in one of the bank robbers. There are lots of action and laughs, some heart tugs, and a subliminal message that it's wrong to steal.

Nobody wanted it. Two years passed, with about twenty rejects. I decided maybe the book needed to be revised. I babysat with friends' four kids—teens and pre-teens—and a couple of their pals. They took turns reading chapters of my manuscript, suggesting things to add or take out, and I noted the words or phrases they stumbled over.

I rewrote it and less than a week later sent it out again. The first place I tried, McGraw-Hill, bought it. Eleanor Nichols, then their juvenile book editor, called saying she normally didn't find anything good in her slush pile but loved my book. She gave me an advance of $1,500, and the book came out in hardcover.

After I gave most of my author's ten free copies of the book to relatives and friends, I sent one to the acquisitions editor at Walt Disney Enterprises. Thinking big, I hoped my book could be made into a movie. But Disney's editor didn't see it that way. He liked it as a book but said it wasn't strong enough for a movie. Discouraged, I gave up the idea of the book's being made into a movie.

But only for about a month. On a rainy Sunday afternoon I was in the public library reading *Variety* and saw a two-page ad for ABC Television. In tiny print in one column was the name of the producer of children's programs for the network. I sent Bob Chenault a copy of *If I'm Lost*, and waited.

About a month later, after a bike ride with my dog, I saw the red light on my telephone-answering machine. Bob Chenault's secretary in Los Angeles had called to ask me to call him back after lunch. Because of the two-hour time difference, I couldn't call him right back, so I waited out the two hours pulling weeds in my back yard; I was too excited to do anything mentally taxing. After all, Chenault wouldn't be calling me long distance to say he hated my book. Or would he?

When I finally reached Chenault, he said he normally didn't even read a published book if it came in without an agent, but his secretary took an interest in the jacket cover and title of my book. She took it home, read it that night, and next morning told him, "You ought to take a look at this one." He did and told me he loved it and wanted to make a two-part ABC Weekend Special for Children out of it.

When it aired, I thought I was going to die of excitement and anticipation. They changed some things, cut out some, added some, and I loved it all. It's run six times now and usually is repeated once a year.

ABC paid about $8,000 for the television rights, 75 percent of which I got; McGraw-Hill got the remaining 25 percent. Every time it runs, I get another $1,250, while McGraw-Hill gets $250.

Then lightning struck again. McGraw-Hill's subsidiary rights editor sold paperback rights to Scholastic Books. McGraw and I split another $6,000 equally. Then I got a two-book contract for a second and third book about Quacky.

Next came *Quacky and the Crazy Curve-Ball* and *Quacky and the Haunted Amusement Park*. Bob Chenault loved *Park* and got me a contract and advance for that to be made into another television movie. But the economy has put those plans on hold for a while.

MOMENTUM BUILDS

Meanwhile, I kept writing magazine articles, because book advances aren't that big and they go fast. Magazines articles keep the cash flow taking care of monthly bills. Most of my magazine sales have been to national magazines a few steps below the top ten or twenty. Smaller magazines pay ten cents a word and sometimes more, but are easier to sell to, and you can sell the editors more often than you can the big magazines.

My first pre-teen nonfiction book, *Laugh, Clown, Cry,* a short biography of Charlie Chaplin, I sold outright to Raintree Ltd./Children's Press. I got about $700 and should have held out for that and royalties.

About then, I met a photographer who knows a lot about astrology. We co-authored a basic guide to astrology for teenagers, *The Universe Is Within You,* and it launched me on my way to selling nearly a dozen more nonfiction books for pre-teens and teenagers. I sent out a short outline and sample chapter of the astrology book to six publishers. The first to offer a contract was Julian Messner, juvenile division of Simon & Schuster.

Since then, I have done most of my teen nonfiction books for Iris Rosoff and Mady Anderson at Messner. My next book for Messner after the astrology book was *Careers in the Animal Kingdom,* in which I interviewed people working with animals at zoos, nature parks, aviaries, etc. That was followed by *It's Women's Work, Too!,* interviews with women in traditionally male occupations such as jet pilot, ship commander, railroad engineer, etc. Then came *Treasure of the Land,* about archaeology in America today and teenagers who are working dig sites from coast to coast.

While doing the Messner books, I queried the editors there about doing a book on UFOs. They had one on that subject, so I tried other publishers with my sample chapter and outline. It led to a contract from Putnam's and a hardcover teenage nonfiction book called *Visitors From Outer Space?*

Then "high-low" books became popular—books written on subjects of high interest to teenagers but with a grammar school vocabulary. Messner gave me contracts to write four of them: *Nature Gone Wild!*, about natural disasters such as earthquakes and typhoons; *The Green Children and Other Aliens*, about teenagers who have reported seeing visitors from outer space; *Paramedics Today*; and *Teens in the Money*, about teenagers in business for themselves who are making big money.

While completing those, Franklin Watts gave me a contract to do a "high-low" nonfiction book for them called *The Black Plague*.

After I completed those books, Messner gave me a contract to do another teenage nonfiction book for their regular trade line, *Undersea Adventures*, about sunken treasure, reclaiming the *Andrea Doria* safes, finding the *Titanic*, searching for Atlantis, etc.

The advances for the books weren't big; they ranged from $1,000 to $3,000. As is typical, half came on signing the contract (or more realistically, several months after signing), and the other half upon acceptance of the completed manuscript. Sometimes there are long waits for the second half of the advance, too.

Making a living off book advances, especially relatively small ones, can be risky. I usually have to supplement advance money by continuing to write magazine articles. Since editors of children's magazines pay very little, either for articles or stories, it is more realistic for me to write articles almost exclusively for grownups' magazines. I've been specializing in articles for the Kiwanis, Elks, Rotary, inflight, motor club, and how-to magazines.

I was getting $100 or so from *Cobblestone* for short historical articles, but got too busy to do much for them. Everything I've ever sent to *Cricket* came back with a form rejection card. At a conference for children's authors recently, I heard the editor from *Cricket* say they return unopened all unsolicited manuscripts. Thanks.

A word about agents. I dropped mine after he told me he had no faith in *If I'm Lost*, and sold several more books without any agent. Then I got a New York agent but when after almost two years she did nothing for me, I dropped her too. Then Mady Anderson at Messner suggested I try Ray Peekner, a Milwaukee agent she had high respect for. Ray and I have been enjoying a very pleasant and successful association for nearly three years now and he has been keeping me very busy and happy.

PERSEVERANCE PAYS

All this article, so far, has been about me and my writing. I wrote it this way because I believe that writing anything for sale, whether it be juvenile novels, nonfiction for young people or adults, or whatever, is about 80 percent perseverance and only 20 percent talent.

Here are some tips on how to persevere:

Be an idea person. Read what others are writing in the fields you want to write and sell in. Send out lots of queries for articles or books, preferably submitting an outline and sample chapter or two for either nonfiction books or novels. Some of it will eventually sell. When you sell to one editor, try to sell him or her as much more as you can.

Keep your manuscript in the mail. I've had enough reject letters to paper a twelve-room house, but it doesn't get me down. If a manuscript bounces, send it right back out that same day to another editor. Turn a "No!" into a "Maybe." Most editors will accept a photocopy of a manuscript, so it's wise to keep the original in your files. The mails frequently are hard on manuscripts, so it's best to hold onto the original and send out a copy. It's always good to let the editor know if it's a multiple submission or not. Some editors don't mind multiple submissions; others won't read them.

Keep writing, even if no one buys. The market has been terrible for the last two years or more, especially for books. Publishers have been using up their backlogs and trimming their lists or putting many book projects on hold for a few years. Now they are finally starting to look again at more new book ideas for both fiction and nonfiction for pre-teens and teenagers. Don't get discouraged. If your manuscript bounces for a couple of years, retire it to your file cabinet for a few months. New editors replace old ones and may like your stuff better. Always remember, your manuscript doesn't have a chance to sell if it stays buried in your file cabinet.

If you want to write for young people, don't look down your nose at the market. Don't consider it only a steppingstone to writing "serious" books for adults. Writing for kids *is* serious business. Editors are just as demanding for kids' books as they are for books for adults, maybe even more so.

I like writing for young people because the subject matter is so varied. I'm an upbeat person and like to write novels and nonfiction books with themes or subjects that can help young people widen their horizons or give them hope. It's a wild and often frightening world out there for kids. It feels great giving them something to read that might steer them toward a career or fire their imaginations.

Writing for young people also is a chance to continue my own learning process. It's great fun researching and interviewing for a new nonfiction book or novel for pre-teens or teenagers.

Another thing I love about writing for young people is dedicating books to them. A nine-year-old boy recently helped me learn about computers for a pre-teen novel I wrote, *Bug Scanner and the Computer Mystery,* for Walker and Company. I've dedicated the book to him; he can't wait to see it and neither can I. What other kind of writing can give a person such satisfaction as writing for young people? I can't think of any.

Good luck with your work aimed at pre-teens and teenagers and young adults. Keep writing, study the market information in magazines and books, keep sending your manuscripts out, and have faith in yourself and your work. I've been freelancing twelve years now, have had thirty-four books published, and still am not rich or famous. But I'm doing something few people can say they're doing. I'm doing work that I absolutely love and making a good living at it.

Additional Resources

Boys' Clubs of America, 771 First Ave., New York, NY 10017. Offers aid in arranging interviews, statistics, information searches, newsletter. List of publications available.

Boy Scouts of America, 1325 Walnut Hill Lane, Irving, TX 75062. Helps arrange interviews, offers annual reports, special photos, brochures, pamphlets, and numerous publications. Often help can be better provided by your local scout council than by the national office.

Camp Fire, Inc., 4601 Madison Ave., Kansas City, MO 64112. Sponsors community and collaborative events for youths; maintains biographical archives and speakers bureau; does research; compiles statistics. Publishes *Leadership Magazine* quarterly, agency profile, manuals, leader guide books, pamphlets, and more.

Children's Art Foundation, P.O. Box 83, Santa Cruz, CA 95063. Maintains 1,000-volume library of children's books and archive of children's drawings, paintings and writings (55,000 works). Sponsors art competitions; presents exhibits of art by children from other countries; conducts research on differences between children's art in America and abroad. Publishes *Stone Soup* (magazine written and illustrated by children) and books written by children.

Children's Book Council, 67 Irving Place, New York, NY 10003. Encourages interest in children's books and literature. Maintains examination library of professional reference works and children's trade books published within the past three years. Offers informational brochures, pamphlets, bibliographies. List of available publications.

Children's Literature Association, c/o Alethea Helbig, English Dept., Eastern Michigan Unviersity, Ypsilanti, MI 48197. Encourages serious scholarship and research in children's literature; provides an outlet for scholarship through conferences and publications; disseminates information about children's literature. Publishes a quarterly newsletter (for members only) and *Children's Literature: An International Journal* (annual).

Children's TV Workshop, One Lincoln Plaza, New York, NY 10023. Research and development laboratory that explores new uses of television and related communications media for educational and informational purposes, both in the U.S. and elsewhere. Creates and produces educational television series, including *Sesame Street, The Electric Company,* and *3-2-1- Contact.* Maintains library. Publishes *International Research Notes* (semiannual) and magazines based on each show.

Council of Interracial Books for Children, 1841 Broadway, Rm. 500, New York, NY 10023. Promotes children's books and other materials which do not project bias based on race, sex, age, or physical handicap. Reviews new books, television programs, films; reports on relevant news and legislation; conducts workshops and courses; administers the Racism and Sexism Resource Center for Educators, which publishes nonracist, nonsexist teaching materials, books, pamphlets, lesson plans, fact sheets, audiovisual materials.

Girls Clubs of America, Inc., 205 Lexington Ave., New York, NY 10016. Offers aid in arranging interviews, statistics, information searches, newsletter. List of publications available.

Girl Scouts of the USA, 830 Third Ave., New York, NY 10022. Helps arrange interviews; offers annual reports, special photos, brochures and pamphlets, numerous publications. Often help can be better provided by your local scout council than by the national office.

Information Center on Children's Cultures, U.S. Committee for UNICEF, 331 E. 38th St., New York, NY 10016. Center includes some 50,000 items, including books, pamphlets, periodicals, films, filmstrips, photographs, games, children's art. Provides mail and telephone reference service; interlibrary loan; book lists of accurate, recommended books for children about children in other lands; exhibits and programs which demonstrate cultural activities of the world's children; other documentation and research assistance as needed.

International Institute for Children's Literature and Reading Research, Mayerhofgasse 6, A-1040 Vienna, Austria. Promotes and evaluates international research in children's literature; sponsors conferences and seminars on problems of juvenile literature. Maintains collections of 6,000 books and 100 periodicals related to technical literature, and 8,000 children's books from all over the world. Publishes *Bookbird* (quarterly), a series of booklets on problems dealt with in children's literature, and lists of recommendations and suggestions for translations. Is developing an international bibliography of technical literature.

International Research Society for Children's Literature, Friendship Library, Fairleigh Dickinson University, Madison, NJ 07940. Promotes research into literature for children and young people, and related fields. Activities cover literature, art, psychology, sociology, education, bibliography, and library science, and include exchange of information, discussion of theoretical questions, and initiation and coordination of research. Publishes annual newsletter.

Media Center for Children, 3 W. 29th St., New York, NY 10001. Serves as information resource for people who want to make use of media, particularly noncommercial media, for children. Services include ongoing evaluations of films and children's responses to them; workshops for teachers, art and museum educators, film programmers, filmmakers; consultations with libraries, museums, schools, and community organizations. Organizes annual free children's film festival and seminars for children's media professionals. Publications include *Young Viewers* (quarterly) and film catalogs, including *Films Kids Like* and *What to Do When the Lights Go On.*

Society of Children's Book Writers, P.O. Box 296, Mar Vista Station, Los Angeles, CA 90066. Acts as a network for the exchange of knowledge among children's writers, editors, publishers, illustrators, and agents. Sponsors regional meetings and national writers' conference. Presents Golden Kite Award and two grants each year. Publishes *Bulletin* (bimonthly) and occasional monographs.

Women on Words and Images, P.O. Box 2163, Princeton, NJ 08540. Authors of "Dick and Jane as Victims," "Channeling Children," and "Help Wanted," united to eliminate sex discrimination in educational materials. Offers slides. Conducts seminars for publishers, educators, feminists, and parents. Publishes assorted materials relating to sexual stereotyping.

Chapter Seventeen

WRITING SPORTS

With customary modesty, *Time* magazine owner Henry Luce once wrote of his then-new (1954) sports magazine, "We have the H-bomb and we have *Sports Illustrated*. These are the two instant symbols of our fears and hopes . . . Peace in America in the mid-twentieth century means enjoyment of life, the pursuit of happiness. It means, in short, *Sports Illustrated*." The importance of sports as perceived by the late Mr. Luce!

He wasn't all that far off target. We live in a nation where sports stars are deified, where a baseball or football strike traumatizes tens of millions of devoted fans and upsets a way of life for months on end. Sport *is* a way of life for millions of Americans, and not merely as spectators. We are participants, too—in tennis, golf, jogging, bowling, hunting, and fishing. The diversity of sports activity continues to grow each year, limited only by human ingenuity and imagination. It follows that there is a wide variety of sports publications; there is at least one publication for every sport: *Archery World, Hoop, Boating, Bowlers Journal, Golf Digest,* and *Tennis,* to scratch the surface.

What does this mean to the sportswriter? It means there are many avenues open in this specialty. You can focus on team sports, especially the big three—football, basketball, and baseball; you can follow the golf tour like Jolee Edmondson, or produce expert coverage of Olympic competition; you can give your readers a taste of cross-country skiing and sailboat racing; you can teach them how to tie flies to tempt brook trout, or how and when to stalk a javelina. You can follow your favorite leisure activities while earning a living.

Sound like fun? Think about what it takes to be a sportswriter.

If you are an armchair quarterback, forget about it. The markets want writers who have been there and who know the score. Just knowing how to play tennis, golf, or racquetball isn't enough; you must understand the sport inside and out if you're to succeed as a freelancer. The moment you try to fake knowledge of any sport, you're in trouble, for the average reader (and most certainly the editor) is probably a participant who can tell when you're winging it.

You might be expected, like Diana Gleasner, to risk limb, if not life, to get first-hand experience of wind-surfing or rappelling. You must have the chutzpah and charm to walk into clubhouses and locker rooms and get interviews out of media-besieged star athletes (Neal

Ashby tells you how it's done). Mastery of photography is greatly desirable, especially for outdoors writers. And today's sportswriters are called upon increasingly to tackle such abstruse topics as sports medicine and ecology.

On the plus side, sportswriting permits a creativity not often found in straight reporting. The great sportswriters, such as Red Smith, John Lardner, Bob Considine, and W.C. Heinz, have given this field an unbeaten legacy of outstanding writing.

MASTER YOUR SPORTS SPECIALTY— AND SUBSPECIALTY
by Hal Higdon

In the basement of my home, positioned between workbench and sprinkler spigot, sit three file cabinets, testimony to a quarter-century of freelance writing. Within the cabinets, probably several hundred folders exist, one for each of my articles. Each folder contains the query letter that initiated the assignment, any other key documents, a copy of the finished article, and tearsheets from the magazine in which it was published. Most subsidiary research material has been purged, otherwise three cabinets would not suffice.

Recently, as I gathered information to write the piece you are reading now, I descended to the basement and riffled through the folders. Included were articles on politics for the *New York Times Magazine,* articles on science for *National Geographic,* and articles on business for *Playboy.* In fact, I was immediately struck by my role as more generalist than specialist. So why am I writing this chapter?

The truth is that, though I fancy myself a generalist, I do specialize by writing many sports articles. And if you were to consider books alone, all but three of my two dozen books (including all those for children) have sports settings. Two of my most successful books fit into the genre: *Pro Football, USA,* which sold more than 300,000 copies in hardcover and paperback, and *Fitness After Forty,* which sold more than 63,000 copies in its original edition. A significant percentage of my income now derives from a contributing editorial relationship with *The Runner* magazine.

Why my interest in sports? Like most boys, I grew up playing sandlot baseball and touch football. And like most boys, I fantasized myself playing in the World Series or Rose Bowl. Unlike most boys, however, I discovered a secondary sport in which my championship fantasies became realities. As a long-distance runner, I have set national records and won world titles. In 1964, I finished fifth in the Boston Marathon.

A lot of my sportswriting has focused on my running, although for many years it was difficult to obtain either frequent or well-paying assignments about that sport. In the fifties and sixties, most editors cared only about baseball and football, the sports of my boyhood fantasies. Only in the seventies did running achieve mass acceptance, as evidenced by the phenomenal sales of Jim Fixx's *The Complete Book of Running*. Published in 1977, it sold more than a million copies in hardcover, both cause and effect of the current running boom. I often tell writing groups that the way to achieve success is spend twenty years cultivating a hobby that becomes an overnight sensation.

But while waiting for lightning to strike, I nevertheless achieved success as a sports specialist.

BE A FAN

To master any specialty, you must care about it. You can't easily fake an interest or expertise in coin collecting or computer technology. The true specialist succeeds because specialization coincides with interest; while reading the newspaper or other source publications, his or her eye is drawn immediately and instinctively to that small paragraph tucked at the bottom of page 58 that might spawn a new article idea. Of course, if your specialty is sports, an entire section of the newspaper screams for your attention, but subspecialties exist within large specialties, and even the sports section contains small paragraphs. Even with the current popularity of running, most major newspapers provide inadequate coverage—one reason why a specialty magazine such as *The Runner* finds an audience eager for news.

One of the problems in writing about sports is its surface banality. Each major league baseball team plays 162 or more games a year, each pro football team 20, and hockey and basketball teams have long seasons somewhere in between those numbers. All games are different, yet all are basically the same. An identical comment could be made about the players: all different, basically the same. So what new is there to write, or read, about?

You would not ask this question if you cared deeply about sports. If you are a fan, the question would not occur to you. To a fan, every action of the field or court—each play action pass or fast break or sacrifice fly—is an event of Significance. *Unless* you are a fan, you probably should be writing about some other subject—like coin collecting or computer technology.

One of the problems in writing about sports is that numerous other writers exist who also happen to be fans and who also read the same sections of the newspaper, including the small paragraphs. Early in my career I used to write for *Sport* magazine, and it took little intelligence to realize that during the baseball season, editor Al Silverman would run at least one article featuring Mickey Mantle and, during football season, one on Johnny Unitas. It was what his readers wanted. During the course of the year, Al probably would receive several dozen queries from aspiring Mantle/Unitas authors, each of them offering slightly differing versions of the basic question: "How about an article on Mickey/Johnny?"

Al would respond politely, and negatively, to most query writers with a form letter. He might well have asked each of them: "What do you want to *say* about Mickey/Johnny?" The freelance writer who could demonstrate that he had something new to say—a fresh angle— about Mickey/Johnny got the assignment. If not, Al (and editors from other magazines seeking similar stories) probably called some trusted professional and told him, "Find something to say!"

On many occasions, I was that trusted professional. One of the advantages of being a specialist is that once you establish a name, editors think of you when they want something written on your specialty. They call with assignments, which profits you in several ways. One, it saves you the time and bother of drafting and distributing query letters that may or may not materialize in work. Two, in recognizing you as the established pro, they often pay more.

BE SOMEONE TO TRUST

But one does not become a trusted professional overnight, in any specialty. When I began freelance writing, I found it easier to sell general articles than those involving sports. Specialists such as Bill Furlong, Bill Surface, or Al Hirschfield worked as sports reporters with newspapers and had better access to hero athletes than I did. By the time an idea for a specific sports article occurred to me, it had already been assigned to them. For a while, it seemed I never would be able to achieve success as a sports writer.

The secret to success proved to be coming up with better ideas. I find I get some of my best ideas while out running. In spring 1967, I was 11 miles into a 17-mile workout, allowing my mind to drift freely. I recently had read Studs Terkel's first bestseller, *Division Street: America*. It suddenly dawned on me: Why not take the Terkel tape-recorded interview technique and apply it to sports? Hardly an innovative idea, it nevertheless worked. A quick query letter to John Blades, then articles editor for the *Chicago Tribune Magazine*, resulted in an assignment.

The "article" (actually an entire section of the magazine) contained interviews with the Chicago Bears' new quarterback, a Green Bay Packers lineman, a minor league player, the Bears' business manager, and an NFL referee. The tape-recorded style was chatty and informational, and you could almost hear the people talking as you read. Because it occupied a lot of space in the magazine (and commanded as much attention), I received a higher-than-usual fee. I also sold reprint rights to the referee interview to a small publication named *Pro Football Digest*.

More important, I saw the possibility of expanding the concept into a book. So did Walter Minton, the top man at G.P. Putnam's Sons. Through my agent, he received a copy of my outline plus tearsheets from the *Tribune* article. We agreed on a book to be named *Pro Football, USA*, mimicking the Terkel title as well as approach. But Walter made an important modification to the approach when he suggested, "Instead of letting the players ramble, why not ask them one specific question: 'How do you play your position?' "

I spent that fall traveling the NFL circuit, seeing numerous games (sometimes two or three a weekend, live and on TV), but mostly talking to players away from the locker room: in their homes, in offices, in restaurants where they could relax. Usually I arranged the interviews well in advance through the team's public relations office. This was in the era before big salaries and pushy agents, and I found most players—even superstars like Joe Namath and Johnny Unitas— quite willing to converse. I later surmised that Walter's key question, which struck to the heart of their techniques as athletes, fascinated them. It focused on an area they thought about a lot, but which was rarely explored during standard postgame interviews focusing more often on the game itself.

The Spinoffs Market

Pro Football, USA appeared in bookstores in November 1968, at a time when interest in professional football was at a peak. It sold out its humble first printing within a few weeks. Alas, by the time the publishers reprinted and got more books to the stores, it was January, the Christmas book-buying rush over, and another football book, Jerry Kramer's *Instant Replay*, had made the bestseller list. Kramer's became the football book everyone wanted to buy that season. Nevertheless, *Pro Football, USA* went through several printings, and the publishers sold reprint rights for a medium-priced children's edition to Grosset and Dunlap and a paperback edition to Tempo Books. I also sold sections of the book to several magazines and used the base of material I accumulated during research to write additional magazine articles over the next few years. Spinoffs can be an important source of income to a freelance writer, unless you get bored (as I often do) regurgitating the same material for an array of lesser-paying publications. A dozen years after its publication, by which time almost all the fifty or so players interviewed in it had retired, I still was receiving royalty income from *Pro Football, USA*.

The book's success also allowed me to launch a series of other sports books for Putnam's in two areas. One was to simply take the tape-recorded interview format and transfer it to another sport. I did follow-up books on auto racing *(Finding the Groove)*, pro basketball *(Find the Key Man)*, and baseball *(Hitting, Pitching, and Fielding)*. None achieved the success of the first, but each allowed me to make additional income by selling sections to magazines or doing spinoff articles from the base subject material. They also helped me establish a reputation as the trusted professional editors turned to when they wanted a sports article written.

The second area of sports books done for Putnam's was for children. Soon after completion of *Pro Football, USA*, Walter Minton suggested I wander down the hall and introduce myself to the firm's juvenile editor, Tom MacPherson. Noting that I lived in Indiana, Tom suggested, "Auto racing books usually sell well. Why don't you write something for us about the Indianapolis 500?"

"I've never seen the Indy 500," I admitted.

Tom didn't give up: "Go down and take a look."

That May, I visited the Indianapolis Motor Speedway, author in search of an angle. It was 1969, a good year to visit the 500, because Mario Andretti won driving a car owned by Andy Granatelli. Andy, owner of STP, had been trying to win at the brickyard for two decades. Mario was the young hot shoe whom everybody soon would want to read about. I still can visualize pudgy Andy, after the checkered flag fell, trotting down pit row to plant a mushy kiss on Mario's cheek. Over the next several years, I would draw on that vision to write several articles about both men.

But I also found my book angle when I realized that drivers and crew spent the entire month of May at the Speedway testing, qualifying, tinkering, but mostly waiting for Memorial Day, the day of the race. The following May, I returned to Indy and spent the month recording every event, listening to the talk in the pits, and inevitably describing what I saw and heard each day. The book was *Thirty Days in May*; it, too, went into several reprint editions and provided royalty income for more than a decade. I followed its success with children's books on drag racing *(Six Seconds to Glory)*, stock car racing *(Showdown at Daytona)*, and a biography of one of the drivers *(Johnny Rutherford, Indy Champ)*. My reputation as an auto racing specialist spread, and I became the trusted professional editors often called when they wanted a story in that area.

PERSEVERANCE PAYS

While writing *Finding the Groove*, I attempted to get an interview with Bobby Unser, the number one driver that year. Most auto racers, particularly those who drive at Indy, live in a cloistered world. Although they have homes scattered around the United States, most also maintain second homes just west of the Speedway. They live together, travel together, party together. They don't take easily to strangers, particularly reporters—who, they suspect (with much justification), don't comprehend what it's like to climb into a car and head down the straightaway at 200 mph, knowing you may get killed on the next turn. If you ever gain their confidence, however, auto racers become friendlier and more open than athletes in other sports. I was attracted to them for this reason.

On several occasions, I approached Bobby Unser for interviews, without luck. It was always possible for a reporter to get a few words out of Bobby, but I wanted a few hours, in front of a tape recorder. Bobby was too much a gentleman to say no, but neither did he say yes. He also had a reputation as a brawler and gave the impression that if you pushed him too far, you might find yourself lying on the ground. He once agreed to an interview in Indianapolis, but when I appeared, he was too harried to give it. Drivers spend a lot of time waiting to work while mechanics tinker with their cars, but when they work, they do so with full attention. It was impossible to get mad at Bobby Unser because he could charm the birds out of the trees, but I was becoming frustrated at my inability to get him on tape.

Finally, we agreed to talk while he was tire-testing for Goodyear in Arizona in November, right up against my deadline. I flew to Phoenix and appeared around noon at the motel where Bobby said he'd be staying. Unfortunately he had not arrived, so I camped in the lobby for several hours, nervously eyeing my watch. I'd hoped to obtain my interview that day and depart on the first plane home. Finally, in the late afternoon, a car roared into the motel parking lot and screeched to a halt. Bobby was at the wheel. He remained in the car for what seemed like several minutes over-revving the engine, apparently trying to make it backfire and blow the muffler. (Auto racers are notorious destroyers of rental cars.) Finally Bobby stomped into the motel and I reminded him of our planned interview. "We'll have dinner together," he suggested. I called the airline to shift my reservation.

When I appeared for dinner, so did a half-dozen other members of

Bobby's entourage. The result was a delightful night of conversation, a lot of insight into how racers lived that would prove valuable later. But I had no chance to use my tape recorder. "Tomorrow," said Bobby as we parted that evening. "We'll do it in the morning." Resigned, I canceled my reservation on the last flight and checked into the motel.

I hoped to obtain the interview at breakfast, or at least before Bobby headed to the track for testing, which I knew would require his undivided attention. He was late appearing and when he did, it was with his girlfriend. He was taking her to the airport. "Climb in," he told me, indicating his car. "After her flight leaves, we'll talk on the way to the track."

We arrived at the airport in 90 seconds. The airport was close to our motel, but not *that* close. Bobby drove as though in the Indy 500, accelerator foot to the floor, cutting each turn at the apex, leaving the smell of burned rubber in our wake. The track where Bobby was testing was maybe ten miles west of town, but I figured at the speed he drove, I'd be lucky to obtain five minutes on tape.

But once Bobby and I were alone, he relaxed and suggested we have breakfast. After a leisurely meal of bacon and eggs, tape recorder running, we climbed back in the rental car and he drove at 20 mph (well under the speed limit) to the track. When we arrived, we sat outside in the parking lot talking for another half hour. He was frank, blunt, pulled no punches, answered every question openly, didn't hesitate to use names. When Bobby finally decided he'd better get to work, I walked into the track with him where the Goodyear technicians, kept waiting, glared at me. I didn't care; I had my dollars-in-the-bank interview. Not only did it make the climactic chapter of my book, but I sold reprint rights for a good fee to *True* magazine, which featured Bobby Unser on its cover. Perseverance had paid off.

Be a Front Runner

Perseverance also paid off when it came to my hobby and current subspecialty in sports, running. While I was writing about Hank Stram in football and Pete Rose in baseball, few people (and fewer editors) cared about the sport of long-distance running. The Olympic Games attracted some attention, but you could sell that idea only once every four years. The Boston Marathon was the only running race that excited the public, but much less than the World Series or Super Bowl. I wrote about running, but mostly for my peers in specialty publications such as *Track and Field News* or *Long Distance Log*, too small for payments.

Even before establishing my reputation, I almost never wrote articles on speculation, and rarely without querying in advance. Nevertheless, after running the 1962 Boston Marathon, I decided to write an article on that event and the people who participated in it, whether it sold to anyone or not. I could always publish in the above-named publications. Two decades ago, only 200 runners appeared to race through Boston on Patriot's Day (a holiday in New England), but half a million spectators usually watched because the price was right. It cost nothing to stand on the curb and cheer the runners, identifying them from the program printed in the *Boston Globe*. After completing my article on the race, I mailed it unannounced to *Sports Illustrated*, whose editors at least knew me from several previous, minor assignments.

Some weeks later, *SI*'s Andy Crichton called to say the magazine had already assigned and purchased an article on the Boston race by another writer. I was reaching for the razor to slit my wrists when Andy continued, "However, yours has so much more insight, we've decided to kill his and run yours." The magazine did insert a few paragraphs from the other author's article, and mentioned him as source for some information retained, but my byline went on the article which they retitled, "On the Run from Dogs and People." (I used that title for a book on running I wrote a half dozen years later.)

The article appeared the week before the Marathon in 1963, and as I ran the race that year, numerous spectators (identifying my number in the *Globe*) shouted that they had read it. The following year, the number of entrants at Boston nearly doubled, and many came to me and said, "I decided to run Boston after reading your article." We didn't know it at the time, but the running boom (which would climax with Fixx's book a dozen years later) had begun. My article in *SI* was only one bit of kindling that ignited the flame.

Meanwhile, I began to achieve success in another specialty area: health. The reason was less related to my interests than to my location. I lived in Chicago before moving in 1964 to Michigan City, Indiana, still only an hour's drive away. Because of being headquarters for a number of health organizations (American Medical Association, American Hospital Association, National Safety Council, etc.), Chicago was an excellent location for a freelancer writing on health, medicine, or related topics, very salable to major magazines. The AMA's monthly publication, *Today's Health* (now defunct), also was a good source of assignments, and its editors favored local writers (just as New York editors favor writers they lunch with). But most of the New York editors recognized that many of the health sources, and stories, existed in Chicago. I became one of the trusted professionals they called upon.

In the mid-seventies, when running became a popular magazine subject, my specialties of health and sports merged. One reason people began to run (I do not differentiate between runners and joggers) was that they realized it was good for their health. By starting an exercise program, losing weight, giving up cigarettes, and changing old dietary habits, they might live longer. Even if they didn't live longer, they could look or feel better. That was why people began to run, but after that beginning, they often realized they enjoyed the sport and would continue in it even if the Surgeon General branded running bad for their health.

I responded with numerous articles on the subject and several books, including *Fitness After Forty*. Running publications began to increase in circulation to over 200,000, and in the competition for readers, upgraded the quality of their writing by seeking trusted professionals. I stood ready, not merely a writer, but also a runner of some stature who could speak from his own experience. I didn't have to hang around a motel lobby waiting for some expert to grant me an interview; I was the expert. When publisher George Hirsch founded *The Runner*, he offered me an attractive monthly retainer to become a regular contributor (my title: senior writer). I now contribute one major article a month, do an occasional column on training, ghostwrite some material for one of the magazine's scientific experts, consult on editorial matters, and serve as a visible spokesman for *The Runner* when I appear at races and clinics. My regular exposure in the magazine also helps me perpetuate my name and reputation, allowing me to charge handsome fees for lectures and appearances.

Because of running's popularity, I have abandoned the sports that occupied my interest as a boy and as a developing writer. I have not attended a baseball game in years. I no longer watch the Super Bowl, preferring to take a long run during its telecast, since there is little traffic on the road; almost everybody but runners watches that game.

And maybe skiers. Already somewhat bored with my current specialty, I have begun to search for new subjects to hold my interest. Recently I have begun to shift some of my attention—both as athlete and writer—into the developing sport of cross-country skiing. When temperatures drop and the snow flies, instead of cursing the weather, I shift from running shoes to ski boots. Right now, only a few ski magazines serve people interested in this sport. But the time may come when cross-country skiing's popularity may boom, and editors of all publications may look around for a trusted professional who knows how to put words together and can meet a deadline. I'll be waiting for them.

HIT TO THE HOLES:
SPORTSWRITER SURVIVAL TIPS
by Al Stump

What ranks first in the arsenal of a self-employed sports reporter? Versatility, I'd say, is foremost. The situation demands someone who is capable of producing magazine or book copy on half a dozen or more of the major games—with professional and college football and basketball, pro baseball, boxing, international tennis, and tour golf leading the list—or your chance of tapping out early in the going is worse than the odds Damon Runyon once quoted on the human race, which was 5-3, against.

Specialization hasn't struck here. Only heirs to money, exacta-ticket winners at the track, and other such lucky people can afford to concentrate on one or two sports.

No one becomes a quick pundit on any of the main, mass-interest American games, of course. Freelancers should have competed in at least one major action sport in their prep school or college days. They need to be widely read and informed in other forms, be it hockey, swimming, track and field, gymnastics, soccer, or horse racing. Sooner or later, an editor may *query you* about a piece on one of these subjects. If you've been personally involved in a "box-office" sport, each with its own regional or national publication—surfing, golf, bowling, skating, skiing, judo-karate, cycling, field and stream, tennis, softball, boating, jogging, and the like—you have an edge. Now you're able to approach editors as a combined writer-doer with inside knowledge and the experience magazines much prefer.

FACING YOUR COMPETITION

In order to survive, however, against competition from all sides—beat reporters of the daily press, magazine staffers, television featurists, and such big-name authors as George Plimpton, Norman Mailer, and James Michener, who occasionally venture into athletics—the freelancer must dig deeper than the rest. Invariably, editors confront you with, "But can you gave us an angle on this guy (or team, owner, official) that no one else has used?"

You meet that tough challenge or, in all probability, you don't get the assignment. For example, recently at *American Heritage,* the distinguished history publication, editors showed an interest in a 1984 Olympic Games piece. But they didn't want an article pegged to the Games' return to the United States after a long absence, the threat of a Communist bloc boycott, or the cost of the event—all aspects well covered in the newspapers and "slick" magazines.

Delving into archives at a sports museum, the concerned writer discovered something never before revealed: that Los Angeles, the host city for 1984, had faced such opposition in the United States, with its breadlines, when it hosted the 1932 Olympics, that the "Depression Games" almost were abandoned. This wasn't headline stuff, but it brought to light a fascinating piece of history right down *Heritage's* alley. A sale followed.

Look for the Fresh Slant

Freelancers must be willing to travel that extra mile to locate fresh slants, new appraisals, hidden information. They must imaginatively look at a star player or sports organization and see beyond the obvious story to what is overlooked or underplayed.

Opportunity is there when an athlete is in trouble—in physical performance, clashes with management, fans' dislike, clubhouse feuding, or chemical addiction. Embattled ballplayers are irresistible to assignment editors—and in long supply. In a time of increasing warfare between more and more emancipated pro and college performers, every other outfielder, power forward, linebacker, and hockey hand is in some sort of brannigan in the 1980s.

That holds true, too, for managers; coaches; NFL, NCAA, NBA, and NHL officials; umpires and referees. Head football coaches last an average of about seven seasons before they're cashiered; big-league baseball managers are fired in droves; pro grid coaches are in, then out. Some are willing to talk about their plight, before and after they're fired.

If you can successfully woo such a subject, negotiating for him to unload his troubles in a few thousand words, the sale is all but automatic. The writer, to begin with, has queried a sports magazine and received the usual "We're interested if you can bring it off." At this point, the writer can tell the subject, "What you have to say will be published, if the story is a strong one. So let's start the interview on that basis."

If a subject's agent or lawyer enters the picture—and frequently does, calling the shots—payment for the interview may be demanded, in advance or on a stipulated later date. Even without an agent, about 50 percent of players want to be paid. One of three things can happen next. One is that the story is dead. Another is that the editor who assigned the article will guarantee $500 or more so you can get your story. Or you might bankroll the money yourself, with a hoped-for refund from the publisher when a top-quality piece has been delivered.

BUILDING YOUR CREDENTIALS

For the sportswriter just breaking in as his or her own boss and demonic self-motivator, the situation may seem hopeless. You need a reputation based on published bylines—or a connection with the headlined subjects in question. And you have neither. Walking in cold without an established name or a pipeline to the subject will work—to quote an old phrase of the trade—in Class B or even Double A, but it won't get you a hearing in the big time.

All of this is by way of saying that independent sportswriting is an extremely perilous, restricted line of work—a tightrope walk. I know of only a few dozen writers in this country who have lasted for twenty or more years in the field. Some left newspaper beats to freelance after acquiring a byline presence. Others started with regional publications and built up to general-interest magazines that buy sports copy, for example, *Esquire, Argosy, TV Guide, Playboy, People, American Legion,* airline and other industry pubs, and the newspaper supplements. From there, in time, they advanced to the small group of nothing-but-sports magazines (and their few number is another hurdle) with the fancy paychecks. Whereas Australia, Germany, Japan, and Italy have many nationally circulated general sports journals, the United States has just *Sports Illustrated, Sport,* and *Sporting News* as top markets, along with the monthly digests, annuals, and specialized pubs covering baseball, football, basketball, boxing, hockey, golf, tennis, bodybuilding, jogging-running, water sports, auto racing and so on.

Some writers make articles about *le sport* only part of their production, blending it into a mix of writing about show biz, action-adventure, the outdoors, aerospace, and even urban problems. Still others are able to combine writing with television and radio commentary. Diversity can help pay the bills.

Almost every metropolitan newspaper has one or two sports staff writers who freelance a piece now and then. Journalists from the *Philadelphia Inquirer, San Francisco Chronicle,* and *Atlanta Journal* regularly win national "best sport story" awards. They have the substantial advantage of working from day to day with famous stars, and although many beat reporters are disliked by the people they cover, there are others who have the trust and confidence of newsmakers. They gobble up a lot of the juiciest assignments.

You see this demonstrated in such collection volumes as *Best Sport Stories,* the annual national prize contest. A typical breakdown of one edition of BSS showed thirty-six articles written by newspaper reporters, five by magazine staffers, and nine by full-time freelancers.

How to Get Launched

Yet some newcomers are bound to find a career in the field, despite all odds. Suggested ways to get launched:

- In high school, or in college, volunteer to keep score or act as umpire/referee; keep notebooks on tactics, strategies, personalities. Write for the city newspaper or surburban weekly, even if unpaid, to pick up experience and credits. You should be on your college newspaper staff, covering each sport in season and getting a byline. This was the particular route I took at a Pacific Northwest university with a fine daily student paper. The spinoff was handling campus games not normally covered by metropolitan Seattle newspapers.

- Take some math courses in school. (Brush up if you're out of school.) Adapt this knowledge to statistics-keeping and hit the magazines with the sort of offbeat facts and figures that fascinate sport "bugs." This could open the door to reporting more than ERAs, TKOs, TDs, and RBIs.

- Obtain a job as a public relations assistant with a college, semi-pro or pro team; work up from "gofer" status to producing press releases, meanwhile gaining exposure to the psyche of the hero athlete and becoming known to editors who view your material as from someone inside the picture.

- Get a wire-service job. Staff veterans often become jaundiced about covering sports and will move over for an interested cub. Sell a magazine piece on the side—then more.

In my case, having played prep and some college baseball helped me break in, long ago, to the *Saturday Evening Post* with a piece on Billy Martin, then a star infielder with the New York Yankees. That article opened another door. I hit the *Post* with football subjects and, because I could honestly say I'd been both a college player and athletics publicist in the past, had traveled with Rose Bowl teams while ballyhooing them, the editors okayed not one, but three projects.

Today that same need for credentials applies.

Background—you've got to have it in some form. If you're not an athlete yourself, you might be the tremendously "hot fan" type of writer who intensely follows sports and can reel off everything from Casey Stengel's middle name to the past fifty World Series winners.

Getting Started in the Bush Leagues

The best way to gain experience is sportswriting in a small or medium-sized town—the springboard for a high percentage of well-known freelancers around today. Here in the "bushes" you learn to score games, recognize the real turning points of contests, do some out-of-town traveling with teams, absorb ballplayers' jargon, and develop a flair with words while meeting deadlines without choking.

Acquiring a press pass and then some seniority, you'll know how to handle yourself if and when you wind up interviewing the Reggie Jacksons, Magic Johnsons, Tom Watsons, and Ken Andersons. At that stage, don't confine yourself to newsprint alone. Go for the major magazine market with sharp, well-rounded, but fairly brief (two pages or so) outline queries. Many daily press beat reporters think they're not good enough for $2,500 checks for one piece of work and don't even try, losing out for simple lack of taking the gamble. Or, still more common, they're too lazy to do double work.

Here's how one freelancer, who makes sports copy a good 75 percent of his output, got started:

Several sales to a $75-$100 small baseball pub in the Philadelphia area; a year later, a sale to *Sport* magazine at $400, which became more articles at $750 within two years; after more articles for *Sport*, a venture into the men's general-interest field of *Argosy* and *Esquire* and, eventually, what was then the leading gent's book, *True,* paying top dollar. But he recognized that ideas that didn't sell to the foregoing could be salvaged for sale to the fraternal organs, such as *Elks* and *American Legion,* and to big-city Sunday magazines. At all times, he kept at least a dozen markets under inquiry, which takes some fast juggling and close knowledge of what editorial boards see as the right copy for their readers. Said freelancer broke down every issue of twenty or more magazines, studying content, thrust, and trends.

Read the Best

However you slip your foot in the door, exhaustive reading of sports literature is essential. A considerable aspect of sports publishing today consists of books—the autobiography, confession, exposé, or writer's straight look at the subject or situation. The titles roll off presses by the dozen, everything from big and better encyclopedias to the tattling of an ex-big league umpire. Crashing this field will take lots of time, but meanwhile, reading everything by such whizzes as Roger Kahn, Harold Seymour, Dick Schaap, Pat Jordan, Roger Angell, Larry Merchant, Ed Linn, or Robert Creamer (naming a mere few of the best) is a guideline to how it's profitably done.

Be ingenious. I'll never forget a young New Yorker without notable credentials named Richard P. Goldman, who produced a profitable book simply by writing to a number of leading newspaper sports columnists and others and saying, "Would you please pick your favorite story of all you've written and allow me to publish it, along with selections of other great writers?" The flattery worked. He landed (without paying for it, so far as I know) thirty-five "favorites" from such writers as Bob Considine, W.C. Heinz, John Lardner, Quentin Reynolds, Westbrook Pegler, Red Smith, and Budd Schulberg. The result, *Sportswriters' Choice,* is a classic in the field.

In sum, you've got to get on base before you can score.

You get on base by sacrificing, hitting to the holes, and never giving up when you strike out (be willing to do as much rewrite as needed, even if it's extensive). But don't steal. Not from anyone. Swiping another writer's language or research will get you the thumb and a rejection slip.

GETTING THE TOUGH INTERVIEW
by Neal Ashby

The sports scene is one of fast action and heroics—one whose characters are impressive physical specimens who can run like deer and throw, bat, and charge like Greek Olympians, who follow a way of life like no other.

It is also a scene strewn with obstacles for writers who are not regularly on the sports beat.

To begin with, you must gain admission to stadiums, playing fields, clubhouses, and press boxes, and access to players, coaches, managers, general managers, and department heads. It isn't always easy.

A writer will find the going easier at the lower level of sports: high school, small college, minor league professional teams. Individuals involved have not been so exposed to the media that they've become bored with being interviewed. They hope to advance in their field and have something to gain by appearing in print. They're flattered to be quoted or have their performances described. Organizations fielding the teams know that publicity will help bring more paying customers to events.

At the major league level, however, college or professional, it gets tougher. Publicity still has value to the schools and team ownerships, but not so much to the individuals. Access to players, particularly famous ones, is especially hard in a time when many command huge salaries, as much as an incredible $1 million a year. Even amateur stars in baseball, football, basketball, and hockey have already been chronicled, photographed, and filmed and are heading toward near-certain big money. Coaches and managers are also well paid, very busy, and concerned about the problems they may face if misquoted or misunderstood by writers.

Be Ready for Avoidance Tactics

Many in high-level sports are friendly and helpful. But in general, these individuals simply don't *need* the sportswriter as they once did to gain recognition and enhance their value to a team. Many are badgered repeatedly for interviews and grow resentful of demands on their time. In addition, as a freelancer, you're not one of those regularly assigned by a publication to cover the teams. You're not around them regularly, well known to players, managers, or front office representatives. You're an outsider.

So the person or persons you want to interview may try to avoid you, or make excuses: "I have to shag some flies now"; "I have to get back to the clubhouse." The latter was employed to dissuade me by Dave Kingman, New York Mets homerun slugger. I think Kingman might have been a little contrite later when I myself was in the Mets clubhouse. His locker was right next to that of Joe Torre, a respected Mets star soon to become the team's manager. Torre greeted me as an old friend, on the basis of interviews I'd had with him that resulted in articles he liked (not that you want to write articles deliberately to *please* an athlete). I thought Kingman looked a little embarrassed.

Or, your interviewee may try to cut your talk short before you've gotten all the necessary information and comment. Or, he may even treat you rudely or disdainfully. I once went up to Chicago White Sox pitcher Jerry Koosman during spring training in Florida for an article for *TV Guide* about postgame interview shows.

"Excuse me, Jerry," I said. (Always say "excuse me" if you don't know them; it's okay to use first names and nicknames.) "My name's Neal Ashby, and I'm doing a piece on . . ."

"You're *who*???" Koosman said, scowling.

"Aaahhh, Neal Ashby, and I'm doing a story on postgame interview shows for . . ."

"You're *what*???" Koosman almost snarled.

The way to surmount these obstacles is to persist politely, about which more later.

It's best to start with a firm assignment from a magazine or newspaper, or a contract with a book publisher. If you can say, "I'm doing a story for *Publication X* on . . ." it will authenticate you. People in sports don't like to waste time on amateurs whose work may never be published—not to say it's *impossible* to get interviews and information without an assignment, but having one gives those involved a far stronger reason to cooperate with you. Your article presumably will bring some attention to the team and arouse spectator interest.

A FREELANCER'S BEST SHOT

What will you write about in sports? Not an account of a game or competition. That's for the regularly assigned staffers.

It might be an assessment of a team's performance, an analysis of why it's been doing so well, or so poorly, with comments from the coach or manager and important players; perhaps some interesting background for a significant sports event or achievement; interviews with or profiles of prominent athletes, coaches, or sports administrators are a staple of sports journalism.

Your best chance for publication is to think of some aspect that the established sportswriters haven't thought of, or had time for: the work and life of the batboy or team trainer, or one of the lowliest members of a team, or an unusual or unlikely interest that a player has away from the playing field. (I once did a magazine article on the gourmet cooking of Rusty Staub, then with the New York Mets in the midst of a twenty-year career as a major league baseball star.)

A Foot in the Door

All right, you have your story concept and, ideally, an assignment, and you're ready to start. Next, find out the name of the team's public relations or publicity representative and call that person. Every college and major professional team will have one; in the case of a minor league team, the general manager or someone in the team office probably will be your initial contact.

Identify yourself as a writer, and describe the piece you want to do in general terms—it's just common sense not to let the precise details of your valuable idea reach other ears. State the publication for which it's targeted. Say what you need: admission to the press box to observe a contest; entrée to the clubhouse to talk with one or more players; an appointment for a longer interview with a specific player, coach, or manager; an opportunity to study the statistics of player or team performance; whatever.

There will be variations, but as a rule the press contact will tell you that a ticket or press pass will be left for you at a certain gate or door, or a gatekeeper will be told to admit you.

If you want an interview, the media contact will consult with your subject, who will choose a time convenient for him. Make it your business to be there at the appointed time. You need your subject more than your subject needs you.

Printed copies of current statistics usually are readily available at the team office.

In the press box, arrive well before game time, to be ready to work and sure not to make waves. Once I got stuck in traffic and reached the Yankee Stadium press box for a New York Giants football game after play had begun and while some exciting action was underway. I was hooted to my ignominious seat down at the end with cries from the regulars to "Sit down!" and "Get out of the way!" No matter how early you arrive, however, never take one of the choicer seats. Those are the preserve of the regulars, and you may be made to feel very uncomfortable if you are found in one. Go down near the end of a row. It will still be a very good seat.

The nonregular should be similarly circumspect in the private haven of the athletes—the clubhouse or dressing room. You will probably recognize those with whom you want to speak and then will be able to approach them respectfully. Or, the publicity representative may introduce you. If neither of the above occurs, you'll have to ask someone to point out your interviewee. It's a little easier to ask a nonplayer, such as a trainer or clubhouse attendant, if possible.

The clubhouse ordinarily has a lighthearted atmosphere—lots of joking and banter. Be ready for anything. When I walked into the dressing room of the New York Giants to interview Sam Huff, the great linebacker, I found him in the center of the room, stark naked.

That scene probably won't be repeated, now that women writers are more or less freely admitted to the inner sanctums of sports. Their treatment is close to equal—except for the occasional sexually oriented catcall from the back of the room.

Use Your Wits—and Know Your Place

Don't push yourself forward when you're not known if you hope to gain quick acceptance. Know your place. Fortunately, I followed that rule when I went to Yankee Stadium in hope of talking with Billy Martin during one of his several terms as team manager. Martin is a volatile man constantly being pressured for interviews. I poked my head into the doorway of his office off the clubhouse and saw that he was chatting informally with *New York Times* columnist Dave Anderson and several other leading sportswriters.

"Can't you see I'm talking to these guys?" Martin called out.

"I see that, Billy," I answered. "Whenever you have a chance, I'll be waiting outside."

A while after the hotshots had left, Martin came to the doorway and said with gruff good nature, "C'mon in." He proceeded to give me everything I asked for. I had paid my dues.

Have your areas of questioning clear in your mind. You'll get a much better response if you keep the interview moving briskly and productively, don't stumble, and are always ready with the next question.

If you meet resistance or lack of interest, stand your ground and keep working. Don't visibly take offense. Press on innocently, as if you didn't notice any discourteous treatment. That's what I did when pitcher Jerry Koosman was giving me a hard time. I just started asking my questions and managed to get him interested in the subject; his turned out to be one of the best segments I got for the story.

Use your wits to get what you need. For my Rusty Staub gourmet cooking piece, the editor had stressed that I must get one of Staub's own recipes. He didn't want to give me one, said he couldn't think of any, and had no more time. I reminded him that he'd mentioned preparing a dinner for then-teammates Tom Seaver and Bud Harrelson.

"Just tell me what your entrée was and how you prepared it," I pleaded.

Staub proceeded to describe a buttery, imaginatively seasoned broiled fish dish that met my needs beautifully.

For another article for which I needed Billy Martin, he had said from his office, "I'll meet you on the bench in a few minutes." Great! Sitting on the New York Yankees dugout bench chatting with Billy Martin! When he joined me, he gave me some good stuff, but only about half of what I needed for a full-fledged piece. Then he said he had to leave. As he got up, I said, "Billy, I need some more time. Can I come back tomorrow?"

"Okay," he said, promptly forgetting the whole matter, I was sure.

So I had to rearrange my schedule and drive twenty miles each way again to Yankee Stadium. I returned early the next afternoon and Martin was alone in his office. He waved me in and gave me as much time as I needed.

And to show what the nonregular can accomplish, that piece (how Martin "runs a game" from the dugout) was reprinted in *Baseball Digest*, usually the province of those who cover the diamond full-time.

(I realize I'm playing a trumpet voluntarily here in recounting my triumphs. I think they're much more instructive than my failures, like the Dave Kingman interview I didn't get.)

If you like sports, then writing about them, despite the difficulties the nonregular encounters, is fun. Who doesn't enjoy having a close rapport, however brief, with fellow humans who excel at what they do?

Just be ready for a challenge.

OUT OF THE ROUGH
AND INTO THE GREEN
by Jolee Edmondson

April 1975. The flowers were blooming, the birds were singing, and I had an uncontrollable itch to be doing something other than what I was doing, namely writing stories about what the mother of the bride wore and Rotary club picnics, for a small-town newspaper.

I should have been content. After all, being features editor of the *Oceanside Blade Tribune,* a thriving daily in a quaint San Diego suburb, was a nice, secure niche. I was 26 and in retirement-pension heaven. But I was frustrated as hell.

One day, as I sat at my desk, staring out the window, I foggily tuned in on a conversation our sports editor was having with his assistants. They were placing bets on who would win the Tournament of Champions, a major golf event being held that week at nearby La Costa Spa and Country Club. Jack Nicklaus was emerging as the favorite until I piped up: "No, Lee Trevino's got it in the bag. This is his kind of golf course—flat with lots of roll, and some of the toughest holes are doglegs to the right, perfect for his natural fade. Also, it's pretty windy out there this week and Trevino's the best wind player on the tour, having learned his game in western Texas."

My awestruck associates asked me where I had gotten this computer readout on Super Mex. I told them my father was a golf pro in Palm Springs, I was weaned on the game, I had won several junior championships, and I had maintained more than a passing interest in the sport. All of which met with a resoundingly incredulous "We didn't know that!" and a few assignments covering local tournaments where Harold Rivers defeats Fred Hollenbacher in an electrifying playoff at Goat Pasture Muny.

LEADING QUESTIONS

That night I got an idea. Why couldn't I combine my writing and knowledge of golf, attend the numerous professional golf events that came to the San Diego area, and sell stories to the leading golf publications? A little freelancing would put a few more designer T-shirts on my back and perhaps help dredge me from my rut.

I decided to put my plan into action by calling Lee Trevino and asking him for an interview that very evening. I correctly assumed that, since the following day was merely a practice round day, he would be spending a long, leisurely evening in one of the executive houses La Costa provides for its visiting luminaries. I dialed the resort's main number and, in a tone that smacked of a weary wife calling her traveling husband, sighed, "Lee Trevino's house, please." No questions. The phone rang.

It took me a while to talk him into granting me an interview. He said he never gave private interviews, that he hated the press, and that he was in the middle of watching a rerun of his favorite TV show, *I Love Lucy.* That's when I started begging. I told him I was a fledgling freelancer, that interviewing him would be the biggest break of my career, that it might help finance my continuing education and down payment on a second-hand vacuum cleaner I had my heart set on, and that my nine-to-five job prevented me from coming out to the tournament during a weekday.

"All right, be here by seven," he said. "Let's get it over with."

The doorbell was answered by a sullen member of Trevino's entourage. "In there," he pointed, and shuffled off to another room.

I found Trevino seated at the end of a baronial dining table, munching on fried chicken from a bucket and wearing a bathrobe that said "Superstar" on the back. A portable television occupied the other end of the table.

"Hi honey," he greeted me, keeping his eyes glued to the screen. "Have a seat."

As the last scene of "Sanford and Son" faded into a commercial, I turned on my tape recorder and Trevino started to talk. Nonstop. As it turned out, he had a lot to get off his chest, and I was a rapt, grateful listener. I just kept the reel turning and my mouth shut, injecting a question or comment only when he paused to gnaw on the Colonel's best. He delivered a three-hour diatribe on his disenchantment, to put it politely, with the sports press, recalling inaccuracies and misquotes that would curl your typewriter ribbon, and divulging locker-room insights into how the pros *really* feel about the newspaper brigade. He was fiery and colorful. To my knowledge, none of this had ever appeared in print. As they say at the *Daily Planet*, I had a scoop.

Every night for the next two weeks I worked on a piece I titled "Teed-Off Trevino." I submitted it to *Golf* magazine and they bought it for $400.

Hitting a Long Drive

My euphoria soon wore off, however, and I was once again at the bottom of the emotions barrel. I realized that I would have to wait eight months before the professional golf caravan rolled into San Diego County again. I was back where I started. I had to make a break for it.

This time I devised a master plan that revolved around taking a wild chance, completely severing my ties with security. I would quit my job, sell my car, buy a camper, pack my typewriter and shaggy dog, and take off in pursuit of the professional golf tour, traveling from tournament to tournament, digging up behind-the-scenes stories and selling them by the truckload to golf magazines.

When I told my friends and relatives about my scheme, they looked at me like I was cuckoo. I reminded them that one must take chances to get ahead in this world. They sort of nodded, but their mouths gaped.

Down That Lonesome Road

Before I took the final plunge, I wrote to *Golf* magazine and *Golf Digest* inquiring about their interest in having a roving reporter on the tour submitting regular columns, truly an innovation. Alas, no go. Their rejections led me to study their mastheads in search of female names, and I found that women golf writers were as prevalent as fairways in Bangladesh. That should have discouraged me, but it only served to fuel my ambition, which now encompassed a new goal: to be the first and only female writer who wrote exclusively about golf.

I collected my last paycheck, sold all my furniture, and went into debt with the purchase of a shiny new Volkswagen camper equipped with an icebox, a sink, a back seat that converted into a bed, a tiny closet, a fold-out table for my typewriter, and cabinets for my notebooks, reference material, tape recorder, etc.

My first destination was the Atlanta Golf Classic, and I gave myself a full week to get there in case I had a blowout or got lost or hijacked. At four o'clock on a misty June morning, I loaded myself, my dog Huckleberry, and a year's supply of cheese sandwiches and granola into my camper, and exchanged choked-up goodbyes with my mother. I moved slowly down the street as Huckleberry raced back and forth in his new home, and before I turned the corner at the bottom of the hill I glanced once more into the rearview mirror and saw the solitary figure of my mother under a street lamp. She was waving and dabbing her eyes with a ball of tissue. I turned the corner. My foot pressed the button that switches the headlights from dim to bright. Everything was so dark in front of me.

Posh Comes to Shove

When I finally reached Atlanta, after enduring sweltering heat through Arizona and New Mexico and traversing the insufferably monotonous continent of Texas, I drove out to the country club, located, of course, in the posh part of town.

Butterflies were having a field day in my stomach, this being my first attempt at squeezing my way into a tournament without the required press badge and parking sticker. Huckleberry was hanging out the passenger window panting and drooling as we made our way past expansive lawns and stately homes toward the tournament entrance. As expected, the guard inquired about a parking decal and asked to see my badge. I gulped and told him they were waiting for me in the press tent. He scratched his head, kept peering inside the camper at Huckleberry, who was now on the back seat frantically chasing his tail, which he always did when we came to a stop, picked up the phone and called the press tent. Oh, Lord. I froze.

"Uh, yeah," he said, "There's a girl here says her credentials are with you people. Julie Edmondson. Yeah." He poked his head out of the booth and motioned me to go on through. It was trite, but I breathed a big sigh of relief.

At the press tent, I told the tournament director that the guard had misunderstood, that actually I had forgotten to send away for my credentials. He looked at me quizzically for a moment and then typed a name tag for my badge and handed me a sticker for my camper. Whew! Gaining admission to each tournament would always be a touch-and-go proposition.

I overslept my first day "on the job." When I stepped out of the camper, the 18th green was already occupied by players and the parking lot was buzzing with traffic and spectators. I walked directly to the press tent to pick up a pairing sheet so I could see whom I wanted to interview and when they would finish their rounds.

The standard press tent at the standard golf tournament is a makeshift set-up with folding chairs and tables—from afar it looks like something Oral Roberts would feel at home in. It is filled with 99.9 percent men, antique typewriters, and a garbage can stocked with ice and soda pop. Most of the time, its inhabitants all sit around and read newspapers, puff on cigars, and slap each other on the back. Not until the tournament leader comes off the golf course do they move into action, their fingers racing over a thousand keys in a thunderous rush to meet deadline.

It took me a long time to build up credibility with my fellow golf writers, not to mention the golfers themselves. They didn't know what to make of me, this blonde in T-shirt and jeans, carrying a canvas sack inscribed "My bag," who chased after pros with a tape recorder and followed the tour in a camper. Was I a groupie or a golfer's ex-wife gathering testimony for increased alimony? I caught the sly glances and was very much aware of the snickers and whispers. A hush fell over the press tent whenever I walked in and bewilderment was the usual reaction to my presence. But I simply went my own way, friendly but not too friendly, and stuck to my work. I made it a policy never to socialize with "the boys" after they filed their stories each evening.

The Rabbit Habit

Anyway, on that initial day, I got my pairing sheet and pursued a number of pros I wanted to interview: I decided to start with a story on the "rabbits"—those rookies who must qualify for each tournament by playing in a qualifying round the preceding Monday. Those who end up in the top half of the field—sixty pros who shoot the lowest scores—

are deemed eligible to play in the tournament proper, Thursday through Sunday. Only when a pro wins a tournament does he become exempt from those miserable Mondays, where survival, not just golf, is the name of the game.

Being a novice pro striving for that first all-important victory is a grueling way to launch a career, especially if the young player has a family to support. Breaking into the top ranks of the professional golf tour means living from week to week on nothing more substantive than hopes and dreams and high-octane fear. It's the furthest thing from a nine-to-five job. There is no guaranteed income, and sponsors are a fickle lot, backing one player one month and switching their financial favors to another, "more promising" newcomer the next. I also wanted to talk to the veterans with rows of trophies lining their shelves and get reflections on *their* hungry years.

Despite the fact that a few of the pros didn't take me seriously, winking and saying, "Sure, sweetie," when I told them I was a writer and ignoring my questions in favor of their questions about what I was *really* doing out there, I collected some decent quotes.

I learned early that it was not mandatory for me to have access to the locker room. Compared to the confined arenas of baseball, football, tennis, etc.—where athletes are whisked from playing field to locker room, having no contact with fans and only selective contact with the media—the golf course is wide open, where pros, press, and spectators mingle. It's a garden party for the otherwise harried sports reporter. What's more, the tournament leaders are always brought directly to the press tent, where they hold court with an Everyman mass of hungry writers following their rounds. No more democratic and opportune environment exists for the sports media than that at a professional golf event. It is the ideal milieu for the female sports journalist who doesn't savor the prospect of demanding locker-room rights.

I staked out my interviews everywhere from the practice putting green to the driving range to the eighteenth green to the grill room to the press tent to the parking lot. As I said, it's a "free society" and even the big-name pros can be found *somewhere* and stopped in their tracks for a few quotes. It's a matter of logistics—after a while you develop a sixth sense on who is going to be where when. One of my favorite stations was right outside the locker room. I just nabbed my subjects as they were going in and coming out, an inevitable routine, I figured. One time a pro, who shall remain nameless, came out of the locker room with nothing but a scant towel wrapped around him and said sarcastically, "I hear you want to interview me." It was obvious he didn't like women reporters and was trying to embarrass me. But I convincingly pretended I was oblivious to his state of semi-disrobement and interviewed him as if he were wearing a tux and top hat. He became so

absorbed in talking about himself that he temporarily forgot his prejudice and gave me some sterling quotes.

At the close of my first day, I did what I would always do—withdraw to my camper for some heavy-duty writing. Sometimes, if my
tape recorder was full, I would leave the golf course early and park in a
shopping center, where I could munch on a sandwich purchased at a
cafe, wait for my clothes to come through the rinse cycle at the laundromat, and pound out a few paragraphs at the same time.

GOLF PROS, GOLF PROSE

So, I had cleared another hurdle. I had made my debut on the tour
without any real snags. My notebook and tape recorder were bulging
with usable material, I hadn't broken out in a cold sweat when I asked
pros for interviews, and I even received a few compliments from reporters who remembered my Lee Trevino story. It looked like I could
indeed inch my way into this tight-knit world.

I sent my story on the rabbits unsolicited to *Golf* magazine, *Golf Digest*, and *Sports Illustrated* consecutively, and it laid an egg on each editor's desk. It seems that topic had been exhausted. But I kept plugging
and eventually learned that golf is a particularly limited sport to cover.
Golf being such an inherently slow, bland game and professional golfers being an unusually reserved lot, catch phrases and fast-breaking
stories are hard to come by. When some desperate sportswriter *does*
come up with an original tag to pin on golf's cardboard-cutout stars, he
is rewarded with tons of plagiarism. Case in point: "Arnie's Army."

An obscure reporter on the *Pittsburgh Gazette* hung that name on
the fanatically loyal legions who followed Arnold Palmer. Before the
blink of an eye, it was devoured by every hard-up golf reporter in the
country. "Arnie's Army" almost immediately became a tired term
avoided by any writer who wanted to impress his editor with a fresh
approach. The trick, in this field especially, is to constantly recycle old
stories with a new twist. It takes a lot of dreary brain work, but it pays
off. For instance, my piece on the rabbits would have sold if I had focused on their wives instead of the players themselves. After all,
what's it like to travel with a man whose livelihood hangs by a thread?
What effects, negative or enduringly positive, does this traumatic in-
auguration into professional golf have on a marriage, a family?

Out of the Fairway, Into the Rough

In the meantime, I suffered a six-month drought. The magazines
were receiving my manuscripts as if they were falling off a conveyor

belt, but none of them sold. I was deeply in debt to my mother and was living on dry granola consumed straight from the box. I lost twenty pounds. On more than one occasion I camped outside the post office in a tournament town, waiting for a money order from home.

Where to sleep was a recurring dilemma. When a KOA was nowhere to be found, I usually ended up parking on a residential street close to the golf course, or behind a hotel, with its ever-available lobby restroom, or, if all else was out of the question, I splurged on a seven-dollar room in the truck-stop section of town.

At the Greater New Orleans Open, I had no alternative at nightfall but to park on a residential street near the golf course. At about two o'clock one morning I was awakened by a flashlight shining in my face. Two policemen were standing outside my camper and telling me to roll down my window, whereupon they ordered me to get out of town by sunrise. When I explained what I was doing, hazily pointing in the direction of the golf course, they thought I was a deranged vagrant. So, in my nightgown and hair rollers, I drove around town until dawn, got dressed and went out to the tournament for another day of freelancing.

In Houston (for the Houston Open), I was almost arrested. Parked in back of a Red Carpet Inn, I was dozing in the middle of the night when the hotel security guard started pounding on my window, commanding me to open up fast. Once again I was in full nocturnal regalia, including chewed-up bedroom slippers. But that didn't stop the guard from dragging me through the lobby and into his office, where he dangled a pair of handcuffs in front of my eyes and told me to confess. He thought I was a hooker soliciting hotel trade.

Hits and Mrs.

Writing is a lonely enough profession without doing it in a confined space in a parking lot in a strange town. Desolation swept over me as I leaned over my fold-out table and stared out the camper window at the Howard Johnson's-McDonald's skyline. I wondered why I couldn't be a "normal" young woman content with a white picket fence around me, a "Mrs." in front of my name and a couple of babies on my knee. I seriously thought about returning to the womb of California. But I didn't.

Two weeks following this lowest of ebbs, I was notified by *Golf* magazine that they had bought one of my stories—"The Flamboyant Twilight of Doug Sanders." It was an interview/profile in which I had incorporated my newfound formula of reviving old stories with an original angle. Everyone in the golf world knew who Sanders was— the tour's flashiest *bon vivant*, with a wildly unorthodox swing that matched his lifestyle. Countless articles had been written about his playboy image, to the point where one more word describing his penchant for good times would certainly have put the entire golf community to sleep. So, I developed an unused slant—a portrait of Sanders as an *aging* swinger. He was, after all, forty-three. Flecks of gray were weaving their way through his hair and his belt buckle was protruding noticeably. What was it like for a man whose very lifeblood was drawn from the fast lane to grow older, slow down? I was in a laundromat in Houston when I got the idea to call Sanders, who is resident pro at a country club about twenty-five miles north of the city. Sanders happily obliged my request for an interview. "Sure, you come on up, sweet thing," he drawled. "Tell me, are you as pretty as your voice?"

"Well, my mother thinks I am."

"That's good enough for me. See you tomorrow."

I arrived at Woodlands Country Club the next day at the appointed hour and met Sanders in his office, where he was doing some light paper shuffling. He stood, kissed my hand ever so debonairly and presented me with an autographed copy of his autobiography, *Come Swing With Me.* Then he announced that he wanted to play nine holes and I could "grill" him "out there." I was accustomed to stationary interviews and approached this talk-while-you-walk method with considerable doubt. But following Sanders around the golf course proved a priceless strategy for gleaning great quotes. This was, after all, his natural environment, where he felt most comfortable. In fact, he was so relaxed and talkative while belting one golf ball after another that I felt like we were a couple of old army buddies having a heck of a good time recapping our days in the trenches or foxholes or whatever. We cruised the fairways in his custom-made golf cart complete with headlights, heater, fan, radio, and ice chest packed with beer, and Sanders fielded my questions about his *maturity* without offense. "Errol Flynn was my kind of dude," he pronounced. "He died of old age at fifty, but he lived." His candor, coupled with my own observations, made for one of the best pieces I have ever turned out.

"Hey, you can really write!" said *Golf* magazine's note that accompanied my remuneration of $400.

Caddies and Daddies

Not long after selling that story, I sold another and then another. My momentum and spirits were picking up. *Golf* magazine, out of sheer sympathy, was providing me with a steady supply of press credentials. And soon I was making a living wage out there, collecting checks for 16 of the 20 articles I produced during that period. *Golf Digest* paid me $500 for a feature I did on Gary Player's loquacious and colorful caddie, Wayne Dyer. (Here again, this was a revised version of the classic caddie story in which that gritty breed of men are depicted as mindless no-mads. *My* theme swerved off that beaten path. Dyer, I proclaimed accurately, was a shrewd businessman who made the most of his strong association with Player and was the forger of a new image for caddies.)

The majority of my manuscripts, however, were purchased by *Golf* magazine, whose possessiveness of me was growing like a man who had just adopted a daughter. My allowance from "Dad" was $400 per story. As I became a more regular contributor, my fee was raised to $500. Now, I am guaranteed $1,000 per 1,000- to 2,000-word article.

In all, I was on the road a year and a half. I covered 22,000 miles and 24 tournaments. I was tired, drained. I wanted to go home, re-group, assess where I had been and think about where I was going. A modicum of satisfaction was certainly mine. After all, I had gone against all odds and emerged with my head above water. My byline had become vaguely familiar to golf fans. And eventually, as my crusty fellow reporters became accustomed to my showing up at every stop along the tour trail and keeping my nose to the margin release, they be-gan to observe my daily entry into their domain with a shrug instead of a raised eyebrow. And when they discovered I could actually construct a publishable paragraph, they became downright respectful. I was confident that my next trip would bring even more succes. I wanted to go on, keep proving myself, see my original plan through, work up to my fullest potential. But was it worth it physically, emotionally, and fi-nancially?

When I returned home, I sat around for two months doing a great deal of nothing. I was into heavy introspection one day when the tele-phone rang. It was the editor of *Golf* magazine announcing that he had entered "The Flamboyant Twilight of Doug Sanders" in the annual competition conducted by the Golf Writers Association of America, that it had won first place, and would I like to come to New York as as-sociate editor of *Golf* magazine? It was a B-movie dream, but it was true.

I spent two years at *Golf* magazine as associate editor, going first class to the tournaments where I had once roughed it like a member of the Donner Party. I stayed in plush accommodations at the world's most beautiful resorts and got a big, bold byline in every issue. I went on to win several more awards from the Golf Writers Association of America and turn out two golf books.

I made it.

I settled into a nice groove as the Lois Lane of golf journalism, drawing a nice salary, accumulating a nice pension—and I got restless. Maybe it was a classic case of spring fever, but I wanted to be doing something other than what I was doing. Something more. I wanted new horizons, new challenges, new realms to conquer. So I quit my job and set up an office in my Manhattan apartment. I am now a freelance writer, New York City style, pounding the pavement with manuscripts falling out of my attaché case, lunching with editors who reject all my story ideas over soup and change their minds over a third martini, trying to block out sirens, horns, bomb blasts at the Cuban Mission around the corner and the shouts of demonstrators, and sweating profusely when the check for a story that appeared five months ago doesn't arrive in time to pay this month's rent.

Although as contributing editor for *Golf,* I continue to stalk an occasional fairway for a recycled story, I'm exploring a new frontier now. The swim upstream has begun again. And I like it that way.

I often reflect on my trip, which seems to have taken place a thousand summers ago, while gazing out my window at a canyon of skyscrapers. And I think about the awesome amount of territory I still have to chart with words. It's a whole different journey ahead of me. I know I'll make it.

BE A SPORT—WRITE A BOOK
by Diana C. Gleasner

I have gray hair and am not fond of heights. Yet two years ago I was dangling spider-like from a rope attached to the tip of a mountain the height of a fifteen-story building. In precise terms I was rappelling from a peak appropriately named the Pinnacle. About halfway down I had quelled terror enough to once again breathe. And think. How did I get into this situation?

My memories were a short course in the vagaries of the freelance business. It all started with the grand idea of writing a how-to book on waterskiing.

The logic of this will appeal. I am a former high school physical education teacher with a specialty in water sports. I have run many a summer camp waterfront and, on a calm day, can muddle across the wake on skis. In addition, our son is, if not an expert skier, pretty darn good. He can do deep-water barefoot starts and tumble turns, and can ski on his elbows and other unexpected body parts. I have watched many of his learning sessions. One needn't be an expert to write how-to books.

Further persuasive reasons for my writing a waterskiing book: I live on a large fresh-water lake within skiing distance of the North Carolina Waterski School, where instructors with impressive credentials give lessons and run sanctioned tournaments. They promised co-operation, including access to the jump and slalom course, for photographs. Final pièce de résistance: My husband is a professional photographer with a variety of excellent sports action shots in his port-folio. We have a boat and offspring willing to pose for how-to photos as well as some of the more esoteric stuff like trick skiing and backward starts.

By now it should be clear how I came to receive a contract for a rock-climbing book.

No Blue Suits

I'm in the business of writing to sell. Both our children are in col-lege. Checks must continue to flow into this house. Pragmatism is the watchword.

I once heard a wise and wonderful man, the late Bill Colby, speak to a workshop session of the Outdoor Writers Association of America. Veteran writer of a multitude of books, Bill made his point well. "Don't sell blue suits to publishers who buy only brown coats." A valuable les-son.

A few years back, I read in *Writer's Digest* magazine that David McKay, the publishing firm, was in the market for how-to books on sports for its juvenile list. So on my annual sell-to-the-editors sojourn, I made an appointment to see that publisher's juvenile editor. At the ready was my sales pitch on the water-skiing book.

The editor politely agreed I would be good for that assignment. But she was looking for a "less affluent" sport, something "an inner-city kid might do" that wouldn't require a boat, skis, gasoline, etc.

Freelancers live by their wits. They must be flexible or they won't survive. Flexibility means meeting the needs of the marketplace. Gin-gerly, this lake dweller started talking inner-city sports.

The editor's nephew had recently gone wild over rock climbing. The last time her nephew went to the "cliffs," the parking lot was full and he had to park half a mile down the road. She thought this sounded like an up-and-coming sport.

I agreed, but felt it imperative to admit I knew nothing about climbing. My admitted ignorance didn't seem to faze the editor, who began talking age level, number of words, and kinds of photographs.

I left promising a proposal and sounding, I hoped, hearty about the specter of learning to climb—which is how I came to be suspended over an abyss contemplating my career.

What am I saying? That there is no logic in this business? Not at all. The lesson here is clear. I was in the right place at the right time to make a sale. I was there because I was out working. I was able to establish a dialogue with the editor because I went in confidently with a good idea and a sound set of reasons for writing a waterskiing book. I had done my homework, and was knowledgeable of the publisher's needs. (After writing for the publishing house's catalog, I had perused it thoroughly.) I established myself as a professional by showing samples of published work and was frank about my nonqualification as a rock climber. Since this was a beginning how-to for a juvenile readership, neither the editor nor I felt my amateur status jeopardized the project.

THE PROPOSAL

I went home, ransacked the library for rock-climbing books, quizzed a master climber at the local outdoors store, and subsequently wrote a formal proposal. The proposal was a standard affair such as is described in detail in Richard Balkin's *A Writer's Guide to Book Publishing*. It included an outline, a zingy chapter on the history of climbing, and a review of competing books in print detailing how mine would be different and/or better. The inactive subject of my sample chapter was no fluke. I had no intention of dangling from rocks and risking life and typing fingers for a proposal. (A full-fledged book contract complete with advance is, of course, another story.) I included a summation of my writing experience, along with factors that would enable me to produce a good book. Since I was a neophyte, I would not assume any knowledge. That, in my opinion, was a plus. I would share the trepidations of fellow beginners and would be able to anticipate their questions and problems. I pointed out that rock-climbing courses were taught in a nearby college and that a fine mountain environment was close at hand for photographic purposes. I zeroed in on the age level and length that fit well with other books in that particular series. This was easy because I had asked the editor to suggest a similar book she thought especially well done, purchased that title, and studied it.

I received a contract and advance on the basis of my proposal, took the course, and wrote the book. I'm glad I did. The research provided my own version of Outward Bound. My instructor's name was Buffalo, and everyone else in my class was twenty-two. Out of deference to my gray hair, I suppose, they politely suggested I go first. I was the first one out of the fire-tower window and first off the Pinnacle.

I turned out to be a lousy climber but can still tie a pretty mean bowline knot. It was a tonic to flee the typewriter for a while and look out over the world. My husband learned to take pictures while he was, quite literally, at the end of his rope. In the unlikely event that anyone ever needs that particular skill, he has it.

When it was announced at my local writers' club that I was doing this book, a handsome young man with a very red face approached me sputtering. The gist of his outrage was soon apparent. He was an expert climber, furious that I should have been given this contract. I admitted my novice status (at rock climbing, not writing) and sympathized. The fact is there are people with more expertise on every subject I tackle.

While my sputtering friend was perfecting his belaying skills, I was home writing, creating a body of work that includes hundreds of magazine articles and more than twenty books. I kept up with professional literature, studied the marketplace and wrote double time so I could afford to fly to New York to peddle my wares. Expertise is one thing; communicating knowledge is quite another. To the best proposal goes the contract. It's easy enough to have an expert check a manuscript later to ensure its accuracy.

I wish I could conclude with some happy statistics about this particular book's sales. Unfortunately, the publisher changed its policy somewhere between acceptance of my manuscript and publication. The juvenile department disappeared. Needless to say, promotion efforts dwindled. *Rock Climbing* remains a curiosity for any future grandchildren we might have. It's not a bad book. I hope all the inner-city kids who read it find transportation to the cliffs and a place to park.

DON'T LET GO

A new writer should not be intimidated by the fact that I went into this experience with a stack of published work. A first book is more difficult to sell, but people do it all the time. My first was sold on the basis of magazine articles I had written. The principles of selling were the same—an analysis of the marketplace and a willingness to write about what the editor wants to publish. After reading of Harvey House's need for collections of biographies on contemporary women in sports, I sent the editor some published articles. I included some on a variety of sports to show I was conversant with the athletic world, along with profiles demonstrating my ability to make people sound lively. I snared that first contract because I got my teeth around the editor's leg and would not let go. I knew I was qualified to do the book and worked hard at convincing him.

There is a snowball effect working in an ongoing career. If you are in the fray, things happen. Because I'd written *Women in Swimming*, I was offered the chance to do *Women in Track and Field*. Because I had an ongoing dialogue with this publisher, I was invited to write *An Illustrated Dictionary of Swimming, Diving and Surfing*, a perfect job for anyone who finds transitions sticky going. Editors tend to typecast writers. This can work for or against you. In this case, I was considered because I had done a book on swimming. No one asked if I had ever been on a surfboard. I haven't. And I know even less about diving.

Lack of experience is no excuse for a slack job. I took my finished definitions to a nearby college swim coach. She was terrifically cooperative and so was her team. Her best divers spent an hour going through the motions of my diving definitions one by one. Most definitions were fine because I had used up-to-date references written by top diving coaches; the few absolutely awful goofs were fixed on the spot. Since the coach would not accept remuneration, I left a donation for the swim team and went home to type my final draft.

Being on a bit of a roll with this particular publisher, I approached him with my water-skiing idea. He yawned. While mentally rummaging through my alternate ideas bag, I listened carefully to his idea of a sports book that would sell.

Wind-surfing!

Luckily, I had several travel writing assignments that took me to Hawaii, the perfect place to master the fine art of sailing on a board. I am pleased to report that wind-surfing is fun. No problem with heights.

I took my lessons on Nawiliwili Bay on the island of Kauai. The setting was splendidly scenic but came with no shark-free guarantee. Most people fall into the water many times while learning to sail on a board. I was no exception, but I was consistently the first in the class to scramble back on the board and try again. They thought I was eager. I was scared. As a result, I conquered wind-surfing in a hurry.

Writing sports books has provided a nice adjunct to my income. Unfortunately, it is not something I can count on for college tuition fees. Perhaps I am writing on the wrong sports. . . .

Oh, I'm not giving up. Eighteen years of freelancing has taught me persistence. If an idea doesn't work one place, it might another. The trick is to keep trying.

Speaking of which—I live on a lake and would love to do a book on waterskiing.

I absolutely refuse to learn to box. But for a fat advance, I might wrestle.

THE WRITER AFIELD—SELLING TO OUTDOORS MARKETS
by Charles L. Cadieux

No one has ever become a millionaire writing for outdoors markets since Zane Grey penned his immortal stuff. And even with the excitement the outdoors offers—battling blue marlin in the Gulf, stalking quail in the Ozarks, facing wolves in Alaska—no one ever had his name become a household word by writing about it. Chances are good that you won't change that.

Before telling you how to write and market outdoors material, I'm going to tell you all the reasons you shouldn't go into this line of work. Then you can't say you weren't warned.

First of all, you shouldn't go into this field because I have entirely too much competition now and I don't need any more.

Hunting and fishing stories were once the sole province of the so-called Big Three—*Field & Stream, Outdoor Life,* and *Sports Afield.* Thirty years ago, when I sold my first feature to *Field & Stream,* I got $200 for it. At that time, the magazine sold for a quarter. Now that the magazine's single issue price is up to a dollar and a half, they pay $400 to $700 for articles. In other words, as the sale price went up 600 percent, the payment for editorial copy went up about 100 percent to 200 percent. But that is not the reason the Big Three are poor targets for the beginning writer.

The Big Three publish about thirty feature articles per month in their combined pages. Some months, 90 percent of their copy is furnished by a dozen writers, recognized authorities who turn out exactly what the magazines want. This is not a criticism of the editors; they are anxious to broaden the list of writers, but they buy the best material that comes in, and these few write the best stuff that comes in. It is tough competition, very tough!

After that depressing summary of the *big* outdoor magazine field, why would anyone try to make a living working for that market? Simple: now the market isn't composed of just the Big Three, but offers opportunities for profitable publication in dozens of magazines that use outdoors stories written to fit their formats. For example, one of the best fishing stories I've ever read was in the *Elks* magazine, not exactly an outdoorsy type of publication. It was written by L. James Bashline and titled "Supper's on the Table."

Trailer Life is certainly not a regular market for hunting and fishing pieces, but they published a story of upland game bird hunting—written around the use of a motor coach as a mobile hunting lodge—and they've printed a dozen of my fishing pieces, all with a recreational vehicle slant.

In the field, we can name *American Hunter,* which pays very well, and *Gray's Sporting Journal,* which pays as high as a thousand bucks for a piece, although they've had financial problems since they began publishing in 1975, and payment may be slow.

What's your field of expertise—salt-water fishing? Try your luck at *Salt Water Sportsman,* whose editors are all "subject matter experts" themselves. You can't sell them a piece about fresh-water fishing—editor Frank Woolner defines fresh water as the stuff cowards put in their bourbon—but a piece about a lesser-known species of salt-water game-fish, about a new or unusual method of luring a salt-water gamefish, or a fact-packed article about a new fishing destination will ring the bell.

Don't drop your plan to write about fresh-water fishing—*Flyfisher, Fly Fisherman's Magazine,* and *Fishing World* are but a few of the many magazines which use this type of material. Regional hunting and fishing magazines abound. Although they don't pay top rates, they are an excellent place to serve an apprenticeship. A complete listing of all such publications is updated annually in *Writer's Market.*

While it's true that none of these magazines can match the $500-and-up figures attainable with the top markets, remember that it's much easier to sell four $300 stories than it is to sell one $1,000 piece.

So Long to Me and Joe?

If you do aim for a top market—or any market—take the time to learn what makes a good outdoors article.

For the last twenty years, the Big Three have insisted they do not want "me and Joe went hunting stories"—while they continued to buy stories about two men who went hunting, or where they went hunting, or how they went hunting. This doesn't mean editors don't know what they want; these three should know exactly what they want. But it means that a hunting trip story should be used as the vehicle to teach a new hunting skill, describe a new hunting area, profile a hunting guide, or give information about a game bird or animal. How can you do this while telling a hunting story? Read several years' back issues—see how the experts do it. I'd recommend reading stories by Erwin A. Bauer, Byron Dalrymple, Norman Strung, Mark Hicks, L. James Bashline, Joel Vance, and J. Wayne Fears. Bauer and Dalrymple have undoubtedly been the biggest sellers over the years. Joel Vance is the best of the new crop, a real artist with the typewriter. Take those authors' writings apart, sentence by sentence. Study how they put a sentence together and ask yourself, "What are they trying to do with each sentence?" How does this sentence contribute to the total effect they are trying to get? How did they open? Close? Was there a surprise along the way? Where did they put that surprise, and what purpose did it serve?

Regional pages are a profitable part of the Big Three. Copy used in these pages is assigned by some of the most knowledgeable editors in the business on the basis of queries that are short, timely, and information-packed. After reading the regional pages in a dozen issues, you'll note that the editor is striving for a regional balance (not too many stories about one state and none about another), and for species balance

(not all about whitetails and none about another), and is working strictly with the seasonal flow of hunting and fishing. After seeing what's
being bought, decide what you can supply to fill in niches in the material needed for a full year ahead. Send in your queries, limited to one
paragraph per idea, and accompanied by photographs, which are an
important selling point. And if you can't take your own photos, you'd
better learn how, or forget the outdoors markets.

NO PICTURES—NO SALES

It is impossible to overemphasize the importance of pictures—lots
of pictures! You'll need them if you go the multiple sales route, the only
way to survive financially. For example, one of my fishing trips to the
Outer Banks of North Carolina resulted in nine separate sales to magazines, which required lots of pictures because you *must not* duplicate
picture submissions! A story about fishing from a mobile fish camp
sold to *Trailer Life;* another about bluefish in the surf sold to *Trailer Travel.* A travel piece, "Introduction to Hatteras," sold to *Southern Outdoors.*
"Ocracoke in October" sold to *Camper Coachman.* Another travel piece,
"Land of Blackbeard," sold to *Southern Outdoors* one month after they
bought the first one. The main story—the only one I had in mind when
I arranged the trip—was titled simply "Hatteras" and sold to *Salt Water
Sportsman,* while "Drum Off Hatteras" sold to *Sea Angler* in far-off Brit-
ain.

But I still needed more pictures, because I consolidated the remaining photographs of the Outer Banks and wrote a roundup piece
about fishing there through the seasons. It sold, and so did another
piece which featured the Outer Banks, about best spots to go fishing
from a recreational vehicle. After that one sold, the idea was expanded
into a small paperback, *Twelve Greatest RV Trips,* which is still selling
nine years later and has earned more than ten thousand bucks.

MULTIPLE SALES—THE NAME OF THE GAME

Every time you go afield to refill the reservoir of ideas about writing about the out of doors, have your sights set on more than one sale.
One article won't pay your expenses. While you're researching the story, take lots of pictures, both black and white and color. Don't go with
strictly color—you'll be ruling yourself out of lots of small markets that
use only black and white. You'll also be ruling yourself out of the aforementioned regional pages in the big mags, for they use only black and
white there also.

One of the secrets to making a buck out of outdoors writing is multiple sales for a single "typewriter-energizing" trip. But there are pitfalls. Hell hath no fury like an editor who sees a similar article of yours in a competing magazine while he is still editing your article for publication in his magazine. Example: I sold a story to *Magazine A* and spent their check in riotous living. Eleven months later, I recycled the idea— with different pictures, different characters, and different fish being caught—but in the same locality. I never stopped to think that *Magazine A* had not yet printed my story. *Mea culpa, mea culpa, mea maxima culpa!*

Because I evidently do not live right, both magazines came out with my stories in the same month. Of course, it was the fault of the editor who sat on a perfectly good story for a year, but it was far more my fault. Never sell similar stories to *competing* magazines unless you wait till the first one has been printed before submitting the second one. In the case just described, I doubt that anyone else noted the similarity— but both editors did, and my relations with them were icy for years.

RULES TO MAKE A LIVING BY

The rules of making a living by writing outdoors stuff for magazines are few, but inflexible:
- Know what you are talking about—because the editors do.
- Take lots of pictures, good pictures, well-thought-out pictures—yes, well-posed pictures. Then take some more.
- Write several, say four or five, stories about each outing, submitting them to noncompeting markets.
- Try your damnedest to develop "outside the outdoors field" markets for your stories about the out-of-doors. *Ladies' Home Journal* might use a piece about trout fishing if it were titled "Fishing for Family Fun" or "Beat the Fishing Widow's Blues (Join Him)." Every publication is a possible market if you can find the angle that suits its format.
- Be prolific! And persistent! Write lots of articles and keep on sending them out. A piece of mine entitled "One Fish's Poison," about chemical rehabilitation of lakes, was rejected thirteen times, then sold to top-paying *Sports Illustrated*.
- Study the market. You should not attempt to write for a publication until you have absorbed its style, taboos, likes and dislikes, and can quote the word lengths it uses for front of the book, middle of the book, and filler stuff.
- Remember that it's easier to sell three small articles for small checks than it is to sell one large article for a big check.
- Never recycle a story idea until after the first one has been published.

- Remember that monthly magazines cannot compete with daily newspapers, so your timely, controversial article (for instance, "The Corps of Engineers Is Ruining the Mississippi") has very little chance to make it with a magazine. Most of the better outdoors magazines have "elder statesmen" in the conservation world who write their controversial stuff—George Rieger of *Field & Stream*, for example.
- "How-to" is still the bestselling theme for any outdoors article.

SET YOUR SIGHTS ON BOOKS

If you are selling magazine articles about the outdoors, sooner or later you'll come up with the bright idea of putting it all between the covers of a book. This must be a good idea, because everybody comes up with it at one time or another. I had written many pieces about the plight of rare or endangered species of wildlife, which led to the book *These Are the Endangered*, still selling well. Goose hunting is a passion with me, so I compiled a book with the novel title of *Goosehunting*. Some of the chapters had been previously published, and I had to get the permission of the magazines that initially published the stories. That was simple. The goose-hunting book is still enjoying a slow but steady sale.

Don't expect to make much money with an outdoors book. I earn at least ten times as much per hour working for magazines as I do when I'm working on a book. Why is this so?

No publisher in this great nation of ours knows how to distribute an outdoors book. Your book may be the best ever written on the subject, and it may draw rave reviews. It may even do well in mail-order sales generated by book reviews. But you won't find it offered for sale in bookstores often enough to finance your fishing trip to Patagonia. Knowing that my *Goosehunting* book was going to get a lot of favorable publicity on television and in the papers in my hometown of Albuquerque, New Mexico, I tried to persuade the manager of the largest bookstore in town to stock the book. He ordered one copy, with a comment that soured me for life: "People who go goose hunting aren't the kind of people who come into bookstores."

I walked across the street and convinced the local sporting goods dealer that the book would sell. He agreed. He sold 161 copies in the five days after the television coverage. This meant that the bookstore manager kicked away 161 times $7.50, or a total of $1,127.

Like it or not, no publisher has a workable method of merchandising the outdoors books to the outdoors-buying public. How can you push your own book?

Promoting Your Book

First of all, cooperate completely with the publisher if he makes any attempt to set up public appearances. *But*—be sure your book is actually offered for sale in the area reached by the public appearance. I am not the only writer of outdoors books who has knocked himself out on a television show only to learn that not one bookstore in the area actually carries the book. When your publisher sets up a public appearance, ask for the names and addresses of the stores that will sell the book. Then, if humanly possible, visit the stores and introduce yourself. Tell them about the public appearance and ask them to watch for it. They appreciate free advertising and will reciprocate by pushing the book after the show.

Second, make sure that you get a good supply of books from the publisher as part of your advance—or as a cash deal if you are more affluent than I usually am. Make sure that everyone you know finds out they can buy the book from you—autographed, no less. If your contract with the publisher allows it, have a letter insert printed which offers the book, by mail, from your home address. I put one of these fliers in almost all of my correspondence. It results in a small but steady flow of orders. Remember that you get 50 percent of the retail price when *you* sell the book, and only 10 percent of the wholesale price when the publisher sells it, even if you generated the sale. The difference between selling it yourself and getting the usual royalty is the difference between filet mignon and Hamburger Helper.

Third, generate your own publicity. Line up your own speaking engagements. Get yourself invited to speak on the subject covered in your book, and plug your book at the same time. Your spouse or other accomplice can sit at a table in the back with a big supply of your books prominently displayed. It's rare for a bookstore to stock more than five copies of an outdoors book—yet you can often sell as many as a hundred copies (and keep the whole retailer's markup yourself) after making a speech to a club or other group.

Fourth, make yourself available to local newspapers and radio and television stations when the book comes out. Pester them, if necessary; they are used to it and even expect it. The "local author" angle works wonders with some media outlets.

Fifth, if your book deals with a subject that might fit into a college classroom course, offer to talk with that class. You'll give the professor a free day, the class will hear something different than usual, and you might generate sales of your book. Do publishers' salespeople work college bookstores? I have noticed that they do, sometimes, but your own visit to a college bookstore will usually sell a bunch of copies. Collegians are inveterate readers.

If you're getting the impression that you *must sell* your own book, then I've succeeded in spreading the truth. If you think selling is demeaning, try some other line of work, not writing outdoors books.

The outdoors field is a lousy place to make a living. I can only name half a dozen who do it without outside income or a profitable sideline such as owning a block of oil wells in North Dakota. But it is a fascinating field, and I wouldn't change for any other job I know about. Well, except maybe for. . . .

GETTING LAUNCHED IN OUTDOORS WRITING
by John W. Malo

Your personal strengths will determine whether you will become a published outdoors writer. Success calls for many stellar qualities, and *perseverance* is just as important as writing skill.

If you live, as most of us do, within a two-hour drive of a large city and surrounding suburban sprawl, you probably seek broader horizons; if you are outdoor-oriented, an active person who takes every opportunity to explore beyond your neighborhood, and are able to express your sensitivities, then freelancing in the outdoors field offers a heartening challenge. Your motivations, born of multiple and diverse drives, keep you at the desk. "Quit" is not in your vocabulary.

The outdoors field of writing is as broad as all life. It can include sauntering along a soft woodland animal path, picking morel mushrooms, identifying birds and flowers, rockhounding, barbed-wire and old-bottle collecting, and on through the old, traditional pursuits— hunting, fishing, boating, tracking, and trapping. The emphasis on these activities has changed from a meat-on-the-table motivation to present-day psychological needs—communing with the land, woods, and waters; pursuing a rare bird or animal; meeting the elements; taking from each outdoor experience the joy of abiding in and appreciating all that is natural, clean, quiet, and eternal.

In the past two decades, outdoors enthusiasts have embraced ever-widening interests: archery, backpacking, bicycling, jogging, motor camping, mountain climbing, parasailing, rafting, and more. Some of these interests are a bit too mechanized for many of us "purists." Whatever their activities, however, outdoors men and women are "doers," not spectators.

Those of you interested in writing about your favorite sport or activity must know, enjoy, and love it, and give it most of your free time and concentration. Only then can you write with passion. Once you become a committed outdoorsman or -woman, your chances of publication will be enhanced by becoming an expert communicator. If you're able to combine your leisure and outdoors recreation writing with photography, so much the better. High-quality action photographs and well-written articles make a package that will capture an editor's attention.

SCAN THE PUBLISHING HORIZONS

There are many markets available to writers in the diversified field of leisure, recreation, and sports. They include:

- Daily large circulation, or weekly neighborhood newspapers (e.g., the outdoors column) cover for participants and spectators alike seasonal sports and recreational activities. There are many subcategories here that have a regional flair: using and enjoying the snowmobile in the snowbelt, the swamp buggy in Everglades country, dune buggies along the seashore, off-road vehicles in the desert. Keep current and report on sports that have a fervent following: community-organized leagues in softball, soccer, football, volleyball, and baseball from Little League to the big leagues.
- Weekly magazine sections of newspapers have a local-color emphasis to them. Reportage deals mostly about events, places and persons in their specific circulation areas. In rural areas, editors give extensive coverage to 4-H clubs, farm auctions, annual fairs, and traditional holiday celebrations. Newspaper magazines welcome seasonal material, human-interest stories, and anecdotes—all with a regional peg.
- Many magazines cover specialized fields ranging from archery to yachting. Name your recreational sport and there's a publication for it—hence a beckoning outlet for every expert who learns to write well. In addition to the major sports, there's growing popularity in boating, scuba diving, camping, fishing, off-road travel, golf, tennis, bicycling, shooting sports, backpacking, mountaineering, skiing, and a lot more.
- General-interest publications are edited for national audiences and carry articles on any subject of interest to a broad spectrum of people. For these publications, the outdoors writer emphasizes the plight of the planet and makes the reader aware of the crucial issues at stake regarding conservation and environmental problems, as well as such issues as population

control, air and water pollution, food production, acid rain, toxic chemicals, and hazardous wastes.

- Photography: Freelancers have many opportunities for both local and national assignments. Slide lectures and film programs are in constant demand, as are filmstrips with accompanying text for sales promotions and school curriculum subjects. Or you can do photojournalism with a striking photo and short essay.
- Outdoors television shows with sparkling commentary continue to get increased time on weekly network and local schedules. Cable television will increase the demand for such programming.

ONE MAN'S ROUTE TO SUCCESSFUL FREELANCING

English was not my best subject when I attended an all-male technical high school. I had no interest in the specifics of grammar and creative writing. Even penning a letter was a chore. Not until college English I and II did I get into writing themes, reading literature and some poetry. The weekly theme assignments, to my surprise, brought favorable comments from profs. Later, as a high school teacher, department chairman, counselor, and assistant principal, my writing skills were constantly used. Freelancing as an avocation, however, came even later.

When I reached age fifty, I was at the top of the hill, and looming ahead—clear and irrevocable—was retirement, the end of a satisfying and fulfilling career. These days most of us have about twenty years of living after retirement. From my observation of oldsters—some happy, most not—I realized that a person must prepare for retirement with a fervor akin to that of the first job. For surely the person who toils till age sixty-five, retires to inactivity, disdains doing things and has no goals doesn't live long enough to enjoy the pension contributions. Thus, the perceptive person prepares for that vital phase of life, looks forward to it, welcomes it. And will enjoy it more if the pension can be augmented by salable writing skills, or any other type of marketable skill for that matter.

So at the age of fifty, while still teaching, I launched an avocational writing career—to test the waters. The inspirations rolled off the typewriter: young-adult sport stories, "naturelogues," environment degradations. All were summarily rejected. I came to see that realization of a misty hope to become published required a helluva lot more than just wishing it. Reality—the exasperating toil, accepting criticism and rejection—came like a sledgehammer blow.

Making a living as a freelancer posed many problems. I'd learned from successful writers that cash flow from royalties was not steady, predictable, or ample enough to support a family. Balancing a budget with income fluctuations was impossible. Thus to hang in there I followed the lead of three fellow faculty members. They had avocations, but stayed with their teaching jobs that guaranteed an adequate salary for basic needs. Two art teachers painted in oils, exhibited, and sold at various art fairs around Chicago. Our music teacher, an excellent cornetist, would fly off after school on Friday to play weekend stands with the Tijuana Brass band. I began to sell articles to small markets. More important, I was building my skills by reading writers' magazines, doing research, attending lectures and workshops, and participating in round-table discussions where we critiqued each others' work. For the four of us teachers, salary paid essential bills, kids' summer camp, sports equipment, uniforms, extensive travel, and college for children.

Now on to becoming a writer of specialized books.

The summer vacation, with its ample block of time, gave me opportunity in the late sixties to enroll in week-long writers' workshops, one at the University of Colorado and two at Colorado Women's College. As a successful high school basketball and baseball coach, I reasoned that writing a novel set in the world of athletics was the way to go. My first evaluation, however, was not encouraging.

The following year at the Colorado Women's College Writer Workshop, Curtis Casewit, a Colorado faculty member, read my improved novel along with some "naturelogues." He was impressed, and after a counseling session that included some in-depth probing of my other background experiences, he, too, said, "Forget the novel for a while. Your canoeing experience, both stateside and in Canada, is the way for you. You're an expert, and publishers will invest in your work."

Two years later the specialist emerged!

In 1969, *Canoeing,* a children's All-Star Sports Book, was published by Follett Publishing Co. Excellent reviews came from *Booklist, School Library Journal, Scouting, Better Camping,* newspapers in Chicago and its suburbs, and media in other states.

Next followed *Malo's Complete Guide to Canoeing and Canoe-Camping,* published by Quadrangle Books (1969) and revised and updated in 1974 by Quadrangle/New York Times Book Co. This title achieved immediate success: over thirty-five favorable reviews; it was bought by the Natural Science Book Club; paperback rights were bought by Collier Books (Macmillan Company) with seven printings; it won a Citation in the Evinrude-Outdoor Writers competition.

Canoeing was clearly my "in," and I wrote fervently on the subject. *Wilderness Canoeing* (Macmillan Company) is now in its third printing, and has over thirty reviews nationwide. This book, along with a story on my work with city youth, won the $1,000 award in the Thermos-Outdoor Writers Association of America national competition in 1973.

Midwest Canoe Trails (Contemporary Books) was written at the request of the publisher as a companion to other trail books. This regional book describes the North American continent's premier waters and the European explorers who traveled them in the 1600s.

Those are but a few of my many titles on outdoors subjects. My writer friends tell me no other person has authored four canoeing books in hardback by major houses.

All this from a kid who disliked high school English.

WRITE YOUR OWN SUCCESS STORY

Getting published requires a long dedication, one that knows more defeats than victories. A writing career—full- or part-time—is not for the weak of heart.

A logical approach to freelancing—the one I took—is to begin on a part-time basis. Read all you can about the writer's craft, join a group, enroll in an evening school creative writing or journalism class, be a constant note-taker on any information relating to the outdoors. The burgeoning notes, ideas, and inspirations can be organized into a file of article subjects to be fine-tuned to salability. Throughout this process, search for an area of specialization, a subject you'll be comfortable with.

Workshops led by stimulating writers or educators are highly motivational, and send you back to the desk with renewed vigor. They make you wonder, too. You meet classmates with lots of talent and ask yourself—if they're not published, how can I be? A budding writer learns early that no workshop, lecture, or textbook can guarantee success. However, these resources, properly mined, can offer direction, motivation, and stir the imagination—all this in company with kindred folk who are traveling the same road.

Against the Odds

I would be remiss if I didn't stress the long-shot odds against a beginner's being published. Some claim these odds are 1,000 to 1, others 500 to 1. Recent stats indicate that of 10,000 unsolicited book manuscripts received by Doubleday, only 5 were published; of 500 manuscripts received by Harlequin, one was accepted.

That's the bad news. But don't stop reading; there *is* some good news. The odds improve when a writer selects nonfiction. Most publishers' profit comes from nonfiction books, and they release about ten such books for each fiction title. A first magazine sale opens the way for similar articles, and it can become a springboard for a book—in fact, you may be asked to do one. In photography, too, once that first photo is sold, confidence is born and momentum started—the ridiculous odds reduced more. If you persevere, you'll come to experience the birth pangs of that first book, a healthy creation, valid and accepted, and you'll feel ten feet tall on top of the world.

Additional Resources

Amateur Athletic Union of the United States, Inc., 3400 W. 86th St., Indianapolis, IN 46268. Provides historical, how-to, and referral information on sports administration and youth sports. Offers aid in arranging interviews, brochures and pamphlets, informational newsletter, photos, press kits, and statistics. Publications include *Media Guide, Code Book*, how-to brochures, and *Info AAU*.

American Auto Racing Writers & Broadcasters Association, 992 N. Pass Ave., Burbank, CA 91505. Conducts contests for top racing stories, photography, broadcasts. Publishes monthly newsletter.

American League of Professional Baseball Clubs, 280 Park Ave., New York, NY 10017. Maintains library and biographical archives on historical ball players; compiles statistics. Publishes annuals: *All Star Guide, American League Red Book, World Series Media Guide*.

Baseball Commissioner's Office, 75 Rockefeller Plaza, New York, NY 10019. Provides comprehensive information related to baseball. Offers aid in arranging interviews, informational newsletter, placement on mailing lists, research assistance, statistics, telephone reference service.

First Interstate Bank Athletic Foundation Sports Library, 2111 West Adams Blvd., Los Angeles, CA 90018. Mailing address: Box 60310, Terminal Annex, Los Angeles, CA 90060. Provides historical information on all sports. Offers bibliographies, biographies, statistics, and information searches. Publications include press and media releases.

Football Writers Association of America, P.O. Box 1022, Edmond, OK 73034. Newspaper and magazine sportswriters covering college and professional football. Publishes *Fifth Down* (monthly, July to December).

Golf Writers Association of America, Inc., 1720 Section Rd., Suite 21, Cincinnati, OH 45237. Editors and writers covering golf for newspapers, magazines, news services. Publishes monthly newsletter, September to June.

National Basketball Association, Olympic Tower, 645 Fifth Ave., New York, NY 10022. Provides comprehensive information covering marketing, promotion, rules, staffing, broadcasting of games, basketball statistics. Offers aid in arranging interviews, biographies, brochures and pamphlets, clipping services, computerized information searches, informational newsletters, placement on mailing lists, press kits, research assistance, telephone reference services. Publications include *NBA Guide, NBA Register, NBA Today.*

National Collegiate Athletic Association, Box 1906, Mission, KS 66201. Offers aid in arranging interviews, brochures and pamphlets, information searches, placement on mailing list, statistics, newsletter, press kits.

National Football League, 410 Park Ave., New York, NY 10022. Offers information and statistics. Publishes annual *Record Manual.*

National League of Professional Baseball Clubs, One Rockefeller Plaza, New York, NY 10020. Offers statistics, information searches, placement on mailing list. Publishes *Green Book* annually, for the press.

National Turf Writers Association, 600 Executive Blvd., Suite 317, Rockville, MD 20852. Newspaper and magazine writers, sports editors and columnists, who regularly write about or publish news of thoroughbred horse racing and breeding. Publishes quarterly newsletter.

Outdoor Writers Association of America, Inc., 4141 W. Bradley Rd., Milwaukee, WI 53209. Compiles market data for members; offers liaison aid in writer assignments. Presents annual awards; conducts surveys for educational and industrial organizations. Publishes a writer's instruction manual, *Outdoors Unlimited* (monthly), *Standard Check List of Common Names for Principal American Sport Fishes, National Directory of Outdoor Writers* (annual).

Professional Golfers' Association of America, Box 12458, Palm Beach Gardens, FL 33403. Provides information on PGA of America programs and activities. Offers aid in arranging interviews, annual reports, bibliographies, biographies, statistics, brochures and pamphlets, information searches, placement on mailing list, newsletter, photos, press kits, films. Publications include *PGA Media Reference Guide* and *PGA Apprentice Program*.

United States Golf Association, Liberty Corner Rd., Far Hills, NJ 07931. Provides information on all aspects of golf, both modern-day and past. Offers aid in arranging interviews, annual reports, bibliographies, biographies, statistics, brochures and pamphlets, placement on mailing list, photos, press kits. Publications include material on golf rules, golf course maintenance, handicapping and course ratings, competitions, general golf literature.

U.S. Harness Writers Association, Inc., P.O. Box 10, Batavia, NY 14020. Maintains hall of fame, placement service, charitable program. Publishes quarterly newsletter.

United States Olympic Committee, 1750 E. Boulder St., Colorado Springs, CO 80909. Provides historical and referral information on the Olympic games. Offers biographies, photos (for sale), placement on mailing lists, research assistance, statistics, telephone reference services. Publications include *The Olympic Games*.

U.S. Ski Writers Association, 7 Kensington Rd., Glen Falls, NY 11801. Promotes skiing and better communication of facts to the public. Presents annual awards for ski writers and top skiers. Publishes *Ski Writers Bulletin* and *U.S. Ski Writers Roster* (annual).

U.S. Tennis Writers Association, 156 Broad St., Lynn, MA 01901. Publicizes tennis and arranges press facilities at tennis tournaments.

Chapter Eighteen

WRITING TRAVEL AND LEISURE

Perhaps no area of specialized writing appeals to newcomers more than travel and leisure. They have immediate visions of all-expense-paid junkets to intriguing spots . . . Tibet or Tonga Tabu, Zurich or New Zealand . . . and a byline, besides! The lure and glamor of travel intrigue readers—and writers—everywhere. And therein lies a problem.

There's a lot of top-notch competition out there. Many outstanding freelancers (seven of them included in this chapter) specialize in travel and leisure. And they'll be the first to tell you that aside from a handful of magazines, the pay for articles isn't what you might imagine. Moreover, it takes experience and perseverance to sell regularly in this field. But if travel and leisure activities appeal to you, this area does offer opportunities to get published while collecting good credits.

For although they may not be the best paying, there *are* quite a few markets in this popular field. Almost every magazine has a column or runs articles on getting away from it all—or at least, escaping the ordinary. Travel-related publications include: inflight airline magazines; trailer, camper, boating, and recreational-vehicle publications; bus and train periodicals; hotel, motel, and resort magazines; and the Sunday magazine section of virtually every major newspaper in the U.S. And of course, consumer, women's, shelter, retirement, and sports publications occasionally feature travel-related articles. Writing travel articles is certainly one of the more exciting nonfiction pursuits, and these pieces can often be done "on the side"—in conjunction with other assignments.

Some travel articles require you to journey no farther than your local library. And any jaunt—even a simple weekend trip to a nearby area—can be developed into a compelling article if you provide the right angle. Area residents searching for gold in the surrounding hills, a stagecoach inn that features entrees from the original menu, snow sculpturing, gravestone rubbings from a two-hundred-year-old cemetery, off-the-beaten-path campgrounds, annual wine festivals, pumpkin festivals, art fairs, firemen's picnics. . . . The possibilities are limited only by your imagination.

This specialty, perhaps more than any other, offers the chance to do what many writers love best: to be keen observers and samplers of experience. Traveling lets you exercise your innate curiosity as you explore new places and meet different kinds of people, describing the sounds, sights, tastes, and smells so readers feel they're there with you. Writers in this field must be able to give honest, objective reports on the places they visit, must often endure hardship—and sometimes even danger—so you need courage, flexibility, and a sense of humor. It also helps to have a good sense of direction; but then again, you never know what great story you may stumble across when and if you happen to get lost. Keep reading to discover what our ASJA veterans have to say about the thrills and chills of this exciting specialty.

"WRITE," THEY SAID
(On Being a Travel Feature Specialist)
by Michael H. Sedge

To think three days ago I was sipping a *prosecco* (sparkling white wine) outside the Caffé Florian in the sun-filled Saint Mark's Square of Venice. It was like a vacation. And the best part was that someone else was picking up the tab.

That's right; I was on a three-day assignment to produce a 500-word travel article on the enchanting, gondola-filled island city. It was an assignment that would eventually cost the magazine a bargain $1100. Because I live in southern Italy, the editors had realized that I could write the feature with half the travel expenses of most writers. Thus, the job was passed to me.

Me! A person who once thought a query was a place where rocks were dug and broken into tiny pieces. A person who had always looked upon writers as "the" select ones, who had always had a secret desire to someday be in that honored group.

Five years ago, I sold my first article. In this morning's mail was a magazine containing published story number 356. If you're a beginning writer, this might sound like a dream come true. And, when I first began, I probably would have agreed with you—especially after receiving my seventieth rejection without having seen my name in print. Now that I have survived the "baptism of fire," as some writers call it, I consider my success more a reward of hard, determined work.

A large percentage of my writing—probably half—has been in the rapidly growing travel field. When I set out to be a writer, I aimed to specialize in photography; because of my location, however, travel editors began to haunt me—to my delight.

I remember the first one. I had sold my second article—a photography piece to *Off Duty* magazine—and was feeling fairly cocky. About three o'clock one afternoon the phone rang. It was Bruce Thorstad, then European editor for *Off Duty,* calling from Germany.

An editor was calling me! Long-distance, no less.

"I've been looking for a writer in your area for some time. Would you be interested in writing a travel guide for the American military?"

Would I! Wow! My head raced at the thought of writing, not only an article, but a whole guidebook.

Needless to say, I did not write the entire booklet. I produced four features for that first edition. But the project became an annual affair that I have written and edited for the past three years.

START WHERE YOU ARE

While my location played a major role in my breaking into travel writing, you don't have to live overseas to get a foot in this specialized door. In fact, there are thousands of markets that I couldn't even consider because they call for "a local slant," "people who know the city first-hand," or "domestic travel only." Beginners should seek out these publications. Newspapers and magazines are constantly looking for travel features that tell their readers where to go on weekends, what to expect, how much it will cost, etc.

One afternoon in a train depot I picked up a national European travel magazine and found a twenty-four-page section on Naples, where I live. This gave me the idea to do something on the city. I did a query and submitted it to the magazine's editor. A week later, the editor called me to say he couldn't use the piece because the topic didn't fit their editorial slant. He advised me, however, to send in some local travel pieces, since they planned to continue the Naples section. Two months later I was writing a monthly "Weekending from Naples" column for the magazine, which is now in its third year.

The moral of the story? Don't wait until you see regular travel features appearing in local newspapers and magazines. By that time the editor has probably already gathered a pool of regular contributors to fill the gap.

Keep Your Eyes Open for Opportunities

Study publications with travel features in mind. For instance, let's say you find a regional magazine that's distributed in the midwestern states of Michigan, Illinois, Ohio, and Indiana. You've looked over the magazine—at least three issues—and found nothing dealing with travel. Yet the publication uses a number of general-interest and family-oriented stories. Next, you notice the advertisers: kitchen products, compact cars, sportswear, and home appliances. With this information you are armed to propose a travel feature geared to the middle-class family on an average—perhaps tight—budget somewhere in one of the four states covered by the periodical. Ideas? Perhaps a venture to one of the state parks along the Lake Michigan coast, a weekend trip to Marriott's Great America fairgrounds in Illinois, or even a trip to the local zoo.

Although these excursions may not contain the high-priced, far-away delights of travel features in the Sunday *New York Times*, they do come under the travel heading and are a great way to break into the field—as well as become a regular contributor to local publications.

You might be scratching your head at this point wondering how a trip to the zoo fits into travel writing. That's probably because you're hung up on the travel concept that has been presented for years by magazines like *Travel & Leisure, Signature,* and *TWA Ambassador.* These (and many other) publications have run some of the finest features on cities like Paris, Rome, Hong Kong, Mexico, Las Vegas, and Madrid—places the average American might see on a once-in-a-lifetime spree. The articles were sophisticated, general, taking in broad aspects of each exotic location.

Details, Details

In the last couple of years, though, editors have changed their style. They realized that Americans no longer wanted to read about things that could be found in guidebooks. They became more concerned with facts. Not, however, the kind found in encyclopedias. Editors saw the high costs of travel as a major concern, even of the nation's upper classes. Magazines suddenly went from "see Europe, you can afford it" concepts to a "see Europe, we'll show you how to afford it" idea.

As David Tykol, managing editor of *International Travel News,* points out in his writers' guidelines, "People [today] like to know how to save money on a trip; places to be sure to see or avoid; the customs one should know in different cultures; what one should not forget to bring along, or leave home; items one should not go home without; the best time of the year to visit; the best way to travel in a certain country (auto, bus, train), and warnings or tips on travel . . . that will make [it] easier, including where to write for more info."

This is the concept behind the new style of travel writing. It holds true for weekly newspaper travel features as well as national million-copy-circulation magazines. Pamela Fiori, editor-in-chief of *Travel & Leisure,* tells potential contributors: "Our aim is to give readers timely, indispensable, and well-written information about restaurants, hotels, shopping, and anything else that helps remove the obstacles of traveling."

In other words, hold the reader's hand. Give step-by-step information. Don't forget important details (prices, times, etc.). And, most of all, tell the truth. If a restaurant is bad, say so! Don't wait until your article appears and the editor receives a letter complaining that Joe's Pizzeria, mentioned in the article, had terrible food.

Travel Pieces for Nontravel Markets

Another change is the rapidly growing market for travel features. If you're a beginner with few (or no) published credits, aiming your queries at the top travel magazines might be like walking into a brick wall. Of course, it is not impossible to sell to these markets. But, unless your idea is so unique that a regular contributor cannot handle it, you will more than likely receive an ego-bruising rejection slip. Editors, in all fields, tend to stick with writers who have proved themselves. They might be contributing editors or simply regular freelancers (stringers). In either case, they are your competitors. I've even had some editors go so far as suggesting story ideas to me that I later discovered were sent to them by other writers.

So how does an unknown travel writer break in? One of the best ways is to try the nontravel markets. They may be general-interest, women's, family, dining, photography, or an array of other magazine categories.

Take for example my article on Venice. The job had been assigned via phone by a Connecticut editor who had gotten my name from another publisher I had worked with in the past. But the interesting thing was that he edited a cooking magazine.

"Mike, what I need is a feature on the city's history, culture, and the eating habits of the people. We've got a thousand recipes that can be plugged in at the end of the story. What we don't have is the meat for a good article."

No market is too far-fetched if you have the right approach. And while on the subject of approach, a few words on the travel-article angle. Many a good writer has failed because he or she lacked a specific story angle. One of the popular anecdotes used to illustrate this is about the travel writer who is about to go on vacation and calls an editor saying: "I'll be in Hawaii next week, do ya want an article?" Well, needless to say, Hawaii is not an angle. If he had called, perhaps, a sports magazine editor and said: "I'll be in Hawaii next week, would you like something on the surfing activities off the coast there?" his chances of an assignment would have increased greatly.

FIND A NEW ANGLE

One of my better-selling articles was a feature that I titled "Erotic Pompeii." There have been hundreds of tourist guides, articles, and books written on this fascinating historical site, yet, with this new angle, I was able to make a profitable sale to *Club International*. Then, a rewritten version sold to *Off Duty, International Daily News, Florida, Italian Bulletin*, and is still making the rounds for reprint rights—all because I found a fresh approach to an old subject, and at the same time discussed an aspect of Pompeii that travelers could not find in guidebooks.

In keeping with this idea, *AMOCO Traveler* editor Susan Ochshore tells writers: "We prefer stories with an interesting angle or new peg: Los Angeles celebrates its bicentennial; a young woman camps out in St. John in search of the real Caribbean; a portrait of an old New England inn."

Another advantage to writing on one aspect of a given location is that it leads to a number of stories—and sales—rather than one. Prolific travel writer Nino Lo Bello, who works out of Vienna, has found this to be true. Following a trip to London, Lo Bello not only had research for an article on the city's theaters, museums, and tourist sites, but also facts that would lead to article sales on London's street musicians, the London Dungeon, and others.

Ho-hum articles that a travel editor will normally pass by often sell if they contain a timely or newsy slant. The day Mount Etna blew its top in 1979, for example, I was on the phone to *Overseas Life*'s managing editor James Kitfield discussing the possibilities of a feature. Kitfield pulled the cover story he had planned for the next month and gave it to me. Along with the check, he wrote: "You can thank Mother Nature for this one."

'Tis the Season

Seasonal articles with a travel slant also sell well if the writer works far enough in advance. In some markets, such as *Adventure Travel, Outside*, and the young, slick publication *Islands*, this means submitting ideas as much as one year in advance. Seasonal travel pieces also sell well to general-interest and women's magazines. Over the past few years I have sold many a story to nontravel magazines (Christmas gifts from Europe; Capri: New Year's for the jet set; Carnevale time in the Mediterranean) using the seasonal peg.

MARKETING MECHANICS

As in any field of writing, the first step is to query, making sure you have a specific slant and are capable of completing the job, if assigned. Photographs, in many cases, are equally important to the well-done travel feature. In fact, over the past few months, I have queried editors—*Adventure Travel, Smithsonian, Outside,* et al.—and been asked to send a selection of photographs for consideration before a final decision was made. So if you have pictures, or can obtain them, it may give the idea more power if you mention this in the query.

Payments for travel features run the gamut. Newspapers will normally pay a flat ten to twenty dollars per article. Military, general-interest, women's, company, and regional magazines generally pay from eight to twenty-five cents a word. In some cases, such as those of the major travel publications, a sliding pay scale is used; some of these publications have been known to pay as high as two dollars and more per word.

Expenses are also a big factor when writing travel pieces and should be considered in the payment arrangement with the publication. In most cases, writers on assignment will have all expenses paid. Beginners, however, who are probably writing on speculation, may have to foot the bills. If you do pay your own way, be sure to save your receipts, as they are work-related and can be deducted for tax purposes.

Happiness Is a Round-Trip Ticket

There are a number of fringe benefits that come with being a travel writer. First, once you're established and begin working for top-paying markets, each job becomes a paid vacation. Second, travel writers, even if the publication isn't picking up the bill, can often receive discounts on travel, hotel accommodations, and even meals. This often means writing to the public relations departments of the representing organizations—airlines, hotels, etc.—with the details of the trip and a copy of the letter that demonstrates that you are, in fact, writing a travel article for a given publication. It is the public relations department's job to look out for their company's image. And if that means helping a struggling writer with discount tickets or free meals, they are more than willing to do so. A few months ago, I read of one airline in the United States that went as far as offering free round-trip transportation to any writer on assignment to a city on their route—and the airline didn't even have to be mentioned in the story. So, no matter how unlikely it may seem, give the PR people a try.

Once you've established yourself in the travel field, opportunities may arise to produce tourist brochures, city guides, or even complete travel books on any number of locations. Since I began working in this specialized field, I've written four city guides, a guide to Mediterranean ports, and a scuba diver's guide; contributed to a backpacking book; and even satisfied my original desire to write on photography, with my *Photographer's Guide to European Museums*.

Here too, the would-be travel writer is encouraged to come up with ideas. One of the best approaches is to outline a travel guide (study other well-done guides for their content, design, layout, and coverage) that could be produced by a local newspaper and be distributed as a supplement. If you can show a publisher that such a guide will bring in revenue from advertising you will probably have an assignment—and be on your way to travel-writing adventures.

HAVE TYPEWRITER, WILL TRAVEL
by Myra Waldo

It's the most glamorous of all writing or journalistic assignments. So everyone thinks. But wait.

Have you ever sat around a jammed airport waiting for a flight that's delayed five hours? (Or maybe more!)

Do you have an unfulfilled desire, a hankering to get up in the middle of the night to catch a 3:30 flight? How does this strike you: sitting on a plane for twenty-two straight hours on a direct flight from New York to Bombay.

In company with most people, you may think that travel writing is the most enjoyable of all activities—the ideal combination of pleasure and work. And in the most fundamental sense, you're absolutely right. I wouldn't change my vocation for anything in the world.

Love to Travel

So, if all this appeals to you as much as it does to me, if you have the stamina—and it *is* tiring—and if you have great patience not knowing when your plane will take off, then join my club.

To begin with, it really helps in this job if you like to travel. Better still, if you really love it in its true sense. Second, it's important to work out your own routine for coping with all the variables, the endless un-predictability and the basic tools of the trade.

WORKING METHODS

Despite this article's catchy title, I long ago gave up the idea of dragging along a typewriter. In fact, I don't even go about with a note-book. It's been my experience that whatever I write into a notebook during the day is not truly retained in the brain. And in the end, that's far more important. For the same reason, I do little photography.

What's the alternative? At night before going to sleep, I write my impressions, review restaurants, evaluate hotels, etc. However, if I have a flight scheduled on the next day, I postpone writing to that time—it's a good way to fill up those hours in the air. Of course, I do have a strange mind (my husband has often pointed that out in a differ-ent context) and I can recall the names, locations, and choice menu items of particular restaurants as far back as ten or fifteen years. I can even recall the arrangement and appearance of hotel rooms I slept in that long ago.

Uppermost in my mind in my dual role as traveler and writer is that I am not the typical tourist. For example, I have been to Hong Kong at least two or three dozen times. Obviously the reader of my guide to the Orient and the Pacific is likely to be seeing that fantastic city quite differently than I am. Thus, it is vital for me to remember that the first-time visitor, in a brief stay, perhaps only three or four days, cannot visit a tiny off-island, however picturesque, if it can be reached only by ferry that will require the better part of a day. It's far more im-portant for me to concentrate on daily practicalities, such as hotels, where to eat and what, sightseeing, and shopping.

With my three travel guides—one each for Europe, South Ameri-ca, and Asia—needing annual updating, it's necessary for me to keep on the move constantly—or so it seems. I used to take long trips. Now I prefer to travel for stretches of about two weeks and then head home to write for two weeks. In the course of a year I average twelve to fourteen overseas flights, and these I try to schedule according to the weather. Obviously it's better in northern Europe from April through October. Australia and New Zealand are best visited during their summer months, which are the reverse of ours. Of course there are some places, Bali or Singapore, for example, where the weather changes scarcely at all the year 'round. And then there are special problems you have to be wise to if you don't want your work hindered—for instance, the torrential rains on the Great Barrier Reef of Australia during Janu-ary and February, even though those are good months for a visit to that country.

TRAVEL TIPS

Over the years, I've also worked out the minimal necessities for survival in my jet-age occupation. When flying, I always take a large substantially built flight bag. Into this go several paperbacks—my insurance against boredom in my moments of much-needed relaxation—quick remedies (including a favorite one for the universal traveler's dread that sometimes sends travelers on more trips to the bathroom than to the local museums), an antinausea preparation, and sundry cosmetics. For me, one essential is a moisturizing face cream; for a man it may be shaving preparations. But it is vital that such items remain in the flight bag with you. They won't do a bit of good in your suitcase, freezing in the baggage compartments that cannot be reached during the flight.

There's also a problem that few people are aware of in present-day flying. The zero humidity in the plane makes it a close second to an Arizona desert. For this reason, I personally limit myself to not more than one glass of wine (no hard liquor), and I drink at least one glass of water or other fluid every waking hour of the flight. This protects me against certain dehydration and its potentially harmful effects. I take precautions to allow for the swelling of feet that invariably occurs during a long flight in the plane's artificial atmosphere. This is why I always wear sandal-type shoes. And also why I avoid wearing any tight garments—whether underwear or outerwear. I've worked out a set of exercises to help keep my circulation closer to normal. Just holding out my legs and making small circles in the air with my feet, frequently walking about the plane, or stretching my arms out full length and clenching and unclenching my fists are easy and helpful.

And then there's jet lag. At this stage of global hopping, my biological clock is so confused that it probably doesn't know what time zone it's really set for. But it is important to realize that if you start a trip exhausted or rundown, jet lag will create a problem that would, if you were in decent shape, be minimal. In any case, make an effort to adjust to the local time condition upon your arrival—including eating and sleeping patterns. Upon your return home—assuming you reach familiar soil at 5 p.m.—no matter how tired, don't give in to the urge to go to sleep immediately, but make a determined effort to stay up until your usual bedtime.

SUCCESS OVER THE LONG HAUL

If after all this you still have a yen to be a travel writer, welcome. But take stock of a few harsh realities. Don't expect to become a bestseller overnight. Or even to get into print your first try. While this profession may be the road to fascinating places, it's no shortcut to riches. Often, travel expenses won't be picked up by your editor. And free tickets and glamorous junkets are more myth than reality.

The important thing is to keep at it. Cull the lists of potential markets and come up with a novel angle geared for the publishing outlet you have in mind. That's a key point, especially if you're writing about well-traveled spots that other writers may already have done to near-death.

But once you make it into print, there's nothing like it. After all these years, I wouldn't trade that sense of accomplishment for anything else.

FREELANCE TRAVEL WRITING
by Robert Scott Milne

If you have envied the glamorous, jet-propelled lives of travel writers and considered becoming one, perhaps you've asked yourself whether travel writing differs from other kinds of nonfiction.

Travel writing is actually *quite* different from the general run of nonfiction. In business reporting, self-improvement pieces, medical articles, stories on scientific developments and so on, reporting must usually be completely objective. Unless you are a top authority on the subject yourself, every opinion must be a quotation from an authority, and you, as the conduit of facts from source to reader, must keep yourself completely in the background. The writing is almost always in the third person, and it's usually awkward if the writer even has to mention him- or herself.

The travel writer, on the other hand, is esteemed by readers not for self-effacing objectivity, but for informed opinions, broad experience, and ability to etch a scene deftly in the reader's mind—along with his or her personal reaction to it.

Recognizing that their function is to lead readers to good travel experiences and tip them off about bad ones, some travel writers call themselves travel critics. This might be generally accepted if it weren't for the fact that the word "critic" is often associated with reviews anathematizing dramatic or literary productions and recording in excruciating detail their absolute barbarities or disasters. When a place or "attraction" is anywhere near that bad, most travel writers simply don't write about it.

Insight and talent with words are thus equally important in travel writing.

The Frenchman Comte Alexis de Tocqueville in 1835 wrote the first major analysis of life in the United States. Called *De la democratie en Amerique*, it describes with an unprecedented degree of insight the remarkably different kind of life being lived in the New World. American insistence upon equality, de Tocqueville shows, affected every facet of life—literature, science, religion, philosophy, the arts, language, business, the family, the military, and manners. He thought our ancestors' manners quite crude, but he foresaw democratic influences causing the emancipation of women.

If you think travel writing concerns itself only with transportation, accommodations, shopping, and recreation in distant places, you might not even recognize de Tocqueville as a travel writer, but his was travel writing of the highest order. He delivered the soul of America to his readers with his rare insight.

The best travel writers are always alert to the subtle emanations of a place and its people. By showing the universal emotions and motivations underlying customs that might seem strange or bizarre, they can link their readers sympathetically to people a world away.

Everything a travel writer *feels* about a place or its people must be seized upon, perhaps examined in detail, but certainly fully realized in words, so that the reader can share the writer's experiences and emotions. Keeping careful notes on a trip is essential, because feelings tend to evaporate or to be overlaid by later events or emotions.

SOME TRAVEL CLASSICS

In addition to de Tocqueville, a few other monumental travel writers must be noted. Homer, whose *Odyssey* was written about 850 B.C., describes not only the fantastic adventures of Odysseus in his twenty-year journey homeward from the Trojan wars, but also gives us a clear picture of much of the Mediterranean world that he visited.

Marco Polo was a man of action who did not intend to be a writer, but took careful notes during his epochal journeys across Asia and in his twenty-four years of service to Kublai Khan. After his return to Venice he commanded part of the Venetian fleet in a war against Genoa. Fortunately for the world, he was captured in 1298 and imprisoned for a year—for during this time he dictated from his meticulous travel journals to the scribe Rustigielo of Pisa. The result was *The Book of Marco Polo*, which revealed the unknown wonders of Cathay to Europe.

Richard Hakluyt of England, who became archdeacon of Westminster and is buried in Westminster Abbey, between 1582 and 1600 wrote several great chronicles of exploration. His *Principall Navigations,*

Voiages, Traffiqves, and Discoueries of the English Nation describes the memorable seaborne expeditions of the English captains to the Americas, the Arctic, the Pacific, and around the world. Although more a scholar than a traveler himself, he inspired much English sea travel in the 1600s. He was one of the planners of the East India Company, and one of his books was written to promote interest in Sir Walter Raleigh's proposed settlement in Virginia.

Guidebooks

John Murray of London is not as well remembered as Karl Baedeker, but should be. The third in a distinguished line of publishers who all bore the same name, John Murray (1808-1892) wrote a series of handbooks on Belgium, France, the Netherlands, and the Rhine.

Karl Baedeker (1801-1859) started a printing plant in Koblenz, Germany, in 1827. He published pocket-size books on Belgium, the Netherlands, and the Rhine, by agreement with John Murray, in 1839. Baedeker's later books covered most of Europe, parts of North America, and the Orient. They were so detailed and complete that the name "Baedeker" came to mean guidebook. Places of greatest interest were marked with one or more stars in Baedeker's guides, so travelers could easily decide what to visit in the time available: "starred in Baedeker" soon meant "well worth seeing." From the beginning, Baedeker published his books in German, French, and English, and thus rapidly became widely read.

Modern Travel Guides

In the twentieth century, Eugene Fodor has succeeded to Baedeker's eminence. Born in Hungary, Fodor was editing travel books by 1936, and began publishing *Fodor's Guides* in Paris after World War II. (He moved his headquarters to the United States in the 1960s.) At last count there were sixty-three *Fodor Guides*, of which sixty-one were being updated annually. Usually, each book is put together by a team of writers, one of whom serves as area editor. A contribution to a *Fodor Guide* is like writing a magazine article, with the possibility of a byline under the chapter title.

Robert C. Fisher, former executive editor of *Fodor Guides*, started his own series, *Fisher's Annotated Guides*, with eight books in 1982. Each of these is by a single author, whose name is on the title page. A distinctive feature is marginal annotations, in red, by Fisher himself, adding information of special interest. Fisher's are the only American-published guides that dare to rate foreign hotels, restaurants, and attractions; they are designed for the sophisticate rather than the first-time traveler.

Arthur Frommer, then a young lawyer, and his wife traveled through Europe on a tight budget soon after World War II, then wrote *Europe on $5 a Day*. The title alone doubtless inspired many planeloads of young Americans to visit Europe. For millions of youths it was the bible of essential information, carried around Europe until it was dog-eared and tattered. With the book's profits Frommer built a publishing house, and he keeps many authors busy writing and updating over forty travel guides. Each book, bylined on the cover, is written by a single author or a team of two. Frommer continues to expand his travel operations, having become a tour operator and hotel impresario as well as a publisher.

Like the Fodor books, Stephen Birnbaum's *Get 'em and Go* guides, and the multivolume guides published by oil companies, are team-written. Temple Fielding's *Fielding's Travel Guide to Europe* and Myra Waldo's *Travel and Motoring Guide to Europe* are another type of guidebook entirely: these books are designed for the American traveler who can afford to live well and does so, who would not deign to consider the bargain-basement travel described by Frommer, and who relies on the taste and preference of Waldo and Fielding to steer him or her to the good life abroad.

Another kind of travel book provides adventure, excitement, and exotic scenes purely for reading pleasure, and not because the reader expects to visit the places or emulate the adventures. Among these are reports of jungle exploration, mountain climbing, Arctic cruising, treasure hunting, visiting lost tribes, archaeological digging, and sailing oceans in small or unusual craft. This escapist nonfiction is for armchair travel—the opposite end of the spectrum from the step-by-step travel instructions of a Baedeker.

Between these two extremes of travel writing are numerous types of books on outdoor life, hunting and fishing, camping, ecology, wildlife, folklore, local crafts, transportation, skiing, boating, historic sites, cruising, flying, gliding, hang gliding, windsurfing, and so forth. Some of these are written merely to amaze or amuse the reader, and others to give practical advice and instruction.

GETTING STARTED

People get into travel writing by many different pathways, as often as not by accident. My own writing career began in Honolulu, where I was a credit manager—a job I had come to detest. I had always dreamed of being a writer, but had done no writing except for high school and college publications. My work hours were eight to five, so I began getting up at four every morning to write. I started with fiction, but soon found myself more attracted to writing articles.

A problem developed with my voice. I moved to New York for treatment, and there worked a year or so with the Scott Meredith Literary Agency evaluating manuscripts and writing detailed reports to authors. At the same time I took writing courses at Columbia University in fiction, articles, and television drama. I spent all my spare time writing magazine articles, and sold a few to low-paying markets. I then returned to Honolulu, where for a year I was assistant editor at the University of Hawaii Press, and wrote at night.

Making a permanent move to New York, I became an assistant editor at *Collier's Encyclopedia,* where I had made myself known by freelancing some articles. I continued moonlighting, and my first sale to a national magazine was the article, "High Credit Standing on a Low Income," based on my credit-managing experience, which I sold to *Modern Bride*—the twenty-second market to which I had sent it (persistence pays).

When my wife and I planned a trip to Jamaica, *Modern Bride* assigned me a honeymoon article on the island, and my pleasure in researching and writing it made me decide to concentrate on travel writing. I did subsequent articles for the magazine on living abroad and on different honeymoon destinations, and gradually broke in with other magazines. (One of the first was the *Atlantic Monthly,* which used to publish travel pieces on "queer places" but no longer does.)

It helps in the travel field, I'm sure, that I majored in languages and can at least read French, Spanish, and German. It helps, too, that my wife, Gaby, is fluent in French, German, and English, and picks up enough Spanish and Italian to get along. She shares my love of travel, and her adventurous spirit makes it easier for me to take on foreign assignments. For example, her fascination with exotic shopping supplies the necessary insight in that area that my total lack of interest deprives me of. Many a traveler complements his or her own observations with those of a spouse or fellow travel writer to get a more rounded picture. (There are many married teams in which one spouse is a travel writer and the other a travel photographer. When both are professionals it is easier for them to travel together on assignment.)

While I was still building my freelance career, Gaby and I flew and drove in various parts of Europe, bought a camper and drove around the U.S. and Canada, and flew to various points in and around the Caribbean. I sold articles to various magazines, to all the major New York newspapers, and to top papers in other cities, but I held on to the security of a steady job, working seven and a half years at *Collier's* and eight and a half as associate editor at *Encyclopedia Americana.*

Finally going out on my own in 1972, I found an office I could rent—implausible as it sounds—in New York's Plaza Hotel, on Central Park South at Fifth Avenue. And that's where I typed this.

One thing that helped me survive was that by 1966 I had published enough articles to be accepted by the Society of American Travel Writers (SATW), where I met many other writers, and travel editors who could buy my articles, at meetings and SATW conventions (held between 1966 and 1972 in Canada, Turkey, Austria, Las Vegas, Finland, Greece, and Tunisia).

Since I took my own office my constant preoccupations have been writing travel articles and traveling, with some major interruptions. When my friend and colleague Eunice Telfer Juckett was asked to write a book on *Opportunities in Travel Careers,* she didn't have time and recommended me as author. I spent half a year writing the book, which I revise every three years.

How I Started a Newsletter

The other major interruption to—or should I say spinoff of—my traveling writing is my newsletter, which now costs me two weeks every month. (I hope to cut that time in half by switching to a personal computer.)

To tell you how it started I must first tell you a bit about the Society of American Travel Writers. SATW has two categories of members, Active and Associate. The Associates, comprising half the membership, are all public relations people in the travel field. The Actives are about equally divided between freelancers and travel editors. About 1974 the freelancers, feeling the need for discussions that would concentrate on their own professional problems and advancement, formed the Freelance Council (FLC) within SATW. The FLC has about a hundred members and holds annual workshops, both abroad and in the U.S., in connection with story-gathering trips.

At the Freelance Council Workshop in Chattanooga in 1977, the chair asked for a volunteer newsletter editor to get out announcements of trips, awards, elections, and other news of particular interest to freelancers scattered about the country. There was a long silence; I meditated on how much time this would take from gainful article writing and finally volunteered, since I was one of the few members in New York, the heart of the publishing world.

I named the publication *Freelance Update* and issued it every two months to the hundred-odd members of the Freelance Council only. I started including market information; soon the newsletter came to be regarded as highly valuable to freelancers. Eventually I was asked by the president of SATW to publish it for the entire organization—everybody wanted it! I changed the name to *Update.*

A great deal of my time was going into the newsletter, however, and no funds were forthcoming, so I was forced to put it on a subscription basis. I changed the name again, to *Travelwriter Marketletter,* so the name would describe its function as accurately as possible. The first subscription issue was in April 1980; the amount of news kept growing rapidly, and in November 1980 I made it a monthly.

Each issue of *Travelwriter Marketletter* has ten pages—the maximum that will fit under the one-ounce first class letter rate. The first section, "Trips," describes travel opportunities being offered to professional travel writers and photographers (usually free and with air transportation provided).

"Marketwatch," the main thrust of the newsletter, is a listing of publication changes—new magazines or newspaper travel sections, suspensions, new editors, increased or reduced rates, editors' requests for coverage of certain areas, slow pay, staff jobs open, etc. Sometimes "Marketwatch" fills nine pages.

"Freelance Achievements" lists published articles and photographs by professional travel communicators. Public relations people find this particularly interesting, because the travel writers who are being published are the ones they want to invite on trips.

Additional sections I use in *TM* when there is space enough are "General News"; "Books," in which I review travel reference books, and some travel books; and "PR World," which notes movement of travel accounts from one PR agency to another, and changes in personnel representing travel accounts.

The response to *Travelwriter Marketletter* has been fantastically favorable. Freelancers depend on it, and write or call me if it's late arriving. Letters of praise arrive frequently. In June 1980 the SATW Freelance Council presented me a special award—an engraved silver tankard—in gratitude for *TM.*

FREE TRAVEL

Do travel writers have offers of free trips? Yes, lots! For years I've been receiving many more offers than I've had time to accept. In *Travelwriter Marketletter* every month I list an average of more than five trips open to travel writers and photographers.

Is it easy to sign up for these trips? Yes, but only if you're a *recognized professional* travel writer. If you've published no travel articles you don't stand a chance, because this is serious business. The sponsor offers you a trip expecting you to write and publish an article about his cruise or resort or airline. He has no right to expect a rave review unless you feel his place or service deserves it, but you are under obligation to try for publication—unless, of course, you feel the place is so bad that it doesn't deserve *any* mention in print. Your obligation to your readers is to write an honest report including your own opinions, whether favorable or not.

Who offers trips? National, regional, and municipal government tourist offices; carriers, including airlines, cruise lines, railroads, and bus lines; resorts and motel and hotel chains; theme parks, caves, and other attractions; regional associations of attractions; tour wholesalers, wilderness trip outfitters—just about every kind of entity that wants tourists. Trip arrangements may be made by media liaison divisions of government tourist offices, public relations personnel of companies, or employees of public relations firms that represent travel operators.

Among reasons for offering a trip are an airline's establishing a new route, a hotel or theme park opening, the completion of new facilities (such as a resort golf course), or a new museum. There are also annual seasonal trips, planned before the beginning of the tourist season so that the writers' articles will appear as the season begins.

Generally such trips are organized for groups of travel writers, so as to make it worthwhile to provide a guide and transportation. An invited group frequently numbers ten to twenty writers, enough to fit comfortably in a bus. These trips are almost never planned at the height of the main tourist season, but before or after, when there are empty hotel rooms and airplane seats. Exceptions are natural events such as cherry-blossom time or fall foliage, and civic events staged only once a year, which the travel writer must cover during the main tourist rush, usually to prepare an article for the following year.

Trips for individual writers are also arranged by sponsors such as state travel bureaus. Typically the writer (and perhaps the writer's spouse) is flown to the state capital. The state travel promotion people will have drawn up a detailed itinerary covering areas interesting to the writer, who is either given a rental car and proceeds alone, staying free at designated hotels, or is passed along from one local travel office to the next and guided through each point he or she will write about.

Ethics

I've mentioned the writer's ethical commitment to write and try to sell an article about a place when given a trip to it, and the greater ethical duty—to readers—to give honest opinions about the place. Actually, travel writers' negative remarks have often been used by tourism people to persuade their higher-ups or the authorities to improve bad conditions. Not infrequently, therefore, tourism directors have thanked travel writers for pointing out deficiencies.

On another ethical front, a few of the country's prominent newspapers have taken the attitude that any sponsored trip has in effect "bought" the writer, and they refuse to buy an article generated by a sponsored trip. This actually bars the professional travel writer from their travel pages. Why? Because payment for travel articles in even the top-paying newspapers is a pittance compared to the cost of travel, and these newspapers refuse to pay travel expenses. This leaves the field to occasional business or pleasure travelers who want to be published, and the papers' own reporters on holiday, or foreign-bureau reporters.

On the subject of sponsored trips, Richard Dunlop, author of numerous travel books and a past president of the Society of American Travel Writers, writes:

"I cannot imagine that any responsible public relations person who works for an honorable client, whether it be a hotel company, airline, state, or foreign government, thinks he can buy a respected travel writer by inviting him on a press trip. Nor would a travel writer of stature go on such a trip if he thought he was being bought. I have always felt free to write exactly what I thought of the areas I visited on press trips."

The same newspapers that reject press trips as unethical accept free tickets to plays, ballets, concerts, and sports events for their theater critics, dance critics, music critics, and sportswriters. They also pay the expenses of any reporter who must travel to cover a story. Their position on freelance stories generated by press trips is, to say the least, quixotic.

TRAVEL WRITERS' ORGANIZATIONS

The Society of American Travel Writers' classes of membership, Active and Associate, are described above. SATW was organized in 1956 with two main goals: to convince publishers that responsible travel journalism is an essential editorial service—an inescapable obligation to readers in this age of rising leisure and discretionary income—and to build joint strength for travel writers in support of their elemental function in the travel industry, as true spokespeople and travel critics for the average reader. Membership requirements for freelancers are designed to admit only professionals who can show a respectable body of work published within the previous year.

The Travel Journalists Guild (TJG) is fairly new. (The organizing meeting was held in Guatemala in 1980.) Its object: "Joint action to strengthen our position in the marketplace." Included in the single class of membership are travel writers, travel photographers, travel film makers, and travelogue lecturers; it is the only national organization restricted to freelance travel communicators. There are about sixty members. TJG has a monthly newsletter, *Guild Guide*, which I edit. It's confidential and restricted to members, because it carries members' current sales reports, with amounts paid for articles and treatment accorded by publishers. TJG takes one or two trips each year devoted (as much as possible) to story gathering. Meeting time is kept to a minimum. Membership requirements are strict, requiring a solid body of professional work.

There are various other local travel writers' organizations and national societies in which travel writing is important. The New York Travel Writers Association is a group of about forty members, both freelance and staff people. They hold monthly luncheon meetings and occasionally hold a grand ball or take a trip. The Midwest Travel Writers Association, centered in Chicago, includes freelance and staff travel writers. The Outdoor Writers of America comprises people who write about hunting, fishing, camping, backpacking, hiking, mountain climbing, wildlife, recreational vehicles, and so forth; much of this also qualifies as travel writing. The American Society of Journalists and Authors shows in its directory of members that one third of its 650-plus members list travel writing among their specialties. Many established travel writers belong to several writers' organizations.

FREELANCE TRAVEL WRITING AS A BUSINESS

Here we come to the crunch. Even though travel articles are important to newspaper and magazine readers, publishers don't pay well for them. One reason is supply and demand. There are thousands of people willing to write travel articles for little or nothing, just to get published. Public relations firms turn out travel stories by the ream and send them free, along with free photographs, to any newspaper or magazine that will print them (sometimes these are written by freelance writers). City newspapers used to buy many travel articles, although they paid little for them. But during the economic slowdown of the mid-seventies, newspapers suffered the same problems as most businesses, and were also faced with paper shortages, labor problems, and fiercely escalating costs. Many of them stopped buying from freelancers; travel editors write their own articles, use free public relations handouts, and get articles from wire services at very low cost.

The recession of the early eighties caused many metropolitan newspapers to merge or go out of business, so this market has been much further reduced. Computerization of editorial offices has also led to some prejudice against articles typed on paper, because they must be "re-keyboarded" into the computer. A few travel writers have gotten around this problem by obtaining personal computers with telephone modems, so the story can be written on the computer and sent by telephone right into the newspaper's computer.

The magazine picture is brighter. Since many people have more free time and increasing disposable income, numerous new magazines are being established to promote travel, fine dining, and a host of leisure activities. Most of these magazines need travel articles. So do all the free magazines such as inflights and magazines for doctors and engineers and students—as do the posh magazines delivered free to the very rich in wealthy enclaves. New magazines seldom pay well for articles, and mortality among them is high, so the writer must be wary.

In sum, freelance travel writing is an insecure business. It takes constant work to make a living, along with good luck in making sales. Some travel writers are able to continue as freelancers only because of inherited income, a spouse's support, or additional work that is more remunerative and dependable.

Here's the bottom line: if you want to be a travel writer just so you can take free trips, you would do better to educate yourself for a high-salaried job so you can afford frequent vacations.

If, on the other hand, you love to travel and to meet people unlike yourself, you have a talent with words, you have good judgment and a desire to inform people about travel opportunities, and you're willing to live without security in order to pursue these goals, travel writing is for you. If you can cope with the problems, it's a fabulous way to live.

TRAVEL WRITING: PROBLEMS, PLEASURES, AND PARAMETERS
by Karen Cure

When I was trying to decide what to do with my life as I graduated from Brown University, I liked the idea of being a freelance writer and decided to direct my efforts in that direction. Andrew Hepburn, a longtime editor who happened to be related to a high school chum, pointed out that it could be a long time between checks and suggested that a regular writing or editing job made a good base for a beginner. I paid attention and developed a plan: I'd spend the summer living at home and saving money so I could afford to return to romantic New England and look for a job on a small-town newspaper. Without a grain of newspaper experience since the ninth grade and no training but a B.A., I imagined that the job search would take a while.

Paying My Dues

What I didn't anticipate was the dearth of summer jobs in Indianapolis, where my parents lived. I was either overqualified or underqualified. The only business that would hire me turned out to be a company owned by acquaintances of my mother. They didn't need someone just for the summer, but by that time I was willing to take anything, and the $100 a week I was offered to work as an executive secretary's secretary seemed princely.

What ultimately set me on my present course (I never did make it to the small-town newspaper) was that my employer was publishing a travel magazine. *Holiday* had just moved to Indianapolis. The office was chaotic, and the only real professional around was managing editor Frederic Birmingham, an old-time magazine man with experience at *Esquire* and *Reader's Digest,* and the patience of a thousand Jobs. As far as my job went, my years of college mattered considerably less than my three years of high school typing. I transcribed memos dictated by the publisher (sometimes as she was falling asleep; she even carried her little Norelco machine into the bathroom). I chauffeured her to beauty shop appointments and drove her kids to and from their friends' houses, picked up dry cleaning, and fetched important personages from the airport—or chicken à la king from a local restaurant for luncheons served to business guests. I set the table and occasionally served the meals (once I even made a tablecloth). And feeling all this very much beneath a Brown University graduate, I also did a lot of moaning and groaning to my parents. But they advised me to stick with it, pointing out that I was learning at least a little about publishing despite my misery—and, in fact, after a few months I got a promotion and traded in my gal Friday job for magazine editorial work.

Launching a Career

Then came a chance to go along on a trip for travel writers, where I met a *Better Homes and Gardens* editor who believed in helping young writers get started. He looked at my work, gave me the chance to do some travel writing for the magazine on speculation—and after my pieces came in to his satisfaction, made the batch of assignments that ultimately gave me the nerve to announce my departure from *Holiday.*

The editor also introduced me to a colleague at *BH&G*'s book division who was looking for a writer to do a book of mini-vacations and, when *BH&G* decided against the project, to yet another colleague at Follett Publishing. *MiniVacations USA* was published in 1976 by Follett. When I got the idea for my second, *The Travel Catalogue,* I went to a former junior editor at *BH&G* Books who was also involved in a book-packaging house (a firm that does the editing, art, and printing on a book, then delivers the finished product to a major house client for bookstore distribution).

That same helpful *BH&G* editor also gave me an introduction to a colleague at the newly established *Diversion* magazine. I wrote one piece for its first editor, another for his successor (after the magazine changed hands), and later—on the strength of my previous work there and on *MiniVacations USA*—for *Diversion's* third editor, Steve Birnbaum. I have been writing for him ever since, not only in his capacity as *Diversion's* editor, but also for a guidebook series that he subsequently developed. In fact, it was Birnbaum who passed on my name to a *TWA Ambassador* editor with whom I've been working happily ever since on a monthly column and occasional features. One thing *does* lead to another.

THERE'S MORE TO TRAVEL WRITING THAN TRAVEL

Whenever I tell people what I do for a living, the usual response is, "You must travel a lot." This isn't necessarily so. The work I'm doing at the moment falls into several distinct categories, and only some of it involves hitting the road.

1. *Editing, revising, and rewriting.*

When Steve Birnbaum inaugurated his travel guide series, I worked with the executive editor to develop a format for the "Diversions" section of the series' roster of vacation ideas organized by subject (backpacking, golf, tennis, resorts, great museums, amusement parks, fishing, and the like), each one described in capsule form. I wrote that section for the U.S. guide and have updated it ever since. In subsequent years, I also edited the "Diversions" section for several of the series' companion volumes.

These projects, though fairly tedious, do provide a great deal of satisfaction. I've acquired considerable abstruse information about out-of-the-way places that are well known to aficionados of this or that, and I love working with the staff. I also enjoy the opportunity that working for a book publisher provides to spend a certain part of each year in an office (although I still keep my own hours—sometimes I work on Saturday and Sunday nights if I've been lazy during the week). The pay is modest by comparison to the pleasures, but the work is steady and the checks are forthcoming almost immediately after the project is completed—a benefit not to be underestimated.

2. *Disneyana.*

When Steve Birnbaum got the contract to produce the official guide to Walt Disney World, he asked me to handle the research and writing—again, on the basis of my previous work with him. The following year, he asked me to write the Disneyland-related sections of a companion guide to the California park. I've also done a number of articles for *Disney News* magazine—feature articles on aspects of the parks, a profile of an important figure in the company, plus sections of the magazine that would be written by a staff writer if *Disney News* had one. These give me the chance to try my hand at different types of writing than I usually do—and I enjoy that.

3. *Roundup articles.*

Drawing on information and ideas from the guidebook research and other sources (depending upon the focus of the article), I occasionally do a "best of" piece. My columns for *TWA Ambassador* generally fall into this category. Designed mainly to tell readers how to get the most out of their stay in various TWA-served cities, each column focuses on one typical business/urban traveler's common need (examples: a place to run or exercise, a hotel that provides service as personal as that at home, an English-language bookstore abroad, the best source for eating-out ideas, the best columnist to read to really catch the pulse of a city), and then tells readers where these needs may best be met in each of a handful of TWA cities, usually four or five cities per column.

4. *Destination articles.*

These are the ones that take me far afield. Sometimes an editor suggests a topic; sometimes I develop the idea myself and try to sell it. The destination may be a place that I want to visit on a weekend, or it may be a location to which an airline, national tourist office, or PR firm has invited me on an all-expense-paid trip designed for travel writers. A few years ago, a photographer colleague and I put together a nine-week trip to the Philippines, Hong Kong, Japan, Malaysia, Singapore, Java, Bangkok, Bangladesh, and northern India, based on assignments obtained from half a dozen different magazines. Originally, we planned our itinerary around a handful of Asian festivals; I then formulated queries and crossed my fingers. The assignments resulted from my queries.

MAXIMIZING YOUR INCOME

Some travel writers seem to do this practically full-time, apparently with great success, but so far I haven't quite figured out how it's possible to make a terrific living at traveling full-time, even if you set your sights at a relatively modest $2,000 a month ($500 per five-day week, $100 per day). Again, the problem is money. Since travel magazines pay anywhere from $200 to $1,500 for articles, you may need several assignments just to pay for your time on the trip (and remember that you can't write two articles on *exactly* the same subject for competing magazines). At the moment, I am sidestepping this whole issue by keeping my traveling to a minimum, but there are other options that I have explored in varying degrees.

For instance, you can write about each location in several ways. After two weeks on the island of Java, I wrote a destination article about the island, a piece on how (and where) to buy batik, and something about a hike to the rim of a volcano. A trip to the Philippines will yield a destination article about the nation as a whole, plus a feature about the Manila Hotel, 100-word shorts on an up-and-coming resort and a distinguished businessman's hotel, a piece about Philippine foods, and another about buying antique oriental ceramics. I might add that while researching all this can be fascinating, a trip designed to yield so much information is a far cry from the relaxing experience that most travelers enjoy in the same place.

It's also possible to sell the same story to several publications. If one magazine buys first North American rights, you can try to place it elsewhere in North America at a later date. Foreign markets are also worth looking into. I haven't had any experience doing this in Europe, but have placed several articles that have run originally in stateside publications with *Silver Kris*, the magazine of Singapore Airlines, which is published in Asia. Newspaper-length destination pieces can be sent to several publications that do not share the same circulation area, and although no single editor pays very well, the checks do add up.

It goes without saying that the more salable a location, the better yield you can get on the trip. You're simply going to get more mileage out of a trip to a destination that you can write about in more different ways. Spending three weeks in Tahiti might be nice, but there are probably more markets for pieces about the destinations you'd visit during three weeks in the Rockies. It's important, I think, to consider the time you spend in each location as an investment rather than as a holiday. Freelancing is a business.

Most of these ploys depend on having markets in the first place—and developing markets takes time, but it certainly can be done.

ATTACKING THE MARKET

When you're starting out, use a book like *Writer's Market* to find out which magazines buy travel pieces. Study six or seven back issues of a magazine to get a feeling for each one's style. Then set out to develop a working relationship with the editor. Work up some ideas for pieces for the publications you've studied. Stick to subjects that you know well—an editor once said to me that in making assignments, she considered not only the proposal but also whether the writer making it was the best person to cover that topic. You are most likely to get a commitment for a piece for which you are uniquely qualified. A woman who asked me for advice not long ago had, on her own, written and published a guidebook to Providence, Rhode Island during her senior year in college. I suggested that she propose stories about aspects of the city to magazines for which she wanted to write.

A perusal of the magazines you want to write for with your particular fields of expertise in mind may give you several ideas. When I was starting out, I made lists of titles of a couple of magazines and then tried to figure out how to take the same approach toward areas that I knew well. You may not be able to write "The Manila Nobody Knows"—but you may be the ideal person to tackle "The Kansas City Nobody Knows." Writers who live in large metropolitan areas like New York, Chicago, San Francisco, and Los Angeles have a wealth of stories in their own back yard; the problem is not to find ideas but to pick just one of them. The competition may be daunting, but bright ideas are always at a premium.

Care and Feeding of Editors

When you're contacting editors, be specific. "I'm going to Cincinnati—can I do anything for you?" is not going to get much of a response coming from an unknown writer. A specific proposal about a specific aspect of Cincinnati—say, the city's enormous Oktoberfest celebration—has a chance. The query should focus on and carefully sketch the story you have to tell in terms that make the editor eager to read your piece. The letter should be as short as you can make it and still get the point across. The editor won't necessarily give your letter the consideration you put into it, and if he or she misunderstands your idea, you might get a refusal for all the wrong reasons.

It goes without saying that the letter should be neatly typed, that spelling should be accurate, and that everything should be proofread. This seems so obvious to me that I would not even have mentioned it were it not for an aspiring travel writer I met a couple of months ago who actually felt that his "art" should excuse him from such burdens. It's also a good idea to enclose some clippings of past work, an SASE to insure their return, and a brief statement about why you'd be a good person to write that story. (Example: "I've written extensively for my college newspaper, and during my senior year researched, wrote, and produced a guidebook to restaurants, shops, hotels, and points of interest in Providence.") If you want to go out on a limb, you might suggest that you'd be willing to do the article on speculation; I can't say this approach would give a writer with no track record extra appeal to just any editor. However, it did work for me and it might for you.

You certainly shouldn't expect a positive response the first time around, so don't get discouraged if the answer is no. A colleague whom I consider very successful told me not long ago that even *he* gets ideas rejected on a regular basis, and by editors he writes for all the time. Reformulate the idea for another magazine and send off a letter. And try again with the first editor. Simply sending frequent queries to an editor can make your name and your style almost as familiar as if you'd been doing assignments; my advice would be to send a new proposal about two to three weeks after the first one had been rejected. Assuming you had a good understanding of what the magazine was using and might conceivably buy from you, I think that this would be an excellent way of getting your foot in the door somewhere. And that's nearly half the battle.

The other half, of course, is delivering the goods. To really make a go of it, you've got to prove to the editor that you're thorough, reliable, accurate, sensitive to the magazine's needs, and easy to work with—so that he or she will feel free to call on you in the future. Therefore, when you do get a first assignment, make sure you understand just what the editor wants (it may be slightly different from what you've suggested—and in fact, even the editor may not be totally aware of what's going to please). Then talk the piece over, perhaps after you've done some research, so that the editor knows exactly what to expect. Then deliver what you've promised. If you anticipate any substantial variation, another phone call might be in order. The best surprise, as they say, is no surprise. Accuracy is vital. If you're asked to supply checking material (your references, sources, notes, quotes), put it in the best possible order, and make sure that your writing is legible.

Follow the magazine's style, if the magazine has one; some allow for more individuality than others, and the style of the *New York Times* travel section differs vastly from that of *Better Homes and Gardens* travel pieces. In every case, however, try to make your writing sparkle. Avoid generalities like "beautiful" and "breathtaking" and concentrate on words that evoke sights, smells, sounds. The best travel article I've ever read was one that Geoffrey Wolff did about Brittany for *Travel & Leisure* a couple of years ago. It's well worth looking up.

Pitfalls—and Pleasures

No matter how good you are, developing markets and getting to the point that you can make an acceptable living at travel writing takes time. One friend of mine started doing travel only about four years ago. He's ambitious and he's worked hard and recently published a book of weekend vacation ideas designed for New Yorkers and took on a rather prestigious radio travel spot. But he still hasn't felt secure enough to quit his full-time job and has to do his traveling on the side. He was able to spend six weeks in the Caribbean this past summer only because he was allowed to take a leave of absence. (Incidentally, to drive home the point that researching travel articles can be very tough indeed, I should mention that he said he got so lonely traveling solo in the land of happy couples that he finally threw in the towel and flew home a couple of weeks early.) Another well-known and no longer so youthful travel writer I know usually makes between $14,000 and $30,000 a year; a really creamy year full of high-paying work not too long ago netted him just under $45,000. This does work out to be more than it would for an employed person—not only because of the tax benefits of being self-employed, but also because during the weeks on the road, meals and most incidentals are taken care of (so that the annual income that does remain may have to cover only six months or so of New York living). But travel writing is not what I'd consider a high-paying occupation. Certainly, the advice I was given as a graduating college senior still holds up: when you're trying to make a go of freelancing, the regular checks that a steady job provides can be awfully useful. Inaugurating that second career means long hours—and not everyone ultimately has the drive to put them in over the required long haul. But the rewards may justify the effort. Even in my bleakest moods, as I contemplate overdue bills and envy friends their big-brother employers and predictable paychecks, I consider myself very lucky to be where I am.

Although I miss the experience of being part of a team, I'm not subjected to office politics either. I do have to live up to my commitments, but I don't have to keep someone else's hours unless I want to. Travel writing gives me the opportunity to sample the world (and even though I'm never able to spend much time in any single spot, that's not so bad). It also gives me the chance to talk with people who are passionately involved in their fields and to acquaint myself with the parameters of their professions—without needing to put in the time to get deeply involved myself with any one subject. For a generalist like me, it's a specialty and a life that can't be beat.

WRITE TO TRAVEL OR TRAVEL TO WRITE
by Bern Keating

Travel writers belong to two schools.
The more easily recognized category includes the journalists who

write to travel. They virtually all have some other source of income—retirement benefits, rental properties, affluent spouses—and are not dependent on their pens for bread and wine. Their primary interest is negotiating free trips and press tours after which they dutifully tap out competent accounts cataloging the sunset views from pre-tested observation sites, the menus touristiques in world-famed restaurants, and unquestionably accurate timetables for the Changing of the Guard. No surprises.

Their product is useful; it fulfills its function, for which the writers must be praised and paid—or at least paid.

TRAVEL WRITERS—TYPE A, TYPE B

There is no denying that a corporal's guard of hustlers do reasonably well as full-time travel writers. But their output is prodigious, their travels more extensive than is comfortable. And the hourly return on their exhausting routines is niggardly—beneath the scorn of a small-town taxi driver. The laborers in that small company of self-supporting travel writers are quite capable of visiting and writing about twenty countries or more in a year. It sounds glamorous till you try it. When you start classifying countries in your mind by the relative cleanliness of the airport toilets, you know that something beautiful has gone out of your life.

No question, the right way to be a travel writer is to marry money and do a comfortable six to eight countries a year. And there is nothing wrong with that. The travel writer who can afford a leisurely pace performs a real service to his readers. He may even have sufficient leisure to find a better lead than the sempiternal "San Banana is a land of contrasts" that curses the output of many hard-pressed workers in the field.

The other type of travel writer is harder to identify. He is far more likely to make his living entirely by writing, which gives him a tougher attitude about expenses, markets, rights, etc. Basically, he does his traveling to pursue research on economic, scientific, political, military or whatever subjects his contract calls for. If he wrote about any country that it is a "land of contrasts," boils would break out on his writing hand.

The travel writer usually has his expenses paid by a sponsoring country, hotel, or airline. The writer who travels in pursuit of the subjects normally has his expenses paid by the magazine hiring him or her. The generalized writer's fees are almost always considerably higher.

Paradoxically, the writer who just happens to travel frequently as part of his research often finds himself in far more exotic outposts than the travel writer.

For instance, I have recently been poking about in forgotten cob-webbed corners of Ireland—not preparing a guide to Dublin or Galway but doing research on digging out ancestral roots in the Old Sod.

Because I speak Spanish, I have spent a month in Chihuahua, Mexico, far back in the Sierra Madre, doing an article on the glamorous subject of soybean extrusion to provide supplementary protein in the diet of the Tarahumara Indians. (The Indians turned out to speak no Spanish, incidentally, so I had to reach them through an interpreter who is also a professor at a Texas school and speaks better English than I do.)

Interest in wildlife conservation got me a month in the Forest of Gir north of Bombay studying the last of the Asian lions.

I am currently dickering to do environmental articles on the rain forest of the Philippines and on the century-long recovery of the Indo-nesian island devastated by the explosion of Krakatoa.

Not once will I call Ireland, Mexico, India, the Philippines, or In-donesia a "land of contrasts." Indeed, I may not even have much to say about sunsets, restaurants, or hotels. Although I shall cover tens of thousands of miles and live in exotic milieux, I shall not write any true travel pieces. I shall be writing about genealogy, food technology, for-estry, and ecology.

But my assignment here is not to write about the writer who hap-pens to travel; it is to write about the travel writer as he is more popu-larly conceived. So I shall address myself to the reader who presumably owns a block of condominiums and a world champion hockey team, and so wants to write only to get a crack at those free trips.

Any reasonably literate and cultured person can succeed as a trav-el writer. It takes no wit or particular charm—indeed, they may be a hindrance to doing the good workaday writing required by this strange craft. What's needed is a pleasant manner and the willingness to trans-mit the minutiae of travel routine that are tedious to record but of un-questioned value to the patient reader and prospective traveler.

BREAKING IN

"Denmark is a land of contrasts," you may feel compelled to write, "with average incomes as low as $20,000 ranging upward to as high as $22,000 annually. The famed Viking physique of the natives averages 5 feet 10 inches with highs of 6 feet 1 inch and lows of 5 feet 8 inches."

Then you go into several paragraphs about the great open-faced sandwiches in "name" restaurants and you list the range of prices in the best hotels. It's all harmless and probably invaluable to a retired couple planning their first trip to Scandinavia.

The first few articles you write will almost certainly have to be done on speculation. Once you have accumulated a small store of tearsheets, however, you'll have only a little difficulty in persuading public relations agencies for client countries and airlines to send you abroad on all-expenses-paid press trips.

It does not take many tearsheets to establish yourself as a promising beginner, but you had better produce more tearsheets to pay for those free trips or you'll find yourself blacklisted, and rightly so. The clients are not shelling out $5,000 trips because they love your pretty brown eyes. They want to see square inches of printed copy.

And that brings up the question of markets. A dismal subject. They have shrunk till the established travel writers of great reputation are fighting for the little space left. Consider them: *Travel & Leisure*, *Signature*, *Travel/Holiday*, *Vista*, perhaps *Friends*, a few automobile club and inflight magazines, some regionals, and a few newspapers paying rates that won't cover your toothpaste and Lomotil bills. *Smithsonian*, *National Geographic*, and *Geo* are not really travel writers' markets: they demand a more skillful and generalized talent.

For the real writer, the subject of travel-writing fees is dreary. Pay is often low and slow, except at the very top like *Travel & Leisure*. For those writers with outside income, of course, poor pay is no problem. All they have to produce is copy; public relations agencies seem happy with generous surface spreads of printed material and apparently are content if it comes from nothing more prestigous than the *Turkey Breeders Gazette*.

Increasingly, the travel writer is expected to take his or her own photographs. Modern 35mm equipment is so nearly foolproof that anybody who can master a screwdriver can work a camera. Photo costs are not included in all-expenses-paid trips, incidentally, and can come to a startling sum if you do not make some early sales.

Do *not* give away your photographs to cinch a sale. They are worth a respectable fee in and of themselves, and you merely encourage the already voracious greed of publishers when you start giving your stuff away.

Those of you readers who do not command princely incomes had better search another field for your careers as writers. Those of you who are assured of paid-up room and board in perpetuity can travel incredible distances in stunning luxury at no cost just by learning the formula and cranking out the bread-and-butter travel articles that will keep the PR people smiling.

WRITING THE TRAVEL ARTICLE
by Jean Ayres Hartley

Travel writing is probably the most pleasant kind of nonfiction to write—and the most difficult to sell. Pleasant, because the research is such fun and can be accomplished in exciting places, rather than just in stuffy libraries. Difficult to sell, because many newspapers and magazines use mostly staff-written travel pieces. Also, it would seem that everyone in the country travels these days and wants to write about it. Jerry Hulse, travel editor of the *Los Angeles Times*, told me he gets over fifty submissions a day on England alone; he won't even look at a piece on England unless it has some unusual or timely angle.

Most of Europe has been covered with millions of words. But this is not to say you can't sell travel and make a living at it. The best way to get started is with the newspapers that have travel sections. They don't pay much—from $35 to $150, but you can sell the very same article to papers in different parts of the country and make as much (or more) on it as you would by selling it to one magazine. Just write "Exclusive your circulation area" on it, and be careful not to overlap.

Go to the library and consult *Working Press of the Nation*. It will give you the addresses and names of travel editors of all the newspapers in the United States. I check only the ones with a circulation of 100,000 or more; if they have a smaller circulation than that they probably can't afford freelancers' stories. At any rate, there are enough large ones to keep you busy.

I don't query newspapers. Editors are so busy meeting deadlines they can't be bothered answering letters or telephone calls. Just send the article.

The more information you have on editors' needs the better. Most of them will send you (for the asking) a schedule of their special editions, which you can aim for at the right time. For instance, the *Los Angeles Times* schedule reads:

March 5	International and Europe
March 26	Alaska
April 23	Canada and Pacific Northwest
May 7	Summer vacations
May 21	Hawaii and Pacific
Sept. 10	Mexico
Sept. 24	Cruises
November 12	Caribbean

Keep your articles moving. If it has been several months since you've written one be sure to update it by calling a travel agent and getting recent rates on airfares, hotels, etc., before you send it out again. Keep a detailed record of where your articles are going.

Photos help sell the article, but it's difficult to know whether the paper uses color or not. Also, postage for photos two ways is expensive, especially if you're sending out a number of them. I often leave out the photographs and enclose a self-addressed stamped postcard with lines on which the editor can easily check if he or she wants photos, and if so, black and white, or color, or if the editor can't use the article at all.

With the price of postage now, it's cheaper to copy a six- or seven-page article for next time you need it than to enclose an SASE. However, once you know what an editor wants you can send the kinds of photographs the publication needs along with the article. It's more attractive this way.

NEWSPAPERS OR MAGAZINES?

Newspapers want short articles, as a rule—not more than 900 words. No first-person articles here (derisively called "Me and Joe"s by the trade). Their readers don't want to know what you did, but what *they* can do, how much it will cost them, how to get there, what the weather is like, what there is to buy, what food there is, where, and how much it costs. I don't mean you shouldn't put yourself into the article at all; readers like to know your reactions and experiences and advice. So put yourself in it for a few lines (e.g., how hot the hot sauce in Guadalajara really is). This will tell the editor that you have really been there, and are not just writing about someone else's experiences, or what you read in a brochure.

I prefer to write for magazines because of the striking design and layout they give my articles—and they generally use several color photos, which pushes the price up. Many magazines that are not travel oriented will have one travel article per issue; this expands your market possibilities tremendously. Travel magazines are few, and the top ones depend on a stable of writers. It's difficult to break into that stable, but if you can find a subject that is so unusual or so off the beaten track that no one has written about it, you can get an editor to take notice.

So, you should plan your travels to the nooks and crannies where the average tourist does not go. I got a lot of mileage out of an article about a hideaway in the Caribbean called Ambergris Cay—just a dot on the map, but it has the peace and quiet and winter warmth and superb fishing that a lot of readers prize. There aren't many hideaways left in this world of universal travel, but if you find one, write it up. I can't tell you what the Changing of the Guard is like, and I'm probably the only American who has gone to London and not visited Westminster Abbey. But I can write about the Isle of Wight, or a terrific little restaurant in Wales that even the taxi driver had never heard of.

Of course you've been told over and over to study the magazines so you'll know just what your target wants. Unlike newspapers, many magazines don't want prices, but lots of description written in a romantic, poetic style. I constantly study travel articles to improve my own writing and get inspiration—it puts me in the swing if I don't know where to start. Make note of what a particular magazine likes—for instance, short or long sentences and paragraphs, frequent narratives, quotes, etc.—and you will be able to please that editor.

Notes from the Field

When I travel I take very complete notes. I record humorous incidents that I use later to give verve to an article. I write down the names and prices of everything, even though I think I may not need them. I note the price of meals and hotels, what we had to eat and how it tasted. I record my impressions of how things feel, sound, and smell. All this helps a great deal when I write about the places. I don't do much on-spot writing because I'm too busy traveling, so I need my notes to recreate the ambience, to return to a particular place or country.

You'll need a lot of research material, which you will pick up along the way. It can get very heavy and bulky; I follow Louise Purwin Zobel's suggestion in *The Travel Writer's Handbook* (Writer's Digest Books, 1980). She says to tuck some large manila envelopes in your suitcase and load them up with this printed information. Then send it home by cheap surface mail. A great idea.

Before I close I want to say a word about discouragement and persistence. Looking back on my writing experience, I can see that I had too much of the former and too little of the latter. When a query or article of mine was turned down I took it personally and thought it was no good and that I couldn't write. But I came to see that editors have many reasons for refusing articles besides their quality. Foremost among these is that they are overstocked: there is simply too much supply for the demand. It's still a buyer's market today. Of course, *all* the writers are not turning out good work, but enough of them are to make you stay on your writing toes. Like all competition, it evokes excellence, so we can be glad for it. Also, editors must keep a wary eye and tight grip on their budgets; they are always too limited. Many times, too, we hit them with an article idea at the wrong time.

One of the keys to opening the doors is persistence. It shows up in the history of many famous writers; one prominent article writer told me he had a hundred rejections before he ever made a sale.

Many times early in my career, after I queried on a subject and got two or three rejections I would discard the idea as probably not worthwhile—only to see an article on that subject somewhere soon thereafter. It took me a while to learn to send it out twenty times, if need be, instead of pitching it into the trash can after two or three tries. Sooner or later, a worthy piece will hit the right editor at the right time.

"WHERE HAVE YOU BEEN?" "OUT." "WHAT DID YOU DO?" "NOTHING."*
(*Or, The Long-Distance Saga of the Travel Writer)
by Kay Cassill

"Her knees are like rubber bands. Her hips are out of control. In spite of everything she still has the heart to want the victory. But, with only 200 yards to go, the body gives out."

Hearing the sportscaster describe a marathon runner about to crawl across the finish line on her hands and knees to wrest second—not even first—place from the jaws of total despair, one naturally thinks of the triumphs and sorrows surrounding highly competitive sports. Yet, when I heard the story my mind was immediately invaded by mental images of a different marathoner—the freelance travel writer.

"If I'm asked to comment on one more hotel room or, indeed, even look at one, I'll scream," an oft-published travel writer recently stated only half in jest. A colleague nodded his head in recognition of the travel writer's bane—the need to admire a certain facility, presumably so he will give the host a plug. It hardly matters if they are little different from thousands of similar settings. He groaned acquiescence:

"We were in an Oriental country recently, one which shall remain nameless. A point came when most of our group just couldn't take any more of being shown only what the tour had planned for us. We played hooky. Just got off the bus on a ruse and hid out for the entire day. They couldn't find us. It was the only way we had of protecting ourselves."

What on earth could these two be bleating about? They were well-established writers. Their specialty was a fascinating-sounding one—travel. They didn't have to join the Army to see the world; they were seeing it courtesy of a country, state, or transportation giant. They'd been wined and dined to a fare-thee-well. They'd been greeted by dignitaries low and high. They'd collected what seemed like tons of printed material about their destinations. What they *hadn't* had was time or, eventually, energy to see those destinations as ordinary travelers; to write well about them they knew they had to finagle some time to experience the places sans guidance.

A UNIQUE—AND DEMANDING—SPECIALTY

Unlike the atmosphere surrounding marathon races, there are few limits or restrictions to the field of travel writing. You can go about it in a myriad of ways, depending on your ultimate goal as your own self-appointed and ever-demanding guide. Nor are successful travel writers in any manner of speaking "ordinary." Those who truly succeed in the field come in all sorts of guises. Their backgrounds are as varied as their interests. Their common denominator, however, is their zest for the new and truly unusual, as well as their ability to dress the commonplace not in purple prose, but in the royal plumage of a great writer's insight. So let me put it bluntly right up front: while it may appear to beginners that specializing in travel writing is easier than concentrating on another area that requires specific training (science or medical writing, for example), it is actually one of the most difficult and exacting. The reason is simple enough. Nearly everyone travels, and all who do have experiences to relate once they return home. But the ability to bring those experiences fully to life for others (and for posterity) is a demanding art.

While much of the travel material printed in today's newspapers and magazines is aimed at the vacation-bound who need to know where and when to go and how much of what to take along, writers should also remember the business traveler, the person on an emergency trip, and the armchair traveler. Certainly for every would-be excursionist who wants to know that the mosquitoes come in sizes marked "large," "extra-large," and "unbelievable," there's also the reader who'll never make the trip to Iquitos except through the eyes of someone like Richard Atcheson. And for that reader the true joy of the trip comes in the act of reading:

". . . I have always enjoyed the fascination of the theoretical jungle; that legendary Green Hell, that primordial wilderness in which all living creatures are singlemindedly engaged in dining on one another twenty-four hours a day. . . . During the elaborate customs procedure, a plump lady approached me across the barrier and said, 'Well, at last you got here. I expected you yesterday. Is Mr. Ellis with you?' I didn't know who she was and nobody had expected me. . . . The terminal was just a tin-roofed shed, baking hot, noisy, and jammed . . . and I figured that if this lady wanted to take responsibility for me, she was welcome. . . . She was attractive, but bitten all over the ankles by mosquitoes. I viewed that with unease, mindful of the caution of an American friend in Lima, who said: 'Gee, Dick, you know it only takes one mosquito.' "

Touristy trepidations about malaria notwithstanding, successful travel writers recognize, too, that next turn in the road always beckoning them onward. Perhaps if travel writers have a common failing it is an "inability to say 'no,' or to recognize when enough is enough," an experienced travel writer reminded me one hot afternoon in mountainous northern Romania. We had run into each other accidentally and sat down to compare notes over lukewarm beer before we each took off again on our separate forays into the unknown. "It's a compulsion unlike any other," he continued, "and no amount of psychiatric help has even begun to touch it."

But the third prerequisite for successful travel writing may be the most important. To do it well one must be able to work hard under any and all conditions and be prepared for the inevitable: those conditions will seldom be as plush or even as ordinarily exciting as they seemed before you arrived. That's not to say that the Australian bush or the vast sweeps of the Arctic or life aboard a cruise ship heading for Rio doesn't offer excitement. Of course, they all do—each its own kind. Yet many times perched smack in the middle of such scenes one finds the travel writer pounding away on his portable typewriter or talking into her tape recorder. This particular piece, for instance, was conceived in New York, Denver, and spots in between; specific notes for it were spoken into a tape recorder on the road between Detroit and Peoria, and it was actually written in four different locations: Providence, Cape Cod, Philadelphia, and Des Moines.

Travel writing, too, is a discipline hard enough to practice without other barriers. Harder yet is the need to face its deadlines with a bad case of writer's block, a not uncommon malaise. One's head may be chock-full of admonitions from editors such as, "I don't want just another travel story about sunny Hawaii or the same old things about Athens we all know." It's then the travel writer stares at the sunset or the Acropolis and thinks, "What in Heaven's name am I supposed to say about all this?"

Which reminds me of the one about the writer who wrote "How to Watch the Indy 500—(Through Your Fingers)." Sports columnist Leigh Montville faced that story head-on, if you'll excuse the phrase.

" 'How will I know when I get there?' 'You'll know.' The traffic jam on 16th Street will run forever. After miles and miles of gray, there will be color. There will be excitement. Have you traveled to the inside of a candied apple? This will be it. Dorothy and her dog, Toto, will be in the car in front. The one with the Kansas plates. There will be more people gathered in one place than you ever thought possible, maybe as many as 400,000. All paying customers. The Goodyear blimp will hang high in the sky."

When a good writer tackles the oft-told story he can still make it come alive. Or, as Montville put it, "I'd say the best way to get there is just drive. Just sit in the car and drive. The road just naturally will take you to the Indianapolis Motor Speedway. HoJo's. Stuckey's. Pennsylvania Turnpike. Pay the toll. Radar trap. All of Ohio. Half of Indiana. Radio stations fade. Radio stations begin. The back hurts. The bladder calls. How much for gas? That much? Just drive."

The Exploratory Urge

I've been striking out on my own ever since, at the age of eighteen months, I scooted across a Boston beach heading for uncharted territory just out of reach of my alarmed parent. True, that particular adventure ended abruptly when my father literally put his recalcitrant toddler on a leash. Now that I think about it, he was probably doing me a favor. By restraining me then he was fostering my love of travel—any travel—once I could get away. Nevertheless, this love of travel has often found me in unusual situations, unfamiliar geography and, occasionally, threatening circumstance. So, I might as well admit it, when I heard the sportscaster describe that marathoner, I didn't really just think about *any* freelance travel writer. I thought for a fleeting instant she was describing *me*. But then, how could she have known that was *exactly* how my muscles were reacting after nearly ten days of nonstop tennis for a travel article about tennis resorts? How could she have been privy to my frantic days and more frantic nights alone behind the Iron Curtain? What sort of visionary was she to have seen me trying to bribe everybody for that room in Sardinia?

Ah yes, Sardinia.

Like a fly returning to a particularly succulent morsel on a picnic table, I've been circling and recircling the Mediterranean over the years. While I usually begin by remembering a specifically pleasurable part of an earlier trip, longing to recapture it, I find I head inevitably if obliquely toward my goal. By nosing about new sections with which I am unfamiliar, I rediscover the smell of the bougainvillea, the garlic, the sundrenched sand, the pines. I almost reinvent that light. I fear if I had attempted to go *directly* back to Bandol or Venice I would have missed what I had come for: their essence. So it seems natural to look back and realize that when I first began to write about travel seriously (i.e., for money), I was actually after other fish to fry. Such a start, by the way, is far from unusual; travel writers often say their initiation into travel writing was accidental as they were on their way to the Indy 500, the search for Big Foot, or to attend the Coronation.

What was I up to? There had been some highly publicized, all-too-successful kidnappings throughout the Mediterranean area and Sardinia especially. The contrast of jet-setters and outlaws cohabiting that island terrain intrigued me. I managed to interest several editors in various aspects of the story and took off, letters of assignment, some addresses, and introductions in my satchel. My preparation, however, had been primarily involved with the banditos; precious little was related to any positive aspects of travel. And Sardinia was new to me. As new as the pleasure palaces of the Aga Khan's resort, the Costa Smeralda. I was far from prepared for the size of the crowd in high season. It was enough that I finally *found* the place after crossing the Sardinian mountains and barren wastes, my rental car threatening to overheat, just as I already had.

On arrival at my destination, I discovered there was certainly no room at any inn. But, I beat the Peugeot to the punch: I boiled over. I twitched. I sputtered. I attempted to cajole. Then, without realizing the threatening impact of my plea, I begged for the police to help. That did it. I was steered to a neighboring village some kilometers away. There I found a Hemingwayesque room—clean, tiny, offering a straw mattress, a mirror the size of a postage stamp, and a window overlooking some ancient train tracks. At least they *looked* ancient and unused. In the dead of night I woke in a fine sweat, the sound of a locomotive swooping down on me. The Costa Smeralda's plush quarters it wasn't; the heart of my travel story it became. Even now I like to fantasize that my village was home territory for the elusive kidnappers, whether or not it was. I was fortunate enough *not* to discover their hiding place. But I did stumble upon enough material for several articles and I plan to use other parts in a novel one of these days, which is the point of my anecdote. By winging it and refusing to land anywhere but on my feet, I managed to more than compensate for my mistakes. The moral: Even the worst blunders can be transposed into blessings if you remain open to the possibilities and always expect the unexpected.

ON BREAKING IN

Among the positive aspects of this specialty are these: (1) being able to see new, exciting, and unusual parts of the world; (2) meeting people in all walks of life; and (3) receiving remuneration and a byline in the process. The negatives, other than those already mentioned, are: (1) discovering jet lag first hand; (2) fighting the many distractions while on the road, yet not missing anything important; (3) a diminishing market for certain kinds of travel writing (which may or may not be temporary); and (4) stiff competition from well-versed, well-connected professionals.

Getting started is relatively easy if you're willing (1) to work hard, (2) to work on speculation, and (3) to pay for your own travel. Since the latter can be expensive, many writers use *any* business travel or family vacation as a springboard to full-time travel writing. Others have carefully laid plans to sell enough stories from one trip to cover expenses, then returned with twice the material needed because they were well-prepared before they left home. But perhaps the best—and least costly—way for the neophyte to begin is by getting that byline without ever going farther than the local library. I often advise students to spend several days looking for ideas for travel-related stories that don't actually require much, if any, travel. Travel service stories, pieces that help readers, usually have much appeal: tips on tipping abroad, famous cons to watch out for while traveling, favorite travel tips of the jet set, how to handle medical emergencies while away, preparing your home (or pet or houseplants) to survive your absence, and so forth. There are many more ideas you'll uncover once you let your mind, instead of your body, roam. And the material for your articles will only be several well-placed phone calls away.

Another way some writers cover their expenses is to band together. When a writer/photographer or writer/writer team joins forces the expenses of car or van are divided, as are the specific territories or interests, so they are not in direct competition with each other. Numerous husband-and-wife travel-writing teams have thus found success—and more fascinating stories—than they would have had they worked alone.

Discover, too, what is essentially in your own backyard. The stories behind a colorful "haunted" house down the street may be old stuff to you because you've heard them all your life. They may be the basis for an interesting travel piece readers across the continent would be delighted with.

Once you have acquired clips of some of your work and perfected your writing skills, you will be in a position to travel on junkets, all expenses paid. When this occurs, new quandaries appear, such as those expressed previously by the two tired professionals, or, as I was recently told, the plight of the travel writer confronted with meal after meal of fish, which she hates. If you have an assignment from an editor, a few phone calls to public relations departments of the areas you want to visit will usually set the ball rolling. Or, if you have begun to publish, be prepared to get a call from some PR person asking if you'd like to join a publicity excursion.

However you get started, though, you'd be well advised to spend time preparing a sensible plan for (1) getting the needed information to write stories irresistible to editors and (2) marketing those stories along your itinerary before you even leave home. Lay out your plan on paper, in detail, and key the stories and their slants to specific markets, then query the editors before you firm up your travel plans. Once you've returned, fire off those stories as quickly as you can turn them out of your typewriter. And for those inevitable ones that don't sell the first time around, have a backup plan—another editor or several— whose stated interest in such a piece you've discovered by poring through *Writer's Market* and other such books.

THE TRAVEL SPECIALIST'S REQUIREMENTS

There is agreement among the best in this field that travel writing is arduous and demanding and that the remuneration may not always be in direct proportion to the work. It calls upon the writer's courage, fortitude, and flexibility. A sense of humor is a decided help. No matter how carefully you plan, things *will* go awry—usually at the worst possible moments. When they do, it's the smart travel writer who looks to them for the heart of the story, as I did in Sardinia.

Perhaps the primary requirement, though, is self-knowledge. Realize what you can and cannot do, what you do and do not like. Wherever you journey, whatever you find, your best, worst, but constant companion will be *you*. If you are in good health, find it easy to deal with the uncommon and uncomfortable, are facile about discarding useless mental baggage when far from home, travel writing will come easy. If you can also put yourself in your readers' places, asking the sorts of questions they'd be asking, your stories will have wide appeal to others.

You'll be requiring a great deal of your senses, since they will help describe the flavor of a place. Learn to pause along the way and to reflect on what they're telling you. Then make note of it. If you've been climbing over the ruins of a once-grand castle and have come away with shin splints and a blank mind, ask yourself about the inhabitants of long ago. What were their lives like? And, although you'll stop at the usual tourist attractions, don't forget the need to see a place the way locals see it: the city hall, the backs of shops, the laundromat, the weekly market, the various modes of travel—from donkey cart to camel, from paddleboat to bus.

Early preparation and rigorous note-taking at the library before leaving home will save you much time—and money—on the road. Not only do you discover what subjects to avoid because they have been most recently covered by others, the out-of-the-ordinary story will usually show itself by such early sleuthing, if you look for it. I find the art, music, and business sections of the library as valuable at such times as the shelves and shelves of travel literature.

Accept that travel writing may become addictive. If not hazardous to your health, it may seem hazardous indeed to your companions' or family's vacation plans. You may tell yourself that you're going to take time off just to relax. But that is more difficult to do than you would imagine. You'll be looking at old, favorite locations with an eye to discovering an unusual travel slant. Your suitcase and car trunk will be jammed with brochures and mementoes. You'll be constantly jotting notes, taking photos, or sketching rough notations of what you've observed. Most of all, you'll ask questions—lots of them—from new acquaintances, strangers slipping off their shoes at the door of a mosque, children sailing toy sailboats in a park—everyone. You'll know that a man whose primary occupation is to stand on a certain street corner in a college town greeting new arrivals at a Big Ten football game has a wealth of opinions and anecdotes for the asking. You'll interview the local celebrity, historian, girl selling tomatoes at a roadside stand, the undertaker. You'll read voraciously and practice the fiction techniques of novelist and short story writer.

Some of the most valuable material I've discovered, other than notes taken prior to my trips, have been those random jottings I made after visiting relatives or old friends—what I call my "Remember Whens." The details others recall about a specific jaunt that I have let memory blur become invaluable when I sit down to write. It doesn't matter if the remembered trip is a family outing to the Black Hills and I'm currently writing about northern Vermont inns. It's often better for the contrast. What matters is the anecdote: my aunt remembers how my sister and I amused ourselves crowded into the old Chevy's back seat, singing childish songs. Suddenly, I not only have a brief story that demonstrates what I want to say, I also have two or three new ideas for a query to an editor. Then, I am reminded that there was a sea of grasshoppers greeting our bare legs as we headed across a patch of sand, that there was frost on the ground as we stretched out on scratchy Army blankets because the motels were full. *Voilà!* Several more handles for stories. Learn to mine such rich veins from oral histories as you go along.

Organizing one's voluminous notes from trips is another bugaboo; I strongly urge you to develop a system that allows you to retrieve the material more than once. Some writers use separate file folders; some use 3x5 file cards; others need a combination of systems. Whatever you choose, be prepared to spend a great deal of time hunting for lost material if you refuse to plan ahead for the volumes of notes you'll be collecting, a frustration none of us needs. You don't have to spend money on fancy systems—shoe boxes properly labeled have been the backbone of many writers' files long after another system could be afforded. But you do need a well-thought-out plan for retrieval. The beginning travel writer, particularly, will want to rely on multiple sales of material, with minor manuscript changes, in order to make financial ends meet. By being able to quickly lay hands on the needed information, you will be making your task much easier.

I've also found that a separate card file for names of people in my specialty is a great asset. I try to cross-reference when necessary and group names according to locations. I thus have a handy stack of cards ready to pop into my briefcase as soon as I know in which direction my next trip is taking me. Also standing at the ready are two versions of my travel desk. One is a vinyl pouch with the bare essentials needed for a two- or three-day trip. The other is an expanded version—a portable file with folders and more desk necessities for those trips when I'm away from the office for any extended length of time.

E.H. Cookridge observed, "No form of public transport has attracted writers in the unique way that the Orient Express did." Like that legendary train, travel writing attracts all kinds of scribblers. One, who told me the following story, had a unique way of checking out his host's facilities. Junketing and partying into the wee hours in Paris had left him a bit under the weather—and perhaps less than completely in control of all of his faculties. Preparing to retire, he noticed a note on his pillow in the five-star hotel where he'd been billeted. When would he like his wake-up call and breakfast delivered? Foolishly, he says, he scrawled "eight twenty-three a.m." Much to his dismay, *precisely* at the requested moment the knock came on his door. "I'd asked for it," he admitted, "so I had to get up and eat it. But it taught me a valuable lesson!"

The most successful travel writers whose work is most lasting learn through experience, and they keep one word—honesty—uppermost in their minds. Whether they are on that all-expenses junket or working their way around the world on a tramp steamer, they must constantly push to unveil the truth about what they see, what they experience. Then, they must struggle mightily to convey that truth in words that, as one author put it, "every cat and dog will understand."

If you do that consistently and stubbornly, yet with grace, you'll find your travel-writing niche along with the best.

Additional Resources

Cruise Lines International Association, % Diana M. Orban Associates, Inc., 60 E. 42nd St., New York, NY 10165. Provides analytical, historical, how-to, referral, and trade information on the history of cruising, cruise lines and their products, how to select a cruise, how travel agents can sell cruises. Offers aid in arranging interviews, brochures and pamphlets, photos, placement on mailing lists, press kits, statistics. News releases, tips, brochures, film, speeches available.

European Travel Commission, 630 Fifth Ave., Rm. 610, New York, NY 10111. The travel commission promotes travel to twenty-three countries in Europe. Provides information on travel, lodging, statistics, restaurants, trends, travel packages. Offers aid in arranging interviews, clipping services, photos, placement on mailing lists, press kits, research assistance, statistics, telephone reference services.

The Leading Hotels of the World, 770 Lexington Ave., New York, NY 10021. An association of 167 deluxe hotels worldwide. Provides advisory, historical, and trade information on hotel accommodations, availability, background, rates, all types of media information. Offers aid in arranging interviews, brochures and pamphlets, photos, placement on mailing lists, press kits, research assistance. Publications include *Corporate Profile of HRI/The Leading Hotels of the World* and *Directory of the Leading Hotels of the World.*

National Park Service, Office of Public Affairs, Rm. 3043, Interior Bldg., Washington, DC 20240. Provides information on areas of the national park system which the service administers. Offers attendance statistics and data on camping, swimming, boating, mountain climbing, hiking, fishing, winter activities, wildlife research and management, history, archaeology, nature walks, scenic features.

National Tour Brokers Association, 120 Kentucky Ave., Lexington, KY 40502. Provides information on the motorcoach tour and allied industries (i.e., hotel, attraction, sightseeing, etc.), governmental proceedings that affect travel industry, association leadership. Offers aid in arranging interviews, annual reports, biographies, brochures and pamphlets, clipping services, computerized information searches, photos, placement on mailing list, press kits, research assistance, statistics. Can assist in arranging familiarization tours for appropriate writers (trips in which a writer travels on an actual tour and recounts his or her experiences). Publications include *Courier* (monthly), *Tuesday* (newsletter), *NTBA Story* (historical), assorted brochures.

Society of American Travel Writers, 1120 Connecticut Ave. NW, No. 940, Washington, DC 20036. Strives to provide travelers with accurate reports on destinations, facilities, and services; encourages preservation of historic sites and conservation of nature. Presents annual awards to honor individuals, organizations or communities championing the cause of conservation, preservation, and beautification in America. Publications include *The Travel Writer.*

Travel and Tourism Research Association, P.O. Box 8066, Foothill Station, Salt Lake City, UT 84108. Provides professional leadership in travel research. Sponsors Travel Research Student Contest and dissertation competition. Provides reference service for travel-research industry to find information sources and solve business problems. Maintains library. Presents Wesley Ballaine Travel Research award. Publications include *Tourism Educator's Newsletter* (bimonthly), *Journal of Travel Research* (quarterly), *Travel Trends in the United States and Canada* (updated in 1981, and *Travel Research Bibliography* (updated in 1980, nine volumes).

Travel Industry Association of America, 1899 L St. NW, Suite 600, Washington, DC 20036. Provides information on government travel, marketing, travel trends and patterns. Offers aid in arranging interviews, annual reports, biographies, brochures and pamphlets, clipping services, informational newsletters, library facilities, placement on mailing lists, press kits, research assistance, statistics, telephone reference services. Publications include *U.S. Travel Roundup.*

Travel Information Center, Cox Road, Woodstock, VT 05091. Provides comprehensive information on all aspects of travel and leisure industry. Offers brochures and pamphlets, computerized information searches, informational newsletters, photos, placement on mailing lists, press kits, research assistance, statistics, telephone reference services. Publications include *Directions* (biweekly newsletter).

Traveler's Information Exchange (Formerly Women's Rest Tour Association), 356 Boylston St., Boston, MA 02116. Provides advisory, historical, and how-to information. Library contains a variety of travel resources, including vintage Baedeker, Cook, Muirhead, and Hare guidebooks, plus 91 years of TIE history. Offers informational newsletters, library facilities, and research assistance. Publications include *The Pilgrim Script* (magazine of travel articles), newsletter (3/year), *American and Foreign Lodging Lists* (for members only, restricted use for others).

United States Tour Operators Association, 211 E. 51st St., Suite 4B, New York, NY 10022. Informs the travel trade, government agencies, and the public concerning activities and objectives of tour operators. Offers meetings and seminars; facilitates and develops worldwide travel. Bestows awards. Publishes quarterly newsletter.

United States Travel and Tourism Administration, Department of Commerce, 14th St. and Constitution Ave. NW, Rm. 1852, Washington, DC 20230. Provides advisory, analytical, how-to, interpretative, referral, technical, and trade information on travel to the U.S., tourism as an American export commodity, the world marketplace. Offers annual reports, brochures and pamphlets, research assistance, statistics.

United States Travel Data Center, 1899 L St. NW, Washington, DC 20036. Provides trade information on travel and tourism research, travel marketing studies. Offers statistics. Publications include quarterly and annual statistical reports.

World Federation of Travel Journalists and Writers, 34 Rue des Archives, F-75004, Paris, France. Travel writers and columnists. Maintains consultative status with UNESCO. Maintains International Documentation Center in Brussels, Belgium. Presents Golden Apple award to cities or districts renovated and facilitating cultural tourism. Sponsors seminars for young travel writers.

World Tourism Organization, Calle Capitan Haya 42, Madrid 20, Spain. Promotes research, technical cooperation, and training of tourist personnel. Sponsors correspondence courses on tourism as well as seminars and symposia. Maintains a Tourist Documentation center containing approximately 20,000 tourist technical publications. Publications include *World Travel-Tourisme Mondial* (bimonthly), *Travel Research Journal* (semiannual), *Travel Abroad* (annual), *World Tourism Statistics* (annual).

Chapter Nineteen

WRITING FOR THE CONSUMER

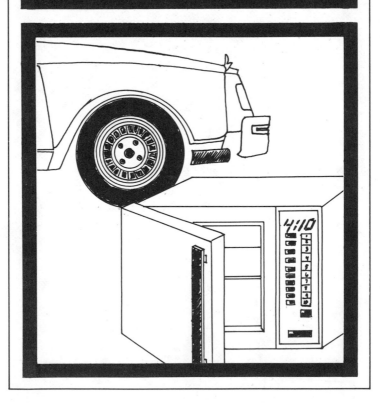

Specialists in the consumerism field are those dedicated writers, protectors of us all, who tell us how to get the most for our hard-earned dollars. Their articles and books give carefully researched and factual advice to buyers of any and all products and services, from home computers and automobiles to laundry detergent and lager beer, from pre-schools and health spas to caterers and electricians. These writers sort through the dazzling array of available products, comparing and contrasting brands, testing and evaluating models, to help consumers make wise purchases. They also do many how-to pieces (e.g., how to do your own auto repairs or build your own solar water heater).

Many of these writers are disciples of Ralph Nader, who challenged the automobile industry on matters of safety, efficiency, pollution, and assorted other ills in the sixties, and who continues to wave the red flag of consumer protest and advocacy. Acting as watchdogs for American buyers, consumerism writers report on everything from the utility executive caught with his hand in the till to toxic materials in children's toys, from fraudulent advertising claims to the physician who "adjusts" his bill to cheat the Medicaid system.

Pick up your newspaper, turn on your television set or radio, glance through any newsmagazine—you'll find news to alert and protect the nation's consumers. Crooked state lotteries, disc jockey payola, nursing-home scandals, price-fixing among powerful businesses—all are grist for the consumerism writer's mill; in fact, such a writer probably broke the story in the first place.

There is no one approach to the matter of consumer protection; there are a thousand and one possible approaches. Consumerism specialist freelancers are employing them all and accomplishing a great deal in our behalf.

TWO BASIC APPROACHES
TO CONSUMER WRITING
by Charlotte Montgomery

My plunge into writing for the consumer market came about this way: before my marriage, I had worked at an advertising agency as a copywriter and found myself fascinated by the way products were devised, designed, packaged, priced, marketed, and, finally, advertised. After marriage, I found myself keeping house, bringing up two children, and doing freelance writing. I had plenty of motivation and concern while observing vast changes take place as an endless list of new products sprang up. This was soon after World War II ended, a period of dramatic development and innovation. Technologies invented during the war opened up whole new industries, such as aerosols. Improvements were coming to plastics, man-made fibers, frozen foods, and "ersatz" items such as margarine. The self-service supermarket, in which many of these were offered, was itself a startling innovation.

Combining my interest in how products originate, how they are sold and serviced, and their effects on the buying public, I wrote a sample column and took it to an advertising trade paper. I saw myself as the voice of the consumer talking to business about what the woman shopper would like to be able to buy, how and why she chooses what she does, and by what new offerings she could be attracted or influenced. (Trade papers are often an excellent place to start a writing career. They aren't concerned about "big" bylines and also, are not apt to be overwhelmed with unsolicited manuscripts. Of course, they don't pay well, but they are a fine place to do an apprenticeship.)

The advertising trade paper to which I took this column had never used a byline or run a column. But my timing was on target because consumerism was just rounding the corner, and coming fast. Accepted at once, this column, called "The Woman's Viewpoint," ran in *Tide* (now defunct) for seven years. This small magazine was widely read in the advertising and publishing worlds, and through it I got assignments from *Nation's Business, Today's Woman, Redbook, Good Housekeeping,* and various others. At the end of seven years, the editor of *Good Housekeeping* persuaded me to change the column's orientation from a trade-paper approach to a general-interest approach, and the column began to appear in *Good Housekeeping,* titled "Speaker for the House." Again, the timing was fortunate because those years had made women extremely aware of the problems of choice among the plethora of competing products, of their rights and privileges in the marketplace, of how easily they could become the victims of fraud and chicanery. They needed a solid base of price and product information to be intelligent consumers and spend their money wisely. I was lucky to be early in this field. Consumerism has since grown at every level, in every direction.

There are two basic (and quite different) ways for a writer to approach writing for the consumer. Either can be used exclusively or they can be combined. I prefer using a blend of techniques, but it takes a certain amount of expertise and practice to meld the two approaches successfully.

The Writer as Educator

The two basic ways are educational and exposé. The educational angle uses the kind of research done by home economics departments of universities, or knowledge acquired by counselors expert in such things as handling debt, how to proceed in a bankruptcy, or what to do if your application for a loan is turned down. An educational story would report on the activities of the Federal Trade Commission, give facts on carpets, cars, cheese, or cough medicine. Newspapers and magazines publish many stories of this kind that are important to the consumer.

The Exposé

The second approach is the exposé, full of angry indignation, the kind of writing that's become popularized by investigative reporting. In this type of consumer writing, the writer lashes out at business, implying that everyone has an angle, that every scheme is a rip-off. This writer doubts the honesty of sweepstakes, of advertising, of warranties, of price comparisons, believing that manufacturers plot a plan to have products break down, that mail orders are held up deliberately.

This kind of writing can be great fun to do. It attracts writers who are witty, acerbic, and sarcastic. Yet it, too, can be dishonest. It's usually vastly exaggerated—allowing for no exceptions, accepting no excuses. Let's say, for example, that a consumer columnist finds it difficult to get at a fountain pen that's enclosed in a plastic bubble and mounted on a card. The exposé writer rants and rails for three paragraphs about the inconvenience and nonsense of such packaging, the need to use a cleaver in order to get your hands on the desired object. The writer would be loath to mellow the story by hinting what anyone might guess, that it would be a good idea to cut the package open with scissors, or that there may be perforations on the back of the card to get it open. Nor does he or she suggest that there are perfectly good reasons for mounting a pen on a card: to increase its visibility as it hangs on display, and to cut down on pilferage. The ever-irritated exposé writer is careful not to see two sides and is especially anxious to blame the Establishment, blind to business justification.

There is some merit in this fist-clenching—the writer will often win smiles and sympathetic nods of approval from readers—but it's also easy for it to become exaggerated and unfair. And rage doesn't help the consumer a bit, doesn't educate or offer a solution. A compromise that usually works is to begin discussion of a subject with some sort of a disclaimer, such as, "I know full well how miserable and frustrating it is to . . ." And then you, if possible, give some solution, a way around the annoyance. For example, suppose you are talking about long waiting lines at bank windows. You could advise people at what hours banks are less busy, and encourage people who don't have to cash their paychecks at a certain hour on a certain day to pick a less busy time. Women who patronize supermarkets know which hours are less crowded, when stocks of meat and produce are apt to be more complete, and that a long weekend is going to send twice as many shoppers to the market on Friday. People can adjust to situations if they are informed intelligently, and are aware that stores have problems too. I tend to take a middle ground, which I hope is more helpful—certainly less prejudiced and more balanced than showing nothing but thorns.

CONTACTS YOU'LL NEED

To write successfully for consumers, solid reference sources are essential. It's important to build up a flow of the most reliable and up-to-date information. This means subscribing to consumer magazines, getting on mailing lists of various federal departments, keeping your eyes and ears open to every trend and nuance. Next, you must make a list of personal contacts at various companies, institutions, trade associations, and consumer groups. I belong to many professional associations. For example, my membership in the Society of Consumer Affairs Professionals is helpful. Their membership list is priceless; knowing who the consumer affairs person is at a wide range of companies is a marvelous tool, not only as a source of information but as a place that will handle individual complaints, in most cases. Make it a point to get to know these people, by mail or telephone. (I like to boast that I have known *three* Betty Crockers!)

People involved in a wide variety of business activities have learned that I am interested in consumer matters and, in consequence, they send me bulletins on many subjects such as nutrition, additives, consumer services, and new regulations and programs. They also send me annual reports, speeches by their top officers, conclusions or summaries of their consumer research, and miscellaneous materials that keep me up to date. And I never spurn public relations releases, which may include a nugget of news to be pursued.

Other sources of information are the *New York Times*, the *Wall Street Journal*, *FDA Consumer* (a magazine published by the Food and Drug Administration), and bulletins from the National Safety Council, the U.S. Consumer Product Safety Commission, and the Federal Trade Commission. I try to keep in touch with a person at various U.S. Departments or agencies, such as Transportation, Treasury, and Consumer Affairs, who knows me by name and will answer questions or suggest where I should go for answers.

Other sources are Better Business Bureaus, who will furnish reports on companies on request, and panels or committees that follow through on consumer complaints on an industry-wide basis. Among those I have dealt with successfully are the Major Appliance Consumer Action Panel (MACAP), a "court of last resort" for problems with large appliances, and other panels having to do with furniture, car repairs, carpeting, and electronic equipment. Cooperative extension services from state universities are invaluable, as are communications offices at many companies. You learn who will be of service, as well as who won't be bothered with simple questions.

GOT ANY IDEAS?

How do you choose what to write about? Naturally, topics have to be of immediate interest as well as newsy. An obvious example would be to write on how to save on your income tax, for March or April publication; write for December publication a warning about possible frauds when shoppers are apt to be careless. Remember, you need to query seasonal ideas six months in advance.

Currently, I think that inflation and the quality of goods take priority in people's minds. But it doesn't stop at that. Variations of these topics are endless. For example, consumers often complain about the limited stock stores carry, with men's shirts offered in "average length" sleeves only, blankets in the same width for double and single beds, and certain sizes of shoes not stocked at all. Every phase of consumerism is an opportunity for annoyance—or understanding and explanation. One young woman said to me, "I like your column. It seems to me every time I am fussing or worrying about something, you write about it." What could be a greater compliment on timing?

Don't Be a Know-It-All

One problem that may arise is your degree of expertise and how much you display it. Personally, I think that "easy does it." You must know what you are talking about, but don't show off, pontificate, or belittle your readers. Foresee what may puzzle them or cause any misunderstanding and clear it up *simply*.

Another trick is to take difficult subjects in steps, if possible. When the Universal Product Codes (UPC) first came out (those masses of little lines designed to be read in stores by electronic scanners), women wanted to know what they were, why they were there, how the consumer could understand them, and so forth. It was a complicated subject and I felt most readers would not "sit still" for the whole explanation at once. So I did it in three different columns. The first time, I showed a picture of a typical UPC. By the third column, consumers knew these codes could be read only by electronic scanners, that they were planned largely to save supermarket operators money, that their consumer benefits were slight, if any, and that consumers wanted items to be priced individually as always.

Timely Plots

Subjects come and go. There will be lots of huff and puff on one topic for a while, then either that peeve passes or better ways are found to handle it. Another set of problems takes its place.

Keep folders on topics. When you see an interesting item in the newspaper, or get a news release, or hear someone talking about a subject, drop a note in the proper folder. You'll be amazed at how soon you'll have information on which to base research, or even enough to write a piece, if you've kept such a file. For example, you would have files on car safety and seat belts, mail-order problems, dangerous fireworks, credit cards and their use and abuse, funeral expenses, work-at-home gyps, where and how to complain about anything, cents-off coupons, carcinogens, postal-service peeves, rebates and refunds, vacation economics, insurance, additives, schemes against the elderly, and more.

Keep in Touch

If possible, encourage mail from readers. There's no better way to find out what's on people's minds than to let them sound off to you about their peeves. Sometimes this can be eye-opening. I recall the flurry of controversy in newspapers and on TV about "truth in packaging." To my surprise, my mail proved that my readers, at least, weren't of the opinion that they were being deceived by packages. They would, however, blow off about lack of convenience and ask, "Why do they say 'Press here to open' when you need a crowbar to get in that box of detergent?"

Mail has started me on consumer crusades. I remember when a woman wrote me that she had made complete summer wardrobes for her three little girls before they went to visit Grandma. She was livid because when she ironed the girls' clothes for the first time, the zippers all melted, making the dresses unwearable. This alerted me to the fact that a well-known manufacturer of zippers was using a plastic which couldn't withstand the heat of an iron. My investigation led to an exposé of the problem and a complete change in the manufacturer's product.

In addition to hearing from consumers by mail, develop other ways to learn what's on their minds. Watch the questions sent to newspaper "Action Lines." I always pay attention to topics that come up during the question period after speeches I make to consumer groups.

One thing to remember is that you aren't necessarily a typical consumer. You must develop an ability to differentiate your personal gripes from those of the average consumer. Some of the major mistakes made by ardent consumer activists have occurred because they assumed they knew better than the public. Or, worse, that their way is the *only* way to think. For example, some activists were demanding washing machines that had only "on" and "off" buttons and no extras or special features. The fact was that such basic machines were being made, but the public didn't like them and wasn't buying them.

Sensitivity to the public is essential; consumer writing demands a "feel." When a new idea or theory comes up, business people often expect it to be instantly liked by the consumer. It takes much, much longer to reach everyday buyers. Take, for example, electronic no-cash banking. As early as 1977, I was asked to talk to a bankers' group about the coming electronic banking age. When I pointed out it would take time and a lot of education and that people who are used to certain banking methods would resent change, this group turned downright antagonistic. They were sold on electronic banking. They wanted it *now*, and they were unwilling to concede the time it would take to be accepted. Because they knew that check-cashing facilities could be set up in supermarkets, they assumed this would happen overnight and every consumer would welcome it. Some ideas are "new" to consumers for years.

Easy Writer

Make your writing easy on the eyes. This has to do with short paragraphs, breaking up the text with quotations, perhaps using a Q-and-A format, quoting a letter from a reader. Another form that's attractive to the eye is lists, and I use them frequently. You can put bullets, numbers, or stars in front of each item. The average reader likes to see something headed "Six ways to cut down the cost of eating out" or some such specific topic. Make information easy to absorb.

In talking to consumers, avoid technical language and difficult words. Use short sentences, clear language, and translate difficult terms into everyday language. Don't be "literary," coy, or obscure.

Where and when your writing appears affects both your style and content. There's a world of difference between a full-fledged article, a monthly column, a weekly, and a daily column. A major article, perhaps on one facet of consumerism, should be as sound as a piece in an encyclopedia, though easier reading. Likewise, smaller articles and monthly columns must be very solid and endlessly researched. They are apt to be clipped and filed and referred to years later. A daily column can be somewhat more ephemeral. You can blow off steam on some subject such as a messed-up department store bill. You can flail your arms, beg for sympathy, imply that the whole world is against you. There's no requirement to give a balanced picture, to explain how the error could have happened, to give the store's side, or to advise any "victim" what action to take.

CONSUMERISM SPINOFFS

My specialization in the consumer field has done well for me. Consumerism is an extremely broad topic, and under that umbrella I have been able (over thirty-five years) to move into peripheral fields of interest such as automobiles, food, and household cleansers as they come to my attention. My specialization has led to many unsolicited assignments. One year, for instance, a large corporation decided to direct its annual report to the woman consumer. They asked me to write the major part of this report. A DuPont magazine was devoting a whole issue to consumerism and came to me to do a piece for it. There have been requests to do special articles for trade papers in fields as diverse as furniture retailing, bakeries, restaurant management, supermarket operation, and automobiles. One large producer of consumer products had me do a series of leaflets that were distributed to millions of people.

Although I have written several books, I have never done one in the consumer field. There have been opportunities to do so but, rightly or wrongly, I felt that this topic was so subject to change (regulations, inventions, even fads) that a book would be out of date before it was in print.

My writing led to speaking engagements. Twice I have given speeches in Europe to international groups—one concerned with consumer advertising and the other with the development of appealing food products. If I wished, I could give a talk a week to women's clubs, consumers' forums, conventions, and the like. Even more financially rewarding, I have done product-consultant work for several of America's most prestigious makers of consumer products. On the "psychic reward" side, I've won a number of awards for service to consumers, and I reap other, intangible rewards from this specialty which aims to help people.

WRITING FOR THE MANY CONSUMER MARKETS
by Dan Ramsey

Q: What do appliances, home-owner insurance, portable toilets, solar equipment, and travel trailers have in common?

A: Over the past two decades, I've helped consumers choose these and other products—and thus been able to afford a few of them myself—as a consumerism writer.

The purpose of consumerism writing is to increase buyer efficiency through practical purchasing. The rewards of this specialty are many: a valued contribution to economic efficiency, a growing market for well-researched writing, and an opportunity to "pay your way" as you develop commercial writing skills.

Most important, consumerism writing offers a hungry outlet for your prose—a hunger that overlooks inexperience in search of knowledge. This editorial hunger gives hope and motivation to the unpublished, helping them overcome natural fear of the writer's most difficult task—sustained application of the seat of the pants to the seat of the chair.

THE IDEA

First comes the idea. A writer is often asked, "Where do you get your ideas?" and usually answers, "Everywhere!" My ideas for consumer articles and books often spring from past experience and future needs. My use of recreational vehicles led to a series of consumer articles for *Camping Journal* on how to buy and efficiently use travel trailers and motor homes. Building a fence recently led to writing *The Complete Book of Fences* for Tab Books. A dream of someday building a log home led to writing two articles and a book on log home construction.

Good ideas also come from other consumers. Our last home was purchased, in part, because of the natural, easy-to-maintain landscaping. The previous owner's efforts and knowledge gave me material for an article on "Easy Care Landscaping" for *110 Better Home Plans* magazine. If a friend is buying a freezer, use his or her experiences and your additional research for the basis of a consumer article or two.

Consumer article ideas come from asking questions: What are people buying? What do they need to know before they purchase? How and where can I learn more?

THE MARKET

Where are you going to sell this great idea? The advantage to this field is that it's needed by nearly every publication from *Accent* ("How to Buy a Tuba") to *ZIP* ("Getting the Most from Bulk Rate").

The first source of market information is your local newsstand. With a notebook and an hour, you can discover what people are reading (translation: what editors are buying), what the advertisers think readers are buying, where to send your masterpiece, and to whom. Also check back issues at the library for ideas on subjects, slants, and editorial needs.

Of course, the bible of writers is *Writer's Market*, the annual book listing the names and needs of more than four thousand markets buying freelance writing. Other sources include *Literary Market Place* and *The Religious Writers Marketplace*. Magazines like *Writer's Digest* and *The Writer* offer monthly updates on how and where to market your consumerism book or article.

To make sure their articles are on target, many writers *query* the appropriate editor to save time and effort. A query is simply an article outline in letter form. Most of my queries are four paragraphs long and include:

- Attention-grabbing opening (often the "hook" that will be used to begin the finished article).
- Subject development (summary of your method or solution).
- Benefits (reasons why this article is important: timeliness, illustrations, expert background, new facts).
- Urge to action ("This article is offered exclusively to *your magazine* on speculation," meaning, "You don't have to buy it until

you see it, but give me the go-ahead and I'll send it post-haste").

Note the proposed length, estimating it by the length of published articles or suggested length in *Writer's Market*. If you have special knowledge on the subject or have published widely in the field, mention it. Otherwise, you don't have to say, "This is my first article." Let the editor judge the finished product on its own merits.

A typical query of mine is appended to this article.

WRITING THE ARTICLE

Mr. Mailman just left a letter from Ed E. Tor of *Water Meter Reader's Digest* saying, "Yes, we'd like to see your article on '10 Ways to Choose and Use Dog Repellent,' on spec." Now what?

It's time to produce.

First, consider the mechanics of the proposed article. That is, if you've been asked to write a 1,200-word article, you certainly don't want to produce one that's 200 or 2,000 words long. With a pica typewriter, double-spaced copy (one-inch margins) produces about 250 words per manuscript sheet. Divide 1,200 by 250 and you get about five. So your article should be approximately five manuscript pages long.

Paragraphs in most consumer publications are typically between 50 and 70 words long, containing a thesis statement, its development, and an example to illustrate the point. Following this guide, you can estimate *roughly* that you will cover four thoughts (paragraphs) per page for five manuscript pages—a total of twenty thoughts on your subject. So, your article outline should include twenty important and interrelated thoughts. That's your article's skeleton.

What does the reader want to know about this subject? The reporter's classic questions—who, what, when, where, why, and how—are appropriate: Who needs this product or service? What should the consumer know before purchasing or using? When should it be purchased? Where? Why should the consumer purchase it? How can the consumer get the greatest value and efficiency from its use?

Next you develop an *approach* to the subject by using the four S's: Subject, Statement, Solution, and Slant. As an example, the subject of this article is "how to write for the consumer." The statement is "consumer writing is an excellent entry-level writing field." The solution is to originate ideas, market the ideas, produce the article, and continually improve your craft. The slant is toward the relatively inexperienced writer.

The first draft of your article is simply putting flesh on your outline skeleton. The thought "solar power is a practical and affordable alternative energy source for homeowners," for example, might become a paragraph reading:

"A student of the sun for thousands of years, man has finally discovered how to harness the power of the earth's nearest star and make it available for use economically. Solar power is becoming a practical and affordable alternative energy source for today's and tomorrow's home owner. In fact, experts predict that by 1985, as many as eleven million homes will be using solar energy."

Once the rough draft is completed, you can go back and verify spelling, improve sentence structure, edit out clichés and excess verbiage, smooth transitions between thoughts (paragraphs), and retype it into final form.

ILLUSTRATING YOUR ARTICLE

Photos and artwork to illustrate your article are available free or at low cost from many sources: trade associations, dealers, wholesalers, or manufacturers. Or, you can shoot your own photos.

Many manufacturers, suppliers, and trade associations are happy to provide professional photos and art on their products in exchange for a credit line. My book on log home construction was almost completely illustrated with art supplied by log home kit manufacturers. You can find a listing of trade associations in the *Encyclopedia of Associations*, available at most libraries, and in *The Writer's Resource Guide*, published by Writer's Digest Books.

You can take your own photos of family, friends, or even strangers purchasing and using the subject of your consumer article. For my easy-care landscaping article, I simply had family members enjoy a picnic in the naturally landscaped yard. People like to see other people in illustrations—even if it's just a hand or a foot. Remember to get signed model releases if anyone in your photos can be recognized.

If you're not handy with a camera, you can often find an amateur photographer through local college classes and photo shops who will furnish low- or no-cost illustrations in exchange for published credit. Or, expected income from your article may justify the cost of a professional photographer. Check with your editor to learn whether the magazine pays for photos and text individually or as a package.

Finally, send your article, making a note of when and to whom. Make out a marketing list for your article so that if it does come back, you'll lose no time in getting it to another editor's desk. He or she is *your* consumer.

Other Markets

Consumer articles can become consumer books, newspaper features, and other literary products. In fact, the easiest way to sell a book on a consumer subject is to sell one or more articles on the subject to recognized magazines first. Two of my books have been sold because of my published articles.

To sell a consumer book, you must first have a subject and a solution that is important to a wide audience of readers. In book publishing, a query is called a *book proposal* and usually includes what will become the introduction and the table of contents of your book. The introduction tells the reader (in this case, the editor) what the book is about, why it is important to the reader, and what benefits or features it offers. The table of contents is a chapter-by-chapter outline including not only chapter titles, which will appear on the actual contents page, but also details of each topic and its treatment. Most book publishers also require a sample chapter, but will often accept a published article on the subject instead.

Many books on nonfiction bestseller lists are actually consumer books written for the widest possible audience—e.g., *Jane Fonda's Workout Book*, *Mastering Rubik's Cube*, and *You Can Negotiate Anything*.

Richard Balkin's *A Writer's Guide to Book Publishing* (Hawthorn/ Dutton) is an excellent source of information on how books are proposed, purchased, and published.

HOW TO WRITE MORE WITH LESS

Part of being a *pro* is being *productive*. That is, a professional consumerism writer must write many articles and books to earn an "average" (i.e., middle-class) income. But even if you're a part-time writer, rules of productivity can be applied to offer you both a better income and increased recognition. Here are a few rules, gleaned from two decades of writing:

- **Keep regular hours.** A regular schedule will make you a regular writer. Test different times of the day to discover which are most creative and efficient for you, but work each day for a specific number of hours or pages to be most productive. Many of my consumer books and articles were written in the early morning hours before heading off to other jobs.
- **Write in regular fields.** Research is much simpler if you specialize in a field you know. If you are a salesperson, write consumer articles about products you sell. If you are a

homemaker, write about home economics, child rearing, and related subjects. Keep current on what's happening, what's needed, and who's buying in your field.

- **Write for regular editors.** Once you've made a sale to an editor, follow up with ideas, queries, personal notes, and enthusiasm. Become a person as well as a writer in the mind of an editor. You'll find yourself getting assignments without queries, faster responses to ideas, and increased payment for accepted articles.

- **Polish lightly.** Precise form and perfect prose are for literature. You are writing to inform and entertain consumers. Polish your writing for smoothness and clarity, then stop. One good outline and two edited drafts are usually enough.

- **Don't take it personally.** Read the so-called rejection slip and you probably won't find the word *rejected* on it. Instead, you will see it as "returned." Nothing personal. They may have too many articles on your subject in stock, or they may be changing editors or ceasing publication, or it may be returned for another reason. Send it to another market within twenty-four hours and get back to work. Needless to say, if an article has been returned with the editor's helpful suggestions as to how it might be revised to make it acceptable—get to work on that revision!

THE WRITER'S WORK-STUDY PROGRAM

Over the past few years, I have directly paid for my fence, tires, flying lessons, travel trailer, and many other consumer products by telling others how to buy and use them. Indirectly, my other consumer articles and books have kept a variable distance between the wolf and my front door.

Most important, the field has offered valuable on-the-job training, in polishing communications and marketing skills toward the goal of becoming a successful professional.

Stephen Wagner, Managing Editor
SCIENCE & MECHANICS Magazine
380 Lexington Avenue
New York, NY 10017

Dear Mr. Wagner:

It's Saturday morning in suburbia and the whole world sounds like one great big lawn mower!

If you're tired of twice-weekly runs across the lawn, constant weeding, sprays and chemicals, there's something you can do. You can begin this weekend by designing and developing your own easy-care landscaping.

The place to start is on paper. After drawing an outline of your lot and penciling in your current landscaping you can use a few easy-to-apply landscaping rules to cut down on the maintenance of your yard. Then you can choose among the many materials available to make your hammock dreams come true: rolled turf, seed grass, rock and gravel, bark dust, fences, annual flowers, herb plants, vegetable garden, ground covers and ornaments. In just a couple of weekends you can transform a full-time maintenance job into an enjoyable couple of hours a week. All you need is easy-care landscaping.

EASY-CARE LANDSCAPING, about 1200 words with illustrations, is offered exclusively to Science & Mechanics Magazine. It can be on your desk within 30 days, on speculation. My "Author's Resume" is enclosed.

Sincerely,

enc: SASE
     Resume

WRITING WHERE ONE THING LEADS TO ANOTHER
by Annie Moldafsky

Consumerism writers are an unrecognized minority.

We do not have an association, trade group, or national society. We are a small group, writing for a large audience served by a declining number of newspapers. However, we can and do make a living wage (depending on the lifestyle to which we've become accustomed), and we have job satisfaction. We know that what we write has direct impact on society. We can and do make a difference in the lives of our readers.

The consumer movement and "consumerism" began to grow in the late sixties. It evolved out of our need for information and our increased awareness that you had to speak up and ask the right questions if you wanted to get any answers. Rachel Carson's *Silent Spring* (published in 1962) alerted us to the negative effects of the "new technology." With this new technology came new materials, new uncertainties, and new decisions.

How would we know, in this rapidly changing marketplace, what was good and what was not? How should we evaluate the trade-offs: environment versus productivity, higher cost versus time saved? What were our rights as citizens and consumers—the users and purchasers of an incredible diversity of products and services? What was government responsible for and to whom?

Virginia Knauer, National Office of Consumer Affairs advisor from 1971 to 1977, felt that American citizens were deprived of access to information simply because they didn't know how to get that information. But with the establishment of the National Office of Consumer Affairs in HEW in 1971, the consumer movement achieved national credibility. Consumers' rights organizations were formed. Ralph Nader raised the flag of consumer protest and also our national consciousness. The citizen's "right to know" became a given. But who would communicate all this knowledge to the public?

Enter the consumerism writer.

Some of us came into the consumerism field because we were experts in a particular area. Herbert Denenberg, former Insurance Commissioner of Pennsylvania—known as "Mr. Insurance"—is one of this group. Sylvia Porter, whose knowledge of business and finance has placed her in the forefront of consumer economists, is another.

Then there were those among us who were already professional writers. When we became frustrated in our everyday war with the "system," we researched the options open to us. Through the time-honored process of gathering and sharing information, we became consumer writers and—more surprising—consumer experts. (One of my friends dismisses the credential of "expert" by explaining, "An expert is someone who knows just a little more about a particular subject than I do.")

WHAT IS CONSUMER WRITING?

Years ago, in my B.C.W. (Before Consumer Writing) period, I attended a fiction-writing class at Northwestern University. There I was told that a good writer should "write from what he knows" and "always take the reader by the hand."

The professional consumer writer does just that. We take everyday information and present it in readable, informative, and easy-to-use form. We take our reader by the hand and show him or her the how-to's: how to save money, time, wear, and tear; how to live better, feel better, do better; how to avoid calamities, catastrophes, and some discomfort.

Several years ago, for example, I wrote a series of articles on health maintenance organizations (HMOs) as an alternative to high-cost medical insurance plans. I interviewed health maintenance organization personnel, professional health-care providers, insurance-plan executives, people enrolled in HMO programs, and those covered by traditional plans.

I compiled a comparative cost and benefit chart to illustrate graphically the positives and negatives of HMO plans and private insurance plans. I "took the reader by the hand" and, with his or her needs in mind, I explained there were alternatives to costly private insurance plans; spelled out all the pluses and minuses of private versus prepaid plans; allowed the reader to share the experiences of men and women who had private plans or HMO memberships; suggested how the reader could evaluate his or her situation to determine which plan was best for him or her.

Remember: the consumer audience is made up of doers. They act on your words. Therefore, the consumer article should include the dollars and cents as well as the typical who, what, where, when, and why.

WHAT DO YOU NEED TO GET STARTED?

First, you must be a *people* person, very aware of and sensitive to the public's needs and interests. You have to *know*— not guess—what's uppermost in readers' minds. What are they talking about? What are they thinking about? What kinds of questions are they asking? What kind of answers can we provide?

Years ago when the economy was upbeat, people were into the good life. They were interested in recreation, retirement, second homes, handicrafts for self-expression, and buying luxuries.

In the current more uncertain economy, people want information about jobs, money management, and less expensive medical and insurance plans. They want to know how to keep their dollar from eroding and how to stretch its buying power.

In order to sell an editor on your story idea, you—the consumerism writer—must know your reader. You must sense the "hot" subject.

Several years ago, one of our friends was burglarized. Another had a small home fire. Both suffered losses because they were not adequately covered by insurance, and they spent many social hours moaning about their hindsight. I listened to their laments and learned from their experiences. I also wrote a three-part series on insurance and appraisals entitled, "You're Worth More Than You Think." The series ran in the Sunday edition of the *Chicago Tribune* and was nationally syndicated by United Feature Syndicate.

The number of reprint requests that followed its publication was amazing. I'd sensed the reader's need to know and was able to successfully answer that need.

WHERE DO YOU GET IDEAS?

A professional freelance writer today must be up to date on business and social trends, scientific research, and world affairs. I purchase and read three daily newspapers: the *New York Times*, the *Wall Street Journal*, and the *Chicago Tribune* (my local paper). I also skim *Crain's Chicago Business* (again, a local paper), *Time*, *Newsweek*, *Barron's*, and *Business Week*, and I try to keep up with *Money*, *Fortune*, *Changing Times*, *Inc.*, *Success*, and some of the women's magazines.

From all this reading, I get a good feeling for what's happening now and what may happen in the near future. I also listen to family, friends, editors, strangers in supermarket checkout lines, people on buses and trains, and lunchers at the next table. Consumerism writers can eavesdrop without embarrassment. Some of the best story ideas may come from a comment you've chanced to overhear.

At a cocktail party, one woman was telling another a "horror story." The first woman's friend, a successful craftsperson, had suddenly developed frightening vision problems. She feared she was going blind. An astute physician, after asking about her activities, realized that the art materials the woman was mixing on her kitchen table were highly toxic. They were actually dissolving her contact lenses and causing her vision problems.

Several days later, during a telephone conversation with an editor friend, I heard about an art teacher who'd become concerned about toxic materials used in school art programs. This art teacher was forming a consumer action group. The two unrelated incidents merged into an article, "Working at Home Can Be Hazardous to Your Health." (True confession time: this article took even longer than usual to write. I became so involved in the "horror" stories that I had to step back and let some time elapse before I could deal unemotionally with the material. After a few months, I was able to deliver a story that was readable, objective, and able to make its point rationally, not hysterically.)

The article, titled "Craft Supplies—Danger Signs," appeared first in *House Beautiful* and was later syndicated to newspapers across the country. The payoff for me came not only in the $800 I earned, but in the satisfaction I felt when hundreds of people wrote in for a pamphlet mentioned in the article. The pamphlet identified the toxic properties of commonly used art materials.

There was another nonmonetary bonus. The art teacher who organized the consumer group received national recognition. She now works with the American Lung Association preparing seminars and materials to alert artists and art teachers to potential dangers arising from misuse of materials.

Some story ideas come out of my files. I am a compulsive article-clipper and I try to file each clipping in an appropriate category for easy retrieval. For instance, under the general heading of *Food*, I have clips on additives, co-ops, generic labels, good buys, new products, super-markets, surveys, and synthetics. Under the general heading of *Retailing*, I have tucked away information on credit, dental services, discount operations, factory outlets, legal services, mail order, merg-ers, research, services, specialty stores, and all the individual files on specific retail establishments. And my files under the three general headings of *Money*, *Women*, and *Writers* are each two feet deep—at least.

Not every consumer story is a big idea breakthrough. But some-times, a simple story idea can generate lots of sales and revenue, if the timing is right.

SPINNING OFF IDEAS

One September, our son went off to college with boxes, bundles, and suitcases filled with worldly goods. Nonetheless, he forgot a "few" things. "Please send," he said. As I mumbled and grumbled through the leftovers, I realized there were parents like me all across America who were faced with the problem of moving out an adoles-cent.

I hired an eighteen-year-old friend of our son, packed a standard box of books and personal belongings, and sent my "researcher" to Greyhound, the post office, and various airlines and package-delivery services to determine the cost of mailing packages.

The researcher spent four hours getting the information and I spent one day writing my article. My cost for the researcher was $20. I sold that same Christmas holiday article, with various modifications and graphs, over a two-year period to the *Milwaukee Journal* ($75), the *Chicago Tribune* ($100), United Feature Syndicate ($35), *Family Circle* ($100), and—with added information on how to mail plants and valu-able one-of-a-kind art works—*House Beautiful* ($300). Total return from a "simple" idea: $605.

The experienced writer learns to save interview notes, too. A year or so after I'd done the package-mailing articles, I dug back into the in-terviews and retrieved some very good quotes that worked well in a furniture-moving piece I was assigned. Well-researched facts and doc-umented quotations can often be recycled from one story to another.

Just be sure to record the date of the interview in your notes, the name of the person interviewed, his or her title at that time, an address, and a telephone number. If the person you interview is articulate and knowledgeable, jot his or her name down in your Rolodex under a broad category designation (e.g., legal, medicine, insurance, etc.) for quick future reference.

CONSUMER RESOURCES AND SOURCES

The consumer story must get the reader involved from the beginning. I try to use a personal anecdote, startling statement, or relevant quotation in my lead to immediately engage the reader.

I also use the most current information I can obtain to give my story immediacy. As a result, I do a great many interviews, usually on the telephone.

For the quotes of "experts," I try to track down qualified people in industry, government, or academia. My membership in the Society of Consumer Affairs Professionals in Business (dues are $100 annually) gives me immediate access to quotable sources in the corporate world. And for good government sources, I often depend on my friends in government. When that approach produces zero sources, I have two back-up measures. The first is to call the nearest Federal Information Center (headquartered in Washington, D.C., with offices in major cities), and the second is to struggle through the current issue of the *U.S. Government Manual*, which lists the names of the people supposed to be sitting at the designated desks in the many departments of government.

One word of caution. Be careful to quote your sources accurately. In these accountability days of "sue you if I can," the freelance professional must be particularly sensitive to the impact of words in print.

To avoid misunderstandings, I tell the person I'm interviewing exactly who I am ("I'm Annie Moldafsky, a professional freelance journalist"), what I'm doing and for which publication ("I'm working on an assignment for *Facts and Figures Magazine*"), and what I'm looking for ("I'd like to ask you a few questions about the XYZ merger and what you feel will be the effects on the future marketing of their wizzo whirly-round."). If the person I'm interviewing asks to have final copy submitted for approval, I cut direct quotations out of the article and deal with the information in a different way. Experience has taught me that people who make this request are insecure about their statements, and it's better to seek other attribution—if you can—than to get involved in a time-consuming, writer-won't-win situation.

When I submit my final article to the publication, I always include a list of all people interviewed and their telephone numbers so the magazine's fact checkers can verify any information directly and immediately. [Editor's note: A number of magazines, in fact, *require* that this information be furnished.]

WHO PUBLISHES CONSUMER ARTICLES?

I think it might be better to approach this question from the minority position. Who does *not* publish consumer articles?

It's amazing to me how many markets there are for the timely, well-written, well-documented consumer article. Every major magazine on the newsstand has, in a one-year period, published at least one major consumer piece. Many of them have regular consumer columns that feature short bits of relevant information.

The writer's aim, of course, is to sell an idea to the publication which pays the most. But sometimes, that publication also demands the most from the writer—like interminable rewrites, or the ultimate giveaway of all rights to your article. You must weigh the options. Sometimes, money *is* the most important factor. But there are periods in your career when a credit will carry a lot of weight, too. A big byline in the Sunday magazine section of your newspaper may be more crucial to your career this year than a small, back-of-the book mention in a major magazine.

It's hard to crack the slick-magazines market on your first try. Many have their favorite in-house consumerism writers. There are hundreds of other markets, however, which pay almost as well, including the "city" magazines, regional publications, and even newspapers. (Pay is from $25 to $150 per article and more for the Sunday magazine section, depending upon the city; the *New York Times Magazine* pays considerably more.)

Then, there are what I call the "second tier" publications. These are external house organs (pay ranges from $35 to $300), association magazines (from $35 to $500), and limited-circulation magazines (from $100 to $700). You can find their names (there are several hundred) in *Working Press of the Nation, Volume Five: House Magazine Directory*, and in the *Directory of Associations*.

Be wary of which rights you sell to a magazine or newspaper. Try to sell one-time or first North American serial rights only. As a consumerism writer, your profits may depend on subsidiary sales down the line. For example, when a magazine assigns you to do an article at $500 to $1,500 on a specific subject (e.g., "The Annual Physical—Does It Really Keep You Well?"), it may take you two weeks just to research it. The payment will just barely cover your time. However, if you sell first rights to that magazine, then sell second rights to newspapers and noncompeting magazines, or use the basic information to develop a working script for a film company, you begin to realize the return from your time investment.

ONE THING LEADS TO ANOTHER AND ANOTHER

Sometimes, an article idea takes on a life of its own and balloons into a book. Several years ago, over lunch with an editor, we decided I would do a five-part series on jobs for his paper. Each part would explore a job sector that showed signs of expanding in the years ahead. The final article would focus on jobs for younger people. My initial payment was $500 for the series, but I resold parts to other newspapers and magazines and earned an additional $600. And I wasn't through. Out of that series came the idea for *Welcome to the Real World, A Guide to Making Your First Personal, Financial and Career Decisions,* published in 1979 by Doubleday.

Consumerism writers who publish books also earn extra professional credentials as well as greater financial security. Every publisher is looking for the hot "how-to" book idea. If you can organize how-to material into a simple, easy-to-read format (e.g., *How to Reduce Fat Knees in Thirty Days)* and your subject is timely, you may achieve instant consumerism writer fame.

But if you're one of the "real" consumerism writers, fame and fortune are not your only goals. Right?

Although we are not a large group, consumerism writers have an awesome responsibility that we take very seriously. We are committed to presenting information that is accurate, well researched, and ready to use. We inform our readers, alert them, and prepare them so that they in turn can make informed decisions about their lives. We help make life more livable for our readers—and in return, we live richer lives.

HOW TO DEVELOP AND MARKET CONSUMER ARTICLES
by Blanche Hackett

Everyone wants to be happy, healthy, and financially secure. My aim as a consumerism writer is to develop and market articles that give my readers advice on how to live more cheaply, comfortably, healthily, and, therefore, achieve more happiness. As a consumerism writer I am the middleperson between the expert and the reader, a writer who offers tactics and techniques on what to look for and what to avoid in the supermarket or with new or used cars, clothing, money, health care, insurance, drugs, toys, vacations, pets, and a wealth of other goods and services.

Initially, travel writing and biography were my specialties, until an editor invited me to stop by her office. She had several articles she wanted written. When I arrived, the editor announced that another writer had dropped in and taken the travel article, but she needed an article on lamb. Lamb, I thought, yuk! While I mentally fumed over my hour's drive, wasted gas, and wasted writing time, she rummaged through a large folder and brought out three books and about half a dozen articles on lamb. It's right there, I thought, it's a piece of cake. And it was. Not only did I learn about grades of lamb, prices, what to look for, what to avoid, how to buy it, store it, and cook it, but I learned to love lamb *and* writing for consumers.

As a writer-librarian in a small town library, I now keep my eyes and ears open not only for interesting travel and biography ideas, but especially for the patrons who pour out their problems at the front desk. There's Virginia, for instance, a recently widowed mother who desperately needs a job and sources of financial aid for her two older children so they can attend college or get job training after high school. Sylvia, who needs a sewing machine, has come to the conclusion that price is the least of her problems in making an intelligent decision. John, a high school drop-out who needs information and help to consider the feasibility of establishing a lawn-care business. And there are the gadflies who see and feel the inequities in schools, health care, jobs, and government and are determined to rally others to their cause. All these people and their problems are raw material for the writer of consumer articles.

As I helped John check *Consumer Reports* for information on fertilizers, sprinkler systems, power mowers, grass seed, and lime, I suddenly imagined millions of us also struggling to produce a decent lawn. After I located every book on lawn care for John, I gave him the address of the local agricultural bureau and college. I also found several books on business education, management, and the address of the Small Business Administration for him. I advised him to send for their pamphlet, "Checklist for Going into Business." Experts in the field were found locally and through referrals. Bill, a second-generation owner of a large garden shop, furthered our education on lawns and the hard work involved in operating a lawn-care business. He also advised what most consumer articles suggest—buy from a qualified retailer who will provide proper service and replacement parts. John took off from there.

I in turn made a phone call to the editor of *Common Cents* (American Consumer Services), and "Do-It-Yourself: Lawn Care" appeared in that publication with "Lawn Care Calendar" as a sidebar. A spinoff, "Fight Inflation—Grow a Garden," was published in *Purpose* magazine. Another article, tentatively titled "Start Your Own Gardening Service," went on a back burner for a magazine that publishes articles for entrepreneurs. (Much later, I heard that John T. bought his own airplane and now flies to Florida for his annual winter vacation.)

Careless, contemptuous service and other consumer frustrations are naturals for consumer articles. I once became livid with rage at the filthy restrooms and mountains of foul-smelling, overflowing garbage in some of our National Park campgrounds. I talked to camp managers, rangers in charge of the campgrounds, and camp workers (mostly students). I questioned fellow campers about the garbage collection and restroom conditions in the other campgrounds they visited. I then compared these conditions with some of the model campgrounds I had seen in New York and Michigan.

As a consumerism writer you are also a gadfly, and if you get paid to help improve conditions for your fellow citizens, that's an extra bonus. I did not query editors before writing this article. I was angry about conditions and I wanted to expose the problem and offer solutions from other campgrounds. The *Reader's Digest* editor who rejected the article explained, "It has been a general principle here never to run pro and con articles unless we can place them back-to-back under the same cover." Next, I submitted it to *American Forests*. The editor there published it under the title of "Are Campers Slobs?" Spinoffs from this research included several articles on excellent campgrounds.

The consumer, personal-experience, and confession articles are all written to give readers definite directions and advice that will resolve their problems and satisfy their needs and desires. The personal-experience article may be about a trip, tour, restaurant, or something out of the ordinary that will make interesting and informative reading. The confession article has always been popular because readers like tales related in a confidential style by a writer confessing frustrations or shortcomings. These articles help consumers by showing how personal problems have been overcome by the person confessing. Even the personality sketch can be a consumer article. For instance, a sketch of Ralph Nader would certainly reveal his major contribution to the creation of the worldwide consumer movement. In this type of article, I aim not only to help the reader operate as a successful consumer, but also to inspire him or her to fight for reform and pursue fair play.

EVERYONE IS A CONSUMER

A look through *Writer's Market* will prove that the consumer article is the mainstay of most mass-market magazines, including *House and Garden, Ladies' Home Journal, Good Housekeeping, McCall's, Working Woman, Working Mother,* and many of the religion, retirement, women's, and young-adult magazines. Editors know that most readers buy magazines largely for advice. Consumer articles answer the following questions: Where can the reader find the best quality, the largest selection, at the best price? What are the special problems or dangers that should be considered before buying or using a service? Who are the experts on this product or service and what is their advice? What are the books, pamphlets, or government bureaus that can give the reader more help and information? As the middleperson between expert and reader, it's your responsibility not only to help the consumer learn about products, insurance, service, or whatever. It's also your responsibility to save the reader time and aggravation seeking help and information. You are the reader's "point," the advance scout. It's possible to sell consumer articles from anywhere in the country. No matter where I am, I keep my eyes and ears open for complaints about defective products, an individual's frustration caused by not knowing enough about a sewing machine or a typewriter or a tour to Europe. I have a simplistic test to determine the salability of an article. I ask myself, will thousands of people be confronted with this problem? If yes, I then ask, can I solve the problem with my article and present options? Will the editors of *Good Housekeeping, Reader's Digest, Mother Jones,* or *Mother Earth News* be interested?

To act as the reader's scout, you not only need to identify her problem. It's equally important to *visualize* the average reader. Often, she is a hurried mother and full-time home manager. Another reader is single, equally hurried, working full-time in the business world. Both have average or below-average incomes. Editors and advertisers know these women intimately. They have researched their interests, education, and income thoroughly. Their recommendations and requirements are crucial to selling my writing. I know these active women need their information quickly, accurately, and in just a few words. (In addition to these women, there are families—neighbors and friends—to whom I direct my articles. I'm always curious to see what magazines these people read. Every magazine is a potential market.)

HOW TO WRITE A CONSUMER ARTICLE

Presently, I'm working for library patrons frustrated over which new automobile to purchase. I begin the research for this difficult and very expensive purchase by examining five years' worth of the *Readers' Guide to Periodical Literature,* jotting down any titles on how to purchase an automobile. I'm always happy when the titles are few or nonexistent, because I can tell an editor that the *Readers' Guide* does not have a current article on the subject. Editors do not repeat a similar story within a short period. I also use the *Readers' Guide* when searching for titles. I not only get ideas, but sometimes just add or subtract words from an existing title and, *voilà*, I have a new title.

According to the Chrysler Corporation, in 1980 women purchased or were registered as owners of 45 percent of the nations' new cars. The women's magazines will naturally want to help the woman driver by publishing more nuts-and-bolts articles.

I have my tentative title, "New Car Buying: Makes—Models—Money." Most of the women's general-interest magazines would probably be interested. I will query *Working Woman, Working Mother, Good Housekeeping, House and Garden, Redbook,* and *Glamour.* I don't attempt an article unless I can list at least six markets for it.

And if any of the magazines I have selected to query has published an article on my subject within the past three years, I cross it off and add another magazine to the list.

After I have read every article I can find about selecting and purchasing an automobile, I read *Motor Trend.* It's packed with facts. Then I read *Consumer Reports* and study the testing done on the cars. What has Ralph Nader written lately on the new automobiles? Does he favor any particular one? Finally, I visit local car experts, the dealers and their mechanics. The working title "New Car Buying: Makes—Models—Money" narrows it down for me and provides focus.

Once I have the basic research finished, a working title and a theme (i.e., What am I trying to prove?), I begin looking for and talking to the experts. Besides the Nader quotes, I will use another organization and authority that will be recognized by most readers. An anecdote by Janet Guthrie, the first woman to compete in the Indianapolis 500, would give authority to the article. Many experts can be found at a local university or in the consumer books and articles published by Ralph Nader and his Raiders. The *Consumer Information Catalog* lists fourteen free federal government publications on the subject of automobiles.

THE RIGHT ANGLE FOR THE RIGHT MARKET

Slanting the subject and query to a magazine is crucial to a sale—if you get your slant right you overcome a major hurdle. I study the style and format of a magazine by reading at least six back issues. (These magazines and newspapers are available at the public library.) When I slant, I aim the article at a specific editor and the magazine's readers. I also try to remember that most people are not interested in problems, *per se*. They are interested in *people* who have problems.

For example, the automobile article, if slanted for *Working Woman*, would aim at an average-income woman like myself. She probably has a family, and reliability, price, and car size would be primary considerations. The same article for *Vogue* would be written for a more affluent woman, and elegance, image, and performance would be more important. I would necessarily analyze Cadillac, Mercedes-Benz, and Lincoln Continental. The same article for *Farm Journal* would be aimed at the ranch and farm woman. Her automobile must be durable, with lots of room and low upkeep. Thus, I would include information and prices for station wagons and pickup trucks. Same subject, but three slants appealing to three different editors and their readers.

Incidentally, when I want to know the readers of a magazine, I study the advertising. I then aim the article at the person who would buy the products advertised in that magazine. Kay Cassill, author of *The Complete Handbook for Freelance Writers*, advises, "If you start piling up rejection slips, it will probably pay you to go back a step and examine the magazine more closely to see if you really understand what the editors are looking for." Most editors immerse themselves in the attitudes and ambitions of their magazine and readers. They're aware of subtle differences between their magazine and the many others that may seem similar at a quick glance.

Editors know that readers are attracted by illustrations. I often hear, "Good pictures will sell me." Writers are frequently asked to provide illustrations for their articles because pictures show simply and attractively what might require hundreds of words to describe. There are many photography books in the library that help the beginning writer-photographer.

Photos also must be slanted to the manuscript to add to its value. Your photo slant is as important as your article slant. Ideally, your pictures should depict part of the article. For instance, photos for an article on hiking for *Modern Maturity* would include mature people wearing sturdy shoes and hiking. The same article for *Seventeen* would portray boys and girls hiking on a well-marked trail. The same article slanted for the travel section of the *New York Daily News* would show and mention New Yorkers hiking in the Catskill Mountains or the nearby Palisades in New Jersey.

When I have illustrations for the manuscript, I casually say something like, "two photographs and a graph are available." The editor always replies, "Good photographs are a definite aid to the sale." Or "Yes, but I'm skeptical. Pix important."

THE QUERY

Once I have an article's title, theme, slant, expert, importance to the reader, and any current or new breakthroughs that will lure the editor into a favorable reply, I query. The query is always addressed to a specific editor by name—usually a top editor. An editor at *McCall's* once said, "A brief query is a great time saver for both writer and editor." That is an understatement! As writer you benefit because the query forces you to make some type of outline. If you can't write a letter stating in detail what your idea is about, you are not ready to write the article. Go back to your source or research. If you can't sell your idea in a query, why bother to write the article? Besides, the editor might not need an article on your subject.

The first paragraphs of my queries are usually similar in this case: "Would you be interested in an article tentatively titled 'New Car Buying: Makes—Models—Money?' " In the second paragraph, I give the statistics of women automobile owners and the importance of giving them nuts-and-bolts information to help them make an intelligent choice. An anecdote or quote by an expert follows, and any new information on the latest research by *Consumer Reports* or Ralph Nader. I close the letter by stating the number of illustrations I have and my credits. The letter is usually one page long.

If I do not like or enjoy a magazine, I don't query it. Obviously, that editor will feel the same way about my writing and ideas. We are not compatible.

When I first write to an expert for information and anecdotes, I briefly explain the nature of my article, the publication for which it's being written, and I give my deadline. On a separate sheet, I list pertinent questions and ask if I may call on such a day and time. I always enclose a self-addressed stamped envelope for the reply. Most people I've interviewed prefer a list of questions. It gives them a chance to do some extra research and, best of all, they can keep copies of their replies. Most experts seem to be considerate of a deadline.

Consumer articles are short, usually 300 to 2,000 words. I try to imitate the style of the other consumer articles published in the magazine I query. One editor actually suggested I "follow the story on page six in the June issue." It's important to give the consumer reader up-to-date information in concise language. Integrity is one of our most important assets. The writing world has experienced too many "clever" writers lately who practice tricks that hurl their articles into print. Unfortunately, some fail to do truthful and accurate reporting. Our readers deserve accurate research. Quotes and anecdotes by experts give authority to the article and make the information more palatable.

Market opportunities abound for the consumerism writer. A quick look at *Writer's Market* will reveal that most of the women's, special-interest, general-interest, consumer-service, weekly-supplement, and city and regional magazines buy consumer articles. Public relations and advertising agencies also often "farm out" writing jobs to freelancers when the agency is overloaded. Other writers in government, business, and industry also prove to be helpful allies. This same network of people will help with interviews and background information.

When the going gets rough, I remind myself that I am in extraordinary company. Criticism and information by muckrakers such as Upton Sinclair, Rachel Carson, Estes Kefauver, and Ralph Nader encourage government and businesss reform. As a result, consumers worldwide are better informed and protected. In his book *Consumer's Guide to Fighting Back,* Morris Bloomstein writes, "As a consumer writer you are prepared to teach your reader to be persistent, loud, and to self-protect."

As the middleperson between the expert and the reader, the consumerism writer must care for the health and the prosperity of his or her readers. Edward Weeks, former editor of *Atlantic Monthly,* said it best: "If he is to be a great writer, which is more than being a successful one, a writer must write about things which matter deeply to him." Amen.

Additional Resources

The Advertising Council, Inc., 825 Third Ave., New York, NY 10022. Produces thirty public service advertising campaigns annually in all media—TV, radio, press, magazines, business press, transit, outdoor advertising. Provides advisory, historical, and referral information about the Advertising Council itself and public service advertising in general. Offers annual reports, brochures and pamphlets, placement on mailing list, newsletter, photos, press kits.

Bureau of Industrial Economics, U.S. Department of Commerce, Rm. 4321, Washington, DC 20230. Provides analytical, interpretative, technical, and trade information on all domestic consumer goods and services industries. Offers research assistance and statistics. Publications include *U.S. Industrial Outlook.*

Consumers' Association of Canada, 200 First Ave., Suite 10, Ottawa, Ontario, Canada K1S 5J3. Offers aid in arranging interviews, bibliographies, statistics, newsletter, placement on mailing list.

Consumer Federation of America, 1012 14th St. NW, Suite 901, Washington, DC 20005. Supplies annual reports, biographies, brochures, booklets, clipping services, information searches, placement on mailing list, newsletter.

Consumers Union, Office of Public Information, 256 Washington St., Mt. Vernon, NY 10550. Offers a variety of consumer publications and counsel on consumer goods and services. Writers must verify definite assignment because of number of requests for information.

Council of Better Business Bureaus, 1515 Wilson Blvd., Arlington, VA 22209. Provides advisory, interpretative, and referral information on mediation-arbitration, charitable solicitations, advertising, industry standards, general consumer information. Offers annual reports, brochures and pamphlets, informational newsletters, statistics. Publications list available.

Discount America, 51 E. 42nd St., Rm. 417, New York, NY 10017. Provides how-to, referral, and trade information on mail-order shopping, discount shopping in general, discount mail-order shopping. Offers aid in arranging interviews, press kits, research assistance, telephone reference services.

Federal Trade Commission, Public Reference Branch, Sixth and Pennsylvania Ave. NW, Washington, DC 20580. The commission, a law enforcement agency, protects the public (consumers and businessmen) against abuses caused by unfair competition and unfair and deceptive business practices; guides and counsels businessmen, consumers, and federal, state, and local officials. Offers reprints, copies of speeches, other pertinent documents. Publications include *News Summary* (weekly).

Food and Drug Administration, 5600 Fishers Lane, Rockville, MD 20857. Provides interpretative, referral, and technical information on regulation and safety of medical products—drugs, vaccines, devices— veterinary feeds and drugs, cosmetics, food. Offers press releases, placement on mailing list, brochures. Publications include *FDA Consumer* magazine, available by subscription through the Government Printing Office.

Office of Consumer Affairs, Consumer Information Division, 621 Reporter's Bldg., Washington, DC 20201. Offers aid in arranging interviews, and government booklets and brochures. Many consumer publications available, such as the *Consumer's Resources Guide.*

Chapter Twenty

WRITING ABOUT BUSINESS AND FINANCE

There are many and varied definitions of just what makes up the "business" and/or "financial" press. Sometimes, there's an overlap with what we call the "trade press" (see Chapter 21) and the "professional press." For our purposes, the business and finance markets are those publications concerned with money management. The focus is on the bottom line.

Business-finance writers provide articles and books for business-people of all kinds, as well as for the general public. They deal with the ways funds can best be earned, spent, budgeted, invested, or saved, and thus provide people with the information they need to build up their net worth, set financial goals, and work to attain them.

Some business-finance freelancers develop specialties within a specialty, becoming experts in tax matters, pensions, social security, stocks and bonds, or real estate. Others may write only about retirement, life insurance, or labor-business relations. Still others, such as Sylvia Porter, may write syndicated columns (and books) that are nuts-and-bolts guides to every aspect of personal and family finances.

In this specialized area, creative marketing really pays dividends. By slanting your article ideas, you can often sell essentially the same material to editors of magazines or journals in many different fields. An example of this approach is a story of how a 50-year-old woman entrepreneur started and manages a successful small business. Such a piece could be offered to *Money* magazine, to periodicals in the industries with which she's involved (e.g., the garment and/or leather industries), to *Dynamic Years,* an "action for independent maturity" magazine published for pre-retirees, as well as to a general women's magazine.

If you can overcome your math anxiety, business-finance writing offers rich rewards. As in all fields, you must first learn the various publications' requirements and who makes up their readership, but this is one specialty where writers are really appreciated. Because there is a great need for information, and few people can convey it effectively, the opportunities for freelancers in this field are almost limitless.

THE DOLLARS AND SENSE OF BUSINESS AND FINANCE WRITING
by Richard Blodgett

I believe business and finance is one of the few specialties in which a capable writer can earn a good living. That's one of the factors that drew me to the specialty in the first place, and it is certainly one of the reasons I have been able to support my family in a reasonably comfortable lifestyle *despite* being a freelancer.

When I began freelancing in 1970 after three regular jobs—reporter for the *Wall Street Journal*, writer for *Business Week*, and, finally, writer at a firm that produces corporate literature—I had no idea of the importance of specialization. Being a freelancer sounded glamorous to me, and the essence of that glamor was writing on all sorts of topics and meeting all kinds of people. But after initially offering myself as a generalist, I soon learned that specialized expertise brings the best assignments—and can be fun, despite my original misgivings. Within three or four years I gravitated to two specialties: business and finance (because of my earlier experience at the *Wall Street Journal* and *Business Week*), and art (because I had a personal interest in collecting).

Today, I write only about business and finance. After our son was born in 1980—and our family's financial needs suddenly escalated—I gave up writing about art because it pays poorly (a change I made happily in return for being a father).

Why specialize in business and finance? What is good about this specialty? What is bad? How much technical expertise and specific financial background do you need?

If business and finance turn you on, I probably don't have to convince you that it's a good specialty. And if you are turned off, you probably wouldn't choose it anyway. So there's no sense in extolling the joys of writing about money and investments. You can make up your own mind.

But I can share some of my experience, and offer advice on fees, markets, and writing style.

GETTING STARTED

The first question often asked by interested writers is, "Do I need a financial background to get into this specialty?" My unequivocal answer is no. I was an English major in college and had no academic background in business or finance—although it's certainly true that my having worked at the *Wall Street Journal* was a plus. I believe I would have succeeded at freelancing anyway, but the *Wall Street Journal* credential brought some initial assignments that might otherwise have been impossible to land.

For the newcomer, what's clearly vital—other than a basic interest in this specialty—is an aptitude for business and finance. (Nobody would expect a writer who feels lost in the kitchen to write about cooking.) Given that aptitude, the best way to learn is by doing—by researching and writing a few articles even if you don't feel totally comfortable with the subject matter at first. You might also want to take a few business and investment courses at a local college or university. But a degree in business is unnecessary. In my twenty years as a financial journalist and writer, I have yet to be asked by an editor about my academic qualifications.

Finally, I am convinced that the best business and financial writers are, indeed, *writers* rather than *technical specialists*. Seldom can the technician who uses jargon transcend that limitation to become a successful writer. Instead, editors are constantly searching for writers who know how to research and interpret technical issues. Take heart if you have heretofore avoided this field because you lacked the technical knowledge.

BASIC INFORMATION—GO TO THE SOURCE

Many financial organizations and government agencies maintain active public relations programs and are anxious to help writers working on financial articles. Examples include Merrill Lynch, Prudential-Bache, and other large brokerage firms; the New York Stock Exchange; banks; the Internal Revenue Service; the Federal Trade Commission; large accounting firms; commodities exchanges; the American Bankers Association; the Insurance Information Institute; the American Council of Life Insurance; the Health Insurance Institute of America; and the Investment Company Institute. In some writing specialties, it's hard to find experts willing to let you pick their brains. In business and finance, the hills are crawling with them.

A warning: don't rely on articles by other writers as source material for statistics, tax rules, and other statements of fact. Some articles are filled with mistakes, and editors can turn icy when they learn you have copied from questionable secondary sources. They even are leery if they learn that you have relied on Sylvia Porter, whose articles are impeccably accurate. Organizations like those listed above *love* to help you find accurate information because they *hate* to see mistakes in financial articles. So don't be shy about pressing such organizations to help you track down good primary source materials.

Also, a number of organizations—including the New York Stock Exchange, the United States League of Savings Associations, the Health Insurance Association of America, the Insurance Information Institute, the Investment Company Institute, and the No-Load Mutual Fund Association—publish annual fact books containing a wealth of authoritative statistical data. These booklets are generally sent free to writers on request. Still further, the Internal Revenue Service media relations department in Washington, D.C. stands ready to review articles on taxes for technical accuracy. The IRS media relations people are very good about sticking to the facts and not attempting to influence the viewpoint of articles you submit for their review. In fact, it's a good idea to attempt to find an appropriate expert to review *any* manuscript that contains technical information or specific financial advice, although you should be prepared to fend off reviewers who—unlike the staff at the IRS—want to purge your manuscript of anything critical or controversial.

MAGAZINE MARKETS—DEMAND IS UP

I see the business and finance field as divided into three major subcategories, each with its own dynamics (including fee structure): magazine articles, books, and corporate ghostwriting.

Because the economy is affecting everyone so greatly, there is enormous demand for business and financial articles: corporate profiles, articles detailing the latest economic trends, advice on how people can better manage their money. Some of the women's magazines, for example, now contain item after item on money and investments. There are also numerous specialized business publications such as *Institutional Investor, Money,* and *Changing Times* that can be good freelance markets.

On the other hand, I am appalled at the low fees paid by many magazines—not just for financial articles, but for nearly any type of article. To me, $400 is not much for an article that takes a week to research and write (particularly when one considers that freelancers must fund their own benefits). Of course, that's the basic problem with freelancing—low magazine fees. I write a monthly column on personal finance for *McCall's,* but other than that, I've done relatively few magazine articles for the last few years because of the generally poor fees.

Nonetheless, writing for magazines may be your most practical entry point into business and finance—if you can afford to get by on a modest income (or at least an income level that seems modest by New York City living standards) for a few years. And the experience and exposure of magazine work *can* lead to book contracts and corporate assignments. So despite the financial drawbacks, there are advantages to writing for magazines.

Additionally, many writers cash in on business and finance magazine pieces by recycling their research—earning multiple fees, for example, by researching an article on money market funds for one magazine and then rewriting the same material for other magazines. This can be particularly effective in business and finance, because you are dealing typically with generalized factual information that can be rearranged for different publications (unlike, say, writing a profile of Leontyne Price for *Opera News* or an article on Texas prisons for *Texas Monthly*—relatively specific material probably hard to sell elsewhere).

Business and financial articles earn anywhere from $200 to $3,000. A few magazines pay freelancers well; generally, these magazines pay well for any article. These include the leading women's magazines, *Playboy*, and *Reader's Digest*. Understandably, competition for writing assignments with these magazines is intense.

Watch Your Writing Style

When I write for magazines, I usually do advice pieces about how people might better manage their money—investments, insurance, financial planning, taxes, and so on. I have strong ideas about how these articles should be written.

First, I'm a firm believer in addressing the reader as "you"—just as I have done in this chapter. Financial information can be dry and impersonal. Using "you" is a way to overcome that dryness and make your articles more lively and readable.

Get to the Point

Second, I believe every financial advice article should have a well-stated viewpoint. Too many articles ramble on without any sense of direction. These articles bore me terribly—and I assume they have the same Morphean effect on most readers. Before putting a single word on paper, think through a theme. In a stock-market piece, for instance, do you want to suggest that this may be a good time to buy stocks? Do you want to warn readers about the dangers of investing? Do you want to let them know how to find a good broker? Pick a theme that most accurately reflects what you have learned through your research and build your article around that theme.

Third, try to offer at least one specific piece of advice on which readers might be able to act. Maybe they should consider opening an

Individual Retirement Account. Maybe they should review their disability income insurance. Maybe they should transfer investments to their children's names to save on taxes. What's the dollars-and-cents payoff for having read your article?

Fourth, keep it simple *and* accurate. Financial information can be highly complex: there are times when absolute simplicity and clarity may have to be sacrificed for accuracy's sake. Accuracy is imperative, since people may spend or invest money based on what you have written. But long technical explanations have no place in general consumer publications. You will have a terrible time getting top-paying magazine assignments if you write in a technical style.

New Ideas from Daily Life

Fifth, develop fresh and timely story ideas rather than pumping out the same limp "evergreens" (why you need a will, how to create a budget, etc.) that are the stock-in-trade of too many financial writers. I admit it's tough to develop new ideas and totally fresh angles on old ideas. You have to be knowledgeable and imaginative; you have to think through current financial trends to their logical conclusions; you have to manage your own money with an eye toward the new opportunities and problems you are constantly facing.

Let me give you an example from my *McCall's* column. Though not a spectacular example, it does illustrate the process by which I developed a particular idea. In early 1982, shortly after a federal law was changed to make Individual Retirement Accounts available to all workers, magazines were filled with articles about IRAs, discussing the new rules and warning about the heavy penalties if you withdrew money from your IRA before you reached age 59½. Many of my friends, I found, weren't opening IRAs because of the penalties. (I love to talk with people about how they manage their money; doing so gives me some of my best ideas.) I, too, was reluctant to open an IRA.

But just how severe were the penalties? As far as I could see, no magazine had explored this question in any depth, and yet it was the key IRA hang-up many of my friends had. I looked into the question and found that you would actually earn bigger profits, despite the penalties, by investing through an IRA and withdrawing your money after five years than by investing the same money in a taxable manner outside an IRA and not having to worry about penalties. It's simply that the tax-free compounding of your profits in an IRA is so great that it overcomes the penalties after a few years. This information made a nice item for my column—an item that contradicted the prevailing wisdom at the time. And I rushed out and opened an IRA myself.

My Rolodex has—in addition to cards listing phone numbers and addresses—another card that I always turn to as I begin my *McCall's* column. That card has four words on it: *short, timely, useful, fresh.* I don't claim to meet those standards in every item I write, but I do think they represent a good goal for all financial advice writers to try to attain.

WRITING BUSINESS BOOKS

As with magazine articles, in recent years a vast market has developed for business and financial books. Again, however, a key issue is the fee.

It is my belief—based on conversations with editors, my own experience, and talking with other writers—that relatively few financial books end up earning much for their authors. Several financial advice books have been runaway bestsellers, including *Sylvia Porter's Money Book* and Douglas Casey's *Strategic Investing.* On the other hand, visit any bookstore and you are likely to find dozens of "me too" financial books (those with nothing to distinguish them from the competition) that are barely selling; the authors of these books seldom earn more than $5,000 to $10,000 for their many months of work.

It is probably unrealistic to expect an advance of more than $4,000 to $5,000 for your first book—unless you have an absolutely smashing idea. You may or may not earn royalties beyond that, depending on how timely and well written the book is, how well it is received by reviewers and the media, and how aggressively your publisher promotes it.

I have written and had published four books. The most I have made from any of them is about $20,000—okay, but not terrific.

The real challenge in writing financial books is coming up with timely, original ideas. To me, there are three elements to timeliness and originality: a fresh idea that strikes a responsive chord with the public; being the first writer to cover that idea in a book; a writing style that presents the idea in bold, straightforward language rather than financial jargon. Such a book stands out from the crowd. Obviously, it's a challenge to meet those three criteria, yet it's by no means impossible.

If you want to grab for the brass ring, Simon and Schuster is by far the leading publisher of financial advice books and does an outstanding job of promoting many of its titles. You might start your search for a publisher with that firm, sending an outline and two sample chapters.

Having asserted at the beginning of this article that business and finance are two of the most lucrative freelance specialties, I may have disappointed you so far by saying that fees for most manuscripts are not high.

But now I come to the writing market where I make quite a nice living—corporate ghostwriting.

THE CORPORATE-FREELANCE RELATIONSHIP

Corporations and their public relations agencies hire freelancers for a variety of writing assignments, including brochures, annual reports, speeches, press releases, and filmstrips. Annual reports are my own particular niche. I also ghostwrite speeches and an occasional brochure.

Corporate work is hard to track down; that's the big problem in entering this market. When writing for magazines, it's easy to identify potential outlets for your work by leafing through various publications to find ones carrying your type of article. It's much more difficult to identify which corporations are looking for freelance help.

Corporations generally locate freelancers by word of mouth. Well-written magazine articles on business topics are one way to gain visibility with corporate executives. Also, you might consider a promotional mailing to large public relations firms and corporate public relations directors. (I have never attempted this and have no idea how well it would work. All my corporate assignments have come by referral.) Many large corporations—such as IBM, Exxon, and Shell Oil—publish quality magazines that sometimes contain articles by freelancers. Writing for these magazines is another possible entry point to the corporate world, although the fees generally are not as high as fees for other types of corporate writing. Still further, if you have any friends who do corporate work, ask them to let you know about any assignments they turn down. [Editor's Note: See also Chapter 21, "Trade, Company, and Professional Journals," for more ideas on how to obtain corporate assignments.]

Once you have cracked this market and have done well on three or four assignments, corporations will begin calling. Many corporations are desperate to find capable freelancers who understand business and can translate complex business concepts into straightforward prose. But I don't want to minimize the difficulty of breaking into this market in the first place.

The Corporate Payroll

When you do get into the market, the fees can be very good. There's an interesting difference in writing for a magazine versus writing for a corporation: a magazine *tells* you what the fee will be, but a corporation generally *asks* what you will charge. If you ask too much, you might not get the assignment. But as a friend of mine says, the worst reason to be chosen for a corporate assignment is that you asked too little, and the best reason to get turned down is that you asked too much.

There's no glory in corporate ghostwriting, only money. So you'd better get enough to make the job worthwhile, or not bother with the assignment.

Besides cash in the pocket, there's another advantage to charging well for your services: corporations actually treat you better when you charge more. If you are inexpensive, there's a tendency to think you are unimportant. And you will get stuck with low fees in the future because your clients will pigeonhole you as a "cheap" writer. But when you charge a lot, you are treated like a prince.

Beginning writers are not necessarily in a position to hold out for high fees. As you build your credentials, however, don't be shy about increasing your rates.

Here is a representative sampling of my own recent fees: annual report for a major corporation, $12,000; very simple annual report for a small corporation, $3,500; speech for a corporate executive, $4,000; brochure for a large consumer products company, $6,000; annual report for a fairly large company, $9,000. Incidentally, I almost always bill in installments: one-quarter or one-third of the total fee when I initially take on an assignment, the remainder over the course of the project. Corporations are used to paying this way. Magazines, by contrast, are seldom willing to pay any money up front.

Deciding What to Charge

In setting your own fees, I suggest you start by determining how much income you need for a year. Divide by 50 for a weekly income need (allowing two weeks for vacation) and then by five for a daily need. Say you list an annual need of $30,000. Dividing by 50 gives you $600, and then by five gives you $120 a day. Then mark up your daily fee by 50 percent or more to allow for contingencies and unpaid time for making contacts and selling. Thus, $120 a day becomes $180. Price jobs on that basis, either charging by the day or—if on a project basis—by trying to determine in advance how many days a project is likely to take. If you have no trouble getting your fees, start moving higher until you encounter serious resistance.

MODUS OPERANDI FOR CORPORATE WORK

Corporate ghostwriting is, in many ways, very different from magazine writing. For example:
- I always take pains to dress neatly and conservatively when

visiting a corporate client. No sports jackets. No unpolished shoes. Appearance is relatively unimportant when doing magazine articles.

- I always submit perfectly typed copy to corporate clients— something I don't usually fuss about when submitting magazine manuscripts.

- Meeting deadlines is important, of course, for both corporate and magazine work. But corporate executives tend to get *very* nervous if you fall behind. Personally, I believe that taking a couple of extra days to "massage" a draft so it's really sparkling is often more important than meeting a deadline and is preferable to turning in copy that's mediocre. However, if you think you might be late, call the client and give advance warning. No surprises, please!

- Then there is the question of number of drafts and being flexible about changes. It's rare that the first draft of a corporate manuscript is accepted by the client without change. Sometimes I do two drafts, occasionally as many as seven or eight. Some writers specify a limited number of drafts. I set no limit and emphasize that I will stay with a project to the end. Corporations appreciate this, and I am able to charge a higher fee—although I take the risk that a given project will drag on far longer than I anticipated.

- Assuming that you intend to go after corporate business, it's important that you be readily accessible to your clients. Corporate executives are under great pressure and often become agitated when they phone and keep getting a busy signal. I suggest you sign up for the telephone company's "call waiting" service if it is available in your area (when you are talking on the phone, a "beep" tells you someone else is calling; you put your current call on hold and switch to the incoming one), or install a second line. A phone-answering machine or answering service is a must.

- The curse of corporate work is to be thin-skinned. You aren't writing the Great American Novel. You are striving to serve a client's needs, and you must be totally flexible about changing copy. Don't get your back up and defend your words and phrasing. Listen to what the client is saying, and be prepared to redraft in a way that responds to the client's concerns.

TYPICAL CORPORATE ASSIGNMENTS

When working on an annual report, I usually gather material for a first draft by interviewing senior executives, including the company president and the head of each operating division. These executives make themselves available and generally talk openly because they want a good annual report. I try to come away from these interviews with a sense of the company's dynamics: objectives, strategies for reaching these objectives, major business opportunities, and most serious problems. I try not to get stuck too far down the corporate pecking order because I am forced then to get my ideas from lower-level officials who lack broad perspective on the company's affairs. Lower-level officials can be very helpful, however, in supplying specific information and briefing me before interviews with senior management.

As for ghostwriting speeches, they are the most challenging of all corporate assignments to me, because a speech is so personal to the individual speaker. It must reflect the speaker's use of language, have pacing, and be interesting and convincing. I absolutely never accept a speechwriting assignment unless I can deal directly with the speaker and tape-record an interview to capture language, phrasing, style, and emphasis.

I am asked sometimes whether there is a conflict between writing for corporations and writing for periodicals. The conflict would arise from quoting or mentioning a corporate client in a magazine piece. I believe a writer must be extremely sensitive to this issue. As a matter of policy, I keep my corporate clients out of my magazine articles. This limits me somewhat when writing magazine articles; there are a few corporations I can never quote. On the other hand, my periodic meetings with the senior executives of these corporations make me privy to business and financial trends in a way that would be impossible as an outsider. So, to a degree, corporate work *helps* me in writing for magazines.

I enjoy working for corporations. I deal with very bright people. I revel in the challenge of organizing a project and keeping it under control. I have to be on my toes at all times. Some projects are exciting and creative. Some, frankly, are not. But nobody ever said life is perfect.

THE PECULIAR JOYS OF BECOMING THE WORLD'S GREATEST SPECIALIST
by Murray Teigh Bloom

A few years after I began freelancing in 1940, I proclaimed the first of a series of Bloom's Laws for magazine writers. My target was a captive student audience—Army, at that—so they had to listen. The law was: A sharp freelancer should be able to pick up three salable magazine article ideas from any Sunday edition of the *New York Times*. A friend, Judith Crist, later helped popularize the law when she taught at Columbia Graduate School of Journalism.

The Second Law descended quietly upon me as I was gathering material for a book that was to become a 1969 bestseller, *The Trouble With Lawyers*. Simply stated: A freelancer can consider himself or herself a specialist if, after reading an article in the *Times* on the subject, he or she can smile indulgently. Why? Because a real specialist would know of the development a week *before* it appears in the *Times*.

The ultimate degree of specialization came to me recently. Again, the test was the *New York Times*. It was a long story in the financial section on International Bank Note, the parent company of American Bank Note. The details in the piece were, of course, long familiar— Bloom's Second Law. But the ascent to the highest degree of specialization came with the realization that I found one major blooper and two minor ones in the article. Nor was it a matter of wrong middle initials: they were real errors. How did I know? What made me so certain? I was the world's greatest writer-specialist on the arcane world of banknote making and selling.

It's not a subject on which to dine. I don't even mention it in the list of specialties that ASJA members opt for in our annual directory: Adventure, Africa, Aging, Alcohol and Drug Abuse, Animals, Antarctica, and so on for eight solid pages. There isn't a whiff of my specialty in the lines I have in *Who's Who*. I certainly can't claim with a smug little smile: a quiet little specialty but a profitable one. Not really. Still, in my head and my files I know more about this strange business than any but a few of the very top executives in the field. And they don't write. Nor do they go in for public relations, handouts, backgrounders, or press conferences. Not to put too fine a point on it: the bank-note world makes the CIA seem like a blabbermouth.

BEING A SUBSPECIALIST

Intense specialists are derided. "People who know more and more about less and less." There was a young historian whose thesis was about weapons used by Homeric warriors. He realized he had acquired too much documentation. Why not limit it to their helmets? He started writing but still had too much to cover. Finally, he decided his true subject was the *plume* the Homeric warriors used. He had created a new, tiny world all his own.

Freelancers can't afford such academic ego trips. We become specialists in medicine, family relations, crime, science, and travel because editors want those subjects. (And to please editors I've written my lifetime quota on those subjects.) But my descent into the secret bank-note world came with innocence aforethought.

Long ago, I'd written some pieces on ingenious money counter-feiters for the old *True* magazine. An editor at Scribner's liked them and wondered if I could get enough yarns together for a book. Thus, *Money of Their Own* became my first book and was brought out in New York and London in 1957. It got fine reviews, and a few readers showed intense appreciation: the book was stolen *four* times from the New York Public Library's main reading room on Fifth Avenue.

One of the chapters dealt with the Portuguese Bank Note Case. This was—and is—an extraordinary, classic white-collar caper in which a leading British bank-note firm, Waterlow and Sons, and the central Bank of Portugal were victimized by a curious assortment of European sharpies led by a bankrupt Lisbon businessman. The Scribner editor loved the story and kept after me to do a book on the case. The trouble was that it required extensive research in Europe, and Scribner's traditional, modest advances simply wouldn't be large enough. Eventually an agreement was worked out with Scribner's and a British publisher, Secken and Warburg, so that there was, in effect, a double advance.

In the many months of research and interviewing—my wife and I spent two months in Lisbon and London—I began learning about the strange ways of the bank-note world, public and private. (Public? That's the United States, with our easily visited Bureau of Engraving and Printing in Washington, D.C. Private? That's how most lesser lands behave when they have their money engraved and printed by firms such as American Bank Note, Thomas de la Rue of London, Enschede of Haarlem, Giesecke Devrient of Munich, and Bradbury, Wilkinson of England.)

Since I was detailing a long-past crime, sources in the trade were willing to talk. But barely so—this is a very close-mouthed bunch. There is much about which to be silent. They have no newsletters, trade papers, or annual conferences to which the press is invited. By the time I finished the book, I knew many details about the bank-note business—just enough to know how little I really knew.

The Man Who Stole Portugal received lovely reviews and had seven foreign editions in the late sixties. It has been optioned four times for films but never made.

The editions of *Portugal* and *Money of Their Own* are long out of print. Over the years, second-hand copies have commanded sizable premiums (thirty and thirty-five dollars) and the books have developed a following among paper-money collectors.

In 1979, during a talk with my agent, I asked if any publisher would be interested in an updated version of *Money of Their Own*. After all, if so many collectors were seeking high-priced second-hand copies, it seemed feasible. He asked me for a set of chapter headings and a brief summary of the kind of updating I'd do. In the list I included a new chapter on the bank-note world, which I labeled "The Brotherhood of Money." He phoned and said the book should be on the bank note world, and the title was great.

The awkward question had to be asked: Was it possible to interview and research sufficiently for such a book? There were no other books, in any language, on the subject, and the clips and magazine bits I had accumulated over the years wouldn't have been enough for a chapter. And even *if* it could be done, who cared? Were there enough readers out there who would pay eighteen to twenty dollars for a book on the curious hidden world of the men who were responsible for turning out the fifty billion pieces of currency the world needs every year? This wasn't a publishing staple.

THE SUBSPECIALIST'S RESEARCH

But what if I still *wanted* to do the book, regardless of cost-effectiveness? This led to the activation of Bloom's Fourth Law: When a subject is very tough to research, when doors are closed and insiders won't talk, on or off, you must *seek out recently retired executives*. They have lots of time, love to talk, and welcome *informed* company. The doldrums of retirement almost always help vitiate the old firm's secrecy rules.

Professional writers don't like to speculate on pieces, let alone books. You go to work in earnest when you have an editor's commitment, a publisher's contract. But there are times to speculate—if you can *afford* to. I could; I had had a national bestseller, *The Trouble With Lawyers,* and I'd miraculously sold my first—and only—novel, *The 13th Man,* to the movies. It was made into a suspense film, *Last Embrace.* There was more than enough to indulge a whim.

I spent the first money on a trip to a well-kept New England farm, where a recent bank-note retiree was living an affluent rural life. He was willing to talk to me because he knew my name; he had my first two books on his shelf. I spent two days with him and he casually suggested another source, another retiree, in England.

Another $750 went into the speculative pot and I went to London via Laker. The British retiree was even more forthcoming. He provided me with diary summaries of his five decades in the business. In addition, through a London friend, I was introduced to a rogue who had once worked for a European bank-note firm and had been fired. He talked freely, even venomously. The rattle of well-hidden skeletons was audible.

When I returned to New York after a week, I knew the book could be researched. I turned in an eighteen-page outline which my agent sent out for bids. Two came in. The best, quite generous—$25,000— was from a major publisher. I was also able to wrangle a sizable travel allowance from a magazine which was interested in some possible article offshoots.

The subsequent travel involved extended trips to Europe, Central and South America, and the West Coast. My task was made easier by my talks with Mr. A in New England and Mr. B in London, and the publication of *The Man Who Stole Portugal*, which most had read.

Inevitably, a catalog of dirty tricks emerged—always performed by the opposition, of course. Marvelous characters began taking full form. Some, such as Rino Giori of Lausanne, possibly deserved books all their own. Giori's very ingenious and expensive intaglio-printing bank-note machines—which 99.99 percent of us could not buy even if we had the money and inclination—did more to change the old bank-note world than anyone since the Sung dynasty emperor who introduced paper money around A.D. 1000.

When I finally finished the book—research, travel, and writing had taken the year I had anticipated—the editor didn't like it. Why? The book world was in great trouble. My publisher was a subsidiary for a foreign publisher who was in financial straits. Mine was a 450-page book, expensive to produce. (Possibly my editor had hoped I would prove the existence of some kind of international conspiracy or something among the bank-note makers.)

WHEN THE PUBLISHER SAYS "NO"

The book now went to the unsuccessful bidder, another major publisher. The editor-in-chief loved it and immediately started editing. It would have to be approved by the new board, but that was a mere detail, he said. It wasn't. The three sales managers on the board declared it a fine book, but questioned who would buy it. Who cared about the men who made the world's money? Two other chief editors wanted the book, too; again, they were overruled by the newly powerful sales managers.

Eventually, the book was taken by a specialty publisher, BNR Press, which turns out books for collectors of paper money and coins. They also decided to reprint my first two books. *Money of Their Own* came out in early 1983 and *Brotherhood*, that summer.

In all, it was not a glorious experience. Admittedly, book publishing was undergoing a great crisis and many contracted books were being turned back by hard-pressed firms. Still, it was the first time a book of mine had been rejected. The original publisher agreed to settle for a small fraction of the advance.

Nearly all book contracts call for the manuscript to be "in form and content satisfactory to the publisher." The trouble is that the deliberately vague terms give unfair advantage to the book publisher in what is, after all, a shared-risk enterprise. All major writers' organizations, including the ASJA, are fighting to eliminate the clause from book contracts. There is very little "hard law" on the subject, but, analogously, the law has held that the advances a commissioned salesman gets are nonrecoverable by the employer.

All this would argue that intense specialization has its financial risks. It does. Right now I'm sure I know more—and have more inside material—about the bank-note world than any writer. It is a peculiar joy. I could talk about it for hours: its characters, crochets, codes, calumnies. But I also realize it is a topic of limited interest. (Yes, I tried, but there's no known way of converting the making of money into how *you* can make money.)

Still, I wouldn't have missed the experience, the listening, the delight in stumbling on hidden crimes, ingenious plots, the double and triple dealing, the unexpected facets of characters. It has become one of my special, private stores of knowledge to which no one else in the writing business comes close. My own intense specialty. A luxury, to be sure, since it isn't likely ever to repay the time and effort I've put into it. But then, freelancing can seldom be factored down to the last dime. There will always be things to write and research which won't actually pay off. There are simply some subjects you *want* to do, because it gives you a special joy. What's the point of being a freelancer if you can't afford that psychic luxury?

WRITING TAX ARTICLES
by Rosalie Minkow

My specialty, business and finance with emphasis on taxation, has a special advantage; although there is great general interest in acquiring information on the subject, few people are competing to write in this field. Why? It would appear that those who have the technical knowledge do not have the time or writing ability. On the other hand, those who have the time or writing ability do not have the technical knowledge.

To write about business, finance, and taxation, you need technical knowledge of these subjects plus the ability to translate the knowledge into simple, direct sentences without losing the accurate intent of the technical language.

SPECIALIZATION BY FIRST-HAND EXPERIENCE

How do you achieve that? Let me talk from my own experience. For some years, I had been writing magazine articles on general subjects. To name just a few, I had written on my hobby of sport boating for boating and Long Island publications; coping with stress for general-interest magazines; author interviews for a Long Island regional magazine; opinion pieces for *Newsday*.

During the income-tax season, I worked for an accounting firm, checking calculations on tax returns—those were the days before most accounting firms used computers, and computations were still being done manually. Checking calculations can be a dreadfully dull task. In order to relieve the boredom, I made a game of trying to figure out why and how the accountant did what he did on the tax return. This led me to ask questions. I was told the answers sometimes; other times, I was referred to the firm's tax library to research the answer myself. In the course of time, I became adept at using its tax library and finding answers. I became so adept that the firm's accountants began to ask me to research problems for them. This reading of tax law gave me a store of knowledge beyond the range of the average layman.

Thus, I had acquired special knowledge. It occurred to me that the general public might be quite interested in what I could tell them about taxes and how to save money on them. I had written on many other subjects, so why not taxes?

A national home and garden magazine had a regular section on money management. I wrote a query to the editor of that section regarding the casualty-loss deduction on income-tax forms. I included what the Internal Revenue Service considered a casualty loss, how to prove your loss, and the extent of the deduction. The query proved to the editor that I had good technical knowledge of my subject and that I was able to transcribe that knowledge into lively, easy-to-understand language without losing the intent of the law. After the success of that sale, I scoured my mind and tax books for other tax topics that would interest the reading public. I found several to sell to the same editor.

The editor was interested in publishing income-tax articles only during income-tax months, however. She felt that her readers wouldn't be interested in tax articles during the rest of the year. Because I had established a liaison with her—she could depend on accurate, well-written copy which met her deadlines—I decided to branch out into other areas of money management that would come under her domain at the magazine.

SPECIALIZATION BY RESEARCH

At this point, I realized that I had to acquire a body of knowledge about business and finance from which I could generate ideas. I paid close attention to items in the business section of the *New York Times*. I subscribed to the *Wall Street Journal*. I went to the local library and read every book in the business and finance sections. Soon, I had enough background knowledge to interview local business and financial people for local and regional publications.

With tearsheets from local markets as proof that I could write further in the field of business and finance, I approached the editor who had used my tax articles. I called her and asked for an appointment. I knew she was busy and my session would be limited, so I prepared a brief but comprehensive presentation on what I was now qualified to do.

I purchased a letter-sized folder with pockets. Into one pocket I put duplicate copies of all the business-finance articles I had done for local markets. In the other pocket was a neatly typewritten list of some twenty-five ideas—described in not more than two or three sentences—which I thought she might be able to use.

In the twenty minutes of our appointment, the editor glanced through the duplicate copies of my work, nodding her approval. Then she scanned the list of ideas, indicating those already assigned by the magazine, those which wouldn't interest the magazine's readers much, and those she could definitely use. "Start with this one," she said, indicating "How to Read a Profit and Loss Statement," and briefed me on the approach she wanted for her readers.

To write "How to Read a Profit and Loss Statement," I contacted several large corporations through their public relations departments, and asked for their profit and loss statements. I also read copiously from accounting books in the local library for explanations of the meaning of each figure and term on the profit and loss statement. Of course, I had to translate the more technical accounting terms into language which the layman could quickly understand. I had the help of an accountant who checked my explanations for accuracy and also read the finished article to ensure that it was technically correct.

Accurate Information Is All-Important

I must emphasize accuracy in writing about taxation, business, or finance. It is extremely important. Your readers are depending on you for information and advice about the way to handle *their* money. An inaccurate statement could mean that someone might lose hard-earned dollars! Always keep in mind that what you say in an article about taxation, business, or finance is often taken literally by readers. On the basis of what you say, your readers may be determining what to do with their money and the possible direction their lives may take—heavy responsibility, not to be taken lightly. Therefore, I strongly urge that everything you write be verified by an expert, be it an accountant, tax lawyer, financial manager, or whoever else is the expert in that particular field of money. Have your article verified *before* you send it to the editor. Few editors are versed in all the areas of taxation, business, or finance. The editor is depending on you, the writer, to hand in accurate copy. The editor is usually not in any position to make technical corrections in your information. Do not assume that if you are hazy on a point the editor will correct it. The information you impart in your article or book is substantially what your readers will get. Misinformation will mislead the average reader, and if an expert happens to read your article or book, and finds inaccuracies, he or she may very well bring that to the attention of your publisher, thus causing you to lose your credibility.

DRY SUBJECTS NEED LIVELY WRITING

When you are writing for a general audience, you must also write lively copy. Read and carefully study money magazines and books for the general audience. The most successful are replete with colorful examples and anecdotes to illustrate their points. It's very important to include specific examples and anecdotes when writing about taxation, business, or finance for the layman. These are heavy subjects. In order to "pull in" your reader, you must lighten up the concrete terms and advice. When interviewing an expert for an article, always ask for specific examples he or she has encountered. Listen in on dinner conversations, cocktail-party chatter, or neighborhood gossip when it deals with money matters. Many a colorful anecdote for an article has been picked up that way.

I branched out from writing solely for home and garden magazines to other magazines that carried articles about taxation, business, and finance. By flipping through magazines in your public library and newsstands, you'll see which magazines carry those types of articles. Note the differences in writing styles. Some magazines favor a tightly written approach. Note the level of vocabulary. It will differ with each magazine's audience. Note the advertisements in each magazine; they will tell you much about the economic level and aspirations of the magazine's readers.

Before you decide to write a query to a magazine, search through two years' worth of back issues to make sure your topic has not been covered similarly in the recent past. You might also notice that some magazines favor certain topics for certain monthly issues. For example, articles about end-of-the-year tax planning will usually appear in the December issue of a magazine. Allowing for the "lead time" of the magazine, you may have to get your query in as much as six months before.

Technical magazines on taxation, business, or finance almost always use professionals in the field. Unless you are a CPA or tax lawyer, you would probably not be writing for tax journals. On the other hand, if you *are* a professional, there is a big market for your writing. The prestige and publicity of being published in professional publications is often of greater value than the dollars, however. Some of them pay nothing but contributors' copies.

Authoring a Book

Perhaps you have already written a number of articles about taxation, business, or finance, and would like to write a book. Browse through your local library and bookstores. Scrutinize published books in your field to see what has been done. You must devise a fresh approach to your topic, outline your proposal in no more than three pages, include a cover letter detailing your credentials to write on the topic and any tearsheets of published articles, and send the package to a publishing house with a line of business books. Mail to only one publisher at a time, and don't be discouraged if you get a "no." Try another publisher.

Don't let the fact that you don't have an agent discourage you. Many books on money topics are sold without agents. The most important point in selling a book idea is that it be unique, solidly researched, and have wide appeal.

Build up a library on your specialty subject. Start with fundamentals such as a good business dictionary, an accounting dictionary, texts on basic economics. There are many government publications dealing with business and finance that can be obtained at reasonable cost. Write to the Government Printing Office and ask to be put on their list for mailings of their catalog of government publications. Call your local Internal Revenue Office and ask them to send you the list of Internal Revenue publications (for a fee).

You can supplement your home library by borrowing from the local library. Colleges and universities will allow you to use their libraries, often for a small (or no) fee. Many of them even have special libraries for taxation, business, and finance materials.

Taking Care of Business

Conditions in the field of taxation, business, and finance are changing every day. Therefore, you must stay informed by reading the business section of a quality daily newspaper such as the *New York Times* or by subscribing to the *Wall Street Journal*. The Sunday edition of the *New York Times* provides a good overall view of the week's business news in its special business section. Good sources for up-to-date information at no cost are the newsletters sent out by insurance companies and stock brokerage houses. Ask to be put on their mailing lists. Your savings and loan or commercial bank also will have a great deal of pertinent literature, yours for the asking.

I use letter-sized file folders to hold newspaper clippings, pamphlets, and so on. On the tabs, I write the general category with which the folder is concerned. If I'm collecting information for a book, each category usually represents a chapter in the book's outline.

Today, more than ever, business, finance, and taxation affect every aspect of our lives. The economics of these subjects have both simple and sophisticated aspects. Readers are clamoring for useful information. There is a bright future for the writer who can write on the most technical level, as well as for the writer who can write on the simplest level.

WRITING FOR THE BUSINESS AND FINANCE MARKETS
by Don German

The annual holiday party held each December by the American Society of Journalists and Authors is always an outstanding affair. It usually takes place in the spacious fiftieth-floor reading room of the McGraw-Hill Building and is literally covered wall-to-wall with nonfiction writers and editors.

An interesting point was revealed at the 1982 party. Standing near the bar with my wife and co-author, Joan, I was talking to several of our members—Julian Block, Dick Blodgett, Grace Weinstein, and Murray Bloom—when Dick said: "Look around. There must be at least a hundred writers here who specialize in psychology and another hundred who specialize in medicine. But when it comes to finance, there aren't many more than the few of us."

His comment was a good one. Business and financial writing is one of the least crowded of the specialty fields. How can *you* succeed at it? That I can't say, but I can and will share the way that Joan and I did.

BACKGROUND

When I was a child, I lived across the street from the Kingsessing branch of the Free Library of Philadelphia. At a time when only movie houses were air-conditioned, the building was always cool and inviting, even during the hot and humid days of a city summer. Best of all, it was filled with shelf after shelf of books. The librarian, Miss Kelly, was a delightful woman who loved books, but who loved children who enjoyed books even more. So, on long afternoons, from about the age of six, I often sat in the library's workroom, repairing torn and worn books with a gum-rubber eraser, a pastepot, and a roll of semi-transparent tape which had to be licked like a long roll of stamps and which dried, curled, and fell off six months later. In the meantime, like a two-legged bookworm, I set out to devour every volume on every shelf. I failed, of course; but I decided, above all things, that I would someday be a writer and add my own books to those shelves.

Years later, I tried studying journalism at Temple University. I quit on the second day, after the professor told me that, because he believed the intelligence level of the average American is that of a twelve-year-old, I would have to write for that level. So I majored instead in public administration with minors in economics, English, and personnel—a background that would help me to become a business writer, although I didn't realize it at the time.

College was followed by marriage, a term as an Army officer, then completion of the executive training program at a major Philadelphia bank. In 1964, when I was working as the advertising and public relations director of the Savings Banks Association of Massachusetts, a representative of a major financial publisher asked me to write a book about bank marketing. Despite initial fears, I agreed to try. I tried, the book was published, and that's where our story really begins.

Joan also had a marketing background. She studied business education at Temple and subsequently worked in several public relations jobs. When I began that first book, our son, Bob, was six, and Joan was bored with being a full-time homemaker. She wanted to join me in my new venture.

Thus, we greeted the book contract with the enthusiasm of the youthfully innocent. Here was our fortune, our future, our dreams! I immediately quit my job, believing that the writers whose books filled the shelves of my childhood library had made enormous sums of money and lived glamorous lives.

Hard Times

I can't recall the amount we grossed on that first bank marketing book, but I do remember that we calculated our earnings to be about ten cents per hour. So to earn grocery money during those first difficult years, we wrote, designed, and sold advertising folders for banks. Joan wrote the copy and did much of the artwork; I supervised the production and handled the selling. But we both felt that Joan should get to know the market as well. Since neither of us wished to risk our best prospects on her then-untried sales techniques, we drove to a strange town where the bankers were unfriendly, unlikely prospects, and I dropped her off, complete with briefcase, and picked her up at day's end. We need not have worried. On her first day, making an impossible sales presentation to a grumpy, elderly Yankee bank vice-president through the barred teller's window of a sleepy little office, Joan sold at least a ten years' supply of folders.

For several years, we struggled to keep going; many times I wanted to call it quits. Jobs in banking were plentiful in those days, and, responding to the commandment, "Thou Shalt Provide," which society then imposed so heavily on men, I gave serious consideration to each of the offers I received. But Joan talked me out of all of them and insisted that we keep trying.

Finally, our first real break came. We were asked if we would serve as the authors/editors of a banking newsletter. We accepted. For the first time as freelancers, this meant a regular monthly check; although stability had not yet arrived, it was on the way. One newsletter led to another and that to another, just as one book led to the next and the next.

Many people ask, "How can you and Joan co-author everything?" The answer is, "We don't co-author everything, just most things." I've written a few books without her, and she's written a few without me. In addition, I write more magazine articles than she does. For books we co-author, we use one of two systems: in some cases, one of us writes the first draft and the other does the rewriting; in other cases, we simply split up the chapters as work assignments and edit each other's copy. It's interesting that, six months after publication, we usually can't tell who wrote what, because our styles have become so similar.

Reasons for Writing

I have a friend who wrote what I consider to be a very successful book, even though he received no advance for it and earned total royalties of less than fifty dollars. When the book was written, the author was one of almost a hundred vice-presidents at a large bank. The book—not an especially good one, as the sales indicated—impressed the president and board of directors of the bank so much that, within six months, my friend was a senior vice-president. His salary doubled. By any standard, his book was a financial, if not a literary, success. So if you're in business and you want to *write for recognition*, that's fine. Publish and get promoted!

On the other hand, you may want to *write for a living*. Joan and I chose to write full-time. Since July 1, 1964, we have not earned any income from a salary; every dime has come from royalties, article fees, or editing fees, with an occasional honorarium for a speaking engagement.

How much can you earn from writing on business and finance? The payment is similar to any other type of nonfiction writing. As we tell people who attend writers' conferences, once you are established, it's an easy way to earn $10,000 a year—but only the top writers earn over $50,000 a year. The pay scale for magazines and books is the same as for other specialties.

MAKING MONEY WRITING ABOUT MONEY

How do you succeed as a business and finance writer? Or considering that there are two of us, how do two people jointly succeed?

It goes without saying that a financial writer must have basic expertise. My first job in the world of business was during high school, as a part-time mail clerk at the Federal Reserve Bank of Philadelphia. In all, I was employed in banking and finance for fourteen years, which included working my way through college at the "Fed," the old First National Bank of Philadelphia, Dun and Bradstreet, and the Insurance Company of North America. After those fourteen years, I began to write about it. The point is, before I began, I knew the language and had developed a wealth of contacts on whom I could call for information. We have kept many of the contacts over the years and added to them; we have built an impressive financial library.

I once calculated that I read ninety-six books to get an undergraduate degree. Now, I read more books than that in a year just to keep up in my field. The point is, to have real expertise, you need more than just an idea on how to make money in investments. You need to keep current in the field through both primary and secondary research.

Fine-Tune Your Writing

The first requirement to write on business and finance for a living seems almost too obvious to state, but at every writers' conference at which Joan and I speak, we see the need to mention it. Realize that *you must be a good writer.* There are literally tens of thousands of people with competent business skills who would love to write; therefore, the beginner must never assume that, because he or she has something special to say, editors will accept poor writing, sloppy manuscripts, or otherwise unprofessional work. Business markets are just as tough to sell to as others. One editor friend told us that she has had too many bad experiences to justify accepting work from people who are experts in a field but who can't write. And one magazine editor admitted that she pays lower fees than she should because she must pay so much for corrections and revisions.

Joan, as I mentioned, majored in business education. She is a fanatic on letter-perfect manuscripts. Until we bought word processors, she insisted that our typist make every page error-free. Now that the electronic brains of our computers have replaced the typist, Joan insists on even neater copy. Has this paid off? You'd better believe it! Like many professionals, we have a reputation for tight, clean copy and for faithfully meeting deadlines. As a result, we receive assignments each year that would not go to careless writers. We sell, on the average, about twelve magazine articles a year, of which eleven come as unsolicited assignments from editors. And this is just a sideline; we don't in any way consider ourselves specialists in writing for magazines. But we get the assignments because our work is accurate, on time, and requires little editing.

Keeping Afloat Financially

The second piece of advice we would offer you as a beginning business and finance writer is to *establish a base of income.* For us, this began as our newsletters and has expanded to include those magazines for which we have become "regulars." For some writers, a base income may come from a monthly column in a magazine; for others, the source may be a weekly column in a newspaper; for still others, it may come from writing advertising copy for a local newspaper or scripts for a radio station. Here's a rule of thumb: *For every ten dollars of total income that you need, have at least five dollars guaranteed from a regular base income of some sort.*

Many beginning writers keep their staff jobs while getting established. This is fine, if you can do it and still write. Joan and I chose to spend all our working time writing and selling our work. This made the struggle greater, but avoided the I'm-too-tired-to-write-tonight syndrome that plagues many beginners striving for creativity after eight hours on the job.

What if you decide to write full-time? There are many base-income opportunities for business writers. A local firm may need a freelance house-organ editor, for example, or a merchants' group may want a consumer newsletter. As a last resort, you can do as Joan and I did with our advertising folders: write and design something that you can peddle just to get started. I gave this advice at a writers' conference a few years ago, and a short time later received a phone call from one of the people who had attended—a minister who wanted to write on a part-time basis. "I wanted to tell you that I started a newsletter for a merchants' group," he said, "and it's working out fine!"

Selling Your Articles

The third bit of advice is *know your market*. This is a stumbling block for many novices, most of whom think immediately of the well-known magazines—99 percent staff-written. Look beyond the "obvious" markets to the many general-interest publications, house organs, and less well-known periodicals. Study *Writer's Market* as if it were scripture. You'll be amazed at the markets that exist beyond the obvious.

The magazine market is diverse. Because trade publications, house organs, and general-circulation magazines all have different requirements, the following is a good way to proceed in order to sell to magazines.

First, make a list of subject areas in which you are qualified to write—insurance, stocks, and budgeting, for example. Then, spend a day or two poring over *Writer's Market*. Read all of it. Using highlighting markers of various colors, mark each publication for which you feel qualified to write with a color to code it for a particular area of expertise. When you have an idea for an insurance article—*voilà!*—every possible market segment is coded blue. When you have a great scheme for budgeting, every possible market is coded yellow.

Marketing Methods

Finally, you have three choices when it comes to selling an article. You may query several publishers with an idea; you may write an article and send it to a particular editor; you may contact various markets in different ways. For example, we know one business writer who writes an article on a specific subject, then makes simultaneous multiple sales to *noncompeting* magazines. He says it works. We've never tried his technique, but we often sell several articles based on the same research, with each article slanted to the respective magazine. In any case, you should always be selling the next article or book while you are working on the current one. One successful writer friend estimates that he spends 25 percent of his time selling his work. From talking to other writers, this seems about average.

Joan and I have had good luck by simply writing to editors of likely magazines, enclosing a detailed bio-data sheet, and asking for future assignments. If you are just getting started, however, it is probably best to send a completed article. In this way, the editor can, at a glance, see your grasp of the subject, your writing ability, your style, and the approach of the article.

While we have many friends who write query letters, we seldom do. But we do use the telephone. With a phone query—or a phoned response to an assignment letter—we can discuss the article, get the editor's ideas up front, and subsequently confirm, with an outline, the form upon which we have mutually agreed. Phone queries allow much greater flexibility than written queries, but you usually have to know an editor well to use this technique.

Magazines may be categorized in many ways. Joan and I break them down according to the fees they pay. Some publications pay $100 or less per article; we know that writing for them is simply not cost-effective. Some pay $2,000 or more per article. However, we have been surprised to find that, because of the time it takes to sell to them, plus the extensive original research often required, it can be just as inefficient to write for these high-paying magazines. We have many professional writer friends who disagree, though.

We shoot, instead, for the middle ground, those magazines that pay $500 to $1,000 per piece. Articles for this market normally take much less time to write, yet these publications often offer excellent editorial backup in terms of copyediting, research assistance, and even in promoting the author.

SELLING BOOK MANUSCRIPTS

Most beginners shy away from the idea of writing a book. Personally I think it is easier to sell a book than an equivalent number of magazine articles. And a book gives you the prestige that opens the doors to other markets. The 2,000-plus publishers in America release about 45,000 books per year. Almost any publisher of trade books will consider a business or finance book with mass appeal, if it has a different angle and will fill a gap in the literature available.

In 1980, Joan and I turned down offers from several publishers to write a book about personal finance. After all, there are many on the market, ranging in quality from awful to excellent. Why reinvent the wheel, even a good wheel? Then, in March 1981, while doing research that involved a careful study of *Books in Print*, we came to a realization. Even though the middle class constitutes most of the population and pays 75 percent of the income taxes, no one had ever written a personal finance book dealing with the specific problems of this group alone. So we drafted a fourteen-page proposal outlining such a book and sent it to our agent. In turn, he had it reproduced and sent copies to twelve major publishers. Within one week, we had seven positive responses; at the end of the two-week auction, three publishers were still bidding. The point is, a good proposal for a book to fill a gap in the market met with instant acceptance.

At this point, a beginning writer might ask, "Do I need an agent?" to which we would reply, of the nineteen books we have had published, three were sold by an agent and two other contracts were negotiated by an agent after we had made the sale. If you are a shrinking violet, an agent is essential. If you live in the backwoods, as we do, he or she is your eyes and ears in New York. But you can get started without an agent, and probably will have to. Few agents will handle an unproved writer.

Book Markets

In addition to trade book publishers (a trade book is a book sold "in the trade," which means general-market works for bookstores), there are professional-book publishers that offer many unique opportunities for business and finance writers. Professional books are those designed for specific markets. They often have specialized sales outlets, the most common of which is direct mail to prequalified prospects. For example, we were recently asked by Warren, Gorham and Lamont to write a complete update and revision of *The Bank Employee's Security Handbook*, which we originally had written in 1971. Because there is a federal law that requires security training for bank personnel, this book meets a very specific need.

Publishers of professional books are especially interested in works on highly selective subjects. To enter this market, you need three basics: knowledge of the subject, excellent research facilities, and good writing skills.

Royalties for professional books, like textbooks, are usually scaled on a different basis from those on trade books. Typically, professional or textbooks earn 10 percent of the publisher's cash received, compared to the standard trade royalties for hardcover books of 10 percent of the retail price on the first 5,000 copies, 12½ percent on the second 5,000 copies, and 15 percent thereafter. But the differential can be more than offset by the price of the book, since professional books usually sell for at least $25 a copy (you would receive $2.50). Prices of $50 a copy are not rare. Also, trade paperbacks traditionally earn royalties of 6 to 7½ percent of the retail price, whereas trade-paper editions of professional books frequently pay the same 10 percent of net as do the hardcover editions.

Writing for Newsletters

Newsletters are perhaps the toughest market to crack, simply because most are self-published or staff-written. Your best bet is either to self-publish or try to join the staff of an established newsletter as a stringer, covering a specific locality or a designated field of expertise. The *Ayer Directory of Publications* can give you a reference point from which to develop a list of editors to contact.

STRIVE FOR ORIGINALITY

Whether you aim for magazine, book, or newsletter markets keep this in mind: what you have to say must be interesting, accurate, and, above all, different. The biggest mistake some beginners make is to read an article and exclaim, "I could have written that!" then try to sell essentially the same piece to the same or a competing editor. Be original!

One final comment. When Joan and I speak at a writers' conference or go to a cocktail party, often someone will say, "But do you ever do any *creative* writing?" The answer is that we do so every day. Both of us write poetry; two of Joan's juveniles are written in verse, and I have sold poems to a few fairly prestigious publications. I am at work on a novel that three publishers are interested in seeing. However, we sincerely feel that no work is more creative than quality writing in the field of business and finance. It requires the same careful research, polished writing ability, and all the other features that go into any good literary production. In the final analysis, we have learned, there are only two kinds of writing—good and bad. And that is true whether you are writing the Great American Novel or copy for the back of a cereal box.

Additional Resources

American Bankers Association, 1120 Connecticut Ave. NW, Washington, DC 20036. Offers aid in arranging interviews, annual reports, biographies, statistics, information searches, placement on mailing list, photos, press kits, publications list.

American Business Press, Inc., 205 E. 42nd St., New York, NY 10017. Member publications represent a "who's who" of the technical production and distribution services of America's industrial community. Offers publication and special research awards.

American Institute of Certified Public Accountants, 1211 Avenue of the Americas, New York, NY 10036. Provides comprehensive information on accounting and auditing. Offers aid in arranging interviews, annual reports, biographies, statistics, brochures and pamphlets, information searches, placement on mailing list, press kits. Most comprehensive U.S. library of published materials on accounting and related subjects. Numerous publications available.

American Management Association, 135 W. 50th St., New York, NY 10020. Arranges interviews; helps obtain data, statistics, list of books for sale. Publications include *AMA Digest*.

American Society of Business Press editors, 435 N. Michigan Ave., Suite 1717, Chicago IL 60611. Conducts research on editorial problems and practices; sponsors seminars; maintains limited placement service. Publishes monthly newsletter and bimonthly *Editor's Notebook*.

American Stock Exchange, 86 Trinity Place, New York, NY 10006. Provides historical, how-to and technical information, including how to become listed on the Amex (i.e., qualifications and paperwork required), market activity, trading information, compliance with securities laws, options market, gold coin trading. Offers aid in arranging interviews, brochures and pamphlets, computerized information searches, photos, press kits, research assistance, statistics.

Associated Business Writers of America, Inc., 1450 W. Havana St., Aurora, CO 80012. Part of the 6,500-member National Writer's Club; anyone writing in business field may join. Sponsors workshops, seminars, contests and a home study magazine writing course. Maintains a 2,000-volume library. Publishes *NWC Newsletter, Flash Market News,* and *Freelancer's Market*.

Department of The Treasury, 15th St. and Pennsylvania Ave. NW, Washington, DC 20220. Offers annual reports, biographies, placement on mailing list, news releases.

Futures Industry Association, 1825 Eye St. NW, Suite 1040, Washington, DC 20006. Provides advisory, analytical, historical, technical, trade information. Offers clipping services, informational newsletter, statistics; educational programs in the form of lecture courses, correspondence courses, seminars, and other activities. Publications include *Commodity Futures Trading Course, Financial Futures Trading Course, Introduction to the Futures Market.*

Institute for Monetary Research, Inc., 1200 15th St. NW, Washington, DC 20005. Offers information searches covering business, economics, industry, monetary questions.

International Association of Business Communicators, 879 Market St., Suite 469, San Francisco, CA 94102. IABC is active in education and research; it sponsors seminars, video teleconferences, annual international conference. Has an accreditation program and placement service for members.

International Executive Association, 122 E. 42nd St., Suite 1014, New York, NY 10017. Offers aid in arranging interviews; supplies statistics, press releases for special events, brochures, pamphlets. Publications include *Sales Executive.*

International Trade Commission, 701 E St. NW, Washington, DC 20436. Provides analytical and trade information covering trade data, economic issues concerning imports; reports in response to legal disputes involving imports and their impact on U.S. economy. Offers aid in arranging interviews, annual reports, biographies, brochures and pamphlets, information searches, placement on mailing list, newsletter, press kits. Publications include an annual report and investigation reports that are issued periodically.

National Association of Bank Women, Inc., 111 E. Wacker Dr., Chicago, IL 60601. Offers aid in arranging interviews, annual reports, bios, statistics, placement on mailing list, photos, press kits, publications.

National Small Business Association, 1604 K St. NW, Washington, DC 20006. Arranges interviews; offers aid in getting statistics, placement on mailing list, newsletter, photos.

Standard & Poor's Corporation Library, 25 Broadway, New York, NY 10004. Provides, "on demand, for a fee," analytical, historical, referral, technical and trade information searches, informational newsletter, research assistance, statistics, telephone reference services. Schedule of services and fees available.

Chapter Twenty-One

WRITING FOR
THE TRADES

It's a cliché, but nonetheless true: every magazine is different. Each appeals to a different audience and has a different set of advertisers. The editorial slants are different; the editors and staff writers are different. Nowhere in publishing is this more true than in the area of trade, company, and professional journals.

You've probably never heard of *Modern Tire Dealer, Airport Press, Footwear Focus, Soybean Digest,* or *Independent Banker.* Not only are these publications different in many respects, but there are more of them than any other kind of magazine. *Writer's Market* typically lists 170 pages of them in more than 70 categories, from "Accounting," "Electronics and Communications," "Library Science," "Petroleum," "Show People and Amusements," to "Water Supply and Sewage Disposal."

Trade journals—such as *Adweek, Iron Age, Datamation, Variety,* and *Women's Wear Daily*—speak to specific industries and aim to help readers in those industries do their jobs better by keeping them informed of trends, suggesting solutions to problems, and offering advice on how to conduct business more profitably. Most professions also have their own magazines, many published by professional societies, e.g., *American Journal of Physics, Bulletin of the American Mathematical Society,* and the *American Bar Association Journal.* And company publications are those magazines or newspapers produced by a single company. Sometimes called "house organs," these may be internal, for employees, or external, for wholesalers or retailers of a company's products. These publications form the largest group of specialized periodicals in the U.S. No one knows exactly how many company periodicals—both external and internal—exist. The best estimate runs around 17,000. And every week, month, or quarter, they go to press and writers are pounding out what they print, and getting paid for it.

If, as most writers are coming to realize, you have to be somewhat specialized to earn a living in the modern world, you must be very well versed in your chosen field to write for these voices of business and commerce. After all, your readers *know* the company, industry, or product lines you're writing about. Yet these periodicals are an excellent market for writers who energetically apply themselves—the trades are not only nearly infinite in variety and number, but are vital links in the American information network.

Here is a vast sea of knowledge that needs to be communicated and a dearth of people who are capable of doing so effectively. Here at last, instead of begging, hat in hand, you the writer are sought after as a highly skilled specialist in working with words. These people *need* you. Another bonus is that writing for the trades can lead to writing for business itself—probably the best-paying writing assignments around. Read what our ASJA specialists have to say, and you'll see that opportunities galore exist in this often overlooked field of writing.

ASSESSING TRADE AND COMPANY PUBLICATIONS
by Marv Wolf

What's the largest group of publishers in North America? A few clues: it's not newspaper chains; it's not magazines; it's not books; it's not newsletters.

Give up? Corporations—both profit and nonprofit—print more newspapers, magazines, newsletters, and books than all the rest of the publishing industry combined. They also produce special publications such as brochures, annual and quarterly reports, plus some hybrids variously described as magapapers or paperzines, which resemble newspapers in format but magazines in content.

The purpose of this paper avalanche is to promote the companies' interests and views on a multitude of subjects to widely disparate audiences, including employees, stockholders, public officials, customers, competitors, contractors, retired employees, and others.

Each of these tens of thousands of publications requires copy—billions of words every year. And while most companies have a writer on the payroll, often the volume of publications or the specialized nature of a one-shot project makes it advisable to hire a freelance writer.

WHO GETS ASSIGNMENTS?

What kinds of writers do corporate publishers hire? As a rule, the larger the corporation, the more specialized its demand. For instance, when I worked as editor-in-chief of a monthly magazine for employees of a leading aerospace manufacturer, we needed a series of booklets on employee benefit plans. And although we probably could have found the time—even if it meant burning some midnight oil—neither I nor my staff had much expertise in the arcane fields of pensions, stock purchase options, health-care plans, and retirement planning.

So, we sought the services of a small firm specializing in trade publications. They hired a pair of freelancers to come in and conduct in-depth research by reading bulging files and interviewing specialists in the corporate personnel department. We then took their first drafts, edited them for consistent style and company buzzwords, and sent them to the corporate legal staff for approval.

Which points to one of the biggest headaches in corporate publications: approvals. If you're writing freelance for *Geo* or the *New Yorker* or *Reader's Digest* or any of the consumer magazines or newspapers, your copy will go through a series of gatekeepers before it is finally published—or rejected. These gatekeepers will be concerned, mostly, with libelous statements, clarity of thought, and grammatical expression. Your copy will be treated with a large measure of respect, and, often, the editors are so good that you'll hardly notice their changes. In most cases, if there is a serious problem with your piece, you'll be given the opportunity to argue your point of view.

Corporations' Modus Operandi

This, however, isn't always the case with corporate publications, and for a variety of reasons. First, it's rare to find a talented editor working on a corporate publication and, even when there is, he or she doesn't have final approval authority. Approvals in the corporate world are usually complex and time-consuming. Often there are as many as a half-dozen individuals in the approval chain and, for important publications such as annual reports (sometimes even for much less visible printing), final approval is retained by the company president or chief executive. For most execs, visibility equals vulnerability. Since most corporations *must* publish an annual report, and it *must* contain certain data, executives assume that everybody who matters will read everything in it. They then make this assumption about everything else published by the corporation, and worry—excessively, I think—about the subtlest nuances.

I point this out not to discourage you from seeking corporate writing assignments, but to prepare you for the work. Corporations tend to be very conservative. They frequently appear humorless because they don't want to offend anyone—and most jokes, however well-intentioned, ridicule someone or something. Even veteran company employees often don't know much about future corporate strategies as conceived at the highest levels. Especially frustrating to the freelance writer on a corporate assignment is the timidity of editors on corporate publications staffs. They'll often blue-pencil a sentence, paragraph, or an entire section of a piece just because they are unwilling to chance their boss's disapproval. So be prepared for heavy-handed editing and sometimes infuriating obliqueness. If you are willing to (and risk losing the account), your best bet on an approval is to request a one-on-one with the senior executive.

Most freelance writing assignments in the corporate world are generated by someone in the public relations department of a company, although the department's *name* may well be something quite different from "public relations." Often, the department is headed by a person with a vice-presidential title; although these officials rarely report directly to the chief executive officer, they usually have a clear idea of what will be acceptable to the top execs. Some major firms have heavily specialized publication staffs with several layers of decision makers. The hierarchy will differ from company to company but, for example, it's common to find a department with separate staffs for *external* public relations (which deals with the media), *internal* publications, *external* advertising, recruiting, financial communications, and community relations (which deals with churches, schools, government, business groups, Boy Scout troops, etc.) Some of the largest companies split these staffs up into widely separated parts of the company; others bunch them under an executive charged with supervision of all company communications.

MARKETING YOURSELF

Wherever you find them in the corporation, none of these communicators is going to offer you an assignment unless they know who you are and what you can do for them. In general, corporations won't give work to new writers unless they have a clear and favorable idea of the writer's capabilities. The easiest way to get an assignment writing a company brochure is to show that you've already written a brochure for someone else. However, if you haven't written a brochure, you may be able to persuade them you have a sufficiently broad background in writing of other kinds, *and some expertise in the subject of the brochure.*

The only way to get in line for corporate writing assignments is to put your name and some demonstration of your skills before the decision makers. One approach is to prepare a mailing including at least a business card and some writing samples, preferably of published work. A modest brochure, listing your areas of expertise and a summary of your writing credits, will help immensely and need not be expensive to produce. I have done several of these, and in each case I've been able to trade my writing skills for a designer's talents, thus reducing the cost of a professional-looking brochure to printing and typesetting.

I've also, more than once, been able to trade a writing job for a printing job. Often a designer would like to have a capabilities brochure—but doesn't want to pay a writer. Or the designer has a client who needs a job designed but also needs copy written.

A writer seeking corporate work can easily assemble a list of several hundred major corporations and the executives who buy freelance writing. The majority of corporate publications staffers in North America are affiliated with a professional society, the largest of which is the International Association of Business Communicators (870 Market Street, San Francisco, California 94102). This organization, with 8,000 members in all fields of corporate and organizational endeavors, publishes an annual directory that lists members by name and is cross-indexed geographically and by industry. It is available by mail for a few dollars.

Another source of corporate addresses is the *National Directory of Addresses and Telephone Numbers,* a trade paperback available in most bookstores. Think of it as a mystery to be solved. Sometimes it's as easy as telephoning and asking whoever answers for the name and job title of the one(s) to see. Other times you write a letter. A good starting point is to ask a "Communications" Department secretary for samples of company publications.

Once contact has been made by phone or mail, the executives usually want to see the writer face-to-face at least once before making an assignment. So, in the beginning, it might be wise to limit your mail or phone contacts to those corporations within convenient driving or public-transportation distances.

You can also generate corporate assignments by approaching corporate editors who must cover factories, sales offices, or other facilities far from company headquarters. Employee publications are often starved for good features on workers at distant locations, as well as on operations and products at these sites. The ability to take good photos to accompany your writing is helpful. I keep a short list of such publications so that when I am to travel outside my local area, I'll contact the editors, tell them my travel plans, and ask for an assignment. While they rarely have a budget for full travel expenses, they usually come up with some expense money. For example, I once had to go to Wisconsin for an ad agency. I contacted a large pharmaceutical manufacturer with a plant and warehouse in Minnesota and told them I was going. They gave me a writing and photo assignment and paid the expense of a stopover in Minneapolis, plus the Los Angeles to Minneapolis to Milwaukee airfare, minus the amount it would have cost to fly directly to Milwaukee. The story was a human-interest feature requiring no special expertise about their company; they saved hundreds of dollars in expenses and got a story they otherwise wouldn't have had.

The Snowball Effect

Experience has shown me that the best way to get a big, juicy corporate assignment—like a company history or a special report—is to demonstrate your competence by taking on a variety of smaller, less exciting writing jobs first. Little things *do* lead to bigger things. If you're willing to be flexible, able to work hard to meet often unreasonable deadlines, are good at handling details, and *always* keep the company's interests paramount, corporate writing assignments can help hone your writing skills while learning about many different kinds of publications and writing styles. And they can go a long way toward keeping the bottom line of your own financial statement in the black.

GETTING PAID

How much should you charge for a corporate job? The fee depends on several factors, not the least of them your time. In general, large corporations won't flinch at paying large fees because they expect the best and know they must pay for it. Your fees depend on your expertise and your experience—these are very different things—and vary from as little as ten dollars an hour to as much as seventy-five dollars or more. (Expertise comes from schooling or education. Experience comes from having applied your skills to a job. My dad, for example, was a junkman for forty years; as a boy, I used to accompany him on weekends and during the summer. One result is that I have *expertise* in recognizing many different kinds of metals and alloys. But I don't have any experience working with metals.)

An easy way to determine rock-bottom rates is to find out the salaries paid to entry-level writers in corporations like your potential market. Convert the monthly salary to an annual figure, then divide by 52 weeks; divide that figure by 40 to get an hourly rate. Then add 50 percent to that figure, which is close to the minimum it costs the corporation to pay Social Security contributions, vacation and sick pay, retirement and bonus pay, and rent on the office space and equipment an employee uses. This should be the *lowest* figure you ask for; you can often get much more. Some companies with experience in hiring freelancers will simply ask your hourly rate and meet it—if, in their judgment, you can carry out the assignment. Smaller firms sometimes require an explanation. In addition to an hourly fee, all out-of-pocket expenses should be paid by the corporation, including auto mileage and meals. If typing paper isn't usually a billable expense, tape cassettes for interviews *are*.

My first corporate job was facilitated by a friend who introduced me to the woman in charge of creative services for a large real-estate chain. She looked at my portfolio of written work and listened to a tape of a radio commercial I had written and produced for my dentist in exchange for dental work. She then outlined the job: writing text for a one-shot magazine for sales agents in the field. She told me that if I wanted the job, she was willing to give it to me on the basis of my portfolio, but that the fee would be negotiated by another person, "our vice-president in charge of money."

While she was out of the office arranging my appointment with the vice-president, I had a whispered conversation with the friend who had introduced me. We hurriedly figured his hourly wage, multiplied that by the number of hours I estimated the job would take, and concluded that $850 would be about what it would cost the company to have him do the job. We agreed that I could ask for $1,200 and they might go along. But on my way downstairs to the vice-president's office, I decided to ask for more, on the theory that I could always come down but not likely ask for more.

Seated in the veep's office and observing his expensive suit, the tasteful art on the walls and his silver coffee service, I was both intimidated and encouraged. After we chatted for a time, he came to the point and asked me how much I wanted for the job. I looked him right in the eye and told him, "I think the job is worth $2,500." He never blinked. "That's about right," he said. "I like a man who knows how to ask for what he thinks he's worth." We shook hands and I went upstairs to begin the first of what proved to be a long series of one-shot writing assignments.

(Before that incident, I had been on the other side of the desk, working for a consumer-finance giant, for a services conglomerate, and for an aerospace company. When I interviewed freelancers, I usually had a budget figure for the total job. It was my practice to select a writer based on an assessment of his capabilities, then tell him how much I had in the budget for the writing. He was free to accept or reject the offer; I never bargained, because I immediately offered the highest figure I could and told the writer so in advance.)

They Want Experts

Writing for company publications offers the writer a chance at a great variety of assignments. It's important to have an area of specialization, however, because the largest companies almost always want to hire not only an accomplished writer but an expert in some field. Corporations frequently use freelancers when the project is long and difficult, and no one in the company has either the time or the special expertise required. Some company publications, notably those of the energy industry, are very well-written, lavishly illustrated magazines that rely almost exclusively on out-of-house contributors. Approaching the editors of these magazines is very much like making a deal wth a consumer publication, and the same techniques for researching and writing apply as well. They often pay as much as the bigger consumer periodicals, although they will just as often try to buy all rights or to get the writer signed to a "work for hire" contract. In California, a new law requires employers to extend all employee benefits, including insurance, workman's compensation, etc., to freelancers signed to work for hire. If the contract specifies work for hire, it's a good bet you can get a higher rate.

Since corporations routinely purchase goods and services from suppliers, they're used to signing contracts for them. But most of these purchases go through a central purchasing authority, and their standard document rarely looks like a literary contract. For this reason, I have developed my own, which is a simple letter in plain English stating what I give and what I get. After accepting an assignment, I usually take out two copies, fill in the blanks, sign both copies, and get the signature of the exec on both. Then we each keep a copy. I've never had anyone refuse to do this, although some are surprised at a few of my provisions. The letter, among other things, provides that unless otherwise agreed I retain copyright to the work, and that I reserve the right to use any nonproprietary information in any other type of writing I may do. Sometimes this gets lined out, but then it's usually good for some additional compensation.

WRITING FOR THE TRADES

Writing for trade publication is a lot like writing for specialty consumer magazines except that, in general, the rates are lower. But so are the standards of editing and the demands for creative approaches, so it's a good place for a beginning writer to break into full-time writing.

Most trade publications serve an industry, and since there are a lot of industries there are quite a few trade journals. Some industries have more than one trade publication; competition is often fierce between them, because they are trying for a very limited pool of advertising dollars.

Trade publications tell who is doing what in the reader's particular field. While articles are often written in the arcane language of a specific business, the content isn't much different from that of a small-town newspaper. So if you can learn the jargon, and have a nose for news, coming up with trade articles isn't terribly difficult.

There are basically two ways to get assignments. The first is to approach an editor, show him you have the requisite writing skills and a working knowledge of the industry, and ask for an assignment. The trouble with this kind of approach is that the editor often doesn't have a ready assignment; he would rather have you suggest one.

The second way is to get a company to pay you to write one. To find out what's going on, you have to talk to people in the industry. Companies' public relations departments are often eager to have their company's story told through trade publications because the readership includes not only competitors, but suppliers, contractors, financial backers, even potential new employees. So the public relations staffs will often cooperate in a big way, providing you with background material, setting up interviews with key people, and helping to clarify jargon. And you can bet they'll steer you away from trouble areas and proprietary information. Quite often your best sources for interesting details are rank-and-file employees who may not know that what they tell you so freely is not something management wants nosed about. But sometimes—more often than you might think—you can finesse this situation by working closely with a decision maker who'll let you generalize the information and say, "More than 1.3 operations per second" but not "1.3762 billion operations per second," or "twice as many as any other computer" but not "20 nanoseconds."

If the company you approach is also a company you have worked for in the past, you already have a basis for mutual respect and trust. You'll have to keep that trust if you expect to work for them again. And one way of killing two birds with one stone is to get the corporation to hire you to write a story intended for a trade publication. (They may even want to reprint it for the benefit of all employees, and that should be worth some kind of additional fee.) The corporation will *pay* you to get them good coverage in a trade magazine that maybe they couldn't get by sending the same information in themselves.

Is this kosher? It is if you tell the trade publication the article was prepared with the assistance of the company. Should you tell them also that you were paid for the writing job? That's up to you, of course. Most freelancers will tell the truth if asked and say nothing if they're not. But be absolutely sure of all facts on anything you send out under your own name.

Since much of the editorial well in trade journals is filled with corporate handouts, the product you present must be qualitatively superior to the handouts. That means digging for hard facts, writing a compelling lead, finding a novel slant to the subject and writing. When you do profiles of industry leaders, you will have to be more objective than the company's handouts might be.

Most trade publications are notorious for low pay and few will offer expenses. But they do provide a way to build writing skills, acquire good contacts within the industry—contacts who may later trust you with important stories—and develop an area of expertise. All of these are important if you intend to move up to writing for business journals like *Forbes* and *Fortune*, where your contacts and expertise make you valuable to cover stories of more general interest.

TRADE JOURNALS:
HOW SPECIALIZED IS SPECIALIZED?
by Ted J. Rakstis

Trade-journal writing has become extremely specialized and sophisticated. If a freelancer is going to succeed in the trades, he or she must select one industry, study all the trade papers regularly, learn the industry's jargon, and develop contacts.

—Barbara Mehlman, executive editor, *Madison Avenue*

The whole idea of having to specialize in trade-journal writing is absurd. The writer who does appliance retailing stories for me is the same one who can walk into a hardware store, a gift shop, a restaurant or wherever and come out with a top story. The skills you learn covering one trade easily can be applied to others.

—James J. Cassidy, Cassidy Associates

These quotes, both from veteran New York trade-journal editors, underscore an ongoing debate within trade circles. Is trade writing just a specialty, or has it become a specialty within a specialty? Can you swing from coverage of one business to another, or should you zero in on one industry and develop a reputation as an expert in a very narrow field?

There's no clear-cut answer, and the pros and cons may confuse the writer seeking direction. Nevertheless, if you're thinking about trying the trades, it's essential to listen to what the experts have to say on the specialist vs. generalist issue.

Today, most of my writing is for consumer magazines, and I contribute regularly to only one trade publication, *Playthings* (toy and hobby industries). But when I began my freelance career twenty-five years ago, almost all my work was for trade journals, covering a broad range of industries. I wrote about bakeries, pharmacies, restaurant-equipment dealers, plumbing contractors, toy stores, audio shops, fast-food outlets, boat dealers, lamp stores, florists, blueprint shops, and on and on through the Yellow Pages.

At writers' conferences over the years, I've preached the gospel of trade writing—either as the best entry-level opportunity into the magazine world or as a specialty that can be cultivated as a steady source of assignments throughout a professional freelance career. While researching this piece, I found that some experts agree with me while others contend I'm living in a yesteryear dreamland.

Dave Kaiser, a fellow ASJA member and long-time trade pro, observes: "My journalism career began as a reporter for daily newpapers, and from there I went on to photography, copyediting, radio newswriting, magazine editing, trade journalism, newsletter editing, and now daily editing. I consider trade journalism the most challenging, the most rewarding, and the place were novice writers will *fail* the fastest."

Ron Derven, a New York-area business freelancer, adds: "To hear the old-timers from the 1940s and 1950s tell it, you just walk into any retail establishment, talk to the owner, snap some pictures, write it up, and send it to an editor. These writers don't make much money today, possibly because they are approaching a changed market in the same old way."

Arguing the other point of view, Louis Alexander, former journalism chairman at the University of Houston and a *Newsweek* correspondent, remarks, "The same trade writing techniques I have always used still work well. There's still a constant need for how-to stories and case histories of successful business practices. It's likely that stories contain some business information more sophisticated than twenty years ago, but it's also likely that such practices are widespread and that writers know about them."

Before analyzing this issue further, let's consider some basics. Why write for trade journals? Quite simply, *because they're there*. *Writer's Market* typically lists more than seven hundred magazines in eighty-one separate trade, technical, and professional fields—and that's just for starters. For one reason or another, many trade journals that buy freelance copy aren't listed in *Writer's Market*.

The only comprehensive compilation of trade journals is the *Business Publication Rates and Data*. It lists every business publication that accepts advertising—an astounding total of 34,000. The index costs $77 (including postage and handling) and may be the best trade-writing investment you'll ever make. It can be ordered by writing to Standard Rate and Data Service (SRDS) at 5201 Old Orchard Road, Skokie, Illinois 60077. (Since SRDS publishes several volumes, be sure to specify that you want the trade-journal index.) If the price is too steep, you'll find the index in most public and college libraries.

WHAT TRADE EDITORS WANT

What are trade editors looking for? Whatever industry they cover, they all want detailed stories on developments within their fields—case-history success articles, new-product information, research and survey reports, stories on finance, customer relations, and any other information that will show their readers how to do a better job and make more money.

When you write for a trade journal, forget momentarily that you're a consumer and pretend you *own* the kind of business you're writing about. For example, if you want to do a piece for *Drug Topics*, look around a drugstore and ask yourself: "What does this guy do that I can copy to increase my profits?" Imagine that you're a pharmacist. Once you begin to think like an entrepreneur, you've mastered the first lesson in trade writing.

I stumbled into a trade field purely by accident and circumstance. With a journalism degree from Michigan State University and a master's in journalism from Northwestern University, I finished college without ever taking a business course. Moreover, I didn't read the business section of anything, because I wasn't interested. I scarcely knew the difference between a retailer and a wholesaler.

After one disenchanting year of newspaper reporting following graduation, I quit my job, confident that all the big consumer magazines would fight to buy my articles. Of course, nobody did. In 1958, after a year of total failure, I finally decided to run a classified ad in *Editor & Publisher*. I received one reply, from a Jerry Steinman, who was managing director of something called Nationwide Trade News Service, Inc.

Steinman was setting up a nationwide stringer network to supply business case-history features to nearly one hundred trade magazines covering diverse industries. He answered my ad but pointed out that assignments probably would be infrequent because of my small-town location in southwest Michigan. When I explained that I lived only forty miles from South Bend and Kalamazoo, seventy-five from Grand Rapids and one hundred from Chicago, he showed a bit more interest.

But at the outset, I knew I was going to have problems. "This is *business writing*," I told myself, "and I don't know the first thing about business." I learned fast, however. I found a few friendly local retailers willing to give me a crash course in the basics of small business—promotion, advertising, displays, purchasing, inventory control, profit margins. I did the same thing with wholesalers to learn the distribution and profit links that connect manufacturers with wholesalers and retailers.

If none of this makes sense, you're in the same boat I was back in 1958. It takes years to learn about retailing—after twenty-five years, I'm *still* learning—but you must begin now if you want to write about it. And, with universal computerization and the spread of national and regional discount and specialty chains, the job is far more difficult now than it was early in my career.

When you go out on your first retail interview, you may hear this kind of terminology: "end-caps," "markups," "SKUs," "loss leaders," "factory-direct," "footballing," "impulse-buying traffic areas," "inventory turns," "big-ticket," "cherry picking," "dating," "low-end," and myriad other bewildering business buzzwords.

(For the curious, "end-caps" are the ends of an aisle display; "markups" indicate the amount added on the wholesale price; "SKUs" are stock-keeping units—the number of different *kinds* of items, with each different piece counted as one (you may have 2,000 cans of Odor-O-No deodorant, but that would be counted as one SKU); "loss leaders" are promotional items or ad gimmicks, sold below cost to get customers into the store; "factory-direct" means that a retailer buys direct from a manufacturer; "footballing" is discounting; "impulse-buying traffic areas" are key spots in a store—near the cash register is a favorite—where promotional merchandise is set up; "inventory turns" are the number of times a year a piece has to be reordered; "big-ticket" items are expensive ones; "cherry picking" means the retailer picks only the items he wants to buy (old Star Wars figures instead of new ones, for instance); "dating" indicates that you order merchandise but don't pay until later in the year; "low-end" means cheap merchandise.)

At the wholesale and manufacturing levels, the task of assimilating industry details becomes even more complex. Indeed, manufacturing processes vary so much by industry category that I usually leave that entire field to others. Nonetheless, I believe that a writer who learns the nuts and bolts of merchandising can move in and out of a number of retail, service, and wholesale areas.

BASIC GUIDELINES TO FOLLOW

- Read about business regularly in your hometown newspaper, the largest metropolitan daily serving your region, the *Wall Street Journal, Business Week,* and whatever trade magazines you hope to write for. If you can't find them in your local library, write to the magazines and ask for sample copies and editorial guidelines.
- Before you send any query letters or try to interview anyone, study a wide range of trade publications in unrelated fields to

see what kinds of articles each publication uses, and who its audience is—retailers, wholesalers, manufacturers, suppliers, or advertisers. If your first effort clearly labels you as an amateur with no business savvy, you lose before you even begin.

• Buy *Writer's Market* and, if you can afford it, the *Standard Rate and Data Service Index* of trade journals, to identify potential markets—and to find out what various markets are looking for.

• Almost every trade journal requires photos as part of an editorial package, so even if it means going into debt, invest in a good 35mm camera with built-in automatic exposure. The best film to use is Kodak Tri-X, the most versatile black and white film for different natural-light situations.

• Keep your car in good condition. Unless you live in a big city and can rely on mass transit, you'll soon learn that profitable trade writing involves travel.

I wish I'd had such a tip list when I got my first call from Jerry Steinman at Nationwide. "I've got a test assignment for you right in your area," Steinman said. "There's a grocer who's got a big new walk-in cooler. Find out why he bought it, what it's done for his business, all that. The magazine is a grocery trade book called *Nargus,* and we'll pay you twenty dollars."

Even as far back as 1958, a twenty-dollar article fee didn't exactly thrill me, and I still hadn't bought a camera. And I knew absolutely nothing about the grocery business, let alone refrigeration. But this was a test. If I blew it, I knew I would be kissing off a broad new field of opportunity.

I studied some grocery trade journals and refrigeration manuals and finally called the grocer for an interview. Without a camera, I hired a professional photographer whom I had to pay, as I recall, fifteen dollars. That left me, after travel and other expenses, in the red.

But the effort paid off. The story sold with a "'good job" note from Jerry, and the assignments began coming in regularly. I bought a secondhand press camera, the bulky box kind you no longer see except in 1930s newspaper movies. (Years later, I finally junked it and bought one of the early 35mm models with automatic exposure, which has forever freed me from the misery of having to use flashbulbs.) Suddenly and most unexpectedly, I was in business on my own as a trade writer.

In those days, Nationwide had an arrangement by which trade editors paid them a basic fifty-dollar fee for a 1,000-word retail case history and four or five usable photos. Nationwide's writers got thirty-five dollars of that and, even though we were averaging only three cents a word, few of us complained. It was a far better deal than we could ne-gotiate on our own, and sometimes Steinman would come up wth a big fifty-two-dollar story or even a blockbuster eighty-five-dollar assign-ment.

I began to turn out three or four articles a week, operating in cities within a radius of fifty to seventy miles from home. Within a year, Na-tionwide gave me the impressive-sounding title of "Chicago-Midwest Field Editor." I was really nothing more than a gypsy journalist with a beat-up car, a typewriter, and a camera. Even so, the title looked good on my business cards and I milked it for publicity in the area daily.

By this time, I had become Nationwide's top producer in the Mid-west, but that very fact created problems. After cleaning out all the nearby cities, I had to travel farther to find stories. It became a matter of hitting a city 100 to 160 or more miles away and pushing hard day and night for three days to come up with eight or nine stories. In trade journalese, this is known as "scorching the earth." Since no trade jour-nals then paid any expenses, scorching the earth also meant scorching my wallet—with hotel, meal, car maintenance, and other substantial cash outlays.

In 1962, Nationwide fell into management disarray, and Jerry Steinman quit to start his own public relations firm. I developed a strong PR retainer account and began to cultivate consumer magazine markets. (A retainer arrangement is one in which the writer is guaran-teed a certain amount of money weekly or monthly in exchange for do-ing whatever work needs to be done. It offers a measure of security, but you must have a good idea of what's going to be involved before you set your rates, or you'll get burned.)

Steinman and I teamed up again in the late 1960s when he edited *Handy Bottle News,* a trade-association publication put out by the Glass Container Manufacturers Institute promoting the use of throwaway beer bottles (now illegal in some states). I profiled a number of restau-rants, taverns, liquor stores, and beer wholesale companies whose owners were willing to give free testimonials on how the new squat no-deposit bottle helped their business. But in 1969, Jerry lost this bread-and-butter account and was in financial distress.

Then he got an idea, the kind that can turn your life around. No-body, he realized, was publishing a beer-industry insiders' newsletter. In 1970, he started *Beer Marketer's Insights* with a goal of grossing $10,000 in the first year. When he sold $7,000 in subscriptions at $25 each within *two weeks,* he knew he was onto something and began turning down other lucrative work. Today, *Insights* is *the* inside news source of the beer industry. Steinman now has thousands of subscrib-ers who pay $117 a year for twenty-four issues, and he and his charm-ing wife, Irene, are living in luxury.

"I was lucky," Jerry told me not long ago. "*Insights* could have been a bust—but I stuck with it and turned down some very good accounts. After years of working with dozens of magazines in dozens of industries with Nationwide, now I'm a specialist publisher. But things could have gone the other way. Writers should keep 'alternative strategy' files—ideas you can fall back on if your first effort flops. That's the real secret of success."

Nationwide is long gone, and I know of no central source where trade writers can get assignments for a variety of magazines, unless they happen to hook up with a publishing house that puts out a dozen or so magazines in different trade areas. But, even there, for reasons I've never understood, I've found that steady work for one magazine rarely leads to assignments for other publications under the company's umbrella.

BE READY TO TRAVEL

Finding trade assignments is now largely a matter of contacting each editor on your own. Unless you live in a metropolitan area, you too may have to go forth and scorch the earth. (One legendary trade journalist of years back had his own small plane and hopped around the country with a collapsible bicycle among his gear.) But no matter where you live, there are trade editors looking for writers with basic business knowledge.

One such editor is Jim Cassidy, head of Cassidy Associates, a small New York marketing-research and communications firm. Cassidy, who has won two Jesse H. Neal Awards for outstanding business journalism, in the early 1960s became the first editor of *Discount Store News* at a time when the discount retailing blitz first began to alter drastically American merchandising practices and shopping habits.

"We had enormous amounts of space to fill around the ads, and we published twice a month," Cassidy recalls. "There were about forty product areas to cover, and I had to find writers in every part of the country. I didn't need experts in any one field; I just needed good general business writers with cameras and cars whom I could 'deep-brief' on what I wanted. I still operate that way. The best trade journalists are what I call 'circuit writers'—people who move around and tell me when and where they're traveling."

Cassidy's anchor client now is Whirlpool Corporation; he produces quarterly magazines for their dealers and service technicians. I worked for Jim for three years in the early 1970s, covering not only dealers but also dealer and service training institutes and new product and other company news. Since I live only twelve country

miles from Whirlpool's corporate headquarters, it was an ideal arrangement while it lasted.

"I use freelancers wherever I can find them," Cassidy explains.
"Since I can pay only seventy-five dollars per printed page, I try to get
every writer a story that will run three or more pages. I've always told
writers, 'I don't pay much, but I pay fast.' When the copy hits my desk,
a down payment goes out immediately, with the balance to come later.
Most freelancers are fed up with the payment-on-publication policies
of many trade books and appreciate my policy."

Unlike some trade editors, Cassidy doesn't mind the time he
spends rewriting. In fact, his crisp, staccato style is so difficult to emulate that I quit trying after my first two or three Whirlpool stories.
"Most writers give me newspaper-type leads on only one angle and
then scatter valuable nuggets of information throughout the piece,"
Jim says. "I take all the key story elements, summarize them in bullet-
style up front, and then let the writer's copy flow. It's still basically his
story; all I change is the lead."

The how-to-do-its of querying, interviewing, researching, and
writing are covered in other chapters of this book. But with the trade
journals you must be much more specific. I'd like to pass on just a few
tips that apply to any publication that pays on a per-page basis.

Write in Detail

First, pack all the detail you can into the story without padding. If
you go in with only a single-angle idea—say, a special dealer promotion or display—keep digging for other story elements. Research the
company's history, its position in the local retail market, strategies to
beat the competition, future expansion plans, and whatever else you
can find. If the businessperson you're interviewing has made any
speeches or written any articles, ask for copies and quote liberally from
them. Then, develop your single idea as the basic piece and use the
other material in two or even three sidebars. While consumer magazine editors often say, "No more than 2,500 words," many trade editors are starving for hard-hitting retail profiles and will tell you, "Write
it for what it's worth." Those extra words mean extra money.

Use Graphics

Second, think visually in every trade piece you prepare. If you
can, present the story in photographic sequence that will lure the editor into adding a photo spread to the text. Overkill with your camera:
take photos of *everything* you think might make a good illustration.

Make sure every picture has people in it and never let them look at the camera. (Don't forget to get signed model releases if the magazine requires them.) To further beef up your graphics, get copies of the dealer's newspaper advertising, direct-mail pieces, window posters, and anything else that can be reproduced in print. Using this technique, I've converted many stories that normally would run only three pages into five-page spreads.

WANTED: STORIES FROM SMALL TOWNS

Jim Cassidy, like virtually every trade editor, is inundated with story leads from the New York, Chicago, and Los Angeles markets. "What I really need are articles from the boondocks," he emphasizes. "When my writers travel for other magazines, I try to find them a strong Whirlpool story that they can pick up along the way. I hitchhike on them whenever I can, and I've bought and reworked many a story simply because it had an 'East Jesus' dateline, a story from a place that nobody ever goes to. I need those stories to show that I'm putting out a nationally balanced book."

The search for "East Jesus" datelines—and almost all trade editors want them—offers encouragement to small-town writers. Says Ron Derven, the New York-area writer I quoted earlier: "I am sometimes jealous of writers who live out in some section of the country where trade editors never travel. They have a wide-open market there and can do articles for many magazines. Often, editors hit the same cities over and over again. They really appreciate a good, clean article from some way-off place."

If you live on a farm, there are many open trade markets. Mike Shulman is an account executive for Dorf/MJH, Inc., a New York public relations firm with several agriculture clients. In his spare time, he freelances for farm magazines. "There are many farming trade journals looking for good freelance copy from the people who know the subject best, the ones who live on farms," Shulman says. "The field is opening up so widely that some journalism schools now are offering special instruction in farm journalism."

Shulman is among those who believe that specialization is the way to go in trade writing, and this point of view has many supporters. Now that we've studied the views of the trade generalists, let's hear from the specialists.

THE WRITER AS EXPERT

"Trade-journal readers have become very sophisticated," says

Ron Derven. "Absolutely all the people who read my stuff know more about the topic than I do. On a regular basis, I write about electronics, material handling, real-estate financing, and pension-fund investment, to name just a few specialty areas. There's no way you can start a freelancing career with those sorts of subjects."

Madison Avenue is a glossy advertising trade journal paying $350 to $500 for "average" freelance articles and up to $1,500 for stories by top ad-agency executives. Executive editor Barbara Mehlman observes: "There's very little chance for freelancers to crack *Madison Avenue* unless they know the advertising business inside out. Our long pieces almost always are staff-written, and our columnists are specialists. For example, Mel Friedman, who writes our 'Videotech' column, has established himself as a television-industry expert and writes regularly for such magazines as *Channels, TV Guide, Dial, On Cable,* and *Cablevision.*" She adds:

"We've had some really bad experiences with freelancers who claimed to have advertising expertise. We once got a query from a writer who proposed a story on how ad agencies use libraries. It sounded like a good idea, and we assigned it. The piece came in with nothing but a lot of elementary quotes strung together. As part of the story, we wanted material on computer data banks, but the writer finally admitted he didn't have the technical know-how to cover that angle. He got paid, but we never used him again."

Although he feels that a competent trade writer can cover many fields, Louis Alexander says he is in demand mostly because of his Texas connection and his knowledge of the energy field. Says Alexander: "If you're writing for laymen, a basic energy story written in simple language will do the job. But for people in the industry, you need to apply the basics to more complex subjects. That means knowing the ins and outs of financing, tax laws, and the typical energy-business practices of top-level corporate officials, which are obviously far more advanced than those of the sales manager or credit manager."

Dave Kaiser lives in Fort Lauderdale and works the sprawling south Florida market for such trade magazines as *CB Quarterly, CB Times-Journal, Florida Golfer, Florida Golf News, Tennis East-West, Tennis Illustrated,* and *Tennis Trade.*

"So far, I've always been in the right place at the right time," Kaiser explains. "When tennis was popular, I worked for four noncompetitive tennis publications at the same time for four years. After the tennis craze died down and two of the magazines went bankrupt, I moved into golf. With citizen's band radios, I was writing about them in the late 1950s, long before they were a national fad. When the CB boom did hit, I was ready with stories for both trade and consumer magazines." He continues:

"Later, I saw the bottom falling out of the CB industry and

switched over to ham radio, which is beginning to get busy. In the meantime, spinoffs are available for overseas sales, since CB just now is getting popular in England. The point is that, if one field begins to stagnate, you've got to move into more lucrative ones as the market dictates."

Kaiser advises all freelance writers to aim first at the best-paying magazine in any field and try to produce enough articles to make the publisher want to put the writer on a retainer basis. If this gambit fails, he advocates "reverse marketing," in which the writer seeks a retainer from a competing magazine. "If the tactic works, fine; if not, you continue with the original magazine," Kaiser concludes. "But from then on, the competition will notice your bylines more often and probably will contact you later with an offer."

Kaiser traces the transformation of trade publishing back to the early 1960s. His analysis: "Trade writing evolved from entry-level freelancing into the tough nut it now is due to sophistication and competition. When publishers were looking for new fields to enter in the 1960s and 1970s, they rushed into many trade areas previously occupied by only one or two other magazines. They often either bought up the assets of an existing magazine or began their own in direct competition. Suddenly, that particular market became deluged with very competitive and highly specialized magazines that needed writing to match. Such writing obviously required more knowledgeable writers who were specialists, or freelancers who were experts in that field, and were paid very well on a retainer basis."

The trend to ultraspecialized trade publications is accelerating. As one example, International Thomson Business Press (ITBP) is based in Radnor, Pennsylvania but is financed largely by North Sea oil money via its British parent company. In March, 1981, ITBP took over Litton Industries' publishing operations, including its medical magazines, for $61 million.

Says ITBP president Richard Groves: "We identified industries we wanted to be in. We like the medical field; people are living longer and the growth of the doctor population is astronomical. In machine tools, we see growth because of the dire need for machinery that can increase productivity. That's why we bought Huebner Publications, with its metalworking focus. A third area is export/import, and in 1980 we bought *Brandon's Shipper* and *Forwarder* in that field."

According to *Madison Avenue,* many other business publishers are spinning off new magazines from established ones to serve new market segments. For example, Chilton Company has launched a series of specialized automotive magazines: *Owner Operator* (1969), *Automotive Marketing* (1971), *The Specialist* (1977), *Truck & Off Highway Industries* (1979), and *Truck Salesman* (1981).

At a time when many magazines are folding, the trade press is thriving. Harcourt Brace Jovanovich Publications (HBJ) has a corporate policy of launching two new ventures a year. Robert Edgell, HBJ chairman, identifies energy and health care as among the fields that look hot in the years ahead. Another major trade house, Miller Freeman Publications, is spinning off into new mining and natural-resources magazines.

The question of generalist vs. specialist trade writing is one that each writer must decide for himself or herself. I think it comes down to this: trade writers can overlap from one business to another if they stick to retailing and other merchandising subjects—that is, the transfer of goods. But once they try to write for such fields as manufacturing, finance, insurance, electronics, and computer technology, they should probably choose one field, become knowledgeable, and stick with it.

As new industries open up, magazines that cover them need writers willing to learn along with others in the business. Perhaps the best current example is the burgeoning field of cable television. Early in 1981, I connected with a new magazine, *Cable Marketing*, whose readers are all upper- and middle-level cable-TV management people. The fact that I'm a cable-TV junkie and know something about the new national satellite networks and pay channels was only a small help; I had to learn a whole new lexicon of technical jargon and marketing theory and practice. Yet I did it and sold seven full-length marketing pieces to *Cable Marketing* in one year. Says *Cable Marketing* executive editor Nicolas Furlotte: "We're open to freelance submissions, and we don't expect our writers to be cable-TV experts. They must, however, have a solid background in sales and marketing."

THE PAY SCALE

As in any magazine category, trade-journal pay rates vary incredibly. Some still pay five cents a word or less, don't pay until publication, refuse to pay expenses, and will look at manuscripts only "on spec." I can't report on these because I don't write for them, and I don't know anyone who does. The better trade magazines now pay ten to fifteen cents a word plus "reasonable" expenses; these are the ones I deal with. Many consumer publications can no longer match the better trade rates, and a solid trade magazine has a much stronger chance of succeeding than a gimmicky new consumer experiment. In a recession economy, magazine purchases often are among the first things chopped out of a family budget. Businesspeople, on the other hand, can't work in a vacuum and *must* read trade journals to ensure economic survival. As one example of corporate longevity, Geyer-McAllister Publications, publisher of *Playthings*, has been in business since 1877.

Appearances Count

If you want to try trade writing, in whatever field you select, remember that first impressions are just as important as basic knowledge and skill. This applies not only to your query letters and manuscripts but also to your personal appearance.

A recent book on freelance writing (*not* published by Writer's Digest Books) offers some of the most disastrous advice I've ever read: "Tennis shoes, faded jeans, a T-shirt—when you're freelancing, your wardrobe doesn't have to be fancy. Other professionals (photographers, politicians, chimney sweeps, salespeople) have to look clean and pressed . . . but not you, freelance writer. People actually expect writers to look a little bohemian."

Contrary to this incredible statement, people who look and smell like skid row bums or inhabitants of a hippie commune are *not* welcome in most business establishments. When you interview businesspeople, wear a conservative suit and tie or an appropriate dress. Even if your interview source should turn out to be a sartorial slob, it's always safe to be overdressed. I know of one major national advertising agency that lost a Fortune 500 industrial account simply because its "creative people" showed up at corporate headquarters wearing T-shirts, jeans, and sandals. The marketing vice-president went into a rage when he saw them, and two weeks later the company assigned all its national advertising to another agency.

Trade Writing as an Occasional Bonus

Although you may not want to devote your entire freelance career to trade journals, they can sometimes generate extra income for minimal effort. For instance, if you're traveling, either on vacation or assignment, take your camera with you and keep your eyes open for unusual store promotions or displays. With an investment of a roll of Tri-X film and half an hour or so of interview time, you could make an easy extra sale. When you get home, find a likely prospect in *Writer's Market* or the *Standard Rate and Data Service* trade index. If your first try doesn't click, keep querying other magazines in the same business until you hit pay dirt.

You may be able to get a trade assignment if you're traveling for another publication in an area where there's a good story, but I have a firm policy of never using one magazine's expense money to finance work for another publication. One way to handle this is to contact an editor, tell him where you'll be and what the story is, and it's highly likely that he'll agree to pay for one night's lodging and several meals.

In this case, the source of your primary assignment pays the travel expense, and the trade editor picks up the tab for your extra day on the road. By checking ahead to see what successful toy and hobby stores are operating in an area I'm covering for another magazine, I've several times been able to earn an extra $250 to $350 from *Playthings,* plus one day's expenses. Furthermore, if you're an expert in another specialty area, look closely into the business aspects of your field and go after those plus sales.

When you run into a good merchandising operation, think beyond just one sale to one magazine. As Dave Kaiser pointed out, he once worked simultaneously for four noncompetitive tennis magazines. But make sure that they are just that—*noncompetitive.* (One might be aimed at retailers, another at wholesalers, and others at manufacturers and parts suppliers.) If you try to sell the same story and photos to two competing magazines, your name may begin to circulate unfavorably throughout the industry you want to cover.

As for reprint opportunities, they're not as abundant in the trades as in the consumer area, but once in a while you can get lucky. Several years ago, a retailing story I wrote for *Mart,* an appliance trade journal, was purchased for reprint in a college business-school textbook. Or, a manufacturer whose product is featured in your story might ask to buy reprint rights for promotional purposes.

BUSINESS IS HOT NEWS

Remember one fundamental fact: business writing today is the hottest field around, and opportunities abound beyond trade magazines themselves. Business writing is covered in depth in another chapter, but trade-magazine experience can prepare you to write on business topics for the better-paying consumer magazines.

Drawing on my knowledge of retailing, for example, in the late 1960s I sold articles on the toy industry and retail give-away games to the *Chicago Tribune Sunday Magazine.* The ever-colorful toy trade also gave me solid material for articles in *Kiwanis, The Lion, Chicago* and two pieces in the now-defunct *Today's Health.* I also came within a pen scribble of signing a bonanza book contract for a vanity biography of an egomaniac toy industry tycoon, but at the last minute decided my sanity was more important than any amount of money.

Magazines such as *Kiwanis, The Lion,* and *Elks* all have business-oriented readers and, once you go through business-writing boot camp with trade publications, your expertise can carry you into broad consumer business writing. Over a period of more than twenty years, I've sold dozens of consumer pieces on such business subjects as shopping malls (when they were still new), trading stamps (when they were red-hot), bankruptcy fraud, small-business bankruptcy, business arbitration, industrial espionage, the culture boom in business, drug abuse in business, why executives need regular vacations, early retirement for executives, the trend toward corporate relocation in small towns, the business side of baseball, the cable-TV phenomenon, fundraising as a big business, and humor in advertising. One *Kiwanis* article, on the temporary-help industry, was reprinted in *Reader's Digest* and enabled me later to sell several originals to that publication.

The trade market, rich and robust, is out there waiting for new talent and ideas. If you decide to try it, good luck—and good business!

WRITING FOR TRADE MAGAZINES
by Alan Caruba

I am the master of the 1,500-word article. I thrive on sidebars. I do my own photojournalism. Editors love me. I know what they want as much as six to nine months in advance. On the average, I have articles appearing in three to five magazines each month.

Sounds like the freelancer's dream, doesn't it? It is.

There's a catch, however. There's always a catch. Few of the magazines I write for ever pay me a dime. How, then, do I manage to satisfy a taste for Cadillacs, travel, wine and good food, fashionable clothes, and the good life?

I go where the money is! In America, the only source of real money lies with Big Business. Even middle-sized business. But *business*, definitely.

Specifically, where trade magazines are concerned, this means writing and "placing" (securing publication of) articles which are underwritten by a corporate or business source. Thus, the magazine gets the article at no cost, while you are paid by your client. This means, of course, you have to understand your client's business and, to some extent, what is newsworthy to the magazine.

Ironically, most writers' greatest weakness is a significant ignorance of business and industry. This extends to the way they conduct the business of writing for a living. Since so many writers have a liberal-arts education, it may seem unfair to berate them for having no business sense, but having no sense at all about how best to use their major money-earning skill is the reason why so many writers simply do not prosper or enjoy the kind of income they deserve.

Too often, writers undervalue their own skills and services.

But let's look at the wonderful world of trade magazines and examine how a freelancer can exploit it to earn a good living without having to suffer the trials of dealing with consumer magazines.

WHAT'S THE DIFFERENCE?

Trade magazines, as the name implies, are business-to-business magazines. They are designed to inform businesspeople how they may better operate their businesses. Who reads them? Management and sales people primarily, also engineers. The object is to spot trends or at least be aware of them and to find ideas they can apply to their responsibilities. The trades are invaluable for selling one's products or services to other businesses.

The Trades Are Booming

Until fairly recently, relatively little hard data was collected about the trade press, but the American Business Press conducts studies of some 2,400 trade publications to track revenue and other trends. To give you an idea of the role trade magazines play, the total estimated revenue for the trades in 1980 was more than $1.9 billion.

For a professional writer, the trade press is virtually a gold mine. First of all, there are so many magazines out there and their need for quality editorial material is endless. I have written for an extraordinarily diverse number of trades ranging from *Restaurant Hospitality* to *Pit & Quarry* to *Pest Control Technology*. I've written for readers in the fields of lodging, restaurants, hospitals, nursing homes, dairies, airlines, laboratories, earth-moving equipment, pharmaceuticals, and marine engineering, to touch on just a few topics.

Am I an engineer? No. Am I a physician? No. Am I trained in hotel or restaurant management? No. Indeed, the only thing I do is write. I am a writer.

Or to put it my way, I package information. I don't have to be an expert in every area I write about. What I do need to know is where to find the experts. I let them provide the information I prepare in the form of magazine articles.

This is quite different from the consumer magazines where, increasingly, just being a writer is not enough. Often, in fact, it helps to be a celebrity of some sort to get published by the consumer magazines. Short of that, one had better have an excellent reputation and super credentials to write for consumer publications. Part of the reason for this is that one is often dealing with an editor who has no such qualifications and, thus, yours become a kind of insurance policy for the editor. "Well, Lester, here, says that the proper nutritional dosage would be . . . and he's written two books on the subject."

Trade Editors Are a Writer's Best Friend

Unlike the editors of consumer magazines, trade editors tend to become solidly entrenched in a single industry and, once a rapport is established, you can return to the same editor year after year with story ideas. In some cases, almost month after month.

Consumer magazines, of course, are locked in a constant struggle for subscribers and off-the-rack readers. This is most evident in the desire of consumer magazines to fill their pages with something "new and exciting" every month. I cringe every time I hear an editor tell a group of writers they're looking for something "new and exciting." There is very little that's truly new and exciting every month and certainly not in topic areas such as diets or how to improve one's sex life. Eat less, touch more are probably the only answers anybody has come up with that matter, but editors tread the same ground year after year, endlessly seeking something "new and exciting."

The trade press wants something else. They want to know about things which will *help their readers function better in their jobs and increase the profits of their companies.* The how-to article is the staff of life to trade magazines, which thrive on useful, applicable information. Case histories of successful operations are an endless source of article material.

There's another major difference between selling to the trades and to consumer magazines. If the article is good—well written and well researched—trade magazine editors will rarely tamper with it. One seldom has this professional satisfaction with consumer magazines, whose editors feel compelled to take a perfectly well-written article and grind it into the literary pablum they feed their readers every month. There are exceptions, yes, but they *are* exceptions.

There is very little protection against this practice, except to assert very loudly up front that you will not have your byline material changed in any fashion without your permission *prior* to publication: "I won't insult you by sending you a piece of junk, Mr. Editor, so don't insult me by turning my work into junk."

The consumer press, of course, is becoming fragmented into an astonishing variety of "vertical" readership categories. This is a plus for any freelancer with a particular specialty. Consumer magazines are now put together on the basis of demographics; they are intended to appeal to a particular age, ethnic, income, or special interest group. Not everybody reads *Yachting* or picks up *Metropolitan Home.* A young girl may start off reading *Seventeen,* move on to *Cosmopolitan*, and end up reading *Redbook* or *Working Woman.* While the fragmentation and presence of many new magazines is a boon in one respect, it also presents a terrible problem to the writer who has geared his article to the "wrong" age group or "wrong" income group. The worst part of this demographic quagmire is that the editors, more often than not, haven't a very good idea of who their readers are. Few editors really bother to sit down and analyze these matters, because they're too harassed with the problems of putting out the next issue or the issue three or four months down the line.

Worse still, consumer magazines tend to use the committee system to decide whether to buy an article or not. Nothing insures blandness and dullness more surely than a committee which may not only do the buying in concert, but may also all want to pass judgment on the text as well.

An Editorial Horror Story

In one case, I was approached by a consumer magazine based on a recommendation that I was an expert in a particular subject area. I am probably the only professional writer in America specializing in structural and ornamental pest control. Don't laugh. Like death and taxes, there will always be cockroaches and rats. My credentials were fine and the article on termites was commissioned.

What I got back from the editors was nothing resembling the text I submitted. In this case, the committee approach had decided that their readers could not possibly survive a lively presentation of the information and had gone to work to reduce it to hash. After all, they reasoned, isn't all the rest of the magazine written to the IQ level of a ten-year-old? To their amazement I refused to let them publish. In the end, in reponse to their pleas, I let them put out their version—complete with their errors based on their ignorance—and accepted a fee for "research and consultation." My name was not to be involved with the published article in any way and I refused to be held responsible for it, not even for the data I provided.

This plain, hardnosed dealing is necessary when the product you're providing carries your personal reputation with it. Remember, once in print, you can't easily retract anything you've said, particularly if someone has changed your words and given them a new, perhaps erroneous, interpretation.

THE ULTIMATE FREELANCER

Writing for the trades requires that you possess some skills beyond just being able to write well. However, if you are less than a very skilled writer, you'd better study your craft and work to improve yourself in every way. Bad writing announces itself faster than day-old fish.

Time was, the freelancer dealt exclusively with editors whose fees for magazine articles made up the bulk of a writer's income. Writers who regularly sold their work to magazines such as the *Saturday Evening Post, Collier's, Pageant,* and *Life* could earn a decent living in the so-called golden age of magazines, when a byline in a handful of highly regarded magazines carried considerable prestige.

Despite the proliferation of magazines today, a writer who depended solely on magazine writing would simply starve to death. The pay is dreadful. It has not, for the most part, increased over rates paid in the 1960s and earlier. Magazines earning several thousands of dollars for a single page of advertising are still paying fees that are in no way comparable for the text that fills the pages between the ads.

Anyone with a lick of sense would ask the obvious question: If I can't earn a living from the magazines, who will pay me to write for them? This brings us directly to the trades. There isn't a business enterprise or industry that doesn't need to communicate news of its products and services. Moreover, within the various corporations and companies that abound, there are men and women who want to advance their careers by having their names on "bylined" articles that give the impression they are deep thinkers.

In one typical situation, I received a call from the director of communications of a major chemical manufacturing company. One of his top executives was on the editorial board of an industry magazine and owed them an article on a management subject. Unfortunately, the man not only didn't know much about the subject, but was vacationing at the very time the article was due. I was called in to write the article in approximately three days' time. This points to an aspect of the freelance writer's life that is virtually a constant: you're rarely given sufficient time to do the job as you'd like, to research an article and to write it. Thus, survival depends heavily on developing the good journalistic skills that permit you to get data quickly and put it on paper swiftly.

It is my view that few of the articles and certainly none of the speeches by businesspeople are actually written by them. There is a world of business to be had for professional writers if they can penetrate the corporate castles.

Getting Your Foot in the Door

Most often, however, entree is achieved via a third party and this tends to be a public relations agency serving a client. Make no mistake about it. The function I have been describing is a public relations service and it is, in most cases, "work for hire." That is to say, you receive a fee and the article belongs to the agency or client underwriting your fee. Unless, of course, you simply assert your copyright by stating on the manuscript that you are selling "First North American Serial Rights Only."

Many public relations agencies need additional or specialized writing talent on which they can call to help service a client. In the early years of independence, I made my availability known to the agencies as well as to corporate directors of public relations, many of whom are now titled directors of communications.

Apart from magazine articles, you may end up writing a whole variety of materials such as brochures, annual reports, advertising copy, and entire newsletters.

In essence, you must become very skilled at self-promotion, and the best way is in the form of direct mailings based on up-to-date lists of who's who in public relations agencies in your geographic area, as well as the who's who of corporate communications executives. The best two sources of information on this are *O'Dwyer's Directory of Public Relations Firms* and *O'Dwyer's Directory of Corporate Communications*, each updated annually and available from J.R. O'Dwyer Company, 271 Madison Avenue, New York, New York 10016. An investment in either or both is well worth it, and can be written off as a tax-exempt business expense.

There are many directories available which can provide "leads" to prospective business. Another excellent one is Gale Research Company's *Encyclopedia of Associations*, which lists thousands of organizations, any one of which might need your writing skills.

Direct-mail promotion to the market of your choice can be a cover letter and a single "fact sheet" listing your professional affiliations, awards, services, and publications where your work has appeared. Or it can be as simple as a postcard reminding people you're around to help.

Sometimes a nice brochure or pamphlet, preferably letter-sized, can prove helpful, but you should look as professional as possible. In brief, you can be as straightforward or as creative as you wish. You can spend as much or as little as you wish. The purpose of direct mail is simply to stimulate an opportunity to work. The more extensive the list, the more likely the opportunity, but sometimes even direct mail doesn't work.

Another approach is to write an article on topics of interest to public relations or corporate communications people which is published in their trade magazines. I regularly seek to be published in magazines serving those areas or industries in which I want to establish a reputation as being knowledgeable.

Frankly, I am wary of space advertising, as it seldom seems to generate business.

Personal contact by phone or socially at business meetings inevitably seems to have the strongest motivational effect. People like to see you personally.

Still another way of keeping in front of your market is public speaking. If you feel comfortable in front of an audience, speech-making is an ideal way to develop your professional reputation and make important contacts that lead to assignments.

You cannot afford to be shy and retiring if you're seeking to be independent as a writer. An aura of expertise and authority is important and allows you to set the parameters of any assignment you undertake. For example, you will want to be reimbursed for travel and lodging if you have to work "in the field," wherever that may be. This is in addition to a *per diem* (daily) fee for the time you spend outside the office interviewing and perhaps taking photos. Such matters have to be set forth candidly—and early—in any discussion.

A rule of thumb that works well for me is that I will generally spend two days in the office for every day spent outside on assignment. Thus, even a one-day trip represents three days' work.

Membership in professional organizations is very important if you are to further your reputation and make contacts that lead to assignments. I belong to several local and national organizations for this purpose alone. In addition, such memberships serve as part of my credentials. Since I rely on the public relations field for assignments, I am a member of the Counsellor's Academy of the Public Relations Society of America and the International Association of Business Communicators.

I want to maintain my reputation as a working journalist, so I also belong to the Society of Professional Journalists. Because I also take photographs while on assignments, I'm a member of the National Press Photographers Association.

Having written a book or two in earlier days, I maintain my membership in the Authors Guild, and as a book reviewer, I am pleased to be a charter member of the National Book Critics Circle.

I am, of course, particularly proud of my membership in the American Society of Journalists and Authors, which puts me in the company of some of the nation's top freelance writers, people whom I admire professionally and personally. I joined the ASJA when it was still the Society of Magazine Writers, and have seen it evolve.

Am I just a compulsive joiner? Not at all. Memberships in these organizations serve as subtle signals of my skills for those who are examining my curriculum vitae. In my case, I offer a regularly updated "Fact Sheet" which succinctly spells out my memberships in these organizations, listings in prominent directories, awards, former affiliations, and a long list of the magazines in which my articles have appeared.

Such a fact sheet is dynamite for locking up assignments.

As you may have guessed, "visibility" is a key factor for staying active and busy.

Another way of achieving visibility is to enter contests where your work has a chance of earning you an award. There are endless contests around. So many, in fact, you can purchase a paperback book published by Facts On File, Inc., called *How to Enter & Win Non-Fiction & Journalism Contests.*

As freelance journalists, it's always important to keep in touch with what's happening in the trade, so I would recommend subscribing to such publications as *Editor & Publisher* (which annually publishes a directory of journalism awards). Other publications you will want to read include *Public Relations Journal, Advertising Age, Marketing Communications,* and *Business Marketing,* to name just a few. There are also excellent newsletters such as *Jack O'Dwyer's Newsletter* on the public relations industry, or the other giant, *Public Relations News.* Reading such publications will provide many valuable bits of information as you seek to sell your skills to those in a position to purchase them.

I often pick up leads as to what agency has acquired a particular account for which I can do work, and I am not hesitant to write a letter indicating just how I can be of help. Every letter I write I also follow up with a telephone call.

If this all sounds like a great deal of time devoted to selling your skills, you're right. Without the sales work, you have no reason to approach the editors of trades with stories you want to "place" with them.

SELL, SELL, SELL

"Placement" is one of the most highly prized talents in the public relations or marketing communications business. It is the ability to sell a story to the editor. You may be a fine writer, but if you stammer and stutter on the phone with editors, you won't last long. You must develop the ability to pick up the phone, call the editor "cold," introduce yourself swiftly, cite your credentials, and get on with the sale. Many times, I sell an article to an editor who has never heard of me prior to the moment we first talk. I consciously think through what I will say to such an editor, trying to give an authoritative quality to my presentation. "Yes, I have a background in restaurant management now for many years and I think this story represents a breakthrough of sorts."

At this point, you may be saying to yourself, "If I have to go through all this to place articles with editors, forget it."

And you'd be right again. The freelancer must live by his or her wits. It's a combination of writing talent and ability (the two aren't the same), plus the willingness to function continually in a sales mode whereby a part of every day is devoted to developing new sales opportunities.

People in the position to hire your skills must be continually informed that you are available. "Continually" may mean just a postcard at the beginning of each year, but whatever you do, the process by which you keep yourself before your "market" is essential to your success or failure.

A salaried job doesn't require you to do much of this at all. You take your orders, you do the work, you get your paycheck. There is a real measure of security in this. On the other hand, there's no real freedom to fully develop yourself in the ways you really want. The flip side of a salary is the fact that you rarely know your total annual earnings for the year ahead.

My aim, of course, is to use all my contacts to continually pull in assignments. These assignments generally lead to writing the magazine articles which the trades will be publishing. Sometimes the articles are used for internal or external corporate publications. Most large corporations publish sophisticated quarterly publications which require top-quality writing and some of the best photojournalism being done in the nation.

Here is a sample of typical article headlines ranging over a variety of subjects about which I have written: "Opening Hotels: Hyatt's Team Makes It Look So Easy!" (Hotel & Resort Industry); "How to Promote Your Business Without Spending a Fortune" (Lawn Care Industry); "Keep Your Campus Pest Free" (American School & University); "The Pointe Resort—From Blueprints to 5-Star in Five Years" (Lodging Hospitality); "New Life for an Old Quarry" (Pit & Quarry); "Tapping a Natural Resource: Female Detailers" (Medical Marketing & Media); and the list could be extended by a hundred more such titles.

The point is, these publications represent extremely diverse industries—ranging from hotels to lawn care companies to pharmaceutical manufacturers. The subjects all relate to the selling of some product or service, even if the titles don't appear to reflect that. Within the text of each article are very specific references to a company or a product which are recommended to the reader.

Yet most large corporations don't have a sufficient number of people on staff to get out and do the nitty-gritty work necessary to provide the articles. Inevitably, the editors of these publications need qualified, trustworthy professional writers.

BEING A PROFESSIONAL

What is trustworthy? It means that you fully account for all your legitimate expenses on the job. It means you know what the editor wants *before* you go a thousand miles to the interview, cover the event, etc. It means you come back into the office and transcribe your taped interview (always put it on tape and transcribe it to insure accuracy and to prove Mr. B actually said what you say he said).

And it means delivering the article swiftly.

Most trade magazines and most writing assignments for free-lancers, as noted, rarely provide a long time frame in which to produce the work. It's important to be *facile*. I was accused of this in my graduating year by an old *Life* magazine editor, Wilson Hicks, who was enjoying semi-retirement supervising student publications at the University of Miami in the late 1950s. He was right. I am facile.

I am quick. I collect the necessary facts as fast as I can. I put them on paper as fast as I can. I usually write an article in a single sitting and I rarely ever rewrite.

Why? Partly because I am very good at my craft. Partly because I am blessed with a mind that can organize a multitude of separate facts. Partly because I tend to conduct interviews in a format that "tells the story" in much the way I will write it and thus the transcription is virtually a rough article in itself. And partly because I don't have the time to linger over and lovingly rewrite everything I have to put into the article.

Why? Because I have to make a living and, at a *per diem* of several hundred dollars, I want to get the job done and get on to the next one. Would it serve me better to waste time and drag out the assignment? Not in the long run. Because those hiring me want to *save* money by using a freelance professional rather than a full-time staff person. If I can bring the job in within a budget that is acceptable to them and the people *they* have to answer to, then I'm making everybody happy!

In my view, the creation of a single article should provide you with a minimum of $500. That's generally about two days' work. An article that requires me to leave the office, travel, gather data and do interviews, come back, transcribe, process, file, and write, should earn at least $1000 and *up*, depending on the time involved.

Now think about this. If I earn $500 a week for fifty weeks, that's an annual income of $25,000. If I earn $1000 a week, with time out for slow periods and a vacation, that's around $40,000 *gross*. Not bad for a freelancer. In fact, damn good.

Now deduct $10,000 to run your office. That's still $30,000 to

$15,000 *net*. No, you're not going to get rich by ordinary standards as a professional writer. Oh yes, some do. Speechwriters generally earn more than other types of writers, but earn it they do because speechwriting requires endless, boring rewrites, and always dealing with committees or others. The others get the credit, too. Me, I like the by-lines on my articles and it is precisely because *my* reputation gives me access to a trade magazine that I am valuable to my clients.

Your reputation as a writer is money in the bank. Much of the work that will eventually come your way will do so because you have built a reputation for quality work, professionally done. You meet deadlines. Your work is clean and ready to go so that editors and others don't have to labor over it. It's well documented, well researched. Your fee is fair and commensurate with a reasonable working budget for an account or corporation. Despite the enormous wealth many large companies have, they generally are extremely vigilant over all expenses and those for outside consultants are the most vulnerable.

TO BEGIN AS A WRITER

Now, if you are at the very beginning of a writing career, here's some advice.

Everyone has to begin sometime. A professional freelance writer can expect to pay his or her dues a lot longer than most other craftsmen and tradespeople. I use these terms purposely because you are not an "artist." You are doing work that is comparable to a plumber or carpenter. I *make* articles. I *construct* them.

Remember my definition of what a professional writer does: "I package information."

There is no one way to learn this craft, but one thing is absolutely necessary. You must write. And write. And write. The more you write, the more skilled you will become and the easier the task of writing will be for you. It may take up to twenty years to become fully at ease in the profession, but by then you will be at the peak of your skills, the prime of your earning power, if you have begun a career in writing after leaving college.

Your apprenticeship might be served on a newspaper. Perhaps a weekly at first—but not for too long because it's underpaid and a trap for those too weak to move upward. Then a daily newspaper where you can learn to work fast, gather information, and get it into print the next day. You will learn to interview *anyone.*

Most people define their lives by the work they do. If you aren't the kind of person who sees dignity in all work and is genuinely interested in why people got into a certain line of work, why it gives them satisfaction, what special talents they bring to it, then get out of the writing business.

The only thing that really counts is *people*. Facts are fine, but it is real people who breathe life into any story. That's why the case history of a person and/or a company is the life's blood of most writing.

So, you will learn to interview, come back to the office, check your notes, and write your story. Journalism is still the bedrock of a professional writer's craft. I may work for public relations agencies or directors of communications, but *the only thing I write is journalism*. The truth.

The only public relations worth anything is the truth. Everything else will, sooner or later, blow up in your face.

That's why there is no conflict in my life as to who pays the bill. I know the magazines can't or won't, so I realistically seek my earnings from those who can.

The great Samuel Johnson was quoted as saying, "No man but a blockhead ever wrote except for money." He was right.

Now, writing does have its therapeutic qualities and I'm all for you taking a crack at a novel, short story, or poetry, but if you intend to earn a living at writing you have to think of it in terms of money. That means deciding how much your *time* is worth, because all you have to sell is time and talent. That means calculating what it costs you to live each month and meet your bills for gas, telephone, postage, clothes, rent, etc. Many writers fail to take a businesslike approach to their craft in this respect.

If you know what it costs you to live and you know what it will take to produce a given piece of work, then you can make a determination of what to charge. And, please, do think about making a *profit* on your time and labor. Add on a respectable percentage to your basic fee so that you will not only respect yourself, but insist that your client respect you, too.

You should apply this principle to your salary requirements for your first jobs, whether they be in newspaper work or perhaps a communications job with a corporation or with a public relations agency. Nothing is worth more than *experience* in the field of writing. *Credentials* are essential to attaining success.

You'll notice I said "jobs" above instead of "job." A successful freelancer has generally worked in a variety of areas ranging from journalism to writing for government or nonprofit agencies, corporations, or public relations firms. The wider your scope of writing experience, the better. I personally think it's a mistake, if you eventually intend to be your own boss, to stay longer than two years or so in any one position. In our fast-paced society, you must be mobile and you should be prepared to travel a bit. Securing employment in different areas of the nation is educational in itself and you will make valuable contacts in these different places which will prove useful in the fullness of time. That's why it's worth cultivating good friends at all levels.

For example, I am always particularly friendly with assistant or associate editors. I cultivate them because, sooner or later, they will grow into editors. I cannot tell you how many times this has happened and resulted in the kind of goodwill that allows me to place articles in their magazines almost at will.

On the other hand, it just makes good sense to be nice to everybody. It's not hard if you develop an open-minded, tolerant attitude. It will help you in life. And don't always listen or contribute to gossip. Everyone has an axe to grind with someone. Make your own judgments about people and keep your own counsel.

As a beginner, your main job is to learn your trade. Stick to that. Do the best work you can and seek appropriate recognition for it. If it's not forthcoming then be prepared to move on. If there is considerable criticism, it means one of two things. Possibly your work is no good and needs improvement. Always get at least one other opinion from as objective a source as possible. Never hesitate to ask a professional writer friend for a review of your work. Most writers are happy to help one another. If your work *is* good, then you're encountering professional fear and jealousy. Or incompetence. Or all three! This is extremely common. Anyone whose own work may look bad beside yours will likely try to transform your work into junk. Fight that with everything in your soul. Do not let your good work—which eventually should appear in print—be turned into junk by those with reasons of their own to make you look bad. Go over their heads if you must.

No one is ever going to hand you anything for free in the writing game. You will always be proving yourself, and you will do it from story to story. Last month's article is already ashes and forgotten. Some people like that kind of constant challenge; it wears others thin. I have always wanted to prove that I'm good at my trade and I never take it for granted that I have over twenty years at it. I am only as good as the piece I have in the typewriter in front of me. Including this one.

A word on "writer's block." It is bunk. It exists only for those who are ill-prepared in their research and, therefore, have nothing to put on the page in the first place.

The true professional cannot wait to attack the blank page as soon as he or she has gathered the data and done all the interviews. Writing should be a thrilling experience, as you know in your heart that you are communicating with that one person who is going to read the words you're putting down.

And it is *one person*.

Writing is a one-to-one form of communication. The magazine

you're writing for may have a circulation of thousands, but you must always write to the one person who is reading your words in that magazine, although that reader may be multiplied by the full extent of its circulation.

That's why you should avoid pontification. You are not necessarily the expert. Your job is to share the knowledge of experts with others. You are a communicator and that should be your primary expertise.

Of course, it helps considerably if you have a body of knowledge, an expertise in a particular subject area or areas that *enhances* your basic skill. In these times, specialization is increasingly a requirement, and this is true as well for the professional writer.

This is also why it is absolutely necessary for a writer who concentrates on trade magazines to develop a knowledge of how business actually functions, either by studying business courses in college or by reading about the subject independently. In this regard, a writer for trade magazines should have a voracious appetite for business news and should study magazines like *Business Week, Inc.,* and others on a weekly and monthly basis. Reading the *Wall Street Journal* or the business section of the *New York Times* is a must.

Writing for the trades means that you are keeping not only abreast of trends, but ahead of them. You must always be asking, what's happending that's *new?* Why is it *better?* What is innovative about it?

Summing Up

While consumer magazines will continue to spring up like daisies, year after year, and have a lot of glamor attached to them, trade magazines go on and on. They carve a niche for themselves and, while some may fail because they're in an overcrowded segment and thus cannot lure sufficient advertising or readership, the old faithfuls among them will endure.

Because of that factor, writing for the trades—once you have secured the corporate or nonprofit sponsorship you require—is a sure way to make a good living at the writing craft. It has its benefits too. One of them is travel.

In a single month in 1982, I traveled to Los Angeles, San Francisco, Seattle, Honolulu, and Las Vegas! All expenses paid!

And the best part is, the more you write, the more you promote yourself, the more work comes to you.

The worst of it is that you can never stop the process of self-promotion and aggressive hustling for assignments. It gets a bit easier as times goes along, but it never gets to be a sure thing.

But it's never dull either. If you are easily bored. If you don't particularly like outside authority directing your work. If you like to grow personally and professionally. If you can mix and mingle with many different types of people and then lock yourself away to do the hard, nitty-gritty work of transcribing, researching, and writing, then you probably have a good chance of being a successful professional freelance writer.

The myth is that you will find security if you take a salaried job and work at it for umpteen years. There is no such thing as security in a society experiencing rapid changes in communications, social and moral attitudes, and cycles of recession and growth.

So why not fulfill yourself in the craft of writing if that is the one thing you do best?

THE BUSINESS OF WRITING . . . FOR BUSINESS
by James Joseph

Perhaps it was predictable.

The more than two hundred preregistrants at the annual "Writing for Today's Markets" conference—conducted by the Southern California chapter of the American Society of Journalists and Authors—had made their choices. Asked to select one among four speaker-panels available during each of the conference's hourly sessions, the overwhelming majority chose panels of special interest to beginning writers.

Predictably, they opted to flock to a panel titled "So You're New to the Game: Freelancing ABCs." Just as predictably, they favored heavily those panels that promised to put them in touch with agents, that offered insight into interviewing and research, local and regional markets ("The Regionals: Markets in Your Own Backyard)."

Yet almost none had chosen the conference's single panel seemingly ready-made and designed for the novice: the panel on writing for business publications—the so-called "trade journals."

Those conference-goers had overlooked—"snubbed" might be more accurate—the challenging, lucrative, multi-marketed, and unlimited opportunities of business writing. And not merely for the more than thirty-five hundred business magazines, but for business itself. Business matters are big business for the nonfiction writer.

BUSINESS IS BOOMING

Some business magazines regularly pay $1,500 and more for an article. That's considerably more than any but a handful of "big name" general (consumer) or specialized magazines pay. Yet relatively few writers seek the paychecks of the business press.

Typically, one Sunday magazine (a newspaper supplement) with more than 14 million circulation reports that it receives "hundreds of queries daily" for the chance to do an article, seldom for more than $450-$500. By contrast, several hundred business publications regularly pay $500 and up and receive relatively few writer queries.

Far higher paying still is business itself.

Business—from local retailers and manufacturers to the Fortune 500 corporate giants—pays handsomely for nonfiction that explains its products, reports its financial status, proclaims a new development or research, announces the formation of a new division, highlights an annual report, or explains to product users how to assemble a product or use it more effectively.

Just as often, and frequently on a continuing contract basis, business looks to freelancers to produce its newsletters, write its executives' speeches, and author the product-familiarization manuals which help its salesmen sell with greater product insight and success.

Veteran nonfiction freelancers such as myself know what many beginning writers do not: nonfiction's big bucks are more likely to be bagged in a corporation's office than in a magazine or book publisher's.

For example, a few years ago a high-technology corporation asked me to devise a course to explain the inner workings of its highly complex products to its worldwide sales staff.

"What we need is a kind of product correspondence course explaining our technology, much as the popular science magazines would explain it," said one of the company's marketing executives.

The job—its research, writing, and art—was no different, nor any more time-consuming, than producing the same length manuscript for one of the leading popular science magazines. What was different was the job price: nearly $15,000, or about $10,000 *more* than most of the big-circulation science magazines would have paid had they, and not a corporation, made the assignment.

Or consider corporate books. Yes, companies do contract books. They are written to trace a company's history, memorialize a famous founder, or explain the development of a product or technology.

It is not unusual for corporations to pay authors $50,000 and up to research and write company books. Additionally, the author often collects royalties if, as is sometimes the case, the book is issued by a trade publisher. In contrast, a recent (1981) Authors Guild survey of its members' book contracts found that nonfiction authors received an average $10,000-$20,000 advance against royalties for undertaking books no more complex or time-taking than the corporate variety. A bare 8.5 percent of authors surveyed received publisher advances exceeding $40,000.

"Business," says a corporate communications insider, "probably buys more nonfiction in all its forms . . . than do all magazines combined."

While some might argue with this assessment, there is no argument that business is a prodigious buyer of nonfiction.

Business Respects Good Writers

More significant to the writer is how business views writers in general and *a writer*, specifically.

Good writers, who produce that which business needs and demands, are prized by corporate management as prized, let's say, as a good engineer or computer programmer. Business management finds all three hard to come by.

Contrast this professional esteem in which writers are often held by business with the downgraded worth of writers by editors of many general and consumer-specialty magazines. One reason for the difference in esteem is frequency and familiarity. Writers in business are a rarity. Writers in an editorial office are commonplace. Moreover, the general magazine editor is himself or herself a "writer"—a writer who, by dint of know-how if not sheer writing talent, has "arrived," has secured a steady job on a magazine staff. Too often, the querying or visiting writer is viewed by the editor as one who has not "arrived." To such an editor, the nonstaffer is "just a freelancer."

Business's view of the writer is a polarity apart. To business management, the freelance writer who submits a proposal to write business nonfiction is an "independent contractor." Many corporations rely heavily on independent contractors to deliver essential specialty services—from computer programming and facility design to writing.

In many cases, business hires the services of independent contractors—whether writers or designers—because it cannot justify, on a regular basis, the staffing (at high corporate salaries) of such skilled and specialized experts. The independent contractor-writer comes to business as a *consultant*—already mantled not only with the esteem that business traditionally holds for the consultant, but with the consultant's clout in job pricing.

Corporate business expects to pay, and pay very well, for consultant-contractor/writer assignments. Virtually the same nonfiction article that pays the writer little more than $150-$250 when purchased by even a major *newspaper,* and seldom more than $350-$950 if sold to a *magazine* (consumer or business publication), may well bring upwards of $1000-$2000 when contracted to a *corporation.*

When approaching business, many writers make a fundamental mistake: *they ask too little for their research and writing time.* Corporations and their well-paid executives are suspicious of any writer or consultant who *underprices* his or her skills. Certainly corporate executives expect to be well paid for theirs, and to pay the writer well for his or hers. What causes many writers to underbid when pricing a corporate nonfiction proposal is the "magazine syndrome." Magazines and their editors are forever trying to pay the writer as little as possible. Corporations are prepared to pay the writer what his or her time, talent, and research perception are *really* worth.

Since a writer's thinking is molded by the "magazine syndrome," many writers approach corporate management prices by magazine pay standards; they'll ask for $600-$1000, about what a magazine would pay for the work. Will he or she get the assignment? Very likely not. At those rates, the writer automatically ranks himself or herself as an $18,000-$22,000-per-year corporate employee—and most certainly not as a consultant who should be earning $45,000 and up. If you price yourself at the lower end of corporate earnings, there is little reason for the hiring executive to rank your savvy and skills any higher than you, by your own underpricing, have ranked yourself.

I have often told company executives straight out, "I doubt very much whether you can afford me."

Invariably, they have—and do.

Corporations *do* because the freelance writer-consultant's bid price for a nonfiction job is almost always a corporate bargain. The company could not get the same work done in-house (by assigning it to one of its own staffers) for less. And, most often, it would cost the company a great deal more. The in-house job, moreover, would likely fall far short of the quality the company is seeking. If it payrolled *that* kind of talent, it would not have called in the freelance writer-consultant in the first place.

Consider the bargain a company buys when it hires you, a nonfiction freelancer, as independent contractor-consultant:

Virtually anyone on its communications staff capable of producing nonfiction of the perception and quality produced by the nonfiction corporate freelancer is earning $25,000-$35,000, and more, a year on the company's payroll.

Roughly, that's $2,100-$3,600 a month. Corporate writings done in-house have a way of stretching into days and weeks. Virtually any major in-house writing project winds up costing a company the salary equivalent of several thousand dollars, or often twice that. The business freelancer can likely get the job done far better in half the time. The business freelancer is a specialist—that's why he or she was offered the job. For another, he or she is accustomed to spending not 40 hours a week (as do most business communications staffers), but perhaps 60 hours or more weekly in fulfilling a business writing contract. Thus, the $1,500-$2,500 a freelancer asks for the job may, in fact, cost the company half what it would expect to pay in equivalent salary. The company, plainly, has bought a bargain. And the business freelancer has earned a consultant's pay.

The Business of Being a Business Writer

How, then, do you launch your career as a a business writer for any of industry's more than 3,500 business ("trade") magazines, for its more general-circulation business publications, or for business itself?

The most obvious launching platform is the query letter. A letter to a business magazine, one of the so-called trade journals, proposes a business-angled article. It capsulizes how and where you intend to research it, the availability of art (photographs, taken either by you or by others), and your qualifications to do the assignment.

Suppose you don't have any "qualifications"?

Well, in fact, you do, if you approach a business publication in a field with which you are (if only peripherally) familiar. Let's say your father is a retailer, and you want to approach a retail business publication. You would be correct to claim qualification that you have grown up in retailing; that your family has been involved in retailing for decades, and that you, as a family member, have studied the business.

Later you may be able to be more specific, citing articles in the field you have published or a college study you made, for example.

But your query letter must be a *selling* letter from the first word of paragraph one. You do not begin a query to *any* editor, business editor or otherwise, with the weak, amateurish question, "Would you be interested in . . .?"

Just this week I queried a number of business magazine editors (in the bicycle and recreation trade), as well as editors of general magazines around the world, on the new "off-road" bicycles.

Typically, my query letter begins:

"A new-breed bicycle—the OFF-ROAD bike—opens to cyclists (and to those who cater to them) a hitherto closed recreational domain: the whole of the out-of-doors. The new high-technology bicycles free the cyclist from bike path and road. So doing, they convert bicycling to what it has never been before—a cross-country sport. The article I propose, "Off-Road Bicycles: New Pedal-Anywhere Bikes," and its color photographs preview the cross-country bicycle which most experts believe will revolutionize cycling . . ."

Reference Sources

Two ready sources put you in touch with business magazines.

One is the annual *Writer's Market*, which lists hundreds of business publications, their rates, article requirements, and editorial contacts.

Far less well known is the highly informative (if you know how to analyze its listings) *Business Publication Rates and Data* monthly, whose nearly 1,600 pages give detailed descriptions of hundreds of business publications. This is not a writer's reference, but rather the essential resource for advertisers and their agencies. It tells potential advertisers about every magazine's most intimate inside information: the kinds of written material it runs, its editorial aims, circulation, and an astounding amount of other in-depth publisher's data.

Business Publication Rates and Data is published by Standard Rate & Data Service, Inc., Skokie, Illinois 60077. An annual subscription costs about $150, but writers have no real need to subscribe. They can ask a local advertising agency for a discarded, month-old copy. Insofar as advertising agencies are concerned, *Business Publication Rates and Data* is "outdated" monthly as new rates are listed. But for writers, even a year-old borrowed or begged copy is current enough.

Still, *total familiarization* with a business publication comes neither from its listings in *Writer's Market* or the in-depth data of *Business Publication Rates and Data*.

Only by studying recent copies of a business magazine—an entire year's issues if you can find them—can you feel the real pulse of the publication and come to know the probable article needs of its editors.

Many libraries—your town's, technical school's, and university's—subscribe to business publications. So, too, do those engaged in businesses covered by specific business publications. Where can you be certain to find any of the dozen business magazines concerned with auto repairs? At virtually any local auto-repair shop. Where to find business magazines concerned with plumbing, heating, and air conditioning? At the local offices and shops of plumbing merchants, contractors, and installers.

Given the often better pay offered writers by the business press, and the heady writing contracts from corporations, why does the novice—like those previously noted conference-goers—ignore one of nonfiction's largest, fastest expanding, and most lucrative multi-markets of business: its publications?

The answers are several. To many novices, the chance to write for a "name" magazine holds far more prestige than writing for—and their bylines appearing in—a company magazine or other business publication. Then, too, many newcomers to writing, as well as some seasoned hands, wrongly believe they are not well enough versed in the basics of business and industry to write for it and its publications. The simple truth is that any able writer and researcher can more easily write for business than for general magazines or newspapers. As for "prestige"? There is nothing more prestigious than a healthy bank account—built from business and business-publication writing.

GEAR UP FOR THE BUSINESS PRESS

How do you make the transition from writing for the business press—for business and trade magazines—to writing for business itself?

There are a number of proven ways:

1. Use industry expertise, gained from writing for business magazines, as a springboard to writing for business itself.

    Let's say you begin to write for many of the magazines in the metalworking field—for business magazines such as *Machine and Tool Blue Book*, *Iron Age*, *American Machinist* or any of two dozen other magazines in the machine production field.

    In researching metalworking articles, you must by necessity visit metalworking plants.

    You not only have a foot in the door; you are *in* the door of plants to which you otherwise might not gain access. And, invariably, the plant people you interview are the same top executives and department heads who hire freelance writers. Sometime during your research, you can mention that you also do writing for businesses in the field, directly. If they like the article when you check it back with them (as every good business writer does), you have *established* your credentials (even if, interestingly, the article may not actually be published for several months). Your in-plant research for a business publication has established your credentials, and often leads to an assignment from the very executives you interviewed for the article.

2. Direct-query businesses, enclosing business press articles you have done in the field.

    Nothing more impresses the business buyer of outside writing than clips from his favorite, and often highly respected and regularly read, trade magazine, by a writer identifying himself as the author of articles the business executive has probably read.

    Typically, the business executive reader may like and admire an article in one of his trade magazines, but scarcely notices its author's byline.

    When you query him with familiar trade magazine clips—familiar because he has probably read the article—you are saying, "I wrote them . . . *I write what you read.*"

    Your clip-credentials speak eloquently for themselves,

and for you. Those clips and the magazine from which they came silently recommend you as an accredited journalist in that particular business/industry field. And you are on your way to writing for business itself.

3. Go where potential business clients go—to industry conferences, shows, conventions, and local association meetings.

Hopeful business writers who complain that business people won't see them, and perhaps not even return their phone calls, expose their lack of ingenuity. You don't need a business invitation—merely a ticket (often at no cost) to any of the convention/trade shows and conferences involving the business fields for which you intend to write. There, in company booths and on the speaker's platform, are hundreds of business executives, sales managers, and production people—out in the open, and no longer behind closed corporate doors.

Business publications in every field of industry and commerce regularly list what conventions, conferences, and shows are being held, and where. If you live in or near a major city, a conference/show in your field of interest is almost sure, this month or six months from now, to come to town. Be there. Get the feel of the industry, if you don't already have it, and solicit business from business.

Likewise, the local chapters of national business societies and associations in your field of business-writing interest often hold regular, usually monthly meetings. Attend them. Ask the chairperson if you may stand up and briefly announce to the chapter's local business executives that you are in the business of writing for business—their businesses.

4. From business magazine columnist, to business book writer, consultant—and more.

A writer friend of mine began, about two years ago, writing computer-use columns, on an every-issue basis, for some two dozen trade/industrial magazines. That led to two books for one of the business-oriented computer-use associations. And those led to a just-signed seven-book contract, with a multi-figure advance, from a major computer consumer-book publisher. And these are leading to highly paid speaking and seminar engagements, remunerative commissions for writing for firms in the computer business, and consulting assignments. He will earn more money this year—and probably for the next decade or so—than any but a very few top "consumer" magazine writers. The difference is, he is earning *his*—from business.

5. Finally, business research, which puts you in touch with top corporations and their experts, leads naturally to business assignments—and top pay.

Typically, I have just launched the business-press oriented *Robomation Report*, a monthly newsletter insert/special feature for industrial and business magazines across a wide spectrum of robot-interested industries around the world.

My daily contact with business leaders, robotic experts and engineers—contacts routine in the research of a project such as *Robomation Report*—has already made me an industry "insider." Obviously, I operate daily on the cutting edge of one of industry's most dynamic trends: toward robomation—industrial automation through the use of robots and robot-operated tools. With this expertise, enhanced day to day, I become a valuable writing asset to any business in, or concerned with, robotics.

Obviously, many of today's established nonfiction writers not only look back fondly on their career-establishing business writing days—but enthusiastically continue to write for business.

I am one of those freelance veterans. My own venture into nonfiction article writing and into business writing may be one of the more unusual demonstrations of career building existent. Quite literally, I launched my career as a lifetime nonfiction freelancer in a single momentous, adventurous, hardworking year—in the "trades" (business trade journals).

Now, more than thirty years later, I have written and photo-illustrated more than thirty-five hundred magazine articles. They have been published by leading magazines around the world (I self-syndicate my major articles globally, in some forty nations and twenty-five languages). I have written twenty-one books, the latest an alternate feature selection for Book-of-the-Month Club and Quality Paperback Book Club. I have done major assignments for business and industry, including a number of respected business newsletters.

Long before graduating from Stanford University, I made two basic decisions: I would pursue freelancing as a lifelong career. And I would *not* begin by making the novice freelancer's numerous errors— the worst among them being to aim, still green as I was at the writing craft, at the major general magazines (which, in those days, included the *Saturday Evening Post, Collier's,* and *American Magazine,* for all of which I eventually wrote).

Instead, not a month out of college, I began as a business writer. And in a most unorthodox way. I loaded my car with typewriter, camera, and luggage, and headed into the Intermountain states (Utah, Montana, Wyoming, and Idaho).

There, I reasoned—in the boondocks, if you will, but exhilarating country—were thriving local businesses and ranches with innovative concepts and methods—business innovations seldom explored and never put to paper. For while most of the few writers I then knew congregated in the major cities (New York, Chicago, Washington, Los Angeles), as did most business-magazine staffers; the fertile hinterlands lay seldom or seriously "business-reported."

I decided to report from the hinterlands.

For that full year—my first as a freelance nonfiction writer-photographer—I roamed the business back country.

I knew not a single magazine editor. I had not a single cashable contact, but I had what every successful nonfiction writer must have: an astute and developing sense of "story"—an instinct for the truly innovative and newsworthy.

I was also, even then, a middling good photographer (I'd been campus news photographer for such national photo feature syndicates as Acme Newspictures and the NEA—Newspaper Enterprise Association). And I was a good writer. All through college I had written and sold articles, some of them to national magazines. I also wrote and self-syndicated a western weekly newspaper column, "Western Round-up."

As a hinterlands business writer, I was the equivalent of a traveling salesman. I would drive into a town, ride around eyeing its businesses, and then head for the office of the local (usually weekly) paper. To its editor I would bluntly explain my mission: to find good local business articles for business magazines. Most of the editors were extremely helpful. Many suggested local business stories. All turned their back-copy files over to me.

Usually, before day's end—every day, seven days a week and across thousands of miles of the West—I had at least one story researched and photographed.

That night, in my motel room, I wrote the article and sometimes, with a portable developing kit, even processed the films (all black and white in those days). I had photo prints made at the local photo shop. And, packaging my text and art, often by late next day I had the article in the mail to an editor I didn't know (but who shortly, I was confident, would be reading an article of business interest to his specialized readers) from an area seldom covered by the magazine or its staff.

In one year I wrote and photographed nearly a hundred hinterland business articles. Even at the then-going poverty rates paid by the then-fledgling business press, I earned more than ten thousand dollars my first freelance "year on the road." And in those days—the early 1950s—ten thousand dollars, while perhaps not a bushel, was a peck of money.

And I had done it without magazine or editor contacts, and with only passing knowledge of the many business and agri-subjects I researched, photographed, and wrote about during that busy-as-thrashing-time year.

I had found a lifelong career in freelancing, in writing for business. And so can you.

Additional Resources

Allied Capital Corporation, 1625 I St. NW, Washington, DC 20006. Provides advisory, analytical, and trade information on investments in small growing businesses, and knowledge of venture capital in the U.S. Offers annual reports and research assistance. Publications include annual report and brochures on venture capital and small business loans.

American Association of Industrial Editors, 802 Kenmore Ave., Buffalo, NY 14216. Publishes newsletters and other special mailings, does analyses of members' publications, has awards program and holds annual meeting. Publishes bimonthly *Editor's Notebook* for members.

American Business Press, Inc., 205 E. 42nd St., New York, NY 10017. (An association of business and merchandising periodicals—about 87 percent classify as industrial.) Member publications represent a "who's who" of the technical production and distribution services of America's industrial community. Membership includes editors and staffers of member periodicals. Offers publication and special research awards.

American Federation of Small Business, 407 S. Dearborn St., Chicago, IL 60605. Provides comprehensive information on economics; labor-management relations; government: executive, legislative, and judicial; demography; international relations; natural-resource development; defense of the free world; and the Marxist threat. Offers aid in arranging interviews, brochures and pamphlets, informational newsletters, library facilities, placement on mailing lists, press kits, research assistance, statistics, and telephone reference services.

Department of Commerce, 14th St. and Constitution Ave. NW, Washington, DC 20230. Offers aid in arranging interviews, annual reports, bibliographies, biographies, statistics, brochures and pamphlets, photos, and press kits. Publications available.

Direct Marketing Association, 6 E. 43rd St., New York, NY 10017. Provides how-to, referral, technical, and trade information in all areas of direct marketing: creative direct response, direct-mail catalogs, telemarketing, samples of successful mail campaigns, statistics, and more. Offers aid in arranging interviews, bibliographies, statistics, brochures and pamphlets, placement on mailing list, press kits (available through the Direct Selling Educational Foundation, at the same address).

National Small Business Association, 1604 K St. NW, Washington, DC 20006. Offers aid in arranging interviews, statistics, placement on mailing list, newsletter, photos.

United States Chamber of Commerce, 1615 H St. NW, Washington, DC 20062. Provides advisory and analytical information on all subject areas in which business deals with government: antitrust, trade policy, regulation, fiscal matters, the economy, economic education, resources and environment, transfer payments, more. Offers aid in arranging interviews, annual reports, brochures/pamphlets, informational newsletters, statistics. Conducts continuing education programs for business executives.

LOOKING TOWARD TOMORROW

With the help of many accomplished writers we have taken you into the stimulating, if perilous, world of freelance writing. These professionals have opened their private work files, offered an astonishing volume and variety of information earnestly and candidly. By now I'm sure the purpose is clear: to help you learn what you need to know about the writing craft, to provide an illuminating and realistic look at the world in which writers daily practice their trade.

Because many potential readers, aspiring to write either part- or full-time in specialized areas, are relatively new at the business, Part I of the book dealt with the nuts and bolts of the writing. Its six lengthy chapters were intended to help newcomers—and experienced writers, too—understand the practices and habits that are basic to a successful writing career—no matter what your interests or specialty.

In Chapter 6, we tried to give you some solid and sensible insights into the age-old question: "Why specialize?" The pros and cons were examined in detail by freelancers who have experienced both sides of the coin.

The remaining chapters were designed to be a relatively painless introduction and guidebook for those who wish to write in any of fifteen major specialty markets. We have explained the genesis and development of these specialties, the range of opportunities within them: what writers need to know about writing for the various general magazines as well as the amazing array of trade, company, and professional periodicals within each specific specialty.

We have shown you the advantages of each area, and the disadvantages: how to work your way in, capitalize on the pluses, work around the minuses, and grow with your own proficiency; how to avoid the pitfalls as you tailor your articles and books to a particular market.

We have tried to be as honest and realistic as possible while allowing you to examine with us our own experiences—the good and not so good—in these many specialized market areas.

Our mutual journey has been a long one. Still, there's one last excursion we must take together: consider the writer's world of tomorrow.

We will look through the glass not necessarily darkly but certainly anxiously, as electronics and MBAs revolutionize the publishing business we once knew. To take us into tomorrow, we've called again on two long-time ASJA members. Here's Margaret Markham's revealing interview with Alvin Toffler on Future Flak.

An Interview with Alvin Toffler on Future Flak

MARKHAM: With mass-circulation daily newspapers in major cities continuing to fall by the way, do you see this medium shrinking to the vanishing point by the next century?

TOFFLER: Not at all. It's true that big-circulation newspapers are losing readership. But this merely parallels a trend that began earlier in the magazine field. The big books have been in trouble just as the big-circulation dailies have. But we've also simultaneously seen the proliferation of small-circulation magazines—regional or special-interest magazines. This same trend is now surfacing in the newspaper field, where we see a burgeoning of community papers, community "shoppers," local special-interest papers, weeklies, biweeklies, all chewing away at the edges of the newspaper market. We are de-massifying all the mass media.

MARKHAM: Will the corner newsstand be a thing of the past by the year 2000, and every home have its own push-button computer to supply news and features to meet individual needs and tastes?

TOFFLER: The question is not "if," but "when." Big cities have already experienced a drop in the newsstand sales with the exodus to suburbia. Assuming all sorts of things, like not blowing ourselves up with "nukes," we may well see a swing to electronic transmission. We're already nearing the limits of the print media and are being pushed to other kinds of delivery systems.

I don't for a moment believe the book and the magazine or the newspaper will disappear within the next generation. They are highly efficient information carriers—for some purposes. But not for all purposes. So they will play a reduced role in a much more diverse ecosystem of information.

MARKHAM: Does this leave the writer out in the cold?

TOFFLER: By no means. Somebody is still going to have to dig up the material and write it, no matter what form it comes out in. Whether audio or video, even print. Or a combination of these. Right now in London, as a matter of fact, you can buy for about $300 a highly versatile gadget that attaches to your TV set. This permits you to select channels that feed print onto the screen like a Reuter's news ticker or special services, like financial quotations, sports information, weather reports, or a variety of special interests like gardening. And all this comes to you in the form of print. The only thing that's needed to turn it into honest-to-God print is a hard-copy printer. But despite all the gadgets, people will still have to collect, interpret, synthesize and write the information.

MARKHAM: Do you see this leading to a complete revolution in reading habits?

TOFFLER: I don't believe we're going to give up reading and writing altogether. But we'll also be communicating our messages in newer ways. Long before the next century—which is not far away—I see us breaking out far beyond the traditional and quite rigid boundaries of the book, the magazine, and the newspaper as we know it today.

If you look far enough down the line, it will even become possible to feed data directly into our skulls by electronic means—that is, by electronic brain stimulation that totally bypasses the intermediate printed stage. We know it is already possible to skip over the crude mechanics of hearing through the ear and the eardrum. We can actually give the deaf the impression of hearing a spoken word. And similar attempts are under way to give the blind the sensation of seeing. Printed words are powerful thought-organizers. But there may be ways around them some day.

Even today, writers are learning new skills. Reporters have learned to use cathode-ray screens and electronic equipment that was unheard of when I worked on a paper. But that's barely scratching the surface. New techniques will make it possible to give the public more varied material in forms and at times of their own choosing. We already have video recorders that allow you to record programs and then play them back at your own convenience. But that's only the most primitive beginning. More important, you can use this equipment to produce your own messages, your own mini-book, a whole show, or what you will. And play them back when you will. This marks a key difference. With Xerox, tape recorders, video recorders, and the like, you can produce your own literature, drama and music and pass it along to others. The line between producer and consumer thus begins to blur. For the first time, message consumers are being given some of the same technology that hitherto was available only to professional message producers.

MARKHAM: How will the writer fit into this somewhat topsy-turvy future?

TOFFLER: The writer may be somewhat less of a specialist in the traditional sense, that is, as a craftsman with lifelong dedication to a single skill. The challenge of the future may lie in switching back and forth among many skills. A writer may turn into a photographer, a video director, perhaps even an artist—not to speak of other things—a consultant, a teacher, a business executive, a scientist, and then a writer again.

I can't visualize this as an insurmountable hurdle for the freelance writer. We have always been less rigidly specialized than the members of any other profession. Most of us have taken a turn in some allied field. We often move for a while into advertising or public relations, or we edit a paper or tackle a novel. Our profession is characterized by more mobility and occupational and mental flexibility than just about any other profession.

If anybody asks me what I am, I conceive of myself as a writer. But while I value that description, I gravitate to other media as well. Like most writers, I welcome a chance to be on a major TV talk show, to lecture widely. Occasionally, I teach. Presumably, we writers care about what we are putting down in words. In the final analysis, we want to persuade others to our views. For me, the ultimate purpose of writing is not just to sell copies, much as I like that. It's to bring about social change. So I see my job extending beyond the actual writing. From the very first, I think of how my book will shape up to meet the needs and dimensions of other media, how it may lend itself to magazine excerpts, TV appearances and the lecture platform. All these are part of an integrated process of communicating the ideas I want to get out front.

MARKHAM: Isn't that getting writers farther away from the written word?

TOFFLER: No. It means the writer must see the written word in a new way, as part of a media environment that affects all of us. The written word is part of a visual, auditory, sensory context. To be really effective, the writer needs to see how the word fits into this environment.

Also, we need to talk about time. I have a theory that bears on this and may have important implications for us as writers. I believe people no longer read as they used to when they had fewer ways of getting information and life went along at a more leisurely pace. There has been a fundamental change in attention span. People read in shorter takes. It's my hunch that, if anybody were to measure it, we'd find uninterrupted periods of reading are considerably shorter than they used to be. And this raises a problem, since not all ideas can be expressed well in short takes.

But there's more to it than this. Information is also coming at people from a wider diversity of media and via many different channels. Language is increasingly diversifying into multiple jargons. Simultaneously, mass society, itself, is de-massifying. For all these reasons, there is an overpowering hunger for synthesis out there.

People are getting modules of information, but very little in the way of frameworks within which to position this knowledge.

For these reasons, I believe that, as never before, the freelance writer's function is to put the world back together again. To make unified sense out of big, discrete chunks of reality. To make a cohesive whole out of bits and pieces of information coming at us from all sides in different forms and shapes. To unify things in larger conceptual pieces than the reader ordinarily perceives. And not to stop there, but to put these pieces into even larger and larger frameworks.

This is a challenge that is both intellectual and psychological, and I see the freelance writer as being in a better position to do this than specialists basically committed to some other field. The key issue is not whether a writer decides to remain at arm's length from a topic and examine it objectively, or whether the role chosen is that of a participant or advocate. So long as the aim is to put the "story" into a conceptual framework, to relate it to the big change forces at work today, I see the writer's role as very powerful. The form in which the material is gathered, the medium selected for getting the story across, are, of course, important. But only to the extent that writers meet the need for cultural synthesis, only to the extent that we help readers make sense of a complex, changing reality, will the freelancer survive usefully into the twenty-first century.

Here are Some Notions of the Book of the Future

1. It is sold "on demand." A master copy of it is kept in a computer bank somewhere. A duplicate is produced as needed. This is close to many existing systems of information retrieval in scholarly libraries.
2. It is a cassette audio-visual tape that connects to your brain with electrodes. You "read" the latest bestseller while relaxing in your commuter monorail train seat on the way to work.
3. It is fed into your home computer from the publisher's computer. You read it on your video display screen. It comes in any language, any size type and any level of language usage you prefer.
4. It is a conventional book, but comes in two editions—one disposable and one permanent, giving buyers the option of getting permanent copies of the books they want to keep.
5. It is a disposable book, but may be scanned with a laser beam and stored in your home computer for retrieval if you want to read it more than once.
6. It is a highly individualized information unit that is fed into your home system. A computer profile of your reading tastes and interests insures that only those books you are likely to enjoy come to your home.
7. It is a cassette that attaches to your television set and gives

you the contents in words and pictures, abridged or complete, depending on your desire for information or simply entertainment.

8. It is a magazine-format, disposable book that comes inserted in your daily newspaper on receipt of your telephone order.

9. It comes in serial form into your home via a personal teletype machine. You pick the books you want to receive.

10. It is a traditional book, well bound and printed, that makes the best use of old and new materials and techniques. This happens when the publishing industry comes to its senses and realizes there is no perfect substitute for a book.

CONCLUSION

For professionals and beginners alike, here's hoping you saw something in Alvin Toffler's crystal ball for tomorrow. Freelancers need all the help they can get merely to survive. Like ideas, we writers suffer a chilling attrition. But like ideas, magazine and book editors still need us. And this gives us a certain scope and flexibility to move in various directions while selling our particular talents.

It's a tough road we travel, stretching from those who are just beginning to those who have been at it for long and lean years. And, for the most part, we travel it painfully and pretty much alone, always looking out for ourselves and sometimes for one another.

We have talked openly about our own cases, our individual experiences, methods that have worked for us.

Nowhere have we said this is the *only* way to write, or the way *you* must write. If we've proved anything by this book, I think it is that many of us follow different, even opposite, procedures. There isn't any best way—Murray Teigh Bloom's system works for him, another system works best for Betty Friedan—and some entirely different one will work for you. Freelance writers have to develop their own routines and approaches.

But before you start to bend or break the basic rules of this business, you must know and understand what they are and why they're there in the first place. Long experience has convinced most professionals that failures in freelancing can usually be traced either to lack of fundamental knowledge about the craft or refusal to use the tools of the trade—or both.

That, in essence, is what we've tried to communicate in these pages—the principles and methods we feel will serve you best as you go about strengthening your natural aptitudes and developing your own distinctive writing style in the field of your choice.

Ultimately, only you can be responsible for your own career. And only *you* can achieve the goal of professional craftsmanship by working diligently at the business of writing. To put it simply, you become a writer by *writing*. There is no other way.

But the rewards, when they come, are sound and satisfying non-fiction articles and books. And a feeling of pride in this unique profession.

ABOUT THE AUTHORS

MARTIN ABRAMSON's nonfiction books include *The Trial of Chaplain Jensen, The Barney Ross Story—Monkey on My Back*, and *The Real Al Jolson*. He writes articles for *Esquire, Family Circle, Geo, Playboy, Reader's Digest, TV Guide*, and the United Feature Syndicate. A former TV writer for NBC, he also wrote for *Stars and Stripes* and has been a congressional press secretary.

LOUIS ALEXANDER is a *Newsweek* correspondent and former journalism chairman at the University of Houston. A former correspondent for the *Wall Street Journal*, he specializes in space flight, business, and energy (especially oil and gas). He is author of *Beyond the Facts*, and has written articles for many regional and national magazines and newspapers.

DAVID A. ANDERTON is author of *The History of the U.S. Air Force, Hellcat, Superfortress at War, Strategic Air Command*, and *Jet Fighters and Bombers*. Formerly European editor and technical editor of *Aviation Week and Space Technology*, he writes for government agencies and for major corporations, specializing in aviation and space, the military, and technology. He is an ASJA Board member.

NEAL ASHBY, former managing editor, *Family Weekly*, and associate editor, *Parade*, has written for many leading U.S. magazines, including *Boys' Life, Family Circle, Family Health, Good Housekeeping, New York News Magazine*, the *New York Times, Parents, Sports Illustrated, TV Guide*, and others. Ashby's work has received awards from the National Education Association and the University of Iowa/Reader's Digest.

CHARLES M. AUSTIN, religion reporter for the *New York Times*, is author of *Let The People Know*. He also covers religion and current events for various leading newspapers and magazines in the U.S. and Europe. He has written for the Religious News Service and the Lutheran World Federation (Geneva, Switzerland). He is a member of the Religious Newswriters' Association.

EUGENE DINIER BALSLEY, author of *Financial Intermediaries in the New Electronic Marketplace* and other books, has written articles for *Industrial Photography, Modern Photography, Photomethods, Training*, and *Travel & Leisure*. He also does audiovisuals, industrial and medical motion pictures, and speechwriting. Former editor of *Business Screen*, he has been associate editor of both *Photomethods* and *Training* magazines.

BEVERLY BARBOUR, author of fifteen cookbooks, including *Cooking With Spirits, Private Recipes from Private Clubs*, and *The Complete Book of Food Preservation*, is food editor of *Club Management*. An international food consultant, TV and radio personality, and lecturer, her syndicated column—"Bev's Bits and Bites"—appears in 186 newspapers. President of Bev-Bar Ltd., she teaches cooking and wine-use techniques to both professionals and amateurs in the kitchens of the Waldorf-Astoria and other major hotels. Also a consultant to the food and beverage industries, Barbour has been honored by the North

American Wine and Food Society, and has received the *Vogue* Fashion Fellowship and a Commandrie des Cordons Bleu de France Silver Spoon Award.

PAMELA BAYLESS, money/careers editor of *Self*, was formerly the special sections editor of *Newsweek International* and is a contributor to many leading U.S. publications, including *Cosmopolitan, Travel & Leisure, Venture, Wall Street Journal*, and *Working Woman*. She is the recipient of a Columbia Journalism School and Correspondents Fund Grant for an Associated Press foreign correspondents internship in Chile. She also does magazine editing, development work, and writes speeches.

IVAN B. BERGER's many articles have appeared in such publications as *Penthouse, Popular Computing, Popular Mechanics, Popular Electronics, Popular Science, Technology Illustrated, Video*, and others. He was senior editor of *Popular Electronics*, electronics and photography editor of *Popular Mechanics*, and presently is technical editor of *Audio*. He is author of the *EIA Guide to Car Stereo*.

CLAIRE BERMAN is author of *"What Am I Doing in a Stepfamily?," Making It as a Stepparent, We Take This Child* and other nonfiction books. A former contributing editor to *New York*, her articles have appeared in *Families, Jewish Living*, the *New York Times, Parents, Redbook, Town & Country, Woman's Day*, and others. She also edits *Adoption Report* and is director of public education for the Child Welfare League of America. She is an ASJA Board member.

SHIRLEY BIAGI is a journalism professor at California State University, Sacramento. She is author of *How to Write and Sell Magazine Articles* and co-author of *Investigating and Interpreting Public Issues*. She has published more than 100 articles in popular periodicals, and also has lectured at the University of California and the University of Hawaii on magazine writing and book publishing.

JULIAN BLOCK, managing editor of the *Research Institute Recommendation* tax newsletter and a former ASJA treasurer, has written magazine articles for such major publications as *Money, Playboy, Better Homes & Gardens, Working Woman*, and *Family Weekly*. He is author of *Tax Saving: A Year-Round Guide* and does columns for several monthly magazines, including *American Bookseller* and *Vogue*.

RICHARD BLODGETT specializes in writing about business, personal finance, and art collecting. He is author of *Photographs: A Collector's Guide, Conflicts of Interest: Union Pension Fund Asset Management, How to Make Money in the Art Market*, and *The New York Times Book of Money*. Formerly a reporter for the *Wall Street Journal* and *Business Week*, he has written for many leading magazines and does *McCall's* "Money Talks" column. He is a former treasurer of ASJA.

MURRAY TEIGH BLOOM, a founder and past president of ASJA, has freelanced since 1940 and written more than 500 magazine articles for most of the major U.S. periodicals. His many books include *Brotherhood of Money; Lawyers, Clients and Ethics; Rogues to Riches;* and the bestselling *The Trouble With Lawyers*. His only fiction book, *The 13th Man*, was recently made into a motion picture.

ANTOINETTE BOSCO is executive editor of the *Litchfield County Times* (New Milford, Conn.) and an award-winning columnist for the National Catholic

News Service. She has written on religion, health, the family, and other topics for many newspapers and magazines. She is author of several books, including *Successful Single Parenting*, *What Do We Really Know About Aging?*, and *Marriage Encounter*. She is a member of the Catholic Press Association.

HELEN BOTTEL specializes in family and marriage relationships, women, and travel. She is author of *Parents' Survival Kit*, *Helen Help Us*, and *To Teens With Love*. Her magazine pieces have appeared in *Family Circle*, *Good Housekeeping*, *McCall's*, *Reader's Digest*, and others. She writes an advice column for the Tokyo newspaper *Yomiuri Shimbun* and is a contributing editor of *Real World*.

BARBARA BRABEC writes and publishes *Sharing Barbara's Mail*, a bimonthly newsletter that evolved from response to her bestselling book, *Creative Cash*. A former publisher and marketing manager of the book division, Barrington Press, she also edited *Artisan Crafts*, which she and her husband published. She authored the *Handcrafts* bulletin published by the Small Business Administration and has written for a number of national magazines, including *Woman's Day*, *Creative Crafts*, and *Changing Times*. She also writes two crafts columns, plus special reports she self-publishes and sells by direct mail.

CHARLES L. (CHUCK) CADIEUX is author of six books, including *These Are the Endangered* and *Goosehunting*. A full-time freelancer, he specializes in environmental issues, hunting, fishing, and conservation, and is an expert outdoor photographer. His articles have appeared in *American Hunter*, *Boating*, *Field & Stream*, *Outdoor Life*, *Sports Afield*, *Trailer Life*, *Trailer Travel*, and *Yachting*. He is a member (and past president) of the Outdoor Writers Association.

JULIE CANDLER is author of the book *Woman at the Wheel*. Former owner of her own public relations firm, she writes for *Advertising Age*, *AAA World*, *Mechanix Illustrated*, *Woman's Day*, and other periodicals. She has received numerous awards for her writing, including the prestigious National Safety Council Public Service Award.

CLAUDIA M. CARUANA's articles and essays have appeared in many newspapers and magazines, such as *American Baby*, the *Chicago Tribune*, the *Christian Science Monitor*, *Consumer's Digest*, and the *New York Times*. A faculty member at St. John's University, she is president of the Deadline Club, the New York City Chapter of the Society of Professional Journalists/Sigma Delta Chi, and associate editor of *Chemical Engineering Progress*.

ALAN CARUBA has spent more than 25 years working at the writer's craft, and has written hundreds of magazine, newspaper, and trade-publication articles. (He estimates he writes a half-million words a year.) Caruba is a frequent contributor to the *New York Times*. His clients represent many of the major Fortune 500 corporations, as well as trade associations and public utilities. Other credits include two nonfiction books, a novel, and a volume of poetry. President of the Caruba Organization, he is a frequent lecturer and speaker on university campuses and to business groups coast to coast. He is also a reviewer and a member of the National Book Critics Circle.

CURTIS W. CASEWIT has published many articles and stories in such magazines as *Holiday*, *True*, *Saturday Review*, and *Coronet*. He has written several successful books, including *Quit Smoking*, *Making a Living in the Fine Arts*, *The*

Mountain World, and *Freelance Writing: Advice from the Pros.* He is a travel columnist for a number of newspapers.

KAY CASSILL's articles on travel, medicine/health, and psychology/behavior have run in *McCall's, Ladies' Home Journal, People, Smithsonian,* and other leading magazines. Her books include *Twins—Nature's Amazing Mystery, The Complete Handbook For Freelance Writers,* and *R.V. Cassill.* She also teaches nonfiction at the University of Rhode Island and Providence College.

KAREN CURE's travel and leisure articles have appeared in most major magazines. Author of *Mini-Vacations USA* and *The Travel Catalogue,* she does a monthly column for *TWA Ambassador* inflight magazine. In addition, she contributes to *Diversion* magazine, and writes—as well as doing editing—for several travel magazines and guidebook series edited by Steve Birnbaum.

GEORGE DEVINE is one of the first laymen to study and teach theology in American Catholic *academe.* He has written a series of sermons from a lay viewpoint, *If I Were To Preach,* published in three volumes. His other theological works include *Transformation in Christ* and *Liturgical Renewal: An Agonizing Reappraisal.* He writes religious-education texts, and his articles have appeared in the *National Observer, The Lutheran, America, Commonweal, Catholic Digest,* and many other top religion magazines. He teaches English and religion at Saint Rose Academy, San Francisco.

CYNTHIA B. DRISCOLL specializes in writing about vegetable gardening, horticulture, children, education, outdoor life, and historical topics. She has written articles for many major publications, including *Alaska Journal, Family Food Garden, Flower and Garden, Harrowsmith, Mother Earth News, North/Nord,* and *Organic Gardening.* She also lectures on gardening, and writes nonprofit grant proposals and company brochures. She is a member of the American Society of Horticultural Science and the Minnesota Horticultural Society and is a Minnesota Master Gardener.

JOLEE EDMONDSON, who specializes in sports writing (particularly golf), personality profiles, and celebrity interviews, is author of *The Woman Golfer's Catalogue* and *The Bear and I: The Story of the World's Most Famous Caddie.* Formerly associate editor, *Golf* magazine, her articles have appeared in *American Way, Inside Sports, Parade, Reader's Digest, Golf, Signature,* and *Vista/USA.* A member of the Golf Writers' Association of America, she has received numerous awards for her writing; her work has been anthologized in *Best Sports Stories, 1977,* published by E.P. Dutton.

JOHN W. ENGLISH teaches journalism at the University of Georgia in Athens. He is author of *Criticizing the Critics* and contributor to *New Journalism* and *Mass News.* His articles have appeared in *American Film, Museum News,* the *New York Times,* and the *Atlanta Journal-Constitution Magazine.* In 1977, he was awarded a filmmaking grant by the National Endowment for the Arts.

GLEN EVANS, author of two nonfiction books and contributor to many others, has written for *Families, Family Circle, Parade, Seventeen,* and *Travel & Leisure.* A former columnist for *True,* he also edited a corporate business magazine and was associate editor of *Missouri Alumnus* magazine. He is on the executive council of both ASJA and the Deadline Club, the New York City Chapter of Sigma Delta Chi/Society of Professional Journalists.

JACK FINCHER's books include *The Brain: Keeper of Life, Lefties, Human Intelligence,* and *Sinister People: The Looking-Glass World of the Left-Hander.* He writes articles for most major magazines and is former San Francisco bureau chief for *Life.* His book *Human Intelligence* won the 1977 American Medical Writers Association Annual Book Award.

LUCY FREEMAN is noted for her writing in the fields of psychoanalysis and psychiatry. A member of the board of directors, National Association of Science Writers, she is author of many books, including *Fight Against Fears, Who Is Sylvia?, Betrayal, Freud Rediscovered,* and *Too Deep For Tears.* Her articles have appeared in most major magazines, and she also does editing work in the mental health field.

BETTY FRIEDAN, author of the bestselling *The Feminine Mystique, It Changed My Life,* and *The Second Stage,* has published articles in most major magazines and won ASJA's Author of the Year Award (1982), presented to a writer whose book, or body of work, has made a significant contribution to American society. In 1979, she won the first Mort Weisinger Award, presented for an outstanding article by a member of the ASJA.

PAUL FRIGGENS, formerly a roving editor for *Reader's Digest,* is co-author of *The Black Hills* and visiting lecturer at the University of Colorado in Boulder. He also conducts *Reader's Digest*-University sponsored seminars and workshops in writing at various colleges around the country.

MICHAEL FROME is a leading author and critic of contemporary environmental and energy policies—public and private—that affect America's resource heritage. He formerly wrote conservation columns for *American Forests* magazine and *Field & Stream* (where he was conservation editor for seven years), and presently contributes a regular column, "Crusade for Wildlife," to *Defenders of Wildlife* magazine. Presently at the University of Idaho as Visiting Associate Professor of Communication and Wildlife Recreation Management, he is author of many books, the latest of which is *The Forest Service: A Profile of History, Policy and Performance.* He won the 1981 ASJA Mort Weisinger Award for his article, "The Un-Greening of Our National Parks."

DON AND JOAN GERMAN are co-authors of many books on money matters, retail banking, and bank marketing, and several books for juveniles. Their most recent success is *The Only Money Book for the Middle Class.* In addition, the versatile couple edits three banking newsletters and writes feature articles for such magazines as *Bankers, Bride's, Compass, Consumer's Digest,* and *Family Weekly.* They also authored the highly successful how-to book, *Make Your Own Convenience Foods.* Joan heads ASJA's Berkshire Hills Chapter.

SARA D. GILBERT is a freelancer who has written for *Good Housekeeping, Ms., Travel,* and other major magazines. She has authored thirteen books and done filmstrips, teaching aids, and considerable ghostwriting. She has worked for Condé Nast, Cowles Communications, ABC News, and WTOP Radio in Washington, D.C. Her awards include the Library of Congress "Best Books" list and the National Science Teachers Association and New York Public Library "teen" lists.

DIANA C. GLEASNER, who specializes in writing about sports, women, the outdoors, and leisure, has written for such magazines as *Better Homes & Gar-*

dens, Boating, Field & Stream, Good Housekeeping, Marathon World, Motorboat, Rotarian, Science Digest, and *Travel.* Presently travel columnist for the *Charlotte Observer,* she is author of a dozen books, including *Windsurfing, Rock Climbing, Sea Islands of the South,* and the *Illustrated Dictionary of Surfing, Swimming and Diving.*

BARBARA GOODHEART writes medical/health articles for both laymen and physicians. Her work has appeared in *Better Homes & Gardens, Companion, Discovery, Family Weekly, Today's Health,* and many other popular magazines and medical publications. She is author of *A Year on the Desert,* and has contributed to several anthologies and textbooks. She also does medical editing and medical audiovisuals. Goodheart is immediate past chairperson of ASJA's Midwest Chapter.

RONALD GROSS, creator of the prestigious Writers in the Public Interest (with support from such well-known journalists and authors as Gloria Steinem, Kurt Vonnegut, Nat Hentoff, Caroline Bird, and John Holt), also conducts Life Planning Seminars at New York University. His award-winning articles have appeared in major magazines and newspapers, and his dozen published books include *The Independent Scholar's Handbook, The Children's Rights Movement, Radical School Reform, Old in America,* and *Individualism.* He lectures extensively on communication skills, education, and civil liberties.

MARVIN GROSSWIRTH has authored many nonfiction books, including the *Mensa Genius Quiz Books, The Heraldry Book, Home Video, Beginner's Guide to Small Computers, The Truth about Vasectomy,* and *Mechanix Illustrated Guide to How to Patent and Market Your Own Invention.* He has written for many publications, including *Argosy, Cosmopolitan, Parents, Personal Computing, 50 Plus, Science Digest* and *SciQuest.* He is past national chairman of Mensa.

ALAN D. HAAS is a freelance "generalist" who has written for many major magazines, including *Coronet, Family Weekly, Look, Mechanix Illustrated, Parade, Popular Mechanics, This Week, True,* and *TV Guide.* He is author of *Welcome Child* and *Profitable Hobbies Handbook,* and his articles have appeared in several anthologies.

BLANCHE HACKETT is a librarian and freelance writer specializing in consumer matters, medicine, and topics of interest to women. Her articles have appeared in such periodicals as *American Heritage, Christian Science Monitor, Family Health, Ford Times, National Geographic,* the *New York Times, Parents, Popular Mechanics,* and *Reader's Digest.* She is a member of the American Library Association.

ALEX HALEY, author of *Roots* and *The Autobiography of Malcom X,* is winner of the Pulitzer Prize and the National Book Award, and has 16 honorary degrees and over 300 other special recognitions. He taught himself to write during a 20-year career in the U.S. Coast Guard, became a magazine writer, and did the first of the now-famous *Playboy* interviews. He spent twelve years researching and writing his classic nonfiction work, *Roots.*

FRANCES HALPERN, author of *Writer's Guide to Publishing in the West* and *Writer's Guide to West Coast Publishing,* has written for *Reader's Digest, Seventeen, Westways,* and other magazines. She also writes the column "Bookings" for the

Los Angeles Herald Examiner and has received awards from California Press Women and National Federation of Press Women.

JEAN AYRES HARTLEY writes on many subjects, including food, family, the outdoors, travel, and leisure. She has written for *Bon Appétit, Camper Coachman,* the *Christian Science Monitor, Elks, Lady's Circle, Modern Maturity, Rotarian,* and several newspaper Sunday supplements and travel sections. She is author of *Clouds in Panama,* and is a member of the California Writers Club.

BARBARA SHOOK HAZEN, author of many children's books, formerly worked as a book editor for Western Publishing, and also was an editor at *Ladies' Home Journal.* She has contributed magazine articles and stories to *Holiday, Saturday Evening Post, Vista/USA* and several other leading periodicals. Her most recent book is *Very Shy.* She is a member of the ASJA Board of Directors.

D.J. HERDA is the author of twenty nonfiction books and contributes to leading U.S. magazines and newspapers. Formerly an articles editor, college writing instructor, and reporter, he specializes in gardening, photography, sports, and human-interest subjects. His most recent books are *The Winds of Kabul, Model Railroading, Model Cars,* and *Bicycle Buyer's Guide.* His gardening books include *Vegetables in a Pot* and *Making a Native Plant Terrarium.*

HAL HIGDON, a freelance writer, has been an ASJA member since 1960. One of the best-known long-distance runners in the world and a regular author of books and articles on that subject, he serves as senior writer for *The Runner* magazine. His work on various subjects also has appeared in *Good Housekeeping, TV Guide, Parade, People, Skiing, Sports Illustrated, Travel & Leisure,* and *Better Homes & Gardens.* He is currently working on a novel, tentatively titled *Falconara,* that traces his wife's family history back eight centuries through Italy to Albania.

GLORIA HOCHMAN's numerous articles in the medicine/health and psychology/behavior fields have won many awards. Her work has been honored by several health foundations, including those representing Easter Seals, arthritis, cystic fibrosis, and lupus. She is director of communications for the Adoption Center of Delaware Valley and an ASJA Board member. She is the author of *Heart Bypass: What Every Patient Must Know.*

ARLINE INGE is articles editor of *Cuisine* and has also held editorial positions with *Bon Appétit, Silver Foxes,* and *Playgirl.* Her articles and special features have appeared in many leading American magazines, including *Architectural Digest, Travel Illustrated, Western's World,* and *Woman's World.* She was formerly director of public relations for the University of Southern California College of Continuing Education.

JOHN H. INGERSOLL was formerly senior editor of *House Beautiful* and senior staff writer for *Housing.* He specializes in writing about light construction, how-to, housing, and science. His articles have appeared in virtually all leading magazines, including *Better Homes & Gardens, Family Circle, Family Handyman, Holiday, House Beautiful, Modern Bride, Omni, Popular Science,* and *Popular Mechanics.* He is author of *We Can Save Ourselves* and *How to Sell a House* and is currently president of ASJA.

JAMES JOSEPH specializes in writing for business, but has written on adventure, science, aviation, and other subjects for virtually every major U.S. magazine and many foreign publications. He is the author of *Car Cures* and *Car-Keeper's Guide*, plus twenty other nonfiction books. He has recently launched a series of writers' marketing seminars under the title "Writer's World." He is chairperson of ASJA's Southern California Chapter.

EVELYN KAYE specializes in families, children, and television and has written for *Glamour, McCall's, Parents,* and others. She is author of many nonfiction books, including *Crosscurrents: Children, Families and Religion.* A former reporter for the *Manchester Guardian* and Reuters News Agency, she was co-founder and first president of Action for Children's Television (ACT); she is currently executive vice president of ASJA and vice president of the Council of Writers Organizations (CWO).

BERN KEATING, president of the Travel Journalists Guild, is author of 25 books, including *Mississippi, Famous American Cowboys, Chopper, Inside Passage,* and *The Flamboyant Mr. Colt and His Six Shooter.* He has written for *Holiday, Travel & Leisure, National Geographic, Playboy,* and *Smithsonian,* among other national magazines. Fluent in Spanish and French, he is also a professional photographer and a winner of the Printing Industry Graphic Arts Award.

KATHRYN LANCE has written articles for leading magazines in the U.S., including *Family Circle, Ladies' Home Journal, Parade, Self, Today's Jogger,* and *Town & Country.* A former associate editor of *Scholastic Voice,* she is the author of six nonfiction books in the health/fitness field, the most recent being *Sports Beauty* and *The Body Team.* She is on the advisory board of the National Jogging Association.

GEORGE DELUCENAY LEON is author of *Energy Forever,* co-author of *Dial 911,* and contributing writer for Reader's Digest Books' *Back to Basics.* Formerly managing editor of *Electronics Products,* he presently is contributing editor of *Sound and Communications* magazine. He specializes in science, technology, energy, and telecommunications and also writes for *Avionics, Popular Electronics, Popular Mechanics, Electronic Warfare,* and *Video Systems News.*

HOWARD R. LEWIS is president of Clinical Communications, Inc., and both editor and columnist of *RN* magazine. Along with his wife, Martha E. Lewis (also an ASJA member), he contributes articles and essays to *American Journal of Psychiatry, Cardiology, Consumer Reports, Family Circle, New England Journal of Medicine,* and *Reader's Digest.* He is author of *The People's Medical Manual: Your Complete Guide to Health and Safety* and other nonfiction books.

PETER R. LIMBURG's many books and articles deal primarily with science and technology. Author of sixteen books, including *Farming the Waters* and *The Story of Your Heart,* and frequent contributor to national magazines, he writes mainly for children and young adults. He is a member of the National Association of Science Writers and Forum of Writers for Young People. He has won four book awards from the National Science Teachers Association and three from the Children's Book Council.

NORMAN LOBSENZ, a past president of ASJA, has written more than 200 articles for major magazines such as *Family Circle, Woman's Day, Redbook,* the *New*

York Times Magazine, Reader's Digest, Redbook, McCall's, and *Good Housekeeping.* He is the author or co-author of numerous books, including bestsellers *Nobody's Perfect, Styles of Loving, No-Fault Marriage,* and, most recently, *Equal Time.*

SUZANNE LOEBL's medical and health articles have appeared in the *New York Times, Redbook, Parents, Science Digest,* and other periodicals and journals. Formerly science editor for both the New York Heart Association and the Arthritis Foundation, she is co-author of several medical books, including *The Nurse's Drug Handbook.* She also was editor of the *Mother's Encyclopedia and Everyday Guide to Family Health.* She is currently secretary of ASJA.

JOHN W. MALO is author of nine books dealing with outdoors skills and recreation/leisure. They include *Fly Fishing for Panfish, Canoeing* (juvenile), *Midwest Canoe Trails, Motor-Camping Around Europe, Snowmobiling: The Guide, Wilderness Canoeing,* and *Complete Guide to Houseboating.* A former teacher and school administrator and a Ford Fellow, his articles have appeared in *Field & Stream* and other national and regional publications. He writes a column, "Earthworks," for his local newspaper in Colorado.

PEGGY MANN's many books include *"Gizelle, Save the Children!," Twelve Is Too Old, The Secret Ship,* and *Ralph Bunche: UN Peacemaker.* Three of her titles have been dramatized for national television, and one received a Peabody Award. She has written and lectured extensively on drug abuse, and also specializes in writing about the holocaust. Her magazine articles have appeared in virtually all leading publications in the U.S., including *Reader's Digest,* the *New York Times, Parade, Redbook, McCall's, Travel & Leisure,* and *Harper's Bazaar.* She is a member of the Dramatists Guild and PEN.

MARGARET MARKHAM, a specialist in medical articles, has contributed to both consumer and professional publications, including *Harper's Bazaar, Parents,* and *Psychiatric News,* and is co-author of *The Breast Book.* She did the interviews with Betty Friedan and Alvin Toffler as executive editor, *ASJA Anniversary Journal* (1978).

PATRICK M. MCGRADY JR., a past president of ASJA, is co-author of the bestseller *The Pritikin Program for Diet and Exercise* (with Nathan Pritikin). He is also author of *The Love Doctors, The Youth Doctors,* and *Television Critics in a Free Society.* He has written articles on medicine, nutrition, and preventive medicine for most major magazines.

CATHERINE LANHAM MILLER is author of *How to Say Yes to Life: A Woman's Guide to Beating the Blahs.* She has contributed to *Dynamic Years, Good Housekeeping, Harper's Bazaar, House Beautiful, Ladies' Home Journal,* and *McCall's.* She also writes a self-syndicated column, "Saying Yes to Life," and is president of Identity, Inc., seminars for women.

ROBERT SCOTT MILNE is publisher of the well-known *Travelwriter Marketletter.* Specializing in guides and encyclopedia articles, he also contributes to leading newspapers and magazines throughout the U.S. He is author of *Opportunities in Travel Careers,* and has contributed to *Exxon Travel Guide, North American Trail Guide,* and *Texaco Travel Atlas.* His newsletter has won an award from the Society of American Travel Writers Freelance Council for excellence in publishing. He is secretary of the Council of Writers Organizations.

HARRY MILT is the author of *Conquer Your Phobia, Alcoholism: Its Causes and Cure, Basic Handbook on Mental Illness,* and *Master Your Tensions.* Former director of information, National Association for Mental Health, and a research writer for the American Cancer Society, his articles have appeared in *Parents, Parade, Reader's Digest, Trends in Psychiatry,* and United Press Features. He also does public relations consulting, specializing in mental health/illness, medicine/ health, and human relations.

ROSALIE MINKOW, who specializes in taxation, money management, and travel, writes for *Better Homes & Gardens, LI Magazine, Newsday, New York Times, Boating,* and *Yachting.* Her books include *Creative Tax Benefits, The Complete List of IRS Tax Deductions* (which has been twice revised), and *Money Management for Women.* She has also taught adult-education writing courses and is currently on the faculty of Hofstra University.

ANNIE MOLDAFSKY's books include *The Good Buy Book, Welcome to the Real World,* and several regional editions of the former. She writes articles and features on consumerism for *Chicago, Prime Times, Self, House Beautiful, Seventeen,* and *Working Mother.* She also does public relations and publicity campaigns, brochures, consulting, lecturing, and radio copy and show production. In addition, her work appears in several major newspapers such as the *Chicago Tribune* and *Milwaukee Journal.*

CHARLOTTE MONTGOMERY has for many years been *Good Housekeeping*'s "Speaker For the House." She also has written consumer and women's-interest articles for *Redbook, Lifetime Living,* and *Tide.* She is author of *Handbook for the Woman Driver* and lectures extensively on consumerism matters. She has received writing awards from the Council of Better Business Bureaus, National Federation of Press Women, and Women in Communications.

TERRY MORRIS, a past president of ASJA, has been published in virtually all writing media. She specializes in human-interest and "as-told-to" stories for such magazines as *McCall's, Family Circle, Redbook, Reader's Digest, Good Housekeeping,* and *New Republic.* She is the author of seven books, including *Just Sixteen; Shalom, Golda;* and *Dr. America: The Story of Tom Dooley.*

BERNIECE ROER NEAL is a contributor to the *New York Times, Washington Post, Woman's Day, Writer's Digest,* and other publications. Her books include *Chicken* and *How to Write Articles.* A former article instructor at Writer's Digest School, she edits and lectures on writing and, with her husband Harry Edward Neal, teaches writing at conferences, workshops, and seminars.

HARRY EDWARD NEAL is the author of thirty-one nonfiction books, including *Before Columbus: Who Discovered America?* and *Nonfiction,* and has contributed articles to *Cosmopolitan, Esquire, Saturday Evening Post,* and many other magazines. He is a former assistant chief of the U.S. Secret Service. He and his wife, Berniece Roer Neal, lecture on and teach writing at writing conferences across the country.

KAREN O'CONNOR writes on religion, juvenile nonfiction, and other topics for many leading periodicals. A writer-consultant for Glencoe Publishing Company, she is author of *Try These on for Size, Melody!, Maybe You Belong in a Zoo!,* and *Contributions of Women: Literature,* among other nonfiction books. She teaches writing at the University of California, San Diego, and does educational writing and consulting. Her honors include the California Press Women Book Award.

SALLY WENDKOS OLDS, a past president of ASJA, has published articles in virtually every major women's magazine, including *Good Housekeeping, Ladies' Home Journal, Mademoiselle, McCall's, Ms., Redbook,* and *Woman's Day.* Her latest books are *The Working Parents Handbook, A Child's World, Human Development,* and *Helping Your Child Learn Right from Wrong.* In 1973, she won the Family Service Association of America's National Media Award, and in 1983, she was a recipient of the ASJA's Mort Weisinger Award.

WALTER OLEKSY, a former *Chicago Tribune* reporter, writes articles and books primarily for teenagers and young adults. He is author of *The Road Runners, Archaeology Today in America, Quacky and the Crazy Curve-Ball,* and 31 other books, both fiction and nonfiction. His articles appear in such magazines as *Boys' Life, Crossroads, Discovery, Kiwanis, Modern Maturity, Reader's Digest,* and *TWA Ambassador.* He is also a professional photojournalist.

VANCE PACKARD, a past president of ASJA, is best known for his books on contemporary America: *Animal IQ, The Hidden Persuaders, The Status Seekers, The Waste Makers,* and *The Pyramid Climbers;* his most recent is *Our Endangered Children.* He has contributed to virtually all of the country's prominent periodicals, including *Atlantic Monthly, Harper's Bazaar, Look,* and the *New York Times Magazine.*

HOWARD PEACOCK is a full-time freelance writer-photographer who specializes in travel, energy, nature, and business topics. His articles have appeared in *Exxon USA, Houston, Fodor's Modern Travel Guides, Texas Highways, American Oil and Gas Reporter, Ultra,* and *Houston Post. Time* commissioned him to write a special nature booklet and *Arizona Highways* picked him for a rarity, an article by a non-Arizonan. Author of *Big Thicket,* he is past president of the Big Thicket Association. He is a member of the International Association of Business Communicators, the National Audubon Society, the Association of Petroleum Writers, and the Texas Folklore Society.

RICHARD QUEBEDEAUX is author of *The New Charismatics II, By What Authority: The Rise of Personality Cults in American Christianity, The Worldly Evangelicals,* and four other books on religion. Educated at the University of California, Los Angeles, he also has a bachelors degree from the Harvard Divinity School, and a Ph.D. in modern history from Oxford University, where he was also a World Council of Churches Ecumenical Scholar at Mansfield College. He is a senior consultant for the New Ecumenical Research Association (NEW ERA). He edited *Lifestyle, Conversations with Members of the Unification Church,* and co-edited *Evangelical-Unification Dialogue.*

TED J. RAKSTIS, winner of ASJA's 1980 Mort Weisinger Award (for "The Poisoning of Michigan," *Reader's Digest,* September 1979), has written award-winning articles for *Kiwanis,* the *Chicago Sun-Times,* the *Chicago Tribune Magazine, Coronet, Cosmopolitan, Discovery, Elks, Pageant, Rotarian,* the *Saturday Evening Post, Today's Health,* and *Writer's Digest.* Specializing in business, sales and marketing, cable TV and other subjects, he also won a 1982 ASJA Special Recognition Award for his article on censorship, "The Great Book Debate" (*Kiwanis*, September 1981).

DAN RAMSEY is the author of fourteen books and articles on consumer subjects for many periodicals including *Camping Journal, Mother Earth News, Plane & Pilot,* and *Today's Homes*. Now a full-time freelancer, his other jobs have included truck driver, factory worker, real estate salesman, radio broadcaster, and newspaper publisher. He is director of Ramsey and Associates, a partnership of writers, editors, and producers specializing in how-to books and articles for the consumer.

BONNIE REMSBERG, in her 20-year career as a journalist, has written more than 900 nonfiction articles and dramatic narratives for most of America's leading magazines, including *Family Circle, Redbook, Ladies' Home Journal, Woman's Day, Good Housekeeping,* the *New York Times Magazine* and *Reader's Digest*. She is author of *Radio & TV Spot Announcements for Family Planning,* distributed by the United Nations and the Ford Foundation to the world's developing countries. She has taught writing courses at the University of Chicago, Northwestern University, Columbia University, and Indiana University. She was won several major journalism awards, and is hostess of "Some of My Best Friends" on Chicago's WMAQ-TV. She is an ASJA Board member.

EDWARD R. RICCIUTI, former curator of publications and director of public relations for the New York Zoological Society, has authored over two dozen nonfiction books. His articles on science, nature, and the environment have appeared in such major magazines as *Audubon, Geo, National Wildlife, International Wildlife, Outdoor Life, Science Digest,* and *Reader's Digest*. He is a member of the board of directors of the Holy Land Conservation Fund and a fellow of the Explorers Club.

ROBERTA ROESCH is author of the successful *There's Always a Right Job for Every Woman, Anyone's Son, Jobs for Weekends,* and *Women in Action*. She has contributed to many magazines, syndicates, and news services and teaches writing at Fairleigh Dickinson University and New Jersey's Bergen and Rockland Community Colleges. She was awarded an Honorary Doctor of Humane Letters degree by Centenary College, and won the top 1980 book award from the National Federation of Press Women. She is a vice president of ASJA.

FLORA RHETA SCHREIBER, award-winning psychiatric writer, also does political profiles. Her books include the bestseller *Sybil, Your Child's Speech,* and her most recent, *The Shoemaker: Anatomy of a Psychotic*. She is a professor of English and speech and has contributed articles to *Good Housekeeping, Family Weekly, Ladies' Home Journal, Modern Maturity,* the *New York Times, Reader's Digest, Redbook,* and *Today's Health*.

NORMAN SCHREIBER, former editor of *Strobe* and publicity writer for Paramount Records, contributes to *Ladies' Home Journal, Travel & Leisure, Village Voice, Camera Arts,* and *Home Video,* among others. He writes the column "Snapshots" for *Popular Photography,* for which he is a contributing editor.

DODI SCHULTZ specializes in medicine, children, and psychology and has written articles for many major magazines, including *Ladies' Home Journal, McCall's, Parents, Parade, SciQuest, Self, Today's Health,* and the *New York Times Magazine*. She has authored or co-authored more than a dozen books, among them *The Mothers' and Fathers' Medical Encyclopedia,* and has received several journalism awards. She is currently a vice president of ASJA.

MORT SCHULTZ, writer for *Family Handyman, Mechanix Illustrated, Popular Mechanics, Reader's Digest,* and many other periodicals, is author of several how-to/crafts books and guides. They include *The McGraw-Hill Illustrated Auto Repair Course* and *Practical Handbook of Painting & Wallpapering.* He writes the well-known column, "Car Clinic," for *Popular Mechanics,* and is a member of the National Association of Home and Workshop Writers and the Society of Automotive Engineers.

MICHAEL H. SEDGE, director of Strawberry Media, is also a contributing editor of *Off Duty.* His expertise is European guidebooks and photography, and he specializes in European travel writing. His articles have appeared in many U.S. and foreign publications, including *Attenzione, Newsweek,* and *Oceans.* His books include *Diver's Guide to Italy, Welcome to the Med,* and *Welcome to Naples.*

CECILE SHAPIRO writes book reviews and specializes in articles on decorative and fine art and housing/architecture. Her work has appeared in *Americana, Art Journal, ARTnews, Victorian Homes, House and Garden Guides, Publishers Weekly, Redbook,* and *Saturday Review.* Her books include *Better Kitchens* and *Fine Prints: Collecting, Buying, and Selling.* She is a member of the New York Book Critics Circle.

ELAINE FANTLE SHIMBERG's articles on women, writing, and popular medicine have appeared in *Baby Talk, Essence, Family Weekly, Glamour, Rx Sports & Travel, Seventeen, Writer's Digest,* and *Woman's Day.* She also writes for many U.S. newspapers and is author of *Two for the Money: A Woman's Guide to Double Career Marriage* and *How to Be A Successful Housewife/Writer: Bylines & Babies Do Mix.* She was formerly co-hostess of the television show "Woman's Point of View."

DOROTHY SIEGEL contributes articles on teenagers, family relations, children, and other topics to many leading magazines, including *Family Circle, Good Housekeeping, Ladies' Home Journal, McCall's, Money, Parents, Reader's Digest, Redbook,* and *Woman's Day.* She is author of *The Glory Road, Winners: Eight Special Young People,* and *The Big Town for Teens.*

ISOBEL SILDEN is a public relations expert whose articles have appeared in *Family Circle, Ford Times, Modern Maturity, Cable Marketing,* and the *Los Angeles Times,* among other magazines and newspapers. Her work appears in several inflight publications. She also contributes to the Australian Consolidated Press.

CIMA STAR, former reporter with the *Rome Daily American* and *International Herald Tribune,* has written articles for leading magazines and journals, including *Cosmopolitan, Family Weekly, Glamour, McCall's,* and the *Journal of International Physicians.* Her specialties include psychology/mental health, food, medicine, and social problems. She is author of *Understanding Headaches* and *Gourmet Dinners in 30 Minutes.*

AL STUMP, former correspondent for *True,* is one of the country's best-known sportswriters. His articles have appeared in *American Heritage, American Legion, Golf Digest, Sports Illustrated,* and many other top periodicals and newspapers. He has also been a contributing writer for *Sport, Esquire,* the *Saturday Evening Post, American,* and *Argosy.* Author of several books, he collaborated on *My Life in Baseball* (Ty Cobb) and *Education of a Golfer* (Sam Snead). Other books include *Champions Against Odds* and *Football Access.*

ALDEN TODD's books include *Finding Facts Fast, Abandoned: The Story of the Greely Arctic Expedition,* and *Justice on Trial: The Case of Louis D. Brandeis.* He is an adjunct assistant professor at New York University, and has written many articles, speeches, and newsletters. He is currently treasurer of ASJA.

ALVIN TOFFLER is author of the bestsellers *The Third Wave, The Eco-Spasm Report, Future Shock,* and *The Culture Consumers;* his most recent is *Previews & Premises.* He has published countless articles in *Fortune, Horizon, Esquire, Reader's Digest, Saturday Review, The New Republic, The Nation,* the *New York Times Book Review, Annals of the American Academy of Political and Social Sciences,* and other leading periodicals and journals. A former associate editor at *Fortune* and visiting professor at Cornell University, he has won numerous writing awards, including the Prix du Meilleur Livre Etranger (France), the McKinsey Foundation Book Award, and *Playboy's* Best Article, 1970.

MYRA WALDO writes a weekly travel column for the *Los Angeles Times* and is author of five annually updated name-above-the-title travel guides, as well as a number of cookbooks; she is president of the Society of American Travel Writers. The distinguished travel writer and radio commentator is also a food and restaurant critic. Her pieces have appeared in most leading American magazines.

MORTON WALKER, D.P.M. (Doctor of Podiatric Medicine), is a full-time freelance medical journalist and author. He has published twenty-one books and over 1200 magazine and medical journal articles. He has received a number of awards. He practiced podiatry for seventeen years before becoming a full-time writer in 1969, has been an editor for the American Medical Writers Association, and taught writing at the University of Connecticut. He specializes in writing on holistic health.

The late **MORT WEISINGER** was a past president of ASJA and a founding member of the Society. He published over 200 articles and was also editor of "Superman." His paperback, *One Thousand & One Valuable Things You Can Get Free,* has sold two million copies. The annual Mort Weisinger Award, recognizing outstanding articles by Society members, honors his memory.

MORRIS A. WESSEL, M.D., is clinical professor of pediatrics at the Yale University School of Medicine and a contributing editor of *Parents.* He also freelances medicine/health articles to many other national publications. He has been published in a number of professional medical journals, and lectures on child care and medical problems.

ARDIS WHITMAN's many articles on religion, psychology, and philosophy have appeared in *Reader's Digest, Ladies' Home Journal,* the *New York Times Magazine, McCall's,* and other leading publications. Her books include *Meditation: Journey to the Self, A New Image of Man,* and *How to Be a Happy Woman.* She lectures throughout the country and has been honored by the National Conference of Christians and Jews with their Mass Media Brotherhood Award.

ELIZABETH FRIAR WILLIAMS specializes in writing about the psychology of women, relationships, and psychotherapy. Author of *Breaking Up and Starting Over* and *Notes of a Feminist Therapist*, she has written articles for *Cosmopolitan, McCall's, Mademoiselle, New Woman,* and others. She is an active member of the American Psychological Association, the New York Academy of Sciences, and the Association for Women in Psychology.

RUTH WINTER, a past president of ASJA, has been published in virtually all major consumer magazines and specializes in health, medicine, and behavior. She is author of *The Great Self-Improvement Sourcebook* as well as many other nonfiction books. The winner of dozens of writing awards and honors, she has thrice been chairperson of ASJA's acclaimed Annual Writers' Conference held in New York City.

MARV WOLF has contributed to many top newspapers and magazines in the U.S. and abroad. Formerly an editor with the Northrop Corporation, Transamerica Corporation, and Avco Financial Corporation, he is author of the book, *Streets of Seoul*. A lecturer on photojournalism at the California State University at Fullerton, he also writes for the Independent News Alliance, *Geo, Asia, New West, Science 83, D, Westways,* and *Los Angeles*. He does copywriting for corporate and advertising agencies across the country.

HELEN WORTH, noted author, feature writer, magazine and newspaper food editor, lecturer, judge in international cooking competitions, and vice-president of Good Taste Products, Inc., has also had her own network television food program. She works as a consultant to major corporations and associations and has developed Brown-Quick, her own unique food product. Worth pioneered college courses on food and drink appreciation, which she taught first at New York City's Columbia University.Her many cookbooks were all book club selections, and she has won Tastemaker Awards. Her books include the *Down-on-the-Farm Cookbook, Shrimp Cookery, Cooking Without Recipes, Hostess Without Help,* and *Damnyankee in a Southern Kitchen.*

MAURICE ZOLOTOW, first president of ASJA (when it was known as the Society of Magazine Writers), has authored many articles and books, including a biography of Marilyn Monroe, *Stage Struck: The Romance of Alfred Lunt and Lynn Fontanne, Shooting Star: The Life of John Wayne, Billy Wilder in Hollywood,* and several novels; his latest is *Confessions of a Racetrack Fiend.*

Suggested Letter of Agreement

originating with the writer (to be used when publication does not issue written confirmation of assignment)

DATE

EDITOR'S NAME & TITLE
PUBLICATION
ADDRESS

Dear EDITOR'S NAME:

This will confirm our agreement that I will research and write an article of approximately NUMBER words on the subject of BRIEF DESCRIPTION, in accord with our discussion of DATE.

The deadline for delivery of this article to you is DATE.

It is understood that my fee for this article shall be $ AMOUNT, payable on acceptance, for which sum PUBLICATION shall be entitled to first North American publication rights in the article.[1] If this assignment does not work out after I have submitted a completed manuscript, a guarantee of $ AMOUNT shall be paid to me.

It is further understood that you shall reimburse me for routine expenses incurred in the researching and writing of the article, including long-distance telephone calls, and that extraordinary expenses, should any such be anticipated, will be discussed with you before they are incurred.[2]

It is also agreed that you will submit proofs of the article for my examination, sufficiently in advance of publication to permit correction of errors.

I hereby warrant that the article will be original and, to the best of my abilities, accurate in all particulars.

This letter is intended to cover the main points of our agreement. Should any disagreement arise on these or other matters, we agree to rely upon the guidelines set forth in the Code of Ethics and Fair Practices of the American Society of Journalists and Authors. Should any controversy persist, such controversy shall be submitted to arbitration before the American Arbitration Association in accordance with its rules, and judgment confirming the arbitrator's award may be entered in any court of competent jurisdiction.

Please confirm our mutual understanding by signing the copy of this agreement and returning it to me.

Sincerely,
(signed)
WRITER'S NAME

PUBLICATION

by _____
    NAME AND TITLE

Date _____

Notes

[1] If discussion included sale of other rights, this clause should specify basic fee for first North American rights, additional fees and express rights each covers, and total amount.

[2] Any other conditions agreed upon, such as inclusion of travel expenses or a maximum dollar amount for which the writer will be compensated, should also be specified.

AMERICAN SOCIETY OF JOURNALISTS AND AUTHORS, INC.
1501 BROADWAY, SUITE 1907, New York NY 10036 • (212)997-0947

American Society of Journalists and Authors Code of Ethics and Fair Practices

Preamble

Over the years, an unwritten code governing editor-writer relationships has arisen. The American Society of Journalists and Authors (ASJA) has compiled the major principles and practices of that code that are generally recognized as fair and equitable.

The ASJA has also established a Committee on Editor-Writer Relations to investigate and mediate disagreements brought before it, either by members or by editors. In its activity, this committee shall rely on the following guidelines.

1. Truthfulness, Accuracy, Editing

The writer shall at all times perform professionally and to the best of his or her ability, assuming primary responsibility for truth and accuracy. No writer shall deliberately write into an article a dishonest, distorted, or inaccurate statement.

Editors may correct or delete copy for purposes of style, grammar, conciseness, or arrangement, but may not change the intent or sense without the writer's permission.

2. Sources

A writer shall be prepared to support all statements made in his or her manuscripts, if requested. It is understood, however, that the publisher shall respect any and all promises of confidentiality made by the writer in obtaining information.

3. Ideas

An idea shall be defined not as a subject alone, but as a subject combined with an approach. A writer shall be considered to have a proprietary right to an idea suggested to an editor and to have priority in the development of it.

4. Acceptance of an Assignment

A request from an editor that the writer proceed with an idea, however worded and whether oral or written, shall be considered an assignment. (The word "assignment" here is understood to mean a definite order for an article.) It shall be the obligation of the writer to proceed as rapidly as possible toward the completion of an assignment, to meet a deadline mutually agreed upon, and not to agree to unreasonable deadlines.

5. Conflict of Interest

The writer shall reveal to the editor, before acceptance of an assignment, any actual or potential conflict of interest, including, but not limited to, any financial interest in any product, firm, or commercial venture relating to the subject of the article.

6. Report on Assignment

If in the course of research or during the writing of the article, the writer concludes that the assignment will not result in a satisfactory article, he or she shall be obliged to so inform the editor.

7. Withdrawal

Should a disagreement arise between the editor and writer as to the merit or handling of an assignment, the editor may remove the writer on payment of mutually satisfactory compensation for the effort already expended, or the writer may withdraw without compensation and, if the idea for the assignment originated with the writer, may take the idea elsewhere without penalty.

8. Agreements

The practice of written confirmation of all agreements between editors and writers is strongly recommended, and such confirmation may originate with the editor, the writer, or an agent. Such a memorandum of confirmation should list all aspects of the assignment including subject, approach, length, special instructions, payments, deadline, and guarantee (if any). Failing prompt contradictory response to such a memorandum, both parties are entitled to assume that the terms set forth therein are binding.

9. Rewriting

No writer's work shall be rewritten without his or her advance consent. If an editor requests a writer to rewrite a manuscript, the writer shall be obliged to do so, but shall alternatively be entitled to withdraw the manuscript and offer it elsewhere.

10. Bylines

Lacking any stipulation to the contrary, a byline is the author's unquestioned right. All advertisements of the article should also carry the author's name. If an author's byline is omitted from a published article, no matter what the cause or reason, the publisher shall be liable to compensate the author financially for the omission.

11. Updating

If delay in publication necessitates extensive updating of an article, such updating shall be done by the author, to whom additional compensation shall be paid.

12. Reversion of Rights

A writer is not paid by money alone. Part of the writer's compensation is the intangible value of timely publication. Consequently, if after six months the publisher has not scheduled an article for publication, or within twelve months has not published an article, the manuscript and all rights therein should revert to the author without penalty or cost to the author.

13. Payment for Assignments

An assignment presumes an obligation upon the publisher to pay for the writer's work upon satisfactory completion of the assignment, according to the agreed terms. Should a manuscript that has been accepted, orally or in writing, by a publisher or any representative or employee of the publisher, later be deemed unacceptable, the publisher shall nevertheless be obliged to pay the writer in full according to the agreed terms.

If an editor withdraws or terminates an assignment, due to no fault of the writer, after work has begun but prior to completion of the manuscript, the writer is entitled to compensation for work already put in; such compensation shall be negotiated between editor and author and shall be commensurate with the amount of work already completed. If a completed assignment is not acceptable, due to no fault of the writer, the writer is nevertheless entitled to payment; such payment, in common practice, has varied from half the agreed-upon price to the full amount of that price.

14. Time of Payments

The writer is entitled to payment for an accepted article within ten days of delivery. No article payment should ever be subject to publication.

15. Expenses

Unless otherwise stipulated by the editor at the time of an assignment, a writer shall assume that normal, out-of-pocket expenses will be reimbursed by the publisher. Any extraordinary expenses anticipated by the writer shall be discussed with the editor prior to incurring them.

16. Insurance

A magazine that gives a writer an assignment involving any extraordinary hazard shall insure the writer against death or disability during the course of travel or the hazard, or, failing that, shall honor the cost of such temporary insurance as an expense account item.

17. Loss of Personal Belongings

If, as a result of circumstances or events directly connected with a perilous assignment and due to no fault of the writer, a writer suffers loss of personal belongings or professional equipment, or incurs bodily injury, the publisher shall compensate the writer in full.

18. Copyright, Additional Rights

It shall be understood, unless otherwise stipulated in writing, that sale of an article manuscript entitles the purchaser to first North American publication rights only, and that all other rights are retained by the author. Under no circumstances shall an independent writer be required to sign a so-called "all rights transferred" or "work made for hire" agreement as a condition of assignment, of payment, or of publication.

19. Reprints

All revenues from reprints shall revert to the author exclusively, and it is incumbent upon a publication to refer all requests for reprint to the author. The author has a right to charge for such reprints, and must request that the original publication be credited.

20. Agents
According to the Society of Authors' Representatives, the accepted fee for an agent's services has long been 10 percent of the writer's receipts, except for foreign rights representation. An agent may not represent editors or publishers. In the absence of any agreement to the contrary, a writer shall not be obliged to pay an agent a fee on work negotiated, accomplished and paid for without the assistance of the agent.

21. TV and Radio Promotion
The writer is entitled to be paid for personal participation on TV or radio programs promoting periodicals in which the writer's work appears.

22. Indemnity
No writer should be obliged to indemnify any magazine or book publisher against any claim, actions, or proceedings arising from an article or book.

23. Proofs
The editor shall submit edited proofs of the author's work to the author for approval, sufficiently in advance of publication, so that any errors may be brought to the editor's attention. If for any reason a publication is unable to so deliver or transmit proofs to the author, the author is entitled to review the proofs in the publication's office.

On "Work Made for Hire": A Statement of Position

Announced April 28, 1978

It has long been the established practice for responsible periodicals, in commissioning articles by freelance writers, to purchase only one-time publication rights—commonly known as "first North American rights"—to such articles, the author retaining all other rights exclusively, and all revenues received from the subsequent sale of other rights reverting to the author.

This practice is affirmed by the Code of Ethics and Fair Practices of the American Society of Journalists and Authors, the national organization of independent nonfiction writers. The philosophy underlying this tradition has been further reaffirmed by the Copyright Law of 1976, which took effect in January of 1978 and states explicitly that copyright is vested in the author of a work and commences at the moment of creation of that work. "Copyright" is, literally, the "right to copy"—i.e., to publish in any form; that right is the author's, transferable only by written agreement and only to the degree, and under the terms, specified by such agreement.

It has come to the attention of the ASJA that certain periodicals publishers have recently sought to circumvent the clear intent of the law by requiring independent writers, as a condition of article assignment, to sign so-called "all rights transferred" or "work made for hire" agreements. "All rights transferred" signifies that the author, the recognized copyright owner, transfers that ownership—and the right to all future revenues that may accrue therefrom—to the publisher. A "work made for hire" agreement specifically relegates the independent writer, so far as the article under consideration is concerned, to the status of an employee, and creates a mythical—but nonetheless presumably legally binding—relationship in which the author agrees to function as a hired hand, while the publisher assumes the mantle of "creator" of the work, with all the rights of ownership vested in the creator under the law.

Both types of agreement clearly presume that the work being produced has an inherent value beyond one-time publication. Both the law and the ASJA Code of Ethics recognize that presumption, and it is the intent of both documents that the transfer of any rights beyond one-time publication take place only as the result of negotiation that assigns a monetary value to each such specific right a publisher seeks to acquire. Both types of agreement described above deny the author's basic role as owner and creator, and seek to wrest from the writer, even before the work has been produced, all future interest in revenues that may derive from that work.

This effort, subverting the intent of the law and contrary to ethical publishing trade practices, is condemned by the ASJA. The demand for blanket assignment of all future rights and interest in an article or other creative work simply *will not be met* by responsible independent writers. Publishers who persist in issuing such inequitable agreements in connection with commissioned works will find that they have done so at the certain risk of losing a healthy flow of superior professional material. The result, for those periodicals, is likely to be a sharp and inevitable decline in editorial quality—an erosion and debasement of the standards on which periodicals must rely in order to attract readers and maintain their own reputations.

INDEX

Other Books Of Interest To Make Your Writing Career More Enjoyable . . . And Profitable.

General Writing Books

Getting the Words Right: How to Revise, Edit, and Rewrite, by Theodore A. Rees Cheney $13.95

How to Get Started in Writing, by Peggy Teeters $10.95

International Writers' & Artists' Yearbook, (paper) $10.95

Law and the Writer, edited by Polking and Meranus (paper) $7.95

Make Every Word Count, by Gary Provost (paper) $7.95

Teach Yourself to Write, by Evelyn Stenbock $12.95

Treasury of Tips for Writers, edited by Marvin Weisbord (paper) $6.95

Writer's Encyclopedia, edited by Kirk Polking $19.95

Writer's Market, $18.95

Writer's Resource Guide, edited by Bernadine Clark $16.95

Writing for the Joy of It, by Leonard Knott $11.95

Magazine/News Writing

Craft of Interviewing, by John Brady $9.95

Magazine Writing: The Inside Angle, by Art Spikol $12.95

Newsthinking: The Secret of Great Newswriting, by Bob Baker $11.95

Stalking the Feature Story, by William Ruehlmann $9.95

Write On Target, by Connie Emerson $12.95

Writing and Selling Non-Fiction, by Hayes B. Jacobs $12.95

Fiction Writing

Fiction Is Folks: How to Create Unforgettable Characters, by Robert Newton Peck $11.95

Fiction Writer's Help Book, by Maxine Rock $12.95

Fiction Writer's Market, edited by Jean Fredette $17.95

Handbook of Short Story Writing, edited by Dickson and Smythe (paper) $6.95

How to Write Best-Selling Fiction, by Dean R. Koontz $13.95

Writing Romance Fiction—For Love and Money, by Helene Schellenberg Barnhart $14.95

Writing the Novel: From Plot to Print, by Lawrence Block $10.95

Special Interest Writing Books

Children's Picture Book: How to Write It, How to Sell It, by Ellen E.M. Roberts $17.95

Complete Book of Scriptwriting, by J. Michael Straczynski $14.95

How to Make Money Writing . . . Fillers, by Connie Emerson $12.95

How to Write a Play, by Raymond Hull $13.95

How to Write and Sell Your Personal Experiences, by Lois Duncan $10.95

How to Write & Sell (Your Sense of) Humor, by Gene Perret $12.95

How to Write "How-To" Books and Articles, by Raymond Hull (paper) $8.95

Mystery Writer's Handbook, edited by Lawrence Treat (paper) $8.95

Poet's Handbook, by Judson Jerome $11.95

Programmer's Market, edited by Brad M. McGehee (paper) $16.95

TV Scriptwriter's Handbook, by Alfred Brenner $12.95

Writing and Selling Science Fiction, Compiled by The Science Fiction Writers of America (paper) $7.95

Writing for Children & Teenagers, by Wyndham/Madison $11.95

Writing to Inspire, by Gentz, Roddy, et al $14.95

The Writing Business

Complete Handbook for Freelance Writers, by Kay Cassill $14.95

How You Can Make $20,000 a Year Writing, by Nancy Edmonds Hanson (paper) $6.95
Jobs for Writers, edited by Kirk Polking $11.95
Writer's Survival Guide: How to Cope with Rejection, Success, and 99 Other Hang-Ups of the Writing Life, by Jean and Veryl Rosenbaum $12.95

To order directly from the publisher, include $1.50 postage and handling for 1 book and 50¢ for each additional book. Allow 30 days for delivery.
Writer's Digest Books, Department B
9933 Alliance Road, Cincinnati OH 45242
Prices subject to change without notice.